FLORENCE ACCESS®

VENICE ACCESS®

MILAN ACCESS®

W9-BQX-308

Northern Italy Orientation

Northern Italy has been increasingly appreciated as an entity in recent years. Just as restaurants around the world have for some time been using the phrase *northern Italian cuisine* almost generically to distinguish it from its tomatoey and garlicky southern counterpart (a surprisingly enduring image of Italy), back in the home country northern Italians have long seen themselves as the more progressive half of their nation: leaders in tourism and culture, an economic power creating modern-day Bragadoccios in the business arena. These latter characters are especially prevalent in **Milan**, the capital of contemporary Italy. Tourism and culture are still best represented by **Venice**, for which all Italians (and indeed most citizens of the world) have a soft spot, and **Florence**, for whose past (if not present) the world shows a continuing respect. Of interest to the visitor to these 3 cities are some of Italy's best hotels and restaurants alongside some of its most famous art and architecture—certainly the best known outside of Rome.

Yet for all of Italy's supposed unity (and that for barely over 100 years), the cities covered in this book have remarkably individual character, which will be discussed in their separate sections. Suffice it to say that the sophisticated Lombard dynamism of Milan, the incredible Byzantine lightness of Venice, and the lucid Renaissance grace of Florence are all enticing aspects of that crucible of man and his achievements known as Italy.

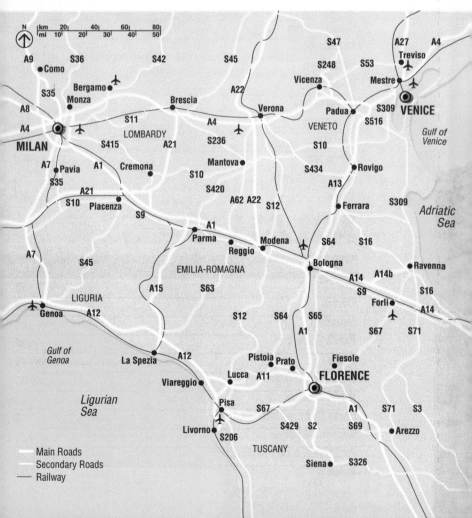

Getting In

General Information Everyone needs a valid passport to enter and leave Italy. Visas are not necessary for stays of less than 3 months; check with the nearest Italian consulate if staying longer. For stays of more than 3 months you are required to register with the local police station once in Italy. When a hotel asks for your passport, it is taking care of this formality for you. If you are not staying in a hotel, you are expected to register yourself each time you change residences, though the Italian authorities are usually fairly *dolce far niente* about enforcing this requirement. There are no innoculations required for Italy, though travelers unaccustomed to the Mediterranean diet and local bacteria might want to bring along Pepto Bismol. Those with special medical needs should check with their doctors about the latest health precautions; in the US you can call the Centers for Disease Control travel information line (404/639.2572, you need a touch tone phone) for up-to-date information. Your physician can provide you with generic prescriptions or a letter explaining any medicines you might be carrying.

Airlines The main gateways to Italy are Milan and Rome, where connecting flights may be made to Milan, Florence and Venice on Italy's domestic airline, **ATI**.

Customs Italian customs officials, though dressed and armed as if for lyric opera, are fairly lax. Occasionally, however (as during periods of international terrorism or the threat thereof), they do choose to reinforce the rules, so here they are: officially you are allowed to bring in up to 1,000,000 lire in Italian currency, 2 still cameras and 10 rolls of film for each, 1 movie camera and 10 rolls of film for it, 1 video camera and 1 cassette for it, 400 cigarettes and 500 grams of cigars or pipe tobacco, 2 bottles of wine and 1 bottle of hard liquor. If you're bringing in any other special equipment or prescription medicines, be sure they have documentation to back them up. From the US, contact the US customs service (202/566.8195) about obtaining the proper forms for equipment; your doctor can provide you with a letter about the medicine.

Check with your local customs service about what you may bring back from Italy.

Scanning Machines Scanning machines in Italian airports shouldn't damage your film; if the film (or you) are especially sensitive, buy lead foil bags to protect it. Remove computer diskettes before your computer passes through the machine and hand them to the inspectors.

Getting Around

Trains The **Italian State Railway** is known as **Ferrovie dello Stato** or **FS**. Even though the trains don't run on time as they did during Mussolini's day, train travel can be a pleasure in Italy, especially if there are no strikes taking place and you've made the increasingly necessary reservation. The fastest train is the *pendolino*, which is first class only and links the cities covered in this guide with many others. The other trains have first- and 2nd-class tickets: in order of efficiency they are the *EuroCity* (EC), an international train; *InterCity* (IC), its domestic equivalent; *rapido*, which operates between major cities; *espresso*, which is somewhat slower than the above; *diretto*, which stops at most stations; and *locale*, which stops at all stations. *Rapido* and faster trains require an additional supplement. There are all sorts of special passes and ever-changing deals—check with a travel agent about them. A word of warning—gassing and robbery occasionally takes place on overnight trains, especially those traveling from north to south. To help prevent it, you can ask the conductor to lock your compartment from the outside—you'll still be able to open it from the inside in case of emergency.

Buses Two bus services connecting most of Italy are **ANAC** (Piazza Esquilino 29, Rome, 06.463383) and **SITA** (Viale dei Cadorna 105, Florence, 055.278611).

Bicycling and Mopeds You can rent bicycles and mopeds in Milan and Florence. See individual cities for particulars.

City Maps The individual city maps collectively called *Tutto Città* have even more detail than the ACCESS® maps and cover extensive ground off the beaten track. Most hotels and bars have a copy on hand.

Driving Members of the European Economic Community can use their countries' drivers licenses in Italy. Others need an International Driver's Permit. Car rental is always cheaper when arranged in advance from abroad. Emergency service is provided by the Automobile Club Italiano (ACI), reached by dialing 116 from any phone.

Walking Walking is the most convenient way of getting around the crowded downtown areas of Italian cities, so bring comfortable shoes. Very few concessions are made to the handicapped.

FYI

Climate and Dress Northern Italy has a fairly moderate climate: though Milan is notorious for its winter fogs, Venice for the chilling winter wind called the *bora* and high water called *acqua alta*, and Florence for its damp winters and ovenlike summers.

You should therefore dress accordingly and comfortably, though note that as in everything Italians are fairly formal and take pleasure in making fun of how foreigners dress. Bare shoulders and shorts are considered inappropriate dress for churches and the street. Faux Anglo has long been considered quite chic in Italy. At the moment a casual look for both sexes of polo shirts in warm weather, quilted jackets in the cooler weather, and Timberland shoes year-round (in addition to immaculate grooming and a well-maintained tan) will have you pass for a native—of Italy, believe it or not.

Crime It is unlikely you'll encounter the Mafia in northern Italy, though it does exist and despite government crackdowns seems to be increasingly in the news; conversely, the famous Italian terrorism is on the wane.

Watch your belongings on crowded streets and public transportation; purse-snatchings and pickpocketings take place, though usually without the violence common in the New World. Also beware of gypsies of all ages, who approach people with astounding tenacity.

If you get into trouble call 113, the emergency number throughout Italy. You can also appoach any one of the various Italian police. Your first choice should be the well-educated and courteous *carabinieri*, who wear dark blue uniforms. *Polizia*, who wear navy jackets and lighter pants or skirts, have a reputation for being a little more hard-boiled. *Vigili urbani*, who wear navy outfits and white bobby's hats, usually concern themselves with traffic violations and petty crime.

Drinking Though wine with meals is common, hard liquor is rarely consumed outside of tourist bars and TV ads, and drunkenness is considered extremely bad form (*brutta figura*).

Drugs Stiff penalties for possession of any amount of narcotics mean you should just say no—easily enough done in Italian, since it's the same word.

English-Language Media Periodicals such as the *International Herald Tribune*, the *Financial Times, USA Today, Time, Newsweek* and *The Economist* are available on newsstands throughout Italy. Telemontecarlo (a Monte Carlo-based private television network accessible throughout Italy) rebroadcasts the CBS Evening News and CNN at various times. The pricier hotels carry live broadcasts of CNN, Skychannel and other cable networks. Radio Vaticano, the Vatican radio station, periodically broadcasts the news in English.

Etiquette Italians love titles, the most popular being *dottore* (*dottoressa* for women) for anyone with a university degree. More specific titles good for both sexes are *ingeniere* (engineer), *architetto* (architect) and *avvocato* (attorney). When in doubt, *dottore* or *dottoressa* will take you further than a simple *signore* or *signora*.

For such a formal culture, it is surprising how agressive Italians can be in public situations. Be prepared for inconsiderate drivers, pushing and shoving at lines in banks and post offices (and no lines at all at bus stops), and the sharp *gomitata* or elbow thrust from innocent-appearing little old ladies in food markets. A stern look accompanied by a firm *prego*? (what gives?) will usually be met with feigned incomprehension on the part of the offender, but he or she will usually back down.

Italian men seem to have no rules of etiquette when it comes to foreign women, and catcalling on the street is common. Squeezing and pinching on crowded buses are referred to as *mano morta* (dead hand—but where it shouldn't be) and *mano lesta* (molesting hand). Use a sharp elbow jab or a good heel kick to get rid of unwelcome attention. We know a woman who carries a hat pin to stick men engaged in *mano morta* on buses; she says they are usually too surprised and embarrassed that they've been challenged to cry out in pain. Ignore the man in the street who tries to pick you up. If you can't shake him, say what the Roman women say: *Crepu!* which roughly translates as *go and die!* Unfortunately, this is a national male pastime.

Food Breakfast is always much more expensive in your hotel. To save lire and get an entertaining sampling of local color, do as the Italians do and have breakfast standing up at the counter of the local coffee bar. The usual choices are *caffè* (espresso), *cappuccino*, or *Hag* (the brand name for the most popular decaffinated coffee) with a *pasta* or pastry.

You pay beforehand at the cashier and take your receipt back to the counter, slapping it down with the customary tip of a 200-lire coin.

Restaurants in northern Italy usually serve lunch between 12:30 and 2:30PM and dinner between 7:30 and 10:30PM. Most are closed one day a week (the day can change, so do call ahead), some time in August, and between Christmas and New Year's. Reservations are usually not required but are a good idea.

The tip (usually around 15%) has been included when you see the words *servizio compreso* or *servizio incluso* on the bill. If not, adding another 15% is generous and should be greatly appreciated. Italians themselves generally leave anywhere from 1000 to 2000 lire per diner on the table.

Mail A recent survey by the European Economic Community showed that the Italian postal service is the most expensive and least efficient in Europe. It does provide mail, telex, telegram and fax services, though you should consider a courier for anything important. Stamps may also be bought at tobacconists. If you would like to receive mail, have the sender mark it *fermo posta* (c/o the post office) or *ufficio postale* in the city in which you will be picking it up for a small fee. If you're passing through Rome, drop off your mail at the Vatican.

American Express offices will hold mail for clients at no fee.

Federal Express and DHL have courier services throughout Italy, though they are staffed by relative novices and are still working out such bugs as picking up and delivering on time.

Medical The **International Association for Medical Assistance to Travelers** (IAMAT) provides a list of English-speaking physicians throughout the world as well as a number of useful publications. Membership is free; you can sign up by contacting the organization at 417 Center St, Lewiston NY 14092, USA, 716/754.4883; 40 Regal Rd, Guelph, Ont. N1K 1B5, Canada, 519/836.0102; 575 Bourke St, 12th floor, Melbourne 3000, Australia; PO Box 5049, Christchurch 5, New Zealand.

Money The Italian monetary unit is the lire. Bills come in denominations of 100,000, 50,000, 20,000, 10,000, 5000, 2000 and 1000 lire; coins in 500, 200, 100 and 50 lire. Avoid changing money at the currency exchange office (*cambio*) in airports and train stations since they charge exorbitant fees. As a general rule, the state-owned travel agency called **CIT** offers good rates at minimal fees. Otherwise, money may be exchanged in travel agencies, banks and hotels at varying exchange rates and fees.

Most shops and restaurants accept major credit cards.

The European Economic Community levies a sales tax (Value Added Tax, called IVA in Italy) of about 19% in Italy. Non-EEC visitors can request exemption on purchases of 575,000 lire and above, and any tax paid can be refunded by mail by showing Italian customs officials your receipt and the merchandise on leaving the country.

Politics Though you may not have a direct interest in Italian politics, you won't be able to avoid it since it's a national pastime and political figures in Italy have celebrity status unknown in most other countries.

Italy's Byzantine and scandal-ridden political system would require a guidebook in itself. The largest party is the **Christian Democrat** party (**Democrazia Cristiana** or **DC**), affiliated with the Roman Catholic Church. Second in popularity until recently was the **Communist** party (**Partito Communista Italiano** or **PCI**, now known as the **Partito Democratico Sinistra** or **PDS**), long independent of Moscow though undergoing a reorganization of its own in the wake of events in the USSR and Eastern Europe. Also politically important are the **Socialists** (**Partito Socialista Italiana** or **PSI**); primarily culturally important are the **Radicals** (**Partito Radicale** or **PR**), good at garnering headlines. (They did so most recently with the election of porn star **Ilona Staller**—aka Cicciolina or Baby Fat—to the camera of deputies.) There are many other political parties in Italy; save learning about them for your next few hundred trips.

Public Bathrooms There are few public bathrooms in Italy. An air of self-confidence and a good sense of direction will help get you into the hotel facilities; otherwise the price of a coffee will entitle you to ask for the *gabinetto* in a coffee bar, though the hygiene is often Third World and you may want to bring your own tissue.

Public Holidays New Year's Day (1 Jan), Epiphany (6 Jan), Easter Monday, Liberation Day (25 April), Labor Day (1 May), Ferragosto or Assumption Day (15 Aug), All Saint's Day (1 Nov), Immaculate Conception (8 Dec), Christmas (25 Dec), St. Stephen's Day (26 Dec)

Religion In case you're from Mars, you may not know that Italians are overwhelmingly Roman Catholic. They are, however, remarkably curious about and accepting of other religions, most of which are represented in Italy. Tuscany and the Veneto have the reputation for being the least tolerant regions in Italy regarding religion as well as race.

Sightseeing Be prepared for crowds of tourists and Italian schoolchildren, especially at major sights and during the summer. Bring a pair of binoculars or opera glasses with you to places with high ceilings or cheek-by-jowl paintings in order to fully appreciate the detailed art and architecture.

Smoking Everyone in Italy smokes, though some hotels and restaurants are now creating non-smoking sections.

Telephones Calling local or long distance from your hotel room usually costs at least twice as much as it would on the outside. The cheapest way of phoning home to the US is to call collect (dial 170 and the operator will arrange it for you) and have someone call you back. If you have an AT&T calling card, you can use it by calling 172.1011 from any phone and you'll be connected to an AT&T operator in the US. MCI users can dial 172.1022. ALLNET subscribers should call 1678.97038. Otherwise, go to the phone company offices, known by the acronyms of **SIP** or **ASST**, and pay cash.

There are 3 kinds of coin phones in Italy, all of which allow you to dial direct anywhere in the world. The small green ones take only an Italian phone slug, called a *gettone*, available at many tobacconists and newsstands. The larger, metallic phones and the orange ones give you a choice of using a *gettone*, a 200-lire coin, or two 100-lire coins. When phones are not working, a red light will come on. A sign reading *guasto* literally means *out of order*, though likely as not the shop owner just doesn't feel like letting people use his phone; try it anyway.

5000- and 10,000-lire prepaid phone cards, which fit into the metal boxes adjacent to the coin phones in many public places, are sold at SIP and ASST offices as well as at tobacconists. The card loses value each time you use it until, finally, the machine eats it up and you must buy another. Clip off the top corner along the dotted line the first time you use it.

Instructions for coin phones:

1. Take *gettoni* or coins out of your pocket or purse.

2. Lift up the receiver; if by any chance it is working, you will hear a dial tone.

3. Put in the coin(s).

4. Dial the number.

5. Answer when spoken to.

6. If you are calling long distance, put in all the coins you think you will need for the entire conversation. When you hang up, press the coin-return button—it's red and halfway down the machine. The unused coin(s) will be returned to you. (Watch the Italians press this button after each call; sometimes they hit the jackpot and get a few extra coins.)

Vocabulary Many Italians speak English, but appreciate the smallest efforts of foreigners to speak Italian. Note that Italian is pronounced exactly as it is written.

In addition to the usual smattering found in any phrasebook, the following expressions should prove useful:

Parla inglese?—Do you speak English?

Non parlo Italiano—I don't speak Italian

Permesso—Excuse me, used when you want to cut through a crowd

Prego—the response to *permesso*

Vada via—Go away, useful for gypsies and other molesters

Aiuto!—Help! (if the above doesn't work)

Già fatto—Already done, an all-purpose phrase for the swamped waiter who forgets he has already taken your order, the harried concierge who has already called you a taxi, etc.

Come sta—How are you?

Buon Giorno—Good morning/afternoon

Buona Sera—Good evening

Arrivederci—Goodbye

Non Capisco—I don't understand

Come si chiama?—What's your name?

Che ora sono?—What time is it?

Dov'è l'albergo?—Where is the hotel?

Dov'è un telefono?—Where is the telephone?

Dov'è il bagno?—Where is the restroom?

Attenzione—Caution!/Look out!

Quanto costa?—How much is it?

Il conto—Bill/check

Sono Vegetariano/a—I am vegetarian

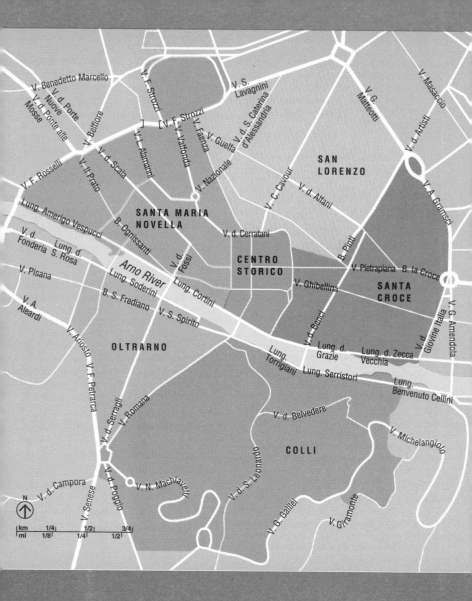

Florence is the proud, petulant sister in the family of Italian cities, and home to some of the greatest works of art in the western world.

FLORENCE*ACCESS*®

Duomo (Cathedral of Santa Maria del Fiore)

Florence Orientation

Florence is the proud, petulant sister in the family of Italian cities, the one who refused to grow up after a precocious youth. Heirs to the birthplace of the Renaissance, Florentines have been criticized for refusing to acknowledge that anything happened after (or even before, though the site was probably settled by the Etruscans and certainly developed by the

Romans) that golden age in civilization. Indeed, the city's primary attraction to the visitor is its wealth of artistic and architectural monuments from the period. Behind the golden-brown stone of the city's churches and palazzi lie some of the greatest works of art in the western world, and some of that stone itself—plain or dressed in other colors—comprises architectural wonders known to every student of the humanities in the world.

With such predecessors as **Michelangelo** and **Leonardo da Vinci** (and the pressures of traffic and tourists who come to discover their legacy), Florentines remain proud at times to the point of rudeness. If you find that happening to you, just remember the Florentine character has been criticized at least as far back as **Dante**, whose Tuscan dialect was adopted as the official Italian language when the country was unified in the last century. And if you listen hard to how the Florentines speak the modern version of *la lingua di Dante*—in an aspirated, countrified way—you may even begin to appreciate the down-to-earth quality that lies beneath all that Machiavellian ceremony and Gucci gloss.

Getting to Florence

Airports

Galileo Galilei airport (050-28088) in **Pisa**, 53 miles from Florence, is the nearest international airport to Florence. It is served by Alitalia, British Airways, Air France and Lufthansa. If you are departing from the airport, you may check in directly at Florence's **Santa Maria Novella** train station. Trains between the airport and the Santa Maria Novella train station run hourly; the trip takes about one hour. There is also taxi service available, which is extremely expensive (about $150 at press time).

The following rental car agencies have offices at the Pisa airport:

Avis	050-42028
Budget	050-45490
Hertz	050-49187
National	050-41017

Service at **Peretola** airport (373498), 2.5 miles from the city, is generally limited to domestic flights, though there are a number of controversial proposals in the works to expand it. The only option for arrival to the city from Peretola is by taxi.

The following rental car agencies have offices at the Florence airport:

Avis	372588
National	318609

Train Station

Florence's central train station is **Santa Maria Novella** (Piazza della Stazione, 278785), smack in the center of town. When buying your train ticket, make sure the train stops at that station and not the **Campo di Marte** station, which is in an inconvenient location on the east side of town.

Getting Around Town

Bicycles and Mopeds

The following agencies rent bicycles and/or mopeds:

Bici-Citta, Stazione Santa Maria Novella (also at: Fortezza da Basso, Piazza Pitti), 499319

Ciao & Basta, Via Alamanni, 213307

Motorent, Via San Zanobi 9r, 490113

Program, Borgo Ognissanti 135r, 282916

Promotourist, Via Bandinelli 43, 701863

Sabra, Via Artisti 8, 576256

Buses

City buses are called **ATAF** and are frequent and efficient. Tickets are available in most newsstands, tobacconists and cafes. They must be purchased before boarding the bus (get on at the front or rear doors, as the center one is for getting off), when you validate them in a little orange machine. The main bus information offices, where English is spoken, are at the entrance to the train station and at Piazza del Duomo 57r.

Driving

Because of the Dantesque rings of traffic zones in Florence, it is not recommended that you use a car.

Taxis

Taxis are plentiful and drivers remarkably pleasant in Florence. They wait at strategic locations around town, may be called by dialing 4390 or 4798, and may occasionally be hailed on the street.

FYI

Addresses

Residences are posted in black numerals on the streets and written as simple numbers; business addresses are posted in red numerals and written by a number followed by an *r* for *rosso* or red.

Consulates

UK, Lungarno Corsini 2, 284133

US, Lungarno Amerigo Vespucci 38, 298276

Hours

Businesses are generally open M 3:30-7:30PM; Tu-Sa 9AM-1PM, 3:30-7:30PM. Food shops are open M-Tu and Th-Sa 9AM-1PM, 3:30-7:30PM; W 9AM-1PM.

Legal Emergencies

Ufficio Stranieri, Via Zara 2, 49771

Medical Emergencies

Misericordia, Piazza del Duomo 20, 212222

Tourist Medical Service, Via Lorenzo il Magnifico 59, 475411

Money

The **American Express** office is at Via Guicciardini 49r, 278751. Another good currency exchange is **Universalturismo** at Via Speziali 7, 217241. Avoid changing money at the airports and train station; the agencies there charge high commissions.

Pharmacies (open 24 hours)

Farmacia Comunale, Stazione Santa Maria Novella 263435

Farmacia Molteni, Via Calzaiuoli 7r, 263490

Farmacia Taverna, Piazza San Giovanni 20r, 211343

Post Office

Poste e Telecommunicazioni, Via Pellicceria, 160. M-F 8:15AM-7PM; Sa 8:15AM-noon

Street Smarts

Pickpockets operate on the buses in Florence. Gypsies harass natives and visitors alike in front of the train station and near the outdoor market of San Lorenzo. Drug dealing is currently concentrated around Via dei Neri.

Telephone

The area code for Florence is 055; outside Italy drop the 0 and just dial 55 after the country code 39 for Italy. The **ASST** telephone at Via Pellicceria (tel. 214145), is open 24 hours.

Tourist Info

Informazione Turistica, just outside Stazione Santa Maria Novella, no phone; and at Via Cavour, tel. 2760382, both daily 9AM-7PM

Ente Provinciale per il Turismo, Via Alessandro Manzoni 16; tel. 2478141; M-Sa 8AM-2PM

English-language cultural events listings include *Florence Concierge Information*, available at the better hotels; and *Florence Today*, available at the tourist information office.

Cuisine

A typical Tuscan repast starts with an antipasto of *crostini* (toasted bread rounds spread wth a chicken liver pâté) or *fettunta* (garlic bread such as you've never tasted it) followed by cured meats such as *prosciutto crudo* (a salty prosciutto), *finocchiona* (a salami seasoned with

fennel seeds) and *salsiccia di cinghiale* (sausage made from wild boar). This is the time to start right in on the local wine—*Chianti, naturalmente*. Don't be surprised if the waiter brings an entire straw-covered flask to the table. You'll be charged only for what you consume (*a consumo*, the arrangement is called), but it's wise to ask for a flask or bottle to be opened then and there, since leftover wines are often mixed. *Chianti* Classico, with the black rooster symbol on the neck of the bottle, is the best known and most common type of the various *Chianti* wines. If you'd rather sample some of the more fancy local vintages, you won't do better than the robust red Brunello di Montalcino. Some other good reds are Carmignano and Vino Nobile di Montepulciano. Of the whites, the dry Vernaccia di San Gimignano is the traditional choice, though the light Galestro has become increasingly popular in recent years.

Primi piatti or first courses can consist of excellent local versions of risotto or variations of pasta dishes available throughout Italy. Particularly Florentine, however, are the soups such as *pappa al pomodoro* (tomatoes, bread, olive oil, onions and basil), *ribollita* (white beans, bread, black cabbage and onions), *carabaccia* (a sweet-and-sour onion soup) and, in the summer, *panzanella* (a salad of tomatoes, onions, vinegar, oil and bread). Before they are eaten, these dishes are often christened with *un C d'olio*—a generous C-shaped pouring of the local olive oil from the ever-present tabletop cruet.

Second to none among the *secondi piatti* or main courses is *bistecca alla fiorentina*—a thick slab ideally of local Chianina beef (though these days most comes from Yugoslavia), grilled over charcoal, seasoned with olive oil, salt and pepper, and served rare. *Trippa alla fiorentina* (tripe stewed with tomatoes in a meat sauce) is also a regional specialty, as are many other roasted meats that go especially well with the *Chianti*. In recent years country dishes such as *cibreo* (a stew of cockscombs and other chicken parts) have been coming out of mamma's closet (or kitchen) and into the restaurants. Main courses are usually served with a *contorno* (side dish) of white beans, sautéed greens or seasonal vegetables such as artichokes, all of which can be drizzled with more of that wonderful olive oil.

Florentine desserts are typically parsimonious. The cheese is the hard *pecorino* (made from ewe's milk), and locals like to go for the even tougher almond cookies called *biscotti di Prato*, which provide an excuse to dunk them in the potent sweet dessert wine called *vin santo*. The current hot dessert is the Piedmontese import *panna cotta*. Literally *cooked cream*, at its best it is nothing more than just that, although it is often thickened with some sort of starch and dressed up with chocolate sauce. Dessert time is also a good opportunity to try some of the seasonal sweets made in Florence—*schiacciata con l'uva* (a grape-covered bread) in the fall, *castagnaccio* (a chestnut-flour cake) in the winter, and *schiacciata alla fiorentina* (an orange-flavored sponge cake topped with powdered sugar) at carnival time.

Tripe stands (the one in Piazza Dante is our favorite) scattered throughout town offer snacks of tripe (cow's stomach) and the more delicate *lampredotto* (cow's intestine); other places, such as Luisa on Via Sant'Antonino, serve salty snacks of fried *polenta* (corn meal mush); pastry shops such as Cucciolo on Via del Corso serve *bomboloni* (deep-fried doughballs filled with custard, chocolate or jam).

Centro Storico

The old city center of all Italian towns is called **Centro Storico** (literally, historical center), but the term is especially meaningful in Florence. While not the palimpsest that Rome is, Florence still offers varying and vivid impressions of all periods from its rich history within its small Centro Storico. To begin with, ancient Roman colonials gave many of the streets their grid pattern. Though only a few columns and capitals remain from those days, some streets have taken on the names of the Roman buildings which once stood on them—the baths were on **Via delle Terme**, the capitol was on **Via del Campidoglio**.

What you will notice most of all in this part of Florence is its medieval aspect. **Palazzo Vecchio**, the **Bargello** and **Ponte Vecchio**, and what remains of the medieval churches and towers, evoke the era of Florence's first stirrings as a powerful force in international commerce. That wealth enabled the great project of the **Duomo** to usher in the Renaissance, which led to the construction of majestic private palazzi. This was followed by a local version of the Baroque in a few churches alongside them.

The next great building boom happened when Florence became, albeit briefly, the capital of a newly united Italy in the last century and the city fathers strived for a monumental look inspired by Haussmann in France, knocking down old buildings and replacing them with more grandiose edifices. Finally, the postwar phenomenon of Italian design has brought about some exciting interior spaces in shops right in the center of Florence. And it's all as easy to see as it is enjoyable, since, happily for the visitor, Centro Storico is now largely a pedestrian zone (though vehicles making deliveries or belonging to residents may still enter), just as it was in the centuries before the advent of the automobile.

Don't worry. There are still plenty of cars and Vespas zooming around the cathedral, giving the Duomo's full-time team of restorers more than enough to keep them busy. But even more intense than the traffic is the concentration of art and architecture, the densest in the Western World. Its effect on visitors is so overwhelming that a Florentine psychiatrist coined the term *Stendhal syndrome* (named after the Grand Tour-era French traveler and connoisseur) to describe the dizziness and depression she observed in one bewildered tourist after another.

Fortunately, there are a number of antidotes close at hand. Besides the legacy of **Leonardo** and **Michelangelo**, a vital part of Florence's heritage are the commercial skills that helped amass the fortunes of the **Medici** and other merchant families. So even here in Centro Storico things that appeal to the purse and palate are interspersed with things that engage the eye and mind. Past and present, it's all Florence.

---

1 Duomo (Cathedral of Santa Maria del Fiore) (begun 1296, **Arnolfo di Cambio**; continued from 1334 under **Giotto**; from 1357 by **Francesco Talenti** and **Lapo Ghini**; dome 1436, **Filippo Brunelleschi**) Brunelleschi's octagonal, red-tile cupola soars above Florence's Duomo, or cathedral, overwhelming the city like the Wizard's balloon in Oz and dominating even the countryside for miles around. According to Renaissance chronicler **Giorgio Vasari**'s *Lives of the Artists*, Brunelleschi won the commission to erect a dome on the base of the candy-colored cathedral by challenging his competitors to make an egg stand up on a flat piece of marble. *So an egg was procured and the artists in turn tried to make it stand on end; but they were all unsuccessful, the account goes. Then Filippo was asked to do so, and taking the egg graciously he cracked its bottom on the marble and made it stay upright. The others complained that they could have done as much, and laughing at them Filippo retorted that they would also have known how to vault the cupola if they had seen his model or plans. And so they resolved that*

Centro Storico

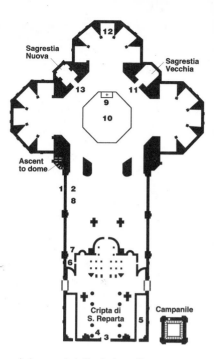

Filippo should be given the task of carrying out the work.... That kind of *egg-o*, and the boldness of Filippo's feat (the first dome in Italy since the Pantheon, which Brunelleschi studied), helped usher in the Renaissance. Other greats of the era to have their say about the dome were **Andrea Verrocchio**, who designed the bronze globe and cross for the top of its lantern, and **Michelangelo**, whose remark that **Baccio d'Agnolo**'s balcony at its base was *a cricket cage* halted construction after only one of its 8 sides was so embellished.

Brunelleschi's cracks *and* wisecracks were as portentious as they were pretentious. A half-millenium later, the dome is riddled with fissures, some due to age and others because modern restorers filled in holes with concrete, blocking the built-in safeguards for expansion and contraction from temperature changes. No one quite knows what to do about it, but should Humpty Dumpty have a great fall, all the authorities' lasers, plumb lines and other measuring devices (some 300 of them make the Duomo the most closely watched structure in the world) will be there to duly record, if not prevent, the event.

The dome overpowers the confection of Tuscan marble (red from the Maremma, white from Carrara and green from Prato—also the colors of the Italian flag) facing the building beneath it. Its original Gothic facade by Arnolfo di Cambio, never completed as with many Florentine churches, was demolished in 1587. The current Neo-Gothic version was put up in the late 19th century, part of the frenzy of construction and destruction when Florence became the capital of the newly united kingdom of Italy. But the richly ornamented **Porta della Mandorla [1]** on the north side, with an *Assumption of the Virgin* **[2]** by **Nanni di Banco** in its pediment, dates from the late Gothic period. Much of the rest of the decoration—indoor and outdoor—is now in the **Museo dell'Opera del Duomo**.

The cathedral has been taken as a metaphor for the Florentine character—showy on the outside, austere on the inside—for despite the directive that it be *più bello che si può* (as beautiful as can be), the interior remains remarkably Spartan. The entrance wall **[3]** has 3 stained-glass

windows made to the designs of **Lorenzo Ghiberti**, better known for (and represented by) the 3-dimensionality of his bronze door reliefs on the Baptistry, and **Paolo Uccello**'s giant clock with the hand going backwards and heads of 4 prophets. Just to the left is **Tino da Camaino**'s almost Minimalist monument to **Bishop Antonio d'Orso [4]**.

In the right aisle, under a bust of Brunelleschi by his adopted son **Buggiano**, is the architect's tomb slab **[5]**, found just beneath its current location during the excavation of the Cripta or **Crypt of Santa Reparata**. The earlier church, built on Roman foundations in the 4th or 5th century, occupied the western third of the present cathedral's nave. The entrance to the site, which has Roman Early Christian relics as well as Gothic tombs and frescoes, is at the first pillar of the right aisle.

Further ahead, across the nave in the left aisle, are 2 works of art taken as tributes to Florentine parsimony, **Andrea del Castagno**'s monument to **Niccolò da Tolentino [6]** and Uccello's monument to **Sir John Hawkwood [7]**. Presumably commissioned as monumental equestrian sculptures, they were instead executed in paint to resemble marble as *trompe l'oeil* frescoes. Following them is a more straightforward, albeit characteristically complicated, Florentine subject, **Domenico di Michelino**'s *Dante Explaining the Divine Comedy* **[8]**.

Inside the cupola are frescoes of *The Last Judgement* **[9]** by Vasari and **Federico Zuccari**. Beneath them is a choir by **Bandinelli** and a crucifix (over the high altar) **[10]** by **Benedetto da Maiano**. The entrance to the **Sagrestia Vecchia** (Old Sacristy) **[11]**, to the right of the altar, is topped by a terracotta lunette of the

Ascension by **Luca della Robbia**. He was also responsible for the 2 terracotta angels in the chapel at the exteme end of the nave **[12]** (it also contains a bronze urn by Ghiberti, holding the relics of St. Zanobius), the terracotta *Resurrection* above the doors to the **Sagrestia Nuova** (New Sacristy) **[13]** to the left of the altar, and for the bronze doors themselves, a unique example of his use of this medium. The doors played a significant role on a dark day in Florentine history, when an event known as the Pazzi Conspiracy took place. That day was Sunday, 26 April 1478, when a group of mad assassins led by the **Pazzi** family (the name means *crazies*) attemped to seize power from the **Medici** family by murdering them in the cathedral at the ringing of the bells at the most sacred moment of the Mass. **Giuliano** died after receiving 29 dagger blows; **Lorenzo** (aka Il Magnifico or the Magnificent) fought off his attackers and took shelter behind della Robbia's doors, which slammed shut with a clang echoing through the enormous space.

Works by Renaissance masters (though admittedly not master*pieces*) and *più bello non si può* notwithstanding, the real beauty of the cathedral interior *is* its expansive space. As a cathedral, it is surpassed only by St. Peter's in Rome, St. Paul's in London and the Duomo in Milan—and it is less cluttered than any of them. If not exactly intimate, at least its empty grandeur is evocative. Above the din of the tourists, it is easy to imagine the Pazzi Conspiracy, or, just a few years later, the fanatic preacher **Girolamo Savonarola** railing to a packed house of 10,000 Florentines for being more worshipful of the ancients than the saints. Today the crowds gather outdoors in the piazza on Easter Sunday to watch **Lo Scoppio del Carro** (the explosion of the cart), a medieval folk event in which an ornately decorated cart is drawn by white oxen into the piazza. At the Gloria, a rocket in the shape of a dove is lit inside at the high altar, traveling the length of the church along a wire attached to the cart, where it sets off a riot of fireworks. The event is meant to recall the days when a flame ignited during the Gloria was then distributed to the townspeople.

The Duomo's enormousness provides the perfect opportunity to explore some of the world's most famous indoor and outdoor space. The 463-step climb to the top along the catwalks and spiral staircases used by the builders provides close-up views of Brunelleschi's dome-within-a-dome structure; from the lantern are panoramas of the sea of Florence's terracotta roofs and monuments in *pietra forte* (strong stone), the local golden-brown stone.
♦ Admission. Daily 7:30AM-6PM. Cupola and Santa Riparata Crypt M-Sa 10AM-5:30PM. Piazza del Duomo. 294514

The **Medici** line became extinct in 1737 with the death of **Grand Duke Gian Gastone de' Medici**, whose fondness for the grape and dissolute young boys called *ruspanti* were court scandals.

2 Campanile (1334-59, **Giotto, Andrea Pisano, Francesco Talenti**) Known locally as Il **Campanile di Giotto**, the tower was actually a collaborative effort. Giotto designed the first story and Pisano and Talenti finished it in visual harmony provided by the same 3 colors of marble that clad the cathedral. (Musical harmony is provided by the bells, named *Grossa, Beona, Completa, Cheirica* and *Squilla*—Big, Tipsy, Finished, Priestling and Shreiker.) The ascent offers views of the city and surroundings, as well as a dumbfounding view of Brunelleschi's

dome. ♦ Daily 9AM-5:30PM, winter; 9AM-7:30PM, summer. Piazza del Duomo

3 Arciconfraternita della Misericordia (Palazzo of the Misericordia) (1575-78, **Alfonso Parigi**; 1781, **Stefano Diletti**) A Florentine tradition dating from the 14th-century plague years, the Misericordia is a charitable organization of volunteers from all walks of life which tends to the sick and needy free of charge, supported entirely by contributions. To preserve their anonymity, members clad themselves in hooded black robes, a custom adopted during the plague of 1630. Inside are statues of *St. Sebastian* and the *Madonna* by **Benedetto da Maiano**, as well as a tabernacle by **Andrea della Robbia**. ♦ Piazza del Duomo 19

4 Loggia of Santa Maria del Bigallo (1352-58, **Alberto Arnoldi**) Originally part of the Misericordia, this organization occupying the palazzo now takes care of beggar children and runs a rest home for the aged. Frescoes depicting religious subjects and acts of charity adorn the inside. ♦ Piazza San Giovanni 1

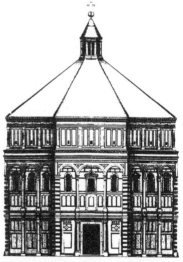

5 Battistero di San Giovanni (Baptistry of San Giovanni) (ca 5th c; south doors 1330, **Andrea Pisano**; north doors 1403-24, east doors 1424-52, **Lorenzo Ghiberti**) **Dante** fondly mentions *bel San Giovanni*, referring to the Baptistry dedicated to Florence's patron

saint. Florentines once flattered themselves by believing it to be an ancient Roman temple of Mars, and although there are Classical elements in the decoration of the green-and-white marble facade and actual Roman columns inside, it dates from much later. The Baptistry is best known for its gilded bronze doors on 3 of its 8 sides (the originals are gradually being restored and displayed in the Duomo Museum, replaced here by copies). The doors were made in the 14th and 15th centuries, the first such work since the ancients. The south doors, by Andrea

Centro Storico

Pisano, combine the Gothic style with the new realism of Giotto. The upper 20 panels tell the story of the life of **John the Baptist**; the lower 8 the cardinal and theological virtues. The north doors are by Ghiberti, who beat **Brunelleschi** in a famous competition held for them in 1401 (their entries are on display in the Bargello). The upper 20 panels here depict scenes from the New Testament (the artist also cast his self-portrait, the hooded head on the left door); the lower 8 represent the 4 evangelists and the 4 doctors of the church. The east doors, also by Ghiberti, were called by the usually cryptic **Michelangelo** *the gates of paradise*. The 10 panels illustrate scenes from the Old Testament, and are surrounded by portrait heads (another one of the artist is on the left door, the fourth from the top on the right side, next to a portrait of his son **Vittorio**) and playful animal motifs.

Inside the Baptistry are mosaics in the vault, made to the designs of **Cimabue** and other artists. A marble pavement of the zodiac surrounds the baptismal font, and the collaborative hands of **Donatello** and **Michelozzo** may be seen in the tomb of **Cardinal Baldassare Coscia**. ◆ M-F noon-5PM; Sa-Su 9AM-5:30PM. Piazza San Giovanni

6 Palazzo Arcivescovile (Archbishop's Palace) (1573-84, **Giovanni Antonio Dosio**) The facade of the archibishop's palace was sliced off to enlarge the piazza in 1895. Its interior courtyard leads to the tiny church of **San Salvatore al Vescovo**, built on the site of a Romanesque church and completely frescoed like pastry from **Scudieri**. For a lower-calorie treat, go around the corner for a look at the Romanesque facade of the original church, part of the palazzo wall facing Piazza dell'Olio. ◆ Piazza del Duomo 3

7 Luisa Via Roma Florence's most international boutique by far, Luisa is the one place in town you're guaranteed to find Kenzo and Comme des Garçons alongside the Italian sartorial maestros for both sexes. ◆ Closed M morning, Su. Via Roma 19-21r. 292130

8 Eredi Chiarini Men may want to do their one-stop shopping here, where the taste in suits, jackets, shirts, trousers, sweaters and accessories winningly combines Anglo-American conservatism with Italian stylishness. ◆ Closed M morning, Su, lunch. Via Roma 18-22r. 284478

9 Raspini The biggest names in Italian and international clothing and shoe design for the whole well-heeled family are here, next to the store's own prestigious label of Florentine leather goods. There are 2 other shops in town, but none outside of Florence, so if Raspini's well-designed and well-crafted style works with yours, this is the best place to take out the wallet. ◆ Closed M morning, Su, lunch. Via Roma 25-29r. 213077. Also at: Via Martelli 5-7; Via Por S. Maria

10 Robiglio Florence's most revered *pasticceria* or pastry shop, Robiglio has been known for over half a century for such goodies as its *torta campagnola*, a rich torte stuffed with fresh and candied fruit. ◆ Closed Su. Via de' Tosinghi 11r. 215013. Also at: Via dei Servi 112r. 212784

11 Facade of San Salvatore al Vescovo (1221) All that's left of a Romanesque church (the rest was remodeled and incorporated into the surrounding bishop's palace). Its green and white marble matches that of the Baptistry and San Miniato al Monte. ◆ Piazza dell'Olio

12 Bottiglieria Torrini This kind of hole-in-the-wall wine shop is an ancient Florentine tradition (historian **Giovanni Villani** tells us that there were 86 such places in the city in the 14th century) and an ideal place for a quick pick-me-up of a glass of *Chianti* with *crostini* (chicken liver pâté on bread rounds) and other snacks. ◆ Closed Su. Piazza dell'Olio 15r. 2396616

13 Beltrami One of the largest of the many Beltrami leather goods shops in town (there is some clothing as well), hence a better selection. ◆ Closed M morning, Su, lunch. Piazza dell'Olio 3r. 213290. Also at: Via dei Calzaiuoli 31r and 44r

14 Max Mara This chain is a favorite of most of our lady friends, who appreciate its bold and well-made line of suits, sweaters, separates, shoes and accessories. ◆ Closed M morning, Su, lunch. Via Brunelleschi 28r. 287761

15 Casa dei Tessuti Bolts and bolts of textiles by Italian designers from A (Armani) to Z (Zegna), as well as other European names, who more than likely had their goods produced in Italy anyway. ◆ Closed M morning, Su, lunch. Via dei Pecori 20-24r. 215961

Restaurants/Nightlife: Red **Hotels:** Blue
Shops/Parks: Green **Sights/Culture:** Black

16 Palazzo Orlandini del Beccuto (redesigned 1679, **Antonio Maria Ferri**) This massive palazzo, owned by a succession of noble Florentine families, has housed the local branch of the **Monte dei Paschi di Siena**, the world's oldest bank, since the beginning of this century. The bank recently restored the palazzo to something of its original splendor, visible indoors in the terracotta floor, white stucco walls and *pietra serena* details, including the only 15th-century wall fountain in Florence. ♦ Via dei Pecori 6-8

17 Old England Stores Florentines, already mad for faux-Anglo, go gaga for the real thing at this shop, stocked with such exotic items as port, sherry, biscuits and a full line of American breakfast cereals as well as a fine selection of British woolens in the back. Expatriate Anglophones may be seen here during the holidays stocking up on plum pudding and cranberry sauce. ♦ Closed M morning, Su, lunch. Via dei Vecchietti 28r. 211983

18 Santa Maria Maggiore (11th c; reconstructed 13th c) One of the oldest churches in Florence, this one has a plain stone facade like many in the city. High up on its old Romanesque bell tower on the Via dei Cerretani side is a late Roman bust of a woman. The interior, redesigned by **Bernardo Buontalenti**, contains a number of artworks, most notably a 13th-century painted wood sculpture of the *Madonna and Child* attributed to **Coppo di Marcovaldo**. ♦ Vicolo di Santa Maria Maggiore 1

19 Scudieri Homemade pastry, including perhaps the best plum cake in Florence, relatively insulated from the noise and confusion of the Duomo. ♦ Closed W. Piazza di San Giovanni 19r. 210733

20 Lo Sport This is the place to pick up that last-minute tennis outfit or clothes for the slopes, Italian-style. There is also the widest possible selection of sporting goods and an ever-popular inventory of faux-Anglo and faux-Austrian woolens (we prefer the soft Italian loden coats to the real thing). ♦ Closed M morning, Su, lunch. Piazza del Duomo 7-8r. 284412. Also at: Lo Sport Due, Piazza dell'Olio 5-7r. 292163

21 Torrini These expensive Florentine jewelers carry international brands such as Rolex as well as their own ultimate souvenir—a reproduction of the florin (the deutschmark or yen of the Middle Ages), with the lily symbol of Florence on one side and the city's patron saint, John the Baptist, on the other. ♦ Piazza del Duomo 9-10r. 284507

22 Fratelli Favilli Florence's finest engravers, the Favilli also specialize in signet rings. They offer etched gold jewelry in their own patterns, and will craft practically any design you bring them. ♦ Piazza del Duomo 13r. 211846

23 Setteclavo For the *appassionato* of classical music, over 50,000 titles are available on vinyl, tape and compact disc. A knowledgeable but respectful staff advises in a multitude of languages, and may be further consulted by mail through its members' club. ♦ Closed M morning, Su, lunch. Piazza del Duomo 16r. 287017

Centro Storico

24 Il Papiro The so-called Florentine or marbelized paper revival began right here with simple sheets of wrapping paper, pencils and boxes. It now extends to desk sets, picture frames, even Venetian masks—a particolored paper chase. ♦ Closed M morning, Su. Piazza del Duomo 24r. 215262. Also at: Via Cavour 24r. 215262

25 Museo dell'Opera del Duomo (Duomo Museum) The town fathers must have anticipated the sputtering and rattling traffic buzzing around the Duomo (reminiscent of Russian bears riding motorcycles in the Moscow Circus as compared with the classical grace of the phenomenon around Rome's Colosseum) when they began relegating works from the Cathedral, Campanile and Baptistry to the administrative headquarters of the **Duomo Works**, open to the public since 1891. A grandiose coat of arms of **Cosimo I de' Medici**, almost opportunistically trying to fill in the void left by the removed sacred decoration, marks the entrance. The courtyard has 2 Roman sarcophagi from the Baptistry, which no doubt fueled the conceit that the building was an ancient Roman temple. There is a marble bust of **Brunelleschi** (attributed to **Buggiano**) in the vestibule. The main sculpture room, the **Sala dell'Antica Facciata del Duomo** (Room of the Old Facade of the Duomo) has a drawing of **Arnolfo di Cambio**'s original facade of the Duomo, as well as many of his sculptures from it by him, **Nanni di Banco, Donatello** and others. Two rooms on the ground floor display Brunelleschi memorabilia, including his death mask and model for the dome. On the mezzanine is **Michelangelo**'s *Pietà*, a late work designed for his own tomb (**Vasari** says that the face of Nicodemus is a self-portrait), later smashed by the master and restored by his pupil **Tiberio Calcagni,** who completed the figure of Mary Magdalen. Upstairs are 2 joyous *cantorie*, one by **Luca della Robbia** and the other by Donatello, whose horrifying *Mary Magdalen*—again, a late work—repents below. The following room contains statues from the Campanile, ending with Donatello's *Habakkuk*, known locally as *Lo Zuccone*, which translates roughly as Pumpkin Head. The **Sala delle Formelle** houses relief panels from the Campanile illustrating spiritual progress. Finally, the **Sala dell'Altare** displays a silver altar for the Baptistry made by such members of the goldsmith's guild as **Verrocchio** and **Antonio Pollaiuolo**, and needlework panels for a tapestry made by craftsmen of the cloth importers' guild to the designs of such artists as Pollaiuolo, **Andrea Pisano** and **Jacopo della Quercia**. ◆ M-Sa 9AM-6PM, winter; 9AM-8PM, summer. Piazza del Duomo 9. 2302885

26 Torre degli Adimali (13th c) During the Middle Ages, Florence was filled with such towers, and even higher ones, as is the Tuscan town of San Gimignano even today. In 1250,

however, the Commune passed what amounted to a zoning law requiring that the height of no tower surpass 100 feet, and that those exceeding that height be truncated. ◆ Via dell' Oche

Within the Torre degli Adimali:

Ottorino ★★$$ Situated in an expansive space within the above-described medieval tower, this popular restaurant has an equally expansive menu of Tuscan specialties (*stracotto a Chianti*, beef cooked in *Chianti* wine), vegetarian dishes (*melanzane alla parmigiana*, the Italian eggplant-and-cheese classic), and such original dishes as *portafoglio Ottorino*, a delicious slice of veal stuffed with parmesan cheese and truffles. ◆ Closed Su. Via dell'Oche 12-16r. 218747, 215151

27 Alessi Paride The Orsanmichele of gastronomy, with 2 different functions on 2 different levels. The ground floor caters to the sweet tooth, selling such seasonal goodies as the dove-shaped Easter cake called *colomba* and the Christmas confections of *pandoro* and *panettone*, along with syrups and liqueurs. Downstairs is the best commercial wine cellar in town, displaying vintages by region, with a decided emphasis on Tuscany. Pick up a bottle of your favorite Brunello here. ◆ Closed W afternoon, Su, lunch. Via dell'Oche 27r. 214966

28 Hotel Brunelleschi $$$
Partially housed in a medieval church and a semicircular Byzantine tower which was once used as a women's prison, this recently opened hotel combines the best of Early Christian and Postmodern with its very upscale ambience in its own secret little piazza. ◆ Piazza Santa Elisabetta. 562068

29 Luisa il Corso The for-women-only version of the mother store on Via Roma, here heavy on the knitwear. ◆ Closed M morning, Su, lunch. Via del Corso 54-56r. 294374

30 Santa Margherita in Santa Maria de' Ricci (1508; facade 1611, **Gherardo Silvani**) An elaborately porticoed little church redone in Baroque style inside in 1769 by **Zanobi del Rosso**. The *Madonna de' Ricci* on the altar is a venerated image. ◆ Via del Corso

31 Zecchi The city's best selection of artists' materials, from paints and brushes to gold leaf and a rainbow of pigments—carmine red made from insects, amber varnish made from fossilized amber, malachite green made exclusively by Zecchi from the mineral, lapis lazuli imported from Afghanistan. ◆ Closed M morning, Su, lunch. Via dello Studio 19r. 211470

32 Pegna The Uffizi of food shops, with window after window and rack upon rack of Italian delicacies from olive oil to to sun-dried tomatoes to porcini mushrooms laid out in well organized, spacious, mouth-watering displays. ◆ Closed W afternoon, Su, lunch. Via dello Studio 8r. 282701

33 Palazzo Salviati (16th c) This imposing palazzo was built on the site of the houses of the **Portinari** family, whose daughter **Beatrice** captured **Dante**'s heart in the nearby **Badia Fiorentina**. Today it houses the **Banca Toscana**, and inside are a 14th-century fresco of the *Madonna and Child with Saints* and 16th-century frescoes by **Alessandro Allori**, including a lively cycle taken from *The Odyssey*. ◆ Via del Corso 6

34 Albergo Firenze $ Of the small, cheap hotels in Centro Storico, this is one of the better ones. What the rooms lack in charm they make up for with cleanliness and a location in the heart of Dante land. ◆ Piazza Donati 4. 214203

35 Cucciolo *Bomboloni*, freshly deep-fried pastries stuffed with custard or jam and dusted with sugar, are the specialty of this unassuming *pasticceria*, which in turn is always stuffed with appreciative Florentines. ◆ Closed Su. Via del Corso 25r. 287727

36 Le Mossacce ★★$$
Florentine restaurateurs have a penchant for giving themselves self-effacing names. This one means *rough*, but it might as well refer to the rustic Tuscan cuisine served alongside such relative rarities in Florence as good lasagne and *spezzatino* (veal in tomato sauce) in these packed premises. ◆ Closed Sa-Su, Aug. Via del Proconsolo 55r. 294361

37 Palazzo Nonfinito (Unfinished Palace) (1593, **Bernardo Buontalenti** and others) Begun for **Alessandro Strozzi**, the palace was never completed to its original scheme. Buontalenti was responsible for the ground floor, **Giovanni Battista Caccini** completed the next 2 to the designs of **Vincenzo Scamozzi**, and **Cigoli** designed the courtyard. Part of the palazzo houses Italy's first anthropological museum (**Museo Nazionale di Antropologia ed Etnologia**), established in 1869 while Florence was still the capital. These days it might as well be called the *unopened museum*, since access to its magnificently musty collection of shrunken heads and the like is the most whimsical of Florence's cultural institutions. ♦ Th-Sa, 3rd Su of month 9AM-1PM; closed July-Sep. Via del Proconsolo 12. 296449

38 Palazzo Pazzi-Quaratesi (1462-72, **Giuliano da Maiano**) A rustic palazzo designed for **Jacopo de' Pazzi**, who lived here but died up the street at the Bargello, where he was hung in 1478 for his instigatory role in the Pazzi Conspiracy. Go inside for a look at the arcaded courtyard. ♦ Via del Proconsolo 10

39 Grand Hotel Cavour $$$ After a seemingly endless renovation, the **Palazzo Strozzi-Ridolfi** (14th century) has finally reopened as a splendid, tastefully modern hotel. Smack in the center of town (as seen from the small roof garden, which has wonderfully intimate views of most of the major monuments), the hotel preserves an air of quiet thanks to the double-paned windows and the fact that its track is slightly less beaten than others. ♦ Via del Proconsolo 3. 210907

40 Casa e Museo di Dante (Dante House and Museum) A shrine, typically Florentine in its parsimony, to **Dante Alighieri**, whose family owned the group of houses (heavily restored) in which this museum of memorabilia has been installed. The lean collection—a few portraits, reproductions of **Botticelli**'s illustrations for *The Divine Comedy*, photos of places associated with Dante, editions of his work—makes one wonder whether the Florentines ever forgave the poet for reviling them. According to tradition, he was born here in 1295. ♦ Free. M-Tu, Th-Sa 9:30AM-12:30PM, 3:30-6:30PM; Su 9:30AM-12:30PM. Via Santa Margherita 1. 283343

41 Pennello ★★$$ Besides the usual Tuscan specialties, here groans an *abbon-dante* (pun intended—the place is also known as **Casa di Dante**) antipasti table filled with olives, salami, prosciutto and other delictables that offer a complete meal in themselves. ♦ Closed M evening, Su. Via Dante Alighieri 4r. No credit cards. 948848

42 Torre della Castagna (1282) A *pietra forte* medieval tower, once the home of the supreme magistrate of the **Priori delle Arti** guild, now housing the **Associazioni Nazionali Veterani e**

Centro Storico

Reduci Garibaldini, veterans of the **Garibaldi** campaigns, whose numbers must certainly be dwindling. ♦ Piazza San Martino 1

43 Pretura (13th c) Take a peek in the courtyard here, the former convent of the **Badia Fiorentina** and now the magistrate's court, for a look at the original facade of the Badia Fiorentina by **Arnolfo di Cambio**. ♦ Piazza San Martino 2

44 San Martino del Vescovo (989; rebuilt 1479) **Dante** supposedly married **Gemma Donati** in the original church on this site, whose plan faced the opposite direction. Inside is lots of *school of* art—school of **Ghirlandaio** frescoes, school of **Desiderio da Settignano** terracotta candelabra, school of **Perugino** *Madonna and Child.* ♦ Piazza San Martino

45 Da Ganino ★★★$$ One of the first of the younger-generation places in Florence to bring back the tradition of *cucina genuina* (in the sense of unpretentious), is Ganino (an understated sign says simply *Vini e Olii*—OK, so it's just a little pretentious). It offers a seasonal menu (year-round items are *risottino verde*, rice infused with spinach, and *strozzapreti strascicati*, *choked priests* or a fusilli-like pasta in a ragu sauce) in a simple setting of just 7 communal paper-covered tables. A few more spill out in the piazza during the warmer months. ♦ Closed Su, Aug. Piazza dei Cimatori 4r. 214125

The **Accademia della Crusca**, founded in Florence in 1583, was the first academy in the world to publish a dictionary of a modern language.

The world is made up of earth, air, fire and water—but there is another element—the Florentines.
Pope Boniface VIII

46 Tripperia ★★★$ *A Firenze c'è una trippaia* went a popular love song to a fetching *vendeuse* of tripe, a Florentine specialty and one of our favorite street eats. The delicacy (cow's stomach), stewed in an herb broth, is sold along with *lampredotto*, the fattiest part of the poor beast's intestine, at this spotless stainless-steel outdoor stand. They are eaten served on waxed paper or in sandwich form, accompanied by the traditional garnish of salt and pepper, ground red pepper, or *salsa verde* (a green sauce of parsley). Blue- and white-

Centro Storico

collar types alike stop by for a snack of either innard. ♦ In front of Via Dante Alighieri 16. No credit cards. No phone

47 I Maschereri The long-dormant Venetian art of mask-making has its Florentine counterpart in this shop, which the owners claim opened in Florence even before Carnival was revived in Venice a few years back. The masks go well beyond the traditional Venetian *commedia dell'arte* characters, and include imaginative designs based on Florentine Renaissance patterns, as well as the kitsch icon of **Michelangelo**'s *David*, and rather drugged-out variations on sun and moon themes. ♦ Via dei Tavolini 13r. 213823

47 Perchè No!... And why not, indeed, try one of the ice creams in this narrow, lively space. One of Florence's oldest ice-cream emporia prides itself on its yogurt-flavored *gelato* and a *semifreddo* (gelato fluffed with whipped cream) version of *zuppa inglese* (made with spongy cookies and liqueur). ♦ Closed Tu. Via dei Tavolini 19r. 298969

48 Paoli ★★$$ Vaulted ceilings frescoed in Neo-Gothic abandon set the amusingly kitsch scene for *atmospheric* dining in the former storerooms of a 15th-century palazzo. It's a bit a matter of style over substance, though the food is substantial enough, best appreciated if one happens to be in a Gothic kind of mood, say having just come from Orsanmichele. The basically Tuscan menu offers such dishes as *pollastrino alla griglia* (grilled chicken), supplemented by Italian staples like *scaloppine alla boscaiola* (veal scaloppine in a spicy tomato sauce) and its very own *taglierini alla Paoli* (pasta with prosciutto, peas and mushrooms in a cream sauce). ♦ Closed Tu. Via dei Tavolini 12r. 216215

49 Cristy An aggressively Postmodern wood-and-glass facade visually grabs you by the collar, only to caress same with an array of soft silk cravats and scarves inside. ♦ Via dei Calzaiuoli 62r. 215085

50 Hotel dei Calzaiuoli $$$ Recently modernized in its dignified 19th-century palazzo, location rather than luxury is the byword of this small, pleasantly furnished modern hotel in the heart of Centro Storico. ♦ Via dei Calzaiuoli 6. 212456

51 Coin The latest Italian department store chain to open a branch in Florence, providing a change of pace from the local mercantile tradition of specialty shops. While not on a par with Macy's or Harrod's, it's a cut above the others, offering a wide selection of its own label of medium-priced clothing as well as cosmetics and other items. ♦ Closed M morning, Su. Via dei Calzaiuoli 56r. 210131

52 Il Granduca This *gelateria* or ice-cream parlor is an atonal symphony of harsh brass and stone design, sweetened by 32 flavors made fresh daily. Among them is a rare Florentine appearance of Sicilian *cassata siciliana*, a creamy white gelato dotted with candied fruits and bits of chocolate. ♦ M-Tu, Th-Su 10AM-midnight. Via dei Calzaiuoli 57r. 298112

53 Beltrami This shop and the Beltrami across the street at Via dei Calzaiuoli 44r (212418) are the 2 original gleaming links in the Italian chain of high-fashion shoes and leather goods for men and women, more interesting than the clothing. Its Florentine origin sets the tone for excellent quality in leather and craftsmanship, as well as some surprisingly imaginative design. ♦ Closed M morning, Su, lunch. Via dei Calzaiuoli 31r and 44r. 214030. Also at: Piazza dell'Olio 3r

54 Orsanmichele Talk about mixed-use architecture. This odd Gothic box, built on the site of the 8th-century oratory of San Michele in Orto, had an even odder function when it was built in the 14th century by **Neri di Fioravante, Benci di Cione** and **Francesco Talenti** (all of whom also worked on the Duomo). The ground floor, which had become a covered market, was converted into an oratory; the upstairs housed a communal granary. The ruling Guelph party assigned the decoration of the exterior, begun in the next century, to various guilds.

Orsanmichele combines the essence of much of Florence in this guild-ed cage: the practicality of using a house of worship to store grain, the glorification of mercantilism in the guild's sponsorship of the decoration, and the early Renaissance genius of the decoration itself. (Not to mention the city's trick of moving its sculptures around in a gargantuan sleight-of-hand game. Many of the originals are now indoors in museums, with copies in the niches here.) Counterclockwise from the far end of Via Calzaiuoli, the sculpture is as follows: Via Calzaiuoli side: [1] **Ghiberti**'s *St. John the Baptist* for the Calimala (cloth importers); [2] **Verrocchio**'s *Doubting Thomas*, with medallion by **Luca della Robbia** above, for the Mercantazia (merchants' tribunal); [3] **Giambologna**'s *St. Luke* for the Guidici e Notai (judges and notaries). Via Orsanmichele side:

[4] **Ciuffagini**'s *St. Peter* for the Beccai (butchers); [5] **Nanni di Banco**'s *St. Philip* for the Conciapelli (tanners); [6] Nanni di Banco's *Four Crowned Saints*, with medallion by Luca della Robbia above, for the Maestri di Pietre e Legname (masons and carpenters); [7] bronze copy of **Donatello**'s *St. George* (marble original in the Bargello) sculpture and relief for the Corazzai (armorers). Via dell'Arte della Lana side: [8] Ghiberti's *St. Matthew* for the Cambio (bankers); Ghiberti's *St. Stephen* (it replaced the statue by Andrea Pisano now in the Duomo Museum), for the Lana (wool guild); [9] Nanni di Banco's *St. Eligius* for the Maniscalchi (smiths). Via dei Lamberti side: [10] Donatello's *St. Mark* for the Linaiuoli e Rigattieri (linen drapers), [11] **Niccolò di Piero Lamberti**'s *St. James the Great* for the Pellicciai (furriers); [12] **Piero Tedesco** or Niccolò di Piero Lamberti's *Madonna della Rosa*, with medallion by Luca della Robbia above, for the Medici e Speziali (doctors and druggists); [13] **Baccio da Montelupo**'s *St. John the Evangelist* (it replaced a 14th-century statue now in the Innocenti Gallery) with medallion by **Andrea della Robbia** above, for the Setaiuoli e Orafi (silk merchants and goldsmiths).

The interior, still used as a church, has stained-glass windows based on designs by **Lorenzo Monaco**, and an elaborate 14th-century tabernacle by **Andrea Orcagna**, surrounding a *Madonna* by **Bernardo Daddi**. For access to the granary, go to the 14th-century **Palagio dell'Arte della Lana** (the exquisite palazzo that once housed the Wool Guild) next door. Crossing over a connecting bridge back to the rooms known as the **Saloni di Orsanmichele**, there are marvelous views of the heart of Florence, once the privilege of medieval mice. ◆ Daily 8AM-noon, 3-7PM. Via dei Calzaiuoli. 284715

55 San Carlo dei Lombardi (begun 1349, **Neri di Fioravante** and **Benci di Cione**; completed 1404, **Simone Talenti**) This simple church, its facade cut into golden *pietra forte* stone like a giant Romanesque cookie, is an oasis of serenity amid the bustle of the pedestrian traffic outside. Inside, its *Deposition* by **Niccolò di Pietro Gerini** was borrowed from Orsanmichele across the street. ◆ Via dei Calzaiuoli, opposite Orsanmichele

56 Vini del Chianti ★★$ Another of Florence's typical watering holes, this one run by 2 brothers whose *Chianti* is accompanied by a wide selection of sandwiches of cheese, salami and various delectable spreads. Souvenir *Chianti* flasks, wrapped in rice straw as in days of old, are also on sale in many sizes. ◆ Closed Su. Via dei Cimatori 38r. 2396096

Unlike the Venetians, the Florentines will never volunteer to show a sight to a passing stranger. They do not care to exhibit their city; the monuments are there—let the foreigners find them.

Mary McCarthy

57 GeCaf The king of coffee is dead, long live the king. Florence's beloved **Caffè Manarese** has been under new management for some time now, but the old signs, strangely shrouded in bubble wrap coverings, burn as brightly as ever. A loyal if confused clientele keeps coming back for snacks of pizza and sandwiches. Better yet is its daily grind of brew and beans, still stored aloft and sent scuttling down the original brass shoots. ◆ Closed Su. Via Arte della Lana 12r. 218934

58 Farmacia Molteni The neon sign in the window of this ancient building says *SEMPRE*

APERTA, meaning if one needs a quick fix of pharmaceuticals any time of the day or night, this is the place. And a lovely one it is too, with 19th-century ceiling frescoes and gilding intact. The *dottoressa* behind the counter says **Dante** studied here when the place formed part of the university, so maybe the Florentine authorities are trying to make up for *keeping him out* by *keeping them open*. ◆ Via dei Calzaiuoli 7r. 289490, 215472

59 Mody Time A bit of timely modern design in old Florence. Mody sells watches by such Italian makers as Lorenz and Sector, along with clever clocks for wall, floor and furniture by L'Eta del Giorno, Anteprima and Vega. The latter's wares are especially attractive, made from marble cut in clever geometric patterns. ◆ Closed M morning, Su, lunch. Via della Condotta 22r. 287029

60 Alessandro Bizzarri The old jars in the shop window (not to mention its name) are an intriguing invitation to Florence's only spice shop, a musty, family-run business which has been selling a medieval mix of spices, gums, extracts and essences since 1842. ◆ Closed M morning, Su, lunch. Via della Condotta 32r. 211580

61 Libreria Condotta 29 In addition to the usual tourist fare, this shop carries an intelligent selection of art books as well as tasteful prints, posters and postcards. ◆ Closed M morning, Su, lunch. Via della Condotta 29r. 213421

62 Badia Fiorentina (Santa Maria Assunta) A 10th-century Benedictine church, remodeled in the 13th century. It was here that **Dante** first saw **Beatrice**, and that **Boccaccio** lectured on Dante (in the present-day **Pandolfini Chapel**, then the site of the church of **Santo Stefano**). The church was rebuilt in the 17th century by **Matteo Segaloni**, who frescoed its ceiling. Also inside are **Filippino Lippi**'s *St. Bernard's Vision of the Madonna* and works by **Mino da Fiesole**, including his monument to **Count Ugo**. ◆ Corner of Via del Proconsolo and Via Dante Alighieri

---

Restaurants/Nightlife: Red   **Hotels:** Blue
Shops/Parks: Green   **Sights/Culture:** Black

63 Bargello (Museo del Bargello or Museo Nazionale) (1255; enlarged 1325; 1345, **Benci di Cione**) This fearful 14th-century palace was Florence's original Town Hall, then the residence of the city's chief magistrate or *Podesta*, then of its police chief or *Bargello*. It was also the site of public hangings, and to make sure the people learned their lesson, artists frescoed gruesome scenes of the executions on the outside walls. Sometimes they were even given public commissions, as when **Andrea del Sarto** was granted the task of depicting the hanging of the Pazzi

Centro Storico

conspirators here (**Botticelli** got to decorate the Palazzo Vecchio with the same subject). **Leonardo da Vinci** made a famous drawing for his own purposes, now in Bayonne, of one of the conspirators hanging from the window, making careful notes about his fashion statement: *tawny cap, black satin vest, black lined sleeveless coat, turquoise blue jacket lined with fox, collar appliquéd with black and red velvet, black hose.*

Today the Bargello houses the most important collection of Renaissance sculpture in the world. Have a look at the arcaded courtyard before going into the ground floor gallery. It contains **Michelangelo**'s *Pitti Tondo, Brutus* and *Drunken Bacchus,* as well as **Jacopo Sansovino**'s response to it, his *Bacchus.* The colorful Mannerist sculptor-goldsmith **Benevenuto Cellini** (whose *Autobiography* is a delightful definition of the pseudo-Italian word *braggadocio*) is here represented by his model for the *Perseus* in Piazza della Signoria as well as *Perseus and Andromeda* from the actual

sculpture's base. He attributed the shape of *Narcissus* to a flaw in the marble rather than an artistic conceit. Also on display are the exquisitely grandiose bust of **Cosimo I** by Cellini and *Victory of Florence over Pisa* by **Giambologna**.

Upstairs in the loggia are Giambologna's *Mercury* and his bronze menagerie made for the Medici. The **Salone del Consiglio Generale** has 2 panels from the Baptistry competition, *The Sacrifice of Isaac* as interpreted by **Filippo Brunelleschi** and **Lorenzo Ghiberti** (the latter artist won). Among the **Donatellos** are *St. George* from Orsanmichele, his marble and bronze *Davids,* this last the first nude since the times of the ancients and in keeping with the Classical appreciation of young male flesh. Young female flesh is represented by **Desiderio da Settignano**'s *Pensive Girl,* equally sweet are the various **della Robbias** in this and the rooms on the next floor. Before ascending, take a look at the large collection of decorative art.

The first room on the next floor has Cellini's *Ganymede* as well as the Roman Baroque sculptor **Gian Lorenzo Bernini**'s bust of **Costanza Bonarelli.** The **Sala di Verrocchio** contains that artist's *David,* a less willowy solution than Donatello's treatment of the subject. In addition to **Antonio Pollaiuolo**'s *Hercules and Antaeus,* the room contains a number of memorable portrait busts, **Mino da Fiesole**'s *Piero de' Medici* being the first in the genre since Roman times. Finally, as its name implies, the **Sala del Camino o dei Bronzetti** houses Italy's finest collection of small bronzes, displayed before a *pietra serena* chimneypiece by **Benedetto da Rovezzano**.
♦ Admission. Tu-Sa 9AM-2PM; Su 9AM-1PM. Via del Proconsolo 4. 210801

Bargello

64 Vinaio Carlo Yet another tiny wine shop for a little tipple with the locals if your elbow is so inclined. ♦ Closed Su. Via dell'Anguillara 70r. No phone

San Firenze

65 San Filippo Neri and San Firenze (design 1715, **Francesco Zanobi del Rosso**; built 1772-75, **Ferdinando Ruggieri**) Any wonder why the proud natives of Florence would corrupt San Fiorenzo to San Firenze? His ancient oratorio stood on the spot now occupied by the church of San Filippo Neri, the left of these twin churches connected by a Neoclassical palazzo, a rare and rather restrained example of Baroque in Florence. On the right is San Firenze, built as an oratorio for the order known as the Filippini, who commissioned the ensemble. Today the palazzo and oratorio are occupied by the **Law Courts**. ♦ Piazza San Firenze

66 Hotel Bernini Palace $$$$ Guest rooms with views of the Palazzo Vecchio, and a frescoed breakfast room where members of Parliament used to meet when Florence was the capital of Italy are 2 of the many niceties of this recently opened, surprisingly sophisticated hotel attracting an upscale crowd of businesspeople and discerning tourists. ♦ Piazza San Firenze 29. 278621

67 Loggia del Grano (1619, **Giulio Parigi**) As you might have guessed by the bust in the middle arch, this space was commissioned by **Cosimo II**. It was originally a granary, but Florentines know it best as the entrance to the movie theater **Capitol Cinema**. ♦ Via dei Castellani, corner Via dei Neri

68 Palazzo Castellani This medieval palace once housed the **Accademia della Crusca** (the Bran Academy), one of those typically esoteric Florentine societies, in this case a linguistic fraternity dedicated to separating the wheat from the chaff in the Italian language. (They would certainly have their work cut out for them in modern-day Florence, home of shops operating *no stop* and *Self Service* restaurants selling *cheeseburghers* and *wurstel*.) The palazzo now houses the **Medici** family's large collection of

scientific instruments, including the lens with which **Galileo** discovered the satellites of Jupiter, which he dutifully named after his Medici patrons. ♦ M, W, F 9:30AM-1PM, 2-5PM. Piazza dei Giudici 1. 293493

69 Palazzo Gondi (1490-1501, **Giuliano da Sangallo**) Another fine monumental Renaissance palace in private hands. Peek into the courtyard to see the fountain and Roman statue, perhaps the spoils from the Roman amphitheater that formerly stood nearby. ♦ Piazza San Firenze 2

Within Palazzo Gondi:

Bar-Pasticceria San Firenze One of the oldest pastry shops in Florence, this one has a tantalizing display of pastries and cookies, including fresh fruit tarts in the warmer months. ♦ M-Sa 7AM-10PM. No credit cards. 211426

70 Piazza della Signoria The piazza has been the center of civic life for centuries, and there's nothing like the sight of 2 elegantly dressed Florentines walking arm-in-arm in deep discussion here to catapult one's spirit back to the Middle Ages. Called an *open-air museum* (though what isn't in outdoor Florence?), the piazza and the **Loggia dei Lanzi** are filled with an impressive collection of monumental sculpture celebrating the schizoid Florentine fascination with tyrants and death to same. From north to south, the assemblage begins with **Giambologna**'s equestrian monument to **Cosimo I** and his attributed bronze figures decorating the base of **Bartolommeo Ammannati**'s **Neptune Fountain**. (Much derided by Florentines, it gave rise to the taunt *Ammannato, Ammannato, che bel marmo hai rovinato!*—what beautiful marble you've ruined!—and to this day is known locally as *Il Biancone*, the Great White One.) Then come copies of **Donatello**'s *Judith and Holofernes* (original inside the Signoria) and his *Marzocco*, the heraldic lion of Florence (original in the Bargello), and **Michelangelo**'s *David* (original in the Accademia), and **Bandinelli**'s *Hercules and Cacus* (original here, since the town fathers don't seem to feel it's worth sheltering from the elements, and most art historians seem to agree).

The piazza was the subject of a recent uproar when it became an open-air quarry. What began as a routine cleaning of its paving stones led to an archeological excavation of a Roman and medieval site beneath. When it came time to repave the piazza, the stones had disappeared, allegedly into the driveways of some wealthy local residents. Furthermore, the stones had been ruined in the cleaning (shades of Ammannati) and no longer fit in place. Florentines wanted to take the opportunity to pave the space in red brick and gray *pietra serena*, as it appears in 15th- and 16th-century paintings, but instead the authorities gave them a literal cover-up—too-perfect rectangular *pietra serena* paving stones which hardly live up to their name. They are the hottest scandal

Centro Storico

since **Savonarola** was burned in the piazza in 1498 (a granite disk, intact for the moment, marks the spot), just a few years after he incited the Florentines to make the original bonfires of their vanities in Piazza della Signoria. ♦ Piazza della Signoria

71 Uguccioni Palace (Palazzo Uguccioni) (1550) **Mariotto di Zanobi** built this palazzo, according to tradition to the designs of **Michelangelo** or **Antonio da Sangallo**. From its balcony, a bust of **Cosimo I** oversees the piazza, including his equestrian monument just below. ♦ Piazza della Signoria 7

72 Il Cavallino ★★★$$ Right on Piazza della Signoria near **Giambologna**'s equestrian monument, Cavallino is not only convenient to the surrounding sights but actually one of the best restaurants in town, serving reliable Tuscan specialties such as the ribboned pasta called *pappardelle* and the juicy steak called *bistecca alla fiorentina* to a clientele of discriminating locals and tourists. It is also one of the few good restaurants in Florence open on Sunday. ♦ Closed Tu evening, W, Aug. Via delle Farine 6r. 215818

73 Raccolta d'Arte Moderna Alberto della Ragione (Alberto della Ragione Collection of Modern Art) A small museum of modern Italian art by artists of local and international reputation. The former include **Ottone Rosai**, beloved by Florentines for his charming views of **Via San Leonardo** (for tourists, the paintings serve as a nice enticement to stroll down the lovely country road); among the latter are a few works by **Giorgio De Chirico, Giorgio Morandi** and **Marino Marini**. ♦ M, W-Sa 9AM-2PM; Su, holidays 8AM-1PM. Piazza della Signoria 5. 283078

74 Bar Perseo If Rivoire is closed or crowded, this is an alternative for coffee or *gelato*. It also sells Brazilian cigarrillos and stamps for the postcards purchased at the newsstand in front. ♦ Closed M. Piazza della Signoria 16r. 2398316

75 Newsstand Besides selling an ample selection of international newspapers and magazines to the tourist throngs, this understandably mercurial *giornalaio* or newsstand also has a nice souvenir video about Florence (constantly being previewed on a monitor) and

stocks the best selection of postcards in the city. There are cards of everyone's favorite Florentine scenes and works of art here, from risqué details of *David*'s anatomy to stigmata on the most pious of saints. ♦ M-Sa 8AM-8PM; Su 8AM-1PM. Piazza della Signoria

76 Palazzo Vecchio (Palazzo della Signoria) (begun 1298, **Arnolfo di Cambio**) This embodiment of the imposing, rustic side to the Florentine character was originally built to house and protect the ministry of the republican government, the Signoria. In 1540, **Cosimo I** brazenly set up house here, moving in from the Medici Palace. After ten years, wife **Eleanor of Toledo** talked him into transferring the official residence to the Pitti Palace. Ever since, it has been known as the Palazzo Vecchio, or Old Palace. Under Cosimo's reign, it was decorated with sycophantic alacrity by **Giorgio Vasari**, who virtually became the court painter. He indiscreetly mythologized the entire Medici line with help from some of the finest artists available, primarily late Mannerists. The modern visitor should exercise more discretion in visiting the palazzo, however, since unless you're a specialist (or worse), it is a waste of energy to try to sample all the often over-ripe fruits of Vasari's labors.

The courtyard contains a copy of **Verrocchio**'s bronze *Putto* in the fountain (the original is upstairs in the **Cancelleria**), surrounded by frescoes of Austria which Vasari commissioned to honor **Francesco de' Medici**'s marriage to **Joanna of Austria**. If you're wondering why the throngs here don't seem to be admiring the works of art but

passing through with disgruntled looks on their faces, it's because the palace now serves its original function as **City Hall**—a more immediate and useful function might be the public toilets in this area.

Upstairs is the **Salone dei Cinquecento**, a gigantic room frescoed with Florentine battle scenes—all victorious, of course. Of more interest are the statues: in the center of the longest wall is **Michelangelo**'s *Victory*; on the opposite wall is **Giambologna**'s *Virtue Overcoming Vice*; and scattered throughout are the almost comically labored *Labors of Hercules* by **Vincenzo de' Rossi**. A door to the right of the entrance leads to the **Studiolo di Francesco I**, which Vasari provided as a hideout for Cosimo I's son Francesco. The walls represent the 4 elements—earth, air, fire and water. (It was Pope Boniface who remarked that the world is made up of 5 elements—the above, plus Florentines.) They are covered with a late Mannerist extravaganza, including **Bronzino**'s portraits of Francesco's mom and dad, Cosimo I and Eleanor of Toledo, at either end of the room. They presumably kept an eye on young Francesco as he meditated over his paintings and bronzes on the subject of science.

Of interest on the next floor are the private apartments of Eleanor of Toledo, among which is a chapel frescoed by Bronzino. The **Cappella della Signoria** contains an *Annunciation* by **Ridolfo Ghirlandaio**, whose father **Domenico** frescoed the **Sala dei Gigli**. (The *giglio*, which means lily but actually depicts an iris, is a symbol of the city, and City Hall marriages downstairs always end with a bouquet of them for the bride.) The Sala dei Gigli dates from before the Medici occupation of the palace and sticks with mere classical and religious subjects. Off it are the sculptures *Judith and Holofernes* by **Donatello** (in the **Sala dell'Udienza**) and Verrocchio's original *Putto* (in the Cancelleria). Before leaving, take the stairs in the Sala dei Gigli to the tower for a guard's-eye view of the Piazza della Signoria. ♦ M-F 9AM-7PM; Su, holidays 8AM-1PM. Piazza della Signoria. 27681

77 Galleria degli Uffizi (Uffizi Gallery) (1560, **Giorgio Vasari**) Originally commissioned as a building for offices (*uffici* in Italian, corrupted to *uffizi* by the Florentines) by **Grand Duke Cosimo I** from Vasari, construction was completed by **Bernardo Buontalenti** under **Francesco I**, who turned the top floor into a museum of art and curiosities and installed artists' and artisans' studios there. Vasari's first architectural commission, the building is a masterful blend of Classical elements with the Tuscanisms of *pietra dura* (a soft, lead-colored stone from nearby Fiesole) and white stucco walls. The Medici family put together the collection, whose strong points are paintings from the Florentine Renaissance as well as works by Flemish and Venetian masters, and an impressive array of antique sculpture. The last of the Medici line, **Anna Maria Ludovica**, donated it to the people of Florence in 1737.

The most important single museum in Italy, the Uffizi is suprisingly manageable, laid out more or less chronologically in a series of human-scale rooms. It is also the most crowded museum in the country. To avoid the squeeze, try to visit it during the lunch hour or late afternoon. Otherwise, be resigned to packs of raucous and enraptured Italian schoolchildren gathered for indoctrination in the national trait of living intimately with great works of art, and, at the other end of the scale, university students clustered around pompous and pedantic art

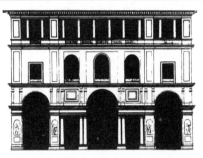

historians—both engaging if distracting subsidiary exhibits in their own right. As with most Italian museums, but particularly frustrating at this one, don't expect every room to be open.

Stop for a look at **Andrea del Castagno**'s frescoes of *Illustrious Men* (mostly Florentines) next to the ticket office in the remains of the 11th-century church of **San Piero Scheraggio**, which Vasari incorporated into his building. Across from the elevator is a fresco of the *Annunciation* by **Botticelli**. Vasari's monumental staircase leads to the prints and drawings department, which usually has an exhibition or two from its rich collection mounted. (If the staircase seems too monumental to the task, take the elevator to the right of it, pretending not to understand the sign that says it's for staff only.)

The painting galleries are on the top floor. Walking from *sala* to *sala* (room to room), don't overlook what may seem to be decorative background elements—lively ceiling frescoes, Flemish tapestries, antique sculpture. The Uffizi is the most conducive place in Florence to the *Stendhal syndrome*, so take a break now and then to gaze out the windows at Florence and the surrounding countryside, or into the courtyard when it is filled with a flower show in the spring.

Highlights of the Galleries:

Sala II Three imposing altarpieces depicting the *Madonna Enthroned* (*Maesta* in Italian) open the show majestically. On the right side of the room is the earliest version, by **Cimabue**. He is considered the father of modern painting, though his panel still shows close ties to Byzantine painting in the Classical stylization of its angels and drapery. In the center of the room is the more realistic (and, for its day, revolutionary) interpretation by Cimabue's alleged pupil, **Giotto**. (*Cimabue thought that he held the field in painting*, writes **Dante** in *Purgatory, but now Giotto is acclaimed and his fame obscured*.) To the left is a work by Cimabue's contemporary in nearby Siena, **Duccio di Buoninsegna**, whose attention to graceful humanity, rich color and surface pattern was seminal in the Sienese school.

Sala III What **Duccio** sowed may be seen here in this room of Sienese pictures. **Simone Martini**'s *Annunciation* is full of grace, whereas **Pietro Lorenzetti**'s *Madonna in Glory* and his

Centro Storico

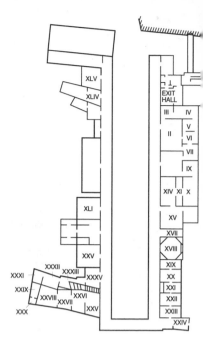

brother **Ambrogio Lorenzetti**'s *Presentation in the Temple* and *Story of St. Nicholas* continue the Sienese preoccupation with surface pattern, here combined with an awareness of **Giotto**'s sense of space and solidity.

Sala IV An assemblage of what used to be referred to as *primitives*. What these panels by followers of **Giotto** as a whole lack in artistic innovation they make up for with the intimate and intense spirituality of the era (the 14th century), their saints performing various empassioned acts before gently glowing gold-leaf backgrounds.

Sala V-VI These 2 rooms bring the Gothic period to a close with **Lorenzo Monaco**'s *Coronation of the Virgin* and *Adoration of the Magi*. In **Gentile da Fabriano**'s treatment of the same subject (*Adoration of the Magi*) across the room, the Gothic marches out with charming pageantry.

Sala VII Recently reevaluated and acclaimed because of the restoration of their frescoes for the **Brancacci** chapel in Florence's **Carmine** church, **Masaccio** and **Masolino**, whose work is seen here in the collaborative *Madonna with Child and St. Anne*, are the trendiest 15th-century artists in this room. But there are other masterpieces, namely a rare picture by **Domenico Veneziano** (*Sacra Conversazione*), *Federico da Montefeltro and Battista Sforza* by Veneziano's pupil **Piero della Francesca**, and the epic *Battle of San Romano* by **Paolo Uccello**. Uccello was obsessed with perspective, a proposition which becomes all the more frightening when you consider that this busy picture, bristling with lances and fantastically colored horses, is but one of 3 panels that once decorated the Medici Palace. The other 2 sections are now in the Louvre and London's National Gallery.

Sala VIII Paintings by **Masaccio**'s pupil **Filippo Lippi** indicate a return to the tender and decorative style of the Gothic period.

Sala IX Paintings by the brothers **Antonio** and **Piero Pollaiuolo**, particularly *The Feats of Hercules* by Antonio, show a strong interest in the Renaissance study of human anatomy. **Botticelli**'s *Finding of the Body of Holofernes* has some of Antonio's energy, though his *Return of Judith* derives more from his master **Filippo Lippi**.

Sala X-XIV **Botticelli**'s—and the Uffizi's—most famous paintings are in these rooms, broken down into one large space. They are *The Birth of Venus* and *Primavera*. The former is a fairly straightforward representation of the goddess of the sea, received by a nymph and the personified wind. *Primavera* (Spring) is a flowery Renaissance interpretation of Classical mythology. (From right to left, Zephyr, Chloe, Flora, the Three Graces and Mercury are all represented.) In addition to the other Botticellis in the room are 2 Flemish masterpieces, **Hugo van der Goes**' *Portinari Altarpiece* and **Roger van der Weyden**'s *Entombment of Christ*, as well as works by **Domenico Ghirlandaio**, **Filippino Lippi** and **Lorenzo di Credi**.

Sala XV Tuscany's own **Leonardo da Vinci** is represented by his sketch for the *Adoration of the Magi*, as well as an attributed *Annunciation* and confirmed angel (the one in profile) in his master **Verrochio**'s *Baptism of Christ*. Other noteworthy works are **Luca Signorelli**'s *Crucifixion* and the *Pieta* by **Perugino**, **Raphael**'s master.

Sala XVII (Access from the Tribune, often closed) Known as the **Room of the Hermaphrodite**, the eponymous sculpture here is a Hellenistic piece placed among other bits of Classical sculpture.

Sala XVIII **Buontalenti** designed this octagonal (like the Baptistry) room, known as *La Tribuna* or The Tribune. It is made of lavish materials that represent the 4 elements—lapis lazuli for air, mother-of-pearl for water, red walls for fire, green *pietra dura* or precious stone floors for earth. It was meant to showcase the highlights of the Medici collection, especially the *Medici Venus*, a Roman copy of a Greek original, which caused longing sighs during the Grand Tour era. It is a veritable temple to Mannerist portraiture of the Medici, by **Vasari, Bronzino** and **Jacopo Pontormo**. Another Mannerist, **Rosso Fiorentino**, painted the delightful little *Musical Angel*, one of our favorite postcards.

Sala XIX Notice **Luca Signorelli**'s *Holy Family* (there's a similar composition by **Michelangelo** in Room 25), and **Perugino**'s *Madonna* and *Portrait of Francesco delle Opere*.

Sala XX German Renaissance painting in all its intensity is exemplified by **Lucas Cranach**'s *Adam and Eve*, and **Dürer**'s treatment of the same subject, as well as his *Adoration of the Magi* and *Portrait of the Artist's Father*.

Sala XXI The beginnings of important Venetian painting are seen here in **Giovanni Bellini**'s *Sacred Allegory*.

Sala XXII More northerners: **Hans Holbein the Younger**'s *Portrait of Sir Richard Southwell*, and **Albrecht Altdorfer**'s *Martyrdom of St. Florian* and *Departure of St. Florian*.

Sala XXIII **Correggio**'s *Rest on the Flight to Egypt* and religious works by his master, the northern Italian painter **Andrea Mantegna**.

Sala XXIV The **Cabinet of Miniatures** is an example of the kind of curiosities collectors collected in times past.

Sala XXV This houses **Michelangelo**'s only painting in Florence, the *Doni Tondo* (a *tondo* or round painting of the Holy Family made for the Doni family), which through its strongly modeled and muscular forms of figures of both sexes shows the artist's clear preference for... sculpture. Its garish colors were meant to disturb, and inspired Florentine painters **Fiorentino** (his violent *Moses Defending the Daughters of Jethro* is in this room) and **Pontormo** to begin working in the style later known as Mannerism.

Sala XXVI A moment of serenity here with **Raphael**'s *Madonna of the Goldfinch*, which owes its restful pyramidal composition to Leonardo. The other Virgin, *Madonna of the Harpies*, is by **Andrea del Sarto**. Raphael is also represented by the *Portrait of Pope Leo X*, a Medici.

Sala XXVII A high-pitched frenzy of early Florentine Mannerism, with **Pontormo**'s vivid *Supper at Emmaus* and **Bronzino**'s *Holy Family*. The movement's counterpart in Siena is represented, albeit weakly, by **Domenico Beccafumi**'s *Holy Family*.

Sala XXVIII A salon of **Titians**, invitingly presided over by the sensuous *Venus of Urbino*. *Flora* and *Eleanora Gonzaga della Rovere* are part of the lustrous and illustrious company.

Sala XXIX Central Italian Mannerism, less spiritual than the Tuscan but equally contorted and distorted, is here typified by **Parmigianino**'s *Madonna of the Long Neck*.

Sala XXX Emilian painting, with works by **Battista Dossi** and **Dosso Dossi**.

Sala XXXI-XXXIV Venetian and French painting. Next to Room 34 is the **Vasari Corridor** (Corridoio Vasariano), built with Vasari's usual fast hand in 5 months to link the Uffizi with the **Pitti Palace** via the **Ponte Vecchio**. Try to get an appointment to make the crossing, which is as much fun in itself as it is to see its display of 17th- and 18th-century works, as well as a gallery of self-portraits extending to the 20th century.

Sala XXXV Umbrian and Venetian painting, also the Venetian-trained **El Greco**.

Exit Hall But there's still more to see in the galleries, so for the moment peek in for a look at the *Wild Boar*, a Roman copy of a Greek original. It was copied again by **Pietro Tacca** for his fountain at the **Mercato Nuovo**. Come back here at the end of the visit for a grand descent down **Buontalenti**'s staircase.

Sala XLI **Van Dyck** and **Rubens**, among them the latter's *Portrait of Isabella Brant*.

Sala XLII The **Sala della Niobe** is named after the Roman sculptures of *Niobe and Her Children*, here ogled incongruously by a collection of 20th-century self-portraits of artists from around the world.

Sala XLIII Back in 17th-century Italy, displayed are some of **Caravaggio**'s earthy and realistic responses to the squeamishness of Mannerism—the mad *Medusa*, decadent *Bacchus* and emotionally charged *Sacrifice of Isaac*. There are also the more bucolic *Summer Diversion* by **Guercino** and *Seaport with Villa Medici* (this villa is at the top of the Spanish Steps in Rome) by **Claude Lorraine**.

Sala XLIV Dutch painting, with 2 self-portraits by **Rembrandt** bookending his early and later years.

Sala XLV The collection ends with a Rococo flourish of paintings by **Tiepolo, Canaletto, Guardi, Chardin** and **Goya**.

To recuperate from this maximum-strength exposure to the *Stendhal syndrome*, take refreshment in the museum bar at the end of the corridor, overlooking Piazza della Signoria from the roof of the Loggia dei Lanzi. ◆ Admission. Tu-Sa 9AM-7PM; Su, holidays 9AM-1PM. Piazzale degli Uffizi. 218341

78 Antico Fattore ★★$$ The *old farmer* of the name doesn't really exist, but his spirit lives on in the rustic country cooking (try the classic Tuscan white-bean soup, *ribollita*) in an informal setting to match. ◆ Closed Sa (summer); M, Su (winter); Aug. Via Lambertesca 1-3r. No credit cards. 261225

Restaurants/Nightlife: Red   **Hotels:** Blue
Shops/Parks: Green   **Sights/Culture:** Black

79 Il Vecchio Armadio If you need to dress like an American for some reason, this is the place.

Centro Storico

This store is well-named (*the old closet*) if your boudoir consists of clothes of the army surplus or *American Graffiti* variety. If that's the look you like—quite stylish among gilded Florentine youth and increasingly difficult to obtain in its country of origin—you're in for some *Happy Days* here. There are also some European goods on occasion. ♦ Closed M morning, Su, lunch. Via Lambertesca 19r. 217286

80 Matassini Friends who have an eye for Bulgari, Cartier and the like tip their hats to the Matassini sisters, who have a knack for knocking off the spirit rather than the letter (hence the lawsuits) of the big-name jewelry designers. ♦ Closed M morning, Su, lunch. Via Lambertesca 20r. 212897

81 Monkey Business
★★$$ Are the giant tusks on the elephant at the entrance of this trendy bar/restaurant an arcane sign that the inventive cuisine inside is Tuscan-inspired? Some dishes  could be pinpointed even more accurately to Florence, such as *risotto alla Brunelleschi*—risotto with funghi porcini mushrooms piled high like the architect's Duomo, covered with prosciutto and ribs of asparagus. Still more nominally local is the *filetto dei fiaccheraio*, named after the carriage-drivers around the corner in Piazza della Signoria—beef filet sautéed in red wine and served with green peppers. ♦ Closed Su. Chiasso dei Baroncelli 11. 288219

82 Loggia dei Lanzi (1376-82, **Benci di Cione, Simone di Francesco Talenti**) On the south side of the Piazza della Signoria is the Loggia dei Lanzi, an arcaded space designed for public ceremonies in the 14th century and last used as such to receive Queen Elizabeth II. **Michelangelo**, with the same eye for symmetry he used to rework Piazza Campidoglio in Rome, once suggested that the loggia be continued around Piazza Signoria. What a wonderful piazza it would be. Now, if they would only bring back those paving stones! Of interest within the loggia are **Cellini**'s *Perseus* (base panels and statuary in the Bargello), which he touchingly writes about making in his *Autobiography*; a Classical lion and its 16th-century copy; and **Giambologna**'s *Rape of the Sabine Women* and *Hercules Slaying the Centaur*. A lineup of Roman matrons brings up the rear. ♦ Piazza della Signoria

83 Rivoire This was Florence's first chocolatier, founded by a Piedmontese from where the sweet vice had dribbled over the Alps from France. It remains the most elegant such emporium in town. Take the harsh edge off the Piazza della Signoria with a cup of hot chocolate topped with luscious whipped cream, or in warmer weather iced chocolate or cappuccino dusted with Riviore's rich cocoa. For those who can't afford to find the tiny boxed Rivoire chocolates on the pillows at the Hotel Excelsior they are also available here. ♦ Closed M. Piazza della Signoria 5. No credit cards. 214412

84 Pineider When Italians present their calling cards, they like to draw a line through their titles to show how modest and well-bred they are, a charming if disingenuous gesture that somehow sums up Janus-faced Italian culture in one swift stroke. The best-bred (and -made) cards in the country come from Pineider, a 6th-generation stationers founded in Florence in 1774. There are branches throughout the country, but this is the flagship store. Through the ages, everyone from heads of state to Hollywood stars has had their names engraved at Pineider. Why draw the line (or *not*) with them? ♦ Closed M morning, Su, lunch. Piazza della Signoria 13r. 284655

85 Erboristeria Palazzo Vecchio One of the widest selections and certainly among the most convenient of the Florentine *erboristerie*, shops which sell medicinal herbs. Hair-restoring shampoos, bust toners, tanning creams (so *that* accounts for all those strangely apricot-juice-faced Florentines) and more—all good for what ails ya. Or what you may *think* ails ya. ♦ Closed M morning, Su, lunch. Via Vacchereccia 9r. 296055

86 Tabasco The town's chic rendezvous spot for the gay crowd, it's a stone's throw from **Michelangelo**'s *David*, whose camp aspect has been adopted as Tabasco's logo. Local lesbian and gay life as witnessed here consists of that combo of refined surface and provincial substance that permeates the Florentine *genius loci*, and it doesn't come cheap. ♦ Tu-F, Su 10PM-3AM; Sa 10PM-4AM. Piazza Santa Cecilia 3r. No credit cards. 213000

87 Oliver The trendiest men's clothing and shoes this side of Milan. Major Italian designers are represented along with Oliver's own line of wool and cotton trousers. ♦ Closed M morning, Su, lunch. Via Vacchereccia 15r. 296327

The **Compagnia del Paiolo**, founded in Florence in the 16th century, was the first cooking academy since the time of ancient Rome. Its membership was limited to 12—all artists, the most famous of whom was **Andrea del Sarto**.

88 Benetton In case you've had the wool over your eyes for the past decade, Benetton is to sheep hair what McDonald's is to cow meat. The Benetton siblings devised a way to make finished woolen goods before applying the dye, thus guaranteeing that their garments could be given the trendiest possible colors in conjunction with the latest market research. The Benetton label now comes in colors everywhere (like *prezzemolo*—parsley—as the Florentines say). This particular shop is geared toward women, but there is a veritable flock of them throughout Florence, and indeed the world. ♦ Closed M morning, Su, lunch. Via Por Santa Maria 68r. 287111

89 Mercato Nuovo (1547-51, **Giovanni Battista Del Tasso**) This *new market* was a 16th-century annex to the old one in what is now **Piazza della Repubblica**, and today still functions as such, filled with stalls selling tourist trinkets (manufacture of the old Italian straw hat, alas, has been moved to Asia). The Florentines call the market the *Porcellino* (piglet) after their nickname for **Pietro Tacca**'s bronze statue of the *Wild Boar* at its south end. Tradition dictates that one rub the beast's nose or toss it a coin to ensure a return to Florence, preferably not to buy a fat pig but some cow innards from the nearby tripe stand toward which the boar's snout points. ♦ Piazza del Mercato Nuovo

90 Libreria del Porcellino Dare to browse in this bookshop, a welcome respite in a heavily trafficked part of town, since the management doesn't discourage it and the selection of books about all aspects of Italian culture—art, food, history, travel, etc., in many languages—warrants it. ♦ Closed M morning, Su. Piazza del Mercato Nuovo 6-8r. 212535

91 Antica Farmacia del Cinghiale This *erboristeria* claims to be over 300 years old. Herbal teas for the insides, herbal fragrances for the outside, and herbal potpourris for the homesite. And there's also a pharmacy. ♦ Closed M morning, Su, lunch. Loggia del Mercato Nuovo 4r. 282128

92 Pollini Their name may mean *chicks*, but instead *chic* is the word for the footwear designed by the 4 (count 'em) Pollini siblings, who hatch sophisticated designs for both sexes, be it the classic men's loafer or the more stylish women's pumps and boots. ♦ Closed M morning, Su, lunch. Via Calimala 12r. 214738

A 16th-century chronicler reported that **Catherine de' Medici**, a member of Florence's most famous family and a notorious glutton, ate so heavily at the marriage of **Mademoiselle de Martigues** that *she just missed kicking the bucket.*

93 Brioni The medieval palazzo that once housed the **Arte della Lana** (the Wool Guild) is now the splendid setting for the Florence home of the famous Roman tailor, whose classic made-to-measure and ready-to-wear men's and women's clothing adds a bit of conservative theatricality to the rational Florentine silhouette. ♦ Closed M morning, Su, lunch. Palagio Arte della Lana, Via Calimala 22r. 295090

94 Piazza della Repubblica (1887) This open space is *not* named after the neon sign at one end proclaiming *La Repubblica*, which is Italy's best newspaper. The piazza was the site of the ancient Roman forum, which later became the **Mercato Vecchio** (Old Market), bordering on Florence's Jewish ghetto at its north end. Florentines still bemoan the 1887 demolition of what was one of the city's most picturesque piazzas, as seen in displays in the **Museo di Firenze com'era**, in spite of the grandiose plaque on the piazza's grand arch referring to the *secolare squallore* (centuries of squalor) in the ancient center of the city that the restoration eradicated. We, on the other hand, like to conjure up those centuries past as we walk in the piazza, perhaps as a way of filtering out its present function as a parking lot surrounded by provincial cafes. Going about our business at the post office beneath the Classical-style loggia paved in colored marbles along the piazza's western edge, we wonder whether patrons of Diocletian's baths might have enjoyed similarly imperial diminishing perspectives. (The baths of ancient Roman Florence were, in fact, nearby on Via delle Terme.) On Thursday, the flower show is reminiscent of the piazza's earlier commerce. And the ever-present save-the-animals lady and her minions collect donations with as much devotion as any medieval mendicant. ♦ Piazza della Repubblica

95 Giubbe Rosse ★$$ The most historic of the piazza's cafes, named after the red jackets still worn (and they *are* a little worn) by the waiters, whose antecedents served Florence's intellectuals a century ago. The atmosphere today is rather more lightweight, with a mediocre restaurant in the back which serves a convincing approximation of an American-style breakfast for the homesick. ♦ Closed Th. Piazza della Repubblica 13-14r. 212280

96 Donnini The best sandwiches and pastry in the smallest of the piazza's cafes, including a nice *budino di riso*, the custardy Florentine version of rice pudding. ♦ Closed M. Piazza della Repubblica 15r. 211862

97 UPIM Floor upon floor of middle-priced merchandise fills this branch, as all branches, of the Italian department-store chain. The clothing is middlebrow, but there is a wide selection of well-designed housewares upstairs. ♦ Closed M morning, Su. Piazza della Repubblica 1r. 298544

Centro Storico

98 Universalturismo This busy travel agency looks like a discreet bank but acts like the trading floor of Wall Street. It does, however, provide a full line of travel services, including the best exchange rate in town at no commission. ♦ M-Sa 9AM-noon, 3-6PM; Su 9AM-noon. Via degli Speziali 7r. 217241

99 Profumerie Aline Those who simply can't go on without their favorite European or American or Japanese brand of cosmetics will most likely find it in this *profumeria*. We remember our amusement when the American men's cologne, *Tuscany*, made its European debut here. ♦ Closed M morning, Su. Via Calzaiuoli 53r. 215269. Also at: Via Vaccereccia 11r. 294976

100 Hotel Savoy $$$ Though its name was changed from Savoia after Italy's rulers from that royal house were politely requested to abdicate (as was Piazza della Repubblica changed from Piazza Vittorio Emanuele II), this hotel retains some of its former glory. It is the oldest and most centrally located if not the grandest of Florence's luxury hotels, with loyal and subdued business travelers hardly stompin' in its faded *fin-de-siècle* facilities. ♦ Deluxe ♦ Piazza della Repubblica 7. 283313

101 Gilli The most elegant of the piazza's cafes preserves the glory days from when it moved here in 1910. Colorful stained glass windows, stucco walls and marble-top tables are matched by Florence's trendiest cocktails (the one currently christened *Bush* is made with bourbon, orange juice and peel and an orange liqueur called *Aurum*) and creamiest *coppe gelato* (the *coppa fiorentina* is concocted out of coffee pudding, chocolate ice cream and whipped cream). ♦ Closed Tu. Piazza della Repubblica 39r. 296310

102 Paszkowski Under the same ownership as Gilli, yet with its own identity. It is the liveliest of the piazza's cafes by night, especially in the warmer months, when it offers crowd-gathering music. The crowd it gathers is a friendly mix of locals and tourists, and the music ranges from oom-pah to provincial pop. ♦ Closed M. Piazza della Repubblica 6r. 210236

Of course it is very dead in comparison [with Paris] but it's a beautiful death....
Elizabeth Barrett Browning

103 Ricordi The best selection of records, tapes, compact discs and sheet music in this part of town. The helpful, young staff is not above naming that tune for you if it's slipped your mind and you hum a few bars. ♦ Closed M morning, Su, lunch. Via Brunelleschi 8r. 214104

104 Gianfranco Ferrè Boutique The Milanese designer's Florence boutique is an apotheosis of high tech, one of the most striking contemporary spaces in the city. A steel spiral staircase connects the stark white men's and women's floors, both framed by the tall arched windows of a 19th-century palazzo. And there are clothes too. ♦ Closed M morning, Su, lunch. Via dei Tosinghi 52r. 292003

105 Al Campidoglio ★★★$$$ Situated as it is in the heart of the city's modern (and ancient) commercial district, this restaurant attracts ladies who lunch, gentlemen who deal, and all combinations thereof. Owner **Franco Spalvier** comes from the *other* Campidoglio city, Rome, by way of Montreal and Miami. He has made some subtle changes lately, maintaining the restaurant's traditions (such as *pollastrino al Campidoglio*, free-range chicken grilled to perfection with just a touch of salt and olive oil) while updating the cuisine (the restaurant has one of the the only steam ovens in town, ideal for poaching salmon and other fish) and the decor (Alinari photos of old Florence line the walls). It is one of the few, and the best, choices for Sunday dining. ♦ Closed Tu, Aug. Via del Campidoglio 8r. 287770

106 Pendini $$ Some people actually enjoy the neon lights on the rooftops above and the hubbub below in the cafes of Piazza della Repubblica, inescapable during the warmer months in the large, pragmatically furnished rooms of this medium-sized former *pensione*, as *its* neon sign proclaims. ♦ Via degli Strozzi 2. 211170

107 Palazzo delle Poste e Telegrafi (1917, **Rodrigo Sabatini** and **Vittorio Tognetti**) The Renaissance-style post office is the place to buy stamps; send mail, telegrams and faxes; and make telephone calls if you're not taking care of such business at your hotel. There are tables upstairs and down for writing out those postcards and cooling those heels. ♦ M-F 9AM-7:30PM; Sa 9AM-1:30PM. Via Pellicceria 212877

108 Caffè La Posta If the post office across the way is crowded, go to this friendly neighborhood bar for your stamps. They also sell simple stationery and tasteful cards and make their own sandwiches fresh daily. The house aperitif (ask for the *aperitivo di casa*—it's made with spumante, Martini rosso, Campari bitter and gin) is guaranteed to send you special delivery. ♦ M-Sa 9AM-7:30PM. Via Pellicceria 24r. 214773

09 Hotel Pierre $$$ Located in a 19th-century building, this recently opened hotel has 39 modern rooms, with double-paned Neo-Gothic windows, ensuring monastic quiet in the center of town. ♦ Via dei Lamberti 5. 216218

10 Passamaneria Valmar This shop is jam-packed with trimmings that make nifty gift items, from a fat gold cord for your favorite club kid's belt to a silk tassel for your great aunt's boudoir, all made with exemplary Italian textiles and workmanship. ♦ Closed M morning, Su, lunch. Via Porta Rossa 53r. 284493

11 Palazzo dei Capitani di Parte Guelfa (14th c; remodeled 15th c, **Filippo Brunelleschi, Francesco Della Luna**; loggia 1589, **Giorgio Vasari**) The Guelph party called in the best artists and architects of the day to work on its headquarters, the earliest Renaissance palazzo in Florence. It discreetly dominates a tiny piazza where one can easily picture political intrigues of the day taking place. Brunelleschi was responsible for the high-ceilinged interior, topped with a coffered ceiling by Vasari.
♦ Piazza di Parte Guelfa

112 Sotto Sotto This unique shop sells intimate wear for men only, including robes, pajamas, slippers and all sorts of under (*sotto*) wear—not to mention such unmentionables as the red briefs and boxers traditionally worn for good luck on New Year's Eve. ♦ Closed M, Su, lunch. Via delle Terme 7r. 296026

113 C.O.I. There's nothing coy about the **Commercio Oreficeria Italiana**, a bustling gold market with the largest selection of merchandise at some of the best prices in town. ♦ Closed M, Su, lunch. Via Por Santa Maria 8r, upstairs. 283970

114 Cirri The delicate Florentine art of hand embroidery is alive and well in this shop, stocked with thousands upon thousands of collars, kerchiefs and lingerie in cotton, silk and linen. ♦ Closed M, Su, lunch. Via Por Santa Maria 38-40r. 296593

115 La Bottega del Gelato Under the same management as the *gelateria* **Perche No!..**, this establishment prides itself on its banana and chocolate flavors. ♦ Closed Tu. Via Por Santa Maria 33r. 296550

116 Mandarina Duck The Florence branch of the Italian chain, known for its trendy, heavy-duty rubber bags and briefcases. ♦ Closed M, Su, lunch. Via Por Santa Maria 23r. 210380

117 Casa-Torre degli Amadei (14th c) This tower, rebuilt after it was destroyed in WWII like most of the immediate vicinity, now houses the conservative jeweler **Ugo Piccini**. Once upon a time, it was the residence of one of the most reactionary families of medieval Florence. The Amadei (the name, ironically, means *love of God*) arranged for the murder of **Buondelmonte dei Buondelmonti**, who had jilted their daughter (see Ponte Vecchio). The Florentines affectionately call this tower **La Bigonciola**, meaning *the tub*, Amadei only knows why. ♦ Via Por Santa Maria

Centro Storico

118 Torre dei Donati Consorti (12th c) And this little tower was affiliated with the Guelph family whose daughter **Buondelmonte** chose. Talk about unfriendly neighbors. The atmosphere here is friendlier these days, since it houses part of the **Hotel Continental**. ♦ Lungarno Acciaioli 2

118 Hotel Continental $$$ One of the few hotels in the area that actually looks out on the Arno, a mixed blessing since the soundtrack to that gorgeous view of the river and the Ponte Vecchio is the racket of cars, Vespas and an endless stream of tourists, the latter the louder. The windows in the modern, comfortable rooms are double-paned, however.
♦ Lungarno Acciaioli 2. 282392

119 Fendi The Roman Fendi sisters women's high-fashion clothing and accessories are represented in Florence by this sartorial embassy. ♦ Closed M morning, Su, lunch. Borgo Santissimi Apostoli 42/48r. 287866

120 Santi Apostoli (11th c; rebuilt 15th-16th c) Legend (and legend only) has it that this Romanesque church was founded by **Charlemagne**. Within its Romanesque interior, partially built with material from the nearby Roman baths, is a 16th-century *Immaculate Conception* by **Vasari**. ♦ Piazza del Limbo

121 Bijoux Cascio This shop specializes in well-crafted imitations—sincerely flattering gold-plated designs set with ersatz stones. ♦ Closed M morning, Su, lunch. Via Por Santa Maria 1r. 294378

122 Gelateria Ponte Vecchio Silvia, the friendly Italian-Canadian proprietress, claims she knows her co-continentals' tastes, and we can't disagree. We like to lick our cups clean of the berry flavors (made only with fruit and water) and the *semifreddo* specialty of *nocciolato* (hazelnut, with whole nuts in the cool, creamy concoction). ♦ Closed W, Jan. Piazza del Pesce 3-5r. 296810

Until the end of the 14th century, Florentine girls were taught to read and write only if they were meant to become nuns.

| **Restaurants/Nightlife:** Red | **Hotels:** Blue |
| **Shops/Parks:** Green | **Sights/Culture:** Black |

123 Santo Stefano al Ponte (documented 1116)
The lower part of the Romanesque green and white marble facade of this church dates from 1233. The interior was rebuilt in the 17th century by **Ferdinando Tacca** and includes his bronze relief *The Stoning of St. Stephen*. (The church itself was reduced to rubble during the German retreat in WWII and damaged in the 1966 flood.) Much of the interior was made for other churches—the elaborate marble staircase by **Bernardo Buontalenti** originally stood in Santa Trinita, the altar by **Giambologna** was

in Santa Maria. The church is usually only open for concerts and occasional exhibitions.
♦ Piazza Santo Stefano al Ponte

124 Buca dell'Orafo ★★$$ Unlike its name implies, one doesn't have to be a goldsmith to afford this typical Florentine trattoria (many such eateries have the typically self-effacing *buca*, meaning hole, in their names), known for its *frittate di carciofo* or artichoke omelets among other simple dishes. ♦ Closed M, Su. Volta dei Girolami 28r. 213619

124 Casa dell'Orafo In this *goldsmith's house* you can watch dozens of jewelers go about their craft, producing what's in store in the shops on the Ponte Vecchio. ♦ Vicolo Marzio 2

125 Hotel Hermitage $$ Again, the tradeoff for in-your-face views of the Ponte Vecchio is the maddening crowd, but there are also quieter rooms in the back and a sunny roof garden facing *centro* in this modest and modern hotel set in a medieval building. ♦ Vicolo Marzio 1. 287216

126 Quisisana e Ponte Vecchio $$ This former *pensione* is where the Florence portions of **E.M.** Forster's *A Room with a View* were filmed. The rooms (reached by taking a heartbreaking old wrought-iron elevator up to the past) have Grand Tour character, and the views extend cinematically on all sides, from the Ponte Vecchio and San Miniato to the Duomo and Centro. ♦ Lungarno Archibusieri 4. 216692, 215046

127 Bruna Spadini Everything from hand-embroidered handkerchiefs to heirloom-quality bed and table linens may be found in this shop, although the price tag may ensure that you leave them there. ♦ Closed M morning, Su. Lungarno Archibusieri 4-6r. 287732

128 Ponte Vecchio (1354, **Neri di Fioravante** or **Taddeo Gaddi**) Florence's *Old Bridge* was so named to distinguish it from the newer **Ponte alla Carraia** upstream, built in thoroughly modern 1220. The Ponte Vecchio crosses the Arno at its narrowest point in the city. It was probably where the Romans built a bridge for the **Via Cassia**, the ancient road which ran through Florence on its way from Rome to what are now Fiesole and Pisa, much more important cities in those days. A statue of *Mars* that once stood at the northern end of the bridge was the scene of a seminal event in the history of

Tuscany. There, on Easter Sunday in 1215, assassins killed **Buondelmonte dei Buondelmonti**, who had spurned his fiancée of the **Amadei** family in favor of a more attractive member of the rival **Donati** clan.

The present bridge and its shops replaced a 12th-century structure swept away in a flood in 1333, events commemorated in a medieval plaque midway across the bridge. Although **Vasari** writes that Taddeo Gaddi reconstructed it, he may have been trying to reinforce his own link with Florentine artistic tradition, since Vasari himself designed the corridor running over it, buying up property on either side of the bridge to do so. (For all his power, he was not able to persuade the **Manelli** family to let him run it through their residence, however, so it twists briskly around the Manelli tower at the Pitti end of the bridge.) The Ponte Vecchio's medieval character persists, albeit dazzling with the glint of gold in its shops. (Medieval spectacle can be fully appreciated watching the **Calcio Storico** parade over the bridge in period garb each 24 and 28 June.) After Vasari built his corridor, **Ferdinand I de' Medici**, annoyed at having to pass over the shops of butchers, tanners and other practitioners of the *vile arts* as he called them, rousted the low-rent tenants and raised the rates. In came the goldsmiths and jewelers whose professional descendants line the bridge today. A tribute to their craft is the bust of the goldsmith/sculptor **Benvenuto Cellini** in the middle of the bridge.

During the German retreat in WWII, the Ponte Vecchio was the only bridge Hitler's troops did not blow up. Instead, they reduced the buildings on either side of it to rubble (which is why Via Por Santa Maria is so modern looking), effectively blocking passage across the Arno. In 1966, the Ponte Vecchio's jewelers were among the first to witness the river's last flood, and played a crucial role in alerting the townspeople. Their shops and Vasari's corridor suffered damage, but the bridge beneath them remained intact.

These days the Ponte Vecchio bustles with upscale shoppers. At night during the warmer months, however, the last hippies in Italy (who seem to have somehow become embedded in the structure in the 1966 flood) congregate in the 2 terraces in the middle, twanging guitars and performing street theater. Our favorite Ponte Vecchio street artist is the Oriental gentleman at the Pitti end of the bridge, whose hair we've watched go from black to white over the years as he sits quietly sketching views of the city.

Jewelers on the Ponte Vecchio come and go (talking not of Michelangelo, but no doubt of Cellini), but the following are likely to stay put for a while:

The *Chianti* wine-producing area around Florence is the largest *Denominazione di Origine Controllata*, or officially designated such area, in Italy and makes the most wine.

■ 29 Ristori Unlike the former tenant of this prime space at the foot of the bridge (**Settepassi**, now on Via Tornabuoni), Ristori makes jewelry with a contemporary feel, though timeless in the cut (and price tag) of its precious stones. The semi-precious stock is equally inventive and, naturally, more reasonably priced, and many settings make bold use of both. ♦ Closed M morning, Su, lunch. Ponte Vecchio 1-3r. 215507

■ 30 Manelli The Marchesi Manelli are descendants of the former inhabitants of the eponymous medieval tower in *pietra forte* at the end of the bridge, noteworthy because the family refused to let **Vasari** run his corridor through it. These days they are more concerned with *pietra dura*, the semiprecious stones they set along with *pietre prezioze* or precious stones in bracelets, necklaces and rings. They are also more oblig-ing, crafting jewelry in whatever designs the client desires. ♦ Closed M morning, Su, lunch. Ponte Vecchio 14r. 213759

■ 31 Rajola Another inventive jeweler who uses precious metals and stones in designs so of-the-moment you won't have to leave them in the safe—chain-snatchers wouldn't believe all that glitters could possibly be real. ♦ Closed M morning, Su, lunch. Ponte Vecchio 24r. 215335

ᴜ. GHERARDI

■ 32 U. Gherardi Gherardi has corralled the coral market in Florence (most of it is produced in Naples), selling buckets of the stuff in pale white, blushing pink and beet red. Check out the cultured pearls and cameos, but watch out for the tortoiseshell, since it won't pass through customs in some countries. ♦ Closed M morn-ing, Su, lunch. Ponte Vecchio 5r. 211809

■ 33 Piccini The Piccini brothers have been crowning heads ever since Queen Elena mar-ried Vittorio Emanuele III at the turn of the cen-tury. Their current designs are on the street level; upstairs are antique pieces the descen-dants of the king and queen could easily have pawned on their abdication. ♦ Closed M morn-ing, Su, lunch. Ponte Vecchio 23r. 294768

■ 34 Melli This shop is completely devoted to antiques, whether jewelry or tea services, Austro-Hungarian and American (Tiffany) silver, statu-ettes and the like—a veritable cavalcade of everything that has made its way across this old bridge through the ages. ♦ Closed M morning, Su, lunch. Ponte Vecchio 44-46r. 211413

■ 35 Cassetti Among the most creative of the bridge's jewelers, Cassetti (they changed the shop's name from **Della Loggia** to their family name a few years ago) was among the first Florentine jewelers to mix precious and semi-precious stones in the same pieces, as well as the Rolex-like combinations of steel and gold. ♦ Closed M morning, Su, lunch. Ponte Vecchio 52r. 296028

Restaurants/Nightlife: Red
Shops/Parks: Green

Hotels: Blue
Sights/Culture: Black

The Davids of Florence

Ever concerned with the triumph over tyranny, Florentines often commissioned artists to address such subjects as Perseus and Hercules, but it is David—slayer of Goliath—who is most closely associated with Florence and most often represented in the city. The **Museo del Bargello** has a large number of *Davids*. **Donatello**'s 2 treatments there are a marble sculpture from 1408 and a bronze made around 1430. **Verrocchio**'s version is also bronze, and dates from before 1476, when it was documented to have been

acquired to decorate **Palazzo Vecchio**. Also at the Bargello is a marble statue begun around 1531 by **Michelangelo**, alternately known as *David* and *Apollo*. Michelangelo's 1501-04 rendition at the **Galleria dell'Accademia** is considered the definitive version, and with copies in front of Palazzo Vecchio and in **Piazzale Michelangiolo**—not to mention the souvenir-stand knockoffs—it has virtually become the mascot of Florence.

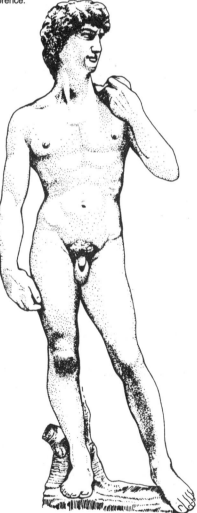

Colli

Even before **Luca Pitti** built his palazzo at the foot of what are now the **Bóboli Gardens**, Florentines have been heading for the hills— *Colli* in Italian—across the Arno. According to a medieval legend, one of the first to do so was the martyr **Saint Minias**, who in AD 250 carried his severed head from Florence's Roman amphitheater to the Mons Florentinus, now the site of th beloved church of **San Miniato**, which beckons from its perch sweetly overlooking the city.

Many have followed through the ages, including **Michelangelo**, who built fortifications around San Miniato to protect Florence from a siege, and the **Medici**, who greatly expanded the already grandiose palazzo begun by Pitti. Others have been great Florentine families such as the **Guicciardini**, **Torrigiani** and **Serristori**, who built palazzi from the Middle Ages onward, and 20th-century *plein-air* painters such as **Ottone Rosai**, who immortalized the landscape of **Via San Lorenzo**, the Florentines' favorite country road.

The Colli continue to provide a bit of country in the city, on **Via San Leonardo** a well as in the panoramic Bóboli, the **Forte di Belvedere** and **Piazzale Michelangelo**

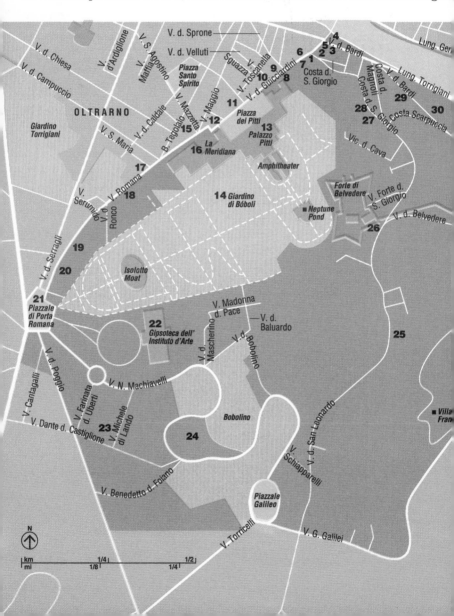

ll ideal spots for a picnic. Even the most famous museum in the area, **Palazzo Pitti**, is uncrowded (though the arrangement of the art is not) compared with other Florentine institutions.

So as not to lose your head like Saint Minias, be forewarned that much of Colli is as hilly as its name implies. Before you begin to explore it, put on some sturdy walking shoes. If they're trendy Timberlands, you may even pass for a native!

1 Santa Felicita (1736, **Ferdinando Ruggieri**) The present Neoclassical structure is a remodelling of a Gothic church, though there has been a church on this choice site since the Early Christian era. The column in its piazza dates from 1381; **Giorgio Vasari** built the portico to support the corridor he designed to run between the Uffizi and Palazzo Pitti in 1564. Inside, the most important sight is the **Capponi Chapel**, perhaps built by **Brunelleschi**. It houses **Pontormo**'s Mannerist masterpiece, *The Deposition*, as well as his *Annunciation* and tondos of the *Evangelists*, worked on in collaboration with his pupil, **Bronzino**.
♦ Piazza Santa Felicita

2 Celestino ★★$$ Smallish and chicish, this bright eatery offers an Italian menu of such

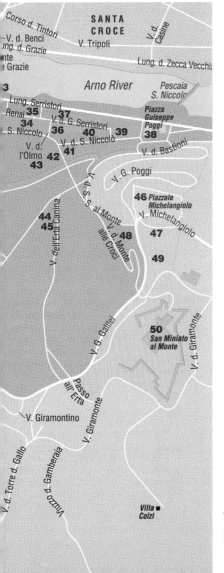

Colli

dishes as *ravioli rose* (in a tomato-and-cream sauce), *scaloppine alla boscaiola* (veal with tomato and mushroom) and *scampi alla pescatora* (shrimp with tomato and garlic). In the warm weather, a few tables spill out into the little piazza for dining *all'aperto*—don't ask to eat *al fresco*, since the expression has now come to mean *in the slammer*. ♦ Closed Su, Aug. Piazza Santa Felicita 4r. 296574

3 La Porcellana Bianca White porcelain is the specialty of this housewares shop. Spots of color among the sea of white dishes, cups and platters include lovely country dish towels and brass-handled stainless-steel cookware.
♦ Closed M morning, Su, lunch. Via de' Bardi 53r. 211893

4 Kenny ★★$ Fast food with a slow view. Besides the price, the saving grace of the grease here—not-bad Italian burgers with names like Kennyburger, Superkenny, Cheesekenny and Fishkenny—is that it's right on the Arno, looking out at the Ponte Vecchio and over to the Uffizi. Less culturally shocking is the **Old Bridge Gelateria** in the same space. It prides itself on its *coppa Firenze* (custard ice cream with whipped cream, strawberries and pineapple) and its *coppa Ponte Vecchio* (a banana split the likes of which you'd never find at Dairy Queen).
♦ Closed M. Via de' Bardi 64r. 212915

5 Madova Florence's prime glove emporium, hands down. The firm makes its own gloves of various leathers, linings and colors—including custom-made sizes—and will ship anywhere free of charge. ♦ Closed M morning, Su. Via Guicciardini 1r. 296526

Restaurants/Nightlife: Red   **Hotels:** Blue
Shops/Parks: Green   **Sights/Culture:** Black

6 Quaglia e Forte The late **Enzo Quaglia** was from Naples, renowned for its delicately carved corals and cameos. Master craftsmen continue that tradition today, as well as reproducing historical jewelry for museums throughout the world. ♦ Closed M morning, Su, lunch. Via Guicciardini 12r. 294534

7 Filatura di Crosa Florence's trendiest yarn shop, which stocks all the latest designer

Colli

skeins in cotton, linen, silk and wool. ♦ Closed M morning, Su, lunch. Via Guicciardini 21r. 289193

7 La Sagrestia ★★$$ The international menu of this comfortable, wood-paneled establishment includes *spaghetti frutta di mare* (with seafood), *filetto alla provenzale* (filet of beef provencale), and crème caramel, along with a special children's section—a rarity in Florence. ♦ Closed M. Via Guicciardini 27r. 210003

8 Pasticceria Maioli This family-run establishment has been making its own pastries for over half a century, so it's no wonder that such delicacies as *budino di riso* (rice pudding tart) and *bignoline* (tiny cream puffs) are turned out with such delicious results. ♦ M, W-Su 9AM-7:30PM. Via Guicciardini 43r. 214701

8 Palazzo Guicciardini (15th c; rebuilt 1620-25 to designs of **Cigoli** by **Gherardo Silvani**) This palazzo was the birthplace of the historian **Francesco Guicciardini**, who lived here from 1482 to 1540. Its elegant courtyard contains a stucco of *Hercules* in the style of **Antonio Pollaiuolo**. ♦ Via Guicciardini 15

8 A. Melozzi Oh, you beautiful doll—Florence's largest and loveliest selection of them for children and collectors alike. ♦ Closed M morning, Su. Via Guicciardini 35r. 216084

9 Freon Some of the most creative costume jewelry in Florence, in a high-tech setting. At last look they were showing chunky pieces of paste stones on flashy metallic backgrounds. ♦ Closed M morning, Su, lunch. Via Guicciardini 118r. 296504

9 Emporium To many, especially after the New York Museum of Modern Art's watershed 197 *Italy: The New Domestic Landscape* show, Ital means design. Though Florence usually doesn't, here you'll find all the big names (Alessi, Kastel, etc.) in small objects for home and office. ♦ Closed M morning, Su. Via Guicciardini 122r. 212646

10 Giulio Giannini & Figlio Marbelized or Florentine paper goods are the specialty of thi 5th-generation shop, which has also been doing custom bookbinding for many of those generations. ♦ Closed M morning, Su, lunch. Piazza Pitti 37r. 212621

11 Pitti Mosaici It's rare to see the younger generations continuing the Florentine tradition of *artigianato* or craftsmanship, but **Ilio de Filippis** has taken up the 16th-century Florentine specialty of *pietra dura* or Florentine mosaic, the inlay of precious and semiprecious stones in jewelry and furniture. ♦ Closed M morning, Su, lunch. Piazza dei Pitti 16r (show room 17r) 282127

11 Caffè This warm, inviting cafe is as old-fashioned in its dark decor as it is in its long list of such mixed drinks as Cuba libres, grasshoppers and stingers. Filled by day with discriminating tourists, and at night with the closest thing in 20th-century Florence to cafe society ♦ Closed M. Piazza Pitti 9. 296241

12 Caffè Bellini The bright, sparkling, expansive option for coffee in Piazza Pitti, offering some of the best cappuccino in Florence as well as a scrumptuous *budino di riso*, the loca rice pudding tart. ♦ Closed Su. Piazza dei Pitti 6/a/r. 212964

12 Taddei Many leather-goods shops in Florenc somehow feel obliged to sell gaudy reproductions of medieval and Renaissance designs, or to dispense with the so-called *Made in Italy* label altogether. Not so this 3rd-generation, family-run business, where the taste level in leather boxes and desk accessories is at as high a level as the craftsmanship. Opens at 7AM. ♦ Closed M morning, Su, lunch. Piazza dei Pitti 6r. 2119139

13 Palazzo Pitti (ca 1457-70, **Luca Fancelli**; enlarged 1558-77, **Bartolommeo Ammannati**; 1620, **Giulio Parigi**; 1640, **Alfonso Parigi**; 1746, 1783-1819, **Giuseppe Ruggieri** and **Pasquale Poccianti**) Florence's largest if not most beloved palazzo was commissioned by the wealthy importer of French cloth, **Luca Pitti**, to keep up with the Joneses, who in his day were named **Medici** and **Strozzi**. Legend has it that Pitti's pitiless ambition called for a plan with windows larger than the doors of the Palazzo Medici and a courtyard that could contain the entire Palazzo Strozzi. (Though the former palazzo was under construction at the time, the latter existed only as a plot of land.) Somewhere between legend and fact is the story that architect Luca Fancelli built the palazzo according to a grandiose plan his master **Brunelleschi** had presented to **Cosimo il Vecchio**. When the Medici rejected it, **Vasari** writes, Brunelleschi *tore the drawing into a thousand pieces in disdain.*

The original palazzo consisted of only the 7 central bays of the present structure, built—as were later additions—out of rough-hewn golden *pietra dura* stone quarried from the **Bóboli Gardens** behind it. Even so, it was most imposing. **Machiavelli** called the palazzo *grander than any other erected in the city by a private citizen,* and Vasari wrote that the view from it was *bellissima,* commenting on how the surrounding hills in the Bóboli made it *almost a theater.*

Work on the palazzo had been at a standstill for decades when **Cosimo I**'s wife, **Eleanor of Toledo**, bought it (not without a sense of courtly triumph, one imagines) from Pitti's impoverished heirs in 1549. From then on, the palazzo became the official residence of the rulers of Florence. The Medici brought in Ammannati, who added wings toward the Bóboli and the courtyard. (He did not ruin any marble here, as the Florentines say of his statue of *Neptune* in

Piazza della Signoria, but instead enlarged the palace with more stone from the Bóboli brought with the help of a mule, whose efforts are commemorated on a plaque in the courtyard.) After Ammannati's interventions, the Pitti, with its grounds, was the most magnificent palace in Europe, a rustic and rambling precursor to Versailles. (It was this version of the palace which Eleanor's homesick granddaughter, known as **Marie de' Medici** when she was married off to **Henry IV** of France, tried to recall when she commissioned the Palais du Luxembourg in Paris.)

Still under the Medici in the 17th century, Giulio Parigi added the 3 bays on either side of the original 7, and his son Alfonso extended the 2 lower floors to their present dimensions. The 2 porticos reaching into Piazza Pitti were added in the 18th century under the Lorraine, giving the palazzo the exterior aspect you see today. Inside, meanwhile, as the Florentine *genius loci* that brought about the Renaissance and the Medici began to wane, the royal rulers looked increasingly beyond the city to embellish the palace with suitably magnificent paintings and decoration. The Pitti became the residence of the Italian royal family when Florence was the capital of Italy in the last century. In this century, **Victor Emmanuel III** gave it to the state. It now houses no less than 7 museums.

Centuries after Luca Pitti commissioned the palazzo, his name lives on in another Florentine institution—the trade shows collectively known as **Pitti Immagine**. Originally Italian fashion shows which took place in the palazzo's **Sala Bianca**, *I Pitti* are now held at the **Fortezza da Basso** and market everything from housewares to international fashion, including the latest versions of those French threads Luca used to import over half a millenium ago. ◆ Admission. Tu-Sa 9AM-2PM; Su 9AM-1PM. Piazza Pitti. 213440

Within Palazzo Pitti:

Galleria Palatina (Palatine Galleries)
Ammannati's monumental 140-step staircase
leads to the most famous section of the Palazzo
Pitti. Its rooms are rich candy-boxes. In keeping
with the taste of the times in which the largely
High Renaissance and Baroque collection was
assembled and hung (from the 17th through
the 19th centuries), paintings are displayed like
chocolates, wrapped in gold frames and set row
upon toothsome row in the elaborately decorated
galleries. To the modern eye it can be more a
visual surfeit than feast—comprising numerous
paintings by **Andrea del Sarto, Raphael, Titian,
Tintoretto, Rubens** and **Van Dyck** among its
hundreds of works—so take care to digest it

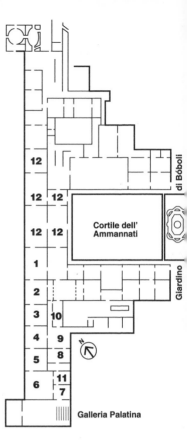

Galleria Palatina

Colli

slowly. Since the non-chronological, non-
geographical arrangement is antithetical to
most art historians, the museum remains relatively free of heavy-handed lecturing. That fact,
coupled with mellow natural lighting from
windows with views of the surroundings,
makes the Palatine one of the most palatable
doses of the *Stendhal syndrome* in Florence.

The first 5 rooms are decorated with **Pietro da
Cortona**'s allegorical ceiling frescoes which give
the rooms their names. In the **Sala di Venere**
(Venus Room) [**1**] are Titian's *Concert, La Bella*
and *Portrait of Pietro Aretino*, as well as
Rubens' *Landscape with the Wreck of Ulysses*
and **Salvator Rosa**'s *Harbor View*. The **Sala di
Apollo** (Apollo Room) [**2**] has more rich Titians
(notably *Magdalen*) and works by **Rosso
Fiorentino**, Andrea del Sarto and the maudlin
Guido Reni, considered the greatest painter of
all time during the Grand Tour days. In the **Sala
di Marte** (Mars Room) [**3**], look for Tintoretto's
Portrait of Luigi Cornaro and the numerous
Rubens paintings. The **Sala di Giove** (Jove
Room) [**4**], used as the throne room, contains
one of the most famous paintings in the gallery,
Raphael's creamy *La Velata*. There are also important works by his master, **Perugino**, as well
as by **Fra Bartolomeo** and Andrea del Sarto.
The **Sala di Saturno** (Saturn Room) [**5**] houses
the painting most singularly identified with the
Pitti, Raphael's *Madonna della Seggiola*, as well
as his other Madonnas and portraits.

Of particular interest in the remaining rooms
are Raphael's *La Gravida* in the **Sala dell'Iliade**
(Illiad Room) [**6**]; **Cristofano Allori**'s *Judith*, a
sensual exception to the cloying Florentine
seicento; the Baroque flamboyance of Pietro da
Cortona's wall frescoes depicting *The Four
Ages of Man* in the **Sala della stufa** (Hot Bath
Room) [**7**]; *stufa* has no mythological signifi-
cance—it means *stove*—but the subjects were
taken from **Ovid**'s *Metamorphoses*); **Cigoli**'s
Ecce Homo in the **Sala di Ulisse** (Ulysses
Room) [**8**]; **Filippo Lippi**'s *Madonna and Child*
in the **Sala di Prometeo** (Prometheus Room)
[**9**]; and **Francesco Furini**'s *Hylas and the
Nymphs*, another exceptional example of the
Florentine Baroque, in the **Galleria Poccetti**

(Poccetti Room) [**10**]. More Florentine Baroque
paintings are in the **Sala Volterrano**
(Volterrano Room) [**11**].

Appartamenti Monumentali (State Apartments) On the same floor as the Palatine [**12**]
this section is often closed. It contains 17th-
century portraits of the **Medici** by **Justus
Sustermans**, 18th-century Gobelins tapestries
and 19th-century decorations commissioned
by the Lorraine.

Galleria d'Arte Moderna (Galleries of Modern Art) Don't be misled by the name of this
section (one flight up), which contains mostly
uninteresting 19th- and 20th-century Tuscan
paintings. The quite notable exception are the
macchiaoli. These *plein-air* painters, whose
name means stainers or blotters, were long
considered the Italian counterpart of the French
Impressionists, but are becoming increasingly
appreciated abroad in their own right.

Museo degli Argenti (Silver Museum) This,
too, is a bit of a misnomer, since rather than
silver, the museum (accessible from the courtyard) is primarily a camp glorification of the
Medici. It is also known for **Lorenzo de' Medici**
collection of precious-stone vases. They
spawned a vogue for *pietra dura* or precious-
stone work so associated with Florence during
the days of the Grand Tour it was known in
English as Florentine mosaic. There are some
examples of it on display here; it reaches its
apotheosis in the **Medici Chapel**.

Meridiana Dwarfed by the Pitti, this *palazzetto* was where **King Victor Emmanuel** chose to stay over the more imposing palace, whose right wing it lies behind. Its **Collezione Contini-Bonacossi** (Italian and Spanish paintings and decorative art), is also dwarfed by that of the Pitti, but works by such artists as **Giovanni Bellini, Paolo Veronese, Tintoretto, Gian Lorenzo Bernini, Goya** and **El Greco** are more than rewarding for those with the stamina. It also houses the **Galleria del Costume**, a costume collection of largely Italian fashion from the mid-18th to the mid-20th centuries.

Museo delle Carrozze (Carriage Museum) This museum, also often closed, is located in the portico extending into Piazza Pitti to the right facing the palazzo. It contains 18th- and 19th-century carriages, primarily from the Lorraine.

14 Giardino di Bóboli (Bóboli Gardens) (begun 1550, **Niccolò Tribolo**; continued 1583, probably **Ammannati** and **Buontalenti**; finished 17th c, **Alfonso Parigi** and others) The *bellissima* view **Vasari** enthused about, the Bóboli are laid out on the hilly slopes behind the Palazzo Pitti. Probably named after the **Bogoli** family, who owned property on the site, the park combines a formal groomed appearance with whimsical Mannerist statuary. Once the private property of the Medici and other courts, its expanses now provide fresh air and soothing views for the Florentine omnibus. Matrons, young lovers, foreign *au pairs* with babies and hippies who seem even more anachronistic than the statues all pass their afternoons in the park with its resident legion of feral cats.

The main entrance is on the left side of the Palazzo Pitti facing it from its piazza. Just inside to the left is **Valerio Cioli**'s statue of **Cosimo I**'s favorite dwarf, *Pietro Barbino Riding a Turtle*, whose image is almost as popular as the *David's*. A gravel path continues to the grotto, designed by Vasari and Buontalenti. It contains copies of **Michelangelo**'s *Slaves* and **Giambologna**'s original *Venus*. As in much of the Bóboli, the Venus room once contained *giochi d'acqua*, surprise jets of water which were the Mannerist

equivalent of water pistols. Rounding the palazzo, the amphitheater extends behind Ammannati's courtyard (both were used to stage court frolics). It is modeled on an ancient Roman circus and contains such authentic Roman relics as a granite basin from the **Baths of Caracalla** and part of an Egyptian obelisk brought to the Eternal City. To the left, towers the red **Kaffehaus**, a semicircular structure with a fanciful dome, built by **Zanobi del Rosso** during the Lorraine as its name implies. It offers refreshment and a terrace with nice views of Florence and Fiesole. From here, a path leads up to the **Neptune Pond**, which surrounds a bronze statue by **Stoldo Lorenzi**. Above it, completing the perspective down to the Pitti, is a colossal statue of *Abun-*

Colli

dance designed by Giambologna and finished by the workshop of **Piero Tassi**. Near it is the **Giardino del Cavaliere**, where the **Museo delle Porcellane**, a museum of European porcelain, has been installed. Its playful **Monkey Fountain** is by **Pietro Tacca**, and its terrace has lovely views of the surrounding slopes. From here a path leads to the **Viottolone**, a spectacular cypress alley studded with Classical and Neoclassical statues. The spectacular path leads downhill to the **Piazzale dell'Isolotto**, the centerpiece of which is Giambologna's **Ocean Fountain**, containing a copy of his *Oceanus*.
◆ Daily 9AM-4:30PM, Jan-Feb, Nov-Dec; 9AM-5:30PM, Mar-Apr, Oct; 9AM-6:30PM, May-Sep. Piazza Pitti. 213440

15 Casa Guidi The poets **Robert** and **Elizabeth Barrett Browning** lived and held court here for 15 years. Here their son, **Pen**, was born. Here Elizabeth developed her romanticized support of the unification of Italy and died in 1861. (She is buried in Florence's Protestant Cemetery.) All that's left of the Brownings' sojourn here is a plaque. The **Casa Guidi Windows,** immortalized in Elizabeth's poem of the same name (*a little child go singing...O bella liberta*, etc.), remain intact. ◆ Piazza San Felice 8

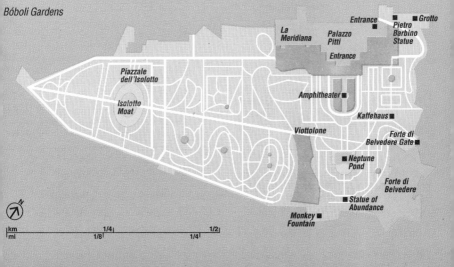

Bóboli Gardens

15 San Felice (1226; facade 1457) **Michelozzo** may have designed the facade to this medieval church, which contains a *Crucifix* and many delapidated frescoes by **Giotto**'s school.
♦ Piazza San Felice

16 Museo La Specola This ancient palace was acquired from the **Torrigiani** family in 1771 by **Grand Duke Peter Leopold**, who added an astronomical observatory (*specola*), giving the palazzo and museum its name. It houses a monument to **Galileo**, the **Tribuna di Galileo**, built in 1841 on the occasion of a scientific conference. Its main attraction, however, is the part of the morbid **Zoological Museum** (also founded by the Grand Duke) which contains graphic wax models of every imaginable part of the human anatomy by **Clemente Susini** and **Felice Fontana**, as well as *memento mori* wax tableaux by **Gaetano Zumbo** representing such upbeat subjects as *The Plague, The Triumph of Time, Decomposition of Bodies* and *Syphillis*. Waxing scientific and philosophical. ♦ M-Tu, Th-Sa 9AM-noon; 2nd Su of month 9:30AM-12:30PM; closed W. Via Romana 17. 222451

17 Annalena $$ This former pensione is housed in a 15th-century *pietra serena* and stucco palazzo given by **Cosimo de' Medici** to a woman named **Annalena**, something of a tragic heroine in Florentine history. Having lost first her husband in a political intrigue and then her son, she became a nun and turned her palazzo into a convent that gave refuge to **Caterina Sforza**, herself the widow of **Giovanni di Lorenzo de' Medici**, and her infant son. The tradition continued under Fascism, when the place harbored political refugees. These days it simply lodges a loyal clientele who appreciate its antiques-furnished rooms and the quiet of the former **Giardino d'Annalena**, now a plant nursery, it overlooks. ♦ Via Romana 34. 222402

Florentines believe that their gastronomic traditions laid the foundation for French cuisine when **Catherine de' Medici** took her chefs with her from Florence upon marrying **Henry II** of France in the 16th century.

18 Hotel Boboli $ A clean if rather plain option for lodgings in the area. Some of its few rooms overlook a bit of green in the back. ♦ Via Romana 63. 2298645, 2336518, 2337169

19 Ficalbi & Balloni *Trompe l'oeil* painting is the specialty of **Stefano Ficalbi** and **Maurizio Balloni**, who decorate everything from large murals to tiny boxes in Neoclassical style. ♦ Closed Su, lunch. Via Romana 49r. 223009

20 Il Barone di Porta Romana ★★$$$ There's nothing baronial about this restaurant, which offers a standard Florentiné menu in a comfortable country setting, with dining in an outdoor garden in the warmer months. ♦ Closed Su. Via Romana 123. 220585

21 Porta Romana (1326) This and a few other gates to the city are remnants of the medieval walls that once surrounded Florence. They lasted from the end of the 12th century until 1865, when, in an effort to modernize the short-lived capital of Italy, they were largely demolished. The boulevards (*viali*) now follow their outline. (The longest sections of remaining walls extend on either side of the Porta Romana.) The road here led to Rome, hence the gate's name. Its portal and fresco of the *Madonna with Child and Saints* date from the 14th century. The large white statue on the grass outside it is contemporary, by **Michelangelo Pistoletto**. ♦ Piazzale di Porta Romana

22 Gipsoteca dell'Istituto d'Arte This curious little museum is reached by following a gravel path from the gate next to a tripe stand popular with students from the art school which houses the museum. Walk through the run-down park filled with dogs and their walkers to the building at the end of the path, formerly the royal stables. The collection consists of plaster casts of famous sculptures (**Michelangelo**'s *David* and *Prisoners*) and even paintings (**Titian**'s *Venus*), quite dusty but supposedly used for didactic purposes by the art academy surrounding it. ♦ By appointment only. Piazzale di Porta Romana 9. 220521

23 Villa Carlotta $$ This small hotel, in a modernized 19th-century palazzo, suits the needs of those who want to stay outside of the hustle and bustle of the center, yet remain in pleasant walking distance from Porta Romana. ♦ Via Michele di Lando 3. 220530

Restaurants/Nightlife: Red   Hotels: Blue
Shops/Parks: Green   Sights/Culture: Black

24 Villa Cora $$$$ A larger, much more luxurious version of the above (in addition to lavish 19th-century decorations and a private garden, it has a strictly 20th-century swimming pool), the Villa Cora attracts a business clientele and local passersby who have come to dine at its restaurant, **Taverna Machiavelli** (below). ♦ Deluxe ♦ Viale Machiavelli 18. 2298451

Within the Villa Cora:

Taverna Machiavelli ★★★$$$ International cuisine is the rule here, supplemented with Tuscan specialties. *Carpaccio* is a popular choice among the many antipasti, as are the Tuscan soups *ribollita* (made with bread, white beans and vegetables) and *pappa al pomodoro* (rich, thick tomato soup). Good old-fashioned lobster thermador goes well with the lavish decor of the restaurant, which opens out onto the pool in the summer. ♦ 2298451

25 San Leonardo (11th c) This little church gave its name to the street where it stands, **Via di San Leonardo**, every Florentine's favorite country road, lined with olive orchards and stone walls. The Romanesque church, restored in 1899 and 1921, contains a lovely Romanesque pulpit moved here from the demolished church of **San Piero a Scheraggio** in 1782. ♦ Via di San Leonardo

26 Forte di Belvedere (1590-95, **Bernardo Buontalenti**) Entered from Costa San Giorgio and occasionally from the Bóboli Gardens, the Forte di Belvedere affords beautiful views of Florence and vicinity from all sides, as its name promises. The rustic fortress was designed to fortify **Grand Duke Ferdinando I de' Medici**'s ego more than anything else—notice the heavy-handed Medici coat of arms. The star-shaped bastions are topped by the **Palazzetto di Belvedere**, designed by Buontalenti in the Mannerist style, with windows set on the sides and decreasing in size on the higher stories; it was the temporary residence of **Grand Duke Ferdinando II de' Medici** during the plague of 1633. The Porta San Giorgio entrance to the Forte has a fresco of the *Madonna and Saints* by **Bicci di Lorenzo** and a relief of *St. George*. There are often indoor and outdoor exhibitions at the site, which also hosts outdoor film screenings in the summer. ♦ Daily 9AM-8PM. Via di San Leonardo. 2342882

27 Spirito Santo (14th c; remodeled 1705, **Gian Battista Foggini**) Stone-faced on the outside, this Baroque church is one of the lightest in Florence inside. It is filled with 17th-century paintings, including *The Glory of St. George* (the church is also known as **San Giorgio**) by **Alessandro Gherardini**, a ceiling fresco. To the right of the altar is a *Madonna and Child with Two Angels*, considered an early work by Giotto. ♦ Costa di San Giorgio

28 Casa di Galileo Galilei Galileo lived in this palazzo, now covered with faded frescoes, and **Grand Duke Ferdinando II de' Medici** used to stop by on his morning walks from the family residence in the Palazzetto di Belvedere. ♦ Costa di San Giorgio 19

29 Il Torchio This *torchio*, or printing press, produces some of the loveliest marbelized paper in Florence, applied to notebooks, boxes, picture frames and other gift items. ♦ Closed M morning, Su, lunch. Via de' Bardi 17r. No credit cards. 2398262

30 Santa Lucia dei Magnoli The interior of this church contains a panel of *Saint Lucy* by the Sienese painter **Pietro Lorenzetti**. ♦ Via de' Bardi

31 Palazzi de' Mozzi (13th c) Three adjacent medieval palazzi once owned by the now-extinct Mozzi family, wealthy bankers who belonged to the Guelph party. **Pope Gregory X** stayed here in 1273 to negotiate a peace, albeit temporary, between the Guelphs and Ghilbellines. ♦ Piazza de' Mozzi

Colli

32 Centro Di Situated in the basement of the **Palazzo Torrigiani**, this hip art bookshop (a favorite of ours) stocks material from many periods in many languages, and has a distinguished small press of its own, specializing in museum and exhibition catalogs. ♦ Closed M morning, Su, lunch. Piazza de' Mozzi 1r. 2342666

33 Museo Bardini A precursor to **Bernard Berenson**, dealer-connoisseur **Stefano Bardini** (1836-1922) built this palazzo out of bits and pieces of other buildings (tearing down a 13th-century church in the process), and filled it with an eclectic collection to match. The result would make a good spread in *Architectural Digest* today, consisting of artworks from Classical and Etruscan pieces to 17th-century Florentine paintings thrown together with the unfailing eye of an uptown interior decorator. ♦ M-Tu, Th-Sa 9AM-2PM; Su 8AM-1PM. Piazza de' Mozzi 1. 2342427

34 Silla $$$ This small hotel is just far enough away from the center of town to be relaxing (the greenery helps) yet within convenient walking distance to most of the major sights. ♦ Via dei Renai 5. 234288

35 Piazza Nicola Demidoff This piazza is named after the wealthy Russian ambassador and philanthropist who lived in Florence from 1773-1828 and died in the nearby Palazzo Serristori. The main feature of the piazza is an elaborate monument, covered with a glass canopy to protect it from the elements, of **Nicola Demidoff** by the Neoclassical sculptor **Lorenzo Bartolini** of allegorical figures of the virtues, which Demidoff was said to personify. ♦ Piazza Nicola Demidoff

36 San Niccolò sopr'Arno (12th c; reconstructed 15th c; additions 16th c) This church has a simple facade, on which the portal and rose window were added during the Renaissance. The interior contains numerous 15th- and 16th-century paintings by minor local artists. ♦ Via di San Niccolò

Tuscans are known by other Italians as *mangiafagioli*, or bean eaters.

Colli

37 Palazzo Serristori (1515; rebuilt 1873,
Mariani Falcani) This palazzo takes its name
from one of Florence's most distinguished
noble families, the Serristori, who gave Italy
numerous men of state, from 15th-century
soldiers to a 20th-century senator. (It is now
best known for its wines, among them *Chianti*
Classico Machiavelli, named for its ancestor,
Niccolò Machiavelli, a clever marketing ploy
which would undoubtedly have pleased him.)
In the 19th-century, family members also became landlords, renting to Russian ambassador **Nicola Demidoff, King of Westphalia
Jerome Bonaparte**, and **King of Naples** and
Spain Joseph Bonaparte, who died here in
1844. Gone are the days of the *grandes fetes*
given by **Countess Ortensia Serristori**:
severely damaged during the 1966 flood, the
palazzo is of interest to the passerby today for
its vast garden. ♦ Lungarno Serristori

38 Porta San Niccolò (1324) An imposing 3-
story medieval tower, built not as a residence but
for defense purposes. ♦ Piazza Giuseppe Poggi

39 Trattoria del Granducato ★★$$ The Grand
Dukes would have felt right at home in this
antiques-furnished trattoria, where the decor
dates from the 15th century. **Natalia** and **Gianni**'s
dishes are equally noble, such as *tortellini
tartufati* (tortellini stuffed with truffles) and
fagiano (pheasant) done the same way. ♦ Closed
M lunch, Su, Aug. Via di San Niccolò 8r. No
credit cards. 2345037

40 Le Sorelle ★★$$ This typically Tuscan
restaurant has a seasonal menu, but you can
always depend on the *spaghetti al pomodoro*
here, prepared perfectly *al dente* and smothered
in rich tomato sauce just like mother—whoops,
the sisters—used to make. ♦ Closed Th. Via di
San Niccolò 30r. 2342722

41 Il Rifrullo This loungy bar/cafe isn't as trendy
as it was when it opened a few years ago, making it all the more pleasant for those who find
Florentine nightlife a bit of a yawn. Instead, it's
settled into the comfortable role of one of the
few decent places in town for a late-night drink,
ice cream, light sandwich or dessert—including

some fine renditions of British and American
fare. ♦ Closed W. Via di San Niccolò 57r.
2342621

42 Gelateria Frilli All the climbing in this part
of town will doubtless make you appreciate the
mounds of homemade ice cream the Frilli
family produces daily in its little grocery store.
Flavors change according to the season, but
year-round treats include *caffè* (coffee),
mousse al cioccolato (chocolate mousse) and
crema (vanilla custard). ♦ Closed W. Via San
Miniato 5r. 2345014

43 Porta di San Miniato A relatively small
medieval city gate which for centuries has provided passage from Florence to the church of
San Miniato, these days via the long staircase
at the end of the street just outside it. ♦ Via San
Miniato

44 La Beppa ★★$$ This homey trattoria offers
home-style cooking—if your home is in the
Tuscan countryside. Particularly good are the
first-course soups (*ribollita, pappa al pomodoro*
minestrone). ♦ Closed W, Aug. Via dell' Erta
Canina 6r. No credit cards. 2342742

45 Jackie O One of the first discos to open in
Florence (you can guess when that was by its
name), Jackie O has made the full swing from
'60s to '60s revival, without missing a chic
beat. ♦ Closed M. Via dell' Erta Canina 24a.
2342442

46 Piazzale Michelangiolo (1873, **Giuseppe
Poggi**) Piazzale means big piazza, and
Michelangiolo is a strange corruption of
Michelangelo, to whom this panoramic piazza
is dedicated. It could just as easily be dedicated
to Cupid, given the amorous Florentines who
park their cars in this postcard-perfect scenic
overlook of the city, famous for its sunsets sil-
houetting cypresses and the major monuments
and rendering the Arno golden as it passes
beneath a succession of bridges. Michelangelo
was originally supposed to be commemorated
here with a museum of all his works in Florence
brought together under one roof in the Loggia
(below). As if that idea weren't ill-advised
enough, architect Poggi devised as a monument
an odd bronze hybrid of some of Michelangelo's
most famous works in Florence, *David* and the
sculptures from the **Medici** tombs—the end
result of which some have called a giant paper-
weight. Under the olive trees to the right of the
piazza is an iris garden. The flower, which
originally in a stylized white and later a red
version became the symbol of Florence, is
celebrated each May in an international iris
show in the piazza. ♦ Piazzale Michelangiolo

47 La Loggia ★★★$$ Instead of architect
Giuseppe Poggi's Michelangelo museum, this
space is occupied by a surprisingly good restaurant for such a touristy location, though it's
a bit of a culinary museum in its own right.
Old-fashioned items such as shrimp cocktail
(swimming in Russian dressing) and
châteaubriand with bernaise sauce appear
alongside such Italian classics as prosciutto

from Parma and *bistecca alla fiorentina*, a thick steak grilled with olive oil and served with wedges of fresh lemon and cracked pepper. Most of the ambitious proposals are successful, and the view certainly can't be beat—ask for an outdoor table, or a window seat in the cooler weather. ◆ Closed W, 2 weeks in Aug. Piazzale Michelangiolo 1. 2342832

48 Gelateria Michelangiolo If it's hot or if you've hiked all the way up to the piazza and need some refreshment, have one of the numerous homemade ice creams here, a hangout for young Florentine roadsters, who also appreciate its pinball parlor. ◆ Closed Tu. Viale Galileo Galilei 2r. 2342705

49 San Salvatore al Monte (1499, **Cronaca**) **Michelangelo** called this simple Franciscan church, high on the hills overlooking Florence, *my pretty little country girl*. No doubt he appreciated the 3 windows on the facade, which used alternating triangular and curved pediments (a Roman convention) for the first time in Florence, just as the columns in the simple interior use alternate orders for the first time locally. ◆ Piazza di San Salvatore al Monte

50 San Miniato al Monte (ca 1018-1207) Florence's most beloved church crowns the highest hill in the vicinity, San Miniato, formerly called **Mons Florentinus**, and it is well worth a detour. It was built on the spot where an early martyr, known in English as **Minias**, according to legend carried his head from the Roman amphitheater across the Arno and up the hill. The geometric green-and-white marble facade (the green is from Prato, the white from Carrara)

ranks with the Baptistry among the finest examples of Romanesque architecture in Florence, embellished with a 13th-century mosaic of *Christ and the Virgin and San Miniato* above the central window. Inside is a 13th-century marble pavement with signs of the zodiac; **Michelozzo**'s 15th-century **Crucifix Chapel**; the 15th-century **Chapel of the Cardinal of Portugal** with a monument to the cardinal, who died in Florence, by **Antonio Rosellino**; an *Annunciation* by **Alesso Baldovinetti**; angels by **Antonio Pollaiuolo**; a terracotta ceiling by **Luca della Robbia**; and a pulpit alive with Romanesque animals. In the crypt, along with the **Reliquary Altar of Saint Minias**, are ancient columns and frescoes by **Taddeo Gaddi**. Monks sing mass here each day

at 5:45PM, 4:45PM in winter. On the church grounds are the **Palazzo Vescovile** (1295, **Andrea dei Mozzi**), built by the bishop of Florence as a summer residence; a bell tower, built on a pre-existing structure (1523, **Baccio d'Agnolo**) and never finished; and fortifications put up by **Michelangelo** barely in time for the 1529 siege of Florence, finished by **Francesco da Sangallo** and others in 1553. ◆ Via del Monte alle Croci 34

Bests

Marchese Piero Antinori
Wine Producer

Via Maggio and its antique shops: walking along, looking and talking with the owners.

Snack at **Procacci** in Via Tornabuoni eating the *panini tartufati* (truffles sandwiches).

Climbing up **Brunelleschi**'s **Cupola del Duomo** around sunset in springtime.

Sales at **Ferragamo** in January, followed by a hot chocolate at **Rivoire** in Piazza della Signoria and a visit at the nearby **Uffizi Gallery**.

Drinks after a hot summer day at the **Loggia** of the **Hotel San Michele** in Fiesole.

A good seat for the **Calcio in Costume** in **Piazza Santa Croce** in June.

A flying lesson above the city of Florence.

Choosing presents at the **Officina Farmaceutica di Santa Maria Novella**.

Dinner with a loud group of friends at **Il Latini**.

Everything about Florence seems to be coloured with a mild violet, like diluted wine.
Henry James

Restaurants/Nightlife: Red   Hotels: Blue
Shops/Parks: Green   Sights/Culture: Black

Santa Maria Novella

Tourism is nothing new to this part of town. As a plaque in **Piazza Santa Maria Novella** states, the area was once called *la Mecca degli stranieri*—the Mecca of foreigners. Indeed, as the plaque reads, **Henry Wadsworth Longfellow** stayed here, as did numerous others. **Henry James** wrote *Roderick Hudson* in a house on **Via della Scala**. **John Ruskin** took his inspiration for *Florentine Mornings* from **Francesca Alexander**, who stayed in a hotel on the piazza. And **William Dean Howells**, **Ralph Waldo Emerson** and **Percy Bysshe Shelley** all sojourned here as well.

Today the most conspicuous contingent of foreigners are the Third World immigrants who congregate in the piazza on weekends. At all times, however, foreigne

7-91 see pg. ##

ntinually pour out of the nearby train station (a masterpiece of Functionalist chitecture) named after the church of Santa Maria Novella to see the sights and tend conferences at **Palazzo dei Congressi** and **Palazzo degli Affari**.

lmost as if deliberately designed to accommodate the foreigners, many of the reets in the area take the form of broad avenues. It is no accident that **Via ornabuoni**, Italy's most elegant shopping street, is filled with shops in the best orentine mercantile tradition. After the Arno, it is the widest and most welcoming (if you can call the somewhat sinister lineup of palazzi welcoming) expanse in e historical part of the city. Almost as wide, if not quite as welcoming because of eir barracks-like buildings funneling a barrage of Vespa mopeds and car traffic, are any of the other streets near Santa Maria Novella. But at least they are more negotile than most parts of Florence, having been laid out as straight and oddly intercting as the lances in **Paolo Uccello**'s painting *The Battle of San Romano* in the ffizi.

nother aspect of the area seems almost to have been predestined to attract a ertain group of foreigners. It is the legacy of its former residents, the **Vespucci** mily, who as merchants and **Medici** vil servants had a great deal of contact ith outsiders. A bridge over the Arno, a

retch of street along it, and chapels in the church of the Ognissanti were all amed after them. And one of its members, **Amerigo**, gave his name not only to e New World but to the Americans who continue to return to this part of lorence to their consulate and their church, not to mention to **Harry's Bar**.

1 Piazza Santa Maria Novella Once used by the Dominicans of the church of Santa Maria Novella for preaching to the multitudes, this piazza was later adapted for public spectacles, including horse races run around the giant obelisks resting on **Giambologna**'s bronze turtles. Today its pervading calm is enlivened at sunset, when the Hitchcockian starlings swoop down into the cypresses in the church cemetery and chatter endlessly into the night.
♦ Piazza Santa Maria Novella

2 Palazzo Pitti Not a misprint. Yes, **Luca Pitti** lived in this relatively humble palazzo before his family went bankrupt building their more famous digs across the river. A plaque on the facade recalls **Giuseppe Garibaldi**'s soujourn when it was a hotel in 1867. Here the unifier of Italy stirred the crowds with the words, *Rome or die*. While not in keeping with the piazza's tradition as a Mecca for foreigners, the speech was in line with the great Dominican preachers who once filled the piazza. ♦ Piazza Santa Maria Novella 21

3 Santa Maria Novella (begun 1246, **Fra Sisto** and **Fra Ristoro**, completed 1360; facade mid-14th c, **Fra Jacopo Talenti**, completed 1470, **Leon Battista Alberti**; remodeled 1565-71, **Giorgio Vasari**) The town fathers erected the present church of Santa Maria Novella on the site of a 10th-century oratorio for the dogmatic, inflammatory Dominican preaching order. Leon Battista Alberti, a true *Renaissance man* (in addition to being an architect and architectural theorist, he was a painter, scientist, musician and playwright) was responsible for finishing the colored-marble, Romanesque-

Gothic facade in Renaissance style, complete with a plug for his patron **Giovanni Ruccellai** emblazoned in Latin along with the date of completion beneath the pediment. As Alberti wrote the first Renaissance treatise on architecture (*De re aedificatoria*), so he designed the facade in the first Renaissance use of his theories of harmonic proportions. The system was remarkably well-named; despite the theorizing, the facade remains pleasingly un-dogmatic if a bit 2-dimensional and Dodge-City-like with what appears to be a false front, like so many Florentine church facades. Alberti was the first to use those scroll-like shapes, known as volutes, on either side of the temple-like upper portion of the facade, and in this case they were meant to mask the nave aisles. Not inappropriately given Alberti's scientific bent, the astronomical instruments were added to the

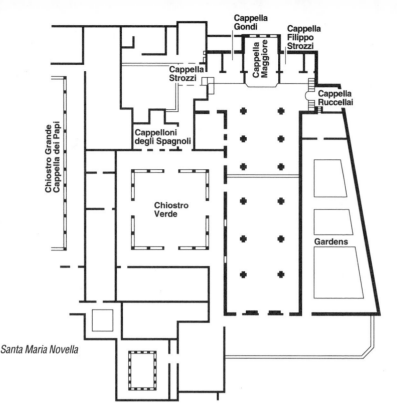

Santa Maria Novella

facade in 1572 by the Dominican **Egnazio Danti**, astronomer to **Cosimo I de' Medici**. The pointed *pietra forte* bell tower to the left of the facade (attributed to Fra Jacopo Talenti) is complemented in visual volume and often surpassed in acoustical volume by the starling-filled cypresses above the old cemetery niches to the right, which are called *avelli* and give their name to the short street along the side.

The vast Gothic interior was richly decorated in the early Renaissance and later refurbished by Vasari, who characteristically whitewashed over a number of frescoes. In the second bay on the right aisle is the 15th-century tomb of **Beata Villana** by **Bernardo Rossellino**. At the end of the right transept is the **Cappella Ruccellai** (Ruccellai Chapel), which has a 14th-century statue of the *Virgin* by **Nino Pisano** and the 15th-century bronze tomb of **Leonardo Dati** by **Lorenzo Ghiberti**. To the right of the altar is the **Cappella Filippo Strozzi**, with a 15th-century tomb of **Filippo Strozzi** by **Benedetto da Maiano** and frescoes from the same period by **Filippino Lippi**. **Boccaccio** chose the chapel (before it was given its present embellishment) as the fictitious meeting-place of the young storytellers at the beginning of *The Decameron*. The high altar has a bronze crucifix by **Giambologna**. Behind it, in the **Cappella Maggiore**, is a 15th-century fresco cycle by **Domenico Ghirlandaio** allegedly depicting the lives of the Virgin and St. John the Baptist, but it is actually a delightful document of everyday life in Florence at the time. The **Cappella Gondi**, to

the left of the high altar, designed by **Giuliano da Sangallo** in the early 16th century, has a 15th-century crucifix by **Brunelleschi**, his only work in wood. The **Cappella Strozzi** at the left end of the transept is frescoed with 14th-century scenes of *The Last Judgement, Paradise* and *Hell* by **Nardo di Cione**, and has an altarpiece by **Orcagna** from the same period. Behind it in the sacristy is a 13th-century crucifix by **Giotto**. Returning to the entrance down the left aisle, the next-to-last pilaster is adorned with a 15th-century pulpit designed by Brunelleschi and executed by his adopted son **Buggiano**. Just behind it is the most popular work in the church, the 15th-century fresco, *Holy Trinity with the Virgin, St. John the Evangelist, and Donors*, by **Masaccio**. ♦ Piazza Santa Maria Novella

4 **Chiostri di Santa Maria Novella** (Cloisters of Santa Maria Novella) (ca 1350, **Fra Giovanni Bracchetti** and **Fra Jacopo Talenti**) The **Chiostro Verde** or Green Cloister takes its name from the green tint which predominates **Paolo Uccello's** 15th-century masterpiece fresco cycle of the *Universal Deluge* (ironically, it was badly damaged during the 1966 flood), as concerned with movement and perspective as his *Battle of San Romano* in the Uffizi but more charged with emotion. The **Refectory** has a 16th-century *Last Supper* by **Alessandro Allori**. The **Chiostro Grande** or Great Cloister is now closed to the public. It is part of the noncommissioned officers' school of the *carabinieri* police—an intriguing proposition since Italy's finest are often the butt of jokes about their intellectual capa-

bilities. (Q. Why do carabinieri always travel in pairs? A. Because one knows how to read, the other knows how to write.) Still, they sometimes understand the visitor's request to see the cloister's **Cappella dei Papi**, frescoed in the 16th century by **Jacopo Pontormo** and **Ridolfo del Ghirlandaio**. The **Cappelloni degli Spagnoli** (Spanish Chapel, so-called because **Eleanor of Toledo**, wife of **Cosimo I de' Medici**, gave her fellow Spaniards burial privileges there) is completely covered with 14th-century frescoes by **Andrea da Firenze** glorifying the Dominican order founded by the Spaniard, **St. Dominic**. Note the symbolic pooches (*domini canes,* Latin for *dogs of God* , is a play on the name of the order) and the famous Dominican saints Dominc, **Thomas Aquinas** and **Peter Martyr** (all of whom preached at Santa Maria Novella) refuting heretics. ♦ Admission. M-Th, Sa 9AM-2PM; Su 8AM-1PM. Piazza Santa Maria Novella. 282187

5 Grand Hotel Minerva $$$ The unassuming facade conceals a very elegant hotel, many of whose 112 rooms have views of Piazza Santa Maria Novella or the church cloisters. Other amenities include a not-bad restaurant serving Tuscan and international food overlooking a quiet private garden, and a rooftop swimming pool for philistines who want to do their laps amid a sea of terracotta roofs and Florentine monuments. ♦ Piazza Santa Maria Novella 16. 284555

6 Officina Profumo-Farmaceutica di Santa Maria Novella This centuries-old *erboristeria* was opened to the public in 1612 by Dominican monks from the church of Santa Maria Novella, who prepared medicinals for local hospitals and such clients as **Catherine de' Medici**. Today the tradition continues with all sorts of exotic products, such as handmade soaps, skin creams, shampoos, liqueurs (the Medici's own

The Muraled Refectories of Florence

Refectories—convent or monastery dining halls—were often painted with murals depicting the *Last Supper*, when Christ ate with his disciples on the night of his betrayal. Florence abounds with such muraled refectories, called *cenacoli* in Italian. Making the rounds of them puts an interesting spin on a visit to the city, combining art history with a meditative experience while providing a tour of some of the city's most characteristic neighborhoods. There are 6 *cenacoli* in Florence. The earliest is in the former refectory of the church of **Santo Spirito** (next to the church of Santo Spirito, where Augustinian monks once supped and a museum is now installed. The fresco was painted by **Andrea Orcagna** around 1360; only fragments remain. **Andrea del Castagno**'s 1450 depiction of the theme in the refectory of the former convent of **Sant'Appollonia** is fraught with dark drama, the rugged-looking apostles intense and self-contained figures beneath equally

Santa Maria Novella

intensely patterned marble background panels. **Domenico Ghirlandaio**'s 1480 *Last Supper* (in the refectory within the cloister next to the church of **Ognissanti** is celebratory in nature, with Christ and the apostles dining on an elaborately embroidered tablecloth and a garden filled with lemon trees and chirping birds in the background. In the refectory of the former convent of **Sant'Onofrio** is **Perugino**'s delicate version of the subject, done with a perspective opening on to a landscape of the artist's native Umbria. In the former abbey of **San Salvi** is **Andrea del Sarto**'s bright and billowy 1516 *Last Supper*, one of the most glorious moments of the High Renaissance in Florence. Finally, **Poccetti**'s late 16th-century rendition of the subject back in another refectory at the former convent of Sant'Appollonia (entrance at Via San Gallo 25) is the last, if not the strongest, treatment of the theme.

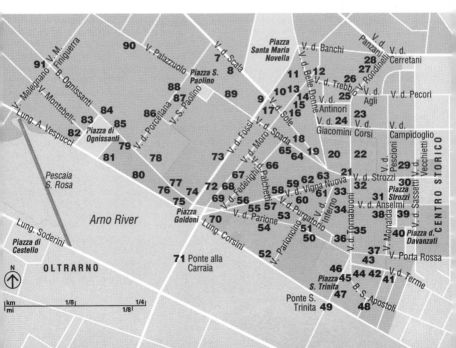

is still sold as *liquore mediceo*), and pungent smelling salts called *aceto dei sette ladri* (seven thieves' vinegar from the plague days when corpse-robbers, each knowing one of its secret ingredients, used it to protect themselves on their gruesome rounds). The monks are gone, but the knockout Neo-Gothic salesroom is presided over with Dominican astringency by the white-coated high priestesses of Florentine *erboristerie*. ♦ Closed M morning, Su, lunch. Via della Scala 16. 216276

7　Hotel Croce di Malta $$$ A very pleasant smallish hotel in a former convent which conserves a feeling of privacy and simplicity in its understated and serene decor, with a touch of modernity in the tranquil garden swimming pool. Its restaurant, **Il Cocodrillo** (★★$$), has a Tuscan and international menu. ♦ Via della Scala 7. 218351, 282600

Santa Maria Novella

8　Caffè Voltaire ★★$$ A high-tech supper club drawing young professional Florentines to a program of jazz, rock, classical and other music and a restaurant serving trendy international Italian dishes such as *carpaccio* and pasta with porcini mushrooms. ♦ Daily 5PM-3AM. Via della Scala 9r. 218255

9　Loggia di San Paolo (1489-96) Built in the style of **Brunelleschi**'s loggia for the hospital of the **Innocenti** in Piazza Santissima Annunziata, and here for the hospital of San Paolo behind it. Its medallions, by **Luca** and **Andrea della Robbia**, depict saints, including a lunette by Andrea illustrating *The Meeting of Saint Francis and Saint Dominic*, which supposedly took place in the hospital. **Il Quadrifoglio**, a florist in a former chapel of the loggia (No. 9/B, 283010) sells little sachets of long-lasting Florentine lavender which make lovely gifts or souvenirs. ♦ Piazza Santa Maria Novella

10　Hotel Roma $$$ This small, crisp hotel reopened in 1988. Its time-honored views of the old monuments of Piazza Santa Maria Novella are seen from efficient and clean rooms. ♦ Piazza Santa Maria Novella 8. 210336

11　The Fiddler's Elbow Just off the green of Piazza Santa Maria Novella is this Irish pub, with recorded Irish background music and real Guinness, Harp and Kilkenny, as well as English cider. Though the pub decor makes it look as though it's been around since James Joyce

came to Italy, in fact it just opened recently, and was an instant hit with Florentines who like to *alzare il gomito* (raise the elbow, to drink rather than fiddle) and foreigners alike. ♦ M-Tu, Th-Su 4:30PM-12:30AM. Piazza Santa Maria Novella 7r. 216056

12　Croce al Trebbio (1308) This cross was erected at the intersection of 3 streets (now 5) where Dominicans inflamed by the preaching of St. Peter Martyr at nearby Santa Maria Novella battled heathen heretics. ♦ Intersection of Via del Moro and Via delle Belle Donne

13　Latteria/Bar Ponticelli This *latteria* or dairy shop is one of the few places open on Sunday for a limited selection of last-minute grocery items and wine when you just don't feel like taking on another restaurant. ♦ M, W-Su 9AM-7:30PM. Via del Moro 61r. 216703

14　Franco Maria Ricci Marchese Franco Maria Ricci's small publishing house is the very definition of esoteric, from his glossy magazines *FMR* and *KOS* to such titles as *Lost Florence* and *Lewis Carroll*, all on sale in the tiny Florence branch of his Milan-based enterprise. ♦ Closed M morning, Su, lunch. Via delle Belle Donne 41r. 283312

15　After Dark Of all Florence's English-language bookshops, After Dark is the most centrally located and has the largest selection of Italy-related material in English. **Norman Grant**, the affable Scottish proprietor, promised us he was expanding his stock of English-language magazine titles (he already carries over 200) and English-language videocassettes. On the European PAL system, the videos make thoughtful gifts for your Anglophone Florentine friends, especially if they understand the expression *couch potato*. There are also lots of artsy postcards, and an extensive gay section. ♦ Closed M morning, Su, lunch. Via del Moro 86r. 294203

16　Spazio Uno This cultural center, much frequented by Florence's Third World population, is best known as the only place left in town that regularly screens art films. Stop in and pick up a program—many of the screenings are in the original language, a rarity in the land of the dubbers' Mafia. ♦ Via del Sole 10. 283389

17　Cellerini One of Florence's finest leather craftsmen, **Silvano Cellerini** prides himself on original creations of bags and suitcases, as well as a limited selection of men's and women's shoes and a collection of Hermès look-alikes. ♦ Closed M morning, Su, lunch. Via del Sole 37r. 282533

17 Buca Mario ★★$$ This downstairs restaurant draws largely a tourist crowd, but if you're comfortable in such surroundings, try the inoffensive versions of Tuscan soups and *bistecca alla fiorentina* (a slab of steak grilled with olive oil). ♦ Closed W, lunch Th, 2 weeks in July. Piazza degli Ottaviani 16. 214179

18 Rafanelli The Bronze Age is going strong at the showroom of these *bronzisti* or bronze-workers, **Enzo** and **Renato Rafanelli**, whose workshop is in the artisan's quarter across the river. Bedsteads, fireguards, doorknobs, knockers and other hand-crafted bronze and copper objects are the dazzling inventory of this unusual shop. ♦ Closed M morning, Su, lunch. Via del Sole 7r. 283518

19 Ideabooks A nice selection of art, photography, design and fashion books as well as posters and postcards in a light and lively, contemporary setting. ♦ Closed M morning, Su, lunch. Via del Sole 3r. 284533

20 Belle Donne ★★$$ The name is not visible from the outside, but this hole-in-the-wall eatery is named after its street, which translates as *beautiful women*, hinting at its shady past. (In fact you'll find a residual contingent of not-so-beautiful women practicing the world's oldest profession on the surrounding pavement.) The restaurant, on the other hand, is popular with younger professionals who work indoors in the chic surroundings, venturing out for a light lunch of soup and salad, or more substantial dinners, eaten communally and followed by some of the best desserts in town. ♦ Closed Sa-Su. Via delle Belle Donne 16. No credit cards. 2382609

21 Giacosa Count Camille Negroni invented the Negroni cocktail (one-third Campari bitter, one-third Martini & Rossi sweet vermouth and one-third gin) here in the 1920s. Today the cafe attracts an upscale crowd of young Florentines for cocktails, coffee and snacks at the bar or the tiny tables. ♦ M-Sa 8AM-7:30PM. Via dei Tornabuoni 83. 2396226

22 Palazzo Corsi (1875, **Telemaco Bonaiuti**) This rambling palazzo was built in the 19th century in place of a 15th-century palazzo by **Michelozzo**, whose courtyard stands invitingly intact within. ♦ Via dei Tornabuoni 16

Within Palazzo Corsi:

Cassetti Glass Porcelain and silver from around the world are the feature of this pricey shop, the only one in Florence authorized to sell the glassware of Venini, the Murano-based concern for whom internationally renowned designers have created beautiful collector-quality pieces. ♦ Closed M morning, Su, lunch. Via dei Tornabuoni 72r. 282387. Also at: Via del Strozzi 7. 210273

Seeber Florence's oldest bookshop (founded in 1865), one of the few in town staffed by actual bibliophiles and especially good for books on Florentine and Tuscan subjects, many of which are in English. ♦ Closed M morning, Su, lunch. Via dei Tornabuoni 70r. 215697

Procacci This family-run stand-up snack emporium is famed for its *panini tartufati* (truffle sandwiches). It also offers delicate concoctions made with salmon, anchovies and cheese, served with local wines and fresh-pressed tomato juice. *Chianti* wines and vinegars, as well as the trendy balsamic vinegar from Modena, are also available for purchase as gifts or souvenirs. ♦ Tu-Su 9AM-7:30PM. Via dei Tornabuoni 64r. 211656

23 San Gaetano (11th c; rebuilt 1604, **Matteo Nigetti**; 1633-48, **Gherardo** and **Pier Francesco Silvani**) San Gaetano has the truest-to-form of Florence's Baroque church facades, complete with billowy statues and imposing coats of arms (Medici, of course). Among the works of art within are *The Martyrdom of St. Lorenzo* by **Pietro da Cortona** and *Crucifix with Saints Mary Magdalene, Francis and Jerome* by **Filippo Lippi**. ♦ Via degli Agli 1

Santa Maria Novella

24 Hotel de la Ville $$$$ A modern hotel in an ancient location, this establishment is quiet and discreet, with one of the most intimate after-hours bars in town. ♦ Piazza Antinori 1. 261805

25 Palazzo Antinori (1461-66, **Giuliano da Maiano**) This rustic palazzo is now property of the **Marchesi Antinori**, known internationally for their wines. In the lovely porticoed courtyard is the **Cantinetta Antinori** (★★$$) where you can sample those vintages along with a light meal of soup or a sandwich at lunch or more substantial Florentine fare at dinnertime. ♦ Closed Sa-Su. Piazza degli Antinori 3. 2392234

25 Buca Lapi ★★$$ Downstairs on the right side of the Palazzo Antinori, Buca (pronounced *boo-ha* in the aspirated Florentine accent) is a typically self-deprecating restaurant name meaning *hole*. This one, papered with faded travel posters, prides itself on its *bistecca alla fiorentina* (the local steak specialty), and its various preparations for artichokes. ♦ Closed Su. Via del Trebbio 1r. 213768

Restaurants/Nightlife: Red	**Hotels:** Blue
Shops/Parks: Green	**Sights/Culture:** Black

26 Il Tricolore The *tricolore* refers to the 3 colors of the Italian flag, and this patriotic boutique sells Italian military and police uniforms and accessories. Much more chic than most such gear, the merchandise ranges from the plumed hats of the *bersaglieri* corps to artfully designed pins and medals, and Italian military watches. ♦ Closed M morning, Su, lunch. Via del Trebbio 4r. 210166

27 Richard Ginori Porcelain produced by the most famous manufacturer in Florence, indeed Italy. The Ginori line began in the 18th century,

Santa Maria Novella

merging in 1896 with the Milanese ceramic firm Richard to create the present partnership. Most of its current production is based on historical patterns, and other internationally known names such as Waterford and Lalique are on sale as well. ♦ Closed M morning, Su, lunch. Via Rondinelli 17r. 210041

28 Bojola Walking sticks, umbrellas, bags and luggage are manufactured with an eye to modern style by this Florentine institution, over a century old. ♦ Closed M morning, Su, lunch. Via Rondinelli 25r. 211155

29 Hotel Helvetia & Bristol $$$$ A recent renovation of this 19th-century hotel (where **Gabriele D'Annunzio, Igor Stravinsky, Luigi Pirandello** and **Giorgio di Chirico**, among others, stayed) fortunately did nothing to change the rich character of one of Florence's—indeed Italy's—finest hotels. Paintings and antiques give the public and guest rooms individual character. ♦ Deluxe ♦ Via dei Pescioni 2. 287814

Within Hotel Helvetia & Bristol:

The Bristol ★★★$$$ Located in the lavish hotel, this restaurant produces equally lavish versions of such local classics as *piccione alle olive nere* (squab with black olives) and *baccalà alla livornese* (dried cod with a spicy tomato sauce). ♦ Via dei Pescioni 2. 287814

30 Principe One of the top clothing stores in Florence, this large emporium specializes in faux-Anglo for men and women, and is also the exclusive agent for Missoni knitwear. ♦ Closed M morning, Su, lunch. Via del Strozzi 21-29r. 216821

30 Yab Yum Florence's oldest discotheque, a vast basement space with large dance floor and 2 bars, still attracts a wide age range of locals and visiting celebs. ♦ Closed M, W, July-Aug. Via dei Sassetti 5r. 282018

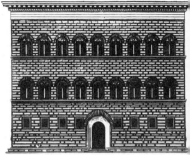

31 Palazzo Strozzi (begun 1489, **Benedetto da Maiano**; completed 1504, **Cronaca** and **Jacopo Rosselli**) Florence's most beautiful Renaissance palazzo was begun as the private residence of merchant **Filippo Strozzi** and continued intermittently as the family was exiled. The great cornice atop the heavily rusticated building was never completed, as may be seen from the Via Strozzi side. The palazzo now houses a number of organizations (such as the **Gabinetto Vieusseux**, a private library and reading room) and is used as an exhibition space. The most prestigious one to take place within it is the **Mostra-Mercato Internazionale dell'Antiquariato**, an international antiques biennial occurring in September on odd years. A fire at an antiques fair in Todi occasioned the hideous practicality of the fire stairs in the otherwise harmonious courtyard. ♦ Piazza Strozzi

32 La Residenza $$ This rambling, charming hotel reflects the personality of the deep-voiced signora who oversees a multilingual staff and a homey kitchen, should you choose to elect the old *pensione* or meal option. Some of the top-floor rooms have balconies overlooking Via Tornabuoni; all can enjoy the intimate glimpse of Centro Storico from the 3rd-floor lounge and Via Tornabuoni from the roof garden. ♦ Via dei Tornabuoni 8. 570093

32 Loggia Tornaquinci This glassed-in loggia by Renaissance architect **Cigola** today is the elegant setting for one of the first (and still the most sophisticated) piano bars to open in Florence, attracting some of the smoothest musicians in town who tinkle the piano as the lights of the city twinkle around you. ♦ Th-Su 10PM-2AM. Via dei Tornabuoni 6. 219148

33 Gucci The world's most famous fashion statement started right here in the firm's flagship store, where the full line of loafers, scarves, luggage and other items blazoned with interlocking G's glistens before the admiring eyes of status-conscious shoppers and the famously condescending sneers of the sales help. ♦ Closed M morning, Su, lunch. Via dei Tornabuoni 73r. 2384011. Also at: Via dei Tornabuoni 57-59r. 264011

33 Mario Buccellati The Florence branch of this Milanese designer, whose talents were praised in the poetry of **Gabriele D'Annunzio**, is still known for delicately handcrafted jewelry and sterling silver objects. ♦ Closed M morning, Su, lunch. Via dei Tornabuoni 71r. 2396579

33 Valentino Ladies who shop and lunch on Via Tornabuoni often combine their outings with a visit to this hairdresser. ♦ Closed M morning, Su, lunch. Via dei Tornabuoni 105r. 212323

34 Tanino Crisci A family-run business that has been crafting fine footwear for the well-heeled of both sexes for 3 generations. ♦ Closed M morning, Su, lunch. Via dei Tornabuoni 43-45r. 214692

GIORGIO ARMANI

34 Giorgio Armani The Florence home of the Milanese designer, known for his sophisticated interpretations of classic American tailoring, loosely cut in lavish fabrics. ♦ Closed M morning, Su, lunch. Via dei Tornabuoni 35-37r. 213819

34 Casadei The hallmark of this elegant women's shoe store is that many of its heels stand proudly high in spite of the highs and lows of trends in footwear. ♦ Closed M morning, Su, lunch. Via dei Tornabuoni 33r. 287240

35 Bijoux Casciou Fabulous fake jewelry. Gold plate and ersatz stones look convincingly like the real thing. ♦ Closed M morning, Su, lunch. Via Tornabuoni 32r. 284709. Also at: Via Por Santa Maria 1r. 2394378

35 Ugolini The firm that once gloved the hands of the Italian royal family continues to provide high quality merchandise in all types of leather for all types of clients, provided they can afford the price that once obliged the noblesse. ♦ Closed M morning, Su, lunch. Via dei Tornabuoni 20-22r. 216664

36 Tornabuoni Beacci $$ A charming (if somewhat noisy) former pensione on the top floors of a 14th-century palazzo, decorated like a house in the Tuscan countryside. It's just as welcoming, and the roof garden is just as sunny. A clientele of regulars requires making reservations well in advance, and one loyal client we know keeps her own mattress in storage here. ♦ Via dei Tornabuoni 3. 212645, 2388377

36 Settepassi-Faraone Florence's oldest jewelers recently moved here from the Ponte Vecchio with great fanfare, hardly necessary since it has been known since the time of the Medici as the most exclusive such enterprise in town. In addition to the diamonds, rubies, emeralds and silver objects, it is the only jeweler to use Oriental pearls in Italy. ♦ Closed M morning, Su, lunch. Via dei Tornabuoni 25r. 215506

37 Hotel Porta Rossa $$ The pleasantly decadent setting of smoked glass and antique furnishings draws a like crowd of English and French. Rooms are cavernous, inviting large parties. Part of the **Palazzo Bartolini Salimbeni**. ♦ Via Porta Rossa 19. 287551

37 La Bussola ★★$$ One of the nicest things about this comfortably modern-looking restaurant is that it's the only place in the center of town open until the wee hour of 2AM. Such dishes as *spaghetti allo scoglio* (made with a fresh seafood sauce) and the grilled meats almost make it worth staying up late. ♦ Closed M. Via Porta Rossa 58r. 2393376

38 Doney ★★$$ When Florence's literary landmark cafe/restaurant on Via Tornabuoni was taken over by a leather shop a few years ago, **Giorgio Armani** bought the fixtures and reopened the place in this space, from which a few tables spill out into the piazza during the warmer months. Frequented by local and foreign ladies who lunch, sip tea or down cocktails, it offers a light Italian menu of fresh ingredients that changes according to season. ♦ Closed Su. Piazza Strozzi 16r. 2398206

39 Palazzo dello Strozzino (begun 1458, **Michelozzo**; completed 1462-65, **Giuliano da Maiano**) **Filippo Strozzi** lived here while overseeing construction of his big place across the piazza. ♦ Piazza Strozzi 2

40 Museo dell'Antica Casa Fiorentina (Florentine House Museum) (14th c) The medieval **Palazzo Davanzati** houses displays of everyday objects used in Florence from the Gothic to the Renaissance periods. From the small courtyard, an elegant staircase leads upstairs to numerous Madonnas (including **Lorenzo Monaco**'s *Madonna and Child with Saints*), textiles, tapestries, chests and other furniture and decorations evocative of the domestic life of Florentine nobility. ♦ Admission. Tu-Sa 9AM-2PM; Su 9AM-12:45PM. Piazza d. Davanzati. 216518

41 Casa-Torre dei Buondelmonti (13th c) This medieval tower belonged to the Buondelmonti family, whose scion Buondelmonte's fickleness touched off the Guelph-Ghibelline conflicts in Tuscany (see Ponte Vecchio). Its street, **Via delle Terme**, preserves some of the aspect it had in the Middle Ages, when it was a mini-Manhattan bursting with towers for that *rvr vw* of the Arno, as an apartment listing in *The New York Times* would say. ♦ Via delle Terme at Chiasso delle Misure

Mannerist architect **Bernardo Buontalenti** is credited with creating the first *gelati* in 1565 for the court of **Francesco I de' Medici**.

42 Toula Oliviero ★★★$$$ The Florence branch of this elegant Veneto-based chain offers well-turned-out Tuscan specialties along with such classic Venetian dishes as *risotto nero di seppia* (made with squid ink), *pasta e fagioli alla veneta* (pasta with dense, soupy *borlotti* beans) and *fegato di vitello alla veneziana* (liver and onions like you've never had it). There are also many fish dishes, including a rare Italian appearance of caviar. The red-velvet decor is ideal for romantic dinners, though business lunchers are given a discount. ◆ Closed M lunch, Su, Aug. Via delle Terme 21r. 287643

42 Da Dante al lume di candela ★★$$$ A romantic, candlelit atmosphere for a pricey dinner for 2, with a menu based on seasonal ingredients, including some of the freshest fish in town. ◆ Closed M lunch, Su, Aug. Via delle Terme 23. 2394566

43 Palazzo Bartolini Salimbeni (1517-20, Baccio d'Agnolo) This palazzo, the first in Florence to embody the principles of the High Renaissance taking place in the Roman architecture of Raphael and Bramante in Rome, was initially criticized for looking more like a church than a residence. (Note the cross-shaped window sashes.) The Salimbeni family motto, *PER NON DORMIRE* (not to sleep—they were no slouches, it seems) and its counterpoint, poppies, appear throughout the palazzo. The small courtyard is decorated with ebullient *sgraffiti*, the 2-tone designs drawn on many Renaissance palazzi. ◆ Piazza Santa Trinita 1

44 La Nandina ★★$$ One of Florence's oldest restaurants has changed hands only twice in the last hundred years. In addition to an international menu are daily Tuscan specials and such staples as *ricotta arrostita* (baked ricotta cheese) and *gallina in odori* (chicken stewed in basil, tomato and other herbs). Huge antipasto table. ◆ Borgo Santissimi Apostoli 64r. 2130

45 Colonna della Giustizia This ancient granite *column of justice*, taken from the **Baths of Caracalla** in Rome, was given to **Cosimo I de' Medici** by **Pope Pius IV** after Medici forces had won the battle of Montemurlo (1537) and established the family's absolute power. The statue on top (1581) is by **Francesco del Tadda**. ◆ Piazza Santa Trinita

46 Santa Trinita (11th c; rebuilt 14th c, possibly by **Neri di Fioravante**; facade 1593-94, **Bernardo Buontalenti**) This Gothic church with a Renaissance facade contains a number of important 15th-century works of art. In the fourth chapel of the right aisle are an altarpiece and frescoes by **Lorenzo Monaco**. The **Cappella Sassetti** (Sassetti Chapel), in the right transept, has frescoes of *The Life of St. Francis* and *The Adoration of the Shepherds*, by **Domenico Ghirlandaio**, filled with rich scenes of 15th-century Florence, including portraits of **Lorenzo the Magnificent** and his sons **Piero, Giovanni** and **Giuliano** (to the right, in front of the **Piazza della Signoria**). The second chapel in the left transept contains the tomb of **Bishop Benozzo Federighi** by **Luca della Robbia**, and in the left aisle is a wooden statue of *Mary Magdalen* by **Desiderio da Settignano**. ◆ Piazza Santa Trinita

Ponte Santa Trinita

47 Palazzo Spini-Ferroni (1289) The greatest of the medieval palazzi in Florence, built as the residence of a family of wool merchants and today housing the shops and offices of their contemporary counterparts. ◆ Piazza Santa Trinita

Within Palazzo Spini-Ferroni:

Ferragamo The flagship store of the famous family-run shoe firm begun by Naples-born **Salvatore Ferragamo**, who came to Florence after a stint in Hollywood, where he became known as *shoemaker to the stars* by shoeing the feet of the likes of Mary Pickford and Douglas Fairbanks. Ever since, Americans have appreciated his family's understanding of their podiatric peculiarities. The rest of the body can also be clad in Ferragamo clothing and accessories, including silk scarves and ties. ◆ Closed M morning, Su, lunch. Via Tornabuoni 16r. 2392123

48 Hotel Berchielli $$$ Don't be put off by this hotel's lobby, a Postmodern apotheosis of polished marble. The rooms upstairs are quieter in all senses, all of them soundproofed and many with views of the Arno. ◆ Piazza del Limbo 6r (other entrance at Lungarno Accaioli 14) 2384061

49 Ponte Santa Trinita (1567-70, **Bartolommeo Ammannati**; reopened 1957) The graceful curves of the Ponte Santa Trinita make it the most beautiful bridge in Florence, maybe even the world. Designed by Ammannati using the curves from Michelangelo's tombs in the Cappelle Medicee, it was built of stone from the Bóboli Gardens. The bridge was blown up during the German retreat at the end of WWII, and painfully reconstructed from as much of the original pieces as could be salvaged and new stone from the original quarry, using the original plans and 16th-century stonecutting tools. The statues at either end represent the 4 seasons, the head of *Spring* retrieved from the river only in 1961 and recapitated with great fanfare. ◆ Piazza Santa Trinita

50 Chiostro del Convento di Santa Trinita (Cloister of the Convent of Santa Trinita) (1584, **Alfonso Parigi** to designs by **Bernardo Buontalenti**) The former cloister of the convent of Santa Trinita is now occupied by the **University of Florence Law School**. In the refectory are 17th-century frescoes of *The Story of Christ* by **Giovanni da San Giovanni** and **Nicodemo Ferrucci**. ◆ Via del Parione 7

Within the Cloisters:

Alimentari Orizi ★★$ There's something comfortably down-to-earth about **Mariano**'s invitingly simple downstairs grocery store in a neighborhood of lavish shops, whether it's the barrel seats used at the lunch counter, or lunch itself, which consists of sandwiches made to order out of such cheeses as mozzarella and *stracchino* and such cold-cuts as prosciutto and *bresaola*. ◆ M-Sa 8AM-7:30PM. Via del Parione 19r. No credit cards. 214067

51 Barretto This night spot, popular with Florence's young professionals, offers light piano music in dark wood surroundings. ◆ M-Sa 6PM-2AM. Closed Aug. Via del Parione 50. 2394122

51 Coco Lezzone ★★★$$$ Though the name of this restaurant is Florentine dialect for *big, smelly cook*, the food is great and aromatic in nothing but a positive sense. The sight of well-heeled Florentines and foreigners packed into the simple white-tile surroundings of this much frequented restaurant is an amusing lesson in radical chic eating. Tuscan specialties (the full range of peasant soups, roast meats accompanied by cannellini beans or cooked or fresh vegetables, pecorino cheese, extensive selection of *Chianti*) predominate. ◆ Closed W dinner, Su; Sa in summer. Via del Parioncino 238r. 287178

52 Palazzo Corsini (1648-56, **Pier Francesco Silvani** and **Antonio Ferri**) A bit of Baroque on the Renaissance underpinnings of this palazzo, the grandest of the many associated with the Corsini family in Florence. Its balustrudes and statuary are not quite as buoyant and ecstatic as their Roman counterparts would be, but even the Corsinis, it seems, felt obliged to make concessions to Florentine parsimony. ◆ Lungarno Corsini 10

52 Corsini pot ★★$$$ The Corsini family has lent its name (and landlordship) to this relatively new restaurant, and we're happy to see that maître d' **Mario Pucci** has lent his grace to its tables. Mario's presence at the old **Doney's** on Via Tornabuoni made it a pleasant place to dish among the dishes, and Corsini pot has something of the light-but-luxurious-lunch air of the legendary establishment. Even such earthy items as *pennette al ragù bianco tartufato* (pasta with white truffle sauce), boar prosciutto and roast kid seem to encourage airy exchanges of gossip among the upscale shoppers and shop owners from the tony surroundings. ◆ Closed M. Lungarno Corsini 4. 217706

53 Silvio ★★$$ Typical Tuscan dishes such as *ribollita* (bread-and-bean soup) and roast meats make this small restaurant a neighborhood favorite. ♦ Closed Su. Via del Parione 74r. 214005

54 Galleria Corsini The greatest private art collection in Florence, put together by **Lorenzo Corsini** (nephew of **Pope Clement XII**—the family has produced a number of religious figures, including a saint), whose idiosyncratic arrangement (a la Palazzo Pitti) includes important works by **Antonello da Messina, Pontormo, Signorelli** and **Raphael**. ♦ By appointment only. Via del Parione 11. 218994

54 Il Bisonte Tanned, undyed leather in casual designs is the hallmark of this shop, which also sells sheepskin jackets and coats. ♦ Closed M morning, Su, lunch. Via del Parione 35a/r. 215722

Santa Maria Novella

54 Bizzanti If you've ever harbored a perverse Pygmalion-like desire to appreciate a statue for more than strictly aesthetic reasons, now is your chance. Bizzanti sells replicas of the world's most famous sculpture, from **Michelangelo**'s *David* to Venuses ripe for blue jeans. While the prices are considerably higher than picture postcards, it's still less of an investment than breaking into the Bargello. ♦ Closed M morning, Su, lunch. Via del Parione 37-39r (other entrance Lungarno Corsini 44-46-48r) 215649

55 Minetta Best selection of hosiery in Florence for men and women, in every color, pattern and fabric imaginable. ♦ Closed M morning, Su, lunch. Via della Vigna Nuova 68r. 287984

55 Antico Setificio Fiorentino Florence was famous for its silk furnishings in medieval times, and more recently **Count Emilio Pucci** helped revive the time-honored art of weaving satins, velvets, brocades, damasks and taffetas in patterns old and new. Artisans produce individual orders of ten yards or more on 17th-century hand looms in the firm's factory on the other side of the Arno (see Oltrano). ♦ Closed M morning, Su, lunch. Via della Vigna Nuova 97r. 282700

56 &C. Florentine designer **Marco Baldini**'s papers have passed the litmus test of inclusion in the New York Museum of Modern Art's gift shop, but here you can pick up the widest possible selections of hand- and machine-made papers on their home turf. ♦ Closed M morning, Su, lunch. Via della Vigna Nuova 82r. 287839. Also at: Via della Vigna Nuova 91r. 215165

57 Caffe Amerini This comfortable, Postmodern-looking cafe attracts a like crowd of shoppers and shop clerks who sit at tiny granite tables and read magazines or groove to an interesting (and loud) selection of background music. A great place for a quick sandwich at lunch, it becomes something of a tearoom in the afternoon, offering dozens of brews and tasty pastries. ♦ M-Sa 8AM-1AM. Via della Vigna Nuova 63r. 284941

57 Ermenegildo Zegna An expensive menswear manufacturing firm known for its top-quality fabrics and stylishly conservative tailoring, here available in what Italians call *total look*, that is, everything from top to toe. ♦ Closed M morning, Su. Piazza Rucellai 4-7r. 211098

58 Palazzo Rucellai (1446-51, **Bernardo Rossellino** to designs of **Leon Battista Alberti**) The first and one of the most handsome of Florence's Renaissance palazzi, built for textile merchant **Giovanni Rucellai**. The family emblem, *Fortune's Sail*, may be seen on the palazzo facade, a classicized and refined version of the rusticated architecture prevalent at the time this was built. ♦ Via della Vigna Nuova 18

Within the Palazzo Rucellai:
Alinari The Alinari archives, primarily known for sepia views of 19th-century Italy and Italian works of art photographed at that time, provide the evocative stock of this shop. Its prints of period photos, loose or mounted on wood, make souvenirs reminiscent of Miss Lavish in **E.M. Forster**'s *A Room with a View*. ♦ Via della Vigna Nuova 46-48r. 218975

Museo di Storia della Fotografia Alinari (Alinari Museum of the History of Photography) Temporary photo exhibitions here draw on the extensive collection of the Alinari brothers, whose shop and archives are in the same building. ♦ Admission. Tu-Su 10AM-7:30PM. Via della Vigna Nuova 16. 213370

emilio paoli

59 Emilio Paoli Though the Florentine art of straw work has all but died out, this shop offers some genuine Florentine goods in an otherwise Asia haystack, namely straw placemats and animals, natural and colored. ♦ Closed M morning, Su, lunch. Via della Vigna Nuova 26r 214596

60 Naj Oleari This Milanese firm specializes in fancifully printed fabrics, which appear on a kaleidoscopic selection of jackets, bags and toys ideal for spoiling your favorite child. ♦ Closed M morning, Su, lunch. Via della Vigna Nuova 35r. 210688

60 Loggia Rucellai (1460-66) Built on the occasion of the marriage of **Giovanni Rucellai**'s son **Bernardo** to **Cosimo Il Vecchio**'s granddaughter **Nannina**. Now glassed-in, it is used for art exhibitions sponsored by the **Societa Alberto Bruschi**. ♦ Via del Purgatorio 12

61 Alex One of the few women's boutiques in Florence with a wide selection of international designers, including Claude Montana, Jean-Paul Gaultier and Thierry Mugler. ♦ Closed M morning, Su, lunch. Via della Vigna Nuova 19r. 214952

61 Enrico Coveri Florence's late native son's line of imaginative clothing continues under his famous label in this flagshop store. Coveri's clothes and accessories brightly cover adults and children alike; the extensive floor space here seems to cover the entire street. ♦ Closed M morning, Su. Via della Vigna Nuova 27-29r. 261769

62 Mario Hairdresser *per excellenza*, catering to a well-dressed and well-heeled crowd of Pitti fashion models and buyers and women who like their style. ♦ Via della Vigna Nuova 22r, upstairs. 2394813, 2398953

63 Filipucci Studio Tricot Yards and yards of yarns in every stripe, designed and used by such leading designers as **Enrico Coveri** and **Gianni Versace**. ♦ Closed M morning, Su, lunch. Via della Vigna Nuova 14r. 215471

64 Cappella Ruccellai (1467) Within this chapel, once part of the church of **San Pancrazio**, is **Leon Battista Alberti**'s 1467 funerary monument to **Giovanni Rucellai**. Called *The Aedicule of the Church of the Holy Sepulchre*, it is a scaled-down version of the eponymous church in Jerusalem. ♦ Via della Spada

65 Museo Marino Marini A permanent one-man show is housed within the deconsecrated 14th-century church of **San Pancrazio**. The man is Marino Marini, who though he was born and died in Tuscany (in Pistoia and Viareggio, respectively) became an international figure in 20th-century art. The show features many examples of his most famous subject, the horse and rider, which he treated with almost Cycladic simplicity and abstraction in bronze and wood sculptures. ♦ Admission. M, W-Su 10AM-1PM, 4-7PM, June-Aug; M, W-Su 10AM-6PM, Sep-May. Piazza San Pancrazio. 219432

66 Il Latini ★★★$$ **Giovanni**, the delightful and diminutive owner of this former *fiaschetteria* or tavern, provides personable companionship to delectable Tuscan dishes that set the standard for the genre, from soup (*ribollita, pappa al pomodoro, zuppa di porri*) to nuts (the almonds in the *biscotti di Prato* cookies offered with the *vin santo* dessert wine at the end of the meal). In between is a Lucullan cavalcade of grilled and roast meats, best accompanied by the white cannellini beans or fresh greens sautéed in oil and garlic. The house wine is an Il Vivaio *Chianti*, specially bottled for Il Latini. ♦ Closed M, lunch Tu, late July, 22 Dec-6 Jan. Via dei Palchetti 6r. 210916

67 Garga ★★★$$$
While Florentine-born owner **Giuliano** has contributed such items as *spaghetti a carciofi* (spaghetti with artichokes) and

agnello saltato in padella (sautéed lamb) to the menu of this lively little restaurant, his Canadian wife **Sharon**'s contribution—cheesecake—needs no translation, even to the local contingent of the polyglot crowd which has come to appreciate the creative cuisine of this lively restaurant. ♦ Dinner only. Closed M, Aug. Via del Moro 48r. No credit cards. 298898

68 Osteria Numero Uno ★★$$$ As the writeups from American and Japanese periodicals proudly displayed at the entrance indicate, this place attracts wealthy tourists. The vaulted-ceilinged rooms are elegant and upscale, the multilingual service is patient and professional, and the Tuscan-based cuisine is palatable and unthreatening. ♦ Closed M lunch, Su. Via del Moro 22. 284897

69 Antico Caffè del Moro Known locally (and even internationally) as *the Art Bar*, this small

Santa Maria Novella

cafe has the best mixed drinks in town, discreetly served in an upscale ambience. ♦ M-Sa 10PM-1AM. Via del Moro 4r. 287661

70 Palazzo Ricasoli (ca 1480) This 15th-century palazzo, built for the Ricasoli family, had the strange name of **Hotel de New York** in the 19th century, when this part of town was known as the Mecca of foreigners. ♦ Piazza Goldoni 2

71 Ponte alla Carraia Originally called the **Ponte Nuovo** or New Bridge to distinguish them from the Ponte Vecchio, bridges on this spot were washed away in a flood in 1274, crushed by a crowd watching a spectacle on the Arno in 1304, destroyed in another flood in 1333, reconstructed by **Ammannati** in 1557, and blown up by the Germans in 1945—sort of a *bridge over troubled waters* in reverse. The current version was put up in the old style after WWII. ♦ Piazza Goldoni

72 Zi Rosa ★★$$ Tuscan cuisine is the basis of the menu in these antique-filled rooms, but if you'd like a change from all that, try *scampi al curry* (curried shrimp) or the *paglia e fieno al prosciutto e panna* (*straw* and *hay*, i.e. yellow and green pasta in a cream-and-prosciutto sauce). ♦ Closed Th. Via dei Fossi 12r. 287062

73 Lisio Tessuti d'Arte Hand-woven furnishings and fabrics in a variety of antique patterns, made in silks and blends that are less expensive but just as finely worked. Silk tassels too. ♦ Closed M morning, Su, lunch. Via dei Fossi 45r. 212430

74 BM Bookshop The wide selection of English-language books (many on Florence and Italy, many others Italian fiction in translation) may be more expensive here than at home, but you can't think of *everything*. On the other hand, the owners of this place just might well *have*—there are also guidebooks, cookbooks, children's books in English and Italian. ♦ Closed M morning, Su, lunch. Borgo Ognissanti 4r. 294575

74 Loretta Caponi Hand embroidery is the famous forte of Loretta Caponi, whose creations embellish kitchen, dining room, bath and bedroom. ♦ Closed M morning, Su, lunch. Borgo Ognissanti 12r. 213668

75 Bruzzichelli One of Florence's most respected antique dealers, **Giovanni Bruzzichelli** has a range of paintings, furniture and objects spanning the centuries. ♦ Closed M morning, Su, lunch. Borgo Ognissanti 31. 2392307

76 Fallani Best Art Nouveau (called *Liberty* in Italy) and Art Deco (called *Art Deco* in Italian) are among the *best*; among the rest are 19th-century European antiques. ♦ Closed M morning, Su, lunch. Borgo Ognissanti 15r. 214986

77 Paolo Romano Antichità Signor Romano, a 3rd-generation dealer whose Neapolitan grandfather started the **Fondazione Salvatore Romano** (see Oltrarno) of Romanesque sculp-

Santa Maria Novella

ture, extends the tradition with his stock of primarily Italian furniture from the 17th to 19th centuries. ♦ Closed M morning, Su, lunch. Borgo Ognissanti 20r. 2393294

77 Palazzo alla Rovescia The story goes that **Alessandro de' Medici**, when asked if he would approve the plans for a balcony on this palazzo, remarked sarcastically *Yes, in reverse*. To many, that would mean *no*, but the literal-minded builder interpreted it as a go-ahead to design it upside-down, as it remains today. ♦ Borgo Ognissanti 12

78 Ospedale di San Giovanni di Dio (1702-13, **Carlo Andrea Marcellini**) This hospital, connected with the nearby church of **Ognissanti**, was funded by the **Vespucci** family. It incorporated the family houses, in one of which **Amerigo** was born in 1454. It contains a fresco by **Vincenzo Meucci** in the vault. Attached to it is Marcellini's remodeled church, **Santa Maria dell'Umiltà**. ♦ Borgo Ognissanti 20

79 Baccus ★★$ This gleaming modern restaurant is perfect for a light plate of pasta (they have 80 different kinds) if you're not in the mood for a serious meal. ♦ Closed Su. Borgo Ognissanti 45r. 283714

80 Harry's Bar ★★$$
This place is affiliated in name only with Hemingway's Harry's in Venice—which is to say, not in price. It's good for the best burger in town as well as a variety of pasta dishes. Harry's is also the quintessence of what Italians are fond of calling an *American bar*, that is, a place that serves mixed drinks. Bartender **Leo Vadorini** is justly proud of his martinis, and

following the tradition of his Venetian counterpart, he invented a cocktail called the *Leonardo*, made with strawberry juice and dry *spumante*. ♦ Closed Su. Lungarno Amerigo Vespucci 22r. 2396700

81 Excelsior $$$$ The grandest of Florence's grand hotels, combining Old World elegance with the relaxed but efficient management of the CIGA chain. The large public and guest rooms, a balance of antique furnishings and such modern conveniences as towel warmers and hair dryers, are made to feel human-scale by the personable and professional staff. ♦ Deluxe ♦ Piazza Ognissanti 3. 2384201

Within the Excelsior:

Il Cestello ★★★$$$ One of the few restaurants in Florence open all week long, and also one of the best. The international menu changes with the seasons, but you'll often find such delicacies as *carpaccio* with truffles and *mille foglie di manzo con parmagiano e pistacchie*, an elaborate dish of beef, parmesan cheese and pistachio nuts. ♦ Piazza Ognissanti 3. 2384201

82 Grand Hotel $$$$ Restored to its former *fin-de-siècle* grandeur just a few years ago by the CIGA chain after a long dormant spell, the Grand Hotel has already acquired its regulars, who claim its smaller size makes for more personalized service than its sister hotel across the piazza. ♦ Deluxe ♦ Piazza Ognissanti 1. 278781

83 Palazzo Lenzi (1470) This Renaissance palazzo is covered with 2-tone stucco designs called *sgraffiti* by **Andrea Feltrini**. It is the home of the **Istituto Francese**, the Florence branch of the **University of Grenoble**, which sponsors a variety of cultural activities including art exhibitions and film series. ♦ Piazza Ognissanti 2

Within the Palazzo Lenzi:

Giotti Bottega Veneta Florence's only outlet for the prestigious leather chain, known for its distinctive woven treatment of the hides. ♦ Closed M morning, Su, lunch. Borgo Ognissanti 3-4r. 2394265

84 Ognissanti (1256; rebuilt 1627, **Bartolomeo Pettirossi**) This church has one of the earliest Baroque facades in Florence (1637, **Matteo Nigetti**). Inside, above the second altar on the right, is **Domenico Ghirlandaio's** fresco *The Madonna of Mercy Protecting the Vespucci Family*. They were parishioners and the boy to the right of the Madonna is probably a portrait of young **Amerigo Vespucci**, whose later voyages (and boastful, perhaps apocryphal, writings about them) gave the New World the name America. In the sacristy is a fresco of *The Crucifixion* by **Taddeo Gaddi** and a crucifix by a follower of his father, **Giotto**. In the left transept is a monk's robe believed to be the one **St. Francis** was wearing while he received the stigmata. ♦ Piazza Ognissanti

---

Restaurants/Nightlife: Red   Hotels: Blue
Shops/Parks: Green   Sights/Culture: Black

84 Refettorio della Chiesa di Ognissanti
(Refectory of the Church of Ognissanti) Three frescoes are to be seen here. *The Last Supper*, by **Domenico Ghirlandaio**, was painted for the space, as may be seen by the clever use of the room's real window as a light source. The other 2 paintings, *St. Jerome* by **Ghirlandaio** and *St. Augustine* by **Botticelli**, originally hung in the church of Ognissanti. ♦ Piazza Ognissanti

85 Palazzo Liberty (20th c, **Giovanni Michelazzi**) Nothing patriotic and no English-snobbery intended by the name of this building. It is one of the few examples of florid Art Nouveau (in Italian, *Liberty* as in Liberty of London) in Florence. ♦ Borgo Ognissanti 26

86 Tredici Gobbi ★★$$ As you may have suspected by its oddball name (it means *thirteen hunchbacks*) this is a quirky restaurant, serving Tuscan and Hungarian specialties, of all things. But like the Austro-Hungarian Lorraine dynasty in Tuscany, they seem quite at home together, and make others feel the same. ♦ Closed M, Su, Aug. Via del Porcellana 9r. 2398769

87 Gianfaldoni The 18th-century art of *sciagliola* is alive and well in this workshop, where the chalklike stone by that name is pressed into artful designs for tabletops and wall hangings that make unique keepsakes. ♦ Closed M morning, Su, lunch. Via del Porcellana 6r. 2396336

88 Sostanza ★★★$$ Known to Florentines as *Il Troia* (the pigsty), this restaurant is hardly bigger than one, and is another case of a radical chic eatery. Pitti fashion dames happily watch as their Fendi furs are inadvertently trimmed during the elaborate slicing-of-the-*bistecca-alla-fiorentina* ritual, along with the workers who still make up a small faction of the clientele. Better than the attitude watching (and you *do* have to be prepared for it) is the food itself, which still includes the best *bistecca* (steak) in town. ♦ Closed Sa-Su, Aug. Via del Porcellana 25r. 212691

89 Amon ★★$ One of the happier (and cheaper) options for ethnic dining in town, this tiny stand-up sandwich shop serves Egyptian specialties on pita bread, freshly baked twice a day (whole wheat only, since the fussy Florentines seem to say *Tut, Tut* to the white variety). One room has a counter where you can order a *shauerma* (like a Greek *gyro* but served, if you want, with a spicier sauce) or a *falafel* (owner **Elkarsh**'s version is made with a puree of white beans instead of the more familiar chick peas). You can then dig into your Egyptian find archeologist-style in the adjoining room, decorated with tongue-in-cheek tomb paintings. ♦ M-Sa noon-3PM, 6-11PM. Via Palazzuolo 26-28r. 2393146

90 Space Electronic One of the first discotheques to open in Florence, Space Electronic retains a number of other firsts. It was the first to use video and laser, and is the first to open at night and the first to close. Its multimedia, light-show decor (with a giant spaceship that makes the rounds of the dance floor) would seem to appeal to aging John Travoltas, but instead the crowd is mostly people in their 20s, consisting largely of American co-eds and the Florentine wolves in chic clothing who have been pursuing them since the days of the Grand Tour. As one of our friends (who should know) says, *Having a foreign accent is an aphrodisiac in Italy*. ♦ Daily 10PM-2AM; closed M, Sep-Mar. Via Palazzuolo 37. 2393082

91 Il Profeta ★★$$ A small, discreet restaurant with an Italian menu of such dishes as *pennette di crema di pomodoro del Profeta* (pasta in a creamy tomato sauce) and *scalloppine campagnola* (veal scallops in a robust tomato sauce). ♦ Closed M, Su. Borgo Ognissanti 93r. 212265

92 Il Contadino ★★$ Good, cheap home cooking is the order of the day here, as witnessed by the fact that the 2 spotless and modern dining rooms are always packed with handsome young men who've just *left* home to do their

military service. ♦ Closed Sa. Via Palazzuolo 71r. 2382673

93 Il Biribisso ★★$$ This small restaurant makes a good *zuppa di cipoll* (onion soup), followed nicely by *stracciatelle* (thinly sliced beef in tomato sauce). ♦ Closed Su. Via dell'Albero 28rm. 2393180

94 Baldini This *bronzista* or bronzeworker is where upper-crust Florentines have their antique furniture refitted with metal accouterments, but it also offers such items as doorknobs, towel racks and other elegant decoration that can be slipped into your suitcase, if not past the metal detector. ♦ Closed M morning, Su, lunch. Via Palazzuolo 99-105r. 210933

95 Hotel Principe $$$ This small hotel is a favorite with visiting Americans, who appreciate its river views and garden, just far enough off the beaten track to be convenient and relatively quiet. ♦ Lungarno Amerigo Vespucci 34. 284848

96 Hotel Kraft $$$ One of the few Florentine hotels with a swimming pool, this peaceful place offers clean accommodations with efficient service and a pleasant roof garden, all relatively removed from the buzzing traffic of the city. ♦ Via Solferino 2. 284273

97 Teatro Comunale (1862, **Telemaco Bonaiuti**; interior 1961, **Alessandro Giuntoli** and **Corinna Bartolini**) This 19th-century theater was burned in 1863, fire-bombed in 1944, and flooded in 1966. But the show goes on, the big one being the **Maggio Musicale Fiorentino**, an international (and internationally renowned) music festival that makes merry not only the month of May, but the rest of the spring as well. ♦ Corso Italia 12. 27791, 2779236

98 Porta al Prato (1284) One of the ancient gates to the city left standing after the wall was knocked down to make way for the *viali* or broad avenues now running in their stead. ♦ Piazzale di Porta al Prato

99 Hotel Villa Azalee $$$ When the azaleas of this small hotel's name are not in bloom, you can appreciate the bamboo and other plants in the garden of this 19th-century palazzo, peacefully situated and pleasantly decorated with lace curtains and handsome antique furniture. ♦ Viale Fratelli Rosselli 44. 214242

100 Il Gourmet ★★$$ A basically Tuscan restaurant that lives up to its name, offering refined versions of such specialties as *crostini* (bread rounds spread with a rough chicken-liver pâté or a vegetable puree), ravioli or tortellini pasta

Santa Maria Novella

stuffed with spinach, and the ubiquitous *bistecca alla fiorentina*, here served as it should be with canellini beans drizzled in olive oil. ♦ Closed Su, Aug. Via Il Prato 68r. 2394766

101 Hotel Villa Medici $$$$ This peaceful and luxurious hotel is partially housed within the **Palazzo Corsini**, which was originally built for **Alessandro Acciaiuoli** by **Bernardo Buontalenti** in the 16th century. Within walking distance of the center of town, the hotel is strangely self-contained, equipped with its own garden, shops, swimming pool, bar and a serviceable restaurant, **Lorenzo de' Medici** (★★$$$), serving an international menu. ♦ Deluxe ♦ Via Il Prato 42. 2381331

102 La Carabaccia ★★★$$ The menu here changes according to season and to the whim of its creative chef, **Graziano**. Besides the titular dish, a type of sweet-and-sour onion soup, such items as *crespelle con funghi o asparagi* (mushroom or asparagus crepes) and *sformato di carciofi* (a vegetable casserole made with artichokes) make regular appearances, as do fish and roasts. As for desserts, the place offers some of the smoothest mousses in town. ♦ Closed M, Su lunch, Aug. Via Palazzuolo 190r. 214782

103 St. James Long-term visitors to Florence appreciate this Neo-Gothic church—which serves the American community—for its weekly rummage sales, where they can pick up the odd appliance they won't be able to use elsewhere, or unload one of their own. During its annual Christmas sale, volunteers serve enough burgers and hot dogs to make the city seem like Kansas City-on-the-Arno. ♦ Via Bernardo Rucellai 13. 2394417

104 Otello ★★$$ A large restaurant with a large menu of all the classic Tuscan dishes from soups to the steak called *bistecca alla fiorentina*, as well as a rare selection of fresh fish dishes. ♦ Closed Tu. Via degli Orti Oricellari 28r. 215819

105 Stazione Centrale di Santa Maria Novella (1935, **Giovanni Michelucci** and other members of the *gruppo toscano*—**Piero Berardi, Nello Baroni, Italo Gamberini, Baldassare Guarnieri** and **Leonardo Lusanna**) Florence's central train station was the first example of Functionalist architecture in Italy and was recently granted the status of a national monument. It is so functional looking, in fact, that when its plans were first made public one critic wrote, *The papers made a mistake, careful! They published the packing crate. The model is inside.* Instead, inside and out the station is filled with intelligent references to the Florentine vernacular, from its *pietra forte* skin to its striped marble pavement and its landscape paintings by **Ottone Rosai** in the cafeteria. Other functional aspects of the station include its always-open pharmacy (just inside the entrance, to the left) as well as a mailbox outside the always-open postal dispatch center (behind *Binario 1* or Track 1) where you can shave a few days off delivery of those important cards and letters.

More recent criticism was caused by the *pensilina* (1990, **Cristiano Toraldo di Francia** and **Andrea Noferi**), a covered platform in front of the station. Its detractors say that, unlike the station, it is function*less*, since it apparently serves mainly to block the view of the entrance to the station (it actually houses booths where bus tickets and tourist information are dispensed), and when Michelucci died in 1990, a few pundits wanted to honor him by blowing up the *pensilina*. But the platform lingers on, an almost deliberately discordant Postmodern appropriation of such Florentine architectural traditions as marble stripes, impassably narrow sidewalks, and a Vasarian propensity to blot out previous architects' work. The final death knell to Michelucci's Functionalism is the fact that the platform severely limits access to a single opening, a convention of military architecture reinforced by a siren that goes off each time pedestrians are given the green light. In its favor, one can say that, er, it sort of *looks* like a train...boat?...Renaissance spaceship? The architects also designed a less assertive small station, the **Terminal di Via Valfonda** (1991), adjacent to the main station. Via Valfonda, incidentally, is bridged by an overpass by **Gae Aulenti** (1991). ♦ Piazza della Stazione

106 Italy & Italy ★$ This was one of the first and the slickest of the *fast* (Italian for *fast food*, gleefully pronounced *fest*) chains to open in Florence. Designed with a trendy Anglo logo (suspiciously similar to Coca-Cola's), tons of travertine and yards of high-tech tubing, it microwaves up the fastest of American and Italian foods. The burgers here are freshly thawed rather than fresh, but they can sometimes serve to nip that onslaught of homesickness in the bun. Pizza (frozen) and pasta (fresh) are also available, and smoking is not allowed, a rarity in the land of Vesuvius. ♦ Closed Tu. Piazza della Stazione 25r. No credit cards. 282885

107 Fountain This marble depiction of *The Arno and its Valley* by **Italo Griselli**, set before the linear **Sala d'Onore**, or reception hall, is a rare and outstanding example of Roman-style Fascist-era art and architecture in Florence. Opposite it, at the end of the covered platform, is a contemporary fountain representing the river Mugnone, which flowed into the Arno near this spot before it was diverted. ◆ Piazza Adua

108 Palazzo degli Affari (1974, **Pierluigi Spadolini**) Another rare example of modern architecture in Florence, this palazzo (in Italy, any building with any pretensions is called a palazzo) has a prefabricated white cement exterior, pierced with upside-down arched windows in dark glass. The modular structure of its insides can be adapted to everything from large receptions to small exhibition spaces. ◆ Piazza Adua 1

109 Palazzo dei Congressi (1969, **Pierluigi Spadolini**) This 19th-century Neoclassical villa by **Giuseppe Poggi** was refashioned by Spadolini, brother of the former Prime Minister of Italy **Giovanni Spadolini**, into a meeting center. His underground auditorium, seating 1000, is celebrated for its perfect acoustics, and as such is occasionally used for concerts and recording sessions. ◆ Piazza Adua 1

110 Fortezza da Basso (1534-35, **Antonio Sangallo**) **Alessandro de' Medici** commissioned this imposing fortress, whose extensive grounds today defend the **Padiglione Espositivo** (1975, **Pierluigi Spadolini**), a modern space hosting trade shows throughout the year, many of them (such as **Firenze a Tavola**, a culinary show) interesting and open to the public. ◆ Viale Filippo Strozzi 1. 49721

111 Hotel Mario's $$ A spotless and tasteful former pensione conveniently located near the station (cleanliness is next to gaudiness), Mario's is popular with Americans in town to see the sights or to attend the trade shows held in the nearby Fortezza da Basso. ◆ Via Faenza 89. 216801

112 Bowling Pin's Club There are those who claim that Italy's pop culture is decades behind the rest of the world's (not to mention its command of English, of which this name is yet another amusing example). What more playful proof than this old-fashioned bowling alley and pool hall, somewhat updated with video games? ◆ Daily 9AM-noon, 3:30PM-midnight. Via Faenza 71. 2381380

113 La Lampara ★★$ Over 80 types of pizza are the hottest ticket at this rambling restaurant, which prepares it in the orthodox method in a wood oven as opposed to the sea of microwaves on which other Florentine pizzerias navigate. ◆ Closed Tu, last 2 weeks in Dec. Via Nazionale 36r. 215164

Restaurants/Nightlife: Red   **Hotels:** Blue
Shops/Parks: Green   **Sights/Culture:** Black

114 San Jacopo in Campo Corboloni (13th c) A lovely little church with a lovely little portico. ◆ Via Faenza

115 Hotel Majestic $$$$ An unobtrusively modern facade in a primarily 19th-century piazza fronts an efficient, modern hotel complete with a piano bar that is a popular late-night watering hole with locals and visiting business travelers. ◆ Via del Melarancio 1. 2384021

116 De'Medici ★★$$ Don't be put off by the seemingly endless expanse of this restaurant, which seems to do things in a big way, beginning with its specialty, *bistecca alla fiorentina*, served in a slab that you know immediately will demand a doggie bag. One room is devoted to a bar and a large selection of light lunches such as pasta or pizza; the other offers an even bigger menu of Florentine favorites. Ambitious as it is, somehow it all works, especially if you

Santa Maria Novella

stick with the simple stuff. ◆ Closed M. Via del Giglio 49r. 21877887

117 Pullman Astoria Hotel $$$ Another clean hotel favored by business travelers and tour groups, this one in a 17th-century palazzo (from which its business-lunch restaurant, **Palazzo Gaddi** [★★$$], takes its name) decorated with modern furniture typical of the French hotel chain. ◆ Via del Giglio 9. 2398095

118 Standa (16th c, **Bartolommeo Ammannati**) This grand palazzo has been converted into a *grande magazzino*, Italian for department store. The Standa chain does best in the housewares department, and is conveniently open *no-stop* (Italian for nonstop) if for some reason you need to pick up a cheese grater or some other item on your lunch hour. ◆ Closed M morning, Su. Via dei Panzani 31r. 2398963

119 Sabatini ★★★$$$ The dean of Florentine restaurants, Sabatini has what is referred to in the New World as *Old World charm*, the kind of place where men feel jacket and tie are in order whether required or not (they're not) and the service is polished and professional. The extensive international menu is ambitious and generally successful. Best choices are Tuscan classics such as *bistecca alla fiorentina* (the local steak specialty), but you won't go wrong ordering such generic Italian dishes as *osso buco* (veal shank), and *saltimbocca* (veal and prosciutto). ◆ Closed M. Via dei Panzani 9a. 282802

120 Hotel Baglioni $$$$ This large, modern hotel is popular with visiting business travelers, either as a place to stay or to participate in the numerous conferences held in the hotel's facilities. Its rooftop restaurant, **Brunelleschi** (★★$$$), is a popular and prestigious spot for a business lunch, offering an international menu amidst sweeping views of the city. ◆ Piazza dell'Unita Italiana 6. 218441

San Lorenzo

The area around **San Lorenzo**, the Medici parish church, is something of a Medici theme park. **Cosimo Il Vecchio**, founder of the dynasty, had **Michelozzo** build the imposing **Palazzo Medici-Riccardi** here, embellished with playful frescoes of the family by **Benozzo Gozzoli** and sycophantic ones by **Luca Giordano** commissioned by later owners. Around the same time, Cosimo commissioned Michelozzo to build the monastery of **San Marco**, keeping aside 2 cells within it for his personal use. Cosimo also founded the collections of manuscripts kept in the library of San Marco as well as in the **Biblioteca Mediceo-Laurenziana**, a library specially commissioned by Medici pope **Clement VII**. The church of San Lorenzo itself, greatly expanded by the Medici and housing the family's last remains in its chapels, epitomizes the beginning and end of the entire dynasty.

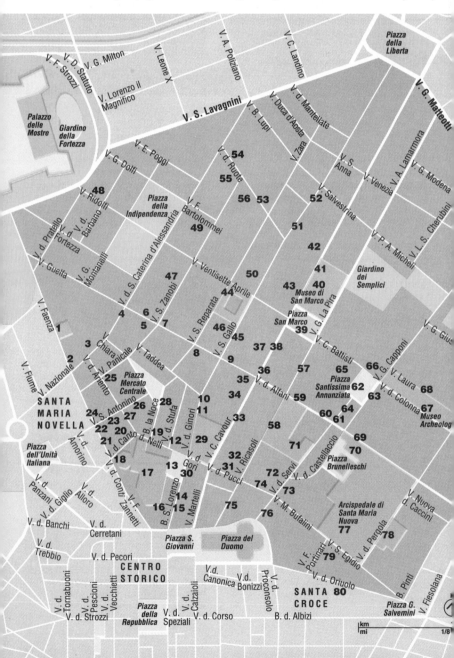

he Medici legacy lives on in a number of noble palazzi which were built in the ea over the centuries. It also continues in varying degrees of monumentality in e surrounding streets, from the numerous coats of arms (they have any number f balls on them—usually 6—giving rise to predictable jokes about Medici atomy) above palazzo entrances to names of cafes and restaurants. Sadly, the mily's original profession as commercial bankers has its modern counterpart in e increasing commercialization of the area with tacky boutiques and pizza arlors. Still, one can't help thinking that **Lorenzo Il Magnifico** (who wrote such nes in praise of love and youth as the famous *quant'è bella giovinezza/che si fugge ttavia*, roughly, how beautiful is youth/which quickly flees) would have enjoyed e large number of university students in the area, and that the livelier members f the Medici family would appreciate the spirit of the bustling indoor food arket and outdoor vendors' stalls in the shadow of San Lorenzo today.

---

1 Cenacolo di Foglino (Last Supper) Similar in composition to the Florentine *Last Suppers* by **Andrea del Castagno** and **Domenico Ghirlandaio**, this treatment of the subject, by **Raphael**'s master **Perugino**, contains a background depicting *The Sermon in the Garden* set in the Umbrian hills. ♦ By appointment only. Via Faenza 42. 286982

2 Il Triangolo delle Bermude This splashy *gelateria*, named after the Bermuda Triangle, offers such adventurous ice cream flavors as rose, whiskey, peanut and rhubarb. ♦ Tu-Su 11AM-midnight; closed M, 15 Jan-15 Feb. Via Nazionale 61-63r. 287490

3 Le Fonticine ★★★$$ When proudly parochial Italians are pressed as to which of their regional cuisines is best, that of Emilia-Romagna usually wins by a nose over Tuscany's. Le Fonticine (named after the 16th-century tabernacle-fountain by **Giovanni della Robbia** on the street outside) is the best of both worlds, as all Italian regions are truly worlds apart. **Bruna Grazia** is from the former region, and each day makes his famous pasta (tortellini, etc.) fresh, with help from daughter **Gianna**. Gianna's husband **Silvano** sees to it that Tuscany is well represented with such standard-setting classics as *bistecca alla fiorentina* (steak), rivalled in season by almost-as-meaty funghi porcini mushrooms. A well-balanced regional menu and wine list make this the best general Italian restaurant in Florence. ♦ Closed M, Aug. Via Nazionale 79r. 282106

4 Giuseppe Bianchi Italian bicycles of all shapes and sizes, with a decided emphasis on the house brand of Florence's oldest manufacturer, are the stock and trade of this shop. If you've been swept up in the national cycling craze, this is your best bet in Florence. Its cyclers' caps, shirts and sweaters make nice gifts too. ♦ Closed M morning, Su, lunch. Via Nazionale 130r. 216991

5 San Barnaba (14th c) This church is another welcome bit of history (note the della Robbia-

San Lorenzo

style lunettes) in a largely 19th-century part of town. ♦ Via Guelfa, corner Via Panicale

6 Arte Cornici If you're a fan of fans, this is the place for you. **Caterina Carola** repairs and restores antique fans and mounts them in frames worthy of the art objects these fashion accessories have become. ♦ Closed M morning, Su, lunch. Via Guelfa 88r. 499452

7 i' Toscano ★★$$ This clean and modern restaurant bases its food on old Florentine recipes. First-course soups are good here, as are the tripe and *bistecca alla fiorentina* (steak). ♦ Closed Tu. Via Guelfa 70r. 215475

8 Cafaggi ★★$$ A roomy restaurant that has been in the same family for decades. Specializing in seafood, it offers such dishes as *spaghetti allo scoglio* (in a seafood sauce) and *frittura di pesce* (breaded and fried fish and shellfish). ♦ Closed M, dinner Su, Aug. Via Guelfa 35r. 294989

9 Trattoria Frosali ★★$$ Another clean and friendly Tuscan restaurant offering well-prepared versions of the standard local fare. ♦ Closed Tu. Via Guelfa 24r. 219201

The Medici

The one family most closely associated with Florence is the **Medici**, who held power interruptedly from the 15th through the 18th centuries and whose ball-studded coats of arms still hang with varying degrees of pomp around the city. The Medici fortune originally came from the banking business founded by **Giovanni di Bicci** (1360-1429). His son **Cosimo Il Vecchio** (1389-1464) rose to power in the government of the Florentine Republic. Cosimo's son **Piero the Gouty** (1416-69) further enriched the family fortune by marrying **Lucrezia Tornabuoni**, daughter of another wealthy Florentine banker, and enriched the family prestige when his illegitimate grandson **Giulio** (1478-1534) became **Pope Clement VII**. Piero and Lucrezia's legitimate son, **Lorenzo Il Magnifico** or the Magnificent (1449-92), began the family tradition of wedding nobility with his marriage to **Clarice Orsini** of the patrician Roman family. Lorenzo Il Magnifico also continued the tradition of commissioning great works of art and was a distinguished man of letters; his powerful presence in the **Neoplatonic Academy** brought together the best minds

of his day and laid the groundwork for the rediscovery of Classical ideals which led to the Renaissance. The family continued its association with the church when Lorenzo's son **Giovanni** (1475-1521) became **Pope Leo X**, and its intermarriage with nobility when the Magnificent's grandson, **Lorenzo II** (1492-1519), became **Duke of Urbino**. Lorenzo II's daughter **Catherine** (1518-89) married **Henry II** of France. After a period of unrest, the family reestablished itself when **Cosimo I** (1519-74) became Duke and then Grand Duke of Florence. His marriage to **Eleanor of Toledo** and the marriage of their son **Francesco I** (1541-87) to **Joanna of Austria** and granddaughter **Maria** (1573-1642) to **Henry IV** of France strengthened ties to royalty while court life grew increasingly dreary under Medici absolute power. On the death of the decadent **Gian Gastone** (1671-1737), the Medici line came to an unglorious finish. Reminders of the dynasty, in addition to numerous works of art and architecture made under their rule, are the numerous Medici coats of arms displayed throughout Florence. The ball motif probably came from the coins on the coat of arms of the bankers' guild with which the family was once linked, reinterpreted as pills as a play on the Medici name, which means *doctors*. One of the balls is often decorated with a French lily symbol of nobility, the *fleur-de-lys*, a prophetic privilege **Louis XI** granted Piero the Gouty early on in the line.

Giovanni di Bicci
(1360-1429)

Cosimo il Vecchio
(1389-1464)

Lorenzo
(1395-1440)

Pierfrancesco
(1430-77)

Piero il Gottoso
(1416-69)

Giovanni
(1421-63)

Lorenzo
(1463-1503)

Giovanni
(1467-1514)

Lorenzo il Magnifico (1449-92)

Giuliano (1453-78)

Maria

Bianca (d. 1488)

Nannina (d. 1493)

Giulio
(1478-1534)
(Pope Clement VII)

Giovanni delle Brande N.
(1498-1527)

Lucrezia
(1470-1550)

Piero il Fatuo
(1472-1503)

Maddalena
(1473-1519)

Giovanni
(1475-1521)
Pope Leo X

Contessina
(1478-1515)

Giuliano
(1479-1516)
Duke of Newport

Lorenzo
(1492-1519)
Duke of Urbino

Clarice
(1493-1528)

Ippolito
(1511-35)
Cardinal

Cosimo I
(1519-74)
Duke, 1537-70
Grand-duke of Tuscany, 1570

Alessandro
(1510-37)
Duke, 1530-37

Catherine
(1519-89)

Francesco I
(1541-87)
Grand-duke, 1574-87

Giovanni
(1543-62)
Cardinal

Lucrezia
(1545-61)

Ferdinando I
(1549-1609)
Grand-duke, 1587-1609

Eleonora
(1567-1611)

Maria
(1575-1642)

Cosimo II
(1590-1621)
Grand-duke, 1609-21

Caterina
(1593-1629)

Carlo
(1596-1666)
Cardinal

Claudia
(1604-48)

Louis XIII of France
(1601-43)

Henrietta Maria
(1609-69)

Ferdinando II
(1610-70)
Grand-duke, 1621-70

Leopoldo
(1617-75)
Cardinal

Cosimo III
(1642-1723)
Grand-duke, 1670-1723

Gian Gastone
(1671-1737)
Grand-duke, 1723-37

Anna Maria
(1667-1743)

10 Piedra del Sol ★★$$ If you want to feel like a *turista* in a different Latin sense, try this elegant Mexican restaurant, part of a chic chain that has other links in Milan and Rome. After a few margaritas in the Renaissance garden, you won't know where you are—or care. But if you do, the menu is as good as any north of the border, and those familiar with the genre can have fun introducing their Florentine friends to a new kind of food for a change. As the Florentines would say in their aspirated accent, *Ay, haramba!* ♦ Closed W. Via de' Ginori 10r. 211427

11 La Ménagère The best housewares shop in Florence, set up like an old-fashioned general store with wooden floors, a long counter and a vintage cash register. It sells everything from the traditional Tuscan glass *fiasco* or flask for cooking beans to Richard Ginori ovenware and china and highly designed Alessi stovetop espresso makers. Don't miss the vast assortment of Guzzini plastic items downstairs. ♦ Closed M morning, Su, lunch. Via de' Ginori 8r. 213875

12 Palazzo della Stufa (14th c) The Stufa or Hot Bath family made enough money running medieval saunas to build this palazzo, where a 16th-century loggia and modern stovepipe openings in the windows of the floor below it apparently still help let off steam. ♦ Piazza San Lorenzo 4

Within the Palazzo della Stufa:
Passamaneria Toscana The best selection of trimmings, including the ever-popular cord tassels (one of the city's most versatile gifts, good for strippers and spinsters alike), in Florence. ♦ Closed M morning, Su, lunch. Piazza San Lorenzo 12r. 214670

13 Mercato di San Lorenzo (San Lorenzo Market) Don't be fooled by the low-rent, almost medieval air of this outdoor clothing and souvenir market, which snakes throughout a number of streets. The simple canvas-covered vendor's stalls, called *bancarelle*, are equipped with electricity, cellular phones and charge-card machines. (Many of the free-spirited vendors themselves are equipped with the most perfect Madison WI accents, one product of their nocturnal trysts with junior-year-abroad co-eds and their guests, who along with Italian and foreign tourists make up the market's clientele.) Best buys are woolens, scarves of all sizes and fabrics, gloves of all leathers and linings, and leather goods. Also be on the lookout (besides for gypsies and other pickpockets) for unusual trends in T-shirts and sweaters. And unlike most other merchants of Florence, they do bargain here. ♦ M 1-8PM; Tu-Sa 8AM-7:30PM. Piazza San Lorenzo and surrounding streets

14 Nuti ★★$$ One of the few places in Florence that serves continuously and doesn't discourage clients from eating only what they want instead of a full-course meal. Some things to want are *penne alla Nuti* (pasta in a sauce of prosciutto, peas and mushrooms) and

cinghiale alla maremanna (a wild boar stew). There is a vast choice of other dishes, from pizza to *bistecca alla fiorentina* (steak). ♦ Closed M. Borgo San Lorenzo 24r. 210145

15 Bata On a street of discount shoe stores, this Italian chain is a step ahead. Inexpensive renditions of this season's trends keep pace with clunky classics for both sexes. ♦ Closed M morning, Su, lunch. Borgo San Lorenzo 34r. 211309

16 Moradei A middle-priced clothing store for middle-class Florentines, but in a city where the bus drivers wear jacket-and-tie and the meter maids' outfits were designed by Emilio Pucci, that's saying something. The sprawling space has the city's widest selection of the tastefully conservative faux-Anglo-American look (with some real UK and US labels mixed in

San Lorenzo

for good measure) that has long fascinated the Florentines. ♦ Closed M morning, Su, lunch. Borgo San Lorenzo 15r. 211468

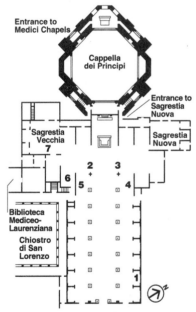

17 San Lorenzo (begun 1419; continued 1442, **Filippo Brunelleschi**; completed 1447-60, **Antonio Manetti**) Built on the site of a church consecrated in 393 by St. Ambrose and enlarged in the Romanesque era, the present exterior is one of the handsomest piles of brick and stone in Italy. When viewed from a few paces behind the shoulders of the silly 16th-century monument to **Giovanni delle Bande Nere** (by **Baccio Bandinelli**) in Piazza San

San Lorenzo

San Lorenzo

Lorenzo, its jumble of curves and angles seems almost Byzantine, a Florentine Hagia Sophia looming over a veritable souk by day, a rich visual backdrop for its heartbreaking bells that ring from **Ferdinando Ruggieri**'s Baroque campanile right into your heart. When the piazza is deserted on Monday morning and at night, it is easy to imagine the cloaked **Medici** and their minions hurrying off to attend to affairs of state or even affairs of the heart.

Financed by the Medici, the great cake of San Lorenzo was never iced (they rejected **Michelangelo**'s model for the facade, now on display at **Casa Buonarroti**), but rather filled with the fruits of the best artists of the era, which become almost too candied for the contemporary palate in the *pietra dura* extravaganza of the **Cappella dei Principi** (Chapel of the Princes). Brunelleschi's interior magnificently lives up to the name of the *pietra serena* (serene stone) used throughout. The inside wall of the facade is by Michelangelo. In the second chapel on the right is a 16th-century *Marriage of the Virgin* [1] by **Rosso Fiorentino**. Just before the transept are two 15th-century bronze pulpits [2, 3] designed by **Donatello**; behind the right one is a 15th-century marble tabernacle [4] by **Desiderio da Settignano**, and behind the left one is a 16th-century fresco of *The Martyrdom of St. Lawrence* [5] by **Bronzino**. In a chapel in the left transept is **Filippo Lippi**'s 15th-century *Annunciation*

[6]; Brunelleschi's harmonious **Sagrestia Vecchia** (Old Sacristy), based on the architectural convention of a circle within a square, is just ahead. It was decorated by Donatello in the 15th century with medallions depicting the life of **St. John the Evangelist**, roundrels of the

Biblioteca Mediceo-Laurenziana

Evangelists, and doors of the **Apostles** and **Martyrs**. To the left of the Old Sacristy entrance is **Andrea Verrocchio**'s 15th-century monument to **Piero** and **Giovanni de' Medici** [7].
♦ Piazza San Lorenzo

Within San Lorenzo:

Chiostro di San Lorenzo (Cloisters of San Lorenzo) A remarkably tranquil break from the bustling market outside, the cloisters (note the views of the Duomo and the dome of the Cappella dei Principi) lead to the **Biblioteca Mediceo-Laurenziana** (Laurentian Library; begun 1524, **Michelangelo**; completed 1578, **Vasari** and **Ammannati**). The *pietra serena* is less serene here in the Mannerist vestibule, which gives a dramatic slant on the Classical elements rediscovered during the Renaissance in anticipation of the Baroque. Things settle down once inside the library, where the Medici motifs on the wooden ceiling are echoed on **Tribolo**'s marble floor. Michelangelo designed the reading benches. Works from the rare book collection (begun by **Cosimo Il Vecchio**) on display include the *Medici Virgil* and autographs of **Petrarch, Poliziano, Machiavelli** and **Napoleon**. ♦ Admission. M-Sa 9AM-1PM. Piazza San Lorenzo. 210760

18 Cappelle Medicee (Medici Chapels) The entrance leads to the **Cappella dei Principi** or Chapel of the Princes (1604, **Giovanni de' Medici** and **Matteo Nigetti**), the Medici mausoleum, which once ranked along with the other monuments as a must-see in Florence—the Graceland of its day. Despite the proto-psychedelic brightness of the mother-of-pearl, lapis lazuli, coral and other *pietra dura* or semiprecious stone materials, the chapel leaves the modern

eye cold, a frozen object lesson in grandiosity. Note the octagonal plan, like the Baptistry, the Tribune room in the Uffizi, and the cupola of the Duomo. By contrast, the **Sagrestia Nuova** or New Sacristy (begun 1521, **Michelangelo**; completed 1555, **Vasari** and **Ammannati**) seems almost restful, though Michelangelo designed it as an uneasy response in part to **Brunelleschi**'s **Sagrestia Vecchia** or Old Sacristy. It contains the tombs of 4 more members of the Medici family—2 Lorenzos and 2 Giulianos. **Lorenzo Il Magnifico** (the Magnificent) and his brother **Giuliano** (killed in the Duomo during the Pazzi Conspiracy), lie in the simple tomb opposite the altar. On top of it is Michelangelo's *Madonna and Child*. The remains of the more grandiose, but less important, 16th-century **Lorenzo** and **Giuliano de' Medici** are in the more elaborate tombs to the left and right, from which Ammannati took the unusual curve for his Ponte Santa Trinita. The tomb of **Lorenzo, Duke of Urbino**, on the left, is crowned with Michelangelo's reclining allegorical statues of *Dawn* and *Dusk*; the tomb of

Giuliano, Duke of Nemours has *Night* and *Day*. Michelangelo is said to have been brooding about the decline of the Florentine Republic when he made these sculptures; whatever his thoughts, some of them may be pondered in remarkably spontaneous fresco drawings in a room beneath the sacristy, discovered a few years ago and now open to the public. ♦ Admission. Tu-Sa 9AM-2PM; Su, holidays 9AM-1PM. Piazza Madonna degli Aldobrandini. 213206

19 Palazzo Bonaiuti (16th c, attributed to **Baccio d'Agnolo**) One of a number of stately palazzi in the piazza, this one with rusticated arches above the entrance and windows.
♦ Piazza San Lorenzo 1

19 Palazzo Inghiarini (16th c) A non-identical twin of its neighbor at No. 1, this palazzo boasts a bust of **Cosimo I** by **Baccio Bandinelli**, whose monument to **Giovanni delle Bande Nere** stands in the piazza below and whose descendants once lived here.
♦ Piazza San Lorenzo 2

Within the Palazzo Inghiarini:

Sergio ★★$ Another typical neighborhood trattoria, in one of the most typical of Florentine neighborhoods. ♦ Closed Su. Piazza San Lorenzo 8r. 330106

20 Hydra ★$ This inexpensive eatery seems to have gotten lost on its way to Miami. Designed to the hilt with a Postmodern entrance through which runs a blue streak of light like a stream, the restaurant draws a younger set of tourists like ducks to neon. Pasta and pizza are the best things on the extensive menu. ♦ Closed M. Via del Canto de' Nelli 38r. 218922

21 Palazzo Riccardi-Mannelli (16th c) Just a bit of local color on this little palazzo, one of many in Florence covered with frescoes in the 16th century, when it was known as Palazzo Benci. The bug-eyed bust above the entrance is a sycophantic tribute to **Francesco I de' Medici**, buried in the colorful mausoleum chapel across the piazza. According to tradition, **Giotto**, the father of modern painting, was born in one of the simple houses from which the palazzo was built. ♦ Piazza Madonna degli Aldobrandini 4

22 Friggitoria Luisa ★★$ This is one of Florence's last remaining *friggitorie*, the hole-in-the-wall eateries that offer fried snacks. (There was once at least a few dozen, as the marble slab above the entrance, *FRIGGITORE NO. 34*, indicates.) Luisa's has made-to-order sandwiches inside, but her best foods are deep-fried street eats available over the curbside counter. Sweets for the sweet include voluptuous *bomboloni* (sugar-dusted custard rolls), *cimballe* (doughnuts) and *crochette di riso* (rice crocettes); saltier fare are the rectangles of polenta. ♦ M-Sa 9AM-7:30PM. Via Sant'Antonino 50-52r. No credit cards. 211630

23 Sieni A bit of gloss amid the dross of the San Lorenzo market, this family-run *pasticceria* is the best in the area and one of the best in Florence. Try any (or better, all) of its cream puffs—*cioccolato* (chocolate), *caffè* (coffee), *nocciola* (hazelnut), *zabaglione* (egg and liqueur) or *crema* (plain custard) or such seasonal treats as *schiacciata* (a flat orange sponge cake dusted with confectioners' sugar) and *castagnaccio* (a cake made with chestnut flour and pine nuts). ♦ Tu-Sa 8AM-7:30PM; closed M morning, Su afternoon. Via dell'Ariento 29r. 213830

24 Fiaschietteria Zanobini As far as we knc this is the only wine shop in Florence that sel wine from its own vineyards by the bottle or the glass. Its label, Le Lame, appears on *Chi-anti* classico and vin santo, a sweet dessert wine. On exceptional years (most recently 1985), the Zanobini family also produces a *C anti* classico riserva called Sorripa, named aft one small tract of its tiny vineyard. ♦ M-Sa 9AM-8PM. Via Sant'Antonino 47r. 2396850

24 Palle d'Oro ★★$ This inexpensive restaurant is popular with neighborhood office work ers, who pack the stand-up lunch counter in the front, so try to come early or late unless you'd like to sit down in the rear with the tourists and pay the service charge. The daily *prin piatti* (first courses) are your best bets for a light but filling lunch, and usually include som sort of pasta, risotto and minestrone. On Frida is *cacciucco*, the tomatoey seafood stew of nearby Livorno. ♦ Closed Su. Via Sant'Antonino 43-45r. 288383

25 Mercato Centrale (Central Market) (1874, **Giuseppe Mengoni**) *Bei harshofini!* is how th greengrocers here sing the praises of their beautiful little *carciofi*, or artichokes, in their aspirated Florentine accents. The hangar-like iron structure was designed by the architect o Milan's stylish Galleria Vittoria Emanuele II. This being Florence, however, it draws a more rustic assemblage of shops and shoppers tha its stylish Milan counterpart. Downstairs are butcher shops selling all types of meat (their proud displays of skinned rabbits, dead pheas ants and decapitated boars' heads are inevitable gross-outs for first-timers), grocers' shops, and an open-air (and what air—both fish and foul!) fish market, many of which still use their booths' original 19th-century marble counters. At the first left corner of the right-hand aisle is **Nerbone** (★★$), a popular if brusque stand-up/sit-down lunch counter offering daily soup and pasta specials along with such salty dishes as *bollito* (fatty beef boiled in broth). Wash it down with the strong wine if you have a cast-iron stomach to match the architecture of the market. Upstairs, refurbished just a few years ago but already showing signs of wear, are slightly seedy displays of fruits, vegetables and local color. ♦ M-Sa 7AM-2PM. Via dell'Ariento

Everyone complains of the noise; with the windows open, no one can sleep.
Mary McCartl

Restaurants/Nightlife: Red   **Hotels:** Blue
Shops/Parks: Green   **Sights/Culture:** Blac

26 Lavanderia Manfredi If you've dribbled spaghetti sauce on your best outfit, have tickets for the Maggio Musicale, and don't want your hotel laundry service to take you for a cleaning, have no fear. The diminutive and *simpatico* **Giuseppe** will make sure you'll have it back clean as a whistle the same day. No matter how good your Italian is, he's fond of asking if you want *starch* and *bleach*, his favorite (and, we suspect, only) English words. ♦ Closed Sa afternoon, Su, lunch. Via Sant'Antonino 66r. 287920

27 La Boutique del Gelato Among the most popular flavors at this ice cream boutique are the *semifreddi* (gelato fluffed up with whipped cream) based on such desserts as *zuppa inglese, tiramisu, chantilly* and *mousse.* ♦ Closed Tu. Via dell'Ariento 14r. No credit cards. 212351

28 Zá-Zá ★★$$ This family-run trattoria is one of the most popular neighborhood places among Florentines and visitors alike. Tuscan classics such as *ribollita* (soup made with white cannellini beans, bread and black cabbage) is served in an informal setting of communal wooden tables and movie-star posters. ♦ Closed Su. Piazza Mercato Centrale 26r. 215411

29 Palazzo Medici-Riccardi (1444-64, **Michelozzo**) This palazzo was commissioned by **Cosimo de' Medici** for the Medici family, who received such visitors as **Emperor Charles VIII** and **Charles V** of France. The corner arches were originally an open loggia, filled in with the first example of the bracketed *kneeling windows* (designed by **Michelangelo**) which became all the rage on Florentine palazzi and to this day enrage tourists who bump into them. The **Riccardi** family had the facade lengthened by 7 windows on the Via Cavour side in the 18th

century. All that remains of the extensive Medici art collection once installed in the palazzo is the **Cappella di Benozzo Gozzoli**. The chapel contains frescoes by 15th-century artist **Benozzo Gozzoli** depicting *The Journey of the Magi*, in which various members of the Medici family take part in a delightful procession through the Tuscan countryside. Upstairs is a 17th-century fresco by **Luca Giordano** of *The Apotheosis of the Medici*, commissioned by the Riccardi family to commemorate the original owners of the palazzo. ♦ M-Tu, Th-Sa 9AM-12:30PM, 3-5PM; Su 9AM-noon. Via Camillo Cavour 1. 27601

30 San Giovanni Evangelista (begun 1579, **Bartolommeo Ammannati**; finished 1661, **Alfonso Parigi the Younger**) A small neighborhood church by a big city architect, restored after WWII along with Ammannati's Santa Trinita Bridge. ♦ Via de' Gori

San Lorenzo

31 Alberti The nicest thing about this TV and hi-fi store is its selection of videos, which the staff says is the largest in Italy. True, you have to have the PAL type of system in order to use them, but they make nice gifts if you have an Italian type of pal. ♦ Closed M morning, Su, lunch. Via de' Pucci 10-20r. 284346. Also at: Borgo San Lorenzo, 45-49r. 294271, 210061

32 Viceversa A sparkling touch of Milanese design here, with Alessi coffee and tea services, Aquilone figurines, and Avant de Dormir tote bags, to name just a few of the better-known names in this signature-obsessed consumer culture. ♦ Closed M morning, Su, lunch. Via Ricasoli 53r. 2398281

Palazzo Medici-Riccardi

33 Teatro della Compagnia Make note of this theater in case you need to come back for a play in what amounts to Florence's theater district. ◆ Via Camillo Cavour 50. 217428

34 Il Papiro One of 4 locations of this shop, which specializes in marbelized or Florentine paper, sold in sheets or in an array of desk and other accessories. ◆ Via Camillo Cavour 55r. 215262. Also at: Piazza Duomo 24r; Via dei Servi 76b/r; Lungarno Acciaiuoli 42r

35 Money Money ★$ Yes, yes this is another place with a trendy Anglo name that's totally meaningless (here they've carried the concept even further with a neon sign pointing to the *DINNER ROOM* downstairs). Most of the American-style fast-food menu items are easily enough understood, except the *tremoney*, which is something like a bacon cheeseburger. ◆ Closed Su. Via Camillo Cavour 61r. 294105

36 Calamai Of the many Calamai novelty-housewares shops in Florence, this one has the largest selection of merchandise. The children's stuff on the ground floor is a bit too cute for

San Lorenzo

words, but downstairs are wonderfully colorful plastic items for throughout the home. ◆ Closed M morning, Su, lunch. 78r Via Camillo Cavour. 214452

37 Biblioteca Marucelliana This library, founded in 1752 with the collection of **Francesco Marucelli**, contains over 400,000 works, among them rare books, manuscripts and prints. ◆ M-F 9AM-1PM, 3-8PM; Sa 9AM-12:30PM. Via Camillo Cavour 43. 210602

ALIVAR

38 Alivar A strikingly modern shop specializing in reproductions of furniture by top modern designers such as Charles Rennie Macintosh and Le Corbusier, all made in its factory just outside of Florence and shipped anywhere in the world. ◆ Closed M morning, Su. Via Camillo Cavour 104r. 2302265

39 Piazza San Marco Italian provincial. This piazza looks like a hundred other piazzas in Italy, and indeed almost anywhere. It is a pleasant place to rest, with the requisite trees, benches, cumbersome monument to an obscure war hero, and the David Lynch detail of the occasional syringe. The administration building of the **University of Florence**, many buildings of which are in the vicinity, is in the piazza at No. 4. ◆ Piazza San Marco

---

Restaurants/Nightlife: Red   **Hotels:** Blue
Shops/Parks: Green   **Sights/Culture:** Black

40 Museo di San Marco (Museo dell'Angelico (Fra Angelico Museum) (1299; enlarged 1437-53, **Michelozzo**) The church and convent of San Marco were built on the site of Vallombrosian and later Sylvestrine monasteries. Dominicans from the nearby town of Fiesole took it over in the 15th century (**Savonarola** became Prior of San Marco before he was dragged from it to his death in Piazza della Signoria), and **Cosimo II Vecchio** financed its expansion, setting apart 2 cells for his own meditations. The decorations of those cells by **Fra Angelico** and his assistants, along with other works by the 15th-century Dominican

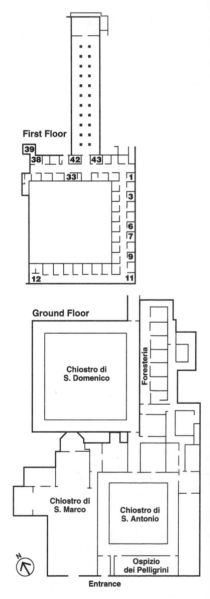

Museo di San Marco

friar-painter, is what draws visitors inside beyond the almost generic facade (1780, **Giocchino Pronti**) today.

Michelozzo's **Chiostro di Sant'Antonino** (Cloister of Sant'Antonino) is reached through the entrance vestibule to the right of the church. The **Ospizio dei Pellegrini** (Pilgrim's Hospice), which once hosted pilgrims, now houses 20 paintings by Fra Angelico, among them *The Madonna of the Linen Guild* and the *San Marco Altarpiece*, which in addition to the church patron saint Mark has representations of the Medici patron saints Cosmas and Damian. The **Sala Capitolare** (Capitolary Room) across the courtyard has Fra Angelico's *Crucifixion* and a *Last Supper* by **Domenico Ghirlandaio** in the bargain. Upstairs is Fra Angelico's *Annunciation* and the monks' cells frescoed by the friar and his assistants. Fra Angelico's hand is most evident in the cells on the left side of the corridor, especially cells No. 1 (*Noli Me Tangere*), 3 (*Annunciation*), 6 (*Transfiguration*), 7 (*The Mocking of Christ*) and 9 (*Coronation of Mary*). Savonarola stayed in cell No. 11 (his portrait by **Fra Bartolommeo** is on right side of the vestibule of cell No. 12), Fra Angelico himself in cell No. 33, and old Cosimo de' Medici in Nos. 38 and 39. The passage between cell Nos. 42 and 43 is where the crowd nabbed Savonarola; beyond it is Michelozzo's harmonious library, today displaying the manuscript collection started by Cosimo. ♦ Admission. Tu-Sa 9AM-2PM; Su, holidays 9AM-1PM. Piazza San Marco 1. 210741

41 Antica Farmacia di San Marco Like the Dominicans of Santa Maria Novella, the Dominicans of San Marco founded a pharmacy, and the wondrous variety of pampering products at this one would have made Savonarola start a pharmaceutical bonfire of the vanities. Creams, soaps, shampoos and eaux de cologne seem even more enchanting amid the antique fixtures. You can also fill real prescriptions here. ♦ Closed M morning, Su, lunch. Via Camillo Cavour 146r. 210604

42 Chiostro dello Scalzo Andrea del Sarto's 16th-century frescoes here include scenes from the life of St. John the Baptist, including remarkable representations of *The Visitation*, *Charity* and *Justice*. ♦ Tu-Sa 9AM-2PM; Su 9AM-1PM. Via Camillo Cavour 69. 472812

43 Casino di San Marco (1574, **Bernardo Buontalenti**) Built as a laboratory for **Francesco I de' Medici**, today this large palazzo is the headquarters of the **Court of Appeals**. ♦ Via Camillo Cavour 57

44 Cenacolo di Sant'Appollonia Andrea del Castagno's 15th-century *Last Supper* fresco unfolds dramatically beneath 3 scenes of the *Passion*. ♦ By appointment only. Via Ventisette Aprile 1. 2870774

45 Palazzo Marucelli (1634, **Gherardo Silvani**) Go through the bizarre doorway of this palazzo (now seat of the law faculty of Florence's university) to see 18th-century frescoes by **Sebastiano Ricci** depicting *Scenes from Roman History, The Labors of Hercules* and *Hercules Ascending Olympus*. ♦ Via San Gallo 10

46 Monastero di Sant'Appollonia (begun 11th c; remodeled 14th c) This former monastery, now housing various departments of Florence's university, has a lovely portal attributed to **Michelangelo**, which leads to a cloister and on to **Poccetti**'s fresco of *The Last Supper* in the former refectory. ♦ Via San Gallo 25

47 San Zanobi ★★$$ **Mariangela** and **Delia**, the 2 sisters who operate this restaurant, pride themselves on their elegant preparations of Florentine dishes old and new, such as the classic *pappardelle al sugo di coniglio* (pasta with a sauce made from rabbit), one of the rarest and best regional pasta dishes. ♦ Closed Su. Via San Zanobi 33r. 475286

48 Don Chisciotte ★★$$ Owner **Walter Viligiardi**'s mother was a cook for the Corsini princes, and he carries on the princely tradition with such dishes as *risotto dell'ortolano* (a

risotto with garden vegetables) and *filetto al sale con salsa alle erbe aromatiche* (filet of beef with an herbed sauce). ♦ Close M lunch, Su. Via Ridolfi 4-6r. 475430

49 Cose Buone ★★$ A Milanese-style *paninoteca* or sandwich shop unusual for Florence, this pretty place offers unusual and tasty sandwich combinations as well as crepes and ice cream. ♦ M-Sa 8AM-1:30AM. Via San Zanobi 63r. 474578

50 Mirò ★★$ Another Florentine *eating club* where you pay a nominal membership fee to join, this restaurant has a lunch menu that changes weekly and a dinner menu that changes every 2 weeks, both featuring herbed-up light Italian staples. The frescoed-ceiling setting is lightened up by the theatrical decor of curtains and lights suspended from guy wires. ♦ Closed Su, Aug. Via San Gallo 57-59r. No credit cards. 481030

51 San Giovanni dei Cavalieri di Malta (begun 14th c) This austere church, which maintains its 14th-century plan though it was remodeled in succeeding centuries, contains a *Crucifix with Mary and St. John* in the apse. ♦ Via San Gallo

In Florence itself the common people...are full of humour and intelligence, though their conceit often acts as a drawback on the latter.

Mary Shelley

Palazzo Pandolfini

52 Palazzo Pandolfini (ca 1520, **Giovanni Francesco** and **Aristotle da Sangallo**) Based on designs by **Raphael**, this elegant palazzo was built for the bishop **Giannozzo Pandolfini**, as the strange inscription under the cornice indicates. Peek through the iron gate to see the statue-studded garden in which the bishop presumably contemplated pressing theological issues of the day. ♦ Via San Gallo 74

San Lorenzo

53 Centro Vegetariano Fiorentino ★★$ This vegetarian restaurant, near part of the University of Florence, is reminiscent of the co-ops that sprang up at universities around the world in the late 1960s. Here you pay a nominal fee to join, then select from the daily menu of specials on a blackboard, pay at the cash register, and take your receipt to the kitchen to pick up your food. The system is a bit of a time warp, but the veggies are fresh and inventive, though purists be warned that they're often combined with eggs and cheese. ♦ Closed M, Sa. Via delle Ruote 30r. No credit cards. 475030

54 Royal $$$ A small hotel in a quiet part of town, made even more peaceful with its thick 19th-century walls and its own little garden. ♦ Via delle Ruote 50-54. 483287

55 La Macelleria ★★★$$ The husband-and-wife team of **Danilo** and **Daniela** do marvelously refined justice to this space's past as a butcher shop with such dishes as *tagliata al pepe verde e rosemarino* (beef with green pepper and rosemary) and extend their talents to land and sea in *riso verde con pignoli al burro di salmone* (green risotto with pine nuts and salmon butter). ♦ Closed Su. Via San Zanobi 97r. 486244

56 Taverna del Bronzino ★★★$$$ Set in a 16th-century palazzo, this antique-filled restaurant offers such palatial dishes as *tortelloni al cedro* (pasta with citron) and *involtini di vitella al sedano e gorgonzola* (veal rolls with celery and gorgonzola, a pungent blue cheese). There is a large selection of *grappa*, the Italian aquavit. ♦ Closed Su, Aug. Via delle Ruote 25r. 495220

57 Galleria dell'Accademia **Michelangelo**'s *David* is the highlight of this gallery. Best see it right away, to dispel the tension. It is at the far end of the gallery, standing majestically in its own room, specially built in the 19th century when it was moved indoors from Piazza della Signoria. Carved from a block of white Carrara marble which had been worked and abandoned by another sculptor, the *David* is a mature representation of the Biblical subject which had been portrayed more youthfully (some say effeminately) by Donatello and Verrocchio, and also represented Michelangelo's coming of age as a sculptor. After you catch your breath, head back to the other works by Michelangelo: *Slaves*, *St. Matthew, The Palestrina Pieta*. There is also a good collection of primitive painting, as well as works by **Alesso Baldovinetti** and **Botticelli**. ♦ Admission. Tu-Sa 9AM-2PM; Su, holidays 9AM-1PM. Via Ricasoli 60. 214375

58 Palazzi Gerini These 2 fused palazzi dominate the street's architecture. The first was designed by **Bernardo Buontalenti** and reworked in the 19th century; the other is attributed to **Gherardo Silvani**. ♦ Via Ricasoli 40-42

59 Opificio Pietre Dure Florentine mosaic, or *pietre dure*, was the art of inlaying semi-precious stone so popular during the days of the Medici Grand Dukes, as seen in the **Cappelle Medicee**. This is its equivalent in a museum, and though to modern eyes it seems precious indeed, it is amusing to see views of Florence in the stuff, like grandiose postcards. There are also examples of it used in various types of furniture. ♦ Admission. M-Sa 9AM-2PM. Via degli Alfani 78. 210102

59 Biblioteca del Conservatorio di Musica Luigi Cherubini Among the collection of the library of Florence's prestigious music academy are ancient instruments as well as violins, violas and cellos by **Stradivarius** and other famed Italian makers. ♦ M-Sa 9AM-noon. Via degli Alfani 80. 292180

Michelangelo's David...The Florentine! The Tuscan pose—half self-conscious all the time.

D.H. Lawrence

When Italy was unified in the 19th century, the dialect used by Florence's most famous literary son, **Dante Alighieri**, was chosen as the national language.

Restaurants/Nightlife: Red **Hotels:** Blue
Shops/Parks: Green **Sights/Culture:** Black

60 La Mescita ★★$ *Mescita* is another Tuscan term for wine shop (like *fiaschetteria*) and this one has quite a mix of wines, Tuscan and otherwise, including fizzy lambrusco wine from Emilia-Romagna. Cheese, salami and a hot dish-of-the-day are also served on inviting granite-topped wooden tables. ♦ M-Sa 8AM-9PM. Via degli Alfani 70r. 296400

61 Robiglio Another branch of this favorite Florentine *pasticceria*, proudest of all of its *torta campagnola*, a cake stuffed with fresh and candied fruit. ♦ Tu-Su 8AM-7:30PM. Via dei Servi 112r. 212784. Also at: Via dei Tosinghi 11r. 215013

62 Piazza Santissima Annunziata Florence's most perfectly proportioned piazza is surrounded by loggias on 3 sides. Within it is some rather less harmonious sculpture—2 strange fountains by **Pietro Tacca** depicting sea creatures (they were destined for the Medici port of Livorno, but were so well liked they remained in Florence), and a pompous equestrian statue of **Fernando I de' Medici**, begun by **Giambologna** and finished by Tacca. The piazza has been the center of folkloric activity in the city for many centuries. Its church's namesake image of the Annunciation, according to legend begun by a monk and finished by an angel, was a popular pilgrimage destination. Annunciation Day used to mark the beginning of the Florentine calendar and is still commemorated with a celebration by city officials and a little fair in the piazza on 25 March. On 8

September children carry lanterns to the piazza from the Duomo down Via dei Servi, which becomes an open-air candyland for the *Festa delle Rificolone* or Lantern Festival. ♦ Piazza Santissima Annunziata

62 Palazzo della Regione (Palazzo Riccardi-Mannelli) (1557-63, **Bartolommeo Ammannati**) This imposing palazzo, an administrative building shared by the province of Florence and the region of Tuscany, is unusual in Florence for its exposed brick. ♦ Piazza Santissima Annunziata

63 Ospedale degli Innocenti Since 1988, part of the facility has been used as a research center by UNICEF. The facade of the foundlings' hospital is by **Brunelleschi**, with medallions by **Andrea della Robbia**. Inside is the **Galleria degli Innocenti**, a gallery which contains works by **Piero di Cosimo, Filippo Lippi** and **Domenico Ghirlandaio**. ♦ Admission. M-Tu, Th-Sa 9AM-2PM; Su, holidays 8AM-1PM. Piazza Santissima Annunziata 12. 2479317

64 Due Fontane $$$ This small, modern hotel takes its name from the 2 bizarre fountains by

Pietro Tacca it faces. Rooms and views are a perfect balance of cleanliness and pleasantness, making this one of the nicest hotels of its size in Florence. ♦ Piazza Santissima Annunziata 14. 280086

65 Loggiata dei Serviti $$$ Like **Due Fontane**, this even smaller and newer hotel faces Florence's most well-proportioned piazza, here from rooms installed in a 16th-century convent. ♦ Piazza Santissima Annunziata 3. 219165, 298280

Piazza Santissima Annunziata

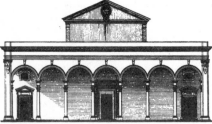

66 Santissima Annunziata (13th c; rebuilt 1444-81, **Michelozzo**) Long one of the Florentines' favorite churches, it is the first choice for upper-crust weddings. The entrance to the church, called the **Chiostrino dei Voti** (Cloister of the Ex-Votos), once held wax ex-votos left by the pilgrims. It has lovely 16th-century Mannerist frescoes. On the right portico wall are a *Visitation* [1] by **Jacopo Pontormo** (he is buried in the **Cappella di San Luca** [Chapel of St. Luke], as is **Benvenuto Cellini**) and an *Assumption* [2] by **Rosso**

San Lorenzo

Fiorentino. At the end of the right wall is **Andrea del Sarto**'s *Birth of the Virgin* [3]. An earlier work, **Alesso Baldovinetti**'s *Nativity* [4] (it contains one of the earliest landscapes in Italian painting), is to the left of the nave entrance. Inside the nave, immediately to the left, is Michelozzo's *tempietto*, which houses the miraculous image of the *Annunciation* [5]. The nave itself is a Baroque extravaganza relieved by **Andrea del Castagno**'s 15th-century *Vision of St. Julian* [6] above the altar and his *Holy Trinity* [7] in the second chapel on the left. At the far end of the circular presbytery is a chancel [8] decorated in the late 16th century by **Giambologna** as the tomb for the sculptor and his fellow Flemish artists working in Florence; left of it is a 16th-century *Resurrection* [9] by **Bronzino**. The **Chiostro dei Morti** (Chapel of the Dead), to the left of the church, contains Andrea del Sarto's masterpiece, the *Madonna del Sacco* [10]; it takes its name from the sack on which St. Joseph is leaning in this representation of the Holy Family. ♦ Piazza Santissima Annunziata

67 Museo Archeologico (Archeological Museum) Highlights of this museum include the **Francois Vase**, a 5th-century BC Greek vase signed by **Kleitias** and **Ergotimus**; a *Mother* figure from the Etruscan town of Chianciano; an important Egyptian collection; a 4th-century bronze *Chimera* restored by **Benvenuto Cellini**; and a 1st-century BC Etruscan *Orator* statue. The top floor contains a jumble of Greek and Etruscan material. ♦ Admission. Tu-Sa 9AM-2PM; Su, holidays 9AM-1PM. Via della Colonna 36. 2478641

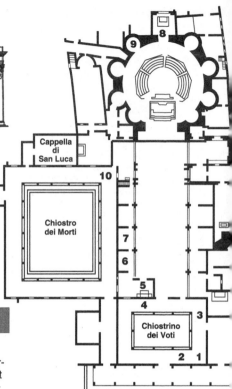

Santissima Annunziata

68 Morandi alla Crocetta $$$ A tiny, quiet hotel furnished with antiques, paintings, icons and medieval manuscripts. The latter accouterment is quite fitting considering the place is housed in a former convent dating from the 16th century. *Housed* indeed, since the Anglo-Italian owners make guests feel they have been welcomed into a private home. ♦ Via Laura 50-52. 2344747

Bests

Marchese Bona Frescobaldi
Editor

Walking at the top of **Forte Belvedere** and looking at the sight of the sunset over the monuments of Florence.

Dinner on a summer's evening with friends at the restaurant **La Loggia** at Piazzale Michelangelo *al fresco*

Strolling along **Via Maggio**, stopping and visiting with the many antique dealers.

Drink a glass of Pomino white wine at the roof terrace of the **Excelsior Hotel** which, in my opinion, is the loveliest terrace in the world!

Reach the **Pitti Palace** from the Uffizi, crossing the Vasari corridor, seeing at the same time the incredible self portrait gallery and the view of the Arno and the city.

Have a *panino tartufato* at **Procacci** in Via Tornabuoni.

Restaurants/Nightlife: Red   **Hotels:** Blue
Shops/Parks: Green   **Sights/Culture:** Black

69 Palazzo Giugni (ca 1577, **Bartolommeo Ammannati**) Ammannati's palazzo has a lovely fresco of the *Allegory of Art* in its courtyard. ♦ Via degli Alfani 48

70 Rotonda di Santa Maria degli Agnoli A rather academic looking octagonal church begun by **Brunelleschi** some time after he went to Rome in 1433. He completed his trip, but not the church, which was restored to its original non-splendor in this century. ♦ Via degli Alfani

71 Palazzo Niccolini (1550, **Baccio d'Agnolo**) This 16th-century palazzo is decorated with 19th-century *sgraffiti*, the 2-tone stucco designs popular during the Renaissance. Go inside to see the 2 courtyards, and if the *portiere* will let you in, you can also admire the 17th- and 18th-century frescoes. ♦ Via dei Servi 15

72 Fior di Loto ★★$$ Despite the lotus-flowering of Chinese restaurants in Florence in recent years, none are on a par with those in the rest of the West. Or with this one, the first and still the best. The names of some of the dishes have been Italianized (the excellent spring rolls appear as cannelloni on the menu), but the fat-free specialties of Beijing remain the same. Finish your meal with some *frutta fritta* (fried bananas, apples, pears or pineapple) and a *grappa* (aquavit) called *mautai*, made with millet. By the way, the Italian word for chopsticks is *bastoncini*. ♦ Closed M. Via dei Servi 35r. 2398235

73 Bartolini A vast array of Italian housewares where high-tack cookie jars are displayed unabashedly alongside high-tech contemporary design by Alessi and others, signed and unsigned. ♦ Closed M morning, Su, lunch. Via dei Servi 30r. No credit cards. 211895

74 Palazzi Pucci These connected palazzi were designed by **Bartolommeo Ammannati** (attributed) and **Paolo Falconieri**. Note the coats of arms of **Cardinal Pucci** and **Leo X**, the latter badly ruined. ♦ Via de' Pucci 2-6

Within the Palazzi Pucci:

Pucci The **Marchese Emilio Pucci** is famous for his sprightly silk patterns, which began adorning the jet set almost as soon as there were jets. Apparently loving a woman in uniform, he then extended his line to brighten the costumes of airline stewardesses and Florence's meter maids, and his silk scarves have become colorfully un-uniform uniforms of young-minded old money and the new rich old guard. Scarves are but the most classic and accessible accessories available in his boutique here, which sells blouses, dresses and *palazzo pajamas*— Pucci's contribution to evening wear of the 1960s. There is a separate entrance for more Pucci clothing, here paired with wine and olive oil from the Pucci estate, at Via Ricasoli 20r (293301). The Marchese Emilio Pucci label graces *Chianti* classico, vin santo (a sweet dessert wine) and sparkling bottles of olive oil. No credit cards accepted for the liquids. ♦ Closed M morning, Su, lunch. Via de' Pucci 6. 283061

75 Teatro Niccolini This 17th-century theater, modern on the inside, is one of the most active in Florence. ♦ Via Ricasoli 5. 213282

76 San Michelino (1660, **Michele Pacini**) Inside this Baroquey church, at the second altar on the right, is a *Holy Family with Saints* by Florentine Mannerist **Jacopo Pontormo**. ♦ Via dei Servi

San Lorenzo

77 Arcispedale di Santa Maria Nuova Florence's oldest hospital was founded in 1287 by **Folco Portinari** (the father of **Beatrice**, **Dante**'s great love). Its portico, perhaps designed by **Bernardo Buontalenti**, contains busts of the **Medici**; inside it are frescoes by the 16th-century artist **Taddeo Zuccari** and 17th-century artist **Pomarancio**. Within the hospital complex itself are the 15th-century church of **Sant'Egidio** and the former monastery of **Santa Maria degli Angeli**, as well as a 15th-century fresco of the *Crucifixion* by **Andrea del Castagno**. ♦ Piazza Santa Maria Nuova

78 Teatro della Pergola (1755, **Giulio Mannaioni**) Court spectacles took place in a wooden theater built on this spot by **Ferdinando Tacca** in 1656, which was rebuilt later in the century. The present 18th-century structure was heavily altered in the 19th century, and gets heavy traffic in the 20th century as one of the city's most active theater houses. ♦ Via della Pergola 12-31. 2479651

79 Museo di Firenze Come'Era This museum recounts the history of the city's growth from the Renaissance on, displaying topographical maps, prints and paintings. Its grounds, the **Giardino delle Oblate**, are peaceful proof that Florence hasn't grown by *too* many leaps and bounds. ♦ Admission. M-W, F-Sa 9AM-2PM; Su 9AM-1PM. Via dell'Oriuolo 4. 298483

80 Teatro dell'Oriuolo Another one of Florence's theaters, this one primarily presenting plays in Italian. By the way, despite the fact that the theater and its street take their name from an old Florentine word for *clock*, don't expect spectacles at this or any other theater in Italy to start on time. ♦ Via dell'Oriuolo 31. 2340507

Santa Croce

The church of **Santa Croce** is where Lucy Honeychurch becomes flustered in **E.M. Forster**'s novel *A Room with a View*, not having brought along her *Baedeker*. Most modern-day frustrations in Santa Croce come from tourists not having brought along their credit cards to the area's numerous leather shops and souvenir stands, while others object to the presence of tourists and shops here in the first place.

Santa Croce has changed from Lucy Honeychurch's time (not to mention that of **Michelangelo**, who lived in the neighborhood as a boy) from a place of lowlife to a place of hard sell. Shady ladies operated in the area between the churches of Santa Croce and **Sant'Ambrogio**, and the debtors' prison once occupied the site of the **Teatro Verdi**. And while much has remained the same (prisons still occupy

its eastern end and drug dealing in Florence currently centers around the otherwise wonderfully animated **Via dei Neri** and **Piazza San Piero Maggiore**), the area is slowly being gentrified. Little antique shops have sprung up around **Piazza dei Ciompi** and throughout the area, **Via Ghibellina** has become something of a restaurant row for all budgets, and other entrepreneurs are opening shops and restaurants in the surrounding streets. And once off the well-trodden tourist track between the parking lots on the *viali* and the leather shops surrounding **Piazza Santa Croce**, the area can still be a rather pleasant place for a stroll, with or without a guidebook.

1 Ruggini A *pasticceria* known for its *crostate* (pies) and *millefoglie* (the rough Italian version of the French pastry *mille-feuilles*, a.k.a. Napoleon). ◆ Daily 8AM-7:30PM. Via dei Neri 76r. 214521

2 Mario ★★$ This *trattoria-rosticceria* is an informal place where you can stand up and eat at the counter or sit beneath the ancient brick vaults. Good home cooking. ◆ Closed M. Via dei Neri 74r. 2382723

3 All'antico Vinaio Another little wine bar, this one famous for its Brunello, the most refined Tuscan wine. It is served by the glass here. ◆ M-Sa 9AM-8PM; closed Su. Via dei Neri 65r. No credit cards. 282738

4 Eito ★★$$ Florence's only Japanese restaurant maintains strict standards, not because the city is so gastronomically cosmopolitan (Florentines, in fact, are notoriously unadventurous in their eating habits), but because of the large groups of Japanese tourists who eat here. ◆ Closed Su. Via dei Neri 72r. 210940

5 San Remigio (13th-14th c) Founded on the site of an 11th-century inn for French pilgrims, this Gothic church has a *Madonna and Child* by a follower of **Cimabue**, who was known as the Master of San Remigio. ◆ Piazza San Remigio

6 Da Benvenuto ★★$ Yet another typically Florentine neighborhood trattoria, with all the wonderful first-course soups and good *bollito misto*, or boiled meats, served with *salsa verde*, a sauce made with parsley and olive oil. ◆ Closed W, Su. Via della Mosca 16r 214833

7 Fiaschetteria Vecchio Casentino Nice atmosphere in this inviting neighborhood watering hole, with its old marble tables and wood bar. There's a large selection of prepared foods, and soothing classical music plays in the background. ◆ M-Sa 9AM-8PM. Via dei Neri 17r. No credit cards. 217411

8 Hotel Balestri $$$ This family-run hotel just underwent a complete renovation, making its rooms (30 facing the Arno and 20 facing a quiet courtyard) among the most modern in Florence. ◆ Piazza Mentana 7. 2146743

9 CarLie's Italian-American smart cookies **Carmel D'Arienzo** and **Elizabeth Nicolosi** have turned the American dream into *la dolce vita* in Italy. Former junior-year-abroad students here, they graduated with

enough business sense to recognize the commercial potential of opening an American-style bakery in Florence. Bank loans, track lighting, and catchy logo and T-shirts later, they've come up with an elegant place that produces authentic cupcakes, cheesecake and cookies hot from the oven. At last sampling, their cake-decorating abilities were still in the learning stages, however. Even the concessions to baking *all'italiana* turn out to be fortuitous—like the Perugina chocolate in the brownies. ◆ Tu-Su 10AM-8PM. Via delle Brache 12r. 215137

10 Piazza dei Peruzzi This evocative little piazza retains the original residences and the name of the medieval banking family, the Peruzzi, whose descendants run leather shops in the vicinity. ◆ Piazza dei Peruzzi

11 Osteria da Quinto ★★$$ Though this downstairs restaurant seems a bit garish and touristy at first, the food usually makes up for it. Quinto could stand for quintessence, since his menu is a paragon of Florentine and Tuscan cooking. Classics such as *baccalà alla livornese* (dried salt cod Livorno-style in a tomatoey stew) are paired with such simple yet inventive dishes as *incavolata*, Quinto's warming concoction of *polenta* (cornmeal mush) with *cavolo nero* (black cabbage). ◆ Closed M. Piazza dei Peruzzi 5r. 213323

12 Migliori This shop stocks a colorful array of terracotta and ceramic housewares and decorative objects from Tuscany and other parts of Italy. ◆ Closed M morning, Su, lunch. Via dei Benci 39. No credit cards. 283681

13 Trattoria del Fagioli ★★$$ Named after a famous buffoon (*Beans*) from the Grand Ducal court who used this spot as his watering hole when it was a simple *fiaschetteria*, this rustic restaurant conserves other Florentine traditions in its cuisine. It offers all the usual Tuscan soups, as well as such dishes as *osso buco* (roast veal shank) and, on Friday, *baccalà alla livornese* (a stew of dried salt cod and tomatoes). ♦ Closed Sa-Su, Aug. Corso dei Tintori 47. No credit cards. 244285

14 Museo Horne (1489, **Cronaca**) Housed in the Renaissance **Palazzo Corsi**, the collection of 19th-century British art historian **Herbert Percy Horne** has a number of paintings by the so-called primitives (**Agnolo Gaddi, Bernardo Daddi, Pietro Lorenzetti, Filippo Lippi**) as well as some interesting Mannerist art (**Domenico Beccafumi** and **Dosso Dossi**). There are also some appealing pieces of decorative art scattered throughout the museum. ♦ Admission. M-Sa 9AM-1PM. Via dei Benci 6. 244661

15 Rigatti $$ Set in the top 2 floors of a 19th-century palazzo (reconstructed on the site of the family houses of **Leon Battista Alberti**), this former pensione is right out of *A Room With a View*. The rooms are furnished with evocative antiques, and the views are of a

Santa Croce

magnolia tree in the courtyard from the dining room and practically all of Florence from the loggia. ♦ Lungarno Generale Diaz 2. 213022

16 Hotel Jennings-Riccioli $$ E.M. Forster's room (#21) with a view (of San Miniato) remains, but alas, has been modernized along with the rest of this family-run hotel, where the period furniture has been relegated to the corridors and public rooms. ♦ Corso dei Tintori 7. 244751

17 Plaza Lucchesi $$$ This comfortably modern hotel is just far enough away from the hustle and bustle of the center of town to be quiet (with the help of soundproof windows) yet retain views of the Arno in front, Santa Croce in the rear. ♦ Lungarno della Zecca Vecchia 38. 264141

18 Biblioteca Nazionale (1911-35, **Cesare Bazzani**) The core of the national library's collection, which has one of the greatest assemblages of incunabula and illuminated manuscripts in the world, comes from the Grand Ducal library. On public view are early editions of **Dante**'s *The Divine Comedy* as well as sculpture by **Giovanni della Robbia** and **Antonio Canova**. ♦ M-F 9AM-6:45PM; Sa 9AM-1PM. Piazza dei Cavalleggeri 1. 244443

19 Palazzo Corsini The elegant (and elegantly barred from public access) courtyard of yet another palazzo belonging to the Corsini family (this one dates from the Renaissance) has 19th-century frescoes by **Gasparro Martelli**. ♦ Borgo Santa Croce 6

20 Palazzo Spinelli-Rasponi The facade and interior courtyard of this Renaissance palazzo are decorated with the 2-tone stucco work known as *sgraffiti*. ♦ Borgo Santa Croce 10

21 Piazza Santa Croce This large, open piazza is lined with stately corbelled palazzi on one side and their gawky poor relations on the other. Both sides are more interesting than the stiff green-and-white marble church facade, added only in the last century, as was the campanile. As the Dominicans preached in the piazza in front of Santa Maria Novella, so the Franciscans preached in the piazza before Santa Croce. This piazza too, was used for public spectacles, including jousts in honor of such noble families as the **Visconti**, **Sforza** and **Medici**. As in centuries past, it is still used as a soccer field by the local urchins (the marble disc dated 1565 in front of the palazzo at No. 21 marks the center line), who daily reenact the ancient rite as if hired by the city to do so. In June a more deliberately historical spectacle, **Calcio in Costume**, takes place in the piazza. Played by medieval rules, the game ends up resembling less its modern equivalent than a Renaissance drawing by Antonio Pollaiuolo as it degenerates into a giant wrestling match with balletic, slightly erotic, overtones. ♦ Piazza Santa Croce

---

Arno Floods
Maledetta e sventurata fossa—cursed and unlucky ditch—is what **Dante** called the Arno River. The Arno has overflown its banks some 70 times since its first recorded flood in 1177. That flood destroyed the **Ponte Vecchio**, which was rebuilt and again destroyed in the flood of 1333, then definitively rebuilt in 1345. Major floods occurred in 1547, 1557, 1740, 1758 and 1844, but the worst ever was the most recent. It took place on 4 November 1966, when the Arno rose 4.92 meters—more than 16 feet. The aftermath of mud mixed with fuel oil flushed out from basement storage tanks engulfed paintings, sculptures, books, manuscripts and other objects. Thousands of such items were extracted from the morass by teams of mostly young volunteers

IL DI 3 NOVEMBRE 1844
L'ACQUA DELL'ARNO
ARRIVÒ A QUESTA LINEA

IL DI 4 NOVEMBRE 1966
L'ACQUA DELL'ARNO
ARRIVÒ A QUESTA LINEA

the Florentines dubbed *angels of the mud* in an atypical fit of gratitude, if with a characteristically ambivalent moniker. Throughout the centuries Florence has commemorated the Arno's inundations, indicating the dates and levels reached by the floodwaters on plaques which may be seen throughout the city.

Cappella Pazzi and Museo dell'Opera di Santa Croce

22 Palazzo dell'Antella (1619, **Giulio Parigi**)
The colorful frescoes on the facade of this palazzo were applied by a team of artists in an astounding 20 days. Ironically, the current restoration of the delicate facade is sure to take much longer. ♦ Piazza Santa Croce 21

23 Cappella Pazzi and Museo dell'Opera di Santa Croce (Pazzi Chapel and Santa Croce Museum) (ca 1430, **Filippo Brunelleschi**) Brunelleschi used the same harmonious circle-in-a-square idea as he did earlier in the Old Sacristy in the church of San Lorenzo here in the freestanding Cappella Pazzi. Despite its name (it means *crazies* in Italian, and actually derives from the family name of its patrons, also known for their role in the notorious Pazzi Conspiracy) it is one of the most peaceful spots in Florence, as are the surrounding cloisters. Decoration of the chapel is by **Luca della Robbia**, who was responsible for the 15th-century tondos of **St. Andrew** over the door and the **Apostles** in the chapel. Brunelleschi may have made the tondos of the **Evangelists**. In the museum, **Cimabue**'s *Crucifixion* has become somewhat of a symbol of the 1966 flood, which totally submerged it and lifted huge patches of paint from its surface. Also on display are **Donatello**'s 15th-century *St. Louis of Toulouse* and a 14th-century *Last Supper* by **Taddeo Gaddi**. ♦ Admission. M-Tu, Th-Sa 10AM-12:30PM, 2:30-6:30PM (3-5PM Jan-Feb, Oct-Dec) Piazza Santa Croce 16. 244619

Restaurants/Nightlife: Red
Shops/Parks: Green
Hotels: Blue
Sights/Culture: Black

24 Santa Croce (begun 1294, **Arnolfo di Cambio**; additions 1560, **Giorgio Vasari**; facade 1853-63, **Niccolò Matas**) This vast church, not quite in keeping with the humble practices of St. Francis, was erected on the site of an earlier church by the town fathers as a showplace as much for the glory of Florence as for the gentle preaching order of the Franciscans. In the former function, Santa Croce contains the tombs and cenotaphs of many of the city's illustrious citizens, a sort of Gothic (then Neo-Gothic) Pantheon. Franciscan principles come through in its fresco decoration by **Giotto** and his pupils, at once vivid and faded.

Within the vast, simple space are an equally vast number of tombs, cenotaphs and works of art. At the first pilaster in the right aisle are **Antonio Rossellino**'s 15th-century tomb of **Francesco Nori** [1], topped by his *Madonna and Child*. In front of it is Vasari's 16th-century monument to **Michelangelo** [2] (buried here). Just ahead is **Stefano Ricci**'s belated 19th-century cenotaph to **Dante Alighieri** [3] (not buried here). Further on is **Benedetto da Maiano**'s 15th-century pulpit with marble reliefs of *Scenes of the Life of St. Francis* [4]; on the wall behind it is **Antonio Canova**'s 19th-century monument to **Vittorio Alfieri** [5], a poet. Further along is **Innocente Spinazzi**'s 18th-century monument to **Niccolò Machiavelli** [6] (buried here), followed by **Donatello**'s 15th-century *Annunciation* [7] in the unusual medium of gilded *pietra serena*, and **Bernardo Rossellino**'s elaborate 15th-century tomb of **Leonardo Bruni** [8], a Florentine statesman.

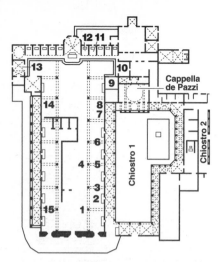

The right transept has the **Cappella Castellani** [9], frescoed with scenes of the lives of saints in the 14th century by **Agnolo Gaddi** and his pupils; and the **Cappella Baroncelli** [10] with wonderfully human 14th-century frescoes of *Scenes from the Life of the Virgin*, the masterpiece of **Taddeo Gaddi**, who also did the cruci-

Santa Croce

fix in the sacristy. The 2 chapels to the right of the chancel, the **Cappella Peruzzi** [11] and the **Cappella Bardi** [12], have 14th-century frescoes by Giotto, damaged in the course of having been whitewashed, uncovered and restored. Another **Cappella Bardi** [13], in the left transept, contains a 15th-century crucifix by Donatello. The left aisle has **Desiderio da Settignano**'s 15th-century lavish tomb of **Carlo Marsuppini** [14], a Florentine statesman, and **Giulio Battista Foggini**'s monument to **Galileo** [15] (buried here). ◆ Piazza Santa Croce

25 I Francescano ★★$$ Named after the humble Franciscan monks who built the nearby church of Santa Croce, this restaurant serves simple Tuscan cuisine to a mostly neighborhood crowd. Among the first courses is the house specialty, *risotto di erbe*, a soupy rice dish made with spinach. Second courses include good meat dishes, *spezzatino* (veal with potatoes) and *bresaola* (smoked beef). ◆ Closed W, Aug. Largo Bargellini 16. 241605

26 Arte del Mosaico Fabio Renai continues the art of *pietre dure*, the inlay of semiprecious stone, so popular during the days of the Medici Grand Dukes. Though elaborate tables and wall-hangings are available (at prices only a Grand Duke could afford), more portable (and affordable) items are the jewelry boxes and cigarette cases. ◆ Closed M morning, Su, lunch. Largo Bargellini 2-4. 241647

Firenze, the most damned of Italian cities, wherein is place neither to sit, stand, nor walk....

Ezra Pound

27 Peruzzi The mercantile tradition of the medieval Peruzzi family continues in this spacious store, laid out to accommodate bewildered tour groups paraded in like cattle to inspect an array of leather goods—bags, clothing, wallets, etc. Groups and goods both would put the Chicago stockyards to shame. ◆ Daily 9AM-7PM. Borgo dei Greci 8-14r, other entrance at Via dell' Anguillara 7-15r. 263039

28 Palazzo Serristori (1469-74) The studied Classical elements of this Renaissance palazzo, more Roman than Florentine, have given rise to various attributions as to its architect, among them **Baccio d'Agnolo** and **Giuliano da Sangallo**. ◆ Piazza Santa Croce 1

29 Leo in Santa Croce ★★$$ Constructed on the site of the former Roman amphitheater, this restaurant retains original columns and capitals from that era and the early Renaissance. Even the atmosphere is somewhat theatrical, with a large international menu catering to tourists. Reliable choices include *risotto ai funghi* (a creamy rice and mushroom dish) and *bocconcini di vitella* (veal with peas and tomato). ◆ Closed M, last 2 wks July, 1st 2 wks Aug. Via Torta 7r. 210829

30 San Simone (14th c) This Gothic church was redone Baroque-style by **Gherardo Silvani** in 1630, but retains some medieval frescoes as well as a terracotta garland in the style of the **Della Robbia** family. ◆ Piazza San Simone

30 Cinema Astor We remember when practically the only movies shown at Florence's English-language uniplex were scratchy prints of *Midnight Cowboy* and *The Graduate*. Happily, though not first-run, the pix now seem to play around the same time their videos come out in the States. ◆ Closed M. Piazza San Simone. 222388

31 Il Pallottino ★★★$$ The eponymous *prima* or first course of this restaurant, *penne Pallotino*, is made with 7 P's—*penne, porri, pancetta, pomodoro, pepperoncino, panna* and *parmeggiano* (*penne* pasta, leeks, bacon, tomato, hot pepper, cream and parmesan cheese), to which we would add more P's for the owner, polyglot purist **Paolo Campani**. Paolo proudly produces perfect propositions of all the Florentine classics, from the typical soups (*ribollita, pappa al pomodoro, zuppa di farro*) to one of the few places in Florence where the *bistecca alla fiorentina* is made with the Tuscan Chianina steer (many of the steaks, alas, come from Yugoslavia). ♦ Closed M, lunch Tu. Via Isola delle Stinche 1r. 289573

31 Vivoli Florence's best-known, and certainly one of the best, *gelateria* can be found by following the discarded paper cups to their well-lit and jam-packed point of origin, a 3rd-generation family business which prides itself on fresh ingredients and its ability to make lip-smacking ice cream out of anything. ♦ Closed M. Via Isola delle Stinche 7r. No credit cards. 292334

32 Acqua al Due ★★$$ This unique restaurant features *assaggi* (tastings). First-course *assaggi* may be rice with gorgonzola cheese, artichokes or *sugo verde* made with green vegetables; and pasta paired with salmon, pumpkin, mushrooms and eggplant. Desserts are given the same treatment, assuming you're still hungry. ♦ Dinner only. Closed M. Via della Vigna Vecchia 40r. 284170

33 Il Viaggio Florence's best shop for maps and travel guides, worthy of the land of Christopher Columbus. ♦ Closed M morning, Su, lunch. Via Ghibellina 117r. 218153

34 Teatro Verdi The neighborhood's ancient theatrical tradition is alive and well here. (The outlines of the Roman amphitheater may be traced by following the curves of Via Torta and Via Bentaccorti a block away.) The modern entrance of Florence's most popular theater leads to a 19th-century interior with a capacity of 3000. ♦ Via Ghibellina 99. 296242

35 La Maremma ★★$$ Tuscany's Maremma district prides itself on its rough and independent spirit, as the rustic decoration of this restaurant, complete with Maremma wagon wheels, bears out. Game is the specialty here (*salsiccia* and prosciutto made from *cinghiale* or wild boar, partridge, etc.), as are the many dishes based on the more generic (but no less substantial) *tartufo* or truffle. ♦ Closed W, Aug. Via Giuseppe Verdi 16r. 244615

36 Palazzo Quaratesi (14th c) Look up at the lovely loggia with Doric columns in this medieval palazzo. ♦ Via Matteo Palmieri, corner Via Ghibellina

37 Salimbeni One of the best art and antiquarian bookshops in the country, which also operates a small press of Italian-interest books. ♦ Closed M morning, Su, lunch. Via Matteo Palmieri 14-16r. No credit cards. 292084

38 Danny Rock ★$$ This nightspot, besides gathering a crowd of Florence's gilded youth, is also the only place in the neighborhood for late-night crepes. ♦ Tu-Su 7:45PM-1AM. Via dei Pandolfini 13r. 2340307

39 Palazzo degli Alessandri (14th c) One of the oldest and most distinguished of the palazzi in the palazzo-populated area. ♦ Borgo degli Albizi 15

40 Palazzo Altoviti (16th c, attributed to **Baccio Valori**) The portrait busts of famous Florentines (**Dante, Petrarch, Boccaccio, Amerigo Vespucci**, etc.) adorning the facade of this

Santa Croce

palazzo earned it the name *Palazzo dei Visacci*, of the ugly faces. ♦ Borgo degli Albizi 88

41 Palazzo degli Albizi (16th c, attributed to **Gherardo Silvani**) The most imposing of the palazzi of the Albizi family, one of many Medici rivals. ♦ Borgo degli Albizi 12

42 I Ghibellini ★★$ A clean and modern place useful for its large selection of inexpensive and decent pizzas in addition to the regular menu. Downstairs is more fun. ♦ Closed W. Piazza San Pier Maggiore 8-10r. 214424

43 Da Paola ★★$ An absurdly small trattoria— there's but one table (for 4) indoors, right next to the stove. During the warmer months, however, Paola places a few tables outdoors so that her home cooking can be enjoyed *all'aperto*. ♦ Closed Tu. Via Matteo Palmieri 37r. No credit cards. 248071

Restaurants/Nightlife: Red   **Hotels:** Blue
Shops/Parks: Green   **Sights/Culture:** Black

Florence is the home of those who cultivate with an equal ardour Mah-jongg and a passion for Fra Angelico.
Aldous Huxley

San Pier Maggiore as it appeared in the 17th century

44 Loggia di San Pier Maggiore (1638, **Matteo Nigetti**) This is one of our favorite pieces of real estate (it can hardly be called a building) in Florence, all that remains of the church of San Pier Maggiore. (It's also called San Piero; Piero is a typically Tuscan diminu-

Santa Croce

tive for Pietro, or Peter.) The church was demolished in 1784, and its former loggia was subsequently altered with uncharacteristic architectural insouciance. Two of its arches were filled in (the one on the left now houses a butcher shop), and a string of flats was built on top of it, the overall effect looking rather more like devil-may-care Baroque Rome than rigid Renaissance Florence. That attitude is carried a bit too far in the piazza before it, which has become something of a haven for drug dealers of late. ◆ Piazza San Pier Maggiore

45 Natalino ★★$$$ One of the few fish restaurants in Florence, Natalino is especially good for such dishes as *spaghetti alle vongole* (spaghetti with clams), *risotto seppie nero* (creamy black rice made with squid ink), *cannelloni di pesce* (tubes of pasta stuffed with fish), and various fish and shellfish on proud display. ◆ Closed Su. Borgo degli Albizi 17r. 289404

46 Sbigoli Terrecotte Terracotta—plain, glazed and painted—is the specialty of this shop, which stocks earthenware from all over Italy, especially Tuscany. ◆ Closed M morning, Su, lunch. Via Sant'Egidio 4r. 2479713

47 Al Tegame Tuscan rustic and other styles of colorfully hand-painted plates, pitchers and planters from throughout Italy stock the shelves of this ceramics store. ◆ Closed M morning, Su, lunch. Piazza Salvemini 7. 2480568

48 Cinema Alfieri Atelier The closest thing Florence has to a French-style cinemathèque, this modern facility screens serious films from all nations—and no Jerry Lewis! It also distributes *Vivil Cinema*, an informative Italian-language circular published by the Federazione Italiana Cinema d'Essai, Italy's art house association. ◆ Via dell' Ulivo 6. 240720

49 L'Enoteca Pinchiorri ★★★★$$$$ This restaurant and *enoteca* or wine cellar provides the most refined dining experience in Florence and is one of a handful of restaurants in Italy to successfully venture forth from the tried-and-true regional formula. Given the sumptuous setting in a Renaissance palazzo (tables are set with Gambellara linen, Ricci di Alessandra silver, Riedel crystal, and delicate flowers) and **Giorgio Pinchiorri**'s liver-boggling selection of thousands of vintages, **Annie Féolde**'s cuisine manages to come off with a minimum of pretense while maintaining a healthy sense of adventure. To be best enjoyed, the restaurant should be approached in like fashion. The various *menu de degustazione* (inspired by fish, Tuscan regional cuisine, or simply by the chef herself, who comes from a long line of French restaurateurs), each course accompanied by a different wine, are the best way of sampling the Pinchiorri cellar. ◆ Closed M lunch, Su, Aug, Christmas week. Via Ghibellina 87. 242757

50 Stazione di Zima ★★$ For a thousand lire you can become a lifetime member of this simple and filling vegetarian restaurant, so near and yet so far from L'Enoteca Pinchiorri. ◆ Closed M dinner, Sa-Su lunch. Via Ghibellina 70r. 2345318

Restaurants/Nightlife: Red   **Hotels:** Blue
Shops/Parks: Green   **Sights/Culture:** Black

50 Casa Buonarroti (Michelangelo Museum) **Michelangelo** did *not* live here (he lived in a house on the corner of Via dell'Anguillara and Via Bentaccorti), but he did buy the land for his nephew **Leonardo**, whose son **Michelangelo Il Giovane** (the Younger) had it decorated. On the death of **Cosimo Buonarroti**, the last of the line, in 1858 it was left to the state, which restored it only in 1964. The space is sometimes used for interesting temporary exhibitions; of the permanent collection of special note are Michelangelo's relief sculptures, *Madonna della Scala* (1490-92, his earliest known work) and *Battle of the Centaurs*. Other works by the master on display are the wooden crucifix (attributed) and his never-completed wooden model for the facade of San Lorenzo. ◆ Admission. M, W-Su 9:30AM-1:30PM. Via Ghibellina 70. 241752

51 Mexcal ★$ Florence's first Mexican-style restaurant has a club atmosphere, serving Mexican-style food but mostly Mexican-style drinks and finger snacks to a young late-night crowd. Live Mexican-style music on Thursday. ◆ Dinner only. M, W-Su 9PM-2AM. Via Ghibellina 69r. No credit cards. 2480609

52 Alle Murate ★★$$
Chef **Umberto Montano** designed the menu for the Metropolitan Opera in New York City, and the one at his restaurant in Florence is just as triumphant. *Orecchiette con le rape* (*little ears* of pasta with turnip greens) is an adaptation of a dish from his native Basilicata; more local in inspiration are his *sformato di verdura* (a vegetable timbale) and *anatra all'arancia* (duck stuffed with parsley and parmesan and served with orange sauce), which Florentines are constantly harping about having been appropriated by the French via **Catherine de' Medici** as *canard a l'orange*. ◆ Dinner only. Closed M. Via Ghibellina 52r. 240618

53 La Baraonda ★★★$$ Given its typically self-deprecating name (which translates as chaos), you would expect to hear the clattering of pots and pans and the whizzing of cleavers and butcher knives being tossed between irate cooks and waiters in this restaurant. But no, it seems we'll never find this operatic restaurant of our dreams. Our disappointment is relieved, however, by the hearty and varied menu prepared by **Elena** and served by husband **Duccio** in the refined dining room. There are always 6 first courses, including homemade *tagliatelle* pasta often served with *ragu alla fiorentina* (made with chicken livers). Of the 6 main courses, you're always sure to find a vegetarian dish and *polpettini in umido* (meatballs made from scratch, not leftovers). Desserts include a *torta di mela* (apple pie) like mother *never* used to make, topped with cream. Unusual is the digestif *nocino*, the walnut liqueur from Emilia-Romagna. ◆ Dinner only. Closed Su, Christmas, 1st week in Jan, Easter, Aug. Via Ghibellina 67r. 2341171

53 Dino ★★★$$$ A modernized Renaissance palazzo sets the tone for likewise modernized historical dishes such as *stracotto del granduca* (beef with garlic, rosemary, almonds, pinenuts, mint and cinnamon) each paired with the owner's selection of fine Italian wines. ◆ Closed M, Su dinner, Aug. Via Ghibellina 51r. 241452

54 Piazza dei Ciompi Woolworkers in medieval Florence, called *ciompi*, were a frustrated and rebellious lot who finally revolted in 1378, winning themselves the right to organize into guilds like the other professions. Their modern counterparts in a sense, surly flea market vendors in simple shacks as opposed to full-fledged antique dealers with glamorous windows, occupy this piazza today, and on the last Sunday of the month hold an outdoor market. At one end of the piazza is **Vasari**'s **Loggia del Pesce** (1567). It once housed a fish market in the center of Florence but is now something of a fish out of water, having been salvaged from the ill-advised urban renewal that created Piazza della Repubblica in the last century and

reconstructed here only in 1955. ◆ Tu-Sa 8AM-1PM, 3:30-7PM; last Su of month 9AM-7PM. Piazza dei Ciompi

55 Caffè Cibrèo An old-fashioned cafe atmosphere prevails in Cibrèo's latest enterprise. Coffee and cocktails may be sampled along with such desserts as homemade cheesecake topped with marmalade made from Sicilian oranges. ◆ Tu-Sa 8AM-1AM. Via Andrea del Verrochio 5r. 2345853

56 Cibrèo Alimentari Wines from the restaurant and olive oil from throughout Tuscany (Antinori, Frescobaldi, San Felice) are sold here along with products from throughout Italy (balsamic vinegar, dried *porcini* mushrooms, sundried tomatoes) and the world (the sight of Paul Newman's salad dressing is always good for a dash of culture shock). ◆ Closed W afternoon, Su, lunch. Via Andrea del Verrocchio 4r. 2341094

56 Il Cibrèo ★★★$$ Named for an old Florentine dish made of chicken giblets and cockscombs, Cibrèo typifies more deliciously than any other restaurant in Florence the relatively recent move to let grandma's recipes out of the closet (or kitchen) and on to the plate. No country bumpkins, **Fabio Picchi** and wife **Benedetta Vitali** have attracted an international clientele (and opened a place in Tokyo) by nonetheless basing their menu on Tuscan country cooking. Regularly occurring antipasti include chicken liver pâté and tripe and chickpea salad. Of the excellent soups (there are no pastas), the one made with *peperoni gialli* (yellow pepper) is our favorite.

If you don't like stuffed chicken necks, there are plenty of other dishes to choose from—rabbit, lamb and pigeon boned and stuffed with seasonal vegetables, proudly presented on sparkling white Ginori china in a refined trattoria setting. Behind the kitchen (entrance at Piazza Ghiberti 35r) is Cibrèo's no-frills, no-reservations restaurant, where many of the same dishes are served on different dishes (institutional rather than museum quality), at much lower prices. ♦ Closed M, Su. Via dei Macci 118r. 2341100

57 Le Campane ★★$$ This bustling place beneath the bells of the church of Sant'Ambrogio prides itself on its homemade ravioli (stuffed with everything from cheese to pumpkin) and huge selection of main courses from all over Italy and the world, including *gran pezzo* (standing rib roast) and *scampi al cognac* (shrimp with cognac). On Wednesday a live band plays music from the 1960s. ♦ Borgo la Croce 87r. 2341101

58 Mercato di Sant'Ambrogio Intended for neighborhood rather than citywide use, the Sant'Ambrogio market is functional compared with its more flamboyant counterpart in San Lorenzo. It houses an inexpensive restaurant along with stands where staples cost less than

Santa Croce

in other shops. Just outside are a few stalls selling fresh farm produce and a rather ragtag assemblage of housewares and clothing. ♦ M-Sa 8AM-1PM. Piazza Ghiberti

59 Cose Cosi A housewares shop carrying a full line of classic porcelain Tuscan ovenware made by **Linea Tuscia**. It features such items as a *fagioliera* for making beans, a boar's head shaped dish for stews, and numerous baking dishes and casseroles. ♦ Closed M morning, Su, lunch. Borgo la Croce 53r. 2343474

60 Sant'Ambrogio (13th c) This site has had churches on it since well before the 13th century, from which the present structure dates. The plain facade was applied in 1888. The interior, redone in 1716, contains a tabernacle by **Mino da Fiesole** housing some miraculous blood, a 15th-century fresco by **Cosimo Rosselli** depicting the bishop and blood in a procession in front of the original church facade, and a 15th-century panel by **Alesso Baldovinetti**, *Angels and Saints*. ♦ Piazza Sant'Ambrogio

61 Hotel J&J $$$ Built in a 16th-century monastery, this hotel still provides an air of peace and tranquility in a just-off-the-beaten-track part of town. Soft modern furnishings, including plenty of pillows, play off of solid wooden ceilings and stonework. ♦ Via di Mezzo 20. 240951

62 Alessi ★★★$$ Giuseppe Alessi's stated aim is to prepare classic Tuscan food at prices everyone can afford. He does so with an almos missionary zeal in this monastic setting, preaching his culinary gospel to devoted initiates while also dishing out exquisite and ever-changing cuisine. Technically the doors are closed to nonmembers, but if you hold up under Alessi's strict scrutiny, you may be accepted (if not exactly welcomed) on the spot ♦ Closed Su, Aug. Via di Mezzo 24-26r. No credit cards. 241821

63 Osteria il Chiasso ★★★$$ Though its name means *uproar*, the noise at this bistro-type restaurant is restricted to the groaning antipasto table and the bubbling *prosecco* win served on tap like in Venice. Three comfortable dining rooms offer a menu that changes every 2 weeks, but maintains such staples as *nicchette del Chiasso* (pasta with carrots, tomato and onion) and *petto di pollo del Chiasso* (breast of chicken in white wine and onion). Desserts are all made on the premises, and should be followed by a glass of one of 60 different kinds of *grappa*, the potent Italian aquavit. ♦ Closed Su, Aug. Via Fiesolana 13r. 242241

64 Hotel Monna Lisa $$$ One of the nicest small hotels in town (the rooms also tend to be small) and one of our favorites, housed in the 14th-century palazzo belonging to the **Neri** family. (Its most famous member, **Saint Philip Neri**, was supposedly born in room #19.) It is now property of the **Dupre** family, whose ancestor **Giovanni**'s sculptures are displayed in this typically Florentine palazzo, with its terracotta floors, white stucco walls and *pietra serena* details. There is also some typically Florentine noise on the street side, so ask for a room with a view of the courtyard or the garden, planted with box hedges and magnolias. ♦ Borgo Pinti 27. 2479751

65 Da Noi ★★$$$ Two former employees of L'Enoteca Pinchiorri opened this cottagey little restaurant, popular with passers-through. The husband's food follows the personalized Franco-Italian line he had at his old job (*tagliatelle* pasta with pâté, rabbit with mint sauce, etc.); the polyglot wife, who knocks herself out trying to make the clientele comfortable

---

Restaurants/Nightlife: Red   **Hotels:** Blue
Shops/Parks: Green   **Sights/Culture:** Black

is responsible for the desserts, her personal contribution being a restrained lack of sweetness. ♦ Closed M, Su. Via Fiesolana 40r. 242917

66 Paperback Exchange As its name implies, this is the place to trade your English-language paperback book (as well as war stories about your travels in Italy) for one of thousands of well-thumbed volumes. Credit for your book is applied to the already-discounted price of your selection. ♦ Closed M morning, Su, lunch. Via Fiesolana 31r. 2478154

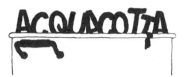

67 Acquacotta ★★$$ The signature dish of this warm Tuscan trattoria is *acquacotta*, not cooked water as its name translates but thick slices of toasted Tuscan bread smothered in vegetable soup and topped with a poached egg. ♦ Closed M, W. Via dei Pilastri 51r. No credit cards. 242907

68 Tempi Futuri Italians are great fans of comic books, as the curious sight of grown men and women avidly reading them on trains and buses bears witness. Here you may begin to see why, as this shop is devoted to rack upon rack of such titles as *Toppolino* (*the little mouse*, none other than Mickey), *Braccio di Ferro* (*iron arm*, or Popeye), *Superman* (Superman), and more esoteric Italian characters with cutesy and/or erotic overtones. Books, posters and postcards on comic-book themes are also available. ♦ M 3:30-7:30PM; Tu-Sa 9:30AM-1PM. Via dei Pilastri 20-22r. No credit cards. 242946

69 Vainio Personalized stationery and calling cards in an imaginative array of colors are the specialty of this print shop. ♦ Via dei Pilastri 18r. 243301

70 Il Cuscussu ★★$$ Florence's only kosher restaurant serves the titular couscous as well as a vegetarian minestrone and roast chicken with herbs, accompanied by kosher wines, including *Chianti*. ♦ Closed M, dinner F, lunch Sa, Su. Via Luigi Carlo Farini 2a. 241890

71 Tempio Israelitico (1874-82, **Mariano Falcini**, **Marco Treves** and **Vincenzo Micheli**) The first stone laid for Florence's synagogue came from Jerusalem; the rest is a fanciful Neo-Moorish pile of intricately carved, particolored stone topped with a copper dome. ♦ Daily 9AM to 30 minutes before services. Via Farini 4. 245252

72 Santa Maria Maddelena dei Pazzi (rebuilt 1480-92, **Giuliano da Sangallo**) The highlight of this church, dedicated to a saint from Florence's own Pazzi family, is **Perugino**'s fresco of the *Crucifixion* in the chapter house. In the church itself are paintings by 17th-century Neapolitan artist **Luca Giordano** (on either side of the high altar) and a modern stained-glass window by **Isabella Rouault** (in the 4th chapel on the right), a hint that the church is now in the hands of French Franciscans. ♦ Donation. Tu-Su 9AM-noon, 5-7PM. Borgo Pinti 58. 2478420

73 Palazzo Panciatichi Ximenes (ca 1499 **Giuliano** and **Antonio da Sangallo**; enlarged 1620, **Gherardo Silvani**) Napoleon slept here in 1796, but long before that it was built by the Sangallos as their own residence. ♦ Borgo Pinti 68

Santa Croce

74 Hotel Regency $$$$ There's something almost volatile about the air of respectability of this small hotel in a 19th-century palazzo. It could be that the colors of the decor have taken William Morris to an almost psychedelic extreme, or that the tranquil green expanse of the Piazza Massimo d'Azeglio outdoors is disturbingly rare for Florence, but if you need to relax, we can't think of a better place without leaving the city. ♦ Piazza Massimo d'Azeglio 3. 245247

Within the Hotel Regency:

Relais Le Jardin ★★★$$$ Well above what you'd expect from a hotel restaurant. In 2 dazzlingly decorated dining rooms (one overlooking a garden, the other with a zodiac painted on the ceiling), chef **Carlo Persia** offers refined regional cuisines from all over Italy. Some recurrent examples are *risotto alla milanese* (a creamy rice and saffron dish from Milan), and *orecchiette con broccoli* (ear-shaped pasta and broccoli, a specialty of Apulia). ♦ Closed Su. Piazza Massimo d'Azeglio 5. 245247

75 Hotel Liana $$$ Housed in a 19th-century palazzo once occupied by the British embassy and now decorated in Art Nouveau style, this hotel has 26 peaceful rooms, many of them facing a garden planted with lonesome pines. ♦ Via Vittorio Alfieri 18. 245303

76 Cimitero degli Inglesi The Protestant or English Cemetery contains the remains of, among others, **Elizabeth Barrett Browning**, **Frances Trollope** and the American preacher **Theodore Parker**. ♦ Piazzale Donatello

Oltrarno

For centuries Florentines have made a distinction between the **Arno di qua** (*this* side of the Arno spreading from its more developed north bank) and the **Arno di là** (*that* side of the Arno along the south bank), also known as the **Oltrarno** or the *other side* of the Arno. Perhaps because of that enduring distinction, based more on attitude than actual distance, the Oltrarno has largely been spared the cutesy shops and greasy pizzerias that have sprung up elsewhere around town.

The Oltrarno embodies Florence in its most palatial and popular aspects. At one end is **Via Maggio** (from *maggiore*, or major), historically its most important street, lined with noble palazzi housing elegant antiques shops. At the other end of the scale is the **San Frediano** area, a tight-knit neighborhood appeciated by outsiders who have strolled its colorful streets or read about it in the late **Vasco Pratolini**'s book *Le ragazze di Sanfrediano* (*The Girls of Sanfrediano*), which beautifully captured the everyday drama of its working-class residents. In between is the **Santo Spirito** neighborhood, where the high- and low-rent aspects of the Oltrarno come together in perfect harmony.

It is easy to see why Florentines have a soft spot for the Oltrarno. Here you can still walk around and hear the hammering of craftsmen next to the peal of bells from the campanile of Santo Spirito. Houses and palazzi alike somehow take on a friendlier air, and even the traffic seems slower and softer in the Oltrarno.

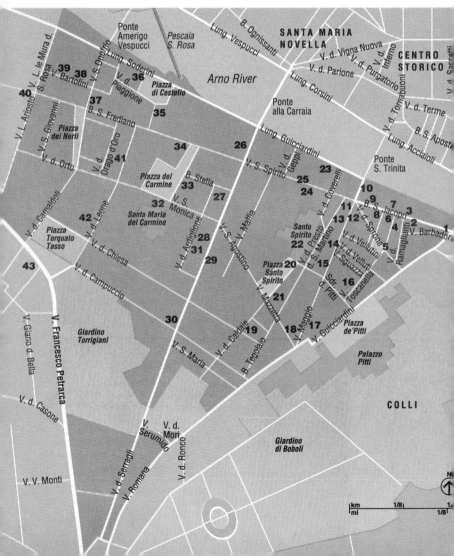

1 Pitti Palace $$$ **Amadeo** and **Mary Ann**, an Italian husband and his American wife, run this hotel, popular with Americans and British. Three of its 40 traditionally appointed rooms have lovely views of the Duomo, as does its roof garden. ♦ Via Barbadori 2. 282257

2 La Luna e le Stelle Women's blouses, dresses, suits and coats custom-made by the talented seamstress **Anna Cei** in the styles of big-name designers. ♦ Closed M morning, Su, lunch. Borgo San Jacopo 17r. 214623

3 Hotel Lungarno $$$$ Modern accommodations amid ancient surroundings. Many rooms at this ever-popular hotel have views of the Arno between its 2 loveliest bridges; others are comfortably installed in a medieval tower. ♦ Borgo San Jacopo 14. 264211

4 Giancarlo Giachetti The crucifix made entirely of horseshoes and blacksmith's nails on one wall of this *bottega*, or craftsman's studio, is testimony to the inventiveness of this young artisan, whose other sculptures include crescent-taloned eagles and fanciful fish. ♦ Closed M morning, Su, lunch. Via Toscanella 3/5r. 218567

5 Nava & Nencini These silversmiths specialize in small birds and animals. They also do custom work, and will faithfully etch each feature of Felix or Fido should you wish a tony tribute to the family pet. ♦ Closed M morning, Su, lunch. Via dello Sprone 4/4r. 283224

6 Mamma Gina ★★★$$
This large restaurant with its large menu used to be largely avoided, but new management has improved the quality of the cooking, largely based on Tuscan classics. Particularly good  are the *minestrone di riso* (a vegetable soup) and *delizie alla Mamma Gina* (beef rolls in a creamy mushroom sauce). Large wine list. ♦ Closed Su, Aug. Borgo San Jacopo 37r. 2396009

7 Flos The Florence branch of the prestigious Italian lighting firm, which sells high-design Flos-brand fixtures with such signatures as Achille Castiglione and Tobia Scarpa as well as lighting by Arteluce. ♦ Closed M morning, Su, lunch. Borgo San Jacopo 62r. 284509

8 Osteria del Cinghiale Bianco ★★★$$
The *cinghiale* or wild boar in the name of this friendly restaurant, set dramatically and charmingly in a medieval tower, appears in such items as antipasti made with gamy boar's sausage and *prosciutto*, and the main course of *cinghiale con la polenta*, boar with cornmeal mush. Another dish appropriate to the setting is *carabaccia*, a sweet-and-sour onion soup. There are also choices that allow for that rarity in Florence, a light lunch, such as the *insalata dello chef*, a chef's salad made with prosciutto, mozzarella, olives and hardboiled eggs. If you're in love, ask to be seated at table 7, in a romantic upstairs alcove. ♦ Closed Tu-W, last 2 weeks in July. Borgo San Jacopo 43r. No credit cards. 215706

8 Cammillo ★★$$ This family-run restaurant prides itself on dishes based on porcini mushrooms and truffles, which appear in such dishes as *taglierini* pasta (all the pasta is homemade here) with mushrooms and *carpaccio* (thinly sliced raw beef) with truffles. Other Tuscan dishes from boar to beet greens round out the menu. ♦ Closed W-Th. Borgo San Jacopo 57r. 212427

9 San Jacopo sopr'Arno (13th c) This Romanesque church has been altered through the ages, giving it a strange Romanesque/ Baroque aspect today. At the entrance to the presbytery are two 14th-century frescoes, a *Pieta* and *Angels Holding the Monstrance*. ♦ Borgo San Jacopo

9 Lo Spillo As its name implies, the point of this specialty shop is pins, which come in all sizes and varieties (brooches, tie pins, lapel pins, stick pins, hat pins, etc.) in case you're

stuck for an unusual gift idea. ♦ Closed M morning, Su, lunch. Borgo San Jacopo 72r. 2393126

9 Angela Caputi If you've just bounced a check buying a designer dress, come here for accessories to the crime. Angela Caputi's imaginative costume jewelry coordinates conspiratorially with the strongest of fashion statements, and she also sells her own line of clothes in an adjacent shop. ♦ Closed M morning, Su, lunch. Borgo San Jacopo 82r. 212972

10 Palazzo dei Frescobaldi (13th c) This is but the oldest of the palazzi associated with the Frescobaldi. The family gave birth to a number of distinguished members (**Dianora**, in fact, was known as *the monster of fertility*, having had some 52 children), including ambassadors, composers, writers and—currently— vintners. ♦ Piazza Frescobaldi 2r

Within Palazzo dei Frescobaldi:

Vera The best Tuscan takeout in town, with a full selection of regional cheeses and lunch meats, soups and salads, breads and mineral waters ideal for an idyllic picnic. ♦ Closed W afternoon, Su, lunch. Piazza Frescobaldi 3r. 215465

Restaurants/Nightlife: Red	**Hotels:** Blue
Shops/Parks: Green	**Sights/Culture:** Black

Giorgio Albertosi Neoclassical antiques, called *impero* from French Empire, are the specialty of this dealer, whose stock usually includes pieces from throughout Europe, with a heavy Italian accent. ♦ Closed M morning, Su, lunch. Piazza Frescobaldi 1r. 213636

11 **Caffè Santa Trinita** A pleasant, modern place for a coffee or sandwich break during or after a day's stroll. ♦ M-Sa 8AM-7:30PM. Via Maggio 2r. 214558

12 **Bartolozzi & Maioli** Fiorenzo Bartolozzi, Italy's finest wood-carver, is best known for his restoration of the famed choir stalls in the Benedictine abbey of **Monte Cassino** after it was destroyed during WWII. These days he and his workshop of master craftsmen continue to carve and gild practically anything imaginable for churches, palaces and other distinguished clients. His 2-floor showroom is filled with his creations great and small, from smiling cupids to fanciful life-sized pythons and ostriches. ♦ Closed M morning, Su, lunch. Via Maggio 13r. 2398633

13 **Guido Bartolozzi** One of Florence's leading antique dealers, Signor Bartolozzi presides over a rambling space filled with furniture, paintings and *objets d'art* ranging from the time of the Medici to Mussolini. ♦ Closed M morning, Su, lunch. Via Maggio 18r. 215602

14 **Luciano Ugolini** Signor Ugolini makes exquisite copper tubs and jugs in patterns

Oltrarno

inspired by the collection of the Museo degli Argenti in the Palazzo Pitti, ideal as planters since their timeless quality works well with practically any kind of decor. ♦ Closed M morning, Su, lunch. Via del Presto di San Martino 23. 287230

15 **Casa di Bianca Cappello** This ancient palazzo, covered with delicate *sgraffiti* decoration by **Poccetti**, was altered by **Bernardo Buontalenti** between 1570 and 1574 for the mistress (later wife) of **Francesco I de' Medici**, the Venetian **Bianca Cappello**, whose family's coat of arms appears above the entrance. ♦ Via Maggio 26

16 **Franceschi** Frames from stately Renaissance style to Minimalist modern are the specialty of this shop. Though meant for paintings, some have been used by our friends for mirrors, making them pretty as a picture. ♦ Closed Sa-Su, lunch. Via Toscanella 34-38/r. No phone

17 **Le Quattro Stagioni** ★★$$ This restaurant, popular with the neighborhood's better-heeled antique dealers, prides itself on its Italian and international menu. *Gnocchi* (tiny potato dumplings) with spinach and ricotta and *gran pezzo* (standing rib roast) are reliable choices here. ♦ Closed Su. Via Maggio 61r. 218906

18 **Il Maggiolino** One of the nicest things about the Art Deco items at this shop is that most of them (jewelry, tableware, toiletries) will fit neatly into your carry-on luggage. ♦ Closed M morning, Su, lunch. Via Maggio 80r. 216660

19 **Prezzemolo** Some of the young and the restless (and rich) Florentines come to this nightspot to play board games (and bored games) in an unusual setting of catacomb-like rooms divided up Italian-style into little seating areas for the local lounge lizards. ♦ Tu-Su 5PM-2AM. Via delle Caldaie 5r. 211530

20 **Piazza Santo Spirito** As grand as Piazza Santa Maria Novella and Piazza Santa Croce are Piazza Santo Spirito, which extends before the Augustinian church of the same name, is down-to-earth. One of the most peaceful spots in Florence, it is shaded by trees, cooled by a splashing fountain, and enlivened by neighborhood vendors, who sell produce weekday mornings. On the second Sunday of the month, it is the setting for an open-air flea market, in which local artisans give demonstrations of their craft. ♦ Piazza Santo Spirito

21 **Bandini** $$ One of the last old-fashioned pensioni in Florence, installed on the 3rd floor of the Renaissance **Palazzo Guadagni** (attributed to **Cronaca** or **Baccio d'Agnolo**). Only 3 of its 10 large rooms have baths, but all have views, either of peaceful Piazza Santo Spirito or the center of Florence. ♦ Piazza Santo Spirito 9. 215308

22 **Fondazione Salvatore Romano** Housed in the old refectory, the only part of the Gothic monastery of Santo Spirito spared by the fire of 1471, is a foundation established by a Neapolitan antique dealer who worked in Florence. Among the works on display are a *Last Supper* and a *Crucifixion* attributed to **Andrea Orcagna**, as well as Romanesque sculpture and other pieces the dealer attributed to **Jacopo della Quercia, Donatello** and **Bartolommeo Ammannati.** ♦ Tu-Sa 9AM-2PM; Su 8AM-1PM. Piazza Santo Spirito 29. 287043

Restaurants/Nightlife: Red   **Hotels:** Blue
Shops/Parks: Green   **Sights/Culture:** Black

22 Santo Spirito (begun 1436, **Filippo Brunelleschi**; finished 1487, **Antonio Manetti, Giovanni da Gaiole** and **Salvi d'Andrea**) The church's 17th-century facade, almost Postmodern in its simplified line, rises like a pale plaster Holy Ghost. Inside is one of Florence's finest Renaissance interiors, fairly faithful to Brunelleschi's original design. (**Vasari**, however, remarked that had it not been for the alterations, Santo Spirito would have been *the most perfect temple of Christianity*, a surprising statement for a man who made such sweeping changes in so many of Florence's interior spaces, this one not included.) In the right transept is **Filippino Lippi**'s 15th-century **Nerli Altarpiece**, which has a depiction of the nearby Porta San Frediano; the left transept has **Andrea Sansovino**'s **Cappella Corbinelli**, which also contains his sculpture. A door beneath the organ leads to **Cronaca**'s 15th-century vestibule and **Giuliano da Sangallo**'s 15th-century sacristy, its octagonal shape based on the Baptistry. ♦ Piazza Santo Spirito

HIGH ALTAR

23 Luana Beni Some of Florence's most noble heads are chopped here—not as revolutionary retribution, mind you, but in the discreet premises of this exclusive beauty salon. ◆ Lungarno Guicciardini 7. 215240, 284885

24 Arredamenti Castorina Florence's antique dealers and restorers come here for the little bits of sculpted wood they use to mend and embellish their frames and furniture. Many of the pieces —putti, geometrical shapes—are lovely objects in and of themselves, and make unusual souvenirs and gifts. ◆ Closed M morning, Su, lunch. Via Santo Spirito 13-15r. 212885

25 Angiolino ★★$$ Another atmospheric Tuscan restaurant, this one in a varnished-wood, yellowed-wall ambience that could have been painted by an Italian Frans Hals. ◆ Closed M. Via Santo Spirito 36r. 2398976

26 Marino Two shifts of fresh-baked bliss at this *pasticceria* or pastry shop. Croissants, plain or filled with jams and custards, emerge from the oven each morning and afternoon into the eager hands of waiting Florentines. ◆ Tu-Sa 8AM-7:30PM; Su 8AM-1PM. Piazza Nazario Sauro 19r. 212657

27 Lamberto Banchi Master bronzeworker Lamberto Banchi does intricate tiny objects

Oltrarno

(frames, paperweights, candlesticks) and larger items (lamps, tabletops) in bronze and copper, as well as repairs antiques in those metals. ◆ Closed M morning, Su, lunch. Via dei Serragli 10r. 2394694

28 Gozzini e Reselli Silver shines in this shop, where affordable small objects such as a *vinometro*, a device for measuring the alcohol content and temperature of your favorite vintage, are among the hand-crafted items by these artisans. ◆ Closed M morning, Su, lunch. Via dei Serragli 44r. 284650

29 Vini e Olii Renzo and Luana Salsi stock a full line of Italian wines and olive oils by such famous names as Antinori, Frescobaldi and Villa Banfi. Other delicacies include truffled olive oil, balsamic vinegars and vinegars made with champagne and fermented apples. ◆ Closed W afternoon, Su, lunch. Via dei Serragli 29r. 2398708

30 Diladdarno ★★$$ The local option for local cuisine in a typical trattoria. All the Tuscan first-course soups (minestrone, *ribollita*, *pappa al pomodoro*) as well as Florentine main courses (*trippa alla fiorentina*, *baccalà*, *osso buco*) are available here. ◆ Closed M-Tu. Via dei Serragli 108r. No credit cards. 225001

31 I Raddi ★★$$ Another typically Tuscan trattoria, this one was recently opened by the Raddi family. Their special pasta sauce, *ardiglione* (made with sausage and a secret blend of herbs) graces *taglierine* pasta as a first course. The main course called *pepposo* is a hearty beef stew (with tomatoes, garlic and red wine) dating from the Renaissance. ◆ Closed M lunch, Su. Via dell'Ardiglione 47r. 211072

32 Santa Maria del Carmine (begun 1268; completed 1476; rebuilt 1782, **Giuseppe Ruggieri** and **Giulio Mannaioni**) The *Carmine*, as it is known locally, was built for the Carmelite nuns and suffered a devastating fire in 1771. Though it destroyed most of the church, the **Cappella Brancacci** was untouched. Recently touched by an extensive and seemingly endless restoration, however, the chapel contains 15th-century frescoes begun by **Masolino**, continued by **Masaccio** and completed by **Filippino Lippi**. Masaccio's contribution was a watershed in the history of art—combining perspective, chiaroscuro and the vivid rendering of human emotions with unprecedented boldness, seminal to the painters of the later Renaissance. Two of Masaccio's sections dominate the entire cycle—the excruciatingly agonizing *Expulsion from Paradise* on the extreme upper left wall, and the serene and noble *Tribute Money* just to its right. Below it, *St. Peter Enthroned* contains a portrait of Masaccio, the figure looking out at the viewer in the group of 4 men at the right of the composition. If you feel like looking at anything else ever again, the left transept of the church contains the 17th-century **Cappella di Sant'Andrea Corsini** with 3 relief sculptures by **Giovanni Battista Foggini**, and the dome has **Luca Giordano**'s 17th-century fresco *The Apotheosis of St. Andrew Corsini*. ◆ Piazza del Carmine

33 Dolce Vita Named after the Fellini film about the sweet life in Rome in the 1960s, this modern-looking nocturnal hangout for Florentine and foreign youth brings a sweet smile, especially when their earnest and urgent interactions take over the parking lot in true Roman fashion. ◆ M-Sa 11AM-1:30AM. Piazza del Carmine. 284595

Florentines claim to have invented fireworks to celebrate their feasts of **St. John the Baptist** and the **Assumption**.

Restaurants/Nightlife: Red   **Hotels:** Blue
Shops/Parks: Green   **Sights/Culture:** Black

34 Carmine ★★$$ One of the most popular trattorias among Florentines and visitors alike (especially during the warmer months when its tables spill out into the piazza), this remarkably warm and friendly restaurant serves a substantial *tagliatelle a funghi porcini* (ribbons of pasta with porcini mushrooms) and filet of beef given the same tasty treatment. ♦ Closed Su, Aug. Piazza del Carmine 18r. 218601

35 San Frediano in Cestello (constructed 1680-89, **Antonio Maria Ferri** to a design by **Cerutti**) A rare Florentine Baroque church, best admired from a distance, when its cupola adds a nice shape to the city's profile. *Cestello* in Italian means *crate*, though in Florence is was a corruption of *Cistercense* or Cistercians, the monks who once inhabited the site. The church's interior decorations, primarily by 18th-century Florentine painters, are inoffensive if uninspiring, though the third chapel on the left has a blissed-out 13th-century *Smiling Madonna*. ♦ Piazza di Cestello

36 Granaio di Cosimo III (1695, **Ciro Ferri** and **Giovanni Battista Foggini**) Built as a granary under the Medici, this wheat bin crate is now used as a military building. ♦ Piazza di Cestello

37 Antico Ristoro di' Cambi ★★$$ The Cambi family has been running this rustic restaurant in an old *fiaschetteria*, or wine shop, for decades. All the Tuscan soups are well-prepared here. If you're feeling adventurous, try the *trippa* (tripe) or *lampredotto* (cow intestine); otherwise, there is an excellent *spezzatino* (beef stewed with tomatoes, potatoes and herbs). ♦ Closed Su. Via Sant'Onofrio 1r. 217134

38 Antico Setificio Fiorentino The Florentine silk manufacturing firm (see Santa Maria Novella) has its factory, staffed by local girls, in this most Florentine section of the city. Open by appointment only, the business may be visited with director **Aldo Marzucchi**. ♦ Via Bartolini 4. 213861

39 Brandimarte Brandimarte Guscelli specializes in fanciful silver. The precious metal is handcrafted into his signature goblets as well as such ordinary objects as cheese graters for the person who has everything. ♦ Closed M morning, Su, lunch. Via Bartolini 18. 218791

Porta San Frediano as it appeared in the 17th century

40 Porta San Frediano (1332-34, **Andrea Pisano**) This towering ancient city gate (part of the old wall is still attached) preserves its original wood and ironwork, to which visitors once hitched their horses. ♦ Piazza di Verzaia

41 Ugolini The brothers **Alvaro** and **Romano Ugolini** carry on a long family tradition as *bronzisti* or bronzeworkers. There specialty is lamps of all types, with a minimum order of 4. ♦ Closed M morning, Su, lunch. Via del Drago d'Oro 25r. 215343

42 La Rucola ★★$$$ Named after the bitter green *rucola* (rocket or arugula in English), this chic trattoria uses the trendy veggie in everything from ravioli to beef. The menu offers 6 first courses and 6 second courses which change daily, based on refined versions of Tuscan cuisine. ♦ Closed M lunch, Su, Aug. Via del Leone 50r. 224002

43 Alla Vecchia Bettola ★★$$ A *bettola* was a sort of prototypical lunch counter in old Florence, a place where peasants ate and ran. You'll want to linger in this trattoria, though. If you think you've finally found a Florentine restaurant without a weird name, just take a look at such pasta garnishes as *rotta in culo* (it has to do with breaking that part of the anatomy upon which one sits) on the menu. The atmosphere is warm and understandably for fun-lovers, and the specialties of tripe and the like are for lovers of the heartiest of Florentine food. ♦ Closed M, Su. Viale Ludovico Ariosto 32r. No credit cards. 224158

Additional Florence Highlights

The following places fall out of the boundaries of the previous chapter maps. We feel they are worth straying from the beaten path for a visit.

1 Museo Stibbert (Stibbert Museum) The Villa Stibbert houses the eclectic collection of **Frederick Stibbert**, a Scottish-Italian who was active in the unification of Italy during the 19th century. That aspect of his life is easily inferred from room after room of displays of arms and armor from East and West, enough to glut any *Camelot* or *Shogun* fantasies. Besides arms, the man also collected furniture, paintings, porcelain, clocks and objects of every sort—most of which are not collecting dust in this oddball, slightly out-of-the-way museum, sure to appeal to obsessive-compulsives of all ages. ♦ M-W, F-Sa 9AM-1PM; Su 9AM-12:30PM. Via Federico Stibbert 26. 475520

Restaurants/Nightlife: Red	**Hotels:** Blue
Shops/Parks: Green	**Sights/Culture:** Black

2 Le Cascine Florentines of all ranks have long loved their public park, so-called because of the **Medici** dairy farms or *cascine* which once occupied the area, extending almost 2 miles along the Arno. Though the park saw its heyday as center of the carriage trade in the last century, the well-heeled still make use of its private tennis courts and swimming pool (as can foreigners); at the other end of the social scale are the ladies of the night (and the men who dress like them) who ply *their* trade along its alleys. Children can ride merry-go-rounds year-round, or take part in the **Festa del Grillo** on Assumption Day (15 August), a festival of crickets which chirp away in tiny cages. On Tuesday morning an open-air market of everything from pigs to Pucci scarves extends west of **Piazza Vittorio Veneto**. Though few visitors

seem to take advantage of the breezy expanses of the Cascine, one who did was **Shelley**, who was inspired to write *Ode to the West Wind* here. At the west end of the park is the **Piazzaletto dell'Indiano**, a little piazza named after the Indian maharaja **Raiaram Cuttaputti**, who died in Florence in 1870 and was cremated nearby, according to the Brahman rite, where the Mugnone river joins the Arno.
♦ Piazza Vittorio Veneto-Piazzaletto dell'Indiano. 360501

3 Ruggero ★★★$$ Owned by a former cook from the tongue-in-chic **Coco Lezzone** restaurant off Via Tornabuoni, the ambience of this rustic eatery is somehow more authentic in its location just outside the city gate. Tuscan first courses take first place here—*pappa al pomodoro* (a thick tomato soup), *ribollita* (a hearty vegetable soup thickened with day-old bread) and *zuppa di farro* (soup made with a kind of wheat). ♦ Closed Tu-W, July. Via Senese 89. No credit cards. 220542

4 Gualtieri A small, family-run *pasticceria* or pastry shop famous for its iris cake, a soft fruit-cake named after Florence's official flower.
♦ Closed M. Via Senese 18r. 221771

5 Omero ★★★$$ A healthy hike or a short cab ride from Piazzale Michelangelo or Porta Romana, Omero offers strictly Tuscan cuisine, from the salami antipasti to pasta with *ceci* (chick peas) and *strasciacata* (*dragged* in meat sauce) to fried chicken, rabbit and brain. The restaurant opens its garden for dinner in the warmer months. ♦ Closed Tu, Aug. Via Pian dei Giullari 11. 220053

6 L'Orologio ★★$$ Named for an old clock that adorned the facade of this riverside restaurant before it was swept away by the 1966 flood, the Orologio offers timeless Tuscan cuisine in addition to such rarities as good *penne al salmona*, pasta with salmon, and the Tuscan version of *osso buco*, veal shank here prepared with a base of tomato and white wine.
♦ Closed Sa dinner, Su, Aug. Piazza Francesco Ferrucci 5. 6811729

7 La Capannina di Sante ★★★$$$ Florence's best fish restaurant, **Signor Sante**'s modestly named *little shack* is appropriately located along the Arno, with tables outdoors during the warmer months. Offerings change according to what he finds at the market that day, but you can always depend on top quality and top dollar. Wines are good,

including *Corvo* from Sante's native Sicily. The kitchen stays open past midnight, when the dining rooms are packed to the gills. ♦ Closed M lunch, Su, 2 weeks in Aug. Piazza Ravenna (Ponte Verrazzano) 688345

8 Cenacolo di San Salvi This *cenacolo* or muraled refectory in the former monastery of San Salvii, now an asylum, houses a magnificent *Last Supper* by **Andrea del Sarto**. The fresco, painted between 1519-25, represents the apogee of the High Renaissance in Florence, as do **Leonardo da Vinci**'s *The Last Supper* (painted between 1495-98) in Milan and **Raphael**'s *School of Athens* and *Disputa* (painted between 1509-11) in Rome. Though Andrea del Sarto is lesser known than the other 2 painters, the third High Renaissance artist, **Michelangelo**, is said to have warned Raphael, *There is a little fellow in Florence who would make you sweat if ever he got a great commission to do* and **Vasari** called del Sarto *pittore senza errori* (painter without fault). *The Last Supper* was the little fellow's greatest commission and is his masterpiece. It embodies the Renaissance principles of solid composition and movement in its figures and drapery at the moment shortly before del Sarto's Florentine contemporaries **Jacopo Pontormo** and **Rosso Fiorentino** were to take movement and color to the disconcerting extreme in the style now known as Mannerism.
♦ Admission. Tu-Sa 9AM-2PM; Su 9AM-1PM. Via di San Salvi 16. 677570

9 Stadio Comunale (1932, **Pier Luigi Nervi**) Florence's soccer stadium (seating capacity 40,000) is a Modernist masterpiece of rein-

Additional Florence Highlights

forced concrete by Pier Luigi Nervi, master of the medium, who designed for it an expansive cantilever roof and widely flying spiral staircase. Beside the stadium rises his **Torre di Maratona** or **Marathon Tower**. ♦ Open during soccer matches. Viale Manfredo Fanti. 572625

10 Villa San Michele $$$$ Just far enough outside of Florence in **Fiesole** for peace and quiet with views of the Duomo anchored above a sea of terracotta roofs, this luxury hotel is named after the former monastery in which it is installed. One of its suites is named after **Michelangelo**, who is said to have designed the villa, though certainly not the Jacuzzi and pool. Its restaurant serves upscale Tuscan cuisine (★★★$$$). Ask for a room with a view of Florence unless you're content to look out onto the countryside or the hotel itself.
♦ Deluxe ♦ Closed Nov-Mar. Via Doccia 4, 50014 Fiesole. 59451

10 Bencista $$$ Just below the **Villa San Michele** in location and well below it in price, the Bencista has the same magnificent views of Florence, here in a country villa setting where guests are asked to take one meal of good home cooking per day. ♦ Via Benedetto da Maiano 4, 50014 Fiesole. 59163

VENICEACCESS®

St. Mark's Basilica

Venice Orientation

Venice is the faded beauty in the family of Italian cities, her blondness now from a bottle and her perfume slightly stale. The city unabashedly thrives on tourism, masks and glass displayed in every shop window and the odor of seafood (and the sea itself) hanging in the air. And while a jaded **Henry James** wrote, *there is nothing left to discover or describe, and originality of attitude is utterly impossible*, romantics can take heart. Time after time, Venice remains the most pleasant city to discover in the world. The theatricality of its buildings and the absence of automobiles give it an ageless (though aging, as pollution from nearby Mestre and damage from the increasing *acque alte* or high water from the Adriatic attest) quality reminiscent of its former epithet *La Serenissima* or Most Serene. The riches brought to the city from the trade routes permitted great commissions in art and architecture from the likes of Titian, Tintoretto, Veronese and Palladio, and have been drawing creative and decadent types from **Casanova** to **Thomas Mann** ever since.

For a people who have seen it all (and at its most excessive) for centuries, Venetians somehow remain chipper, and they will usually be happy to direct you to your destination if you should get lost (and you *should* get lost—it's part of the experience) wandering the maze of the city's streets.

Getting to Venice

Airport

Marco Polo airport (661111) in Tessera, 8 miles from Venice, is the nearest international airport to Venice. It is served by Air France, Alitalia, British Airways, Luftansa and Sabina. A *motoscafo* or water launch service runs regularly between the airport and **Piazza San Marco** in Venice; the trip takes about half an hour. Bus service travels across the mainland to **Piazzale Roma**, from which local transportation is available. There is also water taxi service available, which is extremely expensive (about $100 at press time).

Train Station

Venice's central train station is **Santa Lucia** (Piazza Stazione, 715555). When buying your train ticket, make sure the train stops at that station and not the **Mestre** station across the lagoon on the mainland. One of the most glamorous ways of arriving in Venice is on the **Orient Express**, the fabled train from the romantic age of rail travel. It runs between London, Paris, Venice, Florence, Rome, Salzburg, Vienna, Budapest and Istanbul.

Getting Around Town
(See transit map on inside back cover)

Remember, there are no cars in Venice. Or, as **Robert Benchley** cabled home on his first visit to Venice, *Streets full of water please advise.*

The *taxi acqueo* or water taxi is expensive and will take you anywhere in Venice. Your hotel can arrange for one.

The *motoscafo* is the express water bus, stopping only at a few places along the canals. Tickets are sold at booths marked with the acronym for the city-run system, **ACTV**, at the stops.

The *vaporetto* is the local water bus, stopping at every place along the predestined route. The number 1 travels the entire length along the **Grand Canal**. Tickets are sold at booths marked with the acronym

for the city-run system, ACTV, at the stops.

The gondola is the classic way of seeing the city. Gondoliers gather at strategic places throughout the city (in front of the train station and Piazza San Marco, for example) and will give you an hour's tour and a few serenades for about $50.

The *traghetto* (also called *gondola* by Venetians) is an inexpensive way of crossing the Grand Canal if you are not near a bridge. To do as the Venetians do, just follow signs for *traghetto* or *gondola*, pay a few hundred lire, and you can cross the Grand Canal in a *gondola* on the cheap.

The **Institute of Architecture of the University of Venice** has published *Veneziapertutti*, a free map and guide to Venice designed specifically for disabled travelers. It may be obtained by writing to Assessorato Sicurezza Sociale, Ufficio Inserimenti Sociali, Ca' Farsetti, Commune di Venezia, 30100 Venezia Italy.

FYI

Consulate

UK, Dorsoduro 1051, 5227207

The nearest Australian, Canadian and US consulates are in Milan.

Hours

Businesses are generally open M 3:30-7:30PM; Tu-Sa 9AM-1PM, 3:30-7:30PM; closed M morning, Su. Food shops are open M-Tu and Th-Sa 9AM-1PM, 3:30-7:30PM; W 9AM-1PM; closed W afternoons and Su. Churches are generally open daily 8AM-12:30PM, 3:30-7:30PM.

Legal Emergencies

Ufficio Stranieri, 5200754

Medical Emergencies

Assistenza, 5294517

Money

The **American Express** office is at San Marco 1471, 200844. Another good currency exchange is **Guetta Iaggi**, San Marco 1289, 5208711. Avoid changing money at the airport and train station; the agencies here charge high commissions and should only be used as a last resort.

Post Office

Poste e Telecommunicazioni, San Marco 5554 (tel. 289317), open M-F 8:30AM-6PM; Sa 8:30AM-2:30PM.

Street Smarts

There is relatively little crime in Venice, but watch your bags on the crowded *motoscafo* and *vaporetto*, especially the ones used by tourists.

Telephone

The area code for Venice is 041; outside Italy drop the 0 and just dial 41 after the country code 39 for Italy. The **ASST** telephone at San Marco 5551 (tel. 5333111), open daily 8AM-7:30PM.

Tourist Info

Azienda di Promozione Turistica, calle Rimedio 4421, Castello (tel. 5226110), M-Sa 8:30AM-7PM.

English-language cultural events listings can be found in *Un Ospite a Venezia (A Guest in Venice)*, available at most newsstands.

Cuisine

The city which first brought such civilized eating utensils as the fork and glassware to the table, Venice has a distinguished culinary tradition. Once famed for its sumptuous banquets in which the spices that served as the basis of the republic's economy were worked into elaborate recipes that counted gold leaf among their ingredients, today the main legacy that lives on in Venice's restaurants is the sea.

A full Venetian meal begins with a selection of seafood antipasto, bits of *seppia* (cuttlefish), *scampi* (shrimp), *bottarga* (tuna eggs) or *ostriche alla veneziana* (oysters with caviar). Even landlubbing risotto dishes (the Venetians controlled the Po river valley—the largest rice-growing area in Italy—for centuries) have a special sealike texture in Venice. The natives like them *ondoso*—literally *wavy*, meaning creamier than you'll encounter in other parts of Italy. As *primi piatti* or first courses the variations are many. The most famous is *risi e bisi*, Venetian dialect for rice and peas. After that the sea again takes over, and there are *risotto* dishes made with any of the local fish—or practically all of them, which is what *risotto di mare* is. One of the most unusual risotto dishes is called *risotto di seppie* or *risotto nero*, colored black thanks to the ink of the cuttlefish. Pasta dishes are rare in Venice. The best ones are made with seafood, or combined in the local version of *pasta e fagioli* (pasta and beans), here distinguished by being made with dark *borlotti* beans and a touch of rosemary.

The best-known *secondo piatto* or main course in Venice also has its origins on land. It is *fegato alla veneziana*, or quite simply liver and onions, prepared with a delicacy you'll find nowhere else and often accompanied by the pale *polenta* or cornmeal mush

from the nearby Friuli region. (This is also your chance to try *radicchio* from nearby Treviso as a side dish vegetable.) Another dish made with ingredients from terra firma is *carpaccio*. As served at **Harry's Bar** (proprietor **Arrigo Cipriani** claims to have invented it), the dish is thinly sliced raw beef topped with Parmesan cheese, though fish and other ingredient variations have sprung up all over.

Of course seafood is a natural choice in Venice, and local restaurants do wonders with the humble dried salt cod, called *baccalà*. *Baccalà alla veneziana* is made with onions and anchovy, *baccalà alla vicentina* adds milk and Parmesan cheese, and *baccalà mantecato* is made with olive oil and parsley. *Seppie alla veneziana* is cuttlefish cooked in its black ink and white wine, *Bisato* is eel, served *alla veneziana*, sautéed in olive oil with bay leaves and vinegar or *sull'ara*, baked with bay leaves. There are also seemingly endless local fish, all with unfathomable dialect names. Among the most popular are *bransin* (a type of sea bass) and the tiny soft-shelled crabs called *moleche*.

The most popular wines in Venice are the whites Pinot Bianco and Pinot Grigio, which make an excellent accompaniment with the seafood; and the dry red Merlot, which goes well with the meat dishes. Before, during and after meals, however, most Venetians may be seen sipping *Prosecco*—a light, sparkling white. Meals are often finished with a *grappa* (the Italian aquavit) from nearby Bassano.

An inexpensive alternative to the often unjustifiably pricey restaurants in Venice is the tavern known as the *bacaro*, which serve a wine pick-me-up known as an *ombra* (literally *shadow*, from the days when workmen on the campanile of St. Mark's used to retire into the shade for a spot of wine) along with *cicchetti* or appetizers. These little plates of seafood, vegetables, cheese, prosciutto and the like can be quite filling and are a great place to meet the locals.

Venetian Streets

Wonderful city, streets full of water, please advise is what humorist **Robert Benchley** is said to have cabled home on his first visit to Venice. A waterway in Venice is called a *rio*, but even those streets that are not full of water in this wonderful city need some advice, since they are all in dialect and you won't find translations for them in any dictionary. A *calle* is a principal thoroughfare. A *stretto* is a narrow passageway. A *sottoportego* is a passageway or a covered street. A *ruga* is a street running next to a shop or residence, while a *fondamenta* runs alongside a canal, and a *riva* is an important *fondamenta*. A *lista* is a street that runs in front of a former embassy, and was once a place of diplomatic immunity. A *salizzada* was one of the first paved streets in a parish, while a *rio tera* is a filled-in canal. A *piscina* is a piazza where water once stood. But there are no piazzas in Venice—only Piazza San Marco. What would be called a piazza elsewhere in Italy is known locally as a *campo*, and usually has a well in the center. Venice's wells have since been covered, to prevent the wonderful city from sinking and its many *real* streets becoming full of water.

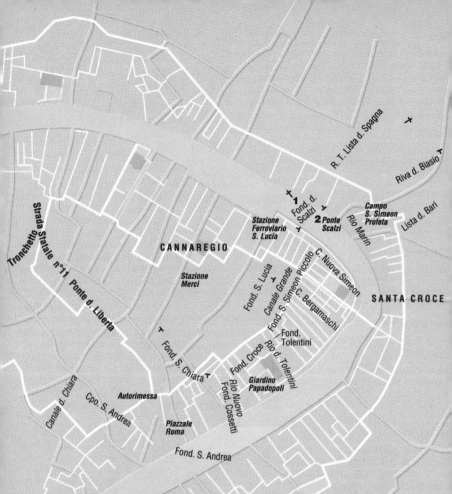

Canal Grande

Whether in high style (and expense) in a gondola or on the cheap in vaporetto No. 1, a ride on the **Canal Grande** or Grand Canal is the perfect, dreamlike introduction to the magic of Venice. The best time to take it from the **Piazza San Marco** towards **Piazzale Roma** is very early in the morning, from 6AM to 8AM, when boats are almost empty and the light is perfect; take it in the opposite direction in the late afternoon. The first time round, just let the fantastic palazzi drift by you reflected in the water and try to believe that this city is real, as have countless visitors from foreign lands and distant times before you. Don't worry about identifying the individual sights on your initial visit—once you've seen the Canal Grande you're sure to return. Many of the places in this chapter are described in further detail elsewhere in this book; check the index for page numbers.

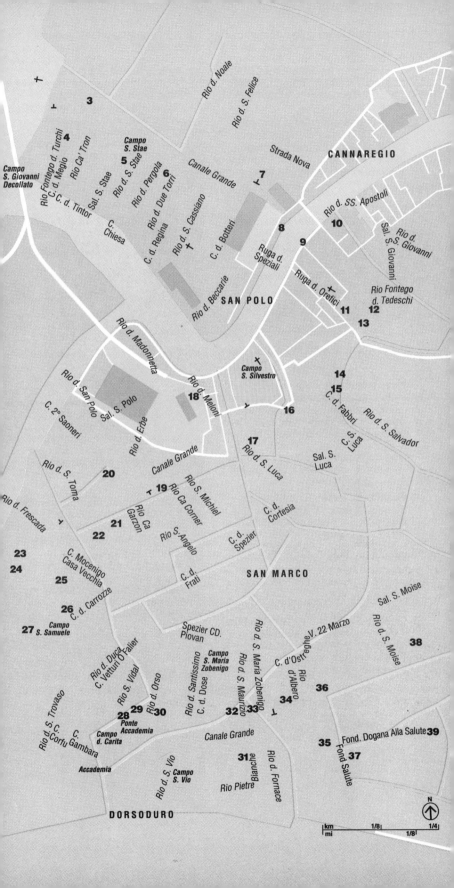

CANNAREGIO

SAN POLO

SAN MARCO

DORSODURO

Campo
S. Giovanni
Decollato

3

4

5

6

7

8

9

10

11

12

13

14

15

16

17

18

19

20

21

22

23

24

25

26

27

28

29

30

31

32

33

34

35

36

37

38

39

Rio d. Noale

Rio d. S. Felice

Strada Nova

Rio Fontego d. Turchi

C. C. d. Meglio

Rio Ca Tron

Campo
S. Stae

Sal. S. Stae

Rio d. S. Stae

Rio d. Pergola

C. d. Tintor

C. Chiesa

C. d. Regina

Rio d. Due Torri

Rio d. S. Cassiano

Canale Grande

C. d. Botteri

Rio d. Beccarie

Ruga d.
Speziali

Ruga d. Orefici

Rio d. SS. Apostoli

Sal. S. Giovanni

Rio d.
S. Giovanni

Rio Fontego
d. Tedeschi

Campo
S. Silvestro

Rio d. Madonnetta

Rio d. San Polo

Sal. S. Polo

C. 2° Saoneri

Rio d. Erbe

Rio d. Meloni

Canale Grande

Rio d. S. Toma

Rio d. Frescada

Rio Ca
Garzon

Rio S. Michiel

Rio Ca Corner

Rio S.Angelo

C. Mocenigo
Casa Vecchia

C. d. Carrozze

Campo
S. Samuele

Rio d. S. Luca

Sal. S.
Luca

C. d.
Cortesia

C. d.
Spezier

C. d.
Frati

C. d. Fabbri

S.
Luca

C.
Luca

Rio d. S. Salvador

Sal. S. Moise

Rio d. S. Moise

Spezier CD.
Piovan

Rio d. Duca

C. Vetturi O Falier

Rio S. Vidal

Rio d. Orso

Rio d. Santissimo

C. d. Dose

Campo
S. Maria
Zobenigo

Rio d. S. Maria Zobenigo

Rio d. S. Maurizio

C. d'Ostreghe

V. 22 Marzo

Rio
d'Albero

Rio d. S. Trovaso

C.
Corfu

C.
Gambara

Ponte
Accademia

Campo
d. Carita

Accademia

Rio d. S. Vio

Campo
S. Vio

Rio Pietre

Rio
Bianche

Rio d. Fornace

Fond. Dogana Alla Salute

Fond. Salute

km
mi

1/8

1/8

1/4

N

1 Chiesa degli Scalzi (17th c) This church, a fine example of Roman Baroque, was built in the 17th century from plans by **Baldassare Longhena**, one of the most celebrated architects of the day (he also designed **La Salute**). The facade was added a few decades later by **Giuseppe Sardi**.

2 Ponte degli Scalzi (1934) A team of city architects built the present bridge, replacing the one built in 1841 by French architect **Neville** in a style which was later judged to be at odds with the rest of the Canal Grande.

Canal Grande

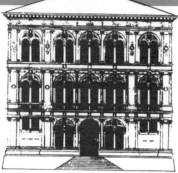

3 Palazzo Vendramin Calergi (15th c) This imposing palazzo, just after the San Marcuola vaporetto stop, was one of the first Renaissance buildings in Venice. It was built by **Mauro Codussi**, who abandoned the Gothic tradition to introduce the new style derived from Florence and Rome. **Richard Wagner** was a guest in the palazzo when he died in 1883. In winter the palazzo is the seat of the **Casino**.

4 Fondaco dei Turchi (Turks' Warehouse) (12th-13th c) A splendid, Oriental-looking building. The elongated supports of the arches and the round medallions in carved stone between them (*patere*) are typical elements of the Byzantine style in Venice. Originally the home of the **Pesaro** family, it was then used by the Turkish community. The facade was rather clumsily restored in the 19th century. The palazzo houses the **Museum of Natural History**.

5 Church of San Stae (1709, **Domenico Rossi**) A fine Baroque facade, remarkable for its balanced architectural and sculptural harmony. The 3 statues at the top represent Christ, Faith and Charity.

6 Ca' Pesaro (begun 1657, **Baldassare Longhena**) One of the most imposing palazzi on the Canal Grande. Although exquisitely Baroque, and in spite of its obvious message of wealth and power, the palazzo respects the Venetian love for ample loggias: on the top floors the facade is mostly columns and arches. Notice the long facade on the side canal—a real luxury, and not a frequent one even among the wealthy patricians of Venice. houses the **Museum of Modern Art** and the **Museum of Oriental Art**.

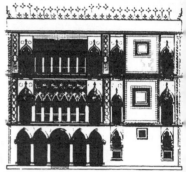

7 Ca' d'Oro (1421-40, **Matteo Raverti**) The most admired example of Venetian Gothic in the city. In Venice, Gothic means pointed arches and elaborate—at times flamboyant—stone decorations, as opposed to the austere Gothic cathedrals in Northern Europe. The top 2 floors here offer an irresistible impression of lightness and grace, in perfect harmony with the water environment. The facade was accurately restored in the 1980s; only the original blue, red and gold trimmings could not be replaced.

8 Pescheria (1907) Notice the open loggia, built in the Venetian Gothic style. A gondola service ferries people across the Canal Grande to shop at this fish market and the adjacent vegetable market.

9 Fabbriche Nuove di Rialto (1552-55, **Jacopo Sansovino**) A long, narrow palazzo erected as part of a general plan to reorganize the Rialto area around the new stone bridge over the Canal Grande. The palazzo houses government offices.

10 Ca' da Mosto (12th-13th c) One of the oldest palazzi on the Canal Grande. The facade dates from the 13th century (the top floors were added later). The 2nd-floor balcony is one of the finest examples of Byzantine architecture in Venice (narrow arches supported by thin columns and round medallions with stone bas-reliefs). Since the early 1980s, the palazzo has been for sale, but potential buyers have been discouraged by the enormous restoration costs.

11 Palazzo dei Camerlenghi (1523-25, **Guglielmo Bergamasco**) Right at the foot of the Rialto bridge, this elegant Renaissance palazzo houses government offices.

12 Fondaco dei Tedeschi (16th c) The Republic of Venice had close commercial ties with Northern Europe. German merchants would buy goods imported by the Venetian navy from the East and store them here before shipping them to their homeland. The palazzo was rebuilt in the Renaissance style after a fire in 1508; the facade was originally covered with frescoes by **Titian** and **Giorgione**. Today the palazzo houses the **Venice Post Office**.

13 Ponte di Rialto (Rialto Bridge) (1588-92, **Antonio Da Ponte**) In the 16th century, the Republic decided to replace the old drawbridge (the only one over the Canal Grande) with a permanent stone structure. The arcades on top were necessary in order to strengthen the structure. Heavy buildings were added on both sides of the bridge to keep the foundations in place.

Ponte di Rialto

14 Palazzo Dolfin Manin (1550, **Jacopo Sansovino**) The ground floor portico of this imposing Renaissance palazzo is a pedestrian walkway. Today the palazzo houses offices of the **Banca d'Italia**.

15 Palazzo Bembo (15th c) A delightful Gothic facade was added late in the 15th century to replace the original Byzantine look of this old palazzo. As in many similar buildings, the top floor was added much later.

16 Palazzo Loredan (13th c) To many a lover of Venice, this palazzo and the one next door (**Ca'**

Canal Grande

Farsetti, 12th c) epitomize the beauty of the Canal Grande as it appeared before the Renaissance moved in with heavier, more imposing facades. The rows of narrow arches supported by thin columns (a Byzantine feature) created a rare impression of lightness and grace, now partly impaired because of the top floors, which were added later. Today the 2 buildings house municipal offices.

17 Palazzo Grimani (begun 1556, **Michele Sanmicheli**) This imposing Renaissance structure was built for one of the leading Venetian families. It is now occupied by the offices of the **Corte d'Appello** or Court of Appeals.

When I went to Venice—my dream became my address.
Marcel Proust

18 Palazzo Papadopoli (16th c, **Giangiacomo dei Grigi**) The palazzo used to belong to the **Tiepolo** family and contained 4 paintings by **Veronese**, now in a museum in Dresden. It was acquired by the Counts Papadopoli, but now belongs to the **Italian Department of Education**.

19 Palazzo Corner-Spinelli (1490, **Mauro Codussi**) A masterwork of the Venetian Renaissance, this palazzo was built in 1490 by Mauro Codussi, who also designed the **Palazzo Vendramin Calergi**.

20 Palazzo Pisani-Moretta (15th c) A fine example of Venetian Gothic, this privately-owned palazzo is currently used for meetings, conferences and carnival balls.

21 Palazzo Garzoni (15th c) This palazzo now belongs to the **University of Venice** and is used by the department of foreign language.

22 Palazzi Mocenigo (16th c) The powerful Mocenigo family had these twin palazzi built in the 16th century. **Giordano Bruno** lived here in 1592 and **George Byron** in 1818. Two more palazzi, one on each side, completed the properties of the Mocenigo in this stretch of the Canal Grande. All 4 palazzi are privately owned and are used as private residences.

23 Palazzo Balbi (16th c) Dating from the late Renaissance, this palazzo belongs to the state and is currently used for administrative offices.

24 Ca' Foscari (16th c) One of the most sumptuous Gothic buildings on the Canal Grande with a great view because of its location at the Canal curve. It belongs to the **University of Venice**.

25 Palazzo Moro-Lin (1670, **Sebastiano Mazzoni**) Also known as the *palazzo with thirteen windows*. The top floor is a later addition.

26 Palazzo Grassi (begun 1718, **Giorgio Massari**) One of the foremost artists of 18th-century Venice designed this building, which was completed after his death. In the 1980s it was acquired by **Fiat Corporation** to be used as a cultural center. It houses expensively mounted art and historical exhibitions visited by thousands each day—the highest number of visitors to any building in Venice except for the Palazzo Ducale.

27 Ca' Rezzonico (17th c) The wealth of the Rezzonico family is illustrated in this sumptuous building, designed by **Baldassare Longhena** and completed by **Giorgio Massari** (top floor). It is now a museum of 18th-century art and furniture.

28 Ponte dell'Accademia (Accademia Bridge, ca 1930) As it is now, this wooden bridge is a *temporary* structure, built to replace a previous iron bridge too reminiscent of the industrial architecture of the 19th century for the tastes of the time. The temporary structure was restored in the 1980s, and most Venetians are convinced that it will remain here for at least a few generations.

29 Palazzo Franchetti An original Gothic building, heavily and not very accurately restored in the 19th century.

30 Palazzo Barbarigo The structure dates from the early Renaissance; the striking mosaics of the facade were added in the 19th century.

31 Palazzo Venier dei Leoni (1749, **Lorenzo Boschetti**) The Venier family intended to compete with the corner palazzo across the Canal, but were never able to go beyond the ground floor. **Peggy Guggenheim** found the unfinished building fascinating and bought it for herself to live in. At her death, it became a museum, the **Peggy Guggenheim Collection**.

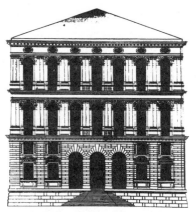

32 Palazzo Corner della Ca' Granda (1537, **Jacopo Sansovino**) The tallest building in the Canal Grande was also one of the first buildings in Venice to express the grandiose ideas of Sansovino, who soon became the official architect of the Republic (also see **St. Mark's Square**).

33 Palazzo Dario (1487, **Pietro Lombardo**) A delightful example of early Venetian Renaissance, this dangerously slanted palazzo was acquired in the 1980s by **Raoul Gardini**, an Italian industrialist, as his Venice residence. Gardini is popular in Venice because of his newly built sailboat, *The Moor of Venice*, which will be competing in the **America's Cup** in 1992.

34 Palazzo Gritti A somber Gothic facade slightly modified in the 19th century. It is one of the great luxury hotels of Venice, with terrace dining right on the Canal.

35 Abbazia di San Gregorio This former abbey, of which a Gothic portal has survived, is now a luxury condominium.

36 Palazzo Contarini-Fasan (1475) Also knows as *Desdemona's palazzo* because of a local legend, this small, beautiful Gothic building is noted for its carved stone balcony. It was restored in the late-1980s and is now a private residence.

37 Chiesa della Salute (1631-81, **Baldassare Longhena**) This is the masterwork of Baldassare Longhena, the great Baroque architect who redesigned the whole complex at the entrance of the Canal Grande. The statue at the very top represents the Virgin Mary dressed as a Venetian admiral. Merchant ships used to stop here for customs upon arrival from all over the Mediterranean and the North Atlantic.

was a great mastery of light and shadow which enabled ntoretto to put into his pictures all the poetry there as in his soul without once tempting us to think that he ght have found better expression in words. The poetry hich quickens most of his works in the Scuola di San occo is almost entirely a matter of light and color.

Bernard Berenson

staurants/Nightlife: Red   Hotels: Blue
ops/Parks: Green   Sights/Culture: Black

38 Ca' Giustinian (1474) The Giustinian family, one of the oldest and wealthiest in Venice, lived in this Gothic mansion, the first on the Canal Grande after the St. Mark's area (the next building, now **Hotel Monaco**, was built in the 19th century). The palazzo belongs to the city of Venice and houses the offices of the **Biennale**, including the headquarters of the **Venice Film Festival**.

39 Punta della Dogana In the 15th century, this was the customs center for all Venetian ships. The long, low building was re-built in the 17th

Canal Grande

century and finished in the 19th. On the tower at the very tip is a large sphere representing the

Gondola! Gondola!

The last private gondola in Venice was owned by the eccentric American art collector **Peggy Guggenheim**, whose gondola rides with her beloved dogs earned her the affectionate epithet *la dogaressa* or the lady doge. Her boat is now in the **Museo Storico Navale**, but you can still get the feeling that the ride and the city are yours alone by hiring a gondola. Just be certain that you insist on the legal fare of 60,000 lire— more after 6PM and on holidays. Then relax as the gondolier makes his way around the network of Venice's canals, singing incongruous Neapolitan songs and crying *a-óe* to alert other gondoliers as he rows his boat with only one oar, using his whole body in a movement as graceful as the gondola itself.

John Julius Norwich

Flying over the city on the way to Marco Polo airport (sit on the *right* of aircraft).

Dinner (in summer) on the raft of the **Gritti**.

Dinner (in winter) before a blazing fire at the **Poste Vecie**.

Lunch (in summer) at **Harry's Dolci**.

Breakfast (in summer) on the **Danieli Terrace**.

Following any of the walks set out in *Venice for Pleasure*, by **J.G. Links**

Mid-morning drink at either of the 2 cafes on the **Campo SS Giovanni e Paolo**.

An excursion to **Torcello** (preferably on a weekday).

The carpaccios at **S. Giorgio degli Schiavoni**.

The **Querini Stampalia Museum**.

The top of the campanile of **S. Giorgio Maggiore**.

The **Church of S. Nicolo dei Mendicoli**.

The food (any time) at **Al Covo**.

Sunday lunch at a fish restaurant in Chioggia.

The Medical Museum in the **Ospedale Civico** (Scuola di S. Marco).

The **Ridotto della Procuratessa Venier** in the Merceria.

San Marco

The most-visited *sestiere* (literally *sixth*, the word refers to the 6 sections of the city) of Venice is **San Marco**. It centers around **Piazza San Marco**, the only square the Venetians deign to call a piazza (the others are called *campo*). **Napoleon** supposedly referred to the piazza as the best drawing-room in Europe, but that characterization could easily be expanded to encompass the world. As it must have during the heyday of the republic of *La Serenissima* (*the most serene*, as Venice was called), Piazza San Marco today provides a drawing-room for people of every size, shape and nationality. They gaze at the sights surrounding the Basilica of San Marco, about which **Henr[y] James** wrote, *If Venice, as I say has become a great bazaar, this exquisite edifice is now the biggest booth.* But there's more to see in San Marco than that exquisite edifice— the **Campanile**, the **Palazzo Ducale**, the **Museo Correr**, **Florian** and **Quadri** cafes, shopping on the **Frezzeria** and the **Mercerie**—though you may be tempted never to leave the piazza itself, caught up in the comings and goings of the bedazzled crowds mimicking the flocks of scraggly pigeons in the air and afoot.

1 Piazza San Marco (16th c, **Jacopo Sansovino**) Piazza San Marco is one of the most beautiful and harmonious man-made spaces in the world. Those qualities can be appreciated during the height of the midsummer tourist season, though there are special times when the sight is even more breathtaking—in the mist of the early morning, the silence late at night, the light

fog that often sets in during the winter, or even during the *acque alte* or high water that occasions the use of wooden planks in order to cross the piazza without getting one's feet wet. But at all times, the square symbolizes and traces the history of Venice, from the 9th century (the Basilica was begun then, and the original Campanile was also erected at that time) through the plan for the piazza as devised by Jacopo Sansovino during the Renaissance and the Neoclassical addition called the **Ala Napoleonica** built under **Bonaparte**, right on to the contemporary era when the piazza was the scene of a notoriously crowded concert by the rock group **Pink Floyd** a few years ago. Through it all the pigeons continue to swoop

(and pollute the monuments), merchants continue to ply their wares, Venetians pause for refreshments at **Caffè Florian**, and bedazzled visitors scratch their heads in awe of the wonder that is Venice. ♦ Piazza San Marco. Vap 1, 2, 34, San Marco or 5, San Zaccaria

2 Basilica di San Marco (begun 9th c) Originally the doges' private chapel, the Basilica of San Marco—**Mark Twain**'s *vast warty bug taking a meditative walk*—is a complex conglomeration of medieval, Classical, Byzantine and Romanesque styles. It was built to house the body of **St. Mark**, stolen from its tomb in Alexandria in an event known as the *traslatio*, which is depicted in a 13th-century mosaic over the far left arch on the exterior. Also noteworthy on the exterior are Romanesque relief carvings on the 3 receding arches of the main entrance, as well as the copies of the gilded bronze horses (originals in the church museum) carted off by **Napoleon** and later returned to the city, and the Gothic carvings of religious figures on the roof. The interior is a beautifully murky and mysterious space, paved with an intricately patterned floor and covered with mosaics dating from the 12th to the 18th centuries. The most important are the 13th-century *Old Testament* scenes in the vaults, the 13th-century *Ascension* in the central cupola, and the *Christ, Madonna* and *Prophets* on the walls of the nave aisles. Also in the Basilica is the **Pala d'Oro**, or golden altarpiece, made of enamels and precious stones from the 10th to the 12th centuries; the **Tesoro**, or Treasury, containing loot from Constantinople (a real prize was the 10th-century icon of **St. Michael**); the 15th-century *iconostasis* or choir screen by the **Masegne** brothers in front of the altar; and the **Cappella dei Mascoli** in the left transept. From the portico is access to the **Museo** or museum, the highlight of which is the cover for the Pala d'Oro painted by **Paolo Veneziano** in 1345. ♦ Admission to Pala d'Oro, Tesoro and Museo. Piazza San Marco. Vap 1, 2, 34, San Marco or 5, San Zaccaria

3 Palazzo Ducale (Doges' Palace) The Doges' apartments, the Assembly Hall and other high officers' headquarters were lodged in this building. Built in the 9th century, it was enlarged and modified many times; its present shape dates from the 15th century, when the side facing the Piazzetta was built, along with the monumental door on the Basilica side. The facade facing the lagoon is the oldest. A capital over a column at the southwest corner bears the date 1344 (marking the completion of the ground-floor loggias). Remarkable sculptures adorn the palazzo's corners: near the bridge on the southeast corner is the *Drunkenness of Noah*, and on the southwest corner *Adam* and *Eve*, all by unknown artists; on the northwest corner is

the *Judgment of Solomon*, attributed to **Jacopo della Quercia**. Over the columns, the capitals are decorated with animals, warriors, men and women, and representations of vices and virtues and human activities. The main entrance is along the Basilica side. The **Porta della Carta** is a Venetian-Gothic masterwork by **Giovanni** and **Bartolomeo Bon**. The figure over the door, on his knees in front of St. Mark's Lion, is **Doge Francesco Foscari**, who led the Republic in the acquisition of new territories on the Italian mainland from 1423 to 1457. In the courtyard, the facades at the south (lagoon side) and west have 14th-century loggias on the 2nd floor; the ground floors were originally just brick walls. In 1602 a city architect named **Bartolomeo Monopola** performed the amazing feat of replacing those walls

with arches and columns by temporarily supporting the structure during construction. The 2 well-heads at the center were cast in bronze in the 16th century. Patricians used to enter through the monumental **Scala dei Giganti** (Giant's Staircase), with its 2 statues of *Mars* and *Neptune*, symbols of Venice's power over land and sea. The interior of the palazzo was reconstructed after a fire in 1574, during which important paintings by **Carpaccio, Giorgione** and **Titian** were destroyed, together with the original woodwork on the ceilings and walls.

Start your visit at the stair leading to the 2nd-floor loggia. From the loggia, another staircase, the imposing [1] **Scala d'Oro**, leads to the **Primo Piano Nobile**, (actually the 2nd floor), home to the Doge's apartments, which are only open for temporary exhibitions. Two small rooms here lead to the [2] **Sala dei Filosofi**, whence a stair leads to the Doge's chapel. Notice the *St. Christopher* by Titian over the door at the stair. The **Sala delle Volte** contains 3 Venice insignias, among them a famous *St. Mark's Lion* by **Vittore Carpaccio**.

From the Scala d'Oro, continue to the **Secondo Piano Nobile** (the 3rd floor). Through the [3] **Atrio Quadrato** (Square Atrium) and the [4] **Sala della Quattro Porte** (Four Door Room) is the small [5] **Anticollegio** room. Here, on the sides of the doors, are 4 paintings by **Jacopo Tintoretto**. On the wall opposite the window is a *Rape of Europe* by **Paolo Veronese**. The next room is the [6] **Sala del Collegio**, where the Doge's cabinet would meet to deliberate and to receive visitors. The ceiling was painted by Paolo Veronese with allegories of virtues and with a famous *Venice Enthroned* (center of ceiling, at the far end). The paintings over the entrance are by Jacopo Tintoretto and those on the right wall are from his workshop. The one over the Cabinet's seats, *Doge Sebastiano Venier Offering Thanks for the Victory of Lepanto*, is by Paolo Veronese. The next room is the [7] **Sala del Senato**, where the Venice Senate used to meet. The Senate was a body of elected patricians in charge of foreign policy and of some domestic affairs. With about 150 members, it was a more agile body than the Maggior Consiglio, the 1200-member legislative assembly which included all male patricians of age. The paintings on the walls and ceiling are minor works—in terms of quality if not size—by Tintoretto and his workshop, **Jacopo Palma il Giovane** and other Mannerist painters. Through the Sala delle Quattro Porte and a small atrium is the [8] **Sala del Consiglio dei Dieci**

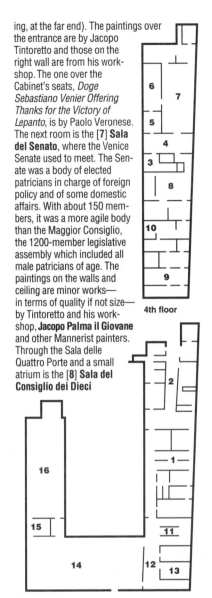

4th floor

3rd floor

(Room of the Council of Ten). This much-feared assembly was in charge of the secret police and of the prosecution of members of the patrician class. Like most secret police, the police in Venice acquired enormous power, particularly in the last days of the Republic's life. Three paintings by Paolo Veronese adorn the ceiling in correspondence with the curved woodwork at the back. The central oval is a copy of *Jupiter Striking Vices with Lightning*, also by Veronese (the original is in the Louvre).

The next 3 rooms [9], reached by going up a few steps, contain a large collection of weapons, mostly from the 16th and 17th centuries, which formed the official armory at the disposal of the Republic's leaders.

San Marco

Usually excluded from the guided visit is the [10] **Saletta dei Tre Inquisitori** (Three Inquisitors' Office), off the room of the Council of Ten. Selected from among the Ten, the Three Inquisitors were the real terror of Venice, particularly in the 18th century. Their trials of real and supposed political criminals were held in secret without the chance of appeal. A small stair led directly from this room to the torture chamber, while a secret corridor led to the **Ponte dei Sospori** (Bridge of Sighs) and the prisons. Inquire at the ticket window for guided tours of these rooms.

Down the stairs at the armory's entrance [11] (**Scala dei Censori**) are the south and west wings of the Primo Piano Nobile. Through the [12] **Andito del Maggior Consiglio**, the tour proceeds to the *lagó*, a veranda with statues of *Adam* and *Eve* by **Antonio Rizzo**, considered to be among the best works of the early Renaissance in Venice. A door on the left wall leads to the [13] **Sala dell'Armamento**. The large, much-damaged fresco here is all that is left of a *Paradise* painted by **Guariento** in 1367. After the fire in 1574, a new *Paradise* was commissioned from Tintoretto (now in the Great Assembly Hall). The remnants of Guariento's work were discovered when Tintoretto's canvas was

Palazzo Ducale (Doges' Palace)

removed for restoration. Back in the Andito, 2 doors open into the grandiose **[14] Sala del Maggior Consiglio** (Great Assembly Hall). Here the patricians met regularly to run the Republic, their numbers varying from 1200 to 2000. They sat in 9 double rows parallel to the long walls of the hall. The Doge and his cabinet sat on the Tribune at the entrance wall. Among the 35 paintings on the ceiling, encased in sumptuous frames, the most noteworthy is Paolo Veronese's *Apotheosis of Venice Crowned by Victory* (at the central oval near the Tribune). Veronese's and Tintoretto's workshops produced most of the other canvasses. Behind the Tribune is Tintoretto's great *Paradise*—the largest painting in the world. It is one of the painter's last works,

and his son **Domenico** and **Palma il Giovane** helped him complete it. A frieze at the top portrays the first 76 Dogi of Venice, up to **Francesco Venier**, who died in 1556. By the way, the view from the windows here is spectacular.

A door at the far right leads through the **[15] Sala della Quarantia Civil Nova** to the last great hall of the palace, the **[16] Sala dello Scrutinio** (Ballet Counting Room), richly decorated with paintings by Palma il Giovane, **Andrea Vicentino, Aliense** and other Mannerist artists. The room is often used for temporary exhibitions. The *Last Judgment* above the Tribune is by Palma il Giovane. Back to the Sala del Maggior Consiglio, a door at the left of Tintoretto's *Paradise* leads back to the staircase and, through a loggia to the Ponte dei Sospiri or Bridge of Sighs, which was built in 1602 to connect the Palazzo with the prisons across the canal (the bridge's name was probably invented by 19th-century travelers). A visit to the prison is included in the admission ticket. ◆ Admission. Daily 8:30AM-7PM. Piazzetta San Marco. Vap 1, 2, 34, San Marco or 5, San Zaccaria. 5224951

4 Molo di San Marco The south side of the Piazzetta, open towards the lagoon, was traditionally the landing pier for patricians, merchants and all kinds of people having business in the area. The pier was once the main entrance into the city. The 2 huge columns marking its sides like an imaginary portal were brought here on boats from Byzantium in the 12th century. They support the statues of *St. Theodor* (the original protector of Venice, later replaced by St. Mark) and a puzzling winged animal, accepted as St. Mark's Lion although it probably is a chimera made in China or Persia (the wings were added in Venice). The most charming aspect of the pier today is the row of gondolas parked along it, furiously rocking all day long from the waves created by the heavy motor boat traffic. In fact, only a few courageous gondoliers (and their unsuspecting passengers) still brave the rough waters of St. Mark's basin. ◆ Piazzetta San Marco. Vap 1, 2, 34, San Marco or 5, San Zaccaria

5 Ponte dei Sospiri (Bridge of Sighs) This elegant bridge owes its melancholy name to the fact that it connected the Doges' Palace with the prisons across the canal. It was built in 1602 and has since figured prominently in countless tales, paintings and movies. ◆ Vap 1 2, 34, San Marco or 5, San Zaccaria

6 Venini Founded in 1921, the Venini glass factory immediately distinguished itself for its innovations in the ancient Venetian glassmaking tradition. The firm introduced new types of glass and contemporary artists produced new shapes. In the 1980s, Venini vases made in the 1950s fetched as much as half a million dollars at auction—30 years from now those prices could well apply to objects on display today. ◆ Closed M morning, lunch. Piazzetta Leoncini 314. Vap 1, 2, 34, San Marco or 5, San Zaccaria. 5224045

7 Torre dell' Orologio **Mauro Codussi**, one of the fathers of the Venetian Renaissance, most probably designed this structure at the end of the 15th century. Its dual purpose was to hold a large clock (which replaced the one that had been on the Basilica) and to mark the entrance to Venice's main wholesale and retail street, appropriately called **Mercerie** (from the Italian word for merchandise). Every hour on the hour the 2 bronze statues on the top of the tower hit the large bell with their long-handled hammers, thanks to a 15th-century mechanism which is still a source of wonder. For a moment, life in the square comes to a halt as everyone watches the 2 Moors—so-called because of the dark color of the bronze they are cast in—majestically pivot around to strike the hour. ◆ Merceria dell 'Orologio 147. Vap 1, 2, 34, San Marco or 5, San Zaccaria

8 Procuratie The name for these buildings means procurator's offices and refers to their function during the Venetian Republic. The procurators were high government officials, and their headquarters next to the Doge's Palace made Piazza San Marco the center of civic as well as religious life in Venice. With your back to the Basilica, the building you see on the right (**Procuratie Vecchie**) was reconstructed

at the beginning of the 16th century to replace a Byzantine structure. **Jacopo Sansovino**, the official architect of the Republic, created the building's final shape by adding the 2nd floor in 1532. Notice that this facade is lighter and less imposing than its counterpart on the other side of the square (**Procuratie Nuove**), also designed by Sansovino and completed a hundred years later by **Baldassare Longhene** (architect of La Salute and the most important contributor to the Venetian-Baroque style). In the first building, Sansovino expanded on the existing first floor (attributed to **Mauro Codussi**) and continued it with thin columns and narrow arches, while on the 2nd floor, built from scratch, he was able to express his personal ideals of Roman-inspired majesty.
♦ Piazza San Marco. Vap 1, 2, 34, San Marco or 5, San Zaccaria

9 Missiaglia Since 1864 the Missiaglia family has been supplying wealthy Venetians and visitors with the best in jewels and gold. Definitely one of the most reliable goldsmiths in town (most items are crafted in their own workshop), Missiaglia excells in sober, classic objects, but keeps an accurate eye on the newest trends in jewelry design. ♦ Closed M morning, Su, lunch. Piazza San Marco 125. Vap 1, 2, 34, San Marco or 5, San Zaccaria. 5224464

10 Ala Napoleonica (1814, **Giuseppe Maria Soli**) In 1797 the young **Napoleon Bonaparte** brought about the end of the Republic of Venice —after a millennium of glory—with a simple letter in which he asked **Doge Ludovico Manin** to resign and open the way for a new, democratic constitution. Pressed by Napoleon's armies at the Republic's borders, the Doge and his men decided to oblige. It was an inglorious end, the only justification of which being that a war would most certainly have ended in defeat for Venice. During their occupation, the French undertook important public works, among them the restructuring on the side of the Piazza opposite the Basilica. **Napoleon's Wing**, designed by the Italian architect Giuseppe Maria Soli, includes a grand staircase and the so-called **Royal Apartments**, with a ballroom which today is part of the **Museo Correr**.
♦ Piazza San Marco. Vap 1, 2, 34, San Marco or 5, San Zaccaria

10 Museo Correr This museum is comprised of 3 sections: the **Collezioni Storiche** or Historical Collections, consisting of 22 rooms on the 2nd floor at the top of the grand staircase with material related to the history of Venice; the **Museo del Risorgimento e dell' Ottocento Veneziano** or Museum of 19th-Century Venice on the 3rd floor; and the **Quadreria** or Collection of Paintings also on the 3rd floor.

The Collezione Storiche includes: maps and views of Venice (in the Galleria); works by **Antonio Canova**, the Neoclassical sculptor (Room No. 1); marbles with various effigies of **St. Mark's Lion** (Room No. 4); documents and images related to the **Dogi** (Room Nos. 5, 6 and 7) with some fascinating bound

commissioni (instructions sent by the Dogi to Venetian ambassadors and other high officers); clothes and portraits of **Patricians** (Room Nos. 8, 9 and 10); Venetian coins from the 12th century (Room No. 11); a scale model of the *Bucintoro*, the gilded boat used by the Dogi for parades (Room No. 14); material related to the history of the **Arsenale** and to Venetian navigation techniques (Room Nos. 15 and 16); weapons (Room Nos. 17 and 18); and documents related to **Doge Francesco Morosino** (Room Nos. 19 to 22).

The Museo del Risorgimento e dell' Ottocento Veneziano covers the history of Venice from 1797 to 1866, focusing on the unsuccessful attempt to gain independence from Austria

in 1848-49. In the Quadreria, a large collection of minor painters documents the evolution of Venetian art from the 13th to the 16th centuries. Included are some works by great masters, such as **Antonello da Messina**'s *Pietá*, painted in Venice; 4 paintings by **Giovanni Bellini** (exhibited next to the works by **Jacopo**, his father, and **Gentile**, his brother); and 2 portraits by **Vittore Carpaccio**, *The Courtesans* (though the women portrayed were most likely not courtesans but members of the Venetian upper class) and the striking *Young Man in a Red Beret*. The museum also contains the original wood dies of **Jacopo de' Barbari**'s famous *Map of Venice in 1500*, an extremely detailed drawing and a valuable source for the reconstruction of the shapes of buildings at that time. ♦ Admission. Daily 9AM-7PM, Apr-Oct; 9AM-4PM, Nov-Mar. Piazza San Marco 52. Vap 1, 2, 34, San Marco. 5225625

10 Pauly Right under the porticoes of the Museo Correr, Pauly's offers a wide selection of glass objects, mostly produced in its own Murano furnace. Vases, chandeliers, drinking glasses and statues come in an incredible variety of shapes. While some pieces would be right at home in a musem, others are less elaborate and more affordable (relatively). The shop has a great reputation for reliability when shipping abroad. ♦ Closed M morning, Su, lunch. Piazza San Marco 72-77. Vap 1, 2, 34, San Marco. 5235484

11 Caffè Florian Definitely the most famous of the Venetian cafes, the Florian was one of the first places in the world to serve that new and exotic drink—coffee. The rooms inside still have the original 18th-century decor, and they are  still patronized by upper-class Venetians, particularly for afternoon tea in the winter. In the summer, a small orchestra plays popular tunes for guests sitting at the outdoor tables sipping expensive coffee and cappuccino. But those in the know take refuge at the counter inside, where they can sip a Bellini cocktail or glass of *prosecco* wine, away from the strains of *O sole mio* and the lambada. Despite the high prices, the Florian is losing money and may soon close its doors, unless the city finds a way to save this Venetian institution. ♦ Closed W. Piazza San Marco 56-59. Vap 1, 2, 34, San Marco or 5, San Zaccaria. 85338

11 Biblioteca Correr Next to Caffè Florian, a door on the **Procuratie** leads to one of the inner courtyards, where an elevator takes scholars and students to the pleas- ant reading rooms of the **Museo Correr**. A friendly staff of librarians helps them find their way through the ancient catalogues, many of

them handwritten. The rich collection of documents and manuscripts was bequeathed in 1830 by the patrician **Teodoro Correr**. A collec- tion specializing in Vene- tian art history was more recently acquired by the library. ♦ 8:30AM- 1:30PM. Piazza San Marco 52. Vap 1, 2, 34, San Marco or 5, San Zaccaria. 5225625

12 Campanile di San Marco (1514, **Bartolomeo Bon**) The highest monument in Venice (325 feet) is one of a number of bell tow- ers on the site which met with disaster over the centuries. On the morn- ing of 14 July 1902, the tower gently collapsed in the piazza; there were no injuries. Many shops around Venice sell what purports to be a photo- graphic record of the event. Unfortunately, no film at the time was fast enough to have captured it, so the image is a picturesque fake. The present, much more sound structure was built immediately after the unfortunate event. Don't miss the wonderful view of Venice from the top. ♦ Admission. Daily 9AM-10PM. Piazza San Marco. Vap 1, 2, 34, San Marco or 5, San Zaccaria. 5224064

12 Loggetta di San Marco (1539-49, **Jacopo Sansovino**) Sansovino designed this structure at the base of the Campanile; the terrace and balustrade in front were added later. The 4 bronze statues in the niches, executed by Sansovino, represent *Minerva, Apollo, Mercury* and *Peace* as symbols of good government. Over them is *Venice Clad as Justice*, accompa- nied by bas-reliefs representing Cyprus and Crete, then part of Venice's empire. Together with the Procuratie and the Library, the Loggetta exemplifies how San Marco was once the gran- diose center of the Republic. ♦ Piazza San Marco Vap 1, 2, 34, San Marco or 5, San Zaccaria

13 Piazzetta San Marco The piazzetta, or little piazza, comprises the space from the Basilica' south side to the lagoon border. It is an inde- pendent square, separated from the piazza by the Campanile. The white marble pavement wa used by the patricians to pace back and forth while their Parliament was deliberating inside the Palazzo Ducale—they would walk on either the east or west side, depending on which one was in the shade. When a young patrician came of age, he was taken here on the family gondola and officially admitted into the com- munity of rulers. ♦ Piazzetta San Marco. Vap 1 2, 34, San Marco or 5, San Zaccaria

14 Museo Archeologico An important collection of archaeological pieces has been temporarily installed in the huge building designed by **Jacopo Sansovino** for the **Biblioteca Marciana** (their final destination is a palazzo under restoration at Santa Maria Formosa). From the 16th to the 18th centuries, many of Venice's patrician fam lies collected archaeological pieces from Rome Greece and the Roman-settled territories bor- dering on the lagoon (Aquileia, Eraclea, Altinum' The **Grimani** family bequeathed its collection t the Republic in the 16th century; other donation followed. The collections of coins, epigraphs, bas-reliefs and statues include many exquisite originals from Greece, particularly from the 5th century BC, and from Rome. Among the most interesting items are a statue of *Demetra* and one of *Athena* (Room No. 4); the *Ara Grimani*, with magnificent sculptures from the first cen- tury BC (Room No. 6); and 3 statues of Gallic Warriors sculpted in Pergamus around the yea 200 BC. ♦ Admission. M-Sa 9AM-2PM; Su 9AM-1PM. Piazza San Marco 17. Vap 1, 2, 34, San Marco or 5, San Zaccaria. 5225978

15 Caffè Chioggia If you're looking for a spler did way to end an evening in Venice, relax at one of the outdoor tables at this cafe, enjoying the romantic music in the company of the Palazzo Ducale in front and the lagoon at the side. ♦ Closed Su and 1 Nov-1 April. Piazza San Marco 11. Vap 1, 2, 34, San Marco or 5, San Zaccaria. 5285011

16 Giardinetti Reali **Napoleon**'s architects designed this small park to replace an existing building so as to permit a view of the lagoon from the Royal Apartments they had created in the Procuratie. Although far from living up to its name, the park offers welcome respite. ♦ Vap 1, 2, 34, San Marco

16 Biblioteca Marciana (begun 16th c, **Jacopo Sansovino**) Sansovino designed this building, but it was completed by his pupil **Vincenzo Scamozzi**. The facade was designed as a continuation of the **Procuratie Nuove** on the Piazzetta, so as to emphasize the architectural unity of the whole compound. The Roman-inspired solemnity of the exterior was intended to visually represent the power and wealth of the Venetian Republic. The building was destined to contain the burgeoning Biblioteca Marciana or Library of St. Mark's, a collection of precious manuscripts and early printed books (*incunabula*). It was built by the Republic around an initial donation by poet **Francesco Petrarch** and by the great humanist **Cardinal Bessarion**. The monumental door (at No. 13) is flanked by 2 large statues of women supporting the vault (carytids). The library is open to the public (entrance at No. 7). General readers (those who arrive before the room fills with high school and college students) are received in a large room on the ground floor. A smaller room on the left is reserved for scholars here to consult ancient books or manuscripts (permission must be granted by the library to do so). The library's best architecture and its most precious collection of manuscripts are reached via the grandiose staircase. Unless temporary exhibitions are being held, permission to visit the rooms upstairs must be obtained from the director's office. ◆ M-F 9AM-7PM; Sa 9AM-1PM. Piazza San Marco 13. Vap 1, 2, 34, San Marco or 5, San Zaccaria. 5208788

17 Harry's Bar ★★★$$$$ Made famous by **Hemingway**, Harry's Bar originally was just a bar, but has now become Venice's most reliable (and expensive) restaurant as well. Colorful owner **Arrigo Cipriani**, son of the original owner, claims that many Venetian specialties were created here—namely the peach juice and spumante cocktail called the Bellini and the raw beef dish called Carpaccio, both named after Venetian painters. Another recommended dish is the *risotto primavera*, made with a variety of vegetables. The see-and-be-seen scene is at its most active between 7 and 9PM. Ask for a table upstairs for a great view of the Canal Grande. ◆ Closed M. Calle Vallaresso 1323. Vap 1, 2, 34, San Marco. 5236797

18 Hotel Monaco and Grand Canal $$$ The Monaco is one of the most attractive hotels in its class. The ground floor rooms have large windows on the Canal Grande in front of La Salute, with bar service and a piano bar at night. Many Venetians stop by for tea or drinks, attracted by the quiet, relaxing atmosphere. The dining terrace, also on the Canal Grande, is open to non-guests as well. ◆ Calle Vallaresso 1325. Vap 1, 2, 34, San Marco. 5200211; fax 5200501

19 Missoni The latest colorful designs created by Milanese **Ottavio Missoni** for men and women are available at this outlet opened by the firm in the 1980s. Look for cardigans, coats, skirts and dresses. Venetians watch for the sales at the end of each season. ◆ Closed M morning, Su, lunch. Calle Vallaresso 1312-B. Vap 1, 2, 34, San Marco. 5205733

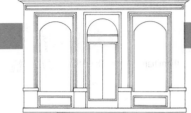

20 La Bottega Veneta The famous high-fashion leather accessories firm started at this shop, before expanding to Madison Ave, Rodeo Dr and 11 other locations, including Tokyo, Paris and Madrid. ◆ Closed M morning, Su, lunch. Calle Vallaresso 1337. Vap 1, 2, 34, San Marco. 5228489

20 Camiceria San Marco A large selection of fabrics and years of experience draw customers to Carmiceria for custom-made shirts at prices comparable to those at good department stores. ◆ Closed M morning, Su, lunch. Calle Vallaresso 1340. Vap 1, 2, 34, San Marco. 5221432

21 Hotel Luna Baglioni $$$ One of the oldest hotels in Venice, the Luna has been completely remodeled. Some of the rooms and all of the suites have original 18th-century furnishings. The Tiepolo Suite has a terrace with a splendid view over the St. Mark's basin; the Giorgione Suite has a terrace with a view over the rooftops. The main conference hall is a masterwork of 18th-century interior decoration. ◆ Calle Vallaresso 1243. Vap 1, 2, 34, San Marco. 5289840; fax 5287160

22 Mario Valentino An elegant outlet of the famous Neapolitan manufacturer of shoes and leather accessories. ◆ Closed M morning, Su, lunch. San Marco 1473. Vap 1, 2, 34, San Marco. 5205733

23 M An antiques store coupled with a workshop for the production of precious velvets handprinted in the style of **Mariano Fortuny**, the Venice-based artist who was all the rage during the 1920s and '30s. Both the antiques and the velvets are of the highest quality. ◆ Closed M morning, Su, lunch. Frezzeria 1651. Vap 1, 2, 34, San Marco. 5235666

The Venetians invented income tax, statistical science, censorship, the gambling casino, the ghetto, and easel-painting.

24 Libreria del Sansovino Very close to Piazza San Marco, this bookstore specializes in art books, including rare and out of print copies, and has a wide selection of books on Venice in English. It also carries the current English-language best sellers—the owner calls them *jet lag* books. ♦ Closed M morning, Su, lunch. Bacino Orseolo 84. Vap 1, 2, 34, San Marco. 5222623

25 Bacino Orseolo Behind the **Procuratie Vecchie**, a canal opens onto this small basin, which is usually crowded with gondolas parked in rows of 4 and 5. The gondoliers and their customers are fun to watch in themselves. ♦ Vap 1, 2, 34, San Marco

San Marco

26 Il Prato Begun as a refined, expensive shop for Carnival clothes and masks, this place has quickly become a successful *curiosity shop*, as its owner calls it. Its latest success are automatons: groups of exquisitely crafted figures that move at the sound of a carillon. Their creator is a certain **Monseur Camus**, who won a World Championship of Automaton Builders in Switzerland. Other marvels include hand-painted eggs and miniature furniture by designer **Ettore Sobrero**. All items are handmade by craftsmen of the highest caliber. ♦ Closed M morning, Su, lunch. Frezzeria 1770. Vap 1, 2, 34, San Marco. 5203375

27 Osvaldo Böhm Antique prints (originals and reproductions), historic photographs and watercolors are available at this reliable shop a few steps from Piazza San Marco. ♦ Closed M morning, Su, lunch. San Moisè 1349-50. Vap 1, 2, 34, San Marco. 5222255

28 Calzature Fratelli Rossetti The highest quality in Italian shoes. Other Rossetti stores are in Paris, London, New York and Singapore. In Venice, there is another outlet in Campo San Salvador near the Rialto Bridge. ♦ Closed M morning, Su, lunch. San Moisè 1447. Vap 1, 2, 34, San Marco. 5220819

The tourist Venice is Venice: the gondolas, the sunsets, the changing light, Florian's, Quadri's, Torcello, Harry's Bar, Murano, Burano, the pigeons, the glass beads, the vaporetto. Venice is a folding picture-postcard of itself.
Mary McCarthy

28 Fendi Luxury leather goods are the specialty of Fendi, but the boutique also carries clothes, umbrellas and gift items. ♦ Closed M morning, Su, lunch. Salizada San Moisè 1474. Vap 1, 2, 34, San Marco. 5205733

29 L'Isola Glass objects made in Murano by the **Carlo Moretti** team, specializing in modern designs. ♦ Closed M morning, Su, lunch. Campo San Moisè 1468. Vap 1, 2, 34, San Marco. 5231973

29 Louis Vuitton The Venice branch of the most famous luggage designer in the world. ♦ Closed M morning, Su, lunch. Campo San Moisè 1461. Vap 1, 2, 34, San Marco. 5224500

30 Chiesa di San Moisè (1668, **Alessandro Tremignon**) Venice is probably the only city in the world with churches consecrated to prophets of the Old Testament (technically included among the Catholic saints): there are churches for Daniel, Zacharias and the Archangel Raphael. St. Moses was built in full Baroque style by Tremignon with funds from the **Fini** family. As in many other Venetian churches, statues of the donors were installed over the portals. Here the family's coat of arms is also sculpted on the pediment. The lavish decorations on the facade have often been compared with stage sets for Baroque operas. Equally controversial is the surprising and sumptuous high altar, a complex sculpture represenating *Moses Receiving the Tablets on Mount Sinai*. ♦ Campo San Moisè. Vap 1, 2, 34, San Marco

31 Hotel Bauer Grünwald $$$ In addition to the modern entrance on Campo San Moisè, the hotel has a Gothic facade on the Canal Grande, with a restaurant and bar on a splendid terrace over the water. Most suites and some rooms are decorated with antiques. Service is excellent. ♦ Campo San Moisè 1459. Vap 1, 2, 34, San Marco. 5207022; fax 5207557

32 Libreria Sangiorgio One of the best bookstores in Venice for reading materials in English. They have a seemingly endless supply of **John Ruskin**'s *The Stones of Venice* and **Mary McCarthy**'s delightful *Venice Observed*, along with **Jan Morris**' *Venice* and **Toby Coles**' collection of quotations on Venice from English and American writers. ♦ Calle Larga 22 Marzo 2087. Vap 1, 2, 34, San Marco. 5238451

Restaurants/Nightlife: Red   **Hotels:** Blue
Shops/Parks: Green   **Sights/Culture:** Black

33 Frette The Frette company, based in Milan, produces high-quality linens for tables, beds and clothing. The Venice shop is one of a dozen throughout the world, including outlets in London, New York, Paris and Beverly Hills. ◆ Closed M morning, Su, lunch. Calle Larga 22 Marzo 2070-A. Vap 1, 2, 34, San Marco. 5224914

34 Hotel Europa and Regina $$$ Right on the Canal Grande, Hotel Europa belongs to the CIGA chain. However, its prices are slightly more affordable than at their Danieli and Excelsior hotels in Venice, while the service is at the same level and the view from the front windows even more attractive. The hotel has 3 terraces for dining along one of the most panoramic points on the Canal Grande. ◆ San Marco 2159. Vap 1, 2, 34, San Marco. 5200477, 800/221.2340 (US); fax 5231523

35 Hotel Flora $$ One of the most charming hotels in its category, the Flora is true to its name with a beautiful garden where breakfast is served when the weather is right. Most rooms are furnished with antiques. ◆ Calle Larga 22 Marzo 2283-A. Vap 1, 2, 34, San Marco. 5205844; fax 5228217

35 Ristorante La Caravella ★★★★$$$$ Elegant and rather formal La Caravella is perhaps the fanciest restaurant in Venice. It specializes in fish, such as *bigoli in salsa*, an old Venetian recipe for pasta with a sauce based on anchovies, and *scampi al porto*, one of the most popular entrees. ◆ Closed W. Calle Larga 22 Marzo 2399. Vap 1, San Marco or Santa Maria del Giglio; Vap 2, 34, San Marco. 5208377

36 Venetia Studium A small store specializing in items created with hand-printed fabric in the style of **Mariano Fortuny**. The lamps, scarves and handkerchiefs are delightful. The store is also connected to a workshop that produces the famous **Delphos** clothes, also created by Fortuny in hand-printed silk. ◆ Closed M morning, Su, lunch. Calle Larga 22 Marzo 2403. Vap 1, San Marco or Santa Maria del Giglio; Vap 2, 34, San Marco. 5229281

36 Casellati Antique Shop One of the oldest and most reliable antiques dealers in Venice. ◆ Closed M morning, Su, lunch. Calle Larga 22 Marzo 2404. Vap 1, San Marco or Santa Maria del Giglio; Vap 2, 34, San Marco. 5230966

37 Libreria Antiquaria Cassini A dealer specializing in old books and prints, with a large clientele and a solid reputation. ◆ Closed M morning, Su, lunch. Calle Larga 22 Marzo 2424. Vap 1, San Marco or Santa Maria del Giglio; Vap 2, 34, San Marco. 5231815

38 Krizia The Milan-based designer opened this boutique in Venice in 1984. Next to the evening clothes, the shop carries a line of casuals called Krizia Baby. ◆ Closed M morning, Su, lunch. Calle delle Ostreghe 2359. Vap 1, Santa Maria del Giglio. 5232162

39 Ristorante Da Raffaele ★★$$ Perhaps a bit too large for personalized service, Da Raffaele is still recommended because of its location along a charming canal, as well as its informal and friendly atmosphere bubbling with the local color of a typical trattoria. ◆ Closed Th. Ponte

delle Ostreghe 2347. Vap 1, Santa Maria del Giglio. 5232317

40 Hotel Gritti $$$$ Traditionally among the most exclusive of the luxury hotels in Venice, the Gritti has a chaste Gothic facade on the Canal Grande with a waterside terrace for drinks and dining. Most of the rooms and suites are furnished with antiques. The atmosphere is one of quiet, understated wealth and old European style. ◆ Campo Santa Maria del Giglio 2467. Vap 1, Santa Maria del Giglio. 794611; fax 5200942

41 Hotel Ala $$$ A comfortable hotel in a renovated building furnished with all the modern necessities in an excellent location close to the city's major sights. ◆ Campo Santa Maria del Giglio 2494. Vap 2, Santa Maria del Giglio. 5208333; fax 5206390

42 Chiesa di Santa Maria del Giglio (1678-83, **Giuseppe Sardi**) This fine example of a Venetian-Baroque church carries to the extreme the Venetian habit of immortalizing the patrician families who financed the construction on the facade. Here the **Barbaros** are represented in 4 statues in the deep niches, while **Antonio Barbaro**, the dynasty's patriarch, looms over the portal between the statues of *Honor* and *Virtue*. The bas-reliefs on the lower facade represent the maps of cities under Venetian domination. Inside, the organ's doors were painted by **Jacopo Tintoretto** with figures of the *Four Evangelists*. ◆ Campo Santa Maria del Giglio. Vap 1, Santa Maria del Giglio

43 Vino Vino ★★$$ Born in the late 1980s as a wine bar with snacks, Vino Vino has quickly become a preferred restaurant for light, informal meals in an elegant atmosphere. It is also one of the few places in Venice open until 1AM. ◆ Closed Tu. Calle delle Veste 2007-A. Vap 1, Santa Maria del Giglio. 5224121

44 Bar Al Theatro ★★$$ Most of the cozy Campo San Fantin is filled in the summer with tables from this old, established restaurant. The service is very professional and the pasta, cooked to order, is available with a large variety of sauces—try the *tagliolini al salmone e caviale* (pasta with smoked salmon and caviar). Among the entrees, a specialty is *cartoccio al Theatro* (a whole fish wrapped up and baked with shrimp and clams). ♦ Closed M. Campo San Fantin 1916. Vap 1, Santa Maria del Giglio or Sant'Angelo. 5221052

45 Teatro La Fenice (1792, **Giannantonio Selva**) A sober Neoclassical facade characterizes this theater, built at the initiative of a group of patricians in 1792. The interior, reconstructed after a fire in 1836, still has most of the original decor and is one of the most elegant performing halls in the world. The theater offers a regular opera season, a symphony season and a number of concerts every year. ♦ Campo San Fantin 1365. Vap 1, Santa Maria del Giglio. Tickets 5210161

46 Legatoria Piazzesi Originally a bookbinding business, this shop branched out decades ago into marbled paper and other kinds of fancy paper objects. There are now many such shops in Venice, but this one remains the most professional and elegant. Notebooks, address and appointment books, desktop items and a large selection of wrapping paper with old Venetian prints make it a great spot for visitors to pick up gifts and souvenirs. ♦ Closed M morning, Su, lunch. Santa Maria del Giglio 2511-C. Vap 1, Santa Maria del Giglio. 5221202

47 Palazzo Zaguri A supremely elegant Gothic palazzo, with one facade on Campo San Maurizio and another along the canal in back. The Zaguri family went broke in the 18th century. **Pietro Zaguri**, one of 2 brothers who last inherited this palazzo, was an intellectual, a free thinker and a close friend of **Giacomo Casanova**, who was often a guest here, as was Mozart's librettist **Lorenzo Da Ponte**, who for a time worked as Zaguri's private secretary. When Zaguri was on his deathbed, his brother, a stern Catholic bishop, had to make a deal with the family creditors in order to keep the palazzo until his death. Now it is occupied by a public grade school. ♦ Campo San Maurizio 2668. Vap 1, Santa Maria del Giglio

48 Antichità Trois This store, in business since 1911, specializes in objects from 18th-century Venice, including lamps, ceramics and paintings. It is also the exclusive agent for the precious textiles produced by the **Mariano Fortuny** workshop, still operating on Giudecca with the original machinery invented by Fortuny. ♦ Closed M morning, Su, lunch. Campo San Maurizio 2666. Vap 1, Santa Maria del Giglio. 5222905

48 Norelene **Nora** and **Elene** sell velvets, silks and cottons that they hand-print in their workshop using the process invented by **Mariano Fortuny** at the turn of the century. However the patterns are original and inspired by painstaking research into the history of Venetian textiles. The fabrics can be used for clothing and interior decorating. Particularly wonderful are the panels printed with designs inspired by St. Mark's mosaics. ♦ Closed M morning, Su, lunch. Campo San Maurizio 2606. Vap 1, Santa Maria del Giglio. 5237605

49 Chiesa di San Maurizio (1806, **Pietro Zaguri**) The Neoclassical facade of this church was one of the last buildings undertaken by the Venetian Republic before its fall in 1797. It was designed by Pietro Zaguri, a patrician and an intellectual who lived in a palazzo on the same campo. The interior is a fine example of Neoclassical architecture, designed by **Giannantonio Selva** (also responsible for Teatro La Fenice). ♦ Campo San Maurizio. Vap 1, Santa Maria del Giglio

50 Il Papiro The technique of marbelizing paper originated in Florence and spread throughout Italy. Florentine-owned Il Papiro is a large store with a huge selection of items made of the paper, including desktop items, lamps, picture frames and even Carnival masks. ♦ Closed M morning, Su, lunch. Calle del Piovan 2764. Vap 1, Santa Maria del Giglio. 5223055

51 Pasticceria Marchini This is a name that makes Venetians' mouths water. Marchini in Venice means the most delicious sweets, whether small pastries eaten in the shop or large cakes taken home for celebrations. A stop for a *cannolo* or a *bigne* is a must. ♦ Closed Tu. Calle del Piovan 2769. Vap 1, Santa Maria del Giglio. 5229109

52 Chiesa de Santo Stefano The space available for the church did not seem sufficient to the Augustinian friars who had it remodeled in the 15th century, so part of the chancel was built on a bridge over the canal in back of the church. The facade is adorned with 2 rose windows and a handsome portal (early 15th century). Inside, the ceiling has the typical Venetian shape of a reversed ships' hull (local master carpenters most likely learned their craft in the shipyards). Of the many monuments to illustrious Venetians here, the most remarkable are inside, among them **Domenico Contarini** (1650) over the portal; **Antonio Zorzi** (1588) on the left side; and **Giacomo Surian** (1493) on the right side. In the **Sacristy** (entrance from the right nave), 3 large canvasses by **Jacopo Tintoretto** hang on the right wall: *The Last Supper, The Agony in the Garden* and *Christ Washing the Disciples' Feet*. On the same wall, notice a *Crucifixion* by **Paolo Veneziano** (1348). ♦ Campo Santo Stefano. Vap 1, Santa Maria del Giglio or Sant'Angelo

53 Campo Santo Stefano One of the largest squares in Venice, Santo Stefano is the cross-roads for the streets leading from the Accademia Bridge to Rialto (north side) and Piazza San Marco (east side). On the east side, the building at Nos. 2802-3 is **Palazzo Morosini** (17th century); the one opposite (No. 2945) is **Palazzo Loredan**, probably the last Gothic palazzo built in Venice. Locals still meet at **Paolin's** cafe (northwest corner, opposite the church's entrance) for drinks in the late afternoon and for cappuccino on Sunday mornings. ♦ Campo Santo Stefano. Vap 1, Santa Maria del Giglio

54 Conservatorio Benedetto Marcello In the Campo Pisani, an extension of Campo Santo Stefano on the southeast side, the **Pisani** family had one of their major palazzi: **Palazzo Pisani**, now occupied by the Venice Conservatory. It is an imposing structure, built between the 17th and 18th centuries. The interior contains 2 courtyards and a handsome ballroom, now used for concerts by the Conservatory's teachers and students. Inquire with the headmaster about visiting. ♦ Campo Pisano. Vap 1, Santa Maria del Giglio

55 Laboratorio di Indorador Signore Cavalier is one of the best among the few Venetians who still practice the art of gilding wood. He creates 17th-century-style frames, chandeliers and sculpture using the technique of that era. ♦ Closed M morning, Su, lunch. San Marco 2863-A. Vap 1, Santa Maria del Giglio. 5238621

56 Ponte dell' Accademia Until the 1840s, the Rialto was the only bridge over the Canal Grande. The structure of the city started to change at that time, with priority shifting to pedestrian traffic over water transportation, and within 10 years, 2 new bridges were built, one near the train station and one at the Accademia. They were designed and built by **A. Neville**, a French engineer who had made a name for himself creating similar structures throughout Europe. Neville built flat, suspended bridges, more fit for the budding industrial cities than for Venice. In the 1930s, his bridges were destroyed. A *temporary* structure was built at the Accademia. It's still here and was restored in the 1980s. ♦ Vap 1, Santa Maria del Giglio or 1, 2, 34, Accademia

57 Palazzo Grassi (begun 1718, **Giorgio Massari**) Built in the 18th century along Classical lines, this palazzo was aquired by **Fiat** in the 1980s and restored by Venetian architect **Antonio Foscari** together with **Gae Aulenti** (designer of Paris' Musee d'Orsay) as a center for international exhibitions. Supported by powerful advertising and by the exceptionally high quality of the exhibitions, it has become the 2nd most popular museum in Venice (after the Palazzo Ducale), with more than 2000 visitors a day. Foscari's and Aulenti's remodeling of the interior is worth a visit in itself. The palazzo has a wonderful view over the Canal Grande and a comfortable cafeteria, run by **Harry's Bar** owner **Arrigo Cipriani**. ♦ Admission. Open only during exhibitions. San Samuele 3231. Vap 2, San Samuele or 1, Santa Maria del Giglio or Sant'Angelo. 5231680

58 Livio De Marchi Signor De Marchi doesn't want to be called a woodcarver but rather a sculptor who works in wood. His whimsical creations are inspired by the most exact, painstaking realism and there is a powerful sense of

movement and life in his objects. The wood clothes hanging on a clothesline seem to move with the wind; and the giant asparagus, the stove and the tablecloth are a source of wonder for those who pass by the windows of his workshop and store. ♦ Closed M morning, Su, lunch. San Samuele 3157-A. Vap 2, San Samuele or 1, Accademia or Sant'Angelo. 5285694

58 Venice Design Art Gallery The gallery specializes in one-of-a-kind objects by contemporary designers, including glass objects by artist **Luciano Vistosi**. Ask to see some of the objects locked in the safe—they include a collection of watches designed by **Marta Marzotto**, the society matron famous, among other things, for her relationship with painter **Renato Guttuso**. ♦ Closed M morning, Su, lunch. Salizzada San Samuele 3146. Vap 2, San Samuele or 1, Santa Maria del Giglio or Sant'Angelo. 5207915

59 Al Bacareto ★★$$ This is one of the few Venetian restaurants that has kept its policy of serving inexpensive meals like mamma used to make at affordable prices in a pleasant, informal setting. A pasta and a salad, or a cutlet with vegetables, make up a tasty meal that won't make your wallet ache. ♦ Closed Sa evening, Su. San Samuele 3447. Vap 2, San Samuele or 1, Santa Maria del Giglio or Sant'Angelo. 5289336

60 Osteria Alle Botteghe ★★$$ Opened in the late 1980s, this cafe specializes in *panini* or Italian-style sandwiches, ideal for a snack before or after a visit to Palazzo Grassi or a performance at La Fenice. Look at the *panini* fillings at the counter and ask for the one that suits your fancy: it could be with eggplant, local salami, a variety of cheeses, or any mixture of the ingredients on display. The sauces are original and tasty—quite a change from the usual mayonnaise and mustard. ♦ Closed Su. Calle delle Botteghe 3454. Vap 2, San Samuele or 2, Santa Maria del Giglio or Sant'Angelo. 5228181

A city for beavers.

Ralph Waldo Emerson

61 Ceramiche Rigattieri An extraordinary variety of artistic ceramics produced in the famous center of **Bassano del Grappa**, an hour north of Venice. The Bassano style has a long and successful tradition to which contemporary artists are very attached. The pieces are typically decorated with flowers and leaves. Look for the reproductions of animals in all sizes and the charming plates decorated with bas-reliefs. ♦ Closed M morning, Su, lunch. Calle dei Frati 3532. Vap 1, Sant'Angelo. 5231081

62 Campo Sant'Angelo (or Sant'Anzolo) This wide square is characterized, like few others in Venice, by an elevated floor in the center, built in order to enlarge the underground cistern, where rainwater was collected for domestic

San Marco

use. The wells at the center (with original well-heads from the 15th century) reached the cistern's bottom, where the water was collected after being filtered by layers of sand and pebbles. Composer **Domenico Cimarosa** died at the Gothic **Palazzo Duodo** (No. 3585). ♦ Campo Sant'Angelo. Vap 1, Sant'Angelo

63 Museo Fortuny Mariano Fortuny was an artist from Catalonia who established himself in Venice, where he acquired this palazzo in the early 1900s. A painter, set designer, clothing designer and textile printer, he charmed all of Europe with his elegant creations. Among his admirers was **Marcel Proust**. The museum illustrates his many activities with a large number of paintings and a precious collection of textiles. ♦ Admission. Closed M. Campo San Beneto 3780. Vap 1, Sant'Angelo. 5200995

64 El Dorador Alfred Barutti's specialty is 18th-century-style gilded woodwork, including frames, lampstands and statues. He also restores old furniture. ♦ Closed M morning, Su, lunch. Campo Manin 4231. Vap 1, Sant'Angelo. 5287316

65 Scala del Bovolo This staircase is often seen in paintings and photographs of Venice because of its unusual and elegant snail shape. It was added to the courtyard of **Palazzo Contarini** at the end of the 15th century in order to permit access to the top floors without going through the interior stairs. ♦ Calle della Vida 4299. Vap 1, Sant'Angelo

66 Ristorante Da Ivo ★★★$$$ The small number of tables here allows Ivo to receive his guests personally and to describe the day's menu the way one would do it with guests at home. Venetian cooking, based on fish, is the specialty. But Ivo is originally from Tuscany, and he can cook meat like no one else in Venice. He prepares the only real *bistecca fiorentina* in town. ♦ Closed Su. Ramo dei Fuseri 1809. Vap 1, Santa Maria del Giglio, Rialto or Sant'Angelo. 5285004

Venice is like eating an entire box of chocolate liqueurs at one go.

Truman Capote

67 Fantoni Libri Arte Originally an outlet of the Electa publishing company (the major Italian art book publisher), this is the best bookstore in Venice for art publications in all languages. ♦ Closed M morning, Su lunch. Salizzada San Luca 4121. Vap 1, 2, 34, Rialto. 5220700

68 Riva del Carbon One of the few stretches of the Canal Grande flanked by a street and allowing pedestrian passage. The name comes from its use as a pier for unloading coal. The presence of city hall, the Bank of Italy and other offices makes this street crowded with Venetians, particularly in the morning (most state and city employees work from 8AM to 2PM). Some of the oldest and most charming palazzi in Venice are located here and can be closely inspected from the pier. At No. 4792 is **Palazzo Bembo**, a Gothic building with remnants of an original Byzantine structure (the frieze on the lower floor); at No. 4172 is **Palazzo Dandolo**, an early-Gothic building with a stone inscription in memory of **Doge Enrico Dandolo**, who headed the 4th Crusade in 1204; and at Nos. 4137 and 4136 are the 2 palazzi **Loredan** and **Farsetti** (city hall offices), which have the original Byzantine ground and first floors (the top floors are later additions). ♦ Riva del Carbon. Vap 1, 2, 34, Rialto

69 Campo San Luca Strategically located between Rialto and St. Mark's, this is one of the busiest squares in Venice. During the day it is the traditional meeting place for real estate agents and middlemen of all kinds, who crowd the **Bar Torino** (famous for the quality and variety of its *tramezzini*, the small sandwiches eaten standing at the counter) and the **Cafe Rosa Salva**, one of the best pastry shops in town. Before and after dinner, the campo is crowded with young men and women—mostly college students—who meet here to gossip and plan their evenings. ♦ Campo San Luca. Vap 1, 2, 34, Rialto

70 Teatro Goldoni Named after the great Venetian playwright of the 18th century, this is the same theater where **Carlo Goldoni** enjoyed some of his successes before moving on to Paris. It was entirely rebuilt in the 1970s and little of the original structure remains. While La Fenice is mostly an opera house, the Goldoni is used for prose performances. ♦ Calle del Teatro. Vap 1, 2, 34, Rialto

71 Bar Al Ponte del Lovo A very busy cafe, well-known in Venice for its terrific drinks and cocktails. It's the best place to try a before-dinner *spritz* (the Venetian mixture of white wine, bitters and seltzer water). An almost invisible stair leads to the 2nd floor, one of the few places in Venice where you can sit and enjoy a chocolate or cappuccino at ease. A handy address in winter and on rainy days. ♦ Closed M morning, lunch. Ponte del Lovo. Vap 1, 2, 34, Rialto. 5251323

Marzato

72 Marzato Amalia and Giuliana Marzato are the hat and accessory wizards of Venice. They personally design their creations in the workshop upstairs, working from antique and modern materials (feathers, pearls, ribbons, lace). In addition to their regular lines, they produce the best tricorns and Carnival hats in town. ♦ Closed M morning, Su, lunch. Calle del Lovo 4183. Vap 1, 2, 34, Rialto. 5226454

72 Scuola di San Teodoro A Baroque facade by **Giuseppe Sardi** decorates this early 17th-century building, now used for temporary exhibitions. ♦ Campo San Salvador. Vap 1, 2, 34, Rialto

73 Fantin One of the best florists in Venice, and a good address to keep in mind for good-bye gifts for your Venetian friends. ♦ Closed M morning, Su, lunch. San Salvador 4805. Vap 1, 2, 34, Rialto. 5226808

74 Chiesa di San Salvador (1534) The facade, cleaned and restored in 1991, is a fine example of Venetian-Baroque (designed by **Giuseppe Sardi**). The interior, by **Giorgio Spavento**, is of great interest because of the attempt to divide the space into perfectly regular 15-foot-square modules. The space between the entrance and the first 2 columns is made of 4 such squares, aligned to form a rectangle. Two identical rectangles, separated by a square, form the side naves. In the central nave, 4 modules form squares under the domes. Multiples of the square's sides also regulate the length of the columns. The result is a perfectly geometrical space—a bit too abstract when compared with the emotional impact of Gothic or Romanesque churches. The 3rd altar in the right nave contains one of **Titian**'s last works, an *Annunciation* painted with a revolutionary, almost Impressionistic technique. At the bottom of the painting he wrote *Titianus fecit fecit*, the repetition of the verb *he did it* perhaps being his answer to the criticism he expected. ♦ Campo San Salvador. Vap 1, 2, 34, Rialto

75 Mercerie This series of narrow streets connecting the Rialto with Piazza San Marco has long been the retail center of Venice and it is still lined with fancy shops. Most of the buildings along the street date back to the 14th and 15th centuries. ♦ Vap 1, 2, 34, Rialto or San Marco

76 Campo San Bartolomeo One of the busiest centers of Venetian life, the campo is enlivened by a graceful monument to playwright **Carlo Goldoni** (built in 1883). The square fills with young men and women every evening, stopping for long chats and making it difficult to pass through—a sign that TV has not completely wiped out social life in Venice. ♦ Campo San Bartolomeo. Vap 1, 2, 34, Rialto

77 Fondaco dei Tedeschi (1505, **Scarpagnino**) Venice's **Central Post Office** has its headquarters in this Renaissance building, where German merchants used to have their offices and storage rooms. The facade on the Canal Grande was originally frescoed by Renaissance artists, including **Titian** and **Giorgione** (some very faded remnants of the frescoes are visible at the **Ca d'Oro Gallery**. ♦ Salizzada del Fontego dei Tedeschi 5554. Vap 1, 2, 34, Rialto

78 Rosticceria San Bartolomeo ★★★$$ Right at the end of the narrow Sotoportego de la Bissa, this is the best place in Venice for prepared foods, to be either taken out or eaten at the counter (more formal dining upstairs).

San Marco

Pastas, risottos, lasagna, roast chicken, *baccalà* and grilled fish keep coming from the upstairs kitchen and are quickly consumed by the many customers. The quality is excellent, much higher even than in many expensive restaurants. The place closes at 9PM and no food is served after 8:30PM. ♦ Closed M. Calle de la Bissa 5424. Vap 1, 2, 34, Rialto. 5223569

79 Al Duca D'Aosta A Venicé institution, this shop carries casual clothing for men and women. ♦ Closed M morning, Su, lunch. Mercerie 4922. Vap 1, 2, 34, Rialto or San Marco. 5204079

80 Cartier The Venice branch of the famous French jewelers seems to sparkle even more brilliantly in the light of the lagoon. ♦ Closed M morning, Su, lunch. Mercerie San Zulian 606. Vap 1, 2, 34, Rialto or San Marco. 5222071

81 Eredi Giovanni Pagnacco This amazing store specializes in original objects created by the best craftsmen in glass and ceramics. Its windows are a constant surprise for Venetians, as they exhibit ever-changing glass reproductions of scenes from life: an orchestra with hundreds of tiny players is one of the most memorable, along with the reproduction of a religious procession in Piazza San Marco. Pagnacco is the exclusive seller of Herend's porcelain in Venice. ♦ Closed M morning, Su, lunch. Mercerie dell'Orologio 231. Vap 1, 2, 34, Rialto or San Marco. 5223704

82 Antichità Dominico An old, fine antiquarian specializing in silver objects and small items easy to pack in a suitcase. Large collection of high-quality prints and early photographs of Venice. ♦ Closed M morning, Su, lunch. Calle Larga San Marco 659-64. Vap 1, 2, 34, San Marco. 5223892

83 Elite The most exclusive store in town for men's clothing, both business and casual. ♦ Closed M morning, Su, lunch. Calle Larga San Marco 284. Vap 1, 2, 34, San Marco. 5230145

Dangerous and sweet-tongued Venice.
Samuel Rogers

Restaurants/Nightlife: Red   **Hotels:** Blue
Shops/Parks: Green   **Sights/Culture:** Black

Dorsoduro

While most visitors are usually drawn to **Dorsoduro** for its art museums, **Accademia** and **Raccolta Peggy Guggenheim**, others have long preferred this largely residential area as a place for their own Venetian residences. Poet **Ezra Pound** had his tiny home here, and it is still inhabited by **Olga Rudge**, his lifelong companion. It stands a few steps from the Canal Grande palazzo where **Peggy Guggenheim** spent the last decades of her life hosting international literati and glitterati. In keeping with the times, Dorsoduro has been home to wealthy industrialists. **Susanna Agnelli**, sister of **FIAT** president **Gianni**, keeps a place here, as does industrialist **Raoul Gardini**. But simple folk will enjoy just strolling around Dorsoduro, especially along its 3 small canals with walkable banks, to take in such unassuming sights as **Campiello Barbaro**, a tiny square that has inspired artists for years.

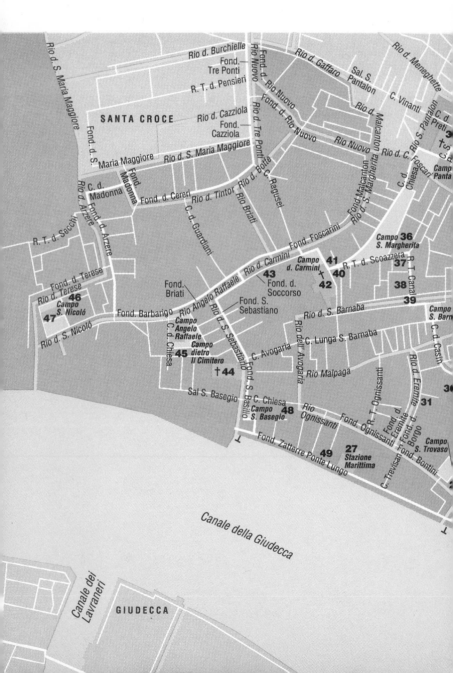

1 Punta della Dogana This was where all ships sailing in with foreign merchandise were examined for customs duties; they would then continue along the Canal Grande and anchor in front of the patrician palazzi, where their cargoes would be unloaded in the ground-floor storage rooms. The whole area was reconstructed beginning in the 1670s as part of a vast plan to redesign the entrance to the Canal Grande, culminating in the church of **La Salute**. Today the area is often deserted, even by tourists, though in the evening it is a favorite stroll for couples looking for an isolated romantic spot. The customs house, between the extreme tip of the island and the church of La Salute, was built in 1677 (NE wing) and in the 1830s (SW wing). The 17th-century tower at the tip

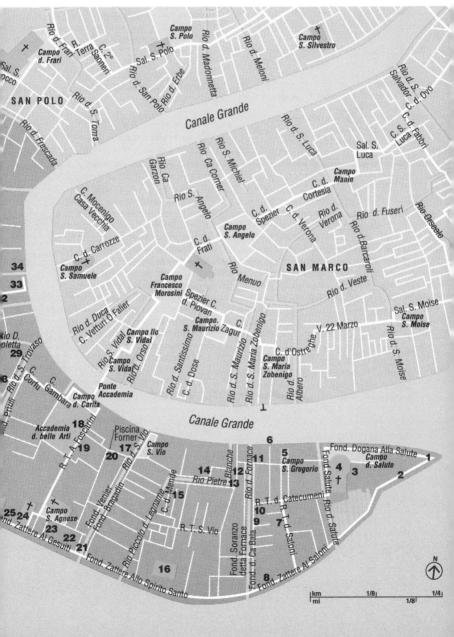

supports 2 bronze giants carrying a gold sphere (the *World*), surmounted by a huge statue of *Fortune*, acting as a wind gauge. Thus the city welcomed its ships with the symbols of its naval power. ♦ Punta della Dogana. Vap 1, La Salute

2 Le Zattere From the tip of the customs house all the way to the western end of Venice (occupied today by the cruise-ship harbor, **Stazione Marittima**), the Canale della Giudecca is flanked by an uninterrupted walk called Fondamenta delle Zattere, or simply Le Zattere. The whole canal bank faces to the south, which makes it a favorite walk for Venetians in the mild winter afternoons as well as on Sunday mornings all year round. Many cafes open onto the street and some have wooden terraces suspended on piles over the water. A cross-section of the population can be seen here catching the sun, sitting at the cafes or walking

Dorsoduro

along eating ice cream. Zattere means *rafts*; and it was in this area that huge barges would land with their cargoes of supplies from the mainland. The Canale della Giudecca, now congested with boat traffic, still offers some memorable sights, such as the boats of the Bucintoro rowing club going out for practice or the large cruise-ships, taller than any buildings in the area, passing by on their way to the harbor at the bank's end. Until the 1960s, a small section of the canal was enclosed by a white and blue fence, creating a swimming pool right in the canal's water, where most Venetians learned how to swim. Today the water of the Canale della Guidecca is polluted, a warning to those interested in swimming. ♦ Fondamenta della Zattere. Vap 5, Zattere or Vap 1, 2, 34, Accademia

3 Seminario Patriarcale (begun 1670, **Baldassare Longhena**) On the Canal Grande side, the building between La Salute and the **Porta della Dogana** was built by Longhena as a school for children of noble families. In 1817, it became the Venice seminary (previously on the island of Murano). Inside is a 17th-century cloister and the **Pinacoteca Manfrediniana**, a collection of minor works of art mostly from the 16th century. ♦ By appt only. Campo della Salute 1-C. Vap 1, La Salute. 5225558

4 Santa Maria della Salute (1630, **Baldassare Longhena**) This church is one of the best examples in Europe of the Baroque concern for large- scale planning (the idea being that not only should a building express its own individual beauty, but it should also work with the surrounding landscape as a whole). In Venice in 1630, the city decided to build a grandiose church in honor of the Virgin of Good Health (*Salute*) to fulfill a vow made during a terrible plague. Longhena was then 26, but his daring project was chosen over those of 11 competitors. The area was of vital importance to Venice, both commercially and aesthetically: it

sat at the entrance of the Canal Grande and was visible from almost any point in Venice. Longhena based his design on a circular plan, and set the whole church above ground on a huge embankment. The dome of his Baroque church was supported by buttresses disguised as stone spirals and topped by a statue of the Virgin Mary dressed as a Venetian admiral. The front of the church, with its imposing staircase and wealth of statues and other stone decorations, faces the Canal Grande. Behind the dome, Longhena built a 2nd, smaller dome flanked by 2 bell towers, creating an elongated shape from the door to the main altar, as in the basilicas. It took more than 50 years to build this wonder of European architecture (Longhena died in 1682, 5 years before completion but one year after the solemn inauguration). In order to support the massive structure, the ground had to be reinforced with more than a million wood piles. Venetian art historicans never fail, when describing La Salute, to compare the courage of the old city government with the timidity and lack of initiative of modern administrations, unable as they are to provide answers to the new needs of the city, and sometimes missing historic opportunities, such as a proposed hospital project by **Le Corbusier** and a conference center by **Louis Khan**, neither of which were ever built.

In contrast with the festive, exhuberant exterior, the interior is sober and reverential. On sunny days, a good deal of light enters the main hall of the church, while the high altar, under the smaller dome, remains shaded and intimate. The 6 chapels open on the sides of the church correspond with the 6 secondary facades on the outside. In the first chapel at the right, look for the *Presentation of the Virgin*, part of the cycle celebrative of the Virgin Mary, originally planned for the church's interior. The high altar, designed by Longhena, surrounds a Greek-Byzantine icon of the Virgin Mary, very dear to Venetians (a war booty taken from Crete in 1672). A small door at the left of the main altar leads to the **Sacristy** (usually closed but shown upon request), with 3 ceiling paintings by **Titian** (ca 1543, influenced by **Michelangelo**). Also by Titian are the *St. Mark Enthroned* at the Sacristy's altar (1512) and the 8 medallions with *Evangelists and*

Easter candlestick from Santa Maria della Salute

Church Doctors around the same altar. On the right wall is *The Marriage at Cana*, usually considered one of the best works by **Tintoretto** (1551). Back in the church, another painting by Titian is at the 3rd altar on the left: *The Descent of the Holy Spirit* (ca 1555, grudgingly executed by the master to replace an identical painting of his, which had been destroyed by a fire). ◆ Campo della Salute. Vap 1, La Salute

5 Campo San Gregorio The church in front of this campo, originally built in the 9th century, was renovated in the 15th century and is now used as a laboratory for the restoration of stone monuments. The beautiful apses are visible from the bridge at the back. At the left side, a wall encloses the garden of **Palazzo Genovese**, a Neo-Gothic building with a facade on the Canal Grande (1892), while a few steps further (No. 172) are still-visible remnants of the old **Abbey of St. Gregory** (now privately owned) with its 14th-century cloister. ◆ Campo San Gregorio. Vap 1, La Salute

6 Traghetto to Santa Maria del Giglio At the end of Calle Del Traghetto is a gondola service that carries people to the other side of the Canal Grande, thus saving a long detour on foot through the **Ponte dell'Accademia** or having to wait for the vaporetto. ◆ End of Calle del Traghetto. Vap 1, La Salute

7 Rio Terrà dei Saloni This wide street was created in the 19th century by filling a canal. The building at the corner of **Rio Terrà dei Catecumeni** (Nos. 107-108) was rebuilt by **Massari** in 1727. For many centuries it was a center for the education of non-Catholics who intended to convert, among them **Lorenzo Da Ponte**, the librettist of **Mozart**. The handsome building at Nos. 70-71 (**Palazzetto Costantini**) dates back to the 14th century and still has the original wood beams over the portico. ◆ Rio Terrà dei Saloni. Vap 1, La Salute

8 Saloni (Magazzini del Sale) The huge building at Nos. 258-266 was built in the 14th century to store the city's salt supplies (salt commerce was one of the city's original sources of wealth). The facades were redesigned in the 1830s, but the enormous storage rooms are still as they were originally planned, capable of holding 45,000 tons of salt. Today they house the boats of a rowing club as well as temporary art exhibitions, often held in conjunction with the **Venice Biennale**. ◆ Fondamenta delle Zattere 258-66. Vap 1, La Salute

9 Pensione Alla Salute Da Cici $$ A comfortable, efficiently run pensione in a great location along a charming canal. ◆ Fondamente de Ca' Balà 222-28. Vap 1, La Salute. 5235404

10 Hotel Messner $$ Clean, pleasant and unpretentious, this small hotel has some rooms with wonderful windows looking out on a canal. ◆ Fondamenta de Ca' Balà 216. Vap 1, La Salute. 5227443; fax same number

11 Cenedese The glass furnace and showrooms of Cenedese, one of the oldest and most prestigious producers of Murano glass, can be seen here. The furnace offers little more than a demonstration of basic techniques (as do all similar furnaces on Murano), but the showrooms are elegant and the pieces on sale range from the most exquisite to more affordable objects for everyday use. The facade of the building (**Palazzo Salviati**) is on the Canal Grande. ◆ Closed M morning, Su, lunch. Campo San Gregorio 175. Vap 1, La Salute

12 Campiello Barbaro This cozy little square is one of the most charming in Venice. The back of **Palazzo Dario** is visible from the bridge, beyond the wall and the small garden. ◆ Campiello Barbaro. Vap 1, La Salute

13 Marangon da Soase On the quiet Campiello Barbaro and near the gentle fountain is the

workshop of a cabinetmaker who restores old furniture and produces gilded wood objects. The name of his shop comes straight from ancient Venetian dialect and means, roughly, *wood carpenter specializing in frames.* ◆ Closed Su, lunch. Campiello Barbaro 364. Vap 1, La Salute

14 Collezione Peggy Guggenheim In 1949 the American millionaire **Peggy Guggenheim** chose this odd one-story palazzo from among the more grand palazzi on the Canal Grande for her home and her extraordinary collection of 20th-century art. It was actually a fateful coincidence that her modern art collection found itself in this *modern* palazzo. As the story goes, the **Venier** family, who built the palazzo, halted construction after completing only the ground floor, apparently after a rival family moved into a larger palazzo across the Canal Grande and pressured them to stop building lest they block their view. The palazzo remains an oddity on the Canal Grande, though it has slowly acquired a beauty of its own. Note the grill at the entrance by **Claire Falkenstein** (1961). The garden contains sculptures by **Alberto Giacometti, Max Ernst, Henry Moore, Jean Arp** and others, along with Guggenheim's tomb. The interior was redesigned as a gallery space for changing exhibitions after her death and is now run by the **Solomon R. Guggenheim Foundation**. ◆ Admission; free Sa after 6PM. M, W-F, Su 11AM-6PM; Sa 11AM-9PM. Calle San Cristoforo 701. Vap 1, La Salute or 1, 2, 34, Accademia. 5206288

The whole course of Venetian art can be seen as a blissful attempt to define Venetian light, until with Tiepolo in the eighteenth century there is only the light left. There is no subject any longer, not even much of a feeling: just the fullness of the light, glittering, searching, flooding everything.

Maurice Rowdon

Restaurants/Nightlife: Red   **Hotels:** Blue
Shops/Parks: Green   **Sights/Culture:** Black

15 Calle delle Mende A walk through the area between this street and Le Zattere (the bank of Canale della Giudecca to the south) is the best way to see why this neighborhood is so dear to foreign lovers of Venice. This is residential Venice at its best. The houses are rarely more than 2 stories high, frequent small gardens are visible, and flower pots line most windows. Quite a few locals still reside in the homes, but they are slowly being driven away by affluent foreigners—in 1991 the apartment prices *started* at 4 million lire a square meter (about $3000 a square yard). On the **Campiello Drio agli Incurabili**, notice the fading fresco of Venice's skyline painted by local painter **Bobo Ferruzzi**. On the **Rio Terrà San Vio**, the small streets on both sides allow access to the buildings between the 2 canals. At the far end of the Rio Terrà (No. 460), a door opens into the former **Convento dello Spirito Santo** (Convent

Dorsoduro

of the Holy Spirit), used today as a high school; visitors are welcome to look at the courtyard and the 16th-century cloister. ♦ Calle delle Mende. Vap 1, 2, 34, Accademia or 1, La Salute

16 Ospedale degli Incurabili The history of this 16th-century building is sort of depressing. It was built for people affected by incurable diseases (mostly syphilis), then used to house abandoned children, and in the 20th century, it was a prison for juvenile delinquents. It now stands semi-abandoned, like many other buildings in Venice, while the city fights over who the future tenants will be: the university (it has more than 30,000 students, with only one dormitory with 150 beds), a hospital, the state, district and city offices, the senior citizens, the youth, the rowing clubs.... Empty buildings and lots are abundant in town, but as soon as is one assigned to a group, a chorus of protests, strikes and legal issues are raised to block the decision. ♦ Fondamenta delle Zattere 423-26. Vap 1, 2, 34, Accademia or 1, La Salute

17 Galleria di Palazzo Cini Piscina del Forner, the palazzo at No. 864, dates from the 17th century. It now belongs to the **Cini Foundation** (see San Giorgio Maggiore) and it houses the **Raccolta d'Arte della Collezione Giorgio Cini**, a collection of some 30 paintings of the Tuscan Renaissance formerly owned by the **Conte Vittorio Cini** and bequeathed by him to the Foundation. Most of the paintings are by minor artists, but they are all exquisite. The collection includes paintings by **Taddeo Gaddi** and **Bernardo Daddi**, a *Guariento*, and a *Madonna* by **Piero della Francesca**. Every year the collection displays a different masterwork on loan from a major art gallery. ♦ Admission. Gallery is open irregularly, usually only in Sep-Oct from 10AM-6PM. San Vio 864. Vap 1, 2, 34, Accademia or 1, La Salute. 5210755 or 5289900

18 Rio Terrà A. Foscarini This unusually wic and straight alley, flanked by a few trees, is a close as Venice comes to a boulevard. It was built in 1863 by filling in a canal in order to facilitate pedestrian traffic to the newly erecte **Accademia Bridge**. The building at Nos. 898 902 houses the **Instituto Cavanis**, a private grammar and high school founded in the 18t century to provide poor children with free ed cation. It's still free, and the quality of educa tion at the school is so high that Venice's upper-crust tries to send their children here. Across from the school, the **Cavanis Fathers** (a small, local monastic order) run an inexpe sive hotel, usually reserved by Catholic grou but theoretically open to anyone. ♦ Rio Terrà Antonio Foscarini. Vap 1, 2, 34, Accademia

19 Ristorante Agli Alboretti ★★$$ The res taurant is run by the same owners as the Hot Agli Alboretti next door. Although the quality the food is excellent, the price level (middle t high) puts it out of reach of most people stay ing at the hotel. ♦ Rio Terrà Foscarini 882-8￡ Vap 1, 2, 34, Accademia. 5230058

19 Hotel Agli Alboretti $$ This hotel is definitely one of the best bets in town. It's comfo able, well-run, and the location is perfect for visits to San Marco and Dorsoduro. Most of the rooms are pleasant (only No. 19 is small and dark). Make reservations in advance. ♦ F Terrà Foscarini 882-84. Vap 1, 2, 34, Accadem 5230058

20 Ristorante Ai Cugnai ★★$$ *Cugnai* mea brothers-in-law, which makes sense since th crowded, colorful restaurant is run by 2 ener getic sisters and their husbands. It started ou as an inexpensive neighborhood hangout, bu word spread quickly (Venetians are always looking for old-time, tourist-free restaurants and cafes) and now has become a favorite or everyone's list. Some of the old spontaneity i gone, in spite of the 2 tireless, down-to-earth sisters. Still rather inexpensive, the restauran specializes in homemade, unpretentious fooc such as bean soup, spaghetti with clams, sar dines and cuttle-fish. They also make wonde ful *gnocchi* and serve a good *prosecco* wine. ♦ Closed M. Piscina del Forner 857. Vap 1, 2, 34, Accademia. 5289238

21 Pensione Seguso $$ Quiet, comfortable a in a great location, this hotel has a loyal follo ing of guests who return again and again for room with a view over the Canale della Giudecca. ♦ Fondamenta delle Zattere 779. V 1, 2, 34, Accademia or 5, 8, Zattere. 522234C fax same number

22 La Calcina $$ Similar to its neighbor, the Pensione Seguso, though perhaps even in a better location. **John Ruskin** lived here when he was writing *The Stones of Venice*. ♦ Fondamenta Zattere 780. Vap 1, 2, 34, Accademia or 5, 8, Zattere. 5206466; fax 5227045

A prevelant style of architecture in Venice is the Gothic style used in many of its palaces. This style is wonderfully sympathetic to the qualities of light and water which characterize the city.

23 Ristorante Alle Zattere ★★$$ This ristorante coasts by on its location as one of only 2 restaurants with a terrace over the Canale della Giudecca. The food is acceptable and the prices reflect the monopoly it has over the canal. But in this case, location is a good enough reason to stop by for lunch or dinner. On hot summer evenings, a gentle breeze blows through the terrace, while rowboats, vaporetti and cruise-ships float along lazily. Many Venetians come here and to Da Gianni next door for pizza and beer and a respite from their hot apartments. ♦ Closed Tu. Fondamenta Zattere 795. Vap 1, 2, 34, Accademia or 5, 8, Zattere. 5204224

24 Chiesa dei Gesuati (Gesuati Church) (1926-43, **Giorgio Massari**) The Gesuati is a local monastic order, different from the Gesuiti (Jesuits). They originally built this church (officially named **Santa Maria del Rosario**) and the

adjacent monastery. In the 17th century the order collapsed and both the church and monastery went to the Dominicans, who proceeded to rebuild the church entirely, trusting the project to Giorgio Massari (see **La Pietà**). The facade is clearly reminiscent of **Palladio** (whose **Redentore** church is visible across the canal). Both churches are flanked by 2 bell towers, but the Gesuati is somewhat more imposing. The canal bank and gondola landing were redesigned to harmonize with the new church, although the effect has been somewhat spoiled by the vaporetto stop in front of the church. The interior is one of the masterworks of the 18th century in Venice, consisting of a single nave, as in La Pietà, with a large chancel behind the altar. Most of the statues are by the ubiquitous and rather uninspiring **Giovanni Maria Morleiter**; but the paintings are among the best by **Tiepolo** and **Piazzetta**. Tiepolo painted the ceiling (1737-39) with the *Institution of the Rosary* (center of ceiling) and with stories from the life of St. Dominick in *St. Dominick Praying the Virgin Mary* (near the chancel). Also by Tiepolo is the altarpiece on the first chapel to the right (*The Virgin Mary with Saint Ladies*), while Piazzetta painted St. Dominick in the next chapel and a splendid St. Vincent Ferreri in the following one (3rd at the right). More frescoes by Tiepolo are on the inside of the apse. A remarkable **Tintoretto** adorns the first chapel the left side: it is a Crucifixion dated 1526, said to have been restored by Piazzetta himself. ♦ Fondamenta Zattere. Vap 1, 2, 34, Accademia or 5, 8, Zattere

25 Ristorante Da Gianni ★★$$ Da Gianni shares the spotlight with **Alle Zattere** as the only restaurants with a terrace over the Canale della Guidecca. Both the food and service are better here (though if you're in town on a hot summer evening and Da Gianni is full, don't hesitate to go next door—the breeze is just as pleasant). Signore Gianni has been running this place for more than 30 years. Many Vene-

---

estaurants/Nightlife: Red   **Hotels:** Blue
ops/Parks: Green   **Sights/Culture:** Black

tians fondly remember the days when the canal could only be crossed by gondola, and Da Gianni, then a seedy wine shop, was a welcome refuge from bad weather. ♦ Closed W. Fondamenta Zattere 918. Vap 1, 2, 34, Accademia or 5, 8, Zattere. 5237210

26 Squero di San Trovaso This small compound, best visible from **Fondamenta Nani** across the canal, is now a national landmark and probably the most photographed and painted sight in Venice. It is one of 3 places that still produces new gondolas in Venice. The 17th-century wooden buildings (home of the owners and hangar for boats), unusual in Venice, were typical of boat builders. They still look like Dolomite mountain homes, and in fact both the wood for the gondolas and the master carpenters often came from that region. Gondolas are still built according to the traditional methods; most other boats, even when in

Dorsoduro

wood, are now coated with plastic to make them more resistant to the elements and easier to maintain. ♦ Campo San Trovaso 1092. Vap 1, 2, 34, Accademia or 5, 8, Zattere

27 Stazione Marittima At the end of the Zattere walk, an unimpressive wooden bridge leads to this cruise ship terminal. The whole area is in terribly bad shape and definitely not worthy of a modern passenger harbor. Dozens of acres of unattractive and vacant buildings cover the southwest tip of Venice. As with the huge Arsenale area, proposals for what to do with the buildings come and go, but so far the city has been unable to decide on a plan of action. An equally dismal fate has fallen upon the **Mulino Stucky**, the strange (for Venice) Neo-Gothic construction looming across the Canal from the terminal. It used to be a flour mill. Abandoned in 1950, it was to become a modern conference center, then a huge youth hostel, but no final decision was ever made. In the meantime, the building has fallen apart, with all the windows broken and pigeons flying in and out. ♦ Fondamenta San Basegio, across the bridge. Vap 5, 8, San Basilio

28 Liceo *Marco Polo* The building at No. 1073 Fondamenta Toffetti, down the **Ponte delle Meraveglie,** was restored in 1980 (facade 18th c, **Andrea Tirali**). Since time immemorial it has housed one of 2 high schools for classical studies in Venice, attended by children of the upper classes. ♦ Fondamenta Toffetti 1073. Vap 1, 2, 34, Accademia

29 Pensione Accademia—Villa Meraveglie $$ It's rare in Venice to find a *real* villa, surrounded by a garden and detached from other buildings. This relatively small hotel is just such a rarity. The halls and rooms are reminiscent of à private home and the prices are surprisingly affordable (for Venice). Breakfast in the canal-side garden is wonderful. Loyal guests keep this hotel booked, so try to make your reservations 2 or 3 months in advance.

30 Libreria Alla Toletta One of the best bookstores in Venice, with a good section on Venice itself, with some books written in English, and an art and photography section that is well worth a look. ♦ Closed M, Su, lunch. Sacca de la Toletta 1214. Vap 1, 2, 34, Accademia or 1, Ca' Rezzonico. 5232034

31 Trattoria Montin ★★★$$ The entrance to this restaurant is on one of the most attractive canals in Venice, **Rio de le Romite**. The dining room walls are lined with paintings by Venetian artists, who have patronized the place since the 1940s. When current owner **Giuliano Montin** was a child, his father ran the place and made it famous. Guidebooks and movies have kept the restaurant in the limelight. The food is excellent and the atmosphere friendly and informal. Try the *pappardelle* (a kind of large fettuccine), *osso buco* and beef filet with green pepper, and among the fish dishes, the *branzino* is worth every lire. Service, under the direction of Giuliano's wife **Midi**, is very professional. Dine in the huge, wonderful garden in the summer. ♦ Closed Tu dinner, W. Fondamenta di Borgo 1147. Vap 1, 2, 34, Accademia or 1, Ca' Rezzonico. 5227151

31 Locanda Montin $ Trattoria Montin also rents 7 rooms above the restaurant, and they are among the best bargains in town, with the only inconvenience being the lack of private bathrooms (there are 4 bathrooms and showers). Two of the rooms have a marvelous view over the canal, with small terraces and beautiful geranium pots. ♦ Fondamenta di Borgo 1147. Vap 1, 2, 34, Accademia or 1, Ca' Rezzonico. 5227151

32 Casa Dè Stefani $ One of the best bets among the inexpensive hotels in Venice, the Casa is conveniently located a few steps from the Ca' Rezzonico vaporetto stop—wonderful you have a lot of luggage to carry. The owners will give you the key to the main door, and after that you are on your own. The interior includes a large and comfortable lobby, while the rest of the decor is typical of Venetian homes of days old: wavy floors (Venetian buildings *move* continuously, due to the soft nature of the ground) slanted doors and, in general, not one perfectly straight line. Even so, the hotel is clean and private. When reserving, make sure you specify a room with or without a bath. ♦ Ca' Rezzonico, Calle del Tragheto 2786. Vap 1, Ca' Rezzonico. 5223337

33 Arianna da Venezia Right in front of the vaporetto stop Ca' Rezzonico is this luxurious shop filled with hand-printed velvet of all sizes shapes and functions, from bed covers, curtains and wall coverings to clothes, carnival masks and book covers. Owner **Arianna de Venezia**—a member of the Venetian aristocracy—hand-prints the fabric herself using a somewhat secret process that was invented in Venice by the Catalan painter **Mariano Fortuny**

a man of enormous influence during the 1920s and '30s. Fortuny's palace is now a museum (see San Marco chapter), and his textile factory is still operating on Giudecca, where da Venezia's velvet is produced. ♦ Closed lunch; Sa-Su by appt only. Ca' Rezzonico, Fondamenta del Tragheto 2793. Vap 1, Ca' Rezzonico. 5221535

34 Ca' Rezzonico—Museo del Settecento Veneziano (Museum of the Venetian 18th Century) This rather imposing building, with its main facade on the Canal Grande, was begun by **Baldassare Longhena** in the 17th century and completed by **Giorgio Massari** in the 18th century. The poet **Robert Browning** died here in 1889. The palazzo is now a museum of 18th-century Venetian art, including furniture, textiles and all kinds of objects one would have seen in a patrician home of that period. On the first of the 2 *noble floors* (*piano nobile*, as opposed to the higher floors, occupied by servants), the large ballroom contains some furniture by the famous woodcarver **Andrea Brustolon**. The ceiling of Room No. 2 was frescoed by **Giambattista Tiepolo** with *The Marriage of Ludovico Rezzonico with Cristina Savorgnan*. More ceilings by Tiepolo are in Room No. 6 (*Allegory of Nobility and Virtue*) and in Room No. 8 (*Fortitude and Wisdom*, a canvas). Room No. 12 is dedicated to Brustolon: the astonishing, extremely elegant furniture was originally conceived for **Palazzo Venier** (the unfinished building now occupied by the Guggenheim Collection). On the 2nd noble floor, Room No.13 contains, among many other paintings, a large canvas by **Giovanni Battista Piazzetta** (*The Death of Darius*). Room No. 14, adorned by a Tiepolo ceiling (*The Triumph of Zephir and Flora*), is called **Sala del Longhi** because it contains some 30 canvasses by **Pietro Longhi**, a Venetian of the late 18th century who delighted in painting scenes from everyday life (*The Morning Chocolate, The Family Concert*). Nothing illustrates the dramatic changes in Venetian life near the loss of independence better than a comparison between these intimate, bourgeois interiors and the triumphant Tiepolo ceilings. In a totally different vein, hints of decadence are also present in the frescoes by **Gian Domenico Tiepoli**, son of Giambattista and himself a first-rate painter. They can be seen in Room Nos. 22 and 23, where they were placed after being removed from the painter's home in the Venice mainland (Gian Domenico had painted them for his own enjoyment). Room No. 29 contains a famous little canvas by **Francesco Guardi**, also a painter of the 2nd half of the century: *Il Ridotto*, which portrays one of the many Venetian gambling casinos. On the 3rd floor is an exhibit of a complete 18th-century pharmacy, restored and moved here after it went out of business in 1909. ♦ Admission. Daily 9AM-7PM. Fondamenta Rezzonico 3136. Vap 1, Ca' Rezzonico. 5224543

35 Crepizza ★★$ Opened in 1990, this restaurant has quickly become a favorite place for pizza and light meals. It is frequented by a mix of students, professionals, yuppies and gondoliers. Pleasant atmosphere, good prices and terrific pizza and crepes (the name is a contraction of the 2 words). ♦ Closed Tu. Calle San Pantalon 3757. Vap 1, 34, San Tomà. Reservations recommended. 5226280

36 Campo Santa Margherita One of the most charming and lively Venetian squares. Neigh-

Dorsoduro

borhood life is centered around this campo—it's lined with food shops, cafes and open spaces where mothers take their children to play. The large building on the east side (Nos. 3003-06) is now occupied by a supermarket, run by the union of shopkeepers in the neighborhood. On the same side is **Al Capon** (★★$$), a restaurant and pensione. An abandoned church sits at the northern end (see the truncated bell tower); it was recently used as a movie theater but is now empty. Some of the houses on the campo are among the oldest and most charming in Venice: the one at No. 2931 (west side) is 13th-century Gothic with original Byzantine elements (such as the 12th-century arch over the main door); a few doors away, the 2 houses at Nos. 2945-62 are 14th-century Gothic. ♦ Campo Santa Margherita. Vap 1, Ca' Rezzonico

37 Ristorante L'Incontro ★★$ Authentic Venetian atmosphere, excellent wine list, and always delicious pasta of the day. Maybe you'll even catch **Paolo**, the main waiter, in a good mood. ♦ Closed M. Rio Terrà Canal 3062. Vap 1, Ca' Rezzonico. 5222404

38 Mondonovo Among the more than 100 mask shops that have mushroomed in Venice since the institution of **Carnival** in the 1970s, Mondonovo is one of the few places left where masks are made with artistic care and respect for tradition. Of the 2 bearded owners, **Guerino** is an art historian and tireless discoverer of old masks, while tall, funny **Giorgio Spiller** is a teacher in an art school. Masks are produced on the premises in a workshop behind the counter. Mondonovo, small as it is, is well-known all over Italy and internationally. They produce masks and other papier-mâché objects for the theater and movies. Among Mondonovo's regular customers is New York's **Bloomingdale's** department store, which features Venetian masks during the Carnival season. ♦ Closed Su, lunch. Rio Terrà Canal 3126. Vap 1, Ca' Rezzonico. 5231607

38 Ca Foscari (15th c) This sumptous Gothic building, one of the most imposing on the Canal Grande, was built for **Doge Francesco Foscari**, one of the outstanding personalities in Venetian political history. It is now the main building of the **University of Venice**. A constant crowd of students and staff move about the building and the courtyard when the university is open—school usually begins in the middle of November, closes for a month in the middle of December, and, after a customary Easter break, is over in the middle of May. ♦ Canal Grande/Rio Nuovo

39 Ponte dei Pugni The name, which means *Bridge of the Fist Fights*, comes from an old tradition (now abandoned) which pitted the residents of **San Nicolò** (a Dorsoduro neighborhood, mostly inhabited by fishermen) against those of **Castello** (mostly Arsenale workers). The champions of both areas used to

hold mock-fights on the bridge, trying to push the opponents into the water. Four footprints still mark the starting places of the opposing fighters. ♦ Ponte dei Pugni. Vap 1, Ca' Rezzonico

40 Pizzeria *Al sole di Napoli* ★$ Friendly and inexpensive, this pizzeria is crowded on summer evenings because of its outdoor tables. Locals gather here when they don't feel like cooking at home. ♦ Closed Th. Campo Santa Margherita 3023. Vap 1, Ca' Rezzonico. 5285686

41 Scuola Grande dei Carmini During the 17th century, the charitable organization of **Santa Maria del Carmelo** (one of many denominations of the Virgin Mary) had some 75,000 people under its wing. The importance of the building today is tied to the extraordinary number and quality of paintings by **Giambattista Tiepolo**. Nine of his canvasses adorn the ceiling of the main hall on the 2nd floor. The central one represents *The Virgin Mary with the Blessed Simon Stock*, and it is considered one of the highest points in Tiepolo's career. A masterwork by **Giovanni Battista Piazzetta**, *Judity and Holofernes*, is in the passageway between **Sala dell'Archivio** and **Sala dell'Albergo**. ♦ Admission. M-F 9AM-noon, 3-6PM; Sa 9:30AM-12:30PM. Rio Terrá Santa Margherita 2616. Vap 1, Ca' Rezzonico

42 Chiesa dei Carmini (begun 14th c) Originally a Gothic church, it was modified in the 16th century by raising the central nave (the rose window on the facade was then partly filled). The rich wood decoration on the interior dates from the 17th century. Within the church are 2 masterworks: in the 2nd chapel at the right is the *Adoration of the Shepards*, one of the last works by **Cima Da Conegliano**; and in the 2nd chapel on the left is *Saint Nicolas, Saint Lucy, Saint John the Baptist and Saint George Killing the Dragon*, one of 3 paintings by **Lorenzo Lotto** in Venice (see Church of San Giovanni e Paolo and Accademia for the oth-

ers), much admired for the coastal landscape at the bottom. Behind the church is the convent of the **Padri Carmelitani**, now used by the **Istituto d'Arte**, which is the main high school for young artisans in the Venice area, specializing in glass, ceramics and textiles. ♦ Campo dei Carmini. Vap 1, Ca' Rezzonico

43 Fondamenta del Soccorso and Fondamenta di San Sebastiano These 2 charming streets, running along 2 canals, lead to the tall, Gothic church of **San Sebastiano**, visible from the corner between the 2 streets. Across the canals is **Palazzo Ariani Pasqualigo**, with its remarkable Gothic windows and an outdoor staircase and now a *scuola elementare* (grade school). ♦ Vap 1, Ca' Rezzonico or 5, 8, San Basilio

44 Chiesa di San Sebastiano (Church of St. Sebastian) (15th c) This church contains a wealth of 16th-century works by **Paolo Veronese**, one of the major painters of the Venetian Renaissance. On the ceiling of the main nave is his *Esther in Front of Ahasuerus*, *Esther Crowned by Ahasuerus* and *The Triumph of Mordecai*. The latter painting could be taken as a manifesto of Veronese's ideas about his art: his aim seems to be a kind of high, refined spectacularity, regardless of the nature of the subject (whether religious or, as in the patrician villas, totally secular). The perspective of the 2 horses in the foreground is striking, as are the twisted column and the top balcony with overlooking ladies. With these paintings, Veronese established himself as the man who could best represent the theatrical, grandiose fantasies of the Venetian nobility in a moment of relentless commercial and political expansion. He also painted the doors to the organ (left wall); the canvas on the main altar (*The Virgin in Glory with Saint Sebastian, Peter, Catherine and Francis*); the 2 large canvasses in the chancel (*Saint Mark and Saint Marcellino*, and the famous *Martyrdom of Saint Sebastian*); the ceiling of the Sacristy (this was his first work here); and, visible from a walk over a stair (ask the custodian to accompany you), 2 frescoes with *Saint Sebastian in front of Diocletian* and another *Martyrdom of Saint Sebastian*. ♦ Campo San Sebastiano. Vap 1, Ca' Rezzonico or 5, 8, San Basilio

45 Ristorante All'Angelo Raffaele ★★$$ This restaurant started as the kind of place where dock workers got drunk and played cards after work. In the 1960s, they added a few basic dishes to the menu, mostly favorite Venetian fish appetizers like octopus, cuttlefish, smelts and sardines, which attracted a different kind of clientele, who ordered the appetizers as whole meals. Along with the new clientele came an expanded menu. Now the back-room card games are history—the space is too valuable—and some of the spontaneity is gone, but the restaurant is still a great place for inexpensive fish dishes. ♦ Closed M. Campo de l'Angelo Raffaele 1722. Vap 1, Ca' Rezzonico or 5, 8, San Basilio. 5237456

46 Casa dei Sette Camini (18th c) This building is a national landmark. It is in need of restoration, but its regularity and striking chimneys give it a simple beauty. The whole neighborhood, once extremely poor, is slowly being renovated as more and more Venetians, lured here by lower prices, discover its quiet, old-fashioned charm. ◆ Campiello Tron 1877. Vap 1, Ca' Rezzonico or 5, 8, San Basilio

47 Chiesa di San Nicolò dei Mendicoli (begun 7th c) A restoration in the 1970s uncovered remnants from as far back as the 7th century, making this one of the oldest churches in Venice. The existing structure was built between the 13th and 15th centuries; the magnificent Veneto-Byzantine bell tower dates from the 11th century; and the facade was redone in the 18th century. The interior, unusually welcoming and intimate, has exquisite 15th-century woodwork. ◆ Campo San Nicolò dei Mendicolo. Vap 1, Ca' Rezzonico or 5, 8, San Basilio

48 Campo San Basilio The building at Nos. 1511-22, separating the campo from the Canale della Giudecca, is an interesting example of a 17th- century housing development. It was conceived as a rental apartment building (4 apartments on each floor). Inside, a small courtyard allows light to enter the back rooms. The triple windows on the 3rd- and 4th floors are typical of popular domestic 17th-century architecture. ◆ Campo San Basilio. Vap 5, 8, San Basilio

49 Ristorante Riviera ★★$$ There may not be a wood terrace over the canal at this restaurant, but the tables set on the banks of the canal are quite pleasant. The chef/owner worked at **Harry's Bar** before opening Riviera, and his training can be seen in the quality of the food and service. The homemade gnocchi, spaghetti, fish and Venetian specialties are all delicious. ◆ Closed M. Fondamenta Zattere 1475. Vap 5, 8, San Basilio or Zattere. 5227621

Masks

With the reinstatement of Carnival a few years ago, the ancient Venetian art of maskmaking has undergone something of a Renaissance. Though the forms are now many and often fanciful to the point of appearing rather drugged-out, there are a few masks with which Casanova would have felt right at home. The classic mask—the angular white form covering everything but the chin, as depicted in the genre scenes of **Pietro Longhi**, is called the *bauta*. Others take their cue from stock characters in the *commedia dell'arte* improvisational theater which originated near Venice—**Pantalone** and **Il Dottore**, the old misers; **Arlecchino** and **Brighella**, the servant buffoons; **Capitano Spaventa**, the *braggadocio*. All the masks are made in a variety of materials, from the original leather and papier-mâché to ceramic. Today they make as authentic a souvenir as Murano glass or Burano lace—if indeed anything about this dreamlike city can be considered authentic.

Dorsoduro

A performance at **La Fenice**. The jewel-box opera house of Europe.

Rialto Market in the early morning. One can imagine the 16th-20th centuries never having gone by. The produce looks like a painting.

An evening stroll on the Zattere. Stop at **Nico's** and **Aldo's** for gelato. The popular promenade of Venice to watch the great liners go by.

Take the Vaporetto No. 1 at the Rialto to the **Lido** and look to the right. Take the No. 1 from the Lido back to the **Piazzale Roma** and look to the left—it's the cheapest and most beautiful tour of the Grand Canal and the palaces of Venice. Take your camera along.

5-star deluxe for great dining—Lunch at the **Cipriani**; a drink at the **Gritti** at twilight and diner on the **Monacco Terrace**; lunch at **Harry's Dolci**; dinner at **Harry's Bar** (save your liras to do any of these).

Fast Food—pizza and tramezzini (finger sandwiches) and great espresso coffee—Stop at any pizzeria for the freshest, crunchiest pizza you ever had. The tramezzini and coffee are found at almost any corner bar. Try it!

San Polo

There's no dearth of art and architecture in **San Polo**. The **Frari** church is, along with **Santi Giovanni e Paolo**, one of the great creations of Venetian Gothic. The **Scuola di San Rocco** houses a breathtaking array of canvases by **Tintoretto**. **Campo San Polo** itself—vast, luminous and elegant—is probably the most beautiful square in all of Venice. Yet for Venetians San Polo is the part of town where *real* people live and go about their daily business. It is the great market area for the whole town. The fruit and vegetable market and the nearby fish market still serve shoppers from throughout Venice—they arrive by vaporetto to buy their weekly food supplies at prices much lower than in their neighborhood shops. The liveliest street is **Ruga Rialto**, parallel to Canal Grande on the west side of the Rialto Bridge. If you look at a map, you'll see an amazing number of narrow, parallel streets between the ruga and the Canal Grande. That's where the market merchants used to have their homes and storage rooms. On the other side of the ruga, a labyrinth of tiny streets hides the best wine shops in town: **L'Antico Dolo, Ai Do Mori, A le Do Spade**. These are real institutions, still packed with Venetians who stop for an *ombra* or glass of wine and a *cicchetto* (the Venetian version of tapas) before lunch or dinner. These Venetians include pensioners, students, teachers, doctors, lawyers and architects—the latter abound in Venice because the university's extensive school of architecture. And though the food booths at the Rialto market are gradually being replaced with stalls selling tourist trinkets, San Polo remains fundamentally human. It is one of the last places on earth where class and money distinctions don't seem to matter, and its wine shops are where human beings are still simply human beings enjoying their city perhaps more than any outsider.

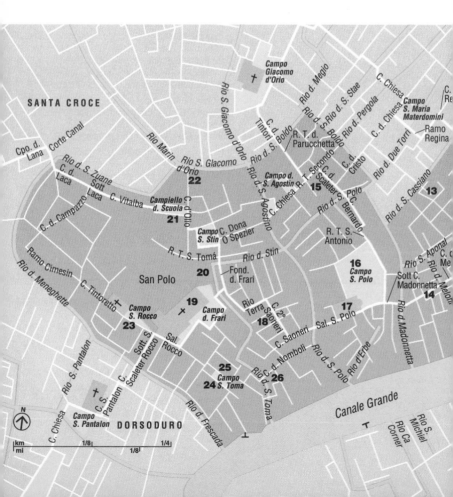

1 Ponte di Rialto (1588-92, **Antonio Da Ponte**) This stone bridge was built at the end of the 16th century, replacing a wooden drawbridge that was too low for ship masts to pass through. Until the 19th century, this was the only bridge on the Canal Grande and the only link between the 3 *sestieri de citra* (on *this* side) and the 3 *de ultra* (on *that* side). Appropriately enough, the architect's name was Antonio Da Ponte (no relation to the painter better known as **Bassano** nor with **Mozart**'s librettist **Lorenzo Da Ponte**). Among the rejected proposals was one by **Antonio Palladio**, now in the city's archives, and one by **Michelangelo**. The sides of the bridge are decorated with high reliefs of the *Annunciation* (16th century). The buildings on the San Marco side, now owned by the city bishopry, are rented as apartments to a few lucky Venetians—lucky because the rental prices are established by a national law, which does not take into account such things as views. On the Rialto side, the city built 2 Renaissance-style palazzi. Coming from the bridge, the palazzo on the right houses the **Camerlenghi** (finance ministry), with prisons on the ground floor, while the one on the left is home to the **Dieci Savi**, 10 magistrates in charge of collecting taxes. ◆ Ponte di Rialto. Vap 1, 2, 34, Rialto

2 Mercato della Frutta Despite the rapid transformation of the rest of the market into a tourist trap, the vegetable market is still very much alive along the Canal Grande, on the bank close to the **Pescheria** or fish market. ◆ Ruga dei Oresi or Ruga degli Orefici. Vap 1, 2, 34, Rialto or 1, San Silvestro

3 Campo San Giacomo (St. James Square) During the daytime, it's hard to see the beauty of this little square, crammed as it is with vegetable stands and shabby canopies. But at night the little church, fondly called San Giacometto by the locals, evokes a time when human size was more important than imperial magnificence. Its 12th-century portico, once common in front of churches, is one of very few left in Venice. The handsome clock on the bell tower has been here since the 15th century. From the early times of the Republic until the 18th century, this square was the Wall Street of Venice. Here the modern banking system was first invented: bankers had their tables on the square or under the nearby colonnade, and they would record transactions in their books,

San Polo

avoiding the transfer of real gold and silver. ◆ Campo San Giacomo. Vap 1, 2, 34, Rialto or 1, San Silvestro

4 Rialta Among the many stores offering *specialità veneziane,* it's rare to come across the exquisite taste, care for detail and originality found in this little shop right under the Rialto's arcades. The necklaces, bracelets, earrings, carnival masks and collectors' dolls sold by Rialta are beautiful and original in design, as are the purses and hats. Some of the glass beads and other materials in the designs are antiques from the '20s and '30s. ◆ Closed M morning. Ruga degli Orefici 56. Vap 1, 2, 34, Rialto or 1, San Silvestro. 5285710

5 Trattoria Alla Madonna ★★$$ One of the few restaurants in Venice serving really fresh fish at decent prices. Alla Madonna is a local favorite, dating back more than 50 years. The eclectic clientele keeps the place lively, the tables filled with everybody from upper-crust Venetians to the gondoliers who park their boats between rides on the nearby stretch of the Canal Grande. Try the risottos and the *granseola* appetizer (a type of crab with deliciously tasty meat). ◆ Closed W. Calle della Madonna 594. Vap 1, San Silvestro. 5223824

6 Gastronomia Aliani ★★★$$ One of the few takeout delis in town, with fancy food items as well as the traditional roast chicken. ♦ Closed W afternoon, Su. Rugheta del Ravano 697. Vap 1, San Silvestro. 5224913

7 L'Antico Dolo ★★$ For the time being, this is still an *osteria*: an old-fashioned wine shop where the owner lines the counter with a pot of hot *musetto* (boiled sausage), a pot of *pasta e fagioli* (bean soup) and a few more popular dishes to go with the carefully selected house wines. A few small tables have now appeared in the narrow space, and table service and more ambitious dishes announce the beginning of a transformation. ♦ Closed Su. Ruga Vecchia San Giovanni 778. Vap 1, San Silvestro. 5226546

8 Ruga vecchia San Giovanni This *ruga* (Venetian for the French word *rue* or street) is narrow and busy, as it's the main connection between the Rialto area and Campo San Polo. Until the 1960s, it was the main shopping street for Venetians, as opposed to the

San Polo

Mercerie near San Marco, where goods and prices are geared toward tourists. But the increased tourist traffic in the San Polo-Rialto area is quickly transforming this ruga as well. Venetians now tend to avoid it, using a parallel, more intricate path to reach Campo San Polo (Calle dei Do Mori to Calle San Matio to Campiello del Sole, all deserted and totally charming). ♦ Ruga Vecchia San Giovanni. Vap 1, 2, 34, Rialto or 1, San Silvestro

9 A le Do Spade ★★$ Workers and shoppers from the nearby vegetable and fish markets and lawyers and clerks from the nearby courthouse have made this *osteria* part of their daily ritual, stopping in for a glass of wine at the counter before heading home for lunch or dinner. The wine list is tremendous, as is the selection of *cicchetti* (small snacks similar to tapas). Order a glass of Chardonnay Brut and the *cicchetti* prepared with bulls neck or goose ham *(prosciutto d'oca)*. The regulars always stand at the counter, leaving plenty of tables for exhausted walkers. ♦ Closed Su. Calle Do Spade 860. Vap 1, San Silvestro. 5210574

10 Ai Do Mori ★★$ Another *osteria* also crowded with Venetians before lunch and dinner, with a good selection of high-quality wines and a long menu of *cicchetti*. A warning for weary feet: there are no tables or chairs here. Customers come in small groups, crowd around the counter, drink their glass of wine and head home—or to the next *osteria* along their way. ♦ Closed W afternoon, Su. Calle Do Mori 429. Vap 1, San Silvestro. 5225401

11 Pescheria This building—with its Neo-Gothic ground floor and Renaissance-style 2nd floor— was erected in the 19th century to provide cover for the colorful and lively fish stands here. Some of the seafood is from local waters—the sardines, which Venetians cook in a variety of succulent ways, some small shrimp, most of the shellfish and the farmed trout. The *branzini* and *orate* are the most expensive items for sale, except for live lobsters. The salmon comes from Norwegian se farms; the sole is mostly imported from Holland; some of the scampi come from Sicily o from Adriatic waters but most are from Norway and Ireland. Most squid and octopus are imported frozen from Thailand and the Canar Islands. ♦ Campo de Le Beccarie. Vap 1, 2, 3 Rialto or 1, San Silvestro, or gondola traghet from Santa Sofia in Cannaregio

12 Antica Trattoria Poste Vecie ★★★$$$ Walk across a small wooden bridge to reach this charming restaurant, where you can dine outdoors in the garden or in the frescoed roo inside. Tradition and perfection are the highe priorities here, and it shows in the food. The black fettuccine (colored with a touch of cutt fish ink) seasoned with crab, shrimp and fres tomatoes is a must; and the filet of dory with cream of artichokes won a national culinary prize in 1990. ♦ Closed Tu. Pescheria di Venezia. Vap 1, 2, 34, Rialto or 1, San Silvestro, or gondola traghetto from Santa Sofia in Cannaregio. 721822

13 Antiche Carampane ★★$$ This restaura generally frequented by locals, is well hidden a labyrinth of tiny *calli*, away from the busy streets of San Polo. The fish is good and the prices are reasonable, thus the largely local clientele and the waiters who sometimes are impatient if you don't speak Italian. ♦ Closed M, Su evening. Calle Carampane 1519. Vap 1 San Silvestro. 5240165

14 da Sandro ★★$ Good pizza at reasonable prices at somewhat crowded tables along the busy *calle* lea ing to Campo San Polo. The place is especially nice in low season, when **Sandro** and his team have more time to entertain customers with dishes more elaborate than pizza. ♦ Closed F. Campiello dei Meloni 1473. Vap 1, San Silvestro. 5234894

15 Trattoria Da Fiore ★★★$$$ The cooking is traditional and sophisticated in this quiet, elegant restaurant frequented by well-off Ven tians as well as visitors. The decor is sober a in impeccable good taste, conducive to relaxe conversation. The menu ranges from fish and meat dishes to a wide selection of original pa tas and risottos. The house wine is excellent. ♦ Closed M, Su. Calle del Scaleter 2202. Vap San Silvestro or 1, 34, San Tomà. 721308

16 Campo San Polo This is the largest square in Venice after Piazza San Marco. When the weather is nice, it is filled with neighborhood life (children, mothers, senior citizens relaxin on the benches in the sun). The curved easte wall of the square was built in the 15th centu with remarkable Gothic palazzi along the ban of a canal which was later filled. For centuries the Campo was used for fairs, outdoor theater performances, even bullfights. Today it is still used for outdoor movies on hot summer evenings. Eight-hundred chairs are fitted around an enormous screen, and people whose windows happen to open onto the campo have no choice but to watch the movies together with other Venetians who have not fled to the seaside. The San Polo summer movies have quickly become a tradition, with people lingering around after the shows, enjoying the cozy feeling of belonging to a small and special community. ◆ Campo San Polo. Vap 1, 34, San Tomà or 1, San Silvestro

17 Chiesa di San Polo (begun 9th c) The rather odd orientation of this church, with the apse facing the square and the entrance cut into one of the sides, is due to the changes the area has undergone during the centuries. The facade originally opened onto a canal. The church has been modified many times since the 9th century: the rose window is Gothic and the exterior is Neoclassical. Inside, don't miss the canvas by **Giambattista Tiepolo** (*The Virgin Appearing to Saint John Nepomuk*, 2nd altar on the left), and, in a separate room (**Oratorio del Crocefisso**), the series of paintings by his son **Giandomenico Tiepolo** representing the stations of a *Via Crucis* (the stations of the cross, Christ's imprisonment, condemnation and crucifixion), with great emphasis on large foreground figures. ◆ Campo San Polo. Vap 1, 34, San Tomà or 1, San Silvestro

18 La Scialuppa This little shop was opened in the late 1980s by a young artist in love with all kinds of Venetian boats, both ancient and contemporary. The astonishing variety of hulls and shapes, adapted to different purposes, is reproduced here in wood models and drawings. Some of the posters on sale are popular because they include the dozen or so most frequent lagoon crafts, still in wide use and recognizable in the canals. ◆ Calle Seconda dei Saoneri 2695. Vap 1, 34, San Tomà. 5289947

19 Chiesa dei Frari (Frari Church) (begun 14th c) *Frari* is a local word for *friars*: all monks are friars, of course, but here the word refers to the members of the **Franciscan** order, as though they were friars *par excellence*. The Franciscans were a more popular order than their rivals, the **Dominicans**: their emphasis was on prayer and poverty, while the Dominicans specialized in learning and education. In Venice the 2 orders tried to outdo each other in the size and elaborateness of their main churches. While the Dominicans were building their grandiose **San Giovanni e Paolo** (see Castello chapter), the Franciscans vastly enlarged the old chapel in their monastery, spending decades in the 14th century integrating the entire old church into the transept of the new one, and still holding services all the while. During this period, the Franciscans owned all of San Polo island, which was at that time mostly marshland, and the order spent centuries filling in the marsh to

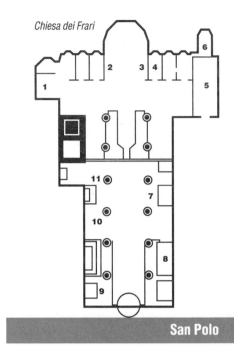

Chiesa dei Frari

make it buildable. Today the order owns only a small part of the area, while the rest is covered with houses, streets and squares.

The exterior of the church they built is sober and mostly unadorned, the most attractive parts being the apses and the bell tower, the 2nd highest in Venice after St. Mark's. The interior, however, is awe-inspiring—in spite of its vast size, it maintains a sense of perfect unity. Like the Dominicans' San Giovanni e Paolo, this church is also a kind of Venetian Pantheon, thickly adorned with the tombs of prominent citizens and with masterworks by the best Venetian artists.

A visit should start with a walk from the back door through the magnificent carved wood choir (the sitting places for the friars, 15th century), to the main altar, where one of the masterworks of all time is awaiting: **Titian's** *Assumption of the Virgin*, painted by the artist when he was in his late 20s. Surpassing **Giovanni Bellini**, Titian introduced new concepts in the composition of figures (the space division in horizontal layers, with the emphatic hands and up-tilted faces of the people pointing irresistibly to the Virgin at the top of an ideal pyramid) and in the use of color. Titian's contemporaries were struck by the Realism in the work: the Virgin *really seems to fly upwards* and the Apostles *show marvel and happiness as if they were alive*, noted **Ludovico Dolce** in 1577. *All painters*, Dolce continued, *tried to imitate this new way, but as they embarked on this totally new territory, they were immediately lost*.

More highlights in the Chiesa dei Frari:

The altarpiece in the Corner Chapel, [1] *St. Mark Enthroned*, is one of the last masterworks of **Bartolomeo Vivarini.** A comparison with the nearby *Assumption* by Titian eloquently shows the progress achieved in Venetian painting during the 42 years that separate the 2 works.

[2] The monument on the left wall of the chancel, the **Tomb of Doge Niccolò Tron** (1476, **Antonio Rizzo**), is considered one of the best examples of Venetian Renaissance sculpture. The Doge is portrayed standing in the central niche, with Charity and Prudence on his sides; he is also sculpted laying on top of his cinerary urn, under a lunette with bas-reliefs of Christ with God the Father and the Angel announcing to the Virgin.

On the right wall of the chancel is [3] the **Monument to Doge Francesco Foscari**, one of the greatest Venetian leaders. Built 20 years before the Tron monument in front, this work shows an interesting mixture of styles: the old Venetian Gothic here gives way to influences of the Renaissance from central Italy.

[4] In the apse, the first chapel at the right of the altar contains a wood sculpture of *St. John the Baptist* by **Donatello**.

San Polo

[5] The **Sacristy** was built in the 15th century with donations from the wealthy **Pesaro** family, one of the most prominent families in Venetian history. Their presence is obvious in this church. The monument on top of the Sacristy's door represents **Benedetto Pesaro**, an admiral in the Venetian navy.

In the small chapel at the left of the Sacristy, [6] the altarpiece is decorated with one of the best paintings by **Giovanni Bellini**: the *Madonna and Child with Four Saints*, in the original carved wood frame.

[7] The statue representing *Saint Jerome* by **Alessandro Vittoria**, a 16th-century sculptor whose works are abundantly present in Venetian churches, is one of the artist's best works.

[8] The 19th-century **Monument to Titian,** by **Luigi** and **Pietro Zandomeneghi**. Titian died during a plague and was probably buried here. The monument was first commissioned from **Antonio Canova**, but was built by the Zandomeneghi, his pupils, after the master's death. It is one of the last examples of Neoclassical sculpture in Venice. Canova's plans for the monument were used by a team of his pupils, including Zandomeneghi, for a monument to Canova himself.

[9] **Monument to Antonio Canova**, built by his pupils in 1827 upon Canova's drawings for the Monument to Titian. The statues on the sides of the pyramid's open door represent the Arts, St. Mark's Lion and Genius. Although Canova's body is in another place, his heart is inside the pyramid, in a vase of porphyry. This entire area is occupied by an imposing Baroque **Monument to Doge Giovanni Pesaro**, based on plans by **Baldassare Longhena**.

[10] *The Pesaro Madonna*, painted by **Titian** in 1526. Here again Titian broke with some of the most venerated rules in composition and use of color. The striking perspective of the painting is explained by Titian's attempt to attract the eyes of visitors walking up the aisle from the church's main door; the 2 gigantic columns in the painting are an ideal continuation of the real columns supporting the church's roof.

Another member of the Pesaro family, [11] **Bishop Jacopo Pesaro**, is buried in the late-Renaissance **Monument to Bishop Jacopo Pesaro**.

On the 3rd floor of this chapel is the tomb of **Claudio Monteverdi**, the composer from Cremona who spent a great part of his life as choir master at St. Mark's. ♦ Campo San Polo Vap 1, 34, San Tomà or 1, San Silvestro

20 Archivio di Stato The Frari Church opens onto a small square along a canal appropriately called **Rio dei Frari**. Walking out of the church, the building on the left used to be part of the large monastery where hundreds of Friars lived. It includes 2 charming cloisters (one attributed to **Sansovino**; inquire about permission to visit at the archive office). Today the building houses the archives of the Venetian Republic. The archives are among the richest and most well-organized in the world. The Doges carefully conserved all kinds of documents related to the city's government. Some 15 million files, some as thick as 10 inches, are stored along many miles of shelves. They tell the story of Venice month by month, often day by day, and include ambassadors' letters and international files that have proved invaluable in the study of the history of Europe. A competent and kind staff welcomes dozens of scholars from all over the world every day. ♦ Campo dei Frari 3002. Vap 1, 34, San Tomà

21 Scuola Grande di San Giovanni Evangelista (Great School of Saint John the Evangelist) The rich and powerful brotherhood named after **St. John** acquired this property early in the 14th century. In 1478, master **Pietro Lombardo**, one of the first architects and sculptors to introduce the Renaissance in Venice, redesigned the little square on the side of the school building and in front of the church. He added the elegant marble portal, decorated with an eagle (the symbol of St. John) and 2 Angels, thus creating one of the first Renaissance environments in town. The brotherhood was housed in the building at the right of the square's entrance (notice the medieval bas-relief representing *The Virgin and St. John Being Adored by the Brotherhood's Members*). The interior was mostly re-done by **Massari** in the 18th century, though the most interesting feature is the splendid staircase designed and built by **Mauro Codussi** in 1498. The building is open to the general public a few times a year, mostly for musical performances. ♦ Campiello della Scuola 2455. Vap 1, 34, San Tomà. 718234

22 Caffè Orientale ★★$$ In 1982, 2 Venetian brothers took over an old wine shop and transformed it into this fancy restaurant. They gave it an Art Deco look using black lacquer and mirrors, and they named it after the Oriental Café, which used to be near St. Mark's Square. **Mario**, the chef, is a devoted lover of old-time Venetian cooking, finding inspiration in Venetian culinary history—and one suspects his mother's recipe file. His mustached brother **Sandro** serves guests with professional grace. He loves Art Deco, and can recite the brand name and history of each chair he has collected for the restaurant. Try to reserve a table on the terrace overlooking the canal. When you're through dining, ask Sandro to call a gondola to take you back to your hotel or to further explore the city. ◆ Closed M. Fondamenta de la Late 2426. Vap 1, 34, San Tomà. 719804

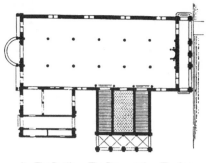

23 Scuola Grande di San Rocco (begun 1515) Most of the great Renaissance architects of Venice contributed to this remarkable building, which epitomizes the stylistic trends of that period: the ground floor was built by **Bartolomeo Bon**, the middle and top floors by **Sante Lombardo** and **Scarpagnino**, and the final touches were added by **Gian Giacomo de' Grigi**. Like its neighboring rival at St. John the Evangelist's, the **Brotherhood of St. Roch** was a powerful association of merchants, storekeepers and other members of the Venetian bourgeoisie whose purpose ranged from assisting the poor to redeeming sinners. When the brotherhood commissioned **Jacopo Tintoretto** to decorate the interior of the building, it tied its name forever to one of the most extraordinary cycles of paintings in the history of Venice.

Start your visit on the 2nd floor. A large door on the left side of the main hall (**Salone Maggiore**, to be visited later) leads to the **Sala dell'Albergo**, the first room decorated by Tintoretto (1565). A majestic *Crucifixion* on the back wall sets the tone for Tintorettos' extraordinary exploits in the compositon of figures, in the use of light and in surprising perspectives. On the ceiling Tintoretto painted *St. Roch in Glory*, the sample work which helped him win the commission for the whole cycle (he competed against a number of painters, including **Veronese**). On the other walls of the room are *Christ in Front of Pilate*, *Ecce Home* and *Christ Carrying the Cross*. Back in the Salone Maggiore, the painting immediately at the right of the door is Tintoretto's *Self-Portrait*. The ceiling was also painted by him, with 21 canvasses depicting *Stories of the Old Testament*, while the New Testament was illustrated in the large paintings on the walls. On the long wall in front of the staircase are *The Nativ-*

ity, *The Baptism*, *The Resurrection*, *The Agony in the Garden* and *The Last Supper*; in front of the altar are *St. Sebastian* and *St. Roch*; on the entrance wall are *The Temptation of Christ*, *The Pool of Bethsheba*, *The Ascension*, *The Resurrection of Lazarus* and *The Miracle of the Loaves and Fishes*. The altarpiece, also by Tintoretto, represents *St. Roch in Glory*. Standing on easels on the sides of the altar are an *Annunciation* by **Titian** and a *Visitation* by Tintoretto; in front of the banisters, also on easels, are 2 youthful paintings by **Giambattista Tiepolo**:

Abraham with Angels and *Hagar Abandoned*. The cycle continues with 8 large canvasses in the ground floor hall (**Salone Terreno**), with stories from the life of the Virgin Mary. These were the last works executed by Tintoretto for the Brotherhood, completed when the painter was nearly 70. They are, starting from the left side: *The Annunciation*, *The Epiphany*, *The Flight into Egypt*, *The Slaughter of the Innocents*, *St. Mary Magdalen*, *St. Mary of Egypt*, *The Circumcision* and *The Assumption*. ◆ Admission. Daily 9AM-1PM, 3:30-6:30PM, Apr-Oct; M-F 10AM-1PM, Sa-Su 10AM-4PM, Nov-Mar. Campo San Rocco 3054. Vap 1, 34, San Tomà or 1, 2, 5, 34, Piazzale Roma. 5234864

24 Pizzeria San Tomà ★★$$ Set in the middle of the charming Campo San Tomà, this wonderful neighborhood restaurant serves great pizza, as well as a number of pastas and Venetian dishes. Good service too. ◆ Closed Tu. Campo San Tomá 2864-A. Vap 1, 34, San Tomà. 5238819

25 Argentiere Sfriso Mario and **Giancarlo Sfriso** are 2 excellent artisans who create elegant silver objects in their laboratory at the back of this store. Their designs are handmade with ancient tools. They vary from expensive vases and trays to affordable little souvenirs such as medals with St. Mark's lion and finely detailed miniature gondolas. ◆ Closed M morning, Su, lunch. Campo San Tomà 2849. Vap 1, 34, San Tomà. 5223558

26 Casa di Goldoni The great Venetian playwright **Carlo Goldoni** was born here in 1707. The small palazzo now houses the **Istituto di Studi Teatrali** (Institute for Theatrical Studies) with a small museum and a Theater Library open to students and scholars. ◆ M-Sa 8:30AM-1:30PM. Calle dei Nomboli 2793. Vap 1, 34, San Tomà. 5236353

Santa Croce

Seven canals come together from Canal Grande toward Campo San Polo in **Santa Croce**, in the center of which is the charming church and campo of **San Giacomo dall'Orto**. Part modern, part ancient, Santa Croce is all rather off the beaten track, making it a pleasant place to get away from the crowds snaking through the rest of Venice.

1 Piazzale Roma The closest automobiles can come to Venice is the Piazzale Roma, built in the 1930s when the railroad bridge over the lagoon was enlarged to permit access by car. This new point of entry into the city radically transformed the Venice street system; the area, peripheral and neglected before, immediately became of vital importance. The ever-increasing tourist traffic further contributed to the transformation, creating challenges which the city is still struggling with. As a result, Piazzale Roma is a chaotic traffic circle where

out-of-town automobiles drive around and around helplessly in search of nonexistent parking places. Many buses still unload their cargo of one-day visitors at the Piazzale, where they are assaulted by vendors of postcards, guidebooks and plastic gondolas. All the streets feeding into the Piazzale are lined with souvenir stands, which makes it hard to pass through. Gondoliers, taxi drivers and all sorts of middlemen offer their services to the puzzled newcomers. In the last months of 1990, the city approved legislation removing the

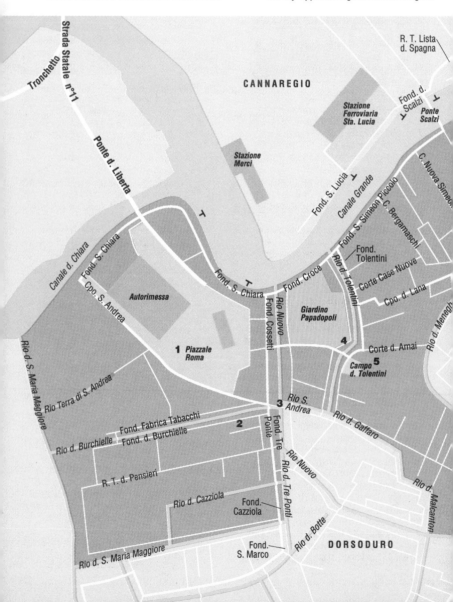

vendors to a new artificial island called **Tronchetto**, hoping that most of the middlemen would either disappear due to lack of customers or—more likely—move on to the newer pasture. Of some architectural interest in the Piazzale is the garage at the entrance (right hand corner), one of the first such buildings in Italy. ♦ Piazzale Roma. Vap 1, 2, 5, 34, Piazzale Roma

2 Trattoria Alle Burchielle ★$ The tables

along the canal make this restaurant one of the most pleasant in the area. **Bruno**, the owner, knows how to select his fish in the morning market, one reason why the place is a preferred lunch spot for gondoliers and water taxi drivers. Stick to the dishes of the day—including fish appetizers and the spaghetti with seafood. ♦ Closed M. Fondamenta Burchielle 393. Vap 1, 2, 5, 34, Piazzale Roma. 5231342

3 Tre Ponti This bridge—actually a group of 3 bridges—is one of the most complex and interesting in Venice. It was completed in 1938, when the opening of Piazzale Roma made it necessary to dig a new canal (appropriately called Rio Nuovo) to join the Canal Grande with the new automobile terminal. The Rio Nuovo, although young, is one of the most battered and fragile canals in the city. The relentless traffic of taxis and *motoscafi* (the water buses of line No. 2) causes constant erosion of the building foundations along the banks. Stretches of the canal are frequently closed to traffic in order to allow urgent repairs to underwater banks, in a frustrating fight against the laws of physics. ♦ Tre Ponti. Vap 1, 2, 5, 34, Piazzale Roma

4 Pullman Park Hotel $$$ In a city where so many hotels are in historic buildings of great architectural interest, it may not make much sense to stop at one which is modern and functional. But the location of the Park, a few steps from the car terminal at Piazzale Roma, makes it convenient for businesspeople and for one- or 2-day visitors. In addition, modernness has some definite advantages: the plumbing is flawless, the doors close properly, the floors are horizontal, and the right angles really measure 90 degrees—a rarity in Venice. Add fine service, a good restaurant, and a pleasant view over canals and gardens, and you will understand why this hotel is often booked to the brim. ♦ Giardino Papadopoli 245. Vap 1, 2, 5, 34, Piazzale Roma. 5285394; fax 5230043

5 Università di Architettura Like many Venetian institutions, the School of Architecture occupies a former convent. This one was built in the early 17th century and includes a pleasant cloister. An interesting feature is the main entrance, designed in the 1950s by Venetian architect **Carlo Scarpa**, a teacher at the school and a major contemporary Italian architect. ♦ Tolentini 191. Vap 1, 2, 5, 34, Piazzale Roma

6 Ponte de la Latte The view is very Venetian from this bridge over the **Rio Marin**, one of the

Santa Croce

most charming canals in town, and over the **Rio di San Giacomo** on the other side of the bridge. Right down the bridge is the pleasant **Caffé Orientale**. ♦ Vap 1, 2, 34, Ferrovia or 1, San Tomà

7 Palazzo Soranzo Capello Readers of **Henry James'** *The Aspern Papers* may remember the dark, labyrinhtine palace where the action took place. It was acquired by the city in 1980 and is currently being restored, while the political forces fight about its future use. ♦ Fondamenta di Ca' Gradenigo 770. Vap 1, 2, 34, Ferrovia

8 Pizzeria Alle Oche ★★$ One of the biggest secrets in Venice. This is one of the best pizza places in town. It's hard to find a free table inside, and much harder to get one in the small outdoor space. But the place is empty until 7PM or so—no Venetian would eat that early. ♦ Closed M. Calle del Tintor 1552-B. Vap 1, San Stae. 5241161

9 Teatro Anatomico The building along the canal at No. 1507 on the southwest corner of Campo San Giacomo was erected in the 17th century as a classroom for medical students to watch the dissection of corpses by their teachers. It fulfilled that function until a fire destroyed it in 1800. It was then reconstructed, though it is currently not open to visitors. ♦ Campo San Giacomo dall'Orio 1507. Vap 1, San Stae

10 Campo San Giacomo dall'Orio (or dell'Orio) Venetians call this campo **Da L'Orio** after a laurel tree (*lauro* or *lorio*) that supposedly once occupied the square. Daily life on the

island of Santa Croce centers around this square and **San Zan Degolá**. The church is run by an active and popular parish priest, who frequently organizes dances, picnics and other events here. ♦ Campo San Giacomo dall'Orio. Vap 1, San Stae

11 Chiesa di San Giacomo dall'Orio (Church of Saint James dell'Orio) (begun 10th c) The handsome exterior of this church, surrounded by the square on all sides, provides a variety of views to passersby. The main entrance is on the facade along the canal (important worshippers used to arrive by gondola); the bell tower dates back to the 13th century, as does the main apse visible at the back; and the other entrance (on the side of the **Anatomical Theater**), was re-done in the 14th century. The interior is characterized by a 14th-century wood ceiling, often used as an example of ancient building techniques; it was built like an upside-down ship hull, a natural process for Venetian carpenters, who were more accustomed to building ships than churches. The Crucifix hanging in front of the main altar is by **Paolo Veneziano**, and it was restored to its golden splendor in 1988. ♦ Campo San Giacomo dall'Orio. Vap 1, San Stae

12 Trattoria Alle Colonnette ★★$ There is nothing exceptional about the quality of the food served in this restaurant, but the pizza is good and the location is simply superb. The tables are outdoors in the little square in front of San Giacomo, right under the medieval bell tower and along a canal. Quiet, charming and inexpensive, it's no wonder that locals flock here. ♦ Closed W. Campiello del Piovan 1461. Vap 1, San Stae. No phone

13 Osteria Alla Zucca ★★$$ A group of women opened this informal, neighborhood place in the early 1970s, when feminism was (justly) raging in town. It has maintained a slightly non-comformist atmosphere, both in the clientele (bearded guru-like men, women reading horoscopes, young and old painters). The focus here is on vegetarian dishes. Quite a few professors from the nearby **School of Architecture** are among the regular customers. ♦ Closed Su. Ponte del Megio 1762. Vap 1, San Stae. 5241570

14 Campo San Zan Degolà A secret spot of the locals, who come to this little square to enjoy its magic beauty, flanked as it is by a narrow canal and adorned by a 10th-century church (the facade was re-done in the 18th century). ♦ Campo San Zan Degolà. Vap 1, San Stae

15 Museo di Storia Naturale (Natural History Museum) See the Canal Grande chapter for a description of this building, which is one of the oldest and most unusual palazzi in Venice. The best way to appreciate the splendid facade is actually from the Canal Grande or from the opposite bank. The museum includes the usual exhibitions of animals, plants and fossils, the highlights being a large dinosaur skeleton found in the Sahara desert in 1973 (the digging was financed and directed by a certain **Signor**

Ligabue, a wealthy Venetian entrepreneur), and the rooms showing animal life in the Venice lagoon. ◆ Admission. Tu-Su 9AM-1:30PM. Salizzada del Fontego dei Turchi 1730. Vap 1, San Stae. 5240885

16 Chiesa di San Stae The name is Venetian dialect for *Sant' Eustachio*. As with most Venetian churches, San Stae was remodeled at various times—the original building dates back to the 12th century. The facade, richly decorated with statues, is one of the finest examples of Venetian Baroque. The interior is particularly interesting for art historians because it includes a wealth of paintings from the first half of the 18th century. The names are not of the most famous (**Camerata, Pittoni, Bambini, Balestra**), but they illustrate the process which influenced painters like **Tiepolo** and **Piazzetta**. Actually a Piazzetta is visible on the lower left of the chancel (*The Martyrdom of St. James*) and a youthful Tiepolo on the lower right (*The Martyrdom of St. Barthelmy*). Next to the Piazzetta is a *Saint Peter Freed from Prison* by **Sebastiano Ricci**, who also painted the chancel's ceiling. Ricci was one of the painters most influential in merging the new trends developed by the Roman Baroque painters with the Venetian tradition of **Veronese**, thus opening the way to the last great season of painting in Venice. The most significant of his paintings are in the **Carmini Church**, the **San Rocco** church and the **Accademia Gallery**. ◆ Campo San Stae. Vap 1, San Stae

17 Centro Studi di Storia del Tessuto e del Costume (Center for the Study of Textile and Clothing History) This unusual center has a large collection of original textiles from the 16th, 17th and 18th centuries, together with a specialized textiles library. Scholars and students can identify the material in the library's files and ask for samples to be brought to their tables. The apartments of **Counts Mocenigo** can also be visited. ◆ Library: Tu-Th 8:30AM-2PM; Apartments: M-Sa 8:30AM-2PM. Salizzada San Stae 1992. Vap 2, San Stae. 721798

18 Campo Santa Maria Mater Domini This delightful little campo is surrounded on one side by a canal and on the other 3 sides by small Gothic palazzi that are among the most charming in Venice. **Casa Zane**, the Veneto-Byzantine-style building at No. 2172, dates back to the 13th century; across from it, at No. 2173, is **Casa Barbaro**, about one century younger; on the 4th side, at No. 2123, is **Palazzo Viaro-Zane**, built early in the 14th century (the 3rd floor was added later). The campo still gives you a glimpse of Venice as it was before the introduction of the Florentine and Roman Renaissance: smaller and more intimate buildings, grace and lightness instead of majestic corpulence. The blacksmith just down the bridge works outdoors in the summer; his ancestors are the cause of the smoky-grayness of the stones around his shop. ◆ Campo Santa Maria Mater Domini. Vap 1, San Stae

19 Museo d'Arte Moderna Ca' Pesaro Early in the 17th century, the wealthy **Pesaro** family acquired 3 adjacent buildings on the Canal Grande and asked the fashionable architect **Baldassare Longhena** to create an imposing palazzo. The result is probably the most successful among the Baroque palazzi in Venice. The facade should be seen from the Canal Grande to appreciate its grandeur and elegance. The building changed hands a few times until **Duchess Bevilacqua La Masa**, the last owner, donated it to the city in 1889. The water entrance, now little used, is marked by stairs as in a building on land. The street entrance leads to a Baroque courtyard and an 18th-century staircase. The Museum of Modern Art occupies the first 2 floors of the palazzo. The bulk of the collection consists of paintings and other works of art chosen from those exhibited at the **Venice Biennale** since its opening in 1895. It's hard to find one known painter of the 20th century who is not represented by a few works in this rich collection (although, of course, not always by his *best* works): **Vedova, Morandi, Boccioni, De Chirico, Sironi, Rosai** are just a few of the Italians, while international painters include **Chagall, Dufy, Kandinski, Klee, Ernst, Klimt** and countless others. ◆ Admission. Tu-Su

9AM-2PM. Fondamenta de Ca' Pesaro 2076. Vap 1, San Stae. 5240695

19 Museo d'Arte Orientale (Museum of Oriental Art) This museum was built around a collection of the **Duke Henry of Bourbon**, a tireless traveler and acquirer of Oriental objects. It specializes in Japanese art (particularly armors and swords), but also includes rooms devoted to India, China and Indonesia. ◆ Admission. Tu-Su 9AM-2PM. Fondamenta de Ca' Pesaro 2076. Vap 1, San Stae. 5241173

20 Hotel Ca' Favretto $$ This small, handsome, 14th-century palazzo with features dating back to the 11th century was owned by **Giacomo Favretto**, a painter in the 2nd half of the 19th century. His house has been remodeled into a hotel, though most of the older features were lost in the process. The interior now looks more like a comfortable, modern hotel than an ancient palazzo. Beautiful Gothic windows overlook the Canal Grande. This is one of the few hotels in the neighborhood, since most visitors prefer to cluster around St. Marks. ◆ Calle del Rosa 2232. Vap 1, San Stae. 721033

21 Osteria Al Non Risorto ★★★$ This old wine shop was bought and remodeled by the son of **Dino Boscarato**, one of Venice's great restaurateurs. In keeping with the shop's tradition, the restaurant is very informal, even slightly bohemian. But class with a capital C is evident in the quality of both the food and service. The side garden is heaven in the summer, scented with the perfume of a large wisteria tree. ◆ Closed Su. Sotoportego de Siora Betina. Vap 1, San Stae. 5241169

Canale d. Sacche

Sacca d.
S. Alvise

Rio d. Riformati

Rio d. Sensa

Secch

Ponte
Moro

Fond. C.
Coletti

Rio d. S. Girolamo

Fond. d. Cappuccine

Rio d. S. Alviso

Campo d.
S. Alviso

Fond. d. Sensa

C. Ferau

C. d. Madonna

Fond. d. S. Giobbe

Ponte d.
Tre Archi

25

Rio d. Torrette

C. d.
Malvasia

C. d.
Capitello

Rio Trast

Fond. d. Ormesini

Campo d.
S. Giobbe

Rio d. Battello

Campo
d. Ghetto

24

Rio d.
Lista

Canale d. Crea

Canale d. Cannareggio

Fond. Savorgnan

Fond. Pescaria

23 22

27 ✝ 26

R. T. Farsetti

Ri
Se

R.
Madda

Canale d. Crea

C. Priuli

Sal. S.
Geremia

Ponte
Guglie

R. T. S. Leonardo

Rio d. S. Marcuola

Rio d. S. Marcuola

Campo
S. Geremia

29

✝
Campo
S. Marcuola

30

28

31

R. T. Lista d. Spagna

Canale Grande

21

34 33

Stazione
Ferroviaria

Fond.
d. Scalzi

32

Ponte
Scalzi

Fond. S. Lucia

Fond. S. Simeon Piccolo

Rio Marin

Rio d. S. Zan Degola

C. Larga

Rio Fontego d. Turchi

C. d. Meglio

C. d. Tintor

Rio d. Ca' Tron

Sal. S. Stae

Rio d.
Pe

SANTA CROCE

Campo d.
S. Giacomo
d'Orio

C.
Chiesa
Ram
Regina

C. d. Chiesa

Rio d. Tolentini

Cpo. d. Lana

Rio d. S. Zuane

C. d. Laca

C. d'Olio

Rio S. Giacomo Orio

C. d.
Tintor

Rio d. S. Boldo

R. T. Secondo

Cpo. Scuola

Rio d. S. Agostino

Rio d. S. Polo

N

km
mi

1/8   1/4

1/8

Cannaregio

Except for the **Ghetto** and the bustling **Strada Nuova, Cannaregio** is largely unknown to the average visitor. This is perhaps why this *sestiere* has preserved its ancient characteristics—and characters. Parallel to the lagoon border on the north side are 3 small canals. It is hard to decide which is more charming or typically Venetian. Houses along them are usually not higher than 3 stories, bridges are tiny and often made of wood, and life goes on largely ignoring the Strada Nuova. These canals run east-west, making them a wonderful place for a stroll at sunset, when a golden light seems to fill the houses, the bridges, the water and the old wooden boats tied along the banks. At sunset, be sure to walk past the church of **Madonna dell'orto** to the vaporetto stop of the same name. It is a lonely stop, with few if any waiting passengers. It sits on the bank of the open lagoon, with **Murano** in front, **Burano** and the *terra firma* in the distance. The sun sets over the lagoon on your left, and a small sea breeze usually ripples the water. On clear days even the local commuters can't stop gazing at the most spectacular sunset in Venice.

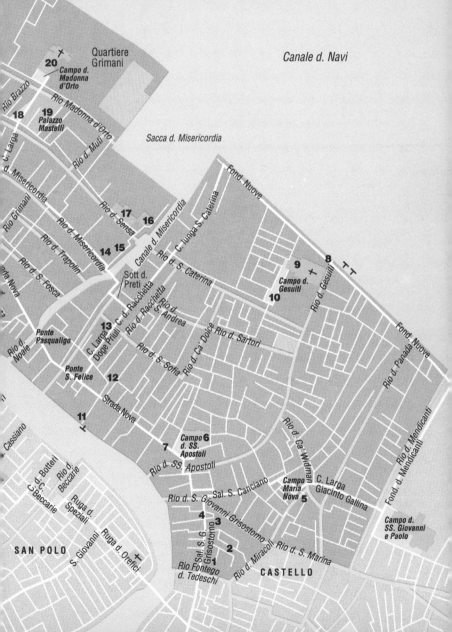

1 Magazzine Generali Coin The name has nothing to do with the English coin; it is pronounced *co-'een* and it is one of those typical Venetian last names ending in *n* because of the fall of the vowel originally at the end. Like Benetton and Stefanel, Coin is the name of a family of entrepreneurs who expanded out of the Venice area to conquer national and international markets. The largest Coin store is in Mestre, just across the lagoon bridge from Venice, while other stores are scattered throughout Italy. The one in Cannaregio, however, is probably the most elegant. It specializes in clothing and beauty accessories. Venetians are fond of it, and visitors should explore it to get an idea of the quality and prices of goods in a middle-to-high end Italian department store. ♦ Closed M morning, Su, lunch. Salizada de San Giovanni Grisostomo 5787. Vap 1, 2, 34, Rialto. 703581

2 Corti del Milion The *Milion* is the title of the book written in French by **Marco Polo** telling the story of his marvelous journeys to the Far East. The house at No. 5845 in the **Corte Seconda del Milion** is the one where Marco Polo was

Cannaregio

probably born in 1254. It has been modified many times over the centuries, but like the other houses in this little square, it preserves an unmistakably Byzantine character. Some of the window frames and columns and all of the round bas-reliefs date back to the 11th and 12th centuries. ♦ Corte Prima del Milion and Corte Seconda del Milion. Vap 1, 2, 34, Rialto

2 Ristorante Al Milion ★★$$ Informal, inexpensive and well-run, this restaurant is popular with Venetians and tourists alike. Some dishes are exactly the same as those you would find in restaurants charging 3 times the price. Try the risotto with arugula and shrimp or the filet of John Dory à la Milion. The house wine is good too. ♦ Closed W. Corte Prima del Milion 5841. Vap 1, 2, 34, Rialto. Reservations recommended. 5229302

3 Chiesa di San Giovanni Crisostomo (1497-1504, **Mauro Codussi**) This church lays at the center of a small island defined by the Canal Grande on the left and by 3 tiny, charming canals on the other sides. This was one of the first areas settled by the founders of the city and one which still maintains traces of its original Byzantine character. The church, however, is pure Venetian Renaissance, since the original structure was destroyed by a fire and entirely rebuilt by Mauro Codussi, the Lombard-born master who changed the face of Venetian architecture by introducing Renaissance

models to replace the late-Gothic tradition (see **San Michele, San Zaccaria** and **Santa Maria Formosa**). The facade has the typical Codussi design, with a full, round arch at the top and 2 half-arches at the sides. Codussi's interior is a masterpiece of clarity and simplicity. On the first altar at the right is one of the last and best paintings by **Giovanni Bellini**: *St. Christopher with St. Jerome and St. Augustine.* The canvas on the main altar is *St. John Chrysostomos with Other Saints* by **Sebastiano del Piombo**, painted by the artist when he was 25 and just before the pope summoned him to Rome and launched his brilliant career. ♦ Salizada de San Giovanni Grisostomo. Vap 1, 2, 34, Rialto

4 Fiaschetteria Toscana ★★★$$$ In spite of the name, which means Tuscan Wine Shop, this restaurant specializes in traditional Venetian cooking. Owner **Albino Busato** is the head of the association of Venetian restaurateurs and a true professional when it comes to food. Service is impeccable and the wine list is one of the best in town. Reservations are a must if you want to sit at one of the coveted tables outside in the little square. ♦ Closed Tu. San Giovanni Grisostomo 5719. Vap 1, 2, 34, Rialto. 5285281

5 Chiesa di Santa Maria dei Miracoli (Church of St. Mary of the Miracles) The particular charm of this small, human-scale

church is its location at the cross-point of 2 of the most handsome canals in Venice. One side of the church, covered with precious marbles, runs directly along the water, creating ever-changing reflections. The facade opens onto a tiny square and an equally small bridge. The creator of this jewel was **Pietro Lombardo**, one of the fathers of the Venetian Renaissance (it is possible that **Mauro Codussi** authored the original plan). Venetian couples love to use this church for weddings: the elegant, cozy interior lends itself perfectly to flowers, while the square in front is a perfect place for guests to arrive and leave on gondolas. ◆ Campiello dei Miracoli. Vap 1, 2, 34, Rialto

6 Chiesa dei Santi Apostoli The relatively high banks of the islands in this part of Venice made them one of the first places to be settled. The foundations of this church date back to the 7th century; however, its present shape is due to a radical renovation in the 17th century. Inside, the first chapel at the right is the **Cappella Corner**, attributed to **Mauro Codussi** and adorned with *The Communion of St. Lucy*, one of **Giambattista Tiepolo**'s best paintings. ◆ Campo Santi Apostoli. Vap 1, 2, 34, Rialto or 1, Ca' d'Oro

7 Strada Nuova The **Campo Santi Apostoli** marks the beginning of this long, wide (for Venice) and unusually straight street. It runs parallel to the **Canal Grande** from Santi Apostoli to **Campo Santa Fosca**, crossing 2 canals and continuing with the relatively wide **Rio Terrá Maddelena** and **Rio Terrá San Leonardo**. The street was designed and built in the 2nd half of the 19th century, and it represents one of the few attempts to rationalize pedestrian circulation in Venice. The problem was the connection of the central Rialto and St. Mark's areas with the new train station, which had joined Venice to the mainland for the first time in the city's history. Among the many proposals, the one that was finally chosen was probably the least damaging for the existing urban structure. Still, it meant the destruction of a large and ancient neighborhood, characterized by tiny alleys and teeming with daily life. All buildings in the way of the new thoroughfare were destroyed, and new facades were erected along its perfectly straight, totally un-Venetian sides. The residents showed their disapproval by refusing to call the new street by the name proposed by its builders, calling it Strada Nuova instead, making this the only Strada (*Street*) in Venice. Today, the steady flow of one-day tourists arriving by train use the Strada extensively; there is a lot of pedestrian traffic toward Rialto in the morning, toward the train station in the afternoon. As a consequence, gift and souvenir shops have proliferated, making this the kingdom of the Venice T-shirt and the plastic gondola. A few yards away, on the side opposite the Canal Grande, the city remains blessedly deserted and perfectly charming, with the old labyrinth of *calli* (the local word for *street*), bridges and porticos. ◆ Strada Nova. Vap 1, Ca' d'Oro or San Marcuola

8 Fondamente Nuove The word *fondamente* is used in Venice for the banks of all canals and of the open lagoon. The borders of the natural islands were—and still are—reinforced with foundations made of wood poles and stone in order to prevent erosion by the waves and tides. The long banks called Fondamente Nuove were built in the 16th century as part of a reclamation effort involving the whole north-eastern part of the city. Way out of the typical tourist tracks (except for the small part used by vaporettos to and from Murano, Torcello and other islands), they constitute a splendid, although somehow melancholy, walk, particu-larly during the long summer evenings. The island right in front, recognizable by its cypress trees, is **San Michele**, site of the Venice cem-etery. Further ahead are **Murano** and, far back, the slanted bell tower of **Burano**. In winter it is not unusual to see all the way to the mainland and to the snow-capped mountains of the Alps. There is a canal along the fondamente for boat traffic. Beyond the canal, marked by the typical wood poles called *bricole*, the lagoon is not deeper than 3 feet, thus motor boats can cross it only at high tide. A walk of an hour along the fondamente is a romantic experience and a way to see the daily rituals of Venetian life—during the day, heavy boats pass by, carrying goods to be distributed all over town, while on Sundays and in the evenings, a surprising number of row boats cross the area, with

Venetians doing their equivalent of jogging. More and more frequent are the flat-bottomed sail boats. These old-fashioned crafts with balanced lug sails are ideal for the flat lagoon waters and have recently been rediscovered by Venetians after a long period of neglect due to the popularity of power boats. ◆ Fondamente Nuove. Vap 5, Fondamente Nuove

9 Chiesa dei Gesuiti (Church of the Jesuits) (13th c) When it was readmitted to Venice after a 50-year banishment in 1657, the Jesuit order took over this church, overlooking the beautiful lagoon toward the cemetery and Murano. The Jesuits then proceeded to rebuild the church according to their well-established standards of grandeur in the international Baroque style they had successfully experimented with in Rome (Chiesa del Gesú), Paris (St. Paul) and all over Europe. The facade is tall and em-phatic, with the Jesuit trademark of columns on 2 levels. It is topped by Baroque statues with limbs reaching toward the sky and typical Baroque poses. But the real magnificence is in the interior, which is decorated with a stunning wealth of marble carved to imitate damasks and draperies. White and green marble covers most of the walls, falling in rich folds like real drapery material and creating an effect which, depending on the viewers' mood, could be thought of as marvelous or kitsch. The canvas on the first altar at the right is *The Martyrdom* *of Saint Lawrence*, a masterwork painted by **Titian** on his return from a trip to Rome (the Classical architecture in the background is not typical of Titian). A recent cleaning, done for the Titian exhibition in Venice and Washington in 1990, brought out the fine details included in this nighttime scene, where the only sources of light are the burning coals under the martyr's body and the divine rays breaking through thick, black clouds in the sky. The painting immediately became famous. A copy was made by Titian himself for **Philip II** of Spain, and a popular engraving, approved by Titian, soon circulated all over Europe. ♦ Campo dei Gesuiti. Vap 5, Fondamente Nuove.

10 Oratorio dei Crociferi The *Crociferi* were an old monastic order that originally owned this entire area, including the square in front of the Oratory, the church, and the large building at the church's right (originally their monastery). The Oratory was an extra chapel. Restored in the 1980s, it contains a cycle of paintings by **Palma il Giovane**, who is considered the heir of **Titian** and the best painter of Venetian Mannerism. Palma's works, which mark the passage between the late-Renaissance and Baroque periods, are found throughout Venice. ♦ F-Su 10AM-noon, Apr-June and Oct; F-Su 4:30-6:30PM, July-Sep. Campo dei Gesuiti 4903-5. Vap 5, Fondamente Nuove. To confirm schedule, call 5200633

Cannaregio

11 Ca' d'Oro e Galleria Franchetti (1421-40, **Matteo Revesti**) The facade of this splendid building, universally considered a masterwork of Venetian Gothic, should be seen from the Canal Grande. In striking contrast with Medieval building principles, the Venetian palazzi have light facades made of carved stone, with ample loggias and open spaces between slender columns. Nothing could be farther from the austere, almost hostile, appearance of the palazzi of Florence, but then leading Florentine families were constantly fighting each other and needed to build their homes like fortresses, while the Venetian constitution guaranteed total peace within the city limits (there are no examples of armed feuds among leading families nor of any popular insurrection during the millenium of the Republic's life). Hence the open loggias, the ample windows and the very fragility of the Venetian facades— perhaps more an act of faith in the Republic than an esthetic choice. In the Ca' d'Oro, the central part of the facade can be seen as a unique window, made precious by the lacework applied to the stones. Originally the facade was decorated in red and blue and trimmed with gold leaf, which gave the palazzo its name, **House of Gold**. The building changed hands a number of times after it was built in 1440, until it was acquired by a Russian prince who presented it to an Italian ballerina in 1840. Later it passed on to **Baron Giorgio Franchetti**, who restored it and

bequeathed it to the city of Venice. The interior was restored again in the 1970s, and in 1991, work has begun to restore the foundations. The **Art Gallery** was built around a central core also bequeathed by Baron Franchetti and reorganized in 1984. On the 2nd floor is an extraordinary collection of early Venetian and Byzantine bas-reliefs in stone, dating from the 11th to 13th centuries. They were used to decorate the facades of public and private buildings, and they exhibit a delightful sense of symmetry and grace. A niche in Room No. 1 contains a famous *St. Sebastian* by **Andrea Mantegna**. Through the splendid, sun-lit ballroom, one can reach the loggia on the Canal Grande and enjoy the view over a long stretch of the Canal and the fish market on the other side. Room No. 3 contains medals and bronzes of the Renaissance and Room No. 6 a fine collection of minor Italian painters, mostly Tuscans. On the 3rd floor, Room No. 9 contains a *Venus at the Mirror* by **Titian**, and 2 remarkable portraits of gentlemen, one by **Tintoretto** and one by **Anthony Van Dyck**. Collected in Room No. 16 are the few remnants of the frescoes which used to cover the **Fontego dei Tedeschi** (Germans' Warehouse) on the Canal Grande. Although barely recognizable, they have an emotional impact on art lovers because they are by **Giorgione** and by Titian, who worked almost shoulder to shoulder on the same facade. Other items of interest on this floor include **Bernini**'s preparatory work for his famous fountain on **Piazza Navona** in Rome and 2 *Views of Venice* by **Francesco Guardi**. ♦ Admission. M-Sa 9AM-2PM; Su 9AM-1PM. Calle Ca' d'Oro 3932. Vap 1, Ca' d'Oro

12 Trattoria Dalla Vedova ★★$$ Old bare wood tables, antique furniture and total informality characterize this most venerable among Venetian *bacari*. The owners have retained the original atmosphere of a working-class wine shop, with ready-made food available at the counter to accompany the drinks. An eclectic group of wealthy Venetians, gondoliers and hard-hats frequent the place. A little English is spoken by the owners, who have been serving tourists for years. Upon entering, check the counter for the choice of food, but ask about what's cooking as well—it may be worth sipping your wine for a few minutes while the risottos, spaghetti or *pasta e fagioli* receive their final touches. The official name of the place, written on top of the door, is **Trattoria Ca' d'Oro**, but all Venice knows it as Dalla Vedova (at the widower's). ♦ Closed Th. Ramo Ca' d'Oro 3912. Vap 1, Ca' d'Oro. Reservations for large groups. 5285324

13 Trattoria All'Antica Adelaide ★★$$ Also informal, this trattoria lost some of its old charm when **Gianni**, the owner's son, brought in brand new wood tables to increase the seating in the large dining room. But in the summer, dining moves outdoors to a lovely courtyard— a decided advantage over the rival **Dalla Vedova** mentioned above. Among the many seafood dishes, we recommend the grilled *mazzancolle* (jumbo shrimp). But the owner, Gianni's mother, is a virtuoso of Venetian cooking, and if money is no object, call her to your table to see what she recommends that day. ♦ Closed M. Calle Racchetta. Vap 1, Ca' d'Oro. 5203451

14 Fondamenta della Misericordia The name of this canal bank changed 5 times before ending in the northwest area called **Sant'Alvise**. A walk along this stretch gives you a glimpse of the quiet, old-fashioned charm of the area. ♦ Fondamenta della Misericordia. Vap 1, Ca' d'Oro or 5, Madonna dell'Orto

15 Scuola Nuova della Misericordia (1583, **Jacopo Sansovino**) The building, unusually tall for this part of town, was designed by Sansovino for a local brotherhood and was never completed. The interior, also by Sansovino, has been neglected by the city—for 50 years, until 1990, the grandiose hall on the 2nd floor was used as a playing field, with seats for hundreds of spectators right under the decaying 16th-century frescoes. A fondamenta along the building's right side leads to the **Ponte dell'Abbazia**, with a charming view over the Canale della Misericordia and the open lagoon at the right. ♦ Fondamenta della Misericordia 3599. Vap 1, Ca' d'Oro

16 Chiesa di Santa Maria Valverde (begun 14th c) The name of this church means Church of Santa Maria in the Green Valley, which derives from the original landscape of this area, which was probably once covered with vegetable gardens. Secluded as it seems to be on the water's edge, with canals in front and on the right side, this small, delightful church used to be the main chapel for the friars of the nearby abbey (see the **Scuola vecchia della Misericordia**). The facade, designed by **Clemente Moli**, is a remarkable example of elegant, sober Baroque architecture. The statue over the portal is not, as one would expect, the portrait of a saint but, more realistically, a monument to **Gaspare Moro**, the patrician who financed the works on the facade. ♦ Campo de l'Abbazia. Vap 1, Ca' d'Oro

17 Scuola vecchia della Misericordia (15th c) The **Brotherhood of Mercy** was an association of laymen connected to the abbey by the same name, which is attached to the Scuola along the canal called **Rio de la Sensa**. The late-Gothic facade of the Scuola, at right angles with the Baroque church of Santa Maria Valverde, completes one of the most pleasant little squares in Venice. Today the Scuola and the connected abbey belong to the city and house one of the most advanced centers for stone restoration in the world. Peep through the small door on the Rio de la Sensa to see the large garden, behind which are the sophisticated laboratories where international experts examine stones and marbles from monuments all over the world, studying their composition and figuring out how to preserve them.
♦ Campo de l'Abbazia 3551. Vap 1, Ca' d'Oro

18 Campo dei Mori (Square of the Moors) Four merchants of Arabic origin—and ancestors of the **Mastelli** family—had their headquarters in this part of town in the 12th century. They are portrayed, turban and all, in 4 statues (3 on the square and one along the prospicient canal).
♦ Campo dei Mori. Vap 1, Ca' d'Oro or 5, Madonna dell'Orto

19 Palazzo Mastelli (Mastelli Palace) The Mastelli family had this palazzo built in the 12th century. Some remnants of the original Byzantine decorations are still visible, but the most admired feature is the large stone camel on the facade along the canal—a reminder of the origin of the family's wealth. On the same facade, a Gothic balcony sits curiously on top of a Renaissance first floor, in an unusual reversal of history. Look at the palazzo from the fondamenta across the canal. ♦ Fondamenta Gasparo Contarini 3527. Vap 5, Madonna dell'Orto

20 Chiesa della Madonna dell'Orto (15th c) This most sober yet pleasing of Gothic churches opens onto a lovely, well-proportioned square along the quiet canal with the same name. The statues in the beautiful niches over the sides represent the 12 apostles. The 4 statues at the very top represent the Virgin Mary and the Four Evangelists. Inside is a surprising wealth of first-class paintings. At the first altar on the right is one of the most beautiful paintings by **Cima da Conegliano**, *St. John the Baptist with Four Saints*, in which the 34-year-old artist, just after his arrival in Venice from his native village of Conegliano, dared to replace the traditional gold background—or the more recent perspectives of Classical buildings—with a landscape of the beautiful hills where he had grown up. The first altar on the left contains a jewel by **Giovanni Bellini**, a *Virgin Mary with Child* which epitomizes Bellini's craft in the painting of Madonnas. On the apse and behind the altar is a group of large canvasses by **Jacopo Tintoretto**, who lived near the church (at No. 3399 on Fondamenta dei Mori) and is buried inside it, in the last chapel on the right. On the left wall of the chancel is Tintoretto's gigantic *Adoration of the Golden Calf*, a painting strangely and dramatically divided into 3 horizontal sections. Behind the

altar Tintoretto painted *The Martyrdom of St. Christopher* and *The Apparition of the Cross to St. Peter*. On the right wall is another huge canvas, *The Last Judgement*, with Christ and the Virgin Mary surrounded by Angels and Saints while a stormy whirlpool carries away the damned souls, with Charon's boat appearing on a background of fire. Tintoretto's *Presentation of the Virgin to the Temple*, on the right side over the door to the last chapel before the chancel, is also dramatically beautiful.
♦ Campo de La Madonna dell 'Orto. Vap 5, Madonna dell'Orto

21 Palazzo Vendramin Calergi (15th c) The facade of this palazzo should be seen from the Canal Grande. It represents the first great achievement of **Mauro Codussi**, the artist who changed Venetian architecture by abandoning the Gothic tradition for the new Renaissance style popular in Florence and Rome. **Richard Wagner** lived in this palazzo and died here in 1883. Today it belongs to the city of Venice and is used in the winter for the Casino (in the summer the Casino moves to the Lido). From October to early May, thousands of gamblers flock to the Casino, one of only 4 allowed by the Italian legislation on national territory. A couple of dozen roulette tables are installed in the Renaissance rooms, with bets from 10,000 lire up; baccarat and black-jack tables are also available. A few water taxis are always stationed at the door at night, ready to take the

Cannaregio

winners to their cars parked on Piazzale Roma—the losers can take a 20-minute walk.
♦ Canal Grande/Fondamenta Vendramin 2400

22 Campo del Ghetto A look at the map shows how perfectly this small island lent itself to housing a community separate from the rest of the city. Heavy doors were built at the end of the only 2 bridges, and they were closed at sunset and reopened on the following morning. Jews in Venice were *assigned* this space in the 16th century and were allowed to move out of it only when young **Napoleon** conquered the Republic. The *ghetto* in the square's name comes from a foundry (*ghetto* in Italian) that was located here. The name spread throughout the world from here. Jews of many nationalities moved to the area, particularly after they were banished from Spain in 1492. They spoke German, Spanish, Italian and a variety of Oriental languages; and though they were accepted as permanent residents, they were subjected to a series of hard conditions and were under constant threat of expulsion. They were not allowed to own any land or buildings; they could not practice any professions except for the sale of used clothes (also medicine, at times); and above all they were obliged to run 3 pawn shops at impossibly low interest rates—an absolute requirement in order to avoid expulsion. The pawn shops took heavy losses and Jewish communities from all over Europe had to chip in frequently in order to keep them open. The

houses on the small island were built around a central square, and as new families came in, extra floors were added to the buildings. Today the square is a wide and peaceful space, ideal for the neighborhood children to play in while mothers watch from their apartment windows. Although many Jewish families still live on the square, only a kosher baker and a couple of souvenir shops are left from the colorful mixture of languages and nationalities that used to fill this area. ♦ Campo del Ghetto Nuovo. Vap 1, San Marcuola

23 Museo di Arte Ebraica (Museum of Jewish Art) Four centuries of Jewish life in the Venice ghetto left important traces, and precious books, tapestries, jewels and sacred articles are collected in this small museum. ♦ Admission. M-F 10:30AM-5PM; Su 10:30AM-1PM; closed on Jewish holidays. Campo del Ghetto Nuovo 2902 B. Vap 1, San Marcuola

23 Synagogues on the Campo del Ghetto Nuovo Of the 5 synagogues in this area, 3 opened directly onto this square. They were the **Sculoa Grande Tedesca** (Great German School), the **Scuola del Canton** (School of the Corner, so-called probably because of its location) and the **Scuola Italiana** (Italian School). They can be visited during museum hours (see the Museo di Arte Ebraica), with a guide provided by the museum. ♦ Campo del Ghetto Nuovo 2902-B. Vap 1, San Marcuola

24 Ristorante All'Antica Mola ★★$$ A few steps from the Càmpo del Ghetto, this used to be an *osteria* (wine shop), strictly for the people of the neighborhood. Transformed into a restaurant in the 1980s, it has kept its old-fashioned character, with large, unpretentious wooden tables, informal service and reasonable prices. The menu is based on traditional Venetian dishes—try the *baccalá alla Vicentina* or the *spaghetti con caparossoli*, a local clam, served in the shell. ♦ Closed Sa. Fondamenta dei Ormesini 2800. Vap 1, San Marcuola or 5, Sant 'Alvise. 717492

25 Ristorante Al Bacco ★★★$$$ At the end of the handsome Fondamenta dei Ormesini (where it changes its name into Fondamenta Cappuccine), this restaurant has grown from a local wine shop into a well-respected ristorante. The atmosphere is still that of an old *osteria*, with uncovered wood tables and wood panels on the walls, but the food is superior, specializing in fish and original pasta dishes. After dinner, take a walk along the canal all the way to La Misericordia: the street is quiet—almost deserted—with long rows of boats tied along the canal and frequent bridges. A small detour will take you to such splendid sites as La Madonna dell'Orto and the church of Santa Maria Valverde. ♦ Closed M. Fondamenta Cappuccine 3054. Vap 1, San Marcuola or 5, Sant 'Alvise. 717493

26 Scuola Levantina This Synagogue is on a little square outside the original island of the Ghetto, on a little piazza called Campiello delle Scuole. The exterior was designed in the 17th century, probably by **Baldassare Longhena**; the interior was decorated with astonishingly beautiful wood carvings by **Andrea Brustolon**, the finest Venetian cabinet-maker of the 18th century. Visits can be arranged at the Museo di Arte Ebraica. ♦ Campiello de Le Scuole 1228. Vap 1, San Marcuola

27 Scuola Spagnola This synagogue, also on the little Campiello delle Scuole, is the largest and most interesting of all. It was redesigned in the 17th century by **Baldassare Longhena**, and the interior decorations are mostly from the 18th century. Visits can be arranged through the Museo di Arte Ebraica. ♦ Campiello de Le Scuole 1146. Vap 1, San Marcuola

28 Palazzo Labia (1720, **Andrea Cominelli**) The wealthy Labia family built this sumptuous home with 3 facades: one on the Canal Grande, one on the Canal de Cannaregio and a 3rd one on the Campo San Geremia. Legend has it that when the palazzo opened, Signore Labia stood at a balcony and proceeded to throw precious pieces of silverware into the canal one by one: *L'abbia o non l'abbia, saró sempre un Labia*, he is reported to have said (*Have it or not, I will always be a Labia*). The interior saloons were frescoed by **Giambattista Tiepolo** and can be visited upon request. Today the palace belongs to the Venice headquarters of RAI, the Italian radio and television network. Production studios as well as offices were installed in the countless rooms, while the Tiepolo halls are frequently used for meetings and conferences —often with protests from the Art Conservation Department. ♦ Campo San Geremia 275. Vap 1, 2, 34, Ferrovia

29 Lista di Spagna The **Spanish Embassy** used to be on this street, at Palazzo Zeno (No. 168). Like most embassies, it was far from the city's center, as though to keep foreigners removed from the Republic's heart (members of the Venetian nobility were forbidden to even to *talk* to representatives of foreign powers, except in an official capacity, and in the theaters and casinos, government spies would denounce patricians simply for greeting or nodding to foreign ministers). The Lista is the most un-Venetian of Venetian streets. It is the only part of town where neon signs are allowed, and the proximity of the train station has turned it into a bazaar for cheap souvenirs. ♦ Lista di Spagna. Vap 1, 2, 34, Ferrovia

30 Hotel Amadeus $$$ This hotel was totally renovated in 1989. It is located 200 yards from the train station and is easy to reach from the garages of Piazzale Roma.  Rooms are large and decorated with 18th century-style furniture. There is also a small private garden and 2 restaurants. The service is impeccable. ♦ Lista di Spagna 227. Vap 1, 2, 34, Ferrovia. 715300; fax 5240841

31 Hotel Abbazia $$ The only shortcoming of this hotel is the tiny alley where its entrance is located—near the side of the train station, it looks a bit depressing at times. But the interior is a pleasant surprise. The hotel was once occupied by a monastery, built in the 19th century for the monks of the Scalzi church. It was totally renovated in 1988. The rooms are in striking contrast with one's idea of a monk's cell—they are large and comfortable. The monastery atmosphere has been skillfully preserved, and a large garden allows for relaxation in the warm weather. ♦ Calle Priuli 66. Vap 1, 2, 34, Ferrovia. 717333

32 Ponte degli Scalzi When the trains started to arrive in Venice in 1841, a bridge over the Canal Grande across from the station became a necessity. French architect **A.E. Neville**, a famous builder of iron bridges and the designer of the **Accademia Bridge**, produced another one of his striking creations: a suspended iron bridge (it was his 38th), reminiscent of such structures as the Eiffel Tower and the Brooklyn Bridge. It contrasted sharply with the Venetian environment, and in 1934 the city decided to demolish it (together with the Accademia Bridge), replacing it with the present structure. At the Accademia, no agreement was reached about style or shape; thus a temporary wood bridge was built and is still there. ♦ Ponte degli Scalzi. Vap 1, 2, 34, Ferrovia

Cannaregio

33 Chiesa degli Scalzi (17th c, **Baldassare Longhena**) The *barefooted friars* are an ancient monastic order which settled in Venice in the 17th century. Their church was designed by Longhena in a style reminiscent of the Roman Baroque; the facade was added by **Giuseppe Sardi** in 1680. The main altar is a Baroque masterpiece, also Roman by inspiration, by **Giuseppe Pozzo**; the ceiling was originally frescoed by **Giambattista Tiepoli**, but was destroyed during WWI bombing. A Tiepolo fresco remains in the vault in the 2nd chapel on the right (*St. Theresa in Glory*), and 2 more, of lesser importance, are in the vault in the first chapel on the left. ♦ Fondamenta dei Scalzi. Vap 1, 2, 34, Ferrovia

34 Stazione Ferroviaria The present structure was erected in 1954 to replace the original station, built under the Austrian domination in 1841. All main vaporetto ines are conveniently located down the steps: on the right is the stop for line No. 1 (Canal Grande to the Lido), on the left line No. 2 (express line to Rialto and to the Lido) and at the far left, after the foot of the bridge, line No. 5 (circular line to Giudecca and Murano). ♦ Fondamenta Santa Lucia. Vap 1, 2, 34, Ferrovia

Venice has been painted and described many thousands of times, and of all cities in the world it is the easiest to visit without going there.

Henry James

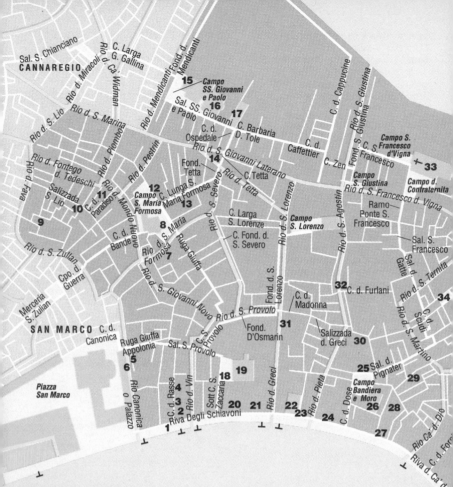

Castello

Castello is the oldest and one of the largest *sestiere* in Venice. More than half of it is taken up by the **Arsenale**, once the main source of its wealth and military power. The densely populated area around the Arsenale was largely built by the old oligarchy to house the Arsenale's workers and sailors at the end of their adventurous lives at sea. The orderly rows of small homes, often embellished with Gothic arches and windows around **Campo Do Pozzi** and on both sides of **Via Garibaldi** are examples of far-sighted urban planning dating from the 13th century. People on the eastern part of Castello still live a quiet neighborhood existence. Bakeries, fish shops and vegetable stands have yet to disappear in favor of shops selling masks or Murano glass, primarily because the train station and parking lots are at the opposite end of town. However it has become an increasingly interesting area for dining. The western part of Castello is rich in palazzi and monuments. It centers around 3 magnificent squares—**San Zaccaria**, **Santi Giovanni e Paolo** and **Santa Maria Formosa**. The narrowness of the land in central Castello makes it very easy to reach the lagoon on both the north and south sides. Perhaps that is why the residents are passionate boat lovers, crowding both banks of the canals with their craft ready to take them to the lagoon islands of **Torcello** and **Sant'Erasmo**.

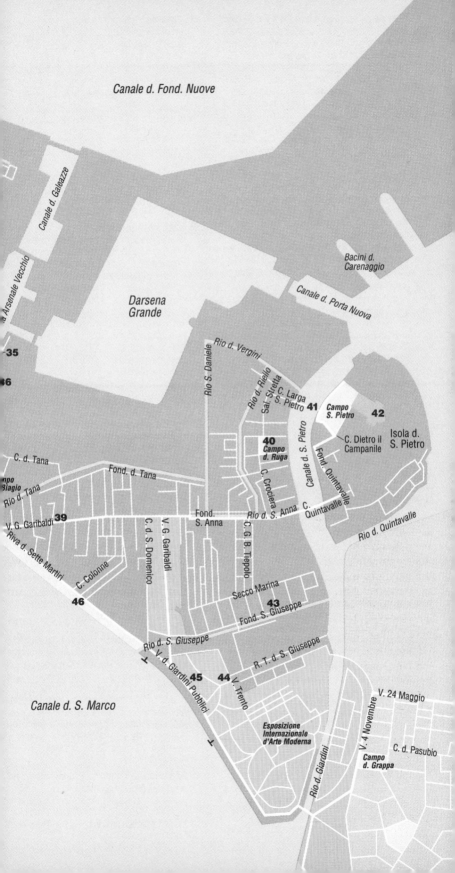

Canale d. Fond. Nuove

Canale d. Galeazze

a Arsenale Vecchio

Bacini d.
Carenaggio

Canale d. Porta Nuova

Darsena
Grande

35

36

Rio d. Vergini

Rio S. Daniele

Rio d. Rielio

Sal. Stretta

C. Larga
S. Pietro

41

Campo
S. Pietro

42

Isola d.
S. Pietro

40
*Campo
d. Ruga*

C. Dietro il
Campanile

Canale S. Pietro

Fond Quintavalle

C. d. Tana

Fond. d. Tana

npo
Biagio

Rio d. Tana

C. Crociera

C.
Quintavalle

Rio d. Quintavalle

V. G. Garibaldi

39

Fond.
S. Anna

Rio d. S. Anna

Riva d. Sette Martiri

C. d. S. Domenico

V. G. Garibaldi

C. G. B. Tiepolo

Secco Marina

46

C. Colonne

43
Fond. S. Giuseppe

Rio d. S. Giuseppe

R. T. d. S. Giuseppe

V. d. Giardini Pubblici

45

44

V. Trento

V. 24 Maggio

Canale d. S. Marco

Esposizione
Internazionale
d'Arte Moderna

V. 4 Novembre

C. d. Pasubio

Rio d. Giardini

Campo
d. Grappa

1 Riva degli Schiavoni and Riva dei Sette Martiri These are the most splendid embankments in town. The *Riva* (bank) extends from St. Mark's Square all the way to the eastern end of Venice. On this bank the Slavonians (*Schiavoni*) were allowed to tie their commercial boats (the *Sette Martiri* stretch derives its name from an episode of the anti-fascist civil war, when 7 partisans were captured and executed by the Germans). There is no better way to experience the peculiar nature of Venice than by taking this 20-minute walk at sunset. Tourists rarely wander beyond the first 300 or 400 yards of the walk; after that, only locals populate the wide banks along the lagoon. Water buses, row boats and enormous cruising ships share the water space. At sunset, lights turn on at the top of the wood poles marking the deep canals in the lagoon flats, while the sun sets magnificently behind La Salute at the Canal Grande's entrance. ♦ Riva degli Schiavoni. Vap 1, 2, 5, 6, 8, 34, San Zaccaria

2 Hotel Danieli $$$$ Set in the 15th-century Palazzo Dandolo, this hotel is the most illustrious in Venice. Opened in 1822, it hosted countless celebrities, including **Honoré de Balzac, Charles Dickens, Gabrielle D'Annunzio** and **Richard Wagner**. In one of its rooms the French author **George Sand** started an affair with an Italian physician, who later became her companion, by stroking his foot while her then-lover **Alfred de Musset** wasn't looking. In 1948 a plain modern annex was added to the hotel, something many Venetians still cannot accept. Suites and waterfront rooms are very comfortable, while some back rooms and those in the

Castello

annex may not be worth the price. The hall is 19th-century Neo-Gothic, a curious feature in Venice. It has a piano bar open to non-guests from 10PM to 2AM. Breakfast on the rooftop terrace is delightful. ♦ Riva degli Schiavoni 4196. Vap 1, 2, 5, 6, 8, 34, San Zaccaria. 5226480; fax 5200208

3 Calle delle Rasse With their open windows filled with fresh fish and live lobsters, the restaurants on this street look very inviting. But be sure to look at the fine print on the menus—many of the prices are listed per hundred grams rather than per portion. ♦ Calle della Rasse. Vap 1, 2, 5, 6, 8, 34, San Zaccaria

4 Bar Penasa A popular watering hole for gondoliers, shopkeepers, passersby and a few tourists in the know. A large variety of *panini* (sandwiches) are displayed at the counter. Good beer and wine, plus espresso and cappuccino. A set of tables and chairs (not always found in Venice's cafes) offers a welcome respite for walkers. ♦ Closed W. Calle delle Rasse 4585. Vap 1, 2, 5, 6, 8, 34, San Zaccaria. No credit cards. 5237202

5 Jesurum The ancient art of making lace used to have its center on the nearby island of Burano. After a long period of decline, it was resurrected on the same island through the efforts of **Michele Jesurum** in the 2nd half of the 19th century. This showroom occupies the premises of a former church built in the 12th century. Next to intricate and expensive laces, the shop sells more affordable items, all handmade. ♦ Closed Su. Ponte Canonica 4310. Vap 1, 2, 5, 6, 8, 34, San Zaccaria. 706177

6 Sant'Apollonia Monastery (13th c) The gem of this compound, a former Benedictine monastery, is the 13th-century cloister, restored in 1969. Its Romanesque style is rare in Venice. The stones around the cloister are mostly fragments of decorations from the original St. Mark's Basilica (9th-11th centuries). On the 2nd floor, the **Museum of Sacred Art** houses a collection of paintings and objects from churches now closed or destroyed. ♦ M-Sa 10:30AM-12:30PM. Fondamenta Sant'Apollonia. Vap 1, 2, 5, 6, 8, 34, San Zaccaria. 5529166

7 Biblioteca Querini Stampalia (Querini Stampalia Library) (early 16th c) The **Querini** were one of the most ancient and powerful families in Venice. In 1207 they became lords of **Stampalia**, an island they conquered for Venice on the Aegean Sea. Among the many branches of the family, the one residing in this palazzo was the richest, although they never had a Doge. The last scion of the family, **Count Giovanni Querini**, bequeathed the building to the city in 1869 to be used as a public library and art gallery. In 1959-63 the ground floor was redesigned by the brilliant Venetian architect **Carlo Scarpa**. The 2nd floor is taken up by the library, an extremely important institution in Venice and the only library open in the evening. Generations of college students have prepared for their examinations by sitting shoulder to shoulder at the ancient tables, ignoring the squeaky floors, the gloomy mythological paintings on the walls, and the sounds of the gondola serenades for tourists drifting in through the giant windows from the canal. On the 2nd floor is a **Pinacoteca** (art collection) specializing mostly in minor Venetian painters and known for its collection of canvasses by 18th-century painter **Pietro Longhi** representing scenes of Venetian life. ♦ Library: M-Sa 2:30-11:15PM; Su 3-6:45PM. Gallery: Admission. Tu-Su 10AM-12:30PM. Campiello Querini 4778. Vap 1, 2, 34, San Marco or Rialto. 5202433

8 Santa Maria Formosa *Formosa* means *very good looking*, with connotations of Junonic plumpness, as was the Virgin Mary who appeared to a Venetian bishop in AD 639, ordering him to have a church built in her name. The present shape of the church is due to **Mauro Codussi**, the great early Renaissance architect in Venice. It is surprising that there are no saints or prophets on the facade, but instead statues of gentlemen, obviously not dressed as religious leaders. They are members of the powerful **Cappello** family who financed the building of the church. The habit of adorning churches with portraits of donors was common in Venice, contributing to the puzzling mixture of sacred and profane elements so typical all over town. The church's interior, after some incongruous modifications in the 19th century, was redesigned according to Codussi's plans in 1921. ♦ Campo Santa Maria Formosa. Vap 1, 2, 34, Rialto

9 Santa Maria della Fava The name of this church may derive from an ancient grocery store, now long gone, specializing in beans (*fava*), or from the last name of a wealthy family living nearby. The building is a fine example of Venetian architecture of the 18th century, a time when, in spite of political and economic decay, the Republic was still investing enormous funds in public and private buildings. At least 49 new churches were built in the 18th century, while many others were restored and modified, most often through private contributions by wealthy families. The final plans for this church were drawn by **Giorgio Massari**, the architect of **Gesuati** and **La Pietà**. The church contains 2 masterworks of 18th-century painting: a *Madonna with St. Filippo Neri* (1727) by **Giambettista Piazzetta** (2nd altar on the left) and a *Virgin as a Child with St. Anne and St. Joachim* (1732) by **Giambettista Tiepoli** (first altar on the right). The former is a product of Piazzetta in his full maturity; the latter is one of the first great works by young Tiepolo. Together they represent the last great flourishing of Venetian painting. The beautiful 18th-century organ is used every Sunday at 10:30AM to accompany the Mass service with Baroque music. ♦ Campo della Fava. Vap 1, 2, 34, Rialto

10 Salizzada San Lio This rather narrow street is busy with locals doing their shopping, as it has been since time immemorial. It still has some good examples of early vernacular architecture. The narrow facade next to the arch at Nos. 5691-5705 is an intact 13th- or 14th-century home; and the small palazzo at Nos. 5662-5672 dates back to the 13th century (the 2nd-floor window to the right of the arch may belong to the 12th century). Each of the buildings may have consisted of 2 turret-like homes united by a pointed arch. The original windows in both buildings have the typical Byzantine shape (round arches pointed at the top and elongated at the base)—a shape which could naturally evolve into the Gothic arch.
♦ Salizzada San Lio. Vap 1, 2, 34, Rialto

11 Calle del Paradiso An example of urban planning of the 15th century, when grace and functionalism didn't seem to be at odds with one another. The 2 rows of homes still have shops on the ground floor. To make the upstairs apartments a bit larger, and also to protect the street from rain, the top floors were made to protrude with a typical Venetian feature called *barbacani*; those on this street are original. The Gothic archways at both ends of the street date from the14th century, and the house on the canal-side features Byzantine windows from the 12th century. ♦ Calle del Paradiso. Vap 1, 2, 34, Rialto

12 Campo Santa Maria Formosa This square, one of the most spacious in Venice, is a real anthology of architectural styles and periods. **Palazzo Vitturi** (No. 5246) is one of the best examples of 13th-century Byzantine architecture; the **Palazzi Doná** (Nos. 6123-6126) include 2 fine Gothic buildings dating from the 14th century; **Casa Venier** (No. 6129) is a delightful Gothic home from the end of the 15th century; **Palazzo Ruzzini-Priuli** (No. 5866) is 16th-century Renaissance. Radial streets connect this pivotal square to key neighborhoods in the city such as Rialto and St. Mark's. It is therefore a busy square, even in the afternoons when the small fruit and vegetable market has closed for the day. ♦ Campo Santa Maria Formosa. Vap 1, 2, 34, Rialto

13 Osteria al Mascaron ★★$$ Friendly and informal, this wine bar serves excellent snacks (*cicheti*) from the counter top. They also make pasta, risotto and entrees. Ask the waiters what's cooking. Patronized by students, intellectuals and a few tourists in the know. ♦ Closed Su. Calle Lunga Santa Maria Formosa 5225. Vap 1, 2, 34, Rialto. 5225995

14 Ponte dei Conzafelzi The small island in front of this bridge (south side) ends at a house surrounded by water on 3 sides. The

Castello

rest of the island is occupied by a former convent, designed by **Andrea Tirali** in 1731 and now used as a high school, located at the opposite end next to the handsome 15th-century Venetian Gothic Palazzo Cappello, once famous for its glorious receptions. The facade of the palazzo is visible only from the canals. ♦ Ponte dei Conzafelzi. Vap 1, 2, 34, Rialto

15 Campo San Giovanni e Paolo This campo is the center of an old and active part of the city, second only to St. Mark's. It was an important crossroads between the large island to which it belongs (extending northwise towards the lagoon, visible from the campo) and a group of busy, intensely populated islands to the south (centered around the **Campo Santa Maria Formosa**).

The north section was reclaimed from the lagoon between the 13th and 15th centuries, and was used especially as a site for convents and charitable institutions. Today it is wholly occupied by the Venice hospital. The latter is a surprising compound, which includes streets, churches and cloisters in a labyrinthine tangle of pavilions where citizens as well as newly-hired nurses and doctors easily get lost. Most of the hospital rooms look out over the lagoon, a quiet and pleasant view, if it weren't for the cypresses of the cemetery island looming ominously on the other side.

The south section, between the street on the side of the church and the parallel canal (Rio di San Giovanni Laterano) was built for low-income residents in the 13th century, with blocks of homes separated by parallel alleys (the oldest is Calle Muazzo, Nos. 6450-6454, with late-Byzantine buildings). As always in Venice, quite a few patrician families had their palazzi next to the low-income developments. Among them was **Palazzo Bragadin** (No. 6480, best seen from the bridge across the canal, with land access in an alley off the Campo Santa Marina), where young **Casanova** lived the best years of his youth under the protection of old **Matteo Bragadin**, who was convinced that the charming young man knew how to consult the spirits in order to forecast the future. Casanova played a similar trick in Paris on the **Marquise of Urfé**, who in turn supported the Venetian adventurer for years until she was rudely awakened by being conned into a mock death-and-resurrection ritual.

The campo is still an important center of local life, with a constant flow of Venetians crossing it in all directions, while in the 2 spacious cafes, groups of old men kill the afternoons playing card games and sipping wine. On the canal at the hospital's side, frequent ambulance launches carry patients to and from the hospital's water entrance. The *pasticceria (*pastry shop*)* in the campo has remained intact from the turn of the century, and the owners proudly serve old-fash-

ioned pastries (most Venetians like the green ones, with pistachio nuts).

The equestrian monument at the center of the campo represents **Bartolomeo Colleoni**, one of the greatest Renaissance *condottieri,* or military heroes, who served Venice for decades until his death in 1475. Colleoni bequeathed most of his considerable wealth to the Republic on the condition of having a monument built in front of St. Mark's. The city government decided that this campo was good enough, perhaps playing on the name of the building at the church's side (**Scuola Grande di San Marco**). But Colleoni was lucky in another sense: the 15th-century monument was trusted to one of the greatest Renaissance sculptors, **Andrea Verrocchio**, who created one of the most admired monuments in Italy (the statue was cast by his pupil **Alessandro Leopardi**).

The building at the left of the church and along the canal is the hospital's entrance. Originally it was the entrance of the Scuola Grande di San Marco, an association of citizens for religious and humanitarian purposes. The 15th-century facade was designed by **Mauro Codussi** and sculpted by **Pietro Lombardo** with his sons **Tullio** and **Antonio**. The splendid *trompe-l'oeil*

marbles represent St. Mark's lion (left side) and 2 episodes from the life of St. Mark (right side). The 15th-century statue by **Bartolomeo Bon** over the portal represents *Charity,* while the winged lion under the top arch was added in the 19th century to replace the original one, destroyed after the French conquest (1797) together with countless similar mementos of the oligarchic republic. You can visit the large hall within the building and—among a crowd of patients and their visitors—study the exhibition of photographs representing the interior of the compound before and after the restorations. You can also explore the compound, though don't be surprised to see patients in pajamas. For visits to the interior of the Scuola (grandiose 16th-century halls, with paintings by **Palma il Giovane, Palma il Vecchio** and **Jacopo Tintoretto**'s son **Domenico**) and to the attached convent, ask the hospital doorman. ♦ Campo San Giovanni e Paolo. Vap 1, 2, 34, Rialto

16 San Giovanni e Paolo (San Zanipolo) (13th-14th c) Owned and run by the Dominican Friars, this church is the largest in Venice, together with Frari, owned in turn by the rival order of the Franciscans. San Giovanni e Paolo is properly called the **Pantheon of Venice**, because from the 15th century on the funerals of the Dogi were held here, and many Dogi were buried here. On the facade, never completed with the planned marble covering, are some of the oldest tombs. Inside the arches on the left side are those of **Doge Jacopo Tiepolo** and of his son, **Doge Lorenzo Tiepolo**. The portal was designed by **Bartolomeo Bon** in the 2nd half of the 15th century. The interior of the church is filled with chapels and monuments and a walk through it is equal to a course in Venetian political and artistic history.

Highlights include:

Monument to Doge Pietro Mocenigo by **Pietro Lombardo**, one of the greatest representatives of the early Renaissance in Venice. Here, as in many other monuments, the war-like attitudes of the Doge are exalted: 6 young warriors stand inside the niches, while the bas-reliefs on the sarcophagus illustrate 2 of his victorious expeditions. The Latin inscription means *the money for this monument came from booty of war.* On top of the sarcophagus, Mocenigo appears in full battle dress. This monument is clearly reminiscent of the equally grandiose one erected at the Frari church by **Antonio Rizzo** in honor of **Doge Niccolò Tron**.

Monument to Marcantonio Bragadin, attributed to **Vincenzo Scamozzi**. Inside the urn is *the skin* of General Bragadin, who was flayed *alive* by the Turks on the island of Cyprus in 1571 after negotiating the free exit of his army. They kept the skin in Constantinople, whence the Venetians stole it. The treacherous flaying is represented in the fresco surrounding the statue.

On the 2nd altar in the aisle is *The Polyptch of St. Vincent Ferreri,* controversially attributed to **Giovanni Bellini** in his youth (ca 1465).

St. Dominick's Chapel, by **Andrea Tirali**, contains *The Glory of St. Dominick*, a masterwork by the 18th-century painter **Giovanni Battisti Piazzetta**.

In the right transept, the stained-glass window was laboriously manufactured in Murano over 50 years (1470-1520) by various artists including **Cima Da Conegliano** (who did the *Virgin*, the *Baptist* and *St. Peter*).

On the back wall, the painting at the right is one of the few works by **Lorenzo Lotto** in Venice. The painting represents *St. Antonino Giving Alms* and corresponds to Lotto's great interest in the world of the underprivileged. The saint in question, a Dominican, had worked on behalf of the poor in Florence in the 15th century. The social content in the painting is rare in 16th-century Venetian art: like most of Lotto's paintings, this one is in clear contrast with the celebrative, grandiose paintings of his contemporaries.

The high altar in the chancel is attributed to **Baldassare Longhena**. **The Monument to Doge Andrea Vendramin**, a collective work of the **Lombardo** family, is one of the best funerary monuments of its period. The top frame is missing, while the 2 Holy Women at the sides are a replacement of 2 statues (Adam and Eve), one of which is in the Metropolitan Museum of Art in New York.

The **Rosary Chapel**, destroyed by a fire in 1867, which also claimed a masterwork by **Titian** (*St. Peter Martyr*) and a *Crucifixion* by **Tintoretto** (a copy of the former can be seen on the 2nd altar in the church's left aisle). On the ceiling, rebuilt in 1932, there are now 3 canvasses by **Paolo Veronese**, previously in another church (*Annunciation*, *Assumption* and *Adoration of the Shepards*). ♦ Campo San Giovanni e Paolo. Vap 1, 2, 34, Rialto

17 Santa Maria dei Derelitti The unusual facade of this church was built in 1674 by **Baldassare Longhena** as an answer to the equally curious facade built by a rival architect at San Moise. The redundant Baroque decorations were meant as a monument to the wealthy donor, **Bartolomeo Cargnoni**. The church is connected to the nearby **Ospedaletto** (No. 6691), one of the 4 orphanages in town where children

were given their musical education. **Pasquale Anfossi**, the author of countless operas in the 18th century, was a music teacher here, as were **Niccolò Porpora** and **Domenico Cimarosa**. The concerts, considered among the best in Europe, were performed in an elegant 18th-century music hall, now part of a nursing home for senior citizens (ask the doorman at the hall next door to the church for permission to visit). ♦ Barbaria della Tole 6990. Vap 1, 2, 34, Rialto

18 Campo San Zaccaria (15th c) The church on this typical Venetian square used to belong to one of the richest Benedictine monasteries in town, founded in the 9th century. It was the preferred monastery for daughters of the noble families to join as nuns. The Doge used to visit it once a year, on Easter day, in memory of the donation by the nuns of a large piece of property to enlarge St. Mark's Square (12th century). There are 8 early Dogi buried inside the church. On the right of the church is the facade of an older chapel and the entrance to the monastery, now the headquarters of the **Venice Carabinieri**. The beautiful 15th-century building at the left was spoiled by the addition of shops on the ground floor. ♦ Campo San Zaccaria. Vap 1, 2, 5, 6, 34, San Zaccaria

19 San Zaccaria (9th c; rebuilt 15th c) The splendid facade was designed by **Mauro Codussi** between 1480 and 1500. Codussi was one of the first architects to break with Gothic tradition in Venice; his facades, widely imitated later, are characterized by a large round arch at the top, supported by 2 half-arches at the sides. His were among the first arches to be seen in

Castello

Venice, which in the late 15th century was still attached to the ogee arches of the Gothic tradition. Codussi brilliantly covered the existing Gothic structure—a central nave with 2 small side aisles—with a set of stone and marble decorations in pure Renaissance style. The facades of the Frari and San Giovanni e Paolo—never covered with stone—give an idea of what San Zaccaria looked like before Codussi's intervention.

The interior marks an important moment in Venice's art history. It is in this church that Renaissance painting made its first appearance in the city, 100 years after the great Tuscan masters had introduced it to Florence and to the world. To see this ground-breaking work, walk along the right aisle and enter the **Cappella di San Tarasio** (Chapel of Saint Tarasius). The paintings in question are the frescoes on the chapel's apse, painted by **Andrea Del Castagno**, a Florentine. Their innovative character is made evident by a simple comparison with 3 polyptychs painted one year later in the same chapel by Venetian masters (**Giovanni** and **Antonio da Murano**, with help from **Antonio Vivarini**), located at the altar and on the 2 side walls. Notice how old-fashioned they seem next to Del Castagno's frescoes.

More than 60 years after Del Castagno, **Giovanni Bellini** painted one of his best known altarpieces for San Zaccaria: the *Virgin Enthroned*, on the 2nd altar in the left aisle. This painting marks a further transition between early Venetian style and the new trends which were to emerge with **Giorgione** and **Titian**. ♦ Campo San Zaccaria. Vap 1, 2, 5, 6, 34, San Zaccaria

20 Hotel Londra Palace $$$$ Most of the rooms have a magnificent view over St. Mark's basin, but some are rather small. The ground floor lobby is comfortable and quiet. ♦ Riva degli Schiavoni 4171. Vap 1, 2, 5, 6, 34, San Zaccaria. 5200533; fax 5225032

21 Pensione Wildner $$ A small, comfortable hotel, run with efficiency by a friendly mamma-like lady. The front rooms have a great view of San Giorgio and the surroundings and are worth reserving in advance. ♦ Riva degli Schiavoni 4161. Vap 1, 2, 5, 6, 34, San Zaccaria. 5227463

22 La Pietà (1745-60, **Giorgio Massari**) This church was built for the nearby orphanage (the facade was added in 1906). Abandoned children were raised in 4 such institutions in town: **La Pietà, I Mendicanti, Incurabili** and

Castello

L'Ospedaletto), where they were taught various professions, among which the most important was music (the word *conservatory* originally meant *place where abandoned children are kept*). Soon the children of the 4 Venice institutions became famous all over Europe for their musical talents, and their concerts were one of the main reasons foreigners visited the city. Many of the great singers of the 17th century were raised in such institutions. Among them was **Madama Ferrarese**, the first interpreter of **Mozart**'s *Cosi fan tutte* and lover of Mozart's librettist, the Venetian **Lorenzo Da Ponte**. Ferrarese was brought up at I Mendicanti, but she eloped in 1780 to marry a young man from Rome and to start a glorious singing career. The young singers and players would perform behind a grill, which made them invisible to the audience. In the 1740s, **Jean-Jacques Rousseau** obtained permission to visit them in the parlor, and was bitterly disappointed by the plain looks of these girls who could sing so celestially. On the tiny alley at the side of the church was the entrance to the orphanage and the spot where children were abandoned. An inscription in stone, still visible in the alley, promised revenge from earth and heaven against parents who abandoned their children. In the

first half of the 18th century, the music teacher at La Pietà was the Baroque composer **Antonio Vivaldi**. He died before construction of the church—therefore the popular appellation *Vivaldi's church* is not appropriate.

The interior, beautifully restored in 1988 with international funds, was conceived more as a concert hall than a church. The unusual oval shape, designed with acoustics in mind, encloses a harmonious, elegant space, with 2 gilt iron grills on the walls behind which stand the singers. The ceiling is a masterwork by **G.B. Tiepoli**, representing the *Triumph of Faith*.

Baroque music concerts are performed inside the church weekly May through September, usually on Monday. ♦ Daily 10AM-noon, 5-7PM. Riva degli Schiavoni 4150. Vap 1, 2, 5, 6, 8, 34, San Zaccaria

METROPOLE HOTEL

23 Metropole Hotel $$$ The space now occupied by this hotel was the concert hall where **Antonio Vivaldi** worked and held his Venice performances. The present building has no special charm, but the hotel's halls and rooms are comfortable and the service is excellent. The view from the front rooms overlooks the water between St. Mark's and the Lido. ♦ Riva degli Schiavoni 4149. Vap 1, 2, 5, 6, 8, 34, San Zaccaria. 5205044

24 Casa di Petrarca (Petrarch's House) The small Gothic building at No. 4146 was given by the Republic as residence to the poet **Francesco Petrarca**, who lived here with his daughter from 1362 to 1367. In exchange, his promised to leave his rare collection of manuscripts to the Republic, which became the core of the **Marciana Library**. In 1367, Petrarch moved to Arquá, a country village in the Venetian hills. The view from the Gothic balcony must have been quite exciting in Petrarch's time: the sailboats coming from abroad would stop right in front for a salute to the city and for customs duties. ♦ Riva degli Schiavoni 4146. Vap 1, 2, 5, 6, 8, 34, San Zaccaria

25 Hotel La Residenza $$ Located on the beautiful and quiet **Campo Bandiera e Moro**, this small hotel is in a Gothic building with a lovely balcony. Behind the balcony is a large breakfast hall, decorated with original 17th-century stuccos and paintings. What the hotel lacks in luxury, it makes up for in comfortable rooms and affordable prices. Reserve at least one month in advance. ♦ Campo Bandiera e Moro 3068. Vap 1, Arsenale. 5285315

26 San Giovanni in Bragora (8th c; rebuilt 1505) **Antonio Vivaldi**, a native of this neighborhood, was baptized in this church in 1678. The main altarpiece (1494, *The Baptism of Christ*) is a masterwork of **Cima da Conegliano**, one of the first Venetian painters to introduce landscape as a background to figures, thereby breaking with early traditions (gold background) and with more recent trends (open loggias or small temples, as in the Bellini at San Zaccaria). Cima's birthplace was, not accidentally, in the beautiful Venetian hills, which he portrayed in his paintings much like his contemporary **Giorgione**, also a native of that area. ♦ Campo Bandiera e Moro. Vap 1, Arsenale

![Al Gabbiano]

27 Al Gabbiano ★★$$ In this area, crowded with mediocre tourist restaurants, Al Gabbiano is a notable exception. The setting is splendid, with the whole basin in full view. The food is prepared with care, and the service is extremely smooth. ♦ Closed W. Riva degli Schiavoni 4120. Vap 1, Arsenale. 5223988

28 Al Covo ★★★$$ Opened in 1986, this restaurant is quickly becoming one of the best in town, thanks to the combined talents of chef **Cesare** and his American wife **Diane**. His passion is for cooking, hers for entertaining and pleasing guests. The menu includes all the typical Venetian specialties: pasta with various fish sauces, shrimp, scampi and local fish, plus brilliant inventions by Cesare, such as an appetizer of fish prepared carpaccio-style. ♦ Closed Tu-W. Campiello de La Pescaria 3698. Vap 1, Arsenale. 5223812

29 La Corte Sconta ★★★$$ Chef **Claudio**, his wife **Rita** and his sister-in-law **Lucia** have been running this restaurant with enormous success for 15 years. In good weather, dining is in an informal but elegant inner courtyard (*corte*). The courtyard is hidden (*sconta*) in the interior of the building. Most people request the house appetizers (seafood in different styles), followed by the *assaggi* of pasta, a *taste* of 3 different pasta concoctions. The seafood is excellent and locally caught, a rarity in Venice. Among the house wines is one of the best *proseccos* to be found in town. ♦ Closed M, Su evening. Calle del Pestrin 3886. Vap 1, Arsenale. 5227024

30 Trattoria Da Remigio ★★★$$ One of the few *trattorie* in town where locals still predominate. The food is cooked with love and care by Remigio's *mamma* back in the kitchen. The homemade *gnocchi* are fabulous (try them with the Gorgonzola sauce); and the fish appetizers are as delicious as those found in the fanciest restaurants at 3 times the price. Service is informal but efficient. ♦ Closed M dinner, Tu. Salizada dei Greci 3416. Vap 1, Arsenale and San Zaccaria. Reservations required. No credit cards. 5230089

31 Collegio Greco e Chiesa del Greci This area was and still is the property of the Greek community in Venice, as it has been since 1526. It is the city's largest foreign community and one of its richest. Even today the compound is a small island of Greek civilization in the middle of Venice. Separated from the rest of the town by a grill and a canal, it is quiet and off the tourist track, although no more than 5 minutes from

St. Mark's Square. The compound includes a **Museum of Icons**, built by **Longhena** in 1578 (one of the largest collections of Oriental icons in western Europe) and the church of **San Giorgio dei Greci** (1539-61), the interior of which is a real triumph of late-Byzantine painting with gold backgrounds. The bell tower (1592) is, remarkably and dangerously, leaning. ♦ Ponte dei Greci 3412. Vap 1, 2, 5, 6, 8, 34, San Zaccaria

San Giorgio dei Greci

32 Scuola di San Giorgio degli Schiavoni The building may look like a church, but it was actually the seat of the corporation (*scuola*) of the **Dalmatian** people, also known as Slavonians (*Schiavoni*). It contains 9 masterworks by **Vittore Carpaccio**, painted between 1501 and 1511 to decorate the hall of the building. St. George was the chosen patron of the association; therefore one of the paintings represents *St. George Killing the Dragon* (2 versions of the same scene are sculpted in stone outside the Scuola: the one on the facade was sculpted in 1552, the one on the canal-side of the building in 1574). St. George, one of the preferred patrons of warriors, was recently removed from the list of Catholic saints because of lack of

proof of his real existence. Two more of the Carpaccio paintings illustrate episodes from the legend of St. George: the *Triumph of St. George* (2nd on the left wall) and *St. George Baptizing the King of Lybia* (front wall, left side of the altar). An episode from the life of St. Triffon, the 2nd patron of the Slavonians, is painted on the other side of the altar (also by Carpaccio). On the right wall are 2 episodes from the Gospel and 3 from the life of St. Jerome (*The Taming of the Lion, St. Jerome's Funeral* and *St. Jerome in His Study*, also called the *Vision of St. Augustine,* all by Carpaccio). For the first time in Italy, Carpaccio depicted religious and mystic subjects in a real, down-to-earth way (note the animals, trees, and clothes on the people) which was a giant step towards the independence of art from religion, which was possible in a city like Venice, run as it was by active, shrewd and earth-oriented merchants. ♦ Tu-Sa 9:30AM-12:30PM, 3:30-6:30PM; Su 9:30AM-12:30PM. Calle dei Furlani. Vap 1, Arsenale or 1, 2, 5, 6, 34, San Zaccaria. 5228828

33 San Francesco della Vigna This Renaissance church is located in an extremely quiet neighborhood, where Venetians go about their daily activity seemingly unaware of being in the middle of a hectic tourist town. The whole area

was redesigned from 1525 to 1540 through an ambitious project by **Doge Andrea Gritti** and architect **Jacopo Sansovino**. It represents a rare example of ancient urban planning. Around the grandiose church, the Gritti residence was rebuilt (No. 2785) and later used as the residence of the Pope's ambassador; small houses were demolished to create the **Campo della Confraternità** (right side of the church); and a bell tower similar to St. Mark's was added. The heavy loggia across the campo is a 19th-century addition. The church was carefully designed by Sansovino according to rigorous Neo-Platonic geometry. The facade was designed by **Andrea Palladio** after Sansovino's death. The interior, sober and solemn, was designed by Sansovino, in collaboration with Doge Gritti and an erudite monk, as an embodiment in stone of the *Harmonia mundi* (the order and proportion found by the Humanists in God's planning of the world), and based on multiples of the number 3. In 1535 the side

Castello

chapels were sold to families of the Venitian nobility, such as **Bragadin, Badoer** and **Contarini**, who vied to tie their names to this monument of Renaissance craft and thought. ◆ Campo San Francesco della Vigna. Vap 5, Celestia

34 Campo Do Pozzi (1350-1400) This campo represents small-scale Venice. The square was planned and built in the 14th century as the center of an island surrounded by 4 canals and adjacent to the Arsenale. The island was inhabited by the Arsenale's workers, a group of choice craftsmen. All of the houses on the campo, except for the one on the south side (rebuilt in 1613), belong to the 14th century; particularly interesting is **Palazzo Malipiero** (Nos. 2684-89). The well-top at the center was sculpted in 1530 with the figure of St. Martin. ◆ Campo Do Pozzi. Vap 1, Arsenale

35 Arsenale Two elegant towers (rebuilt in 1686) mark the water entrance to this astonishingly large compound, the pride of the Republic and the source of its maritime power. More than 16,000 workers could be simultaneously employed in times of need. The Arsenale's origins date back to the 12th century, and its fame was already high at the end of the 13th century, when **Dante** described its activity in a famous .

simile: the damned souls of corrupt politicans were tormented in Hell by immersion in a lake of boiling pitch, with the devils moving about with pointed forks just like those used by Venetian workers to caulk the hulls of their ships. It occupies $1/5$ of the city's total acreage, and is completely surrounded by crenellated walls. It is now a military zone and can be visited only by appointment, which a waiting period of 2 to 3 weeks. Among the precious remnants of the ancient activities are: the sail factory (16th century); the Bucintoro boathouse (16th century; Bucintoro was the ship used by the Doge for public ceremonies); the slips for construction and maintenance of galleass ships (16th century); the Smithies (ca 1390); and the astonishing Cordene buildings, which were more than 300 yards long (14th and 16th centuries) in order to allow the twining of one-piece ropes. Jobs in the Arsenale were coveted and hereditary; the pay was good and the city provided housing for the workers in the surrounding neighborhood. Most of the small homes around the Arsenale date back to the 13th and 14th centuries, although many have been modified countless times. The land entrance, on the side of the left tower, provides access through a flat bridge over a small canal. The Portal was built in 1460 by **Antonio Gambello** and is the first example of the Renaissance arch in Venice. The 15th-century winged lion over the arch is attributed to **Bartolomeo Bon**. The 2 *Winged Victories* were added in commemoration of a great naval victory over the Turks (battle of Lepanto, 1571). Of the 4 lions at the door's side, the one on the left was taken after a naval victory in Athens at Pireus in 168 (on its breast, sides and back it carries a Viking inscription decoded in the 15th century). The first lion on the right was also taken from Athens the same year. The smaller one on its right with its elongated body, was taken from the island of Delos and dates back to the 6th century BC. Little is known about the last and smaller of the lions. ◆ Campo dell'Arsenale. Vap 1, Arsenale

36 Ristorante Da Paolo ★★$$ Few restaurants in Venice can boast a better space for outdoor dining than this informal, unpretentious neighborhood eatery. The Arsenale door is right in front and a quiet canal flows nearby. Few tourists have discovered the place, which fills up on summer evenings with colorful guests from this popular neighborhood. The service may not be very professional, but the spaghetti with clams is as good as anywhere else in Venice, and the pizza is prepared to order. At lunchtime the crowd is much smaller, but the place is equally pleasant, with its large umbrellas shading the fierce sun. ◆ Closed M. Campo dell'Arsenale. Vap 1, Arsenale. 710660

37 Museo Storico Navale (Naval Museum) The building, dating from the 16th century, was originally used by the Republic as a granary. The exhibitions include items related to the recent history of the Italian navy after the national unity (1861) and material collected from the ancient history of the Venetian fleets. There is a large collection of naval cannons from the 16th century on. Room No. 8 contains some interesting models of Venetian ships of the 18th century and one of a *fusta*, a 15th-century warship with 224 oars. Room No. 9 has a splendid model of the last Bucintoro, the ship used by the Doge for parades. The 3rd floor represents the gondolas (history and construction techniques) and other lagoon boats . ◆ M-F 9AM-1PM; Sa 9AM-noon. Campo San Biagio 2148. Vap 1, Arsenale. 5200276

38 Hotel Bucintoro $$ This hotel is in an unparalleled location on the Riva di San Biagio. Most of the rooms enjoy a breathtaking view over the lagoon, with the gardens and the Lido on one side, St. Mark's on the other. Service is friendly, but breakfast a bit scanty. No elevator, but the stairs are not too steep. It is worth reserving in advance for one of the corner rooms. ◆ Riva di San Biagio 2125. Vap 1, Arsenale. 5223240

39 Via Garibaldi This is one of the few areas in Venice where neighborhood life is as it was before the city became a major tourist center. In the morning, a small fruit and vegetable market and a few fish stands are bustling with local shoppers. This colorful street was built by filling a canal, which still flows under its pavement. The whole operation was part of an ambitious project conceived by **Napoleon**'s urban planners during the French occupation (1800-14): they imagined a large and perfectly straight avenue which, like a Paris boulevard, would connect Venice to the mainland, leading right to La Salute. Fortunately, the plan was abandoned with the passage of Venice to Austrian domination (1814-61). ◆ Vap 1, Arsenale or Giardini

40 Campo Ruga Since the 10th century, this campo has been the center of an intensely populated area. The residential neighborhood of today was built in the 14th and 15th centuries. The buildings at Nos. 327 and 329 were rebuilt in the 17th century, and they were probably the homes of well-to-do store keepers. The well-head belongs to the 15th century. ◆ Vap 1, Arsenale or Giardini

41 Ponte San Pietro Many iron bridges similar to this one were built in Venice in the 2nd half of the 19th century. Flat and unattractive, they were in contrast to those in the rest of the city, and many were later demolished (as were **Ponte dell'Accademia** and **Ponte degli Scalzi**). The small lagoon boats double- and triple-parked along the canal are witness to the strong ties still existing between the Venetians and the lagoon: almost every family owns a boat, which they use purely for pleasure, especially on holidays to go fishing or to reach the popular restaurants that have sprung up on the lagoon islands. ◆ Vap 1, Arsenale or Giardini

42 San Pietro di Castello The castle (*castello*) which once existed on this island gave its name to the whole *sestiere*. This island was the first to be inhabited when settlers moved from the

lagoon island of Torcello to the present Venice in the 6th century, and the church was Venice's cathedral up until 1807 (when the title was passed to St. Mark's). The island is like a small, separate country village, and the families that live in the small houses on the side of the church, are undisturbed by the hectic life of the city. The bell tower, now dangerously leaning, was rebuilt in 1596 to plans by **Andrea Palladio**. The interior was totally rebuilt in the 17th century upon Palladian principles. An interesting curiosity is *St. Peter's Chair* on the right aisle. It was created around the 13th century from an Arab stone with inscriptions from the Koran, still visible on the chair's back. ◆ San Pietro de Castello. Vap 1, Arsenale or Giardini

43 Ristorante Da Franz ★★★$$$ A real surprise in the heart of a neighborhood made up of small, unpretentious homes and far from the usual tourist venues. The tables are lined along a quiet and charming canal, a setting that could not be more Venetian. **Franz**, the owner, has had a lot of experience in fine restaurants, and it shows in the excellent food here, especially the fish. When you're ready to leave, you can either catch a vaporetto at the nearby stop (Giardini), or take the splendid 15 minute walk to the St. Mark's area. ◆ Closed Tu. Fondamenta di San Giuseppe 754. Vap 1, Giardini. 5220861

44 La Biennale (Venice Biennial) The public garden at the eastern tip of town was designed in 1895 to house the *Biennale Internazionale d'Arte*, a large art show planned every 2nd year with the purpose of exhibiting contemporary art from all over the world. Twenty-four pavil-

ions are now scattered throughout the garden, representing more than 30 nations. Artists are chosen by committees from their own countries. The Biennale is often controversial—and is meant to be so—and always memorable. ◆ May-Sep on even years. Zona Giardini. Vap 1, Giardini or 2, 34, Biennale. 5289327

45 Monumento all Partigiana (Monument to the Partisan Woman) (1964, **Carlo Scarpa**) Venetian architect Carlo Scarpa designed this unusual, highly moving monument, which was completed with a bronze statue by contemporary sculptor **Augusto Murer**. The monument is set on the lagoon's bank at mid-tide level, so that its steps and the statue itself are subject to immersion at high tide. ◆ Riva del Partigiani. Vap 1, Giardini or 34, Biennale

46 Marinaressa The building with 2 large arches was added in the 1650s at the front of 3 parallel blocks of houses, built in the 15th century as part of a low-income housing project for sailors who had distinguished themselves. Low- income tenants still inhabit most of the apartments, although the ones in the front show signs of fancy—and expensive—restoration. ◆ Riva dei Sette Martiri 1428-60. Vap 1, Giardini

Giudecca

The canal that separates the **Giudecca** from the rest of Venice is only 1000 feet wide, but it is enough to make this island a distinctly autonomous community of some 8000 residents. There are no bridges over the canal, but vaporetto service is regular. Things get a bit complicated in winter, when a thick fog may settle in for hours, making communications nearly impossible. Traditionally a poor community of fishermen and shipyard workers, the Giudecca is changing rapidly. Next to the modest but welcoming homes of the days of old is the most expensive luxury hotel in Venice—the **Cipriani**—and an increasing number of fancy restaurants. A walk along its canal bank is one of the most rewarding experiences you can have in Venice—the city's profile extends from **Dorsoduro** to **La Salute** and **San Marco**, emerging from the water. At night, after a fine dinner at a local restaurant, even waiting for a vaporetto to take you back across the beautiful body of the lagoon in front of **Piazza San Marco** is a delightful experience.

1 Albergo Cipriani (Cipriani Hotel) $$$$
Located at the end of Giudecca, the Cipriani enjoys an incomparable view over St. Mark's and the lagoon. This modern hotel is decorated with great sophistication and taste. The garden and the outdoor facilities abound in flowers, and the swimming pool—the only one in a hotel in Venice—is flanked by an outdoor dining area. In the summer, outside guests are welcome to stop in for a luscious buffet lunch. The hotel runs its own free motorboat service to and from St. Mark's—just ring the buzzer and the boat will arrive in minutes. In 1991 the Cipriani opened an extension called **Palazzo Vendramin dei Cipriani** in a 15th-century building that also has a splendid view over St. Mark's. It includes 9 apartments served by specially appointed butlers. ♦ Giudecca 10, Venezia. 5207744; fax 5203930

2 Chiesa del Redentore (Redemptor's Church) (1577, **Andrea Palladio**) This church was Venice's way of thanking the Lord for the end of a plague, an event which is still

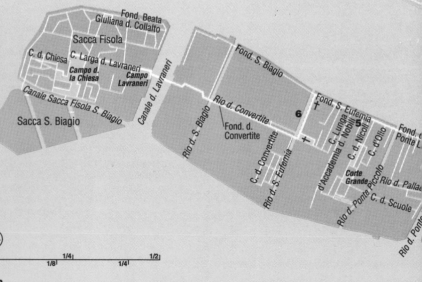

celebrated every year on the 2nd Saturday in July and is called the *notte del Redentore*. A temporary bridge is built over the Canale della Giudecca to allow the traditional pilgrimage to the church. At night, an hour of fireworks over the lagoon attracts enormous crowds from the mainland, while Venetians watch from their boats in the Canale della Giudecca. The rigorous, Classical harmony of the church's facade was one of Palladio's best inventions and was imitated countless times in Venice and all over Europe. The paintings in the interior chapels are designed to illustrate episodes from the life of Jesus, from his birth (first chapel on the right) to the Crucifixion (main altar) and the Resurrection (on top of the dome). ♦ Campo del S.S. Redentore

3 Fondamenta Ponte Lungo A walk along this short street gives you a good idea of Giudecca the way it used to be. The homes are modest but pleasant, and quite a few small fishing boats are tied along the canal. The last building at the left houses a rowing club—the keepers are very kind and won't object to visitors asking permission to enter the premises in order to admire the wide lagoon landscape behind Giudecca. ♦ Fondamenta Ponte Lungo

4 Ristorante Altanella ★★$$ Located on a quiet wooden terrace over the Rio del Ponte Lungo, this restaurant is popular with Venetians because of its homestyle dishes served at affordable prices. Fish dishes are the specialty, particularly those made with such inexpensive fish as sardines, octopus, cuttlefish, mussles and clams—but of course one can have fresh *orata* or *branzino*. ♦ Closed M dinner, Tu. Giudecca 268. Reservations required. 5227780

5 Trattoria Do Mori ★★★$$$ One of many signs of the Giudecca's upgrading was the opening in 1988 of this pleasant restaurant right on the bank of the main canal. The decor is in line with the *trattoria* tradition: old wood

tables, no plastic and a feeling of days old. Chef **Salvatore Meli** is fond of Venetian cooking but often ventures beyond; his pasta is homemade (in the spring, try it with asparagus or artichokes), and his specialties include beef filet *Do Mori* (with nuts, celery, basil and parsley) and fresh salmon *Do Mori* (sautéed in white wine with seasonal vegetables). ♦ Closed Su. Giudecca 588. 5225452

6 Harry's Dolci ★★★$$$ **Arrigo Cipriani**, owner of the famous (and expensive) **Harry's Bar**, opened this annex in the early 1980s. It was supposed to specialize in desserts (*dolci*), but it quickly became one of the town's favorite restaurants—Cipriani class at affordable prices. It offers a full restaurant menu, with such unusual additions as club sandwiches. The canopies along the Canale della Giudecca create a beautiful space for dining outdoors. ♦ Closed M, Su evening, winter. Giudecca 773. 5208337

Glass

Glass has been made in Murano since the end of the 13th century. Much of what is hawked on the island and in Venice—beads and animal figurines—is of little interest, but a few kinds of items stand out as authentic or genuinely creative. Chandeliers, mirrors and replicas of goblets and other items from 16th-century Murano—when the industry was at its peak—are among the most appealing of the many facets of Venetian glassware. Today a few younger people—many of them trained as architects or designers—have been adding a welcome breath of fresh air to Venetian glassmaking with a vast array of contemporary designs based on simple lines or witty interpretations of the glassmaker's art.

Giudecca

Venetian Islands

San Giorgio Maggiore

To anybody approaching Venice from the Lido and the open sea, the Piazza San Marco area is the solemn, triumphant entrance into the Canal Grande. In this grandiose stage setting, the island of **San Giorgio Maggiore** plays an important role, together with the **Palazzo Ducale** and **La Salute**. Architect **Andrea Palladio** was well aware of the overall effect he was creating when he designed the church on the island of San Giorgio.

The island was the property of a Benedictine abbey in the 10th century. The monks still occupy a large part of it, sharing the rest with the **Fondazione Giorgio Cini**, established in 1951 by wealthy **Count Vittorio Cini** in memory of his son **Giorgio**, who died in an airplane crash. The Foundation (entrance near the church, by the boat landing) is one of the most active cultural institutions in Italy. It organizes symposia and

conferences and runs 3 specialized libraries around 2 splendid cloisters, one of which was designed by Palladio. The main staircase was designed by **Baldassare Longhena** in 1644. The libraries are open to the general public—well staffed and never too crowded, they are a pleasure to use.

The church of San Giorgio Maggiore (founded 10th c; reconstructed beginning 1565, Andrea Palladio) faces Piazza San Marco and the Canal Grande entrance. Palladio is at his best in this church—the message is one of quiet, powerful harmony, based on Classical models yet still highly original. The interior contains 2 paintings by **Jacopo Tintoretto**, probably his last works: *The Last Supper* (right wall of chancel) and *The Gathering of the Manna* (left wall of chancel). The impressive bronze above the main altar represents *God the Father over the World Supported by the Four Evangelists*, a work by **Girolamo Campagna**. At the right of the chancel is the entrance to the **Cappella dei**

Morti *(Chapel of the Dead)*, with a *Deposition* by Tintoretto. Still from the chancel, a spiral staircase leads to the *coro invernale (winter choir)*, with *Saint George and the Dragon* by **Vittore Carpaccio**, painted by the master 8 years after his similar work in **San Giorgio degli Schiavoni**. The Benedictine monks meet in the chapel every Sunday at 11AM to sing a Mass with Gregorian chants. The general public is welcome. The San Giorgio campanile (bell tower), much less crowded than St. Mark's, offers a comprehensive view of Venice and of the surrounding lagoon. ♦ Elevator entrance is from the church's chancel; M-F 9AM-12:30PM, 2:30-4:30PM; Su 11AM-12:30PM, 2-4:30PM. Vap 5, 8, San Giorgio

Murano

Less than one mile of water separates **Murano** from the northern shore of Venice (**Fondamente Nuove**). Transportation is provided by vaporetto: line No. 5 runs around the whole city of Venice, with a small detour to circle around Murano as well. It is advisable to board it at **Piazzale Roma** or at the train station, because the trip to Murano (about a half hour from Piazzale Roma) includes some beautiful stretches of the lagoon. From Piazzale Roma, the vaporetto runs through the colorful **Canale0 di Cannaregio** to reach the open lagoon at **Sant' Alvise**; then it coasts along the northwestern banks to Fondamento Nuove, where it heads for Murano. It can also be boarded at St. Mark's—the itinerary is equally fascinating, as it cuts through the **Arsenale** and hits the lagoon at the northeastern tip of Venice. In both cases, you should get off the vaporetto at the first stop in Murano (called **Murano Colonna**) and continue the visit on foot.

The island is famous all over the world for its glass factories, many of which offer a chance to see the glass artists at work. Murano's main street (**Fondamenta Vetrai**) has been taken over by glass souvenir shops, most of them inexpensive and geared towards tourists. The better factories, however, have their shops in downtown Venice as well, and it has been said repeatedly that prices are no better in Murano—on the contrary, they tend to be steeper than in Venice.

Highlights on Murano include:

Museo dell'Arte Vetrario (Museum of Glass Art) The first part of the museum, on Fondamenta Manin and visible across the canal from Fondamenta Vetrai, includes glass objects produced in Murano in the 10th century. To see the 2nd part, continue on Fondamenta Vetrai to the bridge called Ponte Vivarini, then make a right turn at Fondamenta Cavour. This part of the museum contains nearly 4000 Murano glass objects dating back as far as the 15th century. The 16th-century section is particularly rich in precious cups, drinking glasses and painted dishes; the 18th-century section includes some remarkable mirrors. ♦ Admission. Daily 9AM-7PM, 1 Apr-31 Oct;

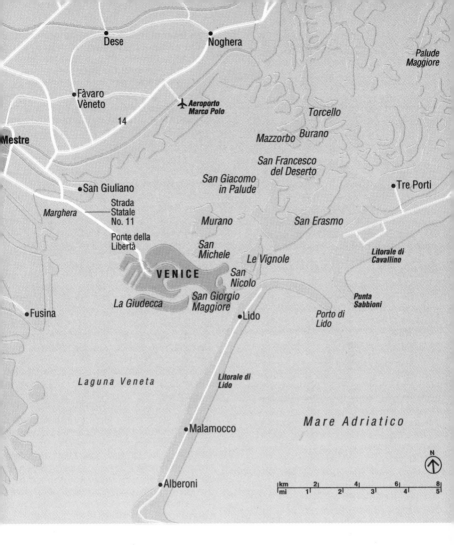

9AM-4PM, 1 Nov-31 Mar; closed 1 May, Christmas and New Year's Day. Fondamenta Giustinian. Vap 5, Murano Colonna. 739586

Chiesa di Santa Maria e San Donato (St. Mary and St. Donato Church) A different Murano from the tourist-oriented glass bazaar awaits you on this magic corner, just a few steps from the Glass Museum. The apse of the San Donato church, beautifully oriented toward a canal, is a masterwork of Venetian medieval art—a simple, handsome Romanesque building with subtle Byzantine influences. The grassy square in front of the church adds to a magic medieval feeling. In the interior, the mosaics on the floor date back to the 12th century, with figures of animals as in the floors of St. Mark's Basilica. The splendid mosaic on the inside of the apse represents the Virgin Mary on a Byzantine-inspired background of gold. The first painting on the left wall represents San Donato and is signed by **Paolo Veneziano** (1310). ♦ Campo San Donato. Vap 5, Murano Colonna

Venice...is my head, or rather my heart quarters.
Lord Byron

Burano/San Francesco del Deserto/Torcello

A trip to these 3 islands is an opportunity to spend a few hours on the quiet landscapes of the lagoon, a totally different environment from the open sea. Public boats depart about every hour from **Fondamente Nuove**. They are large and comfortable, but in the busy tourist season, come in the early morning and leave in the early afternoon to avoid the crowds. This part of the lagoon is at its best at sunset in the summer—though everyone else knows this too (less so in the spring and late fall). The lagoon is surprisingly shallow—one could easily walk, if it weren't for the mud at the bottom. At mid-tide, the depth averages 3 feet; with the tides it can go as high as 5 feet or as low as one or less. The large public boats run through natural canals marked by the typical wood poles called *bricole*; a mistake of manuevering a few yards to either side would cause the boats to run aground in the flats. Smaller crafts, however, run freely through the water, as they have flat bottoms and can move in just a few inches of water.

Burano

Once a fishing community, **Burano** now depends on tourism for most of its income. Lacemaking was revived on Burano in the 10th century and has turned it into *Lace Island* just as Murano became *Glass Island*. Countless shops and stands in the streets and alleys offer all kinds of lace-decorated items—most are machine-made, but you can still find some handmade—thus very costly—items.

In spite of the tourist boom, Burano has maintained the charming character of a small island community. The canals are lined with small lagoon boats, used for fishing and pleasure. It was on one of these boats that the English writer **Frederic W. Rolfe**, known as **Baron Corvo**, spent the last years of his life in the early 1900s working on his novel, *The Desire and the Pursuit of the Whole*. Burano's houses were characteristically painted in bright colors, apparently to make them easy to identify by fishermen returning home; today the local administration contributes to the painting with guidelines and funding. The best way to enjoy a visit here is to walk along the main street, **Via Galuppi**, taking a few random detours along the side canals. Via Galuppi was named after **Baldassare Galuppi**, an 18th-century composer who was born in Burano.

Highlights on Burano include:

Ristorante Da Romano ★★★$$$ At the center of Via Galuppi is this excellent seafood restaurant with a large area for outdoor dining. Ask about the boat schedule after dinner—the trip back to Venice at night is a memorable experience. ♦ Closed Tu. Via Galuppi 211. Vap 12, Burano. 730030

San Francesco del Deserto

Near the church of **San Martino**, a private boat service departs for the enchanting island of **San Francesco del Deserto**. The island houses an ancient Franciscan monastery (it is believed that **St. Francis** stopped here on his way back from the Holy Land). The monks offer tours of their little paradise, which includes beautiful gardens and a 13th-century cloister.

Venetian Islands

Torcello

After Burano, the water bus continues for 20 more minutes to the neighboring island of **Torcello** (many visitors get off at Burano and catch one of the next boats to Torcello). This island can also be reached from Venice by a special taxi service, meant for lunch clients of Torcello's **Locanda Cipriani**; departures are every day at 12:20PM from the bank at St. Mark's in front of **Hotel Danieli**, returning at 3:45PM from Locanda Cipriani.

Torcello was the first lagoon island where the mainland population found refuge from the barbarian invasions in the 5th century. Although other lagoon areas were sparsely populated at the time, it is from this core of settlers that the city of Venice took origin—in the following centuries the Torcello people expanded to Rialto and the islands around it, gradually abandoning Torcello. It was a long process, and in the meantime this small island had become the civic and reli-

gious center of the entire lagoon. The remnants of that period still attract a great number of visitors. Two splendid churches stand side by side on the low, grassy land, surrounded by the lagoon and vegetable gardens. They date back to the beginning of Venice, with a remarkable mixture of Byzantine sumptuousness and naif, almost primitive, imagery. When the area is not filled with tourists, a majestic silence reigns over it—a reminder of the beauty and frailty of all things human. A short walk from the public boat landing along a canal flanked by fields is the former main square of Torcello.

Highlights of Torcello include:

Ostaria al Ponte del Diavolo ★★★$$$ An excellent restaurant specializing in fish and local vegetables. ♦ Lunch M-W, F; closed Th, Sa-Su. Via Chiesa 10-11. Vap 12, Torcello. 730401

Torcello Cathedral (begun 7th c) The Cathedral opens onto a space that used to be the busy center of town, when Torcello had 20,000 residents (today only a few dozen people are permanent residents). An excavation in front of the church shows the foundation of the ancient **Baptistry**, while behind the church, the old bell tower stands intact—dating back to the 11th century and clearly visible from the distant mainland. The Cathedral was reconstructed in 1008 upon an existing structure dating from the 7th century. Some of the material used in the reconstruction was brought over from early Christian buildings abandoned on the mainland when the Barbarians invaded. The interior is reminiscent of the great Byzantine churches of Ravenna. The original 11th-century parts include the capitals, the floor and the 4 splendid marble bas-reliefs in the iconostasis. The mosaic *Madonna and Child* in the apse is a masterwork of the 13th century. Of the same period is the famous mosaic on the interior facade, a *Last Judgment* drawn with Medieval Realism (notice the scene of the *Resurrection of the Dead*, and at the bottom, the *Blessed and the Damned*). ♦ Piazza del Duomo. Vap 12, Torcello

Church of Santa Fosca Next to the Cathedral and surrounded by a Medieval porch with arcades. Across the small square is the **Museo di Torcello** (Torcello Museum), with archaeological material documenting the Roman presence in the mainland communities bordering the lagoon and with material from the early Christian centuries. ♦ Piazza del Duomo. Vap 12, Torcello

Locanda Cipriani ★★★★$$$$ **Arrigo Cipriani**, the founder of **Harry's Bar**, opened this restaurant and tiny hotel in 1946 in a restored 17th-century villa. His idea was to create a place for a wealthy clientele to spend a day or 2 in total isolation, surrounded by the absolute beauty of Torcello. The large garden and outdoor dining area offer a view of the apse of Santa Fosca. The food and service are excellent. The hotel has only 4 rooms, so make reservations at least a month in advance. ♦ Closed Tu, Nov-Feb. Locanda Cipriani. Vap 12, Torcello. Reservations recommended..730150

Trattoria Villa Seicento ★★$$ This restaurant a few steps from the Cathedral started out as a popular, inexpensive place for outdoor lunch but has slowly worked its way up the ladder in both price and quality. The kitchen is still in the hands of the owner's mother, ho continues to cook local fish and vegetables with ve and care. ♦ Closed W. Near Piazza del Duomo. ap 12, Torcello. 730999

an Lazzaro degli Armeni

ne small island of **San Lazzaro degli Armeni** was ven to a group of Armenian monks early in the 17th entury. The monks installed a printing press that ecame famous all over Europe for the quality of its ork. They still run the island and the press. Their brary is exceptionally rich in ancient manuscripts, articularly Armenian. A painting by **Giambattista lepolo** adorns the ceiling of the monastery's entrance all. Vaporetto lines No. 10 and 20 connect the island ith St. Mark's and the Lido. ♦ Monastery daily 3-5PM

he Lido

ine miles long and less than a half-mile wide, the ido is one of 2 thin, fragile islands that separate the goon from the open sea. The other island is called ellestrina and is a continuation of the Lido all the ay to the mainland at Chioggia. On the side toward le sea, the Lido is an uninterrupted stretch of wide eaches covered with fair-colored sand. For this reaon, and because of its proximity to Venice, it became ne of the preferred seaside resorts for the European pper classes beginning in the 17th century. Some of le most luxurious hotels in Italy were built along its hores and are still in business, while the narrow land as built up with villas surrounded by gardens. A special feature of the Lido is the fact that cars are allowed n the roads, which makes the hotels attractive to visirs who travel with lots of luggage and prefer to travel y car. A frequent ferry service carries automobiles to nd from the Tronchetto terminal, near Piazzale Roma, hile St. Mark's square is a beautiful 10-minute aporetto ride away.

hanging into a bathing suit is not permitted in the pen on the Lido beaches; you must rent a cabin for a ay or a half day. The least expensive area to do this is le **Zona A**, at the immediate left of the **Gran Viale** very crowded and often noisy). Much more chic— nd proportionately more expensive—are the luxury abins of **Hotel Des Bains** (at the immediate right of he Gran Viale) and of **Hotel Excelsior** (at the end of he seaside walk). Other beach areas offer intermdiate prices.

lighlights on the Lido include:

listorante Belvedere ★★★$$$ Located at the nding of the vaporetto lines from Venice, this is one f the best restaurants on the Lido. The speciality is sh. Informal but excellent service. ♦ Closed M. Piazza anta Maria Elisabetta 4. Vap 1, 2, 34, Santa Maria lisabetta. 5260115

Gran Viale This colorful boulevard is the main street n the Lido, and the way to reach the beaches on foot rom the vaporetto landings (a 10 minute walk). Most f the outdoor restaurants on both sides of the bouleard cater to tourists looking for a quick bite of pizza nd such. Don't miss the wonderful ceramic baseliefs on the facade of the **Hotel Hungaria** (on the ight half way along the Viale) built in 1906. ♦ Vap 1, , 34, Santa Maria Elisabetta

Hotel Des Bains $$$$ This 4-star hotel was built in 1900 for the European aristocracy and was made even more famous by **Visconti**'s movie *Death in Venice*, based on **Thomas Mann**'s novel. The interior still has the original Art-Deco fixtures. The hotel is surrounded by a large park and includes a swimming pool and an outdoor terrace for lunch. The hotel is now owned by the **Ciga Company** (Compagnia Italiana Grande Alberghi). Free transportation service to and from Piazza San Marco is available every half hour for hotel guests (departure is from **Hotel Excelsior**—a couple of minutes by minibus). ♦ Open early April to late Oct. Lungomare Marconi. Vap 1, 2, 34, Santa Maria Elisabetta. 5265921; fax 5260113

Hotel Quattro Fontane $$$$ This delightful hotel in a villa surrounded by a garden is run with exquisite taste by 2 highly cultivated sisters, who treat the premises like their own home and the guests like personal friends. All of the rooms are decorated with antique furniture. The hotel is close to the Casino and the Movie Festival and 200 yards from the beach, yet it is perfectly quiet. Dining, available also to outside guests, is in the garden among the flowers. Transportation to Venice is available every 20 minutes on vaporetto line No. 2 and/or with Casino Express. ♦ Open early April to late Oct. Via delle Quattro Fontane 16. Vap 2, Casino. 5260227 or 5200726

Hotel Excelsior $$$$ The Excelsior was built at the turn of the century for the posh clientele of the Lido. It is still the most lavish hotel in Venice, with a striking fountain in the main hall and the best rooms directly overlooking the beach. In late August and early September, it becomes the headquarters of the **Venice Film Festival**, and the list of movie stars who have stayed in its suites is long and dazzling. ♦ Lungomare Marconi 41. Vap 2, Casino. 5200201; fax 5267276

Murazzi The name means *rough walls* and refers to the huge stone and concrete boulders which strengthen the median part of the Lido to protect against erosion. At the end of Lungomare Marconi and just after the Hotel Excelsior is this lonely and, in its way, fascinating part of the Lido, a half hour on foot from the main vaporetto landing (also reach-

able by bus). Venetians come here to bathe away from the crowds without having to rent a cabin. Sunset is strinkingly beautiful here, as is the walk back to the vaporetto if you decide to cross the Lido and walk on the lagoon side. ♦ Vap 2, Casino or by bus line A or B from Santa Maria Elisabetta

Lace

While much of what passes for the famed **Burano** lace is imported from Asia, the industry that put the tiny island on the map throughout Europe for centuries (and its product in the trousseau of **Mary Tudor**, among others) is going strong. Revived in the 19th century by **Paolo Fambri** and **Contessa Andriano Marcello**, the Burano lace industry is again flourishing, its school providing the intricate stock for shops on Burano and, most famously, the **Jesurum** near the Bridge of Sighs in Venice.

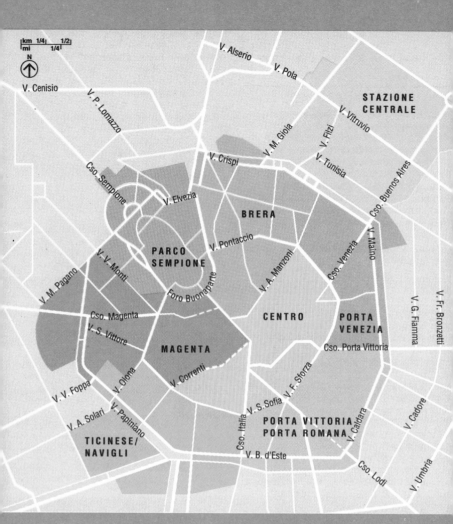

Milan is the center of Italy's –if not the world's– fashion and design industries. It's also the most contemporary city in Italy.

MILANACCESS®

Duomo

Milan Orientation

Milan is the plain, hardworking sister in the family of Italian cities. It is also the most stylish and open-minded. For in spite of its rich past of some Roman and many early-Christian monuments, as well as some excellent art collections, Milan is the most contemporary city in Italy, if not Europe. The center of Italy's (perhaps the world's) fashion and design industries, Milan is also Italy's

economic capital (the Milanese insist their city is the country's *real* capital) and the center of Italy's publishing, television and advertising worlds. Its prosperity ensures that the best of everything is here—shopping and food included, happily for visitors in town for business or pleasure.

Chances are visitors will find themselves here for business, but there is still a wealth of attractions for those coming for pleasure—the above-mentioned museums and monuments and Italy's best-known opera house, **La Scala**, among them. And though Milan may not be beautiful in the sense of many other Italian cities, it is always a delight to find a bit of old architecture mixed in with the modern glass and concrete *palazzi*, or to peek into a courtyard to see how the Milanese nobility once lived—and still do.

Getting to Milan

Airports

There are 2 airports in Milan, and planes will sometimes land at the other if one is fogged in.

Malpensa airport (74852200) is 28 miles from the city and handles intercontinental flights of most major airlines. There is an inexpensive bus service to the **Stazione Centrale**; taxis are considerably more expensive (about $80). Each takes about an hour if the traffic is light.

The following rental car agencies have offices at Malpensa airport:

Avis	868019
Budget	40099322
Hertz	40099000
National	40099351

Linate airport (7485313) is about 5 miles from town and handles all domestic and some international flights. There is bus service to **Stazione Centrale** as well as taxi service, reasonably priced because of the distance involved. Each takes about 20 minutes if the traffic is light.

The following rental car agencies have offices at Linate airport:

Avis	717214
Budget	7610234
Hertz	70200256
National	76110258

Train Station

Milan's central train station is called **Stazione Centrale** (67500). When buying your train ticket, make sure the train stops at that station and not at one of the other stations such as **Lambrate** or **Porta Genova**, which are at less convenient locations.

Getting Around Town

Buses and Trams

City buses and trams go under the acronym of **ATM** and are frequent and efficient. Tickets are available at most newsstands, tobacconists and cafes. They must be purchased before boarding the bus (get on at the front or rear doors, as the center one is for getting off), when you validate them in a little orange machine. The main bus information office, where English is spoken, is underground in the **Piazza Duomo** metro station.

Driving

Because of the heavy traffic and complicated traffic zones in central Milan, it is not recommended that you use a car, bicycle or moped.

Subway

The subway goes under the acronym **MM** (it stands for **Metropolitana Milanese**) and consists of 3 lines. Of most interest to the visitor is line 1, which connects the **Stazione Centrale** to **Piazza Duomo** and **Santa Maria delle Grazie**. Tickets are available at most newsstands, tobacconists and cafes, as well as in vending machines at individual stations.

Taxis

Taxis are plentiful and drivers remarkably pleasant in Milan. They wait at strategic locations around town (such as the train station, **Piazza della Scala**), may be called by dialing 5251, 6767, 8388 or 8585, and may occasionally be hailed on the street.

FYI

Consulates

Australia, Via Borgogna 2, 4565078
Canada, Via Vittor Pisani 19, 6697451

, Via San Paolo 7, 8693442

, Piazza Carlo Donegnani 1, 652841

urs

usinesses are generally open M 4-7:30PM; Tu-Sa
AM-1PM, 4-7:30PM; closed Su. Food shops are
en M 9AM-1PM; Tu-Sa 9AM-1PM, 4-7:30PM;
sed M afternoon, Su. Churches are generally open
ily 8AM-1PM, 4-7:30PM.

gal Emergencies

lizia, Via Fatebenefratelli 11, 62261

edical Emergencies

ssistenza 5511655

oney

e **American Express** office is at Via Brera 3, 85571.
nother good currency exchange is **Banca Cesare**
inti in Piazza Duomo, 88211. Avoid changing money
the airports and train station; the agencies there
arge high commissions and should only be used as
last resort.

harmacy

armacia Stazione Centrale, Galleria delle Partenze,
590735; open 24 hours.

ost Office

oste e Telecommicazioni, Via Cordusio 4, M-F
15AM-7:30PM; Sa 8:15AM-12:30PM, tel.160

treet Smarts

ickpockets operate on buses, trams and crowded
ubways in Milan. Also, beware of the gypsies who
rey on weary tourists, especially those getting off the
rport buses near the train station.

elephone

he area code for Milan is 02; outside Italy drop the
and just dial 2 after the country code 39 for Italy. The
IP telephone at Galleria Vittorio Emanuele II (tel.
211), is open daily 8AM-9:30PM.

ourist Info

nte Provinciale per il Turismo, Via Marconi 1; tel.
09662; M-Sa 8AM-8PM; Su 9AM-12:30PM, 1:30-
PM

fficio Informazioni, Galleria Vittorio Emanuele II; tel.
70545; M-Sa 8:30AM-8:30PM

nglish-language cultural events listings can be found
Night & Day Milano, available in many hotels.

uisine

f all the cities in Italy, Milan offers the best quality
nd most variety of dining, though be forewarned it
lso carries the highest price tag. As the center of the
ountry's food distribution network, Milan gets the
est of Italy's regional ingredients—rice from the
orth, olive oil and beef from Tuscany, pork and pro-
ciutto from Emilia-Romagna, fish from Sicily, fresh
uit and vegetables as well as wine and cheese from
roughout the country—along with such locally
rized imports as Angus beef and Scotch salmon.

In addition to a vast array of regional Italian restaurants serving everything from creamy Piedmontese
specialties to spicy Sicilian dishes (though Tuscan
restaurants are by far the most prolific), Milan boasts
a number of places featuring the rich regional cuisine
of Milan and the surrounding region of Lombardy. A
full Milanese meal might start with cured meats such
as *bresaola* (beef) and *salame milanese* (pork salami),

followed by an antipasto of *nervetti*, a popular salad
made of calf's foot. The *primi piatti* (or first courses)
are numerous. *Buseca* is a tripe soup. *Minestrone* is
a vegetable soup. There are a number of risotto or
cooked rice dishes, the most famous being *risotto alla
milanese*, yellow in color from saffron, which gives it
the local name of *risotto giallo* or yellow risotto.
Almost as popular is *risotto alla certosina*, made with
shrimp, freshwater fish and occasionally frogs. Leftover risotto is often made into *riso al salto*, a pancake
of risotto sautéed in butter. Another popular first
course (as it is in much of northern Italy) is *polenta*,
cormeal mush served with a variety of sauces as a first
course or as an accompaniment to a main course.

The *secondo piatto* or main course most associated
with Milan is *costolette alla milanese*, a veal chop
breaded and fried in butter, served with a lemon
wedge and in the trendier restaurants topped with
tomato and basil. It is usually served with a portion
of *risotto giallo* on the side. Other typical main courses
are *osso buco* (braised veal shank) and *rostin negaa*
(a veal chop braised in white wine). Desserts include
such cheeses as the blue-veined *gorgonzola*, the soft
robiola and *stracchino*, and the hard and pungent
grana. Milan's most famous dessert is Christmas
panettone (though it's increasingly available year-
round), a cake studded with citron, raisins and orange.

Though the Franciacorta district in Lombardy produces palatable and even acclaimed red and white
wines, most Milanese prefer to drink wines from other
regions in Italy. Chianti, Barolo and Bardolino are
popular reds; Pinot Bianco and Pinot Grigio (along
with the ever-trendy Galestro) are usually high among
the whites on the list. Milan's restaurants usually have
a wide selection of *grappa*—the Italian aquavit—as an
after-dinner *digestivo*.

At the other end of the scale, Milan is also known for
its proliferation of fast-food outlets, which fit in neatly
with the city's hardworking lifestyle. The usual international chains such as **McDonald's**, **Wendy's** and
Burger King are all to be found; afficionados of the
genre might want to check out the local versions, particularly **Burghy's**. Another fast-food phenomenon
peculiar to Milan is the *paninoteca* or sandwich emporium, found all over the city. Much more original than
the burger joints, the *paninoteche* pride themselves on
putting together original combinations which are usually entire meals in themselves, more substantial than
the finger sandwiches called *tramezzini* or *sandwich*.

---

*Beastly Milano, with its imitation hedgehog of a
Cathedral, and its hateful town Italians, all socks and
purple cravats and hats over the ear...* **D.H. Lawrence**

Centro

Milan's **Centro** or city center (the densest half of which is covered in this chapter) was enclosed in medieval times by a circular wall and canals or *navigli*. Though the canals have long since been covered up, the boundaries of Milan's innermost circle are still known as the *cerchia dei navigli* or canal ring. Yet apart from the dominating presence of the **Duomo** and the usual scattering of churches, relatively few elements within the *cerchia dei navigli* are historical, and it takes a concerted effort to single them out amid the modern buildings, heavy traffic and bustling crowds. Among the more worthy sights are the stately residences—notably Renaissance and Neoclassical ones—wealthy Milanese commissioned during sporadic building booms. Less genteely, the more recent booms of the extensive bombing of the area during WWII left room for the mostly Modernist construction that so characterizes this and all other parts of Milan today. As its Functionalist appearance suggests, Centro is the heart of Milan's—indeed Italy's—commerce. While most of the business is of little interest to the average visitor, one aspect is of international appeal. The big-name clothing designers who have made Milan the world's major fashion capital have given this small part of the city the largest concentration of status signatures on earth. Most of their wares are dazzlingly displayed on and around the 4 streets—**Via Sant'Andrea, Via Spiga, Via Borgospesso** and **Via Monte Napoleone**—collectively known as the **Quadrilatero**, while the last one is affectionately known as **Montenapo**. Here the names of the patrician families who built the district's discreet palazzi have been virtually eclipsed by their modern-day designer tenants. As contemporary and trendy as the silks and satins shining through the fog in their chic window displays may seem, it is all in keeping within the medieval mercantile tradition and the outline of the very walls which seem to have permanently inscribed the boundaries of Milan.

1 Piazza del Duomo (1865, **Giuseppe Mengoni**) The building boom that swept Italy after the country's unification in the last century has a large echo in Piazza del Duomo. Part of the site had been the center of Milan's civic life since the Middle Ages, and as in Florence's Piazza della Repubblica, a medieval neighborhood was knocked down to expand the space in front of the cathedral, à la Venice's Piazza San Marco. Today the piazza remains the civic center and roughly the geographical center of Milan, the rings of the city's street plan radiat-

Centro

ing like wobbly radar from the vast rectangle of the piazza. Facing the Duomo is an equestrian **Monument to Vittorio Emanuele II** (1896, **Ercole Rosa**), the first king of Italy, backed by proud expanses of billboards and neon, making Piazza del Duomo a rather respectable version of Times Square or Piccadilly Circus. The piazza was torn up for years while a new subway line was being built, and now that construction is completed, it's hard to imagine how the hordes of people you see in the piazza today could ever have negotiated the space while it was cluttered with all that equipment. The masses that pass between king and cathedral include Milanese going about their daily business at their characteristic brisk pace, tourists and schoolchildren gaping at the Duomo, strollers and shoppers headed in and out of the **Galleria Vittorio Emanuele II**, determined flocks of plump Milanese pigeons pecking for a handout wherever it may fall, and the occasional demonstrators expressing their faith or seeking peace or prosperity. Beneath the surface, the piazza is busier than ever now that 2 of Milan's 3 subway lines (at the entrances, its double-M emblem for *Metropolitana Milanese* unconsciously apes the outlines of the Duomo) converge on the spot. ◆ Piazza del Duomo

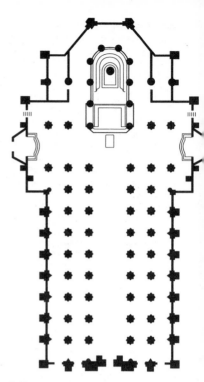

2 Duomo (14th-20th c) Milan's bristly Duomo was begun in 1386 under the progressive dominion of **Gian Galeazzo Visconti** and brought to a hasty conclusion under an impatient **Napoleon** between 1805 and 1813, though the bronze portals of its facade were all completed during this century, the southernmost as recently as 1960. Hence the Milanese expression, *lungo come la fabbrica del Duomo* (long as the building of the Duomo), for something that seems interminable. Its main building material is white marble from the quarry at Candoglia opened by Gian Galeazzo Visconti

Duomo, as it appeared in the 14th century while under construction

and still used today to repair the cathedral. It was first put to use on the apse, the most beautiful and integral part of the cathedral, built between 1386 and 1447 (rose windows by **Filippino da Modena**) in a fairly unadulterated Northern Gothic style. Still more stone was chiseled into a forest of pinnacles and spires sheltering armies of statues, over 3000 in all. Take time to see the trees in the forest, the soldiers in the army, since the statues (of saints and sinners, knights and pilgrims, and fanciful gargoyles held up by wild giants) are surprisingly animated and individualistic. Above it all, the Milanese people's beloved *Madonnina* presides serenely from the central spire on the roof. The *little Madonna*, an 18th-century gilded-copper statue by **Giuseppe Perego**, is actually over 13 feet tall and considered the protectress of the city. It may sound like a quaint idea for sophisticated Milan, but if you take a long look at the *Madonnina* illuminated at night, when she seems to hover in a golden cloud above the darkness and fog, you may begin to believe she's doing her job.

The facade—a conglomeration of Baroque, Neo-Gothic and Neoclassical styles—brings a pout to the mouths of purists. Of its portals, the most interesting is the central one (by **Ludovico Pogliaghi**), depicting the *Life of the Virgin* in a Neo-Gothic style that flows right into Art Nouveau. Atop all the doors are 17th-century bas-reliefs designed by **Giovanni Battista Crespi**, also known as **Cerano**. Even purists' pouty mouths drop open when they enter the cathedral and witness its squat and spiny exterior aspect give way to a soaring smoothness inside. Second in the world only to St. Peter's in Rome in its vastness, the interior is filled with row upon row of columns rising into a haze of incense that is the heavenly counterpoint to the devilish fog frequently sitting watch outside, while stained-glass windows blaze color through the mist.

More color is to be found in the mosaic marble pavement, designed by **Pellegrino Tibaldi** in the 16th century and finished in 1940. Works of art are scattered throughout. In the first bay of the right aisle is the **Tomb of Archibishop Aribert**, by an unknown artist; to the left of it is a marble slab with the inscription, *El principio dil Domo di Milano fu nel anno 1386* (the founding of the Duomo of Milan was in the year 1386), as much proof of the origins of Milan's cathedral as the obscurity of its dialect. In the second bay are the **Tomb of Ottone Visconti** and the **Tomb of Giovanni Visconti**, both by unknown artists. In the third bay is the **Tomb of Marco Carelli**, also by an unknown artist. Against the west wall of the right transept is the 16th-century **Tomb of Gian Giacomo Medici** by **Leone Leoni**. On the east wall of the transept is the Renaissance **Altar of the Presentation in the Temple** by **Agostino Busti**, known as **Bambaia**. Next to it is a decidedly unidealized 16th-century statue *St. Bartholomew Flayed*, skin in hand, by **Marco d'Agrate**. The sculptor tried to dispel some of

his statue's distastefulness by inscribing on it *Non Me Praxiteles sed Marcus Finxit Agrates* (*I was not made by Praxiteles but by Marco d'Agrate*). The ambulatory contains the 15th-century **Monument to Pope Martin V** by **Jacopino da Tradate** and the 16th-century **Tomb of Cardinal Mario Caracciolo** by **Giacomo da Campione**. In the presbytery are a 16th-century high altar and magnificent oak choir stalls by Pellegrino Tibaldi, **Camillo Procaccini** and others. In the left transept is the Gothic Trivulzio candelabrum. Just inside

the main door is a staircase that leads to the paleochristian excavations beneath the church (admission; Tu-Su 10AM-noon, 3-5PM). Outside, on either side of the north transept, are the staircase and elevator that lead to the roof (admission; daily 9AM-5:30PM), for a close-up of the architectural details and delightful statuary and pinnacles as well as the best wide angle of the city and surroundings. If there is no haze or fog, you can see the Alps (including the Matterhorn) and the Appenines across the Lombard plain. ♦ Piazza del Duomo

3 Galleria Vittorio Emanuele II (1878, **Giuseppe Mengoni**) Through a triumphal arch, the Galleria connects Piazza del Duomo to Piazza della Scala, but it is much more than a *galleria* or passageway. Here Giuseppe Mengoni designed a prototypical modern shopping mall: 4 iron-and-glass covered *streets* with Neo-Renaissance facades converging on a central *piazza* topped by an iron-and-glass dome. Though the architect died in a fall from the Galleria's scaffolding a few days before its official opening, his work has lived on with such success that it has become known as *il salotto di Milano* or the drawing-room of Milan. Each day thousands of people gather in or pass through the space, so vast that the authorities have draped netting over the entrances to reduce pigeon traffic. One animal is welcome in the Galleria, however—the bull depicted in the pavement directly beneath the dome. Stepping on the beast's rather publicly exposed privates is supposed to bring good luck.

...the beautiful city with its dominant frost-crystalline Duomo....

John Ruskin

How glorious that Cathedral is! worthy almost of standing face to face with the snow Alps; and itself a sort of snow dream by an artist architect, taken asleep in a glacier!

Elizabeth Barrett Browning

The Cathedral is an awful failure. Outside the design is monstrous and inartistic. The over-elaborated details stuck high up where no one can see them; everything is vile in it; it is, however, imposing and gigantic as a failure, through its great size and elaborate execution.

Oscar Wilde

Within the Galleria:

Bar Zucca The cheery red cordial Campari made its debut in this cafe, when it was called **Camparino**. Most Milanese still know it by that name, and the cafe still retains its original Art Nouveau furnishings, which help make it the most popular such spot in the Galleria. ♦ M-Tu, Th-Su 7:30AM-8:30PM. 873165

Bocca Brusque service but broad selection of art books in this bookshop, the oldest of many in the Galleria. ♦ Closed Su. 871536

Centro

Bernasconi One of the nicest silversmiths in town, with objects in styles ranging from antique to contemporary. ♦ Closed M morning, Su, lunch. 872334. Also at: Via Magenta 22. 867072

Biffi in Galleria ★★$$ A traditional rendez-vous spot for the Milanese, Biffi (under different management from the restaurant **Biffi Scala**) is a fine place for a meal in its ground-floor restaurant (closed Su) or upstairs cafeteria (lunch only; closed Sa-Su), but is even better for a drink in its *outdoor* cafe beneath the dome (M-Sa 7:30AM-midnight), where you can sample the house cocktail, the *slap*, made from grapefruit and pineapple juices with vodka and a splash of curacao. ♦ 8058156

Burghy ★★$ Despite its chic faux-Anglo name and menu of burgers and the like, the Burghy fast-food chain is a thoroughly Milanese phenomenon. Burghys serve as hangouts for the *paninari* (sandwich-eaters), mall rebels *alla milanese*. Actually, they are less juvenile delinquents than fashion plates, affecting such expensive American dress as Pendleton shirts, Levis, Timberland shoes, Burlington socks and Ray Ban sunglasses which they (or *mamma*) can afford it. Because of its location, this Burghy (one of a dozen or so in the city) is particularly popular. The fare, while standard, isn't bad. It's certainly faster and a cut above the other chains in town, **Italy & Italy** (which emphasizes design over dining), and **Wendy's** (which consistently serves stale buns, cold fries and the like, and inevitably claims its milkshake machines are out of order). ♦ M, W-F, Su 10AM-midnight; Sa 10AM-1AM. 86460065

Prada Women's leathergoods are the most popular things in one of Milan's most traditional leather shops, but such items as desk and travel accessories are for everyone. ♦ Closed M morning, Su, lunch. 876979. Also at: Via della Spiga 1. 708636

Luisa Spagnoli Sophisticated women's apparel at reasonable prices. ♦ Closed Su. 863225

CIT The main Milan office of the government-owned **Compagnia Italiana Turismo** travel agency is friendlier and more efficient than other branches in the country, and is a good place to make travel arrangements and cash travellers' cheques, since it doesn't charge commissions and accepts credit cards. ♦ M-F 8:30AM-1PM, 2-6PM; Sa 9AM-1PM. 866661

Il Gabbiano A full selection of *gelato* in fruity and creamy varieties. ♦ M-Sa 7:30AM-8PM. 72022411

Lenci Exclusive and expensive dolls for collectors have made this a doll-lover's paradise for decades. ♦ Closed M morning, Su, lunch. 870376

Savini ★★★$$$ For a taste of Old Milan, no restaurant is better than Savini, as much a city institution as the Duomo or La Scala. The Milanese business types who come to this red-velvet, crystal-chandeliered restaurant like to go for the international  items on the menu, but the surroundings usually inspire us to order such traditional dishes as *risotto giallo* (a soupy rice dish saturated with saffron, so associated with the city it is known throughout the rest of Italy as *risotto alla milanese*), *cotoletta* (breaded and fried veal cutlet known elsewhere as *cotoletta alla milanese*) or *osso buco* (roast veal shank, prepared *alla milanese* with a *gremalada* sauce of lemon peel, anchovies, herbs and spices). There are enough variations on the *risotto giallo* theme alone to have kept us mad about saffron for a number of visits—it can be ordered plain, *con midollo* (with veal marrow), *con tartufo bianco* (with white truffle), and *al salto* (sautéed into a crisp pancake). ♦ Closed Su, Aug. 8058343

Rizzoli The flagship store (this space was designed by **Achille Castiglione**) of Italy's most internationally known chain, part of a publishing empire that comprises books, magazines and *Corriere della Sera*, Milan's daily paper and the closest thing Italy has to a national newspaper (along with *La Repubblica*, partially owned by the rival **Mondadori**). In the basement is the country's largest selection of paperbacks, while of interest to the non-Italian reader are the guidebooks and books on Italian culture, many of which are in English, on the ground floor. ♦ Closed lunch M and Su. 807348

Ufficio Informazione Milan's city tourist information office is so well-organized and forthcoming that the first question you want to ask them is, *Am I really in Italy?* Piled high with printed matter and glowing with touch-sensitive video monitors, the material is backed up by a staff of multilingual city employees. The facilities are most useful for finding out about current art exhibitions, concerts, plays and the like. ♦ M-Sa 8:30AM-8:30PM. 870545

4 La Rinascente Milan's longest established department store with the most widely toted shopping bag, Rinascente is the closest thing in Italy to an American- or British-style department store with 6 floors of decent merchandise, culminating in a cafe on the top floor. Called **Canto Guglie** (it means 100 spires), it has an in-your-face view of the Duomo. ♦ Closed M morning, Su. Piazza del Duomo. 88521

5 Prima Fila ★★$$ A reasonably priced and convenient restaurant serving well-prepared Milanese classics from minestrone and various risotto dishes right through to Gorgonzola cheese. ♦ Closed W, holidays. Via Ugo Foscolo 1. 862020

6 Grand Duomo $$$ Great central location, courteous service and some rooms with a view make this hotel popular with a business and tourist clientele. ♦ Via San Raffaele 1. 8833

7 Casa Svizzera $$$ As efficient as its name (it means *Swiss house*) implies, this no-nonsense hotel gets a loyal business clientele. ♦ Via San Raffaele 3. 802246

8 San Raffaele This little church was commissioned in 1575 by **St. Charles Borromeus** on the site of a medieval church. The facade has been attributed to **Pellegrino Tibaldi**, and more recently to **Galeazzo Alessi**. Inside are 17th-century Milanese paintings: *St. Luke* and *St. Matthew*, by **Ambrogio Figino**, in the right nave; *Supper at the Jews* attributed to **Caravaggio**, on the far wall; *Disobedience of Jonathan* by **Giovanni Battista Crespi**, known as **Cerano**, on the right side wall; and *Dream of Elias*, by **Pier Francesco Mazzucchelli** (known as **Morazzone**), on the left side wall. ♦ Via San Raffaele

9 Caffé Scala A vaguely Viennese-style cafe that attracts a definitely Milanese blend of fashion and designer types. ♦ Tu-Su 7AM-1AM. Via Santa Margherita 14-16. 876847

10 Piazza della Scala More Milanese hustle and bustle at the exit of the Galleria. The piazza's most dramatic moment comes each **Sant'Ambrose Day**, 7 December, dedicated to Milan's patron saint. The date marks the opening of the opera season at **La Scala** across the street, when a motley crowd gathers to gawk at and sometimes jeer the tanned and bejeweled first-nighters. In the center of the piazza is a 19th-century statue by **Pietro Magni** of **Leonardo da Vinci**, who was in Milan in the service of **Ludovico Sforza**. ♦ Piazza della Scala

11 Palazzo Marino (begun 1553, **Galeazzo Alessi**) Commissioned by the Genoese banker **Tomaso Marini,** this handsome palazzo is the work of many hands, some heavier than others. The Renaissance facades facing Via Marino and Piazza San Fedele are by Galeazzo Alessi, but the Piazza della Scala side dates

from 1892 and is by **Luca Beltrami**. That side gives access to Alessi's heavily detailed courtyard, from which may be visited the deeply decorated **Sala dell'Alessi**, seat of the City Council. City government offices also occupy the rest of the palazzo. ♦ Piazza della Scala

12 Piazza San Fedele In this piazza is **Francesco Barzaghi**'s 1883 **Monument to Alessandro Manzoni**, the Milanese author of *I Promessi Sposi* (*The Betrothed*), whose last

communion took place in the church of San Fedele. ♦ Piazza San Fedele

13 San Fedele (begun 1569, **Pellegrino Tibaldi**) This Jesuit church has a cupola designed by **Francesco Maria Ricchino** in 1684, who also did the Baroque sacristy (1624-28), which contains carved wood by **Daniele Ferrari**. ♦ Piazza San Fedele

14 Danese One of the mainstays of Milanese design, this shop carries the work of such great names as **Achille Castiglioni, Bruno Munari, Enzo Mari** and **Angelo Mangiarotti**. ♦ Closed M morning, Su, lunch. Piazza San Fedele 1. 866296. Also at: Via Santa Maria Fulcorina 17. 866019

15 Pellux Luggage, luggage, luggage including the Pellux line of classic leather suitcases. ♦ Closed M morning, Su, lunch. Via Ragazzi del 99. 864104

16 Ravizza Sport Hunting and fishing gear for the Milanese elite. ♦ Closed M morning, Su, lunch. Via Hoepli 3. 803853

17 Hoepli Milan's famous publishing house specializes in its own line of technical manuals on practical and obscure subjects such as painting restoration. ♦ Closed M morning, Su, lunch. Via Hoepli 5. 865446

18 Hotel de la Ville $$$ Great location coupled with service (and for better or worse, some of the rooms) from another era. ♦ Via Hoepli 6. 866609

18 Canoviano ★★★$$$ Sleek eating especially popular with expense accounters. Such dishes as *trittico di pesce al vapore* (steamed fish—whatever's fresh) and *rognoncino trifolato al brandy* (truffled kidney in brandy sauce) speak for the high caliber of this restaurant's cuisine. ♦ Closed Sa lunch, Su, Aug. Via Hoepli 6. 8058472

19 Piazza Meda The piazza features **Arnaldo Pomodoro**'s sculpture *Great Disk*. ♦ Piazza Meda

---

Restaurants/Nightlife: Red   **Hotels:** Blue
Shops/Parks: Green   **Sights/Culture:** Black

20 Casa degli Omenoni (1565, **Leone Leoni**) This *house of the big men* gets its name from the 8 caryatid sculptures by **Antonio Abondio** on the facade. Since 1929 it has been the headquarters of a private club. ◆ Via degli Omenoni 3

21 Palazzo Belgioioso (begun 1772, **Piermarino Piermarini**) A large and stately Neoclassical palazzo for one of Milan's leading families. ◆ Piazza Belgioioso 2

Within the Palazzo Belgioioso:

Boeucc ★★★$$$ A hushed atmosphere

prevails at this most beloved of the old-style Milanese restaurants, an excellent place to sample the city's risotto dishes, *costoletta alla milanese* and a fine selection of fruits, cheeses and desserts. ◆ Closed Sa, Su lunch, Aug. Piazza Belgioioso 2. 790224

22 Museo Manzoniano/Casa del Manzoni This unassuming palazzo housed **Alessandro Manzoni** from 1814 until his death in 1873. Manzoni was the author of the plodding *I Promessi Sposi*, translated in English as *The Betrothed*—a romantic historical novel written in Tuscan dialect as a nod to **Dante** just before the unification of Italy in the 19th century. More important politically than as literature, it is largely derived from **Sir Walter Scott** and is required reading for every school child in Italy, just as every town in Italy has some street or another named after Manzoni. The house is a virtual shrine to the author, containing an exhaustive array of memorabilia. ◆ Tu-F 9AM-12:30PM, 2-4PM. Via Morone 1. 871019

23 Peri Miles of fabrics in this shop, built in the former **Palazzo Crespi**, whose rounded facade traces the outline of a Roman theater which stood on the spot in ancient times. ◆ Closed M morning, Su, lunch. Via Morone 3. 864076

23 Antica Barbiera Colla The ultimate in an old-style men's barber shop. ◆ Tu-Sa 9AM-1PM, 4-7:30PM. Via Morone 3. 874312

24 Giusy Bresciani Lovely millinery (the word comes from Milan, in fact) and other fanciful garb for the ladies. ◆ Closed M morning, Su. Via Morone 4. 708655

25 Museo Poldi Pezzoli Gian Giacomo Poldi Pezzoli was a 19th-century nobleman and collector who decorated various rooms of his Neoclassical palazzo in styles to serve as backdrops for his works of art. Bombed during WWII, the palazzo was subsequently remodeled in accordance with 20th-century exhibition concepts, yet something of the atmosphere of a private collection has nevertheless been maintained. The ground floor has an 18th-century ceiling fresco by **Carlo Innocenzo Carloni**. Upstairs are 3 small rooms, the **Salette dei Lombardi**, with pictures by 15th- and 16th-century Lombard painters. The first of the rooms has a *Madonna and Child* by **Vincenzo Foppa**; in the second are Foppa's *Portrait of Giovanni Francesco Brivio*, *Rest on the Flight to Egypt* by

Andrea Solario, and *Madonnas* by Solario, **Cesare da Sesto** and **Giovanni Antonio Boltraffio**. The **Sala degli Stranieri** has works by **Lucas Cranach** and other foreign artists. The Rococo-decorated **Saletta degli Stucchi** houses a porcelain collection. The **Salone Dorato**, once decorated in a Renaissance style, was badly damaged but still displays the Renaissance works. Among them the profile *Portrait of a Woman* by **Antonio Pollaiuolo**, sometimes attributed to his brother **Piero** (whoever painted her, the bejeweled blonde with the charming overbite has now become the mascot of the museum); **Piero della Francesca**'s *St. Nicolas of Tolentino*; *Madonnas* by **Antonio Vivarini, Andrea Mantegna** and **Sandro Botticelli**; Botticelli's *Lamentation*, *Grey Lagoon* by **Francesco Guardi**, and a *Pieta* by **Giovanni Bellini**. Adjoining the Salone is the **Sala Visconti Venosta**, which contains works from the collection of **Emilio Visconti Venosta**, among them *Madonnas* by **Pinturicchio** and **Bergognone**. Further rooms are the **Sala degli Orologi**, which houses a collection of clocks; the **Sala Nera**, with 6 carved walnut doors, containing paintings and decorative objects; the **Sala dei Vetri Antichi di Murano**, with antique Murano glass; the heavily Neo-Gothic **Gabinetto Dantesco**, intact from the days of Gian Giacomo Poldi Pezzoli; the **Sala del Palma**, so-called because of its 16th-century *Portrait of a Courtesan* by **Palma Il Vecchio**; the **Gabinetto degli Ori**, with a jewelry collection; and finally rooms with works by painters from Venice and the Veneto. ◆ Admission. Tu-F 9:30AM-12:30PM, 2:30-6PM; Sa 9:30AM-12:30PM, 2:30-7:30PM; Su 9:30AM-12:30PM, 2:30-6PM (mornings only Apr-Sep) Via Manzoni 12. 794889, 796334

25 Marcatre A sleek showroom displaying an equally sleek stock of designer goods. ◆ Closed M morning, Su, lunch. Via Manzoni 12. 794514

25 Don Lisander ★★★$$$ Tuscan **Giocchino Coppini** has mastered the Milanese classics from all the risottos to Gorgonzola and other local cheeses in this restaurant, especially pleasant during the warmer months when tables are placed outdoors including a private garden. ◆ Closed Sa dinner, Su, Aug, Christmas-New Year. Via Manzoni 12A. 790130

26 Angelo Radaelli The place where discriminating Milanese buy their flowers. ◆ Closed M morning, Su, lunch. Via Manzoni 16. 76002876

26 Poltrona Frau One of the oldest furniture design producers in Milan, with the newer models designed by the likes of **Marco Zanuso** and **Mario Bellini**. ◆ Closed M morning, Su, lunch. Via Manzoni 20. 796865

27 Grandi Firme As the name implies, designer signatures such as **Yves St. Laurent** and **Guy Laroche** at bargain prices. ◆ Closed Su, lunch. Via Manzoni 26. No credit cards. 780496

28 San Francesco di Paola This Baroque church with the lively facade was only completed in 1891. ◆ Via Manzoni

29 Design Gallery Specializing—guess what?—in contemporary design, this gallery carries **Sottsass** and other international names. ◆ Via Manzoni 46. 797955

30 Leonardo's ★★$$ **Giorgio Cavagliano**'s kitchen is especially praised for its *insalata mille sapore*, a huge *thousand-flavor* salad that many have for lunch. ◆ Closed Sa lunch, Su, holidays. Via Senato 43. 793564

31 Alfio ★★★$$$ **Alfio Bocciardi**, former owner of **Savini**, now runs one of Milan's most famous restaurants, where a groaning anti-pasto table leads to decent risottos and pastas (spaghetti with caviar is one of the most successful) and on to well-prepared fish and game dishes, supplemented in season with truffles and funghi porcini mushrooms. The most interesting wines are from the Piedmont and Trentino regions. ◆ Via Senato 31. Closed Sa, Su lunch. 700633

32 Palazzo del Senato (begun 1608, **Federico Borromeo** and **Francesco Maria Ricchino**) Originally built under Cardinal Federico Borromeo for the **Collegio Elvetico**, this curved-facaded palazzo today houses the **Archivio di Stato** or State Archives. ◆ Via Senato 11

33 Carlton Senato $$$ Friendly and modern, this primarily business hotel (though what hotel isn't in this town?) is also quiet, especially the rooms facing pedestrian Via della Spiga. ◆ Via Senato 5. 798583

34 Sabattini Design objects in silver alloy by **Lino Sabattini** as well as a few other originals and reproductions. ◆ Closed M morning, Su, lunch. Via della Spiga 2. 798449

34 Giuliano Fujiwara A high-design space sets the scene for high-design Japanese clothing.

◆ Closed M morning, Su, lunch. Via della Spiga 2. 792083

35 Prada One of Milan's most traditional venues for ladies' shoes in an appropriately traditional setting where luxurious travel gear is also among the merchandise. ◆ Closed M morning, Su, lunch. Via della Spiga 1. 708636

35 Rondina Ferruccio Fiorentini and other jewelry designers market their wares in this rich space. ◆ Closed M morning, Su, lunch. Via della Spiga 1. 705810

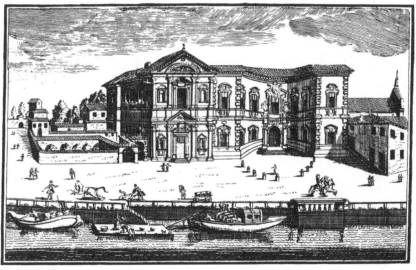

Palazzo del Senato

36 Crottini A small women's boutique featuring big-name designer clothing from casual to formal wear. ◆ Closed M morning, Su, lunch. Via della Spiga 3. 702677

37 Gianni Versace The women's boutique of the designer famed for his original use of rich fabrics. ◆ Closed M morning, Su, lunch. Via della Spiga 4. 705451

38 Bulgari The fortresslike Milan branch protects the heavy-duty jewelry of this Roman designer. ◆ Closed M morning, Su, lunch. Via della Spiga 5. 791651

38 Bottega Veneta The much-imitated hallmark of these leather goods is buttery-soft hides worked into a woven look. ◆ Closed M morning, Su, lunch. Via della Spiga 5. 791651

39 Sharra Pagano Imaginative concoctions of jewelry in semiprecious and faux gemstones. ◆ Closed M morning, Su, lunch. Via della Spiga 7. 709101

Restaurants/Nightlife: Red   **Hotels:** Blue
Shops/Parks: Green   **Sights/Culture:** Black

39 Gio Moretti A high fashion boutique for the whole priviliged family, provided the family fancies **Claude Montana, Gianfranco Ferrè, Gianni Versace**, etc. ♦ Closed M morning, Su, lunch. Via della Spiga 7. 709186. Also at: Via della Spiga 6. 709186; Via della Spiga 9. 780089

39 Club Amici Gran Moda Griffe *Club* means you have to pay a membership fee to join, but once admitted you have access to designer labels of clothing for all sexes at great

Centro

discounts. ♦ M, W, F 4-7:30PM. Via della Spiga 7. No credit cards. No phone

39 Colombo High-fashion leathergoods featuring the best handbags in Milan. ♦ Closed M morning, Su, lunch. Via della Spiga 9. 700184

40 Cose Another boutique full of well-selected designer clothing for women. ♦ Closed M morning, Su, lunch. Via della Spiga 8. 790703

41 Saint Andrew's ★★$$ A trendy stop for shoppers, with the best beef Wellington in town as well as a good Italian menu. The otherwise classic *cotoletta alla milanese* for some reason is called *l'orecchio d'elefante*—elephant ear—here. ♦ Closed Su. Via Sant'Andrea 23. 7931332

42 Carrano Some of the finest footwear in Milan, for men's and women's feet. ♦ Closed M morning, Su, lunch. Via Sant'Andrea 21. 709495

42 Barba's This shop specializes in the kind of casually slick look many men have come to associate with Milanese menswear, and does made-to-order too. ♦ Closed M morning, Su, lunch. Via Sant'Andrea 21. 701426

43 Fendi The Roman sisters have their women's clothing embassy at this address. ♦ Closed M morning, Su, lunch. Via della Spiga 11. 799544

43 Gianfranco Ferrè The designer's men's and women's wear is shown off before a high-tech setting hinting at Ferrè's training as an architect. ♦ Closed M morning, Su, lunch. Via della Spiga 11. 794864

44 Errenuo Giorgio Armani's less expensive, sportier collection for women. ♦ Closed M morning, Su, lunch. Via della Spiga 15. 795575

45 Jean Paul Gaultier Fabulous French women's clothing in a far-out setting designed by the couturier himself. ♦ Closed M morning, Su, lunch. Via della Spiga 20. 780804

46 Diego della Valle Della Valle combines high and casual style with comfort that has made him Milan's hottest shoe designer. ♦ Closed M morning, Su, lunch. Via della Spiga 22. 702423

46 Alberto Subert Some of the more portable items in this antiques store are the 17th-century *paesini* or little landscapes made with semiprecious stones. ♦ M 4-7:30PM; Tu-Sa 9AM-1PM, 4-7:30PM; closed Su. Via della Spiga 22. No credit cards. 799594

46 Adriana Mode One-of-a-kind women's fashion made by **Daniela Gerini** (daughter of the owner) is the specialty of this shop. ♦ Closed M morning, Su, lunch. Via della Spiga 22. 708458

47 Krizia Krizia's fanciful women's wear is set off by a stark monochromatic setting. ♦ Closed M morning, Su, lunch. Via della Spiga 23. 70842

48 Garzanti This new bookshop is chock-full of picture books (art, photography, design, fashion) by its namesake publisher and others. ♦ Closed M morning, Su, lunch. Via della Spiga 30. 794222

49 Mauro Brucoli Antiques, including silver objects and Austro-Hungarian era baubles. ♦ Closed M morning, Su, lunch. Via della Spiga 42. 793767

49 Nica Men's and women's footwear in the trendiest as well as more classic styles. ♦ Closed M morning, Su, lunch. Via della Spiga 42. 706835

49 Gulp Texan-born designer **Sam Rey** displays a penchant for African fabrics in his store. ♦ Closed M morning, Su, lunch. Via della Spiga 42. 76004818

50 L'Utile e il Dilettevole Sort of French and English (therefore very Milanese) country table linens and accessories. ♦ Closed M morning, Su, lunch. Via della Spiga 46. 708420

51 Laura Biagiotti The Biagiotti look in women's wear is frilly and feminine. ♦ Closed M morning, Su, lunch. Via Borgospesso 19. 799659

52 Vetrerie di Empoli The Tuscan town of Empoli is known for its rustic green glass, available here along with more refined breakables. ♦ Closed Su, lunch. Via Borgospesso 5. No credit cards. 76008791

53 Parini Quality foods, many of them such trendy imports as Kellogg's Corn Flakes, but valued Italian olive oil and dried mushrooms among them. ♦ Closed M afternoon, Su, lunch. Via Borgospesso 1. 76002302

54 Bice ★★$$ This restaurant deservedly has an international reputation, with such notables as **Giorgio Armani** and **Gianni Versace** drawn to the Tuscan cuisine. ♦ Closed M. Via Borgospesso 12. 76002572

55 Giulia Schmid *Radica* or briarwood run riot in smoking and travel accessories. ♦ Closed M morning, Su. Via Borgospesso 22. 790251

55 Sebastian Custom-made shoes in a wealth of styles and leathers. ♦ Closed M morning, Su, lunch. Via Borgospesso 18. 780532

56 L'Occhialaio The finest names in international eyewear, as well as the shop's own exclusive line for one-of-a-kind 4-eyes.

◆ Closed M morning, Su, lunch. Via Luigi Rossari 5. No credit cards. 700838

57 Carlo Tivoli The fur flies here, exotically and expensively, but beware of species that customs won't allow back in the USA. ◆ Closed M morning, Su, lunch. Via Santo Spirito 26. 701490

57 Florence Taccani Miles of majolica, most of which is Italian in origin (some is from France and Spain), makes a unique and personal gift, and travels well in your carry-on luggage. ◆ Closed M morning, Su, lunch. Via Santo Spirito 24. No credit cards. 781248

58 Manzoni $$$ A servicable 50-room hotel in the prime location of the city center. ◆ Via Santo Spirito 20. No credit cards. 705697

59 Corrado Irionè Made-to-measure and ready-to-wear furs in this century-old family-run business. ◆ Closed M morning, Su, lunch. Via Santo Spirito 7. 765630

59 Valentino The internationally famed women's designer's Milan shop. ◆ Closed M morning, Su, lunch. Via Santo Spirito 3. 706478

60 Palazzi Bagatti Valsecchi (1878-95, **Bagatti Valsecchi** brothers) Two Neo-Renaissance palazzi with an interconnecting courtyard. ◆ Via Santo Spirito 10

61 Nanni Strada Excruciatingly creative women's clothing based on the principle of fashion as art. Effete and effervescent, it must be seen (and tried on) to be believed. ◆ Closed M morning, Su, lunch. Via Gesú 4. 799708

62 Fendi The famed Roman sister's furs are represented here in their Milanese branch, all cleverly cut and some dazzlingly dyed. ◆ Closed M morning, Su, lunch. Via Sant'Andrea 16. 791617

63 Luciano Soprani Women's wear by designer Luciano Soprani. ◆ Closed M morning, Su, lunch. Via Sant'Andrea 14. 798327

63 Franco Colli Ladies' leather shoes and bags. ◆ Closed M morning, Su, lunch. Via Sant'Andrea 12. 700832

64 Gianfranco Ferrè The *architectural* designer's men's boutique. ◆ Closed M morning, Su, lunch. Via Sant'Andrea 10A. 700385

64 Comme des Garcons Metal, marble and wood create a very Japanese backdrop to the only branch of this Japanese high-fashion boutique in Italy. ◆ Closed M morning, Su, lunch. Via Sant'Andrea 10A. 76000905

64 Cesare Paciotti Stylish shoes with a conservative bent for both sexes. ◆ Closed M morning, Su, lunch. Via Sant'Andrea 8. 701164

64 Palazzo Morando Bolognini (18th c) Within this Baroque palazzo:

Civico Museo di Milano (Museum of Milan) This little museum will give you an idea of what life was like in the city over the centuries with genre paintings depicting street scenes and popular festivals. ◆ Daily 9:30AM-7:30PM; closed last M of month. Via Sant'Andrea 6. 76006245

Civico Museo di Storia Contemporanea (Museum of Contemporary History) Ten

rooms illustrate the history of the city from 1914 to 1945 through artifacts and photographs. ◆ Daily 9:30AM-7:30PM; closed last M of month. Via Sant'Andrea 6. 765006245

Civico Museo di Arte Ugo Mursia (Ugo Mursia Museum) This museum houses the collection of former publishing magnate Ugo Mursia. A great fan of writer **Joseph Conrad**, Mursia collected lots of material related to the sea, such as mastheads, etc. ◆ Daily 9:30AM-7:30PM; closed last M of month. Via Sant'Andrea 6. 76004143

65 Giorgio Armani Men's and women's clothing by the reigning king of Italian fashion. ◆ Closed M morning, Su, lunch. Via Sant'Andrea 9. 792957

65 Trussardi Men's and women's clothing by the designer renowned for his gloves and leather accessories. ◆ Closed M morning, Su, lunch. Via Sant'Andrea 5. 790380

65 Lo Scarabeo d'Oro Unusual jewelry creations made from such exotic materials as antique coins and odd metals like titanium. ◆ Closed M morning, Su, lunch. Via Sant'Andrea 3. 700547

65 Baretto ★★$$ A small and sedate place for a refreshing drink or a shopping lunch, where besides the oysters and caviar, home cooking (*polpettine alla milanese* or Milanese meatballs) is the order of the day. ◆ M-Sa 10AM-midnight. Via Sant'Andrea 3. 781255

66 Sevigne Good china at better prices than at most shops in the area. ◆ Closed M-F lunch, Su. Via Sant'Andrea 1. No credit cards. 793250

66 Guido Pasquali Oddball shoes for women. ◆ Closed M morning, Su, lunch. Via Sant'Andrea 1. 701645

66 Marisa **Marisa Lombardi**'s boutique brings together top women's designers as well as a collection of sweaters made just for her. ◆ Closed M morning, Su, lunch. Via Sant'Andrea 1. 799225. Also at: Via Cino del Duca. 791054

67 Bagutta ★★$$ The Tuscan cuisine that began when the restaurant was founded by **Alberto Pepori** in 1926 is still going strong here, as is the literary prize (Italy's first) begun here as well. ◆ Closed Su. Via Bagutta 14-16. 76000902

68 Albrizzi Adalberto Cremonese produces the chicest paper and paper products in Milan. ◆ Closed M morning, Su, lunch. Via Bagutta 8. No credit cards. 76001218

69 Paper Moon ★★$$ A lively *pizzeria* with an international reputation. Its *quattro stagione* (4 seasons, made with 4 kinds of cheese) pizza makes the perfect light lunch after some heavy shopping. ◆ Closed Su. Via Bagutta 1. 792297

70 Palazzo Taverna (1835, **Ferdinando Abertolli**) A handsome residence from the last

Centro

century, this stately palazzo houses:

Ricordi The main shop of Italy's best-known music publishers, where the recordings are augmented by books and sheet music. ◆ Closed M morning, Su, lunch. Via Monte Napoleone 2. 701982

Mila Schön Elegant separates for women are what Mila Schön is best known for, but there are also accessories, perfumes and china here. (The men's line at Via Monte Napoleone 6, same hours and telephone number). ◆ Closed M morning, Su, lunch. Via Monte Napoleone 2. 701803

GUCCI

Gucci The Milan branch of the Florentine firm long famous for its loafers but now updating its look a little. (Leathergoods at Via Monte Napoleone 5, same hours, 5456621). ◆ Closed M morning, Su, lunch. Via Monte Napoleone 2. 799955

Nazareno Gabrielli Interesting silver objects on sale alongside diaries, leathergoods and jewelry. ◆ Closed M morning, Su, lunch. Via Monte Napoleone 2. 76006561

71 Santini e Dominici Top fashion shoes at less than top prices. ◆ Closed M morning, Su, lunch. Via Monte Napoleone 1. 76001958

71 Pederanzi Diamonds are your best friends in this jewelry shop, run by 2 dazzlingly charming brothers. ◆ Closed M morning, Su, lunch. Via Monte Napoleone 1. 701728

71 Pirovano Made-to-measure ladies' eveningwear and luxurious fashion accessories. (Couture shop at Via Monte Napoleone 8, 702571.) ◆ Closed M morning, Su, lunch. Via Monte Napoleone 1. 702473

71 Missoni Colorful knits for men and women, especially in sweaters, are the trademark of this shop. ◆ Closed M morning, Su, lunch. Via Monte Napoleone 1. 790906

71 Fratelli Rosetti Men's and women's shoes for those for whom money is no object. ◆ Closed M morning, Su, lunch. Via Monte Napoleone 1. 791650

71 Fausto Santini Lots of trendy leather for men and women's feet at relatively affordable prices. ◆ Closed M morning, Su, lunch. Via Monte Napoleone 1. 701958

72 Salvatore Ferragamo The Florentine shoemaker's ladies foothold in Milan, with clothing and accessories as well. ◆ Closed M morning, Su, lunch. Via Monte Napoleone 3. 700054

72 Fontana Arte Some of the best one-stop shopping for museum-quality Italian design by all the famous names. ◆ Closed M morning, Su, lunch. Via Monte Napoleone 3. 791089

72 Tanino Crisci Famous footwear for both sexes. ◆ Closed M morning, Su, lunch. Via Monte Napoleone 3. 791264

72 Lario 1898 Shoes and leathergoods for men and women. ◆ Closed M morning, Su, lunch. Via Monte Napoleone 3. 702641

73 Mario Buccellati Delicate jewelry in this family-run shop. ◆ Closed M morning, Su, lunch. Via Monte Napoleone 4. 702153

73 Valeriano Ferrario Handmade shoes for men and women. ◆ Closed M morning, Su, lunch. Via Monte Napoleone 6. 790928

74 Trabucco High-tech jewelry for high rollers. ◆ Closed M morning, Su, lunch. Via Monte Napoleone 5. 792856

74 Faraone The Milan branch of Florence's most famous jeweler. ◆ Closed M morning, Su, lunch. Via Monte Napoleone 7A. 5456256

75 Philippe Daverio A contemporary gallery showing such international art superstars as **Sandro Chia**. ◆ Closed M, Su. Via Monte Napoleone 6A. 7600148

75 Cova The traditional stop for pastry in a discreet setting frequented by those who can afford to shop in this area. The coffee is better than the tea. ◆ M-Sa 8AM-7:30PM. Via Monte Napoleone 8. No credit cards. 700578

75 Martignetti Pearls and coral are the seaworthy specialties of this jeweler. ◆ Closed M morning, Su, lunch. Via Monte Napoleone 10. 701509

76 Larusmiani Anglo-Italian menswear of all types for budgets of only one—limitless. ◆ Closed M morning, Su, lunch. Via Monte Napoleone. 706957

76 Pisa Milan's largest selection of watches and—more affordably—watchbands to fit all major names. ◆ Closed M morning, Su, lunch.

Via Pietro Verri. 791998

76 Gianni Versace The fabric-conscious designer's men's boutique. ♦ Closed M morning, Su, lunch. Via Pietro Verri. 790281

76 Lorenzi The cutting edge in cutlery, as well as pipes and such housewares as espresso makers. ♦ Closed M morning, Su, lunch. Via Monte Napoleone 9. 792848

76 Venini The famous Venetian glassmaker's Milan branch stocks the firm's complete line of sleek and traditional collectible wares—pricey vases, plates and bowls. ♦ Closed M morning, Su, lunch. Via Monte Napoleone 9. 700539

77 Casolari A perfume shop that stocks a fine selection of British goods. ♦ Closed M morning, Su, lunch. Via Pietro Verri 2. 791937

78 Ermenegildo Zegna Men's tailoring and ready-to-wear with an emphasis on evening wear. ♦ Closed M morning, Su, lunch. Via Pietro Verri 3. 795521

78 Manhattan Unlike its island namesake, the music at this piano bar is a romantic combination of Italian and French love songs as interpreted by **Enzo Scianna**. ♦ M-Sa 6PM-3AM. Via Pietro Verri 3. 793566

78 Cravatterie Nazionali Ties in all fabrics, colors and patterns. ♦ Closed M morning, Su, lunch. Via Pietro Verri 5. 76004208

79 Il Salumaio di Montenapoleone After you've shopped until you drop, stop in here for a few delicious food items—cheeses especially make a nice upscale snack. ♦ Closed M morning, Su, lunch. Via Monte Napoleone 12. No credit cards. 701123

79 Coiffeur Greco A relatively reasonable ladies' hairdresser who gives a 10% discount Tuesday-Thursday. ♦ Closed M, Su. Via Monte Napoleone 12. No credit cards. 791834

79 Divarese Sensible shoes for both sexes with a touch of whimsy. ♦ Closed M morning, Su, lunch. Via Monte Napoleone 12. 790280

79 Lorenz Clocks and watches by such designers as **Richard Sapper**, whose *Static* steel clock won Lorenz the prestigious *Compasso d'Oro* design award. ♦ Closed M morning, Su, lunch. Via Monte Napoleone 12. 794232

80 Eskenazi Milan's leading expert in Oriental art and antiques. ♦ Closed M morning, Su, lunch. Via Monte Napoleone 15. 76000022

81 Beltrami Men's and women's shoes of the famous chain. ♦ Closed M morning, Su, lunch. Via Monte Napoleone 16. 702975

81 Clara Antonini Some of the most reasonable pricetags in the area are attached to Clara Antonini's women's wear. ♦ Closed Sa, Su. Via Monte Napoleone 16. 780788

82 Ronchi Finely crafted men's shoes and ladies' slippers. ♦ Closed M morning, Su, lunch. Via Monte Napoleone 18. 706270

83 Alexander-Nicolette Conservative shoes for both sexes. ♦ Closed M morning, Su, lunch. Via Monte Napoleone 19. 701886

84 Salvatore Ferragamo The men's boutique of the Florentine designer of shoes, clothes and accessories. ♦ Closed M morning, Su, lunch. Via Monte Napoleone 20. 706660

85 Marithe et Francois Girbaud High design

(by the SITE group of New York) accentuates that element of the clothing in this boutique. ♦ Closed M morning, Su, lunch. Via Monte Napoleone 26. 76006027

85 Albanese & Mauri Trendy footwear for men and women. ♦ Closed M morning, Su, lunch. Via Monte Napoleone 26. 706027

86 Dal Vecchio Silversmiths with an untarnished reputation for contemporary design as well. ♦ Closed M morning, Su, lunch. Via Monte Napoleone 29. 708740

87 Galtrucco Tailored Galtrucco menswear as well as clothes by such names as **Ermenegildo Zegna** and **Claude Montana**. ♦ Closed M morning, Su, lunch. Via Monte Napoleone 27. 702978

87 Aldovandi Conservative men's shoes and more fashionable ladies' footwear. ♦ Closed M morning, Su, lunch. Via Monte Napoleone 27. 784256

87 Saporiti The place to see the entire collection of the famous design firm, whose furniture has been upholstered by such designers as **Missoni**. ♦ Closed M morning, Su, lunch. Via Monte Napoleone 27. 709109

87 Luca Trendy leather shoes and handbags for men and women. ♦ Closed M morning, Su, lunch. Via Monte Napoleone 27. 791115

87 Tecno The designer showroom features furniture by Centro Progetti Tecno. ♦ Closed M morning, Su, lunch. Via Monte Napoleone 27. 79041

88 Alle Antiche Armi Antique swords and daggers are the intriguing specialty of this shop. ♦ Closed M morning, Su, lunch. Via Bigli 24. No credit cards. 792318

89 Casa Olivazzi (17th c) A stately old residence from the days when people could still afford to live in the area. ♦ Via Bigli 21

90 I Regali di Nella Longari If you're stuck for a gift and don't have time to shop for one, trust Nella Longari's exquisite taste in everything from picture frames to tea services. (Her antiques shop is at Via Monte Napoleone 23, 790317.) ♦ Closed M morning, Su, lunch. Via Bigli 15. 782066

Restaurants/Nightlife: Red	**Hotels:** Blue
Shops/Parks: Green	**Sights/Culture:** Black

91 Palazzo Bigli-Poni (facade 19th c) A palazzo has occupied this spot since the times of the **Sforzas**, which can be seen by taking a peek at the **Bramante**-influenced courtyard. ◆ Via Bigli 11

92 Etro Fabulous fashion accessories in lush fabrics. ◆ Closed M morning, Su, lunch. Via Bigli 10. 795203. Also at: Vicolo Fiori 17. 807768

93 Tabak Furs with a contemporary cut. ◆ Closed M morning, Su, lunch. Via Bigli 4. 795017. Also at: Via Brera 4. 89010155

Centro

94 Truzzi The best place in town for made-to-measure men's shirts, with pajamas and suits to boot. ◆ Closed M morning, Su, lunch. Corso Matteotti 1. No credit cards. 700568

94 Dom More variety than anywhere in the city for porcelain, crystal and silver. ◆ Closed M morning, Su, lunch. Corso Matteotti 3. 793410

95 Elam **Achille Castiglioni** designed this showroom for furniture by all the top Milanese designers. ◆ Closed M morning, Su, lunch. Corso Matteotti 5. 79984

96 ICF Another well-designed designer showroom, this one featuring objects by Milanese designers historic and contemporary. ◆ Closed M morning, Su, lunch. Corso Matteotti 7. 76000583

96 Sant'Ambroeus Another of the chic places for a snack after shopping in the area, be it tea or Campari accompanied by delicate pastry. ◆ M-Sa 8AM-7:30PM. Corso Matteotti 7. 700540

96 Alessi The whole line of design objects, including the famous tea kettles designed by **Aldo Rossi** and **Richard Sapper**. ◆ Closed M morning, Su, lunch. Corso Matteotti 9. 795726

97 Mario Valentino The late clothing designer's Milan shop. ◆ Closed M morning, Su, lunch. Corso Matteotti 10. 781659

98 Moroni Gomma This shop has the strange specialty of rubber, which comes in boots, coats, containers and everything else imaginable. ◆ Closed M morning, Su, lunch. Corso Matteotti 14. 316641

98 Maestro Geppetto The largest selection of toys in the city, including the lovely wooden Pinocchio dolls made by the fictional Geppetto. ◆ Closed M morning, Su, lunch. Corso Matteotti 14. 791212

99 Petronio One of Milan's most prestigious made-to-measure men's shirtmakers. ◆ Closed M morning, Su, lunch. Corso Matteotti 20. 792084

100 Neglia A nicely chosen selection of men's clothing by all the famous names. ◆ Closed M morning, Su, lunch. Corso Venezia 2. 795231

100 Il Vendoro Service is sacrificed for savings at this gold market, where 18K items come in all varieties and there's a little silver on the side for good measure. ◆ Closed Su. Corso Venezia 2. 794107

101 Santini ★★★$$$ British-style decor provides the backdrop for Veneto-style cuisine (*pasta e fagioli* or rice and beans, *fegato alla veneziana* or liver and onions) at Japanese-style prices. ◆ Closed M, Aug. Corso Venezia 782010

102 Alla Pelle A huge selection of fashionable bags of good value for the money. ◆ Closed M morning, Su, lunch. Corso Venezia 5. 79117. Also at: Corso Venezia 9. 705247

102 Leoni Milanese insist this take-out place offers the best roast chicken and meat in the city. ◆ Tu-Su 9AM-7:30PM. Corso Venezia 7. 76000762

103 Seminario Arcivescovile (begun 1565) A number of architects worked on the Archibishop seminary. **Vincenzo Seregni** began it in 1565 it was taken over by **Pellegrini** in 1577; **Aurelio Trezzi** began the courtyard in 1602, th work on which was taken over by **Fabio Mangone** in 1608. ◆ Corso Venezia 11

103 Komlan Extremely avant-garde fashion. ◆ Closed M morning, Su, lunch. Corso Venezi 11. 7600271

103 Brigatti Milan's leading sports store, great for standard items or such souvenirs as bicycl shirts, pants and caps. ◆ Closed M morning, Su, lunch. Corso Venezia 15. 76000273

104 De Padova The very spare designer showroom which features the works of Italian designers as well as the firm's own reproductions of Shaker furniture. ◆ Closed M morning Su, lunch. Corso Venezia 14. 76002925

105 Mercantini Michela Inexpensive furs, if you want to haggle. ◆ Closed Su. Corso Venezia 8 (one flight up) No credit cards. 702521

105 Casa Fontana Pirovano (15th c) This rare Milanese Renaissance palazzo has been attrib uted variously to both **Bramante** and **Bramantino**. ◆ Corso Venezia 10

106 San Babila This Romanesque basilica was badly restored in the 19th and 20th centuries. ◆ Piazza San Babila

107 Piazza San Babila The column in this piazza (1626, **Giuseppe Robecco**) is surmounted by the lion symbol of the ancient quarter of Porta Orientale. The outdoor stand in the piazza is known for its cheap, well-designed costume jewelry. ◆ Piazza San Babila

108 Valextra Leather desk accessories at steep prices for discerning gift-givers. ◆ Closed M morning, Su, lunch. Piazza San Babila 1. 705024

108 Coppola A high-design hairdressing salon fo high-design women. ◆ Closed M morning, Su, lunch. Piazza San Babila 1. 76004074

109 Donini *Gin rosa* (pink gin) is just one of the beverages available at this bar/cafe, which also has sandwiches and ice creams for a passing snack. ◆ M-Sa 8AM-8PM. Galleria San Babila 4B. 700461

10 Picowa Kitchen accessories from practical to high-design. ♦ Closed M morning, Su, lunch. Piazza San Babila 40. 794078

11 Flos Higher-design lighting fixtures. ♦ Closed M morning, Su, lunch. Corso Monforte 9. 701641

12 Artemide One of Milan's leading lighting design shops. ♦ Closed M morning, Su, lunch. Corso Monforte 3. 76006930

13 Quattrifolio High-design lighting fixtures. ♦ Closed M morning, Su, lunch. Via Santa Cecilia 2. No credit cards. 781498

14 Magnolia Bargain children's clothing galore, for members only, but you can become one on the spot. ♦ Closed Sa afternoon, Su. Via Visconti di Modrone 11. No credit cards. 795168

15 Caracalla Bathroom accessories by leading historic and contemporary designers. The shop is named in honor of the famous ancient Roman baths. ♦ Closed M morning, Su, lunch. Via Cerva 19. 76002195

16 Palazzo Bolagnos (18th c) Nice, inviting courtyard in this old palazzo. ♦ Via Borgogna 8

17 Christie's The Milan outlet for the international auctioneers, where showings and sales take place with increasing regularity. ♦ Closed Su, lunch. Via Borgogna 9. 794712

18 Arflex High-design furniture by one of Milan's most important postwar firms. ♦ Closed M morning, Su, lunch. Via Borgogna 2. 76005972

19 Simon International Dino Gavina, who went on to found Knoll International, began by producing furniture under the name of Simon International. Other Simon designers on display here are Pier Giacomo Castiglioni and Meret Oppenheim. ♦ Closed M morning, Su, lunch. Via Durini 25. 796322

20 Palazzo Durini (1643, Francesco Maria Richini) An ornate Baroquey palazzo built for a wealthy Milanese silk merchant. ♦ Via Durini 24

In the Palazzo Durini:

Emporio Armani Less expensive but equally stylish clothing for men, women and children by the maestro of Milanese clothing design, Giorgio Armani. ♦ Closed M morning, Su, lunch. Via Durini 24. 709030

121 Franco Maria Ricci Effete publications on esoteric subjects. ♦ Closed M morning, Su, lunch. Via Durini 19. 7702

122 Bar Prada The most pleasant and practicable option for coffee, drink, pastry or light lunch in the immediate surroundings. ♦ M-Sa 8AM-9PM. Galleria Strasburgo 3. 798425

122 Gruppo Industriale Busnelli Designer furniture augmented by such fashion-turned-fabric designers as Nicola Trussardi. ♦ Closed M morning, Su, lunch. Galleria Strasburgo 3. 709428

123 Cassina The most singularly spectacular of Milan's design showrooms, carrying products signed by Italians and such international names as Frank Lloyd Wright and Le Corbusier. ♦ Closed M morning, Su, lunch. Via Durini 18. 790745

Centro

123 Caffé Moda Durini An American-style shopping mall with the difference being it's full of affordable Milanese-style clothing. ♦ Closed M morning, Su, lunch. Via Durini 14. 791188

124 Peppino ★★$$ Tuscan Peppino has been replaced by Alberto Besuti, who has added Apulian chef Gaetano Schiavoni in the kitchen to augment the Milanese-Tuscan standards with some southern specialties such as the tiny ear-shaped pasta called *orecchiette*. ♦ Closed F, Sa lunch, July. Via Durini 7. 781729

124 Joaquin Berao A tiny jewelers featuring highly original, almost sculptural, designs. ♦ Closed M morning, Su, lunch. Via Durini 5. 76003993

125 Arcando Exclusive custom-made men's and women's footwear with a tradition dating from 1919. ♦ Closed M morning, Su, lunch. Via Durini 4. 780791

126 B&B Office furniture in a matching high-tech setting. ♦ Closed M morning, Su, lunch. Corso Europa 2. 76009306

127 Palazzo Litta Cusini (15th c) This old palazzo was given a showy renovation in the 17th century. ♦ Corso Europa 16

127 Carrano Due The less-expensive line of the usually more expensive shoemakers, with an appeal to the young and young-at-heart of both sexes. ♦ Closed Su, lunch. Corso Europa 18. 799031

128 Ribes Rosso Cheap costume jewelry. ♦ Closed Su. Corso Europa 22. 781680

129 Fiorucci A huge shop featuring the outrageous clothing and accessories of Elio Fiorucci. ♦ Closed M morning, Su. Galleria Passarella 1. 708033

130 Benetton One of the myriad shops of the highly successful purveyor of woolen goods for both sexes. ♦ Closed M morning, Su. Galleria Passarella 2. 794749

130 Sisley Benetton's slightly more upscale sister store, with woolen and other goods again for the whole family. ♦ Closed M morning, Su. Galleria Passarella 2. 704043

130 Marco A well-stocked newsstand with an international selection, good for a browsing break. ♦ Closed M morning, Su. Galleria Passarella 2. 795866

131 San Carlo al Corso (1839-47, **Carlo Amati**) A strangely Pantheon-like church in the fashionable Neoclassical style of the mid-19th century. ♦ Piazza San Carlo

Centro

132 Zebedia More men's shirts (from casual to formal) than you can shake a stick at, with a faithful clientele of tomboys as well. ♦ Closed M morning, Su. Corso Vittorio Emanuele II 37B. 792078

133 Ercolesi The best place for pens and writing supplies in the city. ♦ Closed M morning, Su, lunch. Corso Vittorio Emanuele II 15. 76000607

133 Bocci The place to come if you're on the go, since its specialty is luggage and travel accessories in all shapes, sizes, colors and fabrics. ♦ Closed M morning, Su, lunch. Corso Vittorio Emanuele II 15. 790839

133 Panca Women's shoes with panache. ♦ Closed M morning, Su, lunch. Corso Vittorio Emanuele II 15. 793673

134 Hair Studio Mario A fashionable makeup studio which, in fact, does the makeup for such fashion shows as **Krizia**, **Missoni**, **Versace** and others, and counts leading Italian show folk among its regulars. ♦ Closed M, Su, lunch, M. Via San Pietro all'Orto 2. 791631

135 Santa Lucia ★★$$ If you're into Italian celebrity-spotting, this decent restaurant becomes all the more exciting, since actors often come here after the theater to sample the Milanese menu. ♦ Closed M, Aug. Via San Pietro all'Orto 3. 793155

136 Eve A garden of Eden for bags in all colors, shapes and sizes with a contemporary look. ♦ Closed M morning, Su. Via San Pietro all'Orto 9. 706450

136 Gabbianeli Designer tiles, perhaps a little heavy toting for an entire bathroom but sometimes interesting as trivets and the like. ♦ Closed M morning, Su, lunch. Via San Pietro all'Orto 11. 791886

137 Linea Lidia Women's shoes of high quality and price. ♦ Closed M morning, Su, lunch. Via San Pietro all'Orto 17. 791660

137 Pomellato Bold and modern jewelry as well as table settings, leathergoods, and men's and women's accessories. ♦ Closed M morning, Su, lunch. Via San Pietro all'Orto 17. 706086

137 Enrico Coveri Colorful and playful men's and women's wear by the late Tuscan designer. ♦ Closed M morning, Su, lunch. Via San Pietro all'Orto. 701624

138 Palazzo Spinola (1580-97, **Martino Bassi**) One of the older residences in the area, this one suffered like much of Milan from bombing during WWII and was faithfully reconstructed by **Antonio Cassi Ramelli**. ♦ Via San Paolo 10

139 Charleston ★★$ A pleasant spot for a light lunch of pizza or a more substantial selection from the regular menu. ♦ Closed M, Aug. Piazza Liberty 8. 798631

MaxMara

140 MaxMara Ladies love the well-designed, colorful and well-made selection of clothing from casual to business attire for which this chain is famous. ♦ Closed M morning, Su, lunch. Corso Vittorio Emanuele II. 708849

141 Mondadori Three floors of books under the auspices of Italy's largest publisher, carrying the Mondadori imprint along with many others. ♦ Closed M morning, Su. Corso Vittorio Emanuele II 34. 705832

142 Pollini Fashionable footwear for men and women. ♦ Closed M morning, Su, lunch. Corso Vittorio Emanuele II 30. 794912

142 Stefanel Benetton's leading competitor offer's a somewhat jazzier version of clothing for a slightly younger clientele. ♦ Closed M morning, Su. Corso Vittorio Emanuele II 28. 780721

143 Messaggerie Musicali A huge selection of musical recordings in all forms as well as music publications make this Milan's best-loved music store. ♦ Closed M morning, Su, lunch. Galleria del Corso 2. 781251

144 SEM Fashion chameleons for both sexes offering the latest generic styles at some of the lowest prices in the city. ♦ Closed Su, lunch. Corso Vittorio Emanuele II 8. No credit cards. 793892

145 Borsalino Perhaps the most famous hatmaker in all Italy, with headgear for men and women alike. ♦ Closed M morning, Su. Corso Vittorio Emanuele II 5. 8690805

146 Fratelli Freni Stop in for coffee and pastry or some of the fanciful marzipan concoctions these Sicilian brothers have brought from their native island to the city. ♦ M-Tu, Th-Su 8AM-midnight. Corso Vittorio Emanuele II 4. 804871

146 Di Bernardi Miles of hosiery and gloves for women. ♦ Closed M morning, Su. Corso Vittorio Emanuele II 4. 872130

147 L'Omm de Preja This ancient stone sculpture (it means *l'uomo di pietra* or *man of stone* in Milanese dialect) of a Roman emperor stands solemnly amidst the hustle and bustle of the street. ♦ Corso Vittorio Emanuele II

148 Piazza Beccaria The monument in the center of this piazza (bronze copy of a 19th-century marble by **Giuseppe Grandi**) is to **Cesare Beccaria**, an 18th-century Milanese jurist and philosopher, who gave his name to streets and piazzas throughout Italy. ♦ Piazza Beccaria

49 Ai Bersaglieri A sculptural monument by **Mario Robaudi** *To the Bersaglieri*, Italy's beloved black-plumed crack military division famed for running rather than walking at all times. ♦ Via Verziere

50 PAB Ladies' made-to-measure for a mature (but not necessarily richer) clientele. ♦ Closed Su, lunch. Via Merlo 1. 76006142

51 Colonna del Verziere Francesco Maria Richini and son **Domenico**'s column is topped with a statue of Christ the Redeemer by 17th-century sculptor **Gaspare Vismara**. ♦ Largo Augusto

52 Santo Stefano Maggiore (begun 1584, **Giuseppe Meda**) An imposing church of primarily historical interest, since **Galeazzo Maria Sforza** was assassinated from its medieval antecedent in 1476. ♦ Piazza Santo Stefano

52 San Bernardino alle Ossa This medieval church was worked on by **Andrea Biffi** in 1679, **Carlo Giuseppe Merlo** in 1750 and **Ferdinando Reggiori** in 1937. Its **Cappella Ossario** is decorated with bizarre human bones and a 1695 fresco of *The Triumph of Souls* by **Sebastiano Ricci**. ♦ Piazza Santo Stefano

53 Piazza Santo Stefano The busy piazza has a statue of poet **Carlo Porta** by **Ivo Soli**. ♦ Piazza Santo Stefano

54 Piazza Fontana This large expanse is a product of WWII bombing. In the center is a Neoclassical fountain by **Giuseppe Franchi**, from which the square takes its name. ♦ Piazza Fontana

54 Telerie Ghidoli Textiles and fabrics in all forms at all prices. ♦ Closed Su, lunch. Piazza Fontana 1. No credit cards. 72022880

54 Palazzo Archivescovile The archbishop's palace has occupied this site since medieval times. The present structure dates from after the sack of Milan by **Barbarossa**, rebuilt in 1174. The palazzo's most important enlargement dates from 1565, when **St. Charles Borromeus**, Archbishop of Milan, commissioned **Pellegrino Tibaldi** to design its **Cortile della Canonica** or rectory courtyard, which has 19th-century statues of *Moses* by **Antonio Tantardini** and *Aaron* by **Giovanni Strazza**; the other courtyard, **Cortile dell'Archivescovado**, has statues of **St. Ambrose** and St. Charles Borromeus. The interior of the palazzo, decorated with paintings and tapestries, is accessible only with special permission. ♦ By appt. Piazza Fontana 2. 85561

Within the Palazzo Archivescovile complex:

Scuderie dell'Archivescovado The archibishop's stables are also attributed to **Pellegrino Tibaldi**. ♦ Entrance Via delle Ore 3

54 Palazzo del Capitano di Giustizia (begun 1578, **Piero Antonio Barca**) This imposing building, historically the seat of the Milan court, today houses city offices. ♦ Piazza Fontana

155 Palazzo Reale (1771-78, **Giuseppe Piermarini**) Medieval city offices and, later, residences of the **Visconti** and **Sforza** rulers once occupied this site. It reverted to its administrative role under the Spanish and Austrian rulers, the latter of whom commissioned Giuseppe Piermarini to transform it into its present aspect. Sections of Piermarini's extensive palazzo were demolished under Fascism to make way for an office building behind it and the **Arengario** beside Piazza Duomo. Its Neoclassical interior was destroyed by bombs

during WWII and then refurbished into modern spaces for museums and temporary exhibitions, though the room called the **Sala delle Cariatidi** was left in ruin as a sort of permanent anti-war memorial. ♦ Piazza Duomo

Within the Palazzo Reale complex:

Museo del Duomo (Cathedral Museum) Highlights of the museum include a 15th-century tondo of the *Eternal Father* (Sala I); a 15th-century marble statue of **Gian Galeazzo Visconti** (Sala II); 15th-century statues of saints and prophets (Sala III); a 14th-century state of **St. Peter** (Sala V); 15th-century statues of **Galeazzo Maria Sforza** and an *Angel* (Sala VI); a Byzantine embossed metal *Crucifix* and *Madonna and Child with Two Angels* (Sala VII); 15th-century saints (Sala VIII); choir stalls (Sala IX); 16th-century tapestries and a painting by **Jacopo Tintoretto** of *Christ at the Temple* (Sala XI); 17th-century sculptural models (Sala XII); liturgical objects (Sala XX, to the left of Sala XII); terracotta models for the *Madonnina* statue atop the Duomo and 18th-century marble statues (Sala XIII); 19th-century Neoclassical sculpture (Sala XIV); models of the Duomo (Sala XVI); and models of the Duomo portals (Sala XVII). ♦ Admission. Tu-Su 9:30AM-12:30PM, 3-6PM. Piazza Duomo 14. 860358

Civico Museo d'Arte Contemporanea (Civic Museum of Contemporary Art) In its contemporary art museum (known as CIMAC in the acronym-obsessed museum world) as elsewhere, Milan has a loopier view of history than most cities. It stretches the commonly accepted definition of the beginning of contemporary art as the end of WWII back to Futurism, a movement given its name in an article by **Filippo Marinetti** in 1909. Contemporaneously, the museum compresses the definition to comprise only Italian artists. Well, some of Marinetti's words are remarkably contemporary (*We wish to glorify war*...), and where better than Milan to exhibit the works of artists who extolled the virtues of machines and motion before WWI knocked that notion out of them forever. Works by Futurists **Umberto Boccioni, Carlo Carrà, Giacomo Balla**and **Gino Severini**—the highlights of the collection —are on display in Salas XXI and XXII. Beyond those, the museum is still the best lesson on the development of 20th-century Italian painting in Italy. Canvases by the Paris-influenced **Amadeo Modigliani** and Gino Severini (Sala XXIII), the so-called metaphysical paintings of **Giorgio De Chirico** (Sala XXIV and XXV), and the volumetric landscapes and still-lifes of **Giorgio Morandi** (Sala XXIX), are among the more internationally recognized works on display. Also represented are those contemporary painters who subscribe to the going zeitgeist that futures are more important than Futurism. ♦ Daily 9:30AM-7:30PM; closed last M of month. Piazza Duomo 12. 62083219

Centro

San Gottardo in Corte (1330-36, attributed to **Francesco Pecorari**) This medieval church is noted for its octagonal campanile. The interior, redone in Neoclassical style, contains a damaged 14th-century **Giottoesque** fresco of the *Crucifixion* and the Gothic **Tomb of Azzone Visconti** (reconstructed 1930), who commissioned the church. ♦ Via Pecorari

156 Arengario (1939-56, **Enrico Griffini, Pier Giulio Magistretti, Giovanni Muzio, Piero Portaluppi**) One of these 2 Fascist-era marble buildings houses the **Ente Provinciale di Turismo** or **EPT**, where you can pick up maps and information about current events and other activities. ♦ M-Sa 8AM-8PM; Su 9AM-12:30PM, 1:30-5PM. Via Marconi 1. 62083106

157 Piazza Diaz The piazza contains a sculpture *To the Carabiniere* (one of Italy's police forces, considered by the general public to be much less abstract than the sculpture implies) by **Luciano Minguzzi.** ♦ Piazza Diaz

157 Nepentha Club ★★$$ Dancing and dining (champagne, caviar, etc.) amid Milan's most *perbene* (upper crust) club kids. ♦ Closed Su, Aug. Piazza Diaz. 804837

158 Croff A great place for inexpensive and well-designed housewares. ♦ Closed M morning, Su, lunch. Piazza Diaz 2. 862745. Also at: Corso Buenos Aires 19. 200747; Corso Vercelli 10. 432160; Corso XXII Marzo 25. 733403

158 Tino Fontana ★★$$ One of the nicer dining options in the area, offering a solid Milanese menu with such flourishes as *tagliata di manzo in salsa balsamica* or beef in balsamic vinegar sauce. ♦ Closed Su, Aug, Christmas week. Piazza Diaz 5. 860598

159 Casa della Penna This *house of pens* has all the major international brands, including Italy's own Pelikan brand, as well as some antique writing instruments. ♦ Closed M morning, Su, lunch. Via Dogana 3. 807115

160 Galtrucco Elegant fabrics for furnishings and apparel as well as ready-to-wear for men and women. ♦ Closed M morning, Su, lunch. Piazza del Duomo 2. 876256

160 Pikenz Furs with markdowns during sale periods and discounts on showroom models. ♦ Closed Su, lunch. Piazza Duomo 2. 3452231

161 Lirico (1778, **Giuseppe Piermarini**) The interior of Milan's largest theater was renovated in 1939 by **Renzo Gerla** and **Antonio Cassi Ramelli.** ♦ Via Larga 14. 866418

162 Palazzo Greppi (1776, **Giuseppe Piermarini**) Within this stately palazzo is a ballroom (also by Giuseppe Piermarini) with a 1790 ceiling painting of *Jove and Ganymede* b **Andrea Appiani.** ♦ Via Sant'Antonio 12

163 Sant'Antonio Abate (1582, **Dionigi Campazzo**) This 14th-century church was rebuilt in the 15th century (from which its cam panile dates) and again in the 16th century. Th interior is decorated with 17th- and 18th-century paintings. Among them are *St. Andrew Avellino* by **Francesco Cairo**, in the second chapel on the right; *Adoration of the Magi* by **Pier Francesco Mazzucchelli** (known as **Morazzone**), on the right wall of the transept; *Adoration of the Shepherds* by **Ludovico Carracci**, on the left wall of the transept; a *Nativity* by **Annibale Carracci**, on the left wall of the presbytery; and a *St. Cajtean* by **Giovanni Battista Crespi** (known as **Cerano**). ♦ Via Sant'Antonio

164 Beretta A restaurant supply warehouse where you can also find industrial-design objects for your home, kitchen or dining room ♦ Closed M morning, Su, lunch. Via Bergamin 5. 58304131

164 Anaconda Old-fashioned craft techniques applied to modern jewelry made from semiprecious stones and more unusual materials like mother-of-pearl and wood. ♦ Closed M morning, Su, lunch. Via Bergamini 7. 58303668

165 Odeon ★★$$ **Mario Denti**'s restaurant offers a fine Italian menu with a few French touches like a silken chocolate mousse. ♦ Closed M, Aug. Via Bergamini 13. 58307418

166 Cantina Piemontese Trattoria ★★$ An old-fashioned trattoria serving such hearty Italian fare as prosciutto and melon, *pasta e fagioli* and a nice selection of cheese. ♦ Closed Sa lunch, Su, Aug. Via Laghetto 11. 784618

167 Ospedale Maggiore (begun 1456, **Antonio Averulino**, known as **Filarete**) Originally built as Milan's main hospital (it still has some administrative offices here), this sprawling palazzo now houses the humanities department of the **Università Statale** or state university, though it is also affectionately known as **Ca' Granda**, Milanese dialect for *big house*. Commissioned by **Francesco Sforza**, the hospital became a civic project which lasted, typically, hundreds of years.

Funds were raised privately and publicly, largely though contributions made during the **Festa del Perdono** (from which the street takes its name), held 25 March on odd years.

Filarete's Renaissance plan consists of 2 sections, each divided into 4 courtyards and furnished with an elaborate plumbing system connected to the nearby *naviglio* or canal. The right wing was completed under Filarete's direction; then **Guiniforte Solari** continued the construction in a more conservative Gothic style, as seen in the windows of the facade, though the heavy cornice is pure Renaissance. A number of other architects continued the work, adding the Baroque entrance (designed by **Fabio Mangone** and **Francesco Maria Richini**) with 17th-century statues of *St. Charles* and *St. Ambrose* by **Gian Battista Bianco** and an *Annunziation* by **Gian Pietro Lasagna**, and doubling Filarete's plan for a central courtyard (by **Francesco Maria Richini**). Heavily damaged during WWII, it was restored by **Piero Portaluppi** and **Liliana Grassi**.

Within the Ospedale Maggiore:

L'Annunziata This 17th-century church has a 17th-century *Annunciation* by **Giovanni Francesco Barbieri**, known as **Guercino**.

Quadreria dei Benefattori (Benefactors' Painting Gallery) The collection consists mostly of stiff portraits of hospital benefactors, but the portrayees include everyone from **Francesco Hayez** to **Carlo Carra**. ♦ By appt. Via Festa del Perdono. 58307002

168 Olivetti Milan's most famous brand of office furniture has had such designers as **Ettore Sottsass** and **Michele De Lucchi** apply their talents to its wares. ♦ Closed M morning, Su, lunch. Largo Richini 6. 85064450

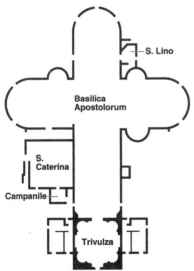

S. Lino

Basilica Apostolorum

S. Caterina

Campanile

Trivulza

169 San Nazaro Maggiore (founded 4th c) Founded by **St. Ambrose**, this church was altered through the centuries and restored to its Romanesque appearance after it was bombed in WWII. It contains **Bramantino**'s Renaissance **Cappella Trivulzio**, the octagonal mausoleum of the Trivulzio family (**Gian Giacomo Trivulzio** was the marshall of **Louis XII** of France), who lay in black stone sarcofagi in the niches. ♦ Corso di Porta Romana

170 NCA Sinigaglia Housewares at good value. ♦ Closed Su, lunch. Corso di Porta Romana 7. 8058590

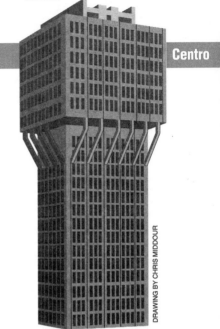

Centro

DRAWING BY CHRIS MIDDOUR

171 Torre Velasca (1958, **Studio BBPR**, including **Gian Luigi Banfi, Lodovico Belgoioso, Enrico Peressutti, Ernesto Nathan Rogers**) Named after the pre-existing piazza built by 17th-century Spanish governor **Juan de Velasco**, the Torre Velasca is contemporary Milanese architecture at its best, intelligent yet not lacking in a sense of humor. 20 office stories are topped with a 6-story residential section resting on reinforced-concrete corbels, openly exposed structural elements which refer back to the Duomo. The overall effect is wry and impressive, combining the medieval creepiness of the Castello Sforzesco with the delightful cheap thrills of 1950s space-monster movies. ♦ Piazza Velasca 5

172 Palazzo Acerbi (17th c) This noble former residence has a relaxing courtyard for a bit of respite from this busy part of the city. ♦ Corso di Porta Romana 3

173 Palazzo Annoni (1631, **Francesco Maria Ricchino**) One of the more impressive former residences in the area, with a relaxing courtyard. ♦ Corso di Porta Romana 6

174 Mixed-Use Complex (1951-56, **Luigi Moretti**) A sweeping building Milanese architect **Ernesto Rogers** compared to a ship's sail. ♦ Corso Italia

175 Sant'Eufemia This ancient church was given a Neo-Gothic facelift in the last century. ♦ Piazza Sant'Eufemia

176 San Paolo Converso This church and a no-longer-extant convent replaced some bordellos on this site beginning in 1549 thanks to the patronage of the good countess **Ludovica Torelli di Guastalle**. **Giovanni Battista Crespi** (known as **Cerano**) designed the facade in the 17th century. The inside is rich in *trompe l'oeil* architectural frescoes by the **Campi** brothers—**Antonio, Giulio** and **Vincenzo**. Now deconse-

crated, the church has been somewhat sadly relegated to use as an exhibition space; its cloister met a more glamorous end, having been used as a recording studio by such singers as **Maria Callas** and **Mina**, who has been called *the Italian Barbra Streisand*. ♦ M 3-7PM; Tu-Sa 10AM-12:30PM, 3-7PM. Corso Italia

177 Alivar Reproductions of modern furniture by **Aalto, Breuer, LeCorbusier, Macintosh** and others at less-than-collector prices. ♦ Closed M morning, Su, lunch. Via della Chiusa 10. 58101096

178 San Lorenzo Maggiore (founded 4th c) One of the most important churches from Milan's heyday as the capital of the Western Roman Empire, San Lorenzo has maintained its quatrefoil plan despite having been remodeled several times over the centuries, making it a stylistic hodgepodge of everything from Romanesque to Neoclassical. What unifies it is its hugeness, its vast interior surmounted by the largest cupola of any church in Milan. The most important chapel within San Lorenzo is the **Cappella di Sant'Aquilino**, reached though the atrium on the right as you face the altar (admission). The chapel contains ancient mosaics and a sarcophagus said to hold the remains of Byzantine empress **Galla Placidia**. Near and dear to the hearts of the Milanese, the church is the site of a particularly elaborate religious procession on 29 January, the feast day of **St. Lawrence**. ♦ Corso di Porta Ticinese

179 Colonne di San Lorenzo Maggiore (4th c) Sixteen Corinthian columns, perhaps the remains of an ancient temple, today provide an uncharacteristically Milanese—indeed rather Roman in both historic and contemporary senses—backdrop for spirited soccer games by day and loungy Milanese teenagers by night. A copy of a bronze statue of the **Emperor Constantine** (who, you'll recall, was responsible for the Edict of Milan in 313 AD) imperially oversees it all. ♦ Corso di Porta Ticinese

179 Porta Ticinese Medievale (12th c) Not to be confused with its Neoclassical counterpart of the same name, this medieval city gate is closer to the city center, when Milan's walls held a tighter grip on the city. ♦ Corso di Porta Ticinese

180 San Vito da Nino ★★$$ Nino Musella makes nicely Frenchified Italian food such as risotto with Champagne and chocolate souffle ♦ Closed M, Aug. Via San Vito 5. 8377029

181 Palazzo Stampa di Soncino (begun ca 1534) This type of house/tower was once a common sight among the nobles of northern Italy. ♦ Via Soncino 2

182 L'Ulmet ★★★$$$ Such refined dishes as *ravioli d'anatra al burro e timo* (duck-filled ravi pasta with butter and thyme), *dorso di conigl alla Vernaccia* (saddle of rabbit with Vernaccia wine) and a wide selection of mousses (*ciocc lata amara* bitter chocolate, *bianca* white chocolate and *caffe* or coffee) make this refine restaurant a favorite of the Milanese. ♦ Closed Su, M lunch, Aug. Via Disciplini. 8059260

183 Fortura International brand-name toys at a discount. ♦ Closed Sa afternoon, Su. Via Olmetto 10. No credit cards. 861670

184 Palazzo Archinto This former residence today houses city offices. ♦ Via Olmetto

185 Profumeria Mario Galli International cosmetics at a discount. ♦ Closed M-Sa afternoons, Su. Via Amadei 11. No credit cards

186 Palazzo Recalcati (begun 16th c) The courtyard part of this palazzo dates from the 16th century; other parts were added in the following 2 centuries. ♦ Via Amadei 8

186 Palazzo Mazenta The former residence of one of Milan's oldest families. ♦ Via Amadei 2

187 Primavera Inexpensive clothing for both sexes at bargain prices. ♦ Closed Su, lunch. Via Torino 47. 792662

188 Standa This long-established department store chain (modeled on the English, it was called Standard until foreign words were forbidden under Fascism) is perhaps more down market than the others in the clothing department, but is a good place for basic home furnishings and grocery items. ♦ Closed M morning, Su, lunch. Via Torino. 871425

189 Sant'Alessandro (begun 1601, **Padre Lorenzo Binago**) There's a little bit of Rome in this church, built on a central plan (like Bramante's and Michelangelo's plan for the Vatican) with a cupola and 2 domed campanile Begun on the site of a Romanesque church, a number of architects, including **Francesco Mari Richini**, carried out Padre Binago's project, finished off with a Rococo facade in the 18th century. The somewhat dark interior is rich in 17th-century works, including a *Beheading of John the Baptist* by **Daniele Crespi** in the third chapel of the left nave. ♦ Piazza Sant'Alessandr

189 Scuole Arcimboldi (1663, **Lorenzo Binago**) One of the nicest Baroque buildings in Milan. ♦ Piazza Sant'Alessandro 1

190 Piazza Missori This piazza has **Riccardo Ripamonti**'s equestrian monument to the Italian general as well as the open-air remains of the Romanesque church of **San Giovanni** in Conca. ♦ Piazza Missori

Sant' Alessandro

191 Al Guanto Perfetto The *perfect glove* here can be looked for amid the leather creations by the hands of all the top designers. ◆ Closed M morning, Su, lunch. Via Mazzini 18. 875894

192 Palazzo Erba Odescalchi (16th c, attributed to **Pelligrini**) Another stately former residence with an inviting courtyard. ◆ Via Unione 5

193 Libreria Unione Half-price books, including art books in English. ◆ Closed M morning, Su. Galleria Unione 3. No credit cards. 877304

194 Latteria Unione ★★$ A great place for a quick light lunch of changing daily pasta specials or sandwiches. ◆ Closed M afternoon, Su, lunch. Via Unione 6. No credit cards. 874401

195 Santa Maria presso San Satiro (1480, **Donato Bramante**) This small complex in the middle of a busy business district contains some of Milan's most important medieval and Renaissance architecture behind its 19th-century facade. The site was originally occupied by a basilica the **Archbishop Ansperto** built to honor **St. Satirus, St. Ambrose's** brother, in the 9th century. In the 13th century an image of the *Madonna* in the basilica miraculously drew blood when it was stabbed. Soon after it also drew crowds, so to accommodate them and commemorate the miracle, it was decided to enlarge the church. Most of the old basilica was demolished, and in its place Bramante erected the present Renaissance church. Though in the form of a *T*, the church appears to be shaped like a proper cross from the inside, thanks to Bramante's trick of making a perspective relief behind the high altar (where the miraculous image of the *Madonna* is displayed) to create the illusion of a presbytery. Also of note is Bramante's octagonal bapistry (on the right of the nave), which he originally designed as the sacristy, decorated with a terracotta freize of *putti* and busts of men made by **Agostino de' Fondutis** in 1483 to Bramante's designs. Just as interesting are the remains of medieval San Satiro, reached through the left transept.

Thought to originally have been Archbishop Ansperto's chapel, it contains traces of Byzantine frescoes of *Saints and the Madonna and Child* as well as columns topped with Early Christian and Romanesque capitals. It is now called the **Cappella della Pieta** because of its 15th-century terracotta statue of the *Pieta* by **Agostino de' Fondutis**. Bramante retained the chapel's Greek-cross shape in its interior, though outside he simplified its lines by enclosing the structure in a typically cylindrical wall. The 10th-century campanile was also part of the original basilica, and together with the Campanile dei Monaci at the basilica of San Lorenzo, served as the prototype for bell-towers throughout medieval Lombardy. ◆ Via Torino

196 Casa del Formaggio The **Peck** food empire's cheese store (*house of cheese*) where hundreds of cheeses from throughout Italy (a few from other countries) may be sampled—one is tempted to try them all at one sitting! ◆ Closed M afternoon, Su, lunch. Via Speronari 3. 800858

197 Fiordipelle Original, well-crafted bags and jewelry at affordable prices. ◆ Closed M morning, Su, lunch. Via Speronari 8. 871069

198 Savinelli The nicest pipe shop in Milan, best appreciated for its own Savinelli line. ◆ Closed M morning, Su, lunch. Via Orefici 2. 876660

199 La Furla Fashionable bags from the Bologna-based firm. ◆ Closed M morning, Su. Via Orefici 11. No credit cards. 8053944

200 Loggia degli Osii (1316, **Scoto da San Gemignano**) One of Milan's oldest pieces of architecture, this loggia was restored in 1904 and now houses private enterprises. ◆ Piazza Mercanti

201 Palazzo dei Giureconsulti (begun 1561, **Vincenzo Seregni**) This palazzo has been much altered through the ages, primarily in the last century when it was remodeled and sliced up by the city's modern street pattern. ◆ Via Mercanti

Magenta

Though much of it lies within the *cerchia dei navigli* which defines the historic center of the city, the most appealing aspect of this part of Milan is the less congested residential quarter centered around **Corso Magenta**. The broad boulevard leads past the innermost ring to the second one, known as the **Viali** or **Bastioni**, which traces the 16th-century Spanish walls. Laid out as recently as the 19th century, the Magenta area abounds with tree-lined streets, boutiques and cafes, and stately apartment buildings. In addition to boasting one of Milan's most prestigious residential neighborhoods, the Magenta area also contains a number of important churches, including **Sant'Ambrogio** (after the Duomo, the church most singularly connected with historical and popular Milanese culture) and **Santa Maria delle Grazie** (where one of the most famous works of art in the Western world, **Leonardo da Vinci**'s *The Last Supper*, is housed). Interspersed with a delicious variety of shops and restaurants, the monuments make Magenta one of the most manageable and pleasant places for a boulevardier to sample the more subtle and upscale charms of Milan.

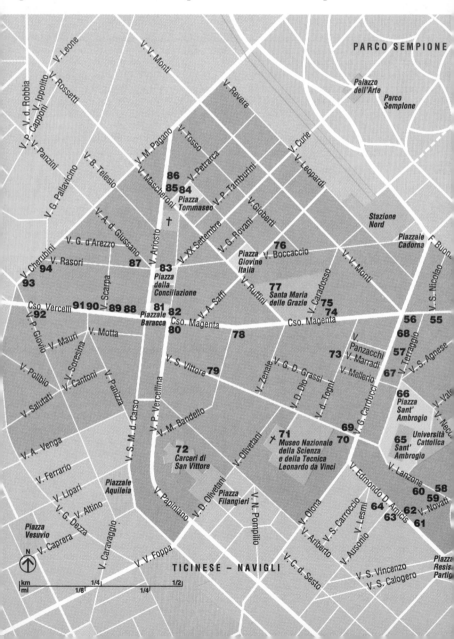

1 Riccardo Prisco A large selection of women's apparel by Prisco and other designers, especially useful for putting together a coordinated working wardrobe. ♦ Closed M morning, Su, lunch. Via Orefici. 878032

2 Bottega del Maiale The *salumeria* or pork butcher of Peck, whose restaurant and gourmet shops are a mini-empire in the vicinity. ♦ Closed M afternoon, Su, lunch. Via Victor Hugo 3. 8053528

2 Garbagnati In a neighborhood of specialty shops, Garbagnati has more *pane* than you can shake a breadstick at, including seasonal treats celebrating Christian and Jewish religious traditions. ♦ Closed M afternoon, Su, lunch. Via Victor Hugo 3. 860905

3 Gastronomia Peck Milan's most famous gourmet shop where prepared pasta, meats, pâté and salads make for the chicest office or outdoor picnicking in the city. ♦ Closed M afternoon, Su, lunch. Via Spadari 9. 871737

4 Peck ★★★$$$ French chef **Daniel Drouaidaine** sees to it that the largely business crowd that frequents this bright and bustling restaurant gets some of the most varied yet not-too-surprising cuisine in the city. Pasta, meat, fish, wine and dessert are all consistently well-prepared (his *paglia e fieno* shows that he is one of the few Frenchmen who understands *les pâtés*, and the two menus (*tradizionale* or traditional and *degustazione* or tasting) have kept us coming back for years. ♦ Closed Su, Aug. Via Victor Hugo 4. 876774

4 Bottega del Vino Peck's snacks are washed down here with more than 200 varieties of wine. ♦ Closed M morning, Su, lunch. Via Victor Hugo 4. 861040

4 Passarini *Gelato* time! One of the richest treats at this ice-cream parlor is *cioccolato gianduia* (chocolate hazelnut) topped with a generous helping of whipped cream. ♦ M-Tu, Th-Su 8AM-10PM. Via Victor Hugo 4. 800663

5 Giovanni Galli Outstanding among the confectioner's goodies here are the *paste di mandorle* or almond paste confections in the fanciful forms of fruits and vegetables. ♦ Closed M afternoon, Su, lunch. Via Victor Hugo 2. 800087

6 Rosticceria Peck's rotisserie grill is just the place to put together a picnic of plump fowl or spit-roasted meat, and there are pastas and veggies to round out your meal. ♦ Closed M afternoon, Su. Via Cantu 3. 8693017

7 L'Ambrosiana (begun 1603, **Lelio Buzzi**) This institution of higher learning was founded in the early 17th century by **Cardinal Federico Borromeo**, cousin of **St. Charles Borromeus**, to further the cause of Roman Catholic orthodoxy through scholarship during the threat of Protestantism. It is still a private foundation associated with the Roman Catholic church. The Ambrosiana was once made up of various academies, the most important of which remaining are the **Biblioteca Ambrosiana** and the **Pinacoteca Ambrosiana**.

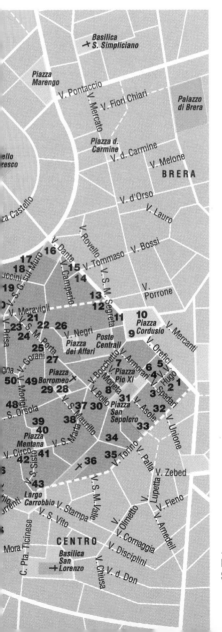

Restaurants/Nightlife: Red   **Hotels:** Blue
Shops/Parks: Green   **Sights/Culture:** Black

Within L'Ambrosiana:

Biblioteca Ambrosiana (Ambrosiana Library) **Cardinal Federico Borromeo**'s men combed the civilized world to come up with the core collection of 30,000 books and 15,000 manuscripts for his library, since grown to 750,000 volumes and 35,000 manuscripts. Some of its rarer treasures include the *Ilias Picta*, a 5th-century Byzantine manuscript; rare editions of **Virgil, Dante** and **Boccaccio**; and the *Codex Atlanticus*, over 1000 pages of technical drawings by **Leonardo da Vinci**. Its hallowed halls are decorated with sculpture of learned men and wealthy benefactors, among them a bust of **Byron** by Neoclassical sculptor **Bertel Thorwaldsen**. ♦ M-F 9AM-4:30PM; Sa 9AM-noon. 86451436

Magenta

Pinacoteca Ambrosiana (Ambrosiana Picture Gallery) Originally donated by **Cardinal Federico Borromeo** to the Ambrosiana's now-defunct fine arts academy (transferred to the Brera under the Hapsburg rule), this is now the most important art collection in Milan after the Pinacoteca di Brera and the Cicivi Musei del Castello Sforzesco. Alas, it will be closed for restoration for the next few years, so here's a quick rundown of what you're missing: **Leonardo da Vinci**'s only portrait in Italy, *Portrait of a Musician*; **Caravaggio**'s only still-life in the world, *Basket of Fruit*; works by **Botticelli, Ghirlandaio, Titian**and **Jan Brueghel**; and the huge cartoon or preparatory drawing for **Raphael**'s *School of Athens* fresco in the Musei Vaticani—artistic ambrosia turned forbidden fruit! ♦ Piazza Pio XI 2. 800146

8 Gran Duca di York $$ Old-fashioned comfort in tastefully decorated—if not sleek—Milanese rooms at almost old-fashioned prices. ♦ Via Moneta 1A. 874863

9 Banca d'Italia (1907-12, **Luigi Broggi** and **Giuseppe Nava**) A Beaux Arts building, with a somewhat academic look, which makes sense since the architects taught at the Brera Academy. ♦ Piazza Edison

10 Piazza Cordusio This piazza, connecting the cathedral to the Castello Sforzesco, has a sculpture of Milanese poet **Giuseppe Parini** by **Luigi Secchi** and **Luca Beltrami**. ♦ Piazza Cordusio

10 Palazzo della Borsa (1898-1901, **Luigi Broggi**) Milan's academic-looking stock market building today houses a large post office. ♦ Piazza Cordusio

11 Libreria Mondadori An open space designed by San Francisco's **Landor Studio** is filled with this book, record and video store owned by **Mondadori**, where you can also have coffee or cocktails. ♦ Closed M morning, Su, lunch. Piazza Cordusio 2. 72001457

12 La Mozzarella Napoletana The titular Neapolitan mozzarella (fresh buffalo-milk cheese) is but one of many items (pasta and cold cuts are others) on sale in this food shop. ♦ Closed M afternoon, Su, lunch. Via Santa Maria Segreta 2. 8050417

12 Sin This after-hours club keeps the latest (or is it earliest?) hours of them all, and is a great place for après-disco breakfast. ♦ Tu-Su 2AM-7AM. Via Santa Maria Segreta. No phone

13 Prenatal The children's clothes of this Italian chain are bolder in design than the cutesy-poo stuff inspired by the sacchrine side of the Italian character seen in many children's shops. ♦ Closed M morning, Su, lunch. Via Dante 7. 802535

14 La Citta del Sole High-quality toys of all types, notably the shop's own line, called Il Leccio, of wooden items. ♦ Closed M morning, Su, lunch. Via Dante 13. 806068

15 American Bookstore English-language books—some of which are out of print in their native lands—from mostly American publishers are the specialty of this shop. ♦ Closed M morning, Su, lunch. Via Manfredo Camperio 16. 870944

16 Santa Maria della Consolazione This church, also called **Santa Maria al Castello** because of its proximity to Castello Sforzesco, dates from the 15th century but was completely renovated in the last century. Inside, in the 3rd chapel on the left, are some nicely decaying frescoes attributed to **Daniele Crespi** depicting *St. Peter Martyr* and *St. Charles*. ♦ Via San Giovanni sul Muro

17 I Quattro Mori ★★$$ **Sisto** and **Lina Arrigoni** put a lot of care into their food—pasta is produced on premises, meat and fish is fresh (often personally picked up from the farm by Signor Arrigoni, and desserts are homemade. The outdoor garden is one of the most pleasant spots in Milan during the warmer months. ♦ Closed Sa lunch, Su, Aug. Via San Giovanni sul Muro 2. 870617

18 La Dispensa di Gualtiero Marchesi Local food impresario Gualtiero Marchesi here markets his line of gourmet foods, such as extra-virgin olive oil and balsamic vinegar. ♦ Closed M afternoon, Su, lunch. Via San Giovanni sul Muro 6. 72000948

19 Vecchia Milano Old Milan, indeed, is what you'll see in the furnishings of this *profumeria*, where cosmetics take second place to Empire-style cabinets and counters as well as frescoed ceilings. ♦ Closed M morning, Su, lunch. Via San Giovanni sul Muro 8. 873651

20 Tibidabo Well designed clothing from casual to dressy for both sexes on a budget. ♦ Closed Su. Via San Giovanni sul Muro 18. 873439

Santa Maria alla Porta

21 La Colonna ★★$ Some of the best value on Milanese risottos, tripe and veal cutlet, especially on the lower-priced lunch menu. ♦ Closed Sa, Su, Aug. Via Santa Maria alla Porta 10. 861812

22 Santa Maria alla Porta (begun 1652, **Francesco Maria Ricchino, Francesco Castelli**) The parochial church happens to be a nice little Rococo number. ♦ Via Santa Maria alla Porta

23 Marchesi A favorite cafe for the local upper crust to sip Campari or cappuccino in an opulent wood-paneled setting. ♦ Tu-Su 7AM-11PM. Via Santa Maria alla Porta 13. 862770

24 Gian Carlo Ricco The best Neoclassical antiques in this most Neoclassical of cities. ♦ Closed M morning, Su, lunch. Via Santa Maria alla Porta 11. 875956

25 Torre Gorani Another medieval tower spared from the bombs of WWII. ♦ Via Gorani

26 Teatro Romano Fragmented remains of the ancient Roman theater beneath the **Borsa Merci** or Stock Exchange. To see them, contact the **Camera di Commercio**, Via Meravigli 9B. ♦ Via San Vittore al Teatro 14

27 Biscione $$ A small and modern hotel, popular with Italian stockbrokers and business-people, especially quiet at night except for the discotheque. ♦ Via Santa Maria Fulcorina 15. 879903

28 Statues For no apparent reason, someone has asssembled a group of statues from a Tuscan villa under a portico for all to enjoy. ♦ Piazza Borromeo

28 Piazza Borromeo This piazza has **Dionigi Bussola**'s Baroque statue of Milan's own **St. Charles Borromeo**, the aristocratic Archbishop of Milan. ♦ Piazza Borromeo

28 Palazzo Borromeo (15th c) A lovely old palazzo with Gothic arches dressed in terra cotta, and unusual 15th-century frescoes depicting games such as Tarot popular at court at the time on the ground floor. ♦ Piazza Borromeo 7

29 La Parete ★★$$ A Belle Epoque restaurant with unusual, creative dishes such as *lumache fritte* or fried snails. ♦ Closed Sa, Su, Aug. Christmas week. Via Borromei 13. 867355

30 Era l'Ora Wonderful old watches (Rolex, Patek Philippe) and not-so-wonderfully new prices. ♦ Closed M morning, Su, lunch. Via del Bollo 3. 867436

31 Piazza San Sepolcro Hard to tell, but Milan's Roman forum once occupied this piazza and the adjacent block taken up by the Ambrosiana. The statue, by **Costantino Corti**, is of Ambrosiana founder **Federico Borromeo**. ♦ Piazza San Sepolcro

31 San Sepolcro (founded 1030) This church has been dedicated to a number of saints throughout the centuries, and considerably altered architecturally. Its most interesting aspect is its 11th-century crypt, which contains a painted terracotta sarcophagus decorated with a *Pietà* that probably influenced the one in San Satiro. ♦ Piazza San Sepolcro

32 CIP Rock-bottom prices on rocks of the semi-precious stone and costume jewelry variety. ♦ Closed Sa lunch, Su. Via Torino 22. No credit cards. 860333

During the Middle Ages, the *consiglio grande* or parliament of Milan was made up of all those who produced their own bread or wine.

Restaurants/Nightlife: Red	**Hotels:** Blue
Shops/Parks: Green	**Sights/Culture:** Black

33 San Sebastiano (begun 1577, **Pellegrino Tibaldi**) This votive church was commissioned by **St. Charles Borromeus** following the plague of 1576. Pellegrino Tibaldi's circular plan was carried out by a number of architects, the last being **Fabio Mangone**, who completed the project in the early 17th century. The interior is best viewed for its architecural plan than for its art, most of which dates from the 18th to 20th centuries. ◆ Via Torino

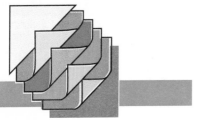

34 Papier A fine assortment of paper made by the French firm **Marie Papier**. ◆ Closed M morning, Su, lunch. Via San Maurilio 4. 865221

35 La Bottega del Tutu Classic ballet and exercise wear in a high-tech setting. ◆ Closed M morning, Su, lunch. Via Torino 48. 875363

35 Cagliani & Croci All the knits by the big-name designers (Coveri, Krizia, Trussardi, Valentino). ◆ Closed M morning, Su, lunch. Via Torino 46. 800096

36 San Giorgio al Palazzo (founded 750) Another ancient church radically transformed through the ages, this one's present aspect is that of a Neoclassical facade (by **Francesco Crose**) fronting a Neoclassical interior (by **Luigi Cagnola** and **Alfonso Perrucchitti**). In the 3rd chapel on the right are paintings by **Bernardino Luini**, a *Deposition, Flagellation, Crowning of Thorns*, and *Crucifixion*. ◆ Via Torino

37 Santamarta 6 ★★$$ **Gianni** and **Dade** add to a regular Milanese menu the robust cooking of Sardinia, rich in roast meats (*capretti* or roast kid) and hearty cheeses (*pecorino* ewe's milk cheese) and best washed down with a heavy wine such as Doragli, supposedly the strongest table wine in Italy. ◆ Closed Th, Sa, Aug. Via Santa Marta 6. 872798

38 Palazzo Salvatico (16th c, **Cesariano** and **Cristoforo Solari**) This stately palazzo's Classical references (columns, arches) are a result of the architects' interest in architectural theorist **Vetruvius**. ◆ Via San Maurilio 19

39 Longobardo ★★$$ **Pino Birolini**'s new restaurant offers some of the most reasonably priced *cucina creativa* or creative cuisine, such as lasagna with prosciutto and porcini mushrooms, and truffled beef. ◆ Closed Sa lunch, Su, Aug, Christmas week. Piazza Mentana 8. 860036

There are plenty of dwarfs all over Italy, but it did seem to me that in Milan the crop was luxuriant.
Mark Twain

40 Piazza Mentana The monument here by **Luigi Belli** is called *To the Garibaldini of Mentana*, commemorating a historic battle by **Giuseppe Garibaldi**. ◆ Piazza Mentana

41 Civico Studio Museo Francesco Messina (Francesco Messina Studio Museum) Housed in the former church of **Sisto** (of remote origin, it was rebuilt in the early 17th century), this museum houses t work of Francesco Messina, a contempora representational sculptor who works in Mil ◆ Daily 9:30AM-7:30PM. Via San Sisto 10. 871036

42 Meazza Haute hardware, with the latest designs in nails, screws, hinges, etc. ◆ Clos M morning, Su, lunch. Via Circo 1. 872418

43 Museo Alchimia A showroom for furnitu by the renowned Alchimia studio. ◆ Closed M morning, Su, lunch. Via Torino 68. 86922

44 Bussi Paint the town red or whatever color you like from the best selection of paints, brushes and paper in the city. ◆ Closed M morning, Su, lunch. Via del Torchio 1. 808732

45 Sabor Tropical The *tropical flavor* of this night spot comes from the Caribbean and South American music played in a theatrica setting of toy toucans and the like and Milar versions of tropical drinks. ◆ Tu-Su 10PM-2AM. Via Cesare Correnti 10B. 8690380

46 Palazzo Visconti (1589-91, **Giuseppe Meda**) An imposing palazzo whose 2 order of windows on the facade take their inspiration from **Galeazzo Alessi**'s **Palazzo Marin** ◆ Via Lanzone 2

47 Santa Maria Maddelena al Cerchio (12th c) This convent was built on the old Roman circus and its cloister retains a timeless tranquility. ◆ Via Cappuccio 3

48 Palazzo Belgioioso (18th c) One of the earliest of the stately residences that helped give this part of Milan its best addresses. ◆ Via Morigi 9

Within the Palazzo Belgioioso:

Pellini Donatelli Pellini recently designed accessories line for **Karl Lagerfeld**, but here she's on her own with an imaginative collect of jewelry in often inexpensive materials. ◆ Closed M morning, Su, lunch. 8690178

49 Fac-Simile The neighborhood's contempo rary art gallery in a refinedly raw setting remi niscent of New York's SoHo. ◆ Closed M, Su lunch, M. Via Morigi 8. 8055341

50 Torre dei Morigi This brick tower dates from medieval days. ◆ Via Morigi

51 La Brisa ★★$$ French chef **Christian Delemas** adds a Gallic touch to Milan's resta rant scene from *soupe a l'oignon* to *quiche* and *coq au vin* if those Alps look too imposir to make the crossing. ◆ M 4-7:30PM; Tu-Sa 9AM-1PM, 4-7:30PM; Via Brisa 15. 872001

Milan is a giant, nightmare city. **Dylan Thomas**

52 Falliva Panizza Well-wrought jewelry giving a touch of originality to traditional shapes in a turn-of-the-century setting. ♦ Closed M morning, Su, lunch. Corso Magenta 5. 804829

52 Provera Pietro and **Aurelia Provera** are the third generation in charge of this *enoteca* or wine bar, where the better sipping centers around wines from the northern Italian regions of Piedmont, Friuli, the Veneto and Alto Adige. ♦ Closed M morning, Su, lunch. Corso Magenta 7. 8050522

52 Bardelli Men's and women's executive dressing in authentic and imitation Anglo-American styles, from Burberry-style tartans to Ralph Lauren rep ties. ♦ Closed M morning, Su, lunch. Corso Magenta 13. 806813

52 Curiosita Esotiche These *exotic curiosities* —objects and fabrics from around the world— might not seem so exotic to those who lived through the Third World crafts boom of the 1960s and '70s, but it's a nice place to pick up an Indian print or brass ashtray for your Milanese friends. ♦ Closed Su, lunch. Corso Magenta. No credit cards. 876693

53 Civico Museo Archeologico (Civic Archeological Museum) The city's ancient Greek, Etruscan and Roman archeological collections are housed in an evocative Benedictine monastery. Its courtyard appropriately includes 2 Roman towers from when the city was known as **Mediolanum**, one square and the other presciently polygonal. The museum's Greek holdings span examples of 3rd-millenium BC Cycladic statuary through 2nd-century BC vases from Magna Grecia, the colonies of *Greater Greece* in what is now southern Italy. Etruscan objects include ceramics and a 2nd-century BC sarcophagus from Tarquinia showing a reclining female figure. Roman artifacts include the 4th-century AD *Trivulzio cup*, the 4th-century AD *Parabiago patera*, and 1st- to 3rd-century AD portrait busts from Roman Milan. ♦ Daily 9:30AM-7:30PM; closed last M of month. Monastero Maggiore, Corso Magenta 15. 8053972

54 Palazzo Litta (1645, **Francesco Maria Richini**) An opulent Baroque palazzo with a rich Rococo facade (1743-60, **Bartolomeo Bolli**) and no less than 3 indoor courtyards. ♦ Corso Magenta 24

Magenta

55 Valentina Ladies' shoes by the **Carrano** house, with the same care but lower price tags than the shoes in their namesake shop. ♦ Closed M morning, Su, lunch. Corso Magenta 27. 871193. Also at: Via San Pietro all'Orto 17. 782520; Corso Europa 18. 799031

56 Buscemi A music-lover's paradise, the quiet half selling classical and the livelier portion devoted to the rest. ♦ Closed M morning, Su, lunch. Corso Magenta 31. 804103

56 Figus Bags and belts, mostly well-crafted leather, by the firm's own artisans, but canvas too. ♦ Closed M morning, Su, lunch. Corso Magenta 31. 807485

57 Ella Classic women's tailoring, especially successful in the blouse department. ♦ Closed M morning, Su, lunch. Via Terraggio 28. No credit cards. 8671115

58 Profumeria Raimel Scents and bath products at $1/5$ to $1/3$ off. ♦ Closed M morning, Su, lunch. Galleria Borella. 875332

59 Lanterna ★★$$ **Massimo Santini** serves refined versions of all the Italian standards in this neighborhood haunt. ♦ Closed M lunch, Su, Aug. Via Novati 2. 8052497

60 Pilgio Modern-design jewelry in precious and semiprecious metals and stones with such abstractly ethnic twists as feathers and elephant skin. ♦ Closed M morning, Su, lunch. Via Lanzone 23. 806964

61 Pierre $$$ One of the newer hotels in town, the Pierre prides itself on its combination of high-tech facilities and down-to-earth personal service. ♦ Via Edmondo De Amicis 32. 8056221

Restaurants/Nightlife: Red	Hotels: Blue
Shops/Parks: Green	Sights/Culture: Black

187

62 Entropia This relaxed club has a small snack menu, best sampled when exhibitions and other cultural events take place in the space. ♦ M, W-Su. Via Edmondo De Amicis 34. 867639

63 Marri Architect and art supplies with true Milanese style, combining sleek design with functionalism. ♦ Closed M morning, Su, lunch. Via De Amicis 47. 8373121

64 R&G Falzone Piles of women's designer clothing in large sizes at small prices. ♦ Tu-Sa 3-7:30PM. Via Edmondo De Amicis 51. 89403714

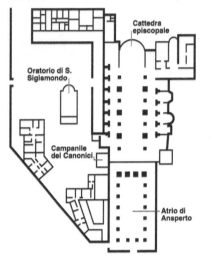

65 Sant'Ambrogio The brick basilica of Sant'Ambrogio was founded on a cemetery in 386 by **Ambrose**, the Bishop of Milan who later became the city's patron saint. (He must have known something, since he immediately named the church in his honor.) Enlarged in the 9th and 11th centuries, its plan became the basis of all Romanesque church architecture in Lombardy. Heavily restored in the 19th century, the church was again restored following bombing during WWII. Not only important artistically and historically, Sant'Ambrogio is also closely connected with Milanese popular culture. Besides the bustling *O Bei O Bei* market held in the surroundings on 7 December, *Ambrogiano*, like *Meneghino*, has become a synonym for *Milanese*.

The exterior atrium of the church dates from the 12th century. The campanile on the right, called the **Campanile dei Monaci** or monks' campanile, dates from the 9th century and is the oldest in Milan. The one on the left, called the **Campanile dei Canoni** or canons' campanile, is from the 12th century. Inside, religious and other material, including recordings of Ambrosian chant made in the church, are for sale. Among the most noteworthy works of art are a magnificent pulpit reassembled from 11th- and 12th-century fragments; 5th-century mosaics of Ambrose and other saints in the dome; a richly detailed 9th-century gold-and-

silver high altar with a 12th-century ciborium the sanctuary; more ancient mosaics, reset in the 10th century and restored over the years, the apse; and a crypt containing a shrine housing the remains of Saints Ambrose, Gervase and Protasius. A door in the crypt leads to **Bramante**'s unfinished *Portico della Canonica* (dating from 1499), which in turn leads to the **Museo della Basilica di Sant'Ambrogio**. The church museum houses a collection of art and artifacts associated with the long history of Sant'Ambrogio, including mosaic and wood fragments, tapestries, frescoes and a missal which belonged to **Gian Galeazzo Visconti**. ♦ Admission to museum. M, W-Sa 10AM-noon, 3-5PM; Su 3-5PM; closed Easter, Aug, 24-26 Dec. 872059

65 Università *Cattolica del Sacro Cuore* Milan's prestigious private university was founded in 1921, incorporating 2 cloisters built by **Bramante** in 1498, his last work in Milan. ♦ Largo Gemelli 1. 88561

66 Piazza Sant'Ambrogio The square and streets surrounding the church of Sant'Ambrogio are most animated on **St. Ambrose Day** (7 December), when they are transformed into a sprawling outdoor market called *O Bei O Bei*. Of medieval origin, the even takes its name from the cry the vendors use (*Oh beautiful!*) to draw attention to their merchandise, everything from cheap snacks and trinkets to antique furniture. The sculpture in the piazza, a monument to the Milanese soldiers of WWI, is by **Adolfo Wildt**. The column in the piazza is of Roman origin, probably put in place in medieval times, when Saint Ambros restored many of the city's monuments.

67 Openhouse This bipartite club is divided into a *zona talk* or talk area, where light conversation matches the light menu, and a *zona fun* o fun area, where live music and dancing takes place. ♦ M-Sa 10PM-3AM. Via Giosue Carducci 25. 879389

68 Bar Magenta This Art Nouveau bar gets an artsy New Wave crowd of young people, especially on weekends. ♦ Tu-Su 8AM-midnight. Via Giosue Carducci 13. 8053808

68 Il Vaso di Pandora An eclectic blend of evening wear, objects and the shop's own line of paper boxes. ♦ Closed Su, lunch. Via Giosue Carducci 13. No credit cards. 8053859

68 Boccondivino ★★$$ Succulent *prosciutto* ham and a mouthwatering selection of regional cheeses from throughout Italy are some of the finer ingredients that make up the menu of **Luigi Concordati**'s restaurant, which offers a wine-tasting menu as well. ♦ Closed Su, Aug, Christmas week. Via Giosue Carducci 17. 864640

After being invited to a 50-course dinner given for the marriage of **Violante Visconti** o the **Duchess of Chirenza** in 1368, friar **Galvano Fiamma** attacked the Milanese as *magni commestores* or big eaters.

69 Palazzo Viviani Cova (1915, **Adolfo Coppedè**) A unique Milanese example of the fanciful residential architecture of Adolfo Coppedè, better known for his work in Rome. This building is an eclectic blend of fortressy elements with some almost Moorish Roman-esque touches. ♦ Via Giosue Carducci 36

70 Antica Trattoria ★★$$ A place to sample the flavorful cuisine of Trieste, especially evident in the fruity wines and rich, strudely desserts, made under the watchful eye of **Anna Loy**. ♦ Closed Sa lunch, Su, Aug. Via San Vittore 13. 468355

71 Museo Nazionale della Scienza e della Tecnica Leonardo da Vinci
(National Science Museum) Housed somewhat incongruously in the former Benedictine monastery of **San Vittore** (it dates from the 11th century), Italy's national science museum was just refurbished and more than ever sings with the industrial spirit of the city in place of monastic chant. The museum takes its name from a core collection of models of machines and instruments based on drawings by **Leonardo da Vinci**, each one accompanied by a reproduction of the original drawing and a modern technical drawing of the model. Land, air and sea machinery for war and peace and a wealth of specialized instruments give insight into the scientific side of Leonardo's genius. After that, we can see what Leonardo and others wrought as we watch the seeds of the Industrial Revolution sprout, grow and burst forth before our very eyes. Room after room of didactical displays include everything from a medieval jeweler's workshop to printing presses, astronomical instruments, musical instruments, photographic and cinematic equipment, radios, computers, cars, trains, boats and planes, with a few saints and Madonnas thrown in for good measure. This is the Italian science museum, after all. ♦ Admission. Tu-Su 9:30AM-4:50PM. Via San Vittore 21. 48010040

Within the museum complex:

Museo Navale Didattico Comunale Some 4000 pieces are on display in this naval museum, which includes models of Italian ships as well as exotic and historical vessels from around the world. ♦ Tu-Su 9:30AM-4:50PM. Via San Vittore 21. 4817270

72 Carcere di San Vittore (1864-79, **Francesco Lucca**) Milan's prison is laid out in a 6-spoked

floor plan with an almost unintentionally whimsical fortresslike entrance. ♦ Piazza Gaetano Filangeri 2

73 Il Giardino di Leonardo Occasional finds of designer objects turn up at this used furniture shop. ♦ Closed Su. Via Aristide De Togni 10. No credit cards. 8058614

74 La Vetraia di Maria Virginia Bonanni Postwar and contemporary glass objects from vases and ashtrays to dishes and the like. ♦ Closed M morning, Su, lunch. Corso Magenta 52. 8901052

75 Attilio Nosari Grace Well-designed menswear, including off-the-rack at competitive prices, and made-to-measure at prices a little less than elsewhere. ♦ Closed Sa afternoon, Su, lunch. Via Caradosso 2. No credit cards. 4818545

76 Casa Donzelli (1903-04, **Enrico Donzelli**) An imaginative, budding Art Nouveau residence—one in a series built in this middle-class residential area. ♦ Via Gioberti 1

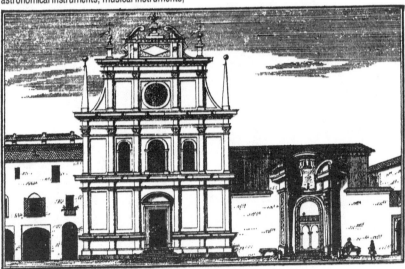

Museo Nazionale della Scienza e della Tecnica Leonardo da Vinci

189

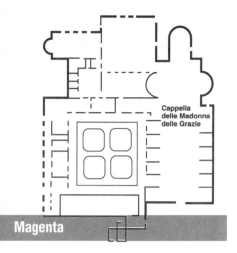

Cappella
delle Madonna
delle Grazie

77 Santa Maria delle Grazie (1466-90, **Guiniforte Solari**) **Bramante** added the tribune and dome to this Dominican church. In its left nave is the **Cappella delle Madonna delle Grazie**, a chapel which contains a venerated image of *Our Lady of Grace* by a 15th-century Lombard painter. The chapel next to it has a 16th-century painting of the *Holy Family with St. Catherine of Alexandria* by **Paris Bordone**. The **Chiostrino** or cloister and **Sagrestia Vecchia** or old sacristy are attributed to Bramante.
◆ Piazza Santa Maria delle Grazie

In the Refectory:

Cenacolo Vinciano Even though it is the most famous painting in the world and has bee reproduced ad nauseum on everything from calendars to dish towels, it is still possible to look at **Leonardo da Vinci**'s *Last Supper* with fresh eye. This is partially because the delicate painting, done at a famously slow pace (betwee 1495 and 1498), is being completely cleaned an even slower pace. Also, its unexpected movie-screen size is impressive enough to silence the most chattering spectators—well, most of them anyway. We are in Italy, after all (It has the opposite effect of Leonardo's *Mona Lisa* in the Louvre, which inevitably elicits a chorus of *It's so small!* in various languages.) The first work of the High Renaissance, *The Last Supper* depicts the moment Christ drops the dinner conversational bomb, *Verily I say unto you, One of you which eateth with me shall betray me.* (*Mark 14:18*) The Savior sits serenely as the apostles, grouped in threes, take it from there, exploding in a flurry of the sort of physical and psychological reaction which fascinated Leonardo. He was also concerned with technique, here experimenting unsuccessfully with tempera on plaster, which started deteriorating in Leonardo's own time and suffered from bad restorations over the centuries. Compare it to the true or *buon fresco* technique (water-based paint applied to wet plaster) of the *Crucifixion* by **Donato da Montorfano** on the opposite wall, which was painted in 1495 (Leonardo did the kneeling fig ures of **Ludovico il Moro** and family in 1497) and is remarkably well-preserved. As expansive as it is, *The Last Supper* is also inch-for-inch the most expensive piece of art you can see in Italy, the ticket being as high as for the entire Galleria degli Uffizi in Florence or Musei Vaticani at the Vatican. Verily!
◆ Admission. Tu-Sa 9AM-1:15PM, 2-6:15PM; M, Su and holidays 9AM-1:15PM. Piazza Santa Maria delle Grazie. 4987588

78 San Carlo Another favorite neighborhood *pasticceria* or pastry shop, nicely animated on Sundays when **Biffi** is closed, for a cappuccino and croissant. ♦ Closed M morning, Su, lunch. Via Matteo Bandello 1. 4812227

79 Casa Candiani (1882-85, **Luigi Broggi**) A wonderfully fanciful and eclectic Neo-Renaissance residence by one of Milan's leading 19th-century architects. ♦ Via Matteo Bandello 20

80 Biffi One of Milan's most traditional tea-rooms, where matrons favor *panettone*, the Milanese citrus-studded cake that dates from medieval days. ♦ Closed Su. Corso Magenta 87. 4395702

81 Piazzale Baracca The monument to aviation hero **Francesco Baracca** is by **Silvio Monfrini**. ♦ Piazzale Baracca

82 Casa Laugier (1905-06, **Antonio Tagliferri**) Viennese Seccesionist details on a traditional residence using a panoply of stone, brick, cement and ceramic. ♦ Corso Magenta 96

83 Piazza della Conciliazione The abstract sculpture in this piazza is the 1972 *Gesto per la Liberta* (Gesture for Liberty) by **Carlo Ramous**. ♦ Piazza della Conciliazione

84 Pupi Solari Pupi picks out the best of Milan's top designers—from Romeo Gigli to Enrica Massei—for woman and children in her well-trodden boutique. ♦ Closed M morning, Su. Piazza Tommaseo. 463325

85 Eve Contemporary-looking fashion handbags as well as shoes, belts and luggage. ♦ Closed M morning, Su, lunch. Via Mascheroni 12. 4696922

86 Ariosto $$$ An Art Nouveau mansion-turned-hotel, Ariosto offers modernized accommodations in a homey setting. The best rooms overlook the tree-planted courtyard. ♦ Via Ariosto 22. 490995

87 Bazaar Carrano Fashionable shoes for men and women, a little later in the season and lower in price. ♦ Closed M morning, Su, lunch. Via Rasori 4. 4390588

88 Coin Well-wrought woolens and men's shirts are among the most eye-catching items in this department store chain. ♦ Closed M morning, Su, lunch. Corso Vercelli 8. 432160

88 Rosabianca Perfumes and makeup in all international brands. ♦ Closed M morning, Su, lunch. Corso Vercelli 8. 4395696

89 Casa Croff Casual contemporary housewares in bold colors and functional designs are the hallmark of this Italian chain. ♦ Closed M morning, Su, lunch. Corso Vercelli 10. 463373

90 Gusella Tasteful and well-tailored clothes for spoiling your favorite child. ♦ Closed M morning, Su, lunch. Corso Vercelli 14. 4814144

91 Gemelli One-stop upscale shopping for the whole family's fashion needs by top-line designers as selected by **Sergio Gemelli**. ♦ Closed M morning, Su, lunch. Corso Vercelli 16. 490057

92 Bassetti Linens in classic and fashion colors. ♦ Closed M morning, Su, lunch. Corso Vercelli 25. 4396518

93 Torrefazione Vercelli The neighborhood coffee bar where the enticing aroma of freshly roasted beans permeates the air. Coffee can be sipped and beans can be slipped into your suitcase as an aromatic souvenir. ♦ M-Sa 7:30AM-8:30PM. Via Cherubini 2. No phone

94 La Casa del Cinghiale *The house of the wild boar* predictably sells pigskin bags and accessories in absolutely unpredictable colors and designs. ♦ Closed M morning, Su, lunch. Via Mario Pagano 69A. 4984597

Milanese Design

Fostered by the strongest industrial culture within Italy, design in Milan began to develop in the 1930s with such early names as **Gio Ponti** and **Ernesto Rogers**, trained architects who applied Bauhaus-influenced and other Modernist principles to their concepts for everyday objects. Following WWII, Milanese design began to take off when the **Triennale** design exhibitions resumed just as Milan became Italy's definitive industrial capital. (An equally important event these days is the **Salone del Mobile**, a furniture trade fair held at the **Fiera di Milano fairgrounds**.) During the postwar period **Gae Aulenti, Mario Bellini, Cini Boeri, Rodolfo Bonetto**, the **Castiglioni** brothers (**Pier Giacomo** and **Livio**), **Joe Colombo, Vittorio Gregotti, Vico Magistretti, Enzo Mari, Bruno Munari** and **Marco Zanuso** came into prominence. Many of their efforts were celebrated in the landmark exhibition *Italy: The New Domestic Landscape* at New York's Museum of Modern Art in 1972, which helped establish international recognition for Milanese design. After that, such groups as **Alchymia** (whose alchemy derives from such diverse sources as Constructivism and Pop Art) and **Memphis** (so-called because the eponymous **Bob Dylan** song got stuck as its originators were trying to come up with a name for the group, and known for its deliberately jarring forms and colors) came into being. In 1983 the **Domus Academy**, Italy's first postgraduate design school, was founded and helped to institutionalize Milanese design ideology. Lately, the scene has settled into an almost conservative Modernism, but new trends and old polemics should ensure that other tricks are up the Milanese designers' Armani-clad sleeves. Admired from afar in the pictures if not the often unintelligible words of such specialized publications as *Domus* and *Modo* as well as the more general-interest design magazines *AD, Casa Vogue* (both offshoots of American publications) and *Abitare*, Milanese design can be sampled firsthand in the showrooms concentrated in the heart of the city.

Restaurants/Nightlife: Red   **Hotels:** Blue
Shops/Parks: Green   **Sights/Culture:** Black

Parco Sempione

At the beginning of the last century, a grandiose project for theaters, meeting halls, government and financial buildings, thermal baths, a customs house, and a Pantheon was conceived for Milan in the area around **Castello Sforzesco**, which Napoleon had occupied with troops and military accouterments. Called the **Foro Bonaparte** or Bonaparte Forum in honor of the French emperor, the project died along with Napoleonic rule in Milan. It remains in name only in the form of the broadly curving avenue called Foro Bonaparte, but something of its civic spirit has come to pass in the **Parco Sempione**, a public park behind Castello Sforzesco. On its grounds are an exhibition pavilion, a public library, a sports arena, an aquarium, an arch of triumph, and an equestrian monument to Napoleon. Of most interest to the visitor is Castello Sforzesco itself, which thankfully today is filled with art rather than soldiers—including some of Milan's most important museums, among which the **Civiche Raccolte d'Arte Antica**, where **Michelangelo**'s *Rondanini Pietà* is displayed. More than any other park in Milan, Parco Sempione provides pleasant respite from the hustle and bustle of the city, its broad vistas and rambling terrain as relaxing as the occasional surprise of contemporary sculpture is stimulating.

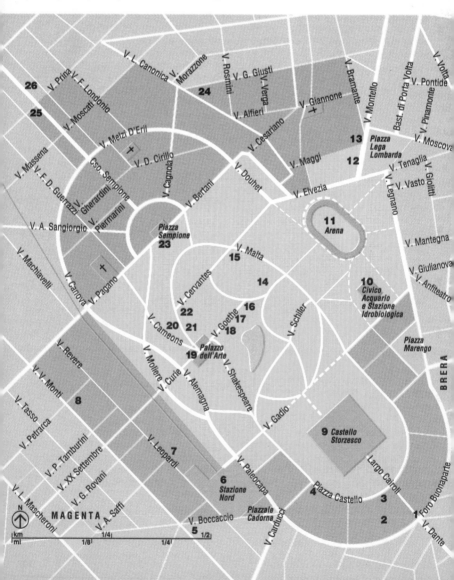

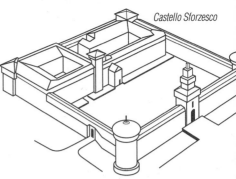

Castello Sforzesco

1 **Largo Cairoli** The confluence of streets before **Castello Sforzesco** is dominated by Sicilian sculptor **Ettore Ximenes'** 1895 equestrian monument to **Giuseppe Garibaldi**, the *Hero of Two Worlds* who after fighting in Uruguay returned to Italy to play a key role in the 19th-century unification movement known as the **Risorgimento**. ♦ Largo Cairoli

2 **Teatro Dal Verme** (1872, **Giuseppe Pestagalli**) This 19th-century opera house, which was the scene of the premiere of **Leoncavallo**'s *Pagliacci* directed by **Arturo Toscanini** among other events, is now used for concerts sponsored by the city. ♦ Largo Cairoli

3 **L'Appassionata** ★★$$ **Beppe Cardile**'s romantic restaurant has candles and roses on every table and serves such refined dishes as *filetto di sogliola al balsamico con salsa di basilico e pinoli* (filet of sole with balsamic vinegar and basil sauce with pine nuts) well into the night, often accompanied by live entertainment. ♦ Closed M, Aug. Piazza Castello 1. 878516

4 **Castelli** The showroom of the renowned office furniture design firm whose *Plia* chair is in the collection of New York's Museum of Modern Art. ♦ Closed M morning, Su, lunch. Piazza Castello 19. No credit cards. 870257

5 **Coeugh** A great place for takeout, specializing in such Milanese classics as risotto and *costoletta alla milanese* (breaded veal cutlet) as well as more historical Milanese and Lombard dishes going back to the 18th century. ♦ Tu-Sa 8AM-midnight. Via Vincenzo Monti 16. 48195468

6 **Stazione Nord** This train station, reconstructed internally in 1956, serves the communities lying to the north of the city. ♦ Piazzale Luigi Cadorna. 8511608

7 **Centro della Seta** A factory outlet for **Mantero**, which makes scarves and ties in tasteful Italian and faux-Anglo patterns. ♦ Closed Su, lunch. Via Leopardi 26. 4394075

8 **Stivaleria Savoia di Ballini** Originally bootmakers to the Italian royal family, this shop now makes boots and other exquisite equestrian accessories for those who can afford it. ♦ Closed M morning, Su, lunch. Via Petrarca 7. 463424

9 **Castello Sforzesco** (14th-20th c) Milan's brick fortress is a 20th-century reconstruction of a 19th-century reconstruction of a 15th-century reconstruction of a 14th-century construction. Originally built by the **Visconti**, it takes its name from **Francesco Sforza**, who in the 15th century commissioned **Giovanni da Milano** to rebuild the castle after it had been sacked. His son, **Galeazzo Maria Sforza**, moved the court here and hired **Vincenzo Foppa**, **Cristoforo Moretto** and **Benedetto Ferrini** to decorate the interior. Under **Ludovico il Moro**, **Bramante** possibly worked on the castello and **Leonardo**

da Vinci became resident court genius, adding further decorations and designing court frolics. When the Sforza were replaced by Spanish rulers in the 16th and 17th centuries, the castle was surrounded by heavy bastions in the form of a 12-pointed star to make it an impregnable fortress. At the arrival of **Napoleon** the star fell and the castle became a military barracks for years. Its association with despots made the castello a symbol of repression, and proposals

Parco Sempione

called for its destruction following the unification of Italy. Instead it was decided to restore the castle to its approximate appearance under Francesco Sforza and fill it with cultural institutions, the civic equivalent of putting a carnation down the gun barrel. Nevertheless, the castello was hit heavily during the WWII bombing of Milan, which gave the prestigious architectural firm **Studio BBPR** an opportunity to redesign the museum spaces in the interior.

Within the Castello Sforzesco:

Civici Musei del Castello Sforzesco (Civic Museums of Castello Sforzesco) The museums are entered beneath the central tower, the **Torre Filarete**, originally built by Filarete in 1452. The expansive main courtyard (concerts are held here in the warmer months), the **Piazza d'Armi**, contains remains of various buildings gathered from throughout the city. At its far end is the **Corte Ducale**, from which the **Civiche Raccolte d'Arte Antica** (Civic Collection of Ancient Art) is entered. The first section of this collection is the **Raccolta di Scultura** (Sculpture Collection), displayed on the ground floor. In Sala I is a 6th-century Byzantine marble head said to be a portrait of the **Empress Theodora**; Sala II has the 14th-century **Tomb of Bernabo Visconti** by the sculptor **Bonino Campione**; Sala VII is decorated with 17th-century frescoes and tapestries; Sala VIII has some heavily restored decorations by **Leonardo da Vinci**; Sala XV contains the 16th-century **Tomb of Gaston de Foix** by **Agostino Busti** (called **Bambaia**) and the highlight of the entire museum, the 16th-century *Rondanini Pietà*, **Michelangelo**'s last work. (the piece, once part of the collection of the noble Roman Rondanini family, was bought by the city as a sort of civic status symbol in 1952.) The marble sculpture is an almost Gothic-looking meditation on death, deeply moving in its abstract, unfinished state. Upstairs, after a huge collection of mostly northern Italian furniture from the 15th to the 18th centuries, is the **Pinacoteca** (Painting Gallery). Highlights include 15th-century *Madonna* paintings by **Filippo Lippi, Giovanni Bellini** and **Andrea Mantegna** (all in Sala XX); 16th-century Lombard paintings of *The Martyrdom of St. Sebastian* by **Vincenzo Foppa,** *Madonna* by Foppa, *Pietà* and *The Alms of St. Benedict* by **Ambrogio Bergognone,** *Noli Mi Tangere* by **Bramantino,** and *Polyptich* by **Cesare da Sesto** (Sala XXI); the16th-century *Spring* in the style of **Archimboldo** (Sala XXIV); and the 15th-century *Poet Laureate* by Giovanni Bellini and *Portrait of a Youth* by **Lorenzo Lotto** (Sala XXV). From here, a loggia leads to the upper floor of the section of the fortress complex called the **Rocchetta.** In it is the **Civiche Raccolte d'Arte Applicata** (Civic Collection of Decorative Art), which includes Chinese porcelain from the 7th to the 18th centuries and Italian majolica from the 15th to the 18th centuries (Sala XXX); 18th- and 19th-century French and Austrian porcelain

Parco Sempione

(Sala XXXI); and ivories and precious metal objects (Sala XXXII). Downstairs is the **Museo degli Strumenti Musicale** (Musical Instruments Museum), which includes violins by **Antonio Stradivarius** and **Giuseppe Guarnieri** (Sala XXXVI). In the basement of the Rocchetta are the prehistoric Lombard and ancient Egyptian holdings of the **Civiche Raccolte Archeologiche** (Civic Archeological Collections). ♦ Daily 9:30AM-7:30PM; closed last M of month. Piazza Castello. 62083940, 62083947

10 Civico Acquario e Stazione Idrobiologica (1906, **Sebastiano Locati**) Milan's Art Nouveau civic aquarium (note the statue of **Neptune** by **Oreste Labo** on the facade), rebuilt after it was destroyed during WWII, contains some 50 tanks filled with creatures of the deep. ♦ Daily 9:30AM-7:30PM; closed last M of month. Via Gadio 2. 872847

11 Arena (1806, **Luigi Canonica**) Milan's Neoclassical sports arena, shaped like a Roman amphitheater, has a capacity of 30,000—too small for major-league soccer games but large enough for small-scale soccer and the other sporting events. ♦ Parco Sempione

12 Vecchia Arena ★★$$ **Lino** and **Mariapia**'s cozy restaurant prides itself on its *risotto giallo* (made with saffron) and *risotto al salto* (fried crisp) among other Milanese specialties. ♦ Closed M lunch, Su, Aug, Christmas week. Piazza Lega Lombarda 1. 3315538

13 Nuova Arena ★★$$ The foreign influence of the Egyptian owners of this eatery can be sampled in such dishes as *bocconcini al curry con riso pilaf* (curried beef with rice pilaf), adding an unusual (for Milan) twist to an otherwise inventive Italian menu. ♦ Closed M, Aug. Piazza Lega Lombarda 5. 341437

14 Monumento a Napoleone III This equestrian monument was made by **Francesco Barzaghi** in 1881. ♦ Monte Tordo

15 Biblioteca Parco Sempione (1954, **Silvio Longhi** and **Ico Parisi**) A small branch library in the park, outside of which is a 1954 abstract cement sculpture by **Francesco Somaini** called *Grande Motivo.* ♦ Monte Tordo

16 Accumulazione Musicale e Seduta A 1973 cement and metal piece by witty French artist **Arman.** ♦ Viale Goethe

17 Teatro Continuo A cement and painted-steel sculpture by **Alberto Burri.** ♦ Viale Goethe

18 Bagni Misteriosi A 1973 sculpture by metaphysical artist **Giorgio De Chirico.** ♦ Viale Goethe

19 Palazzo dell'Arte (1932-33, **Giovanni Murzic**) This Modernist building is also known as the **Triennale** since it hosts Milan's renowned design exhibition, the Triennale, every 3 years. At other times it is used as the site of temporary exhibitions. ♦ Viale Alemagna 6. 8900728

Within the Palazzo dell'Arte:

Old Fashion Club Slightly proper in ambience if not in the grammar of its name, this 1950s-style nightclub has a live orchestra for ballroom dancing. ♦ Tu-Su 10PM-2AM. Viale Alemagna 6. 8056231

20 Torre del Parco (1932, **Cesare Chiodi, Gio Ponti, Ettore Ferrari**) This steel-tube tower structure dates from the Palazzo dell'Arte. ♦ Viale Alemagna

21 Storia della Terra This 1973 abstract sculpture is by **Antonio Paradiso.** ♦ Viale Guiglielmo Shakespeare

22 Chiosco Scultura This 1973 abstract sculpture is by **Amelio Roccamonte.** ♦ Viale Guiglielmo Shakespeare

23 Arco della Pace (1838, **Luigi Cagnola**) This Neoclassical triumphal arch is decorated with sculptures of the *Chariot of Peace* by **Abbondio Sangiorgio,** *4 Victories* by **Giovanni Putti,** personifications of the Po and Ticino rivers by **Benedetto Cacciatori,** the Adige and Tagliamento rivers by **Pompeo Marchesi,** and other 19th-century sculpture and bas reliefs. ♦ Piazza Sempione

24 Europeo $$$ A small and modern accommodations option near the park, in the heart of Milan's very un-Chinatownlike Chinese district where only the names on the doorbells indicate the residents' nationalities. ♦ Via Luigi Canonica 38. 344041

25 Former Fascist Headquarters (1938-39, **Gianni Angelini, Giuseppe Calderara, Tito Varisco**) This building, designed as the local headquarters for the Fascist party, is one of the purist extant examples of Fascist-era Modernist architecture in the city. ♦ Corso Sempione 25

26 Casa Rustici (1933-35, **Giuseppe Terragni**) This apartment building is the best example of International Modernist architecture in the city. ♦ Corso Sempione 36

Brera

Named after **Palazzo Brera**—a convent now housing a number of institutions including the **Pinacoteca di Brera**, one of Italy's finest museums—the Brera was until relatively recently one of the most proudly low-rent districts in Milan. Back in the 19th century, **Via San Fermo** was the first neighborhood in Milan expressly developed for public housing, and at the turn of the century it was the center of Milan's bohemian life. Even today the art school within Palazzo Brera helps maintain a cafe-society air in the area, though you can be sure its students can't afford to do their shopping in the boutiques that have sprung up in its streets or even the flea market held on the 3rd Saturday of the month on **Via Fiori Chiari** (though bargains still turn up at the outdoor market

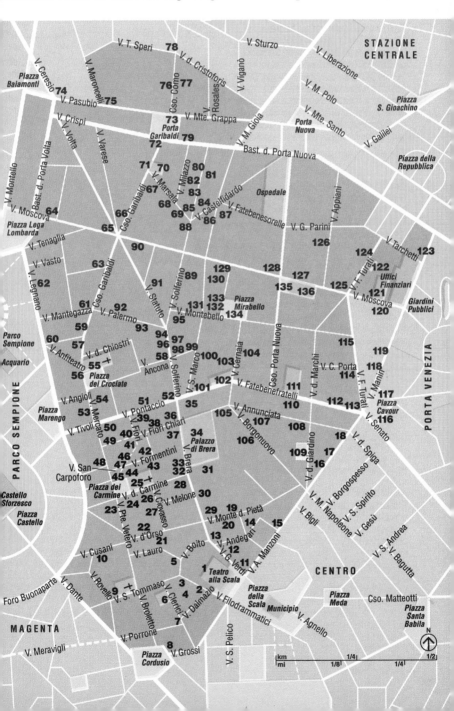

in **Piazza Mirabello** Monday and Thursday mornings). This route also incorporates such elegant sights as **Teatro della Scala** and a few palazzi on **Via Manzoni**, but the stroller will find the gentrified Brera just as upscale. Whether tripping down its cobblestone streets for shopping and sightseeing by day or stepping out in its bars and clubs by night, the Brera is perhaps the single most pleasant neighborhood in Milan.

1 Teatro alla Scala (1776-78, **Giuseppe Piermarini**; reconstructed 1945-46, **Luigi Lorenzo Secchi**) At first glance, the Neoclassical exterior of one of the world's great opera houses seems surprisingly un-grand. Once inside its horseshoe-shaped wooden interior, however, it is easy to imagine the precipitously rising boxes and balconies filled with gentry giving one another the eye, eating, playing cards, carrying on romantic or political intrigues (as

Brera

they did when Milan was subjugated by **Napoleon** and the Austro-Hungarian rulers), and occasionally even paying attention to the stage. Among the many works to have premiered here were **Vincenzo Bellini**'s *Norma*, **Giuseppe Verdi**'s *Otello* and *Falstaff*, **Amilcare Ponchelli**'s *Gioconda*, and **Giacomo Puccini**'s *Turandot*. Severely damaged by Allied bombs during WWII, the theater was rebuilt largely thanks to the efforts of **Arturo Toscanini**, who under Fascism had emigrated to the US, where he raised funds for the reconstruction. Other kinds of bombs have fallen in the postwar years, since the theater began a policy of introducing less traditional works into its regular repertoire, from **Alban Berg**'s *Wozzeck* to **Robert Wilson**'s production of **Giacomo Manzoni**'s *Dr. Faustus*. Opera season at La Scala runs from 7 December to July; concert season is September through November. Though non-subscription tickets are hard to come by, hotel concierges can often produce them if you sing a convincing enough aria and see to it that their efforts are applauded with palm grease. ◆ Via Filodrammatici 2. 86460035

Within the Teatro alla Scala:

Museo della Scala (La Scala Museum) An opera fan's Valhalla, the museum contains room after room of operatic memorabilia, a large part of it centering around **Giuseppe Verdi**. Of more general interest are the bust of tenor **Niccolo Taccardini** by Neoclassical sculptor **Antonio Canova** and objects from ancient Greek and Roman theater, including a Greek drinking vessel covered with scenes from the popular theater. The ticket to the museum will also let you take a peek at the theater. ◆ Admission. M-Sa 9-11:30AM, 2-3:30PM (5:30PM May-Oct) 8053418

2 Biffi Scala ★★★$$$ This historic restaurant has been given a light touch in its Postmodern decor and menu, though such Milanese classics as *risotto al salto* (crisp fried risotto) and *costoletta milanese* (breaded fried veal cutlet) are as deliciously rich as ever. As perfect for a business lunch as it is for after-Scala supper. ◆ Closed Su, Aug, 25 Dec-6 Jan. Via Filodrammatici 2. 866651

3 Palazzo Visconti Aimi (17th c) One of the few relatively unchanged patrician palazzi in the area. ◆ Via Filodrammatici 10

4 El Toulà ★★★$$$ The Milanese link in this Italian restaurant chain adds a local accent (Milanese minestrones and risottos) to the Veneto-based cuisine. Expense-accounters appreciate the sea of fish dishes that has always been a hallmark of the chain, and the dessert chef here is out of this world. ◆ Closed Su, Aug. Piazza Paolo Ferrari 6. 870302

5 Finarte Milan's leading auction house usually has a pre-sale showing or 2 going on at this space. ◆ Closed Su, lunch. Piazzetta Bossi 4. 877041. Also at: Via Manzoni 38. 790436

6 Palazzo Clerici (18th c) The former residence of Milanese nobleman and statesman **Antonio Giorgio Clerici** is one of the finest examples of a patrician villa in Milan. Typically unostentatious on the outside, its granite doorway leads to 2 courtyards, from the second of which ascends a monumental staircase. The vault above it has a fresco formerly attributed to **Giovanni Battista Piazzetta**, now to **Mattia Bortoloni**. Upstairs, in the **Galleria degli Arazzi** (which has lovely 17th-century Flemish tapestries portraying scenes from the life of Moses) is the showpiece of the palazzo, a magnificent frescoed ceiling by **Gian Battista Tiepolo**, his last work in Milan. It depicts the chariot of the sun, driven by Mercury, illuminating the world. Deities of land, sea and sky are bathed in a beautiful pastel light in this masterpiece of Rococo ceiling decoration. Two other noteworthy rooms in the palazzo are the **Salone degli Specchi** (a mirrored hall) and the **Salottino Dorato** (a small room covered with gold decorations). The palazzo now houses the **Istituto per gli Studi di Politica Internazionale** (Institute for the Study of International Politics), whose permission is necessary for a visit. ◆ By appointment only. Via Clerici 5. 878266

Restaurants/Nightlife: Red   Hotels: Blue
Shops/Parks: Green   Sights/Culture: Black

7 Champagneria ★★$$ Caviar, oysters, sweets and such foods that go well with champagne make up the giddy menu of this bubbly spot. ◆ Closed Su, holidays. Via Clerici 1. 800862

8 Roxy Value-for-money neckwear (ties, scarves, Ascots) make up the well-designed merchandise in this well-designed shop. ◆ Closed Su, lunch. Via Tommaso Grossi 10. 874322

9 Piccolo Teatro One of Milan's leading cultural institutions (the interior was designed by **Marco Zanuso**) presents Italian-language plays, but the strong direction by **Giorgio Strehler** transcends the language barrier along with the 4th wall. ◆ Via Rovello 2. 877663

10 Rovello ★★$$ An intimate setting where pastas are expertly prepared and paired with such inventive ingredients as saffron and salmon. Main courses are equally creative, and desserts—including the house chocolates— are large and sublime. ◆ Closed M afternoon, Su, lunch. Via Rovello 18. 864396

11 Milano Libri In a city where books mean business like everything else, it's a treat to walk into **Anna Maria** and **Giovanni Gandini**'s bookshop. The selection of material on theater, fashion, design and photography is intelligent, and browsing is actually encouraged. Milano Libri is the closest thing the city has to a literary scene, done with more style than anywhere else we can think of. ◆ Closed M morning, Su, lunch. Via Giuseppe Verdi 2. 875871

11 Wal-Mar Woolen sweaters and such at a discount. ◆ Closed Su, lunch. Via Giuseppe Verdi 2. No credit cards. 860214

12 Suntory ★★$$$ If you have a lire for Japanese food, this is your best bet in town. All the standards, sometimes amusingly translated into Italian—tempura, for example, appears on the menu as *fritto misto*. ◆ Closed Su, 10 days in Aug, Christmas. Via Giuseppe Verdi 6. 862210

13 San Giuseppe (1630, **Francesco Maria Ricchino**) This octagonal church contains a 17th-century canvas depicting the *Marriage of the Virgin* by **Melchiorre Gherardini** on the left altar. ◆ Via Giuseppe Verdi

14 Fontana dei Tritoni This Triton fountain by **Alessandro Minali** has statues by **Salvatore Saponaro**. ◆ Via Romagnosi

15 Sawaya & Moroni Design objects for home and office by William Sawaya, Luigi Serafini, Adolfo Natalini, Charles Jencks, Borek Sipek, Michel Graves, Prando and Rosso, Katsuo Shinoara, Marco Mencacci and others. ◆ Closed M morning, Su, lunch. Via Manzoni 11. 874549

15 Frette One of Italy's (and the world's) best-known linen shops. Frette began just outside of Milan in the town of Monza, and over the past century has graced some of the world's best addresses with its luxurious sheets, towels, bathrobes and comforters. ◆ Closed M morning, Su, lunch. Via Manzoni 11. 864339

16 Pennisi Antique jewelry at all-too-modern prices. ◆ Closed M morning, Su, lunch. Via Manzoni 29. 862232

17 Centro Domus
Recently renovated (1989, **Ermanno Ranzani** and **Gigi Spinelli**), this space hosts exhibitions and sells publications  (including its namesake *Domus*, the Italian design magazine) and prints selected by **Studio Marconi**. ◆ M 4-7:30PM; Tu-Sa 9AM-1PM, 4-7:30PM; closed Su. Via Manzoni 37. 6598227

18 Palazzo Borromeo d'Adda (19th c) The driving force behind this stately Neoclassical residence was architect **Gerolamo Arganini**, who had his hand in the building between 1820 and 1825 before it was again altered. ◆ Via Manzoni 39-41

Within the Palazzo Borromeo d'Adda:

Fiumi Milan's finest watch and clock shop, where timepieces tick and clang in the opulent setting of the original turn-of-the-century silks and velvets. ◆ Closed M morning, Su, lunch. Via Manzoni 39. 6599074

19 Banca del Monte di Lombardia Milan's most upscale pawn shop (run by a bank) often holds auction sales of orphaned family furs and jewels. ◆ Via Monte di Pieta 5. 88861

20 Casa Beccaria **Cesare Beccaria**, the 17th-century Milanese economist and jurist who is primarily known throughout Italy as someone the streets are named after, was born and died here. ◆ Via Monte di Pieta 6

20 Cassa di Risparmio delle Provincie Lombarde (1868-72, **Giuseppe Balzaretto**) The reference in this 19th-century palazzo is to the imposing palazzi of Renaissance Florence. ◆ Via Monte di Pieta 8

21 La Porcellana Bianca A white dream of porcelain objects, all in the sparkling non-color. ◆ Closed M morning, Su, lunch. Via dell'Orso 7. 8050557. Also at: Via Statuto 11. 6571560

21 Blackout Lighting fixtures in that kind of design you've come to expect in Milan. Major names are Fontana Arte, Artemide, O Luce, Quattrofolio, Leucos, Lumina and Traconi. Coincidentally, at the same address as **La Porcellana Bianca**. ◆ Closed M morning, Su, lunch. Via dell'Orso 7. 873073

22 Centro Botanico Plants and related potpourris, fragrances, even paper and posters in botanical themes, are the root of this shop, a marketing concept developed by the enterprising **Naj Oleari** brothers whose whimsical fabric designs are featured in 2 other shops in the vicinity. ◆ Closed M, Su, lunch. Via dell'Orso 16. 873315

23 Gelateria Toldo The cool option for *gelato* in this neighborhood, with seasonal flavors displayed in 2 cases—one for fruit, the other for milk-based treats. ◆ M-Sa 9AM-11PM. Via Ponte Vetero 11. 872517

24 Mac Borse No, not a hamburger chain, rather a shop that makes stylish bags from the cow's outside. ◆ Closed M morning, Su, lunch. Via Ponte Vetero 22. 807947

25 Santa Maria del Carmine (begun 1400, **Bernardo da Venezia**) This church has been much altered over the centuries. After a collapse, the original structure was rebuilt in Gothic style around 1456. After some Baroque additions, it was again remodeled between

Brera

1826 and 1839 under the direction of **Giuseppe Pestagalli** and given a Neo-Gothic facade in 1180 by **Carlo Maciachini**. The last renovation was done in 1912 by **Ambrogio Annoni**. The art inside is pleasant enough to look at if not important historically, dating from the 15th to the 19th centuries. ◆ Piazza del Carmine

26 La Bitta ★★$$ Dark wood paneling and crisp linen set the scene for **Giuseppe Pelliccia**'s Italian-French restaurant, which features such creations as *gnocchi alle pescatrice* (potato dumplings seafood). ◆ Closed Sa lunch, Su, Aug. Via del Carmine 3. 879159

27 Consolare ★★$$ Politicos and show folk frequent this restaurant, run with great charm by **Gianni** and **Rosanna**, whose fresh flowers complement the fresh interpretations of Italian favorites such as *spaghetti al cartoccio con crostacei* (seafood spaghetti). ◆ Closed M, Tu lunch, Aug. Via Ciovasso 3. 8053581

27 Galleria Seno A well-designed gallery (lighting by **Castiglioni**, table by **Sottsass**) where the works of **Albers** and **Matta**, among others, are shown. ◆ Closed M, Su, lunch. Via Ciovasso 11. 8058064

28 Toselli Italian Neo-Expressionist painters such as **Paladino** and **DeMaria** are among the artists in the stable of this blue-chip gallery. ◆ Via del Carmine 9. 8050434

29 Ponte di Brera **Silvano d'Auria** is the piano man at Milan's oldest and swankest jazz club. ◆ Tu-Su 9PM-1AM. Via Brera 2. 876723

Stendhal lived in Milan for 7 years and described them as *the flower of my life*. He asked that his tombstone be inscribed, *Henri Beyle, Milanese.*

30 Naj Oleari Whimsical fabric designs in patterns ranging from airplanes to eyeglasses for the young and young at heart, often made into such items as bags and umbrellas. ◆ Closed M morning, Su, lunch. Via Brera 8. 800633. Also at: Via Brera 5

30 Pelligrini Art supplies, catering to the students at the nearby Brera Art Academy. ◆ Closed M morning, Su, lunch. Via Brera 16. 8057119

30 Il Diaframma **Lanfranco Colombo** runs Milan's first photography gallery, showing contemporary and historical work. ◆ Via Brera 16. 8056814

30 Fornasetti Imaginative design objects from teacups to bicycles by one of Milan's foremost such *maestri.* ◆ Closed M morning, Su, lunch. Via Brera 16. 8050321

31 Piazzetta Brera Behind the fence in this little piazza is a monumental sculpture of **Francesco Hayez** (once president of the Brera Academy) by **Francesco Barzaghi**. ◆ Piazzetta Brera

32 La Forma e Anima della Materia A large abstract metal sculpture by Milanese artist **Teodoro Antonio Franz Sartori**. ◆ Via Brera

33 Palazzo Cusani This opulent palazzo has 2 rich Rococo facades—one on Via Brera (1715-17, **Giovanni Ruggieri**) and one in the rear (1775-90, **Giuseppe Piermarini**) which make one of the most distinguished residences in the neighborhood. ◆ Via Brera 13-15

34 Palazzo di Brera (1651, **Francesco Maria Richini**) The present Neoclassical palazzo is an enlargement of a 14th-century college belonging first to the prosperous Umiliati religious order and later to the Jesuits, who commissioned architect **Martino Bassi** to enlarge it in 1591 before the last expansion in the 17th century. The courtyard, in the tradition of the Jesuit colleges in Rome (Collegio Romano) and Pavia (Collegio Borromeo), has as its centerpiece a monumental bronze statue of **Napoleon** as the nude god Mars by **Antonio Canova**. Students at the **Accademia di Belle Arti**, the prestigious fine arts academy within the palazzo, have been known to make use of the statue for less than monumental purposes such as draping it with manifestos or spray-painting slogans on it.

Behind Napoleon in the Palazzo di Brera complex

Pinacoteca di Brera (Brera Picture Gallery) As the bronze statue in the courtyard suggests **Napoleon** had a monumental role in establishing the collection of the Brera, founded under Hapsburg rule in the late 18th century. Under his rule, thousands of works of art were confiscated from all over northern Italy and brought to the Brera, which has the best collection of northern Italian painting in the world. It is quite extensive, so be prepared for that feeling of faintness from cultural overload called the *Stendhal syndrome*, particularly appropriate here since Milan was the French traveler and connoisseur's favorite city. The effect is somewhat lessened by the fact that entire sections of the museum are often closed, something else to watch out for.

♦ Admission. Tu-Sa 9AM-1PM; Su 9AM-12:30PM. Via Brera 28. 808387

Highlights of the Brera:

Sala I This long corridor was formerly called the **Corridoio degli Affreschi** because it contained the museum's fresco collection. Today it displays 2 by **Vincenzo Foppa**, the most important painter in Milan in the 15th century before Leonardo da Vinci arrived from Florence. They are a *St. Sebastian* and a *Madonna and Saints*, both from the church of Santa Maria di Brera. Also on display are a series of *Self-Portraits* from the 16th-century **Palma Il Giovane** to the 20th-century **Umberto Boccione**.

Sala II This small room has 14th-century frescoes of religious subjects, attributed to **Giovanni da Milano**, showing that Tuscan painting had begun to influence northern Italian artists by mid-century.

Sala III The next 3 rooms, along with **Sala XVII**, show the bulk of Napoleon's booty. These 3 concentrate on Venetian painting, with its celebration of drama with shimmering light and a warm palette. It is introduced spectacularly in Sala III with 3 paintings by the 16th-century painter **Paolo Caliari** (known as **Veronese**), *The Last Supper, Christ in the Garden* and *The Baptism of Christ*. Other important works from 16th-century Venice are **Lorenzo Lotto**'s *Pietà* and **Paris Bordone**'s *Baptism of Christ*. Compare them to the gentler light of the altarpiece by 16th-century Lombard painter **Gerolamo Savoldo**.

Sala IV Three distinct styles of Venetian Mannerist painters, who like their counterparts in Florence and Rome were concerned with manipulating the human figure to often grotesque proportions, may be compared in this room. Here are **Veronese**'s sumptuous *Saints Anthony, Cornelius and Cipriano*, **Jacopo Bassano**'s gentle *St. Rocco Visiting the Plague Victims*, and one of the most famous paintings in the museum, **Jacopo Tintoretto**'s dramatic *Finding of the Body of St. Mark*. One of 4 paintings done on the subject of Venice's patron saint for the Scuola Grande di San Marco in Venice (the other 3 are in the Accademia in Venice), it depicts the saint halting grave robbers who have discovered his body.

Sala V Back at the beginning of the 16th century in Venice, the subject of St. Mark was taken up by **Gentile Bellini** in *The Preaching of St. Mark*. Finished by the artist's brother **Giovanni**, the painting supposedly represents

the saint before the church of St. Euphemia in Alexandria, but the Bellinis have clearly used Piazza San Marco in Venice as their inspiration, populated with an exotic cast of Arabs, camels and giraffes.

Salas VI-VII These 2 rooms contain frescoes of *Armed Men*, the only surviving paintings by the Renaissance architect **Donato Bramante** and another highlight of the museum. Attributed variously to Bramante and **Bramantino** is the *Christ at the Column*.

Sala VIII 14th- and early 15th-century painting is on display here, including **Gentile da Fabriano**'s polyptych, **Ambrogio Lorenzetti**'s *Madonna and Child*, and their northern Italian contemporaries, **Giovanni da Milano**'s *Judging Christ* and **Stefano da Zevio**'s *Adoration of the Magi*.

Ala Nuova Off Sala VIII is the entrance to the Ala Nuova or new wing, which houses the Brera's collection of painting from 1910-30. In the corridor are *Head of a Woman* and *Portrait of Moise Kistling* by **Amadeo Modigliani**; the Futurist

Rising City and *Brawl in the Galleria* by **Umberto Boccioni**; and the Cubist-influenced *Rhythms of Objects* by **Carlo Carrà** and *The North-South* by **Gino Severini**. The galleries of the Ala Nuovo have 3 Metaphysical paintings by Carlo Carrà: *The Metaphysical Muse, Mother and Son* and *The Enchanted Room*. Following those are *Still Lifes* by **Giorgio Morandi**. The section reaches a crescendo with a series of canvases by Futurist painters, whose aim was to depict machines and motion: Boccioni's *Elasticity, The Drinker, Dynamism of a Human Body, Lancers Loading*; **Giacomo Balla**'s *Automobile, Laughing Brush, Spring* and *Patriotic Demonstration*; Carrà's *Nocturne in Piazza Beccaria* and *Horse and Horseman*; Gino Severini's *Bus* and *The White Dancer*; **Mario Sironi**'s *Trenches, White Dancer* and *Little Dancer*.

Salas VII-XVII From Ala Nuova, go back through Sala VII to Sala VII to continue the visit. These rooms contain 15th- and 16th-century paintings from Lombardy and Piedmont, including portraits of *Francesco Sforza* and *Bianca Maria Sforza* (Sala VII); *Portrait of a Youth* by **Ambrogio da Predis** (Sala XIII); and the *Altarpiece* by **Vincenzo Foppa** (Sala XVII).

Sala XVIII Another of the most famous paintings in the Brera, **Andrea Mantegna**'s gravely foreshortened *Dead Christ*, lying with his feet in the viewer's face while the women grieve in the background, is in this room. Also on display are canvases by the 15th-century artist **Carlo Crivelli**, characteristically Venetian in their decorative detail (*Madonna of the Candle*) and richness (*Coronation of the Virgin*).

Sala XIX Two *Madonnas* and a *Pietà* by the Venetian Renaissance painter **Giovanni Bellini** are the highlights of this room.

199

Sala XX Look for **Mantegna**'s *Madonna* and the Ferrarese Renaissance painter **Francesco Cossa**'s *St. Peter* and *St. John the Baptist*.

Sala di Piero della Francesca e di Rafaello This recently rearranged room (formerly Sala XXIV-XXVI) has the 2 most famous paintings in the museum: 15th-century Tuscan painter **Piero della Francesca**'s severe *Madonna with Saints and Angels Adored by Federico da Montefeltro*, with its attention to architecural detail, and **Raphael**'s delicate *Betrothal of the Virgin*, an early work (1504) showing the influence of his master, **Perugino**, in its balanced composition.

Sala XXVII Gerolamo Gegna's 16th-century *Madonna and Child with Saints* is the highlight of this room.

Sala XXVIII Dedicated to the Bolognese **Carracci** family, who painted in the late 16th and early 17th centuries, this room displays *The Canaanite* by **Ludovico Carracci**, *The Samaritan at the Well* by his cousin **Annibale Carracci** and *The Adultress* by Annibale's

Brera

brother **Agostino**.

Sala XXIX Dedicated to **Caravaggio** and his followers, this room is dominated by his subtly dramatic *Supper at Emmaus*, painted in 1606. Caravaggio's spiritual influence can be seen on **Battistello Caracciolo**'s *The Samaritan at the Well*, which in fact was attributed to the master when it was acquired by the museum in 1820.

Sala XXX The influence of his master, **Ludovico Carracci**, combined with the chiaroscuro of **Caravaggio**, may be seen in 17th-century Bolognese painter **Guercino**'s *Repudiation of Hagar* in this room.

Salas XXXI-XXXIII Foreign paintings are displayed in these rooms, including a *Last Supper* by **Peter Paul Rubens** and *Madonna and Child with Saints* by **Anthony van Dyck** (Sala XXXI); a *Tryptych* by **Jan de Beer** (Sala XXXII); and *Portrait of a Young Woman* by **Rembrandt** (Sala XXXIII), all 17th-century works.

Sala XXXIV A 17th-century *Madonna* by **Pietro da Cortona** and 18th-century *Madonna* by **Gian Battista Tiepolo** are here.

Salas XXXV-XXXVI 18th-century Italian painting, including **Canaletto**'s *View of the Grand Canal*, **Giovan Battista Piazzetta**'s *Rebecca at the Well*, and **Giovanni Maria Crespi**'s *A Fair*.

Sala XXII and Sala XXXVII-XXXVIII Used for temporary exhibitions.

Also within the Brera:

Biblioteca Nazionale di Brera Founded by **Maria Theresa** of Austria in 1770, the National Library today has over1 million volumes. Among its most notable works is the 11th-century

manuscript of **St. Ambrose**'s *Hexaemeron* and the papers of **Alessandro Manzoni**. ◆ M 1:30-7PM; Tu-Sa 9AM-2PM. 861270

Osservatorio Astronomico Founded in 1763, the astronomical observatory is the seat of Milan's city weather service. ◆ 86460135

Orto Botanico The Brera's expansive but run down botanical garden is closed to the public.

Within the Palazzo di Brera:

Pinacoteca Bar A high-design cafe (it was commissioned by the design magazine *Abitare*) serving light snacks to help you recover from a heavy morning at the museum. ◆ Via Brera 28. 866431

35 The Body Shop Lotions and creams galore in the Milan branch of this British chain. ◆ Closed Su. Via Brera 30. No credit cards. 8690112

35 Jamaica The 1960s-style decor remains in this cafe, though the artists and intellectuals who frequented the place at that time have been replaced by the Nouveau-Bohemian types who've discovered the Brera. ◆ M-Sa 8AM-midnight. Via Brera 32. 876823

36 Roberta & Basta Antiques, with a specialty in Empire and Art Deco from Italy and France. ◆ Closed M morning, Su, lunch. Via Fiori Chiari 2. 861593

37 Marzot & C. Furniture and lighting design by such great names as **Mario Botta** and **Artemide** in this showroom. ◆ Closed M morning, Su, lunch. Via Fiori Chiari 3. No credit cards. 871828

37 Franco Sabatelli A very Florentine-looking artisan-type shop specializing in picture frames in all shapes and sizes. ◆ Closed M morning, Su, lunch. Via Fiori Chiari 5. 8052688

37 Decomania Art Deco antiques, with an emphasis on Italian contributions to the movement by **Gio Ponti** and the like. ◆ Closed M morning, Su, lunch. Via Fiori Chiari 7. 808027

38 Momus Extreme chic in this piano bar-restaurant, where the quality of the people-watching often exceeds that of the food. ◆ Tu-Su 9PM-1AM. Via Fiori Chiari 8. 8056227

38 Baldan Imaginative custom-made jewelry by **Maria Grazia Baldan**, who works antique pieces such as Chinese coins into whimsical settings. ◆ Closed M morning, Su, lunch. Via Fiori Chiari 14. 808714

39 Etro Paisley prints, especially nice on velvet pillows but also in a variety of fabrics and accessories. ◆ Closed M morning, Su, lunch. Vicolo Fiori 17. 807768

40 Starry ★$$ One of the less-expensive dining options in the area, especially if you stick to the pizzas. ◆ Closed M, holidays. Vicolo Fiori. 869309

41 Miro American-style 1970s music revisited and appreciated if not quite fully understood at this club. ♦ Tu-Su 9PM-1AM. Vicolo Fiori 2. 8760116

42 Poly's A Parisian-style piano bar where you can get a plate of pasta at midnight. ♦ Daily 9:30PM-2:30AM. Via Formentini 5. 8053492

43 Club Due Another longtime Brera hangout, this one featuring live jazz until the wee hours. ♦ Via Formentini 2. 873533

44 Patuscino A club attracting a thick middle-aged crowd to live loungey music. ♦ Tu-Su 9PM-1AM. Via Madonnina 2. 807264

45 L'Oro dei Farlocchi Very unusual gift items, mostly antique British knickknacks. ♦ Closed M morning, Su, lunch. Via Madonnina 5. 850589

45 Angela Caputi The Milan branch of the imaginative costume jewelry and swimsuit designer whose home shop you can find in Florence. ♦ Closed M morning, Su, lunch. Via Madonnina 11. 807384

45 Makeup Studio Diego della Palma's fashionable beauty parlor in this most fashionable of neighborhoods in this most fashionable of cities. Yes, they do the makeup for all the fashion shows. ♦ Closed M morning, Su, lunch. Via Madonnina 15. 876818. Also at: Via Agnello 19. 874080

46 M. Bardelli Cashmere, Cotton & Silk No translation necessary of this shop's name, which offers highly designed men's clothing in all the above fabrics. ♦ Closed M morning, Su, lunch. Via Madonnina 19. 8056426

46 Patuscino Another one of the neighborhood's tiny, crowded clubs good for a late-night plate of pasta after everything else has closed. ♦ Closed M. Via Madonnina 21. 807264

46 Montmarte This little club is almost as Parisian in its lively, bubbly spirit as its name implies. ♦ Tu-Su 9PM-1AM. Via Madonnina 27. 807747

47 Rimessa Fiori Romantic and sophisticated womenswear by Milanese designer **Luisa Beccaria**. ♦ Via San Carpoforo 9. 876840

48 Brera Art books galore. ♦ Closed M morning, Su, lunch. Via Mercato 3. 865885

49 Idea Bijoux One of the rare places for costume jewelry in Italy. ♦ Closed Su. Via Mercato 20. 876878

49 La Torre di Pisa ★★$$ Tuscan food, including the famous white bean soup called *ribollita*, tucked into by a fashionable crowd of models, actors and journalists. ♦ Closed Sa lunch, Su, Aug. Via Mercato 26. 874877

50 Erboristeria Novara The place in Milan to buy homeopathic medicinals by **Dr. Alessandro Novara** as well as the ancient-formula products of the famed Florentine *erboristeria* Farmacia Santa Maria Novella. ♦ Closed M morning, Su, lunch. Via Pontaccio 19. 870547

50 Rodolfo II Newish collectors items, with an emphasis on Art Nouveau and Deco jewelry. ♦ Closed M morning, Su, lunch. Via Pontaccio 19. 800636

51 Palazzo Crivelli (1658-1705) A handsome, simple residence typical of the neighborhood. ♦ Via Pontaccio 12

52 Spelta Ladies' shoes, of the casual variety. ♦ Closed Su, lunch. Via Pontaccio 2. 8052592

52 Lucia Ladies' handbags, of the fashionable variety. ♦ Closed M morning, Su, lunch. Via Solferino. 867708

52 Drogheria Solferino A contemporary men's and women's clothing shop (international threads) in an old drug store. ♦ Closed M morning, Su, lunch. Via Solferino 1. 878740

53 Surplus American-style used clothing with a glamorous spin in the top hats and tails. ♦ Closed Su, lunch. Corso Garibaldi 7. 8693696. Also at: Corso Garibaldi 39. 800987; Via Castaldi 41. 222353; Via Mancini 1. 5459719; Corso di Porta Ticinese 101/103. 8353916

54 Al Teatro Cocktails and recorded music for a crowd that comes from the theater across the street. ♦ Tu-F 7AM-2AM; Sa-Su 3PM-2AM.

Brera

Corso Garibaldi 16. 864222

55 San Simpliciano This church, which dates from Early Christian times, was restored to something approximating its original state in the last century. The restoration mainly involved getting rid of the Baroque additions, leaving the meditative impression we see today. Even more peaceful is the adjacent convent, whose **Chiostro Grande** makes for a pleasant break in the day's activities. ♦ Piazza delle Crociate

56 Nicol Caramel Maternity clothes à la Milanese, meaning well-designed and functional. ♦ Closed M morning, Su, lunch. Piazza San Simpliciano 7. 807880

57 Dodo The Milan branch of a Florentine shop specializing in hand-painted accessories and gift items, such as toys, boxes and the like. ♦ Closed M morning, Su, lunch. Corso Garibaldi 55. No credit cards. 8058269

58 La Nazionale ★★$$ A lively mix of students from the Brera and a few area *rampanti* or young professionals are the clientele of this restaurant, which serves a light menu of salads and crepes. ♦ Closed Sa lunch, Su. Via Ancona 3. No credit cards. 6572059

59 Rossignoli Bicycles, accessories and nifty racing gear. ♦ Closed M morning, Su, lunch. Corso Garibaldi 71. No credit cards. 804960

60 Murnik Andrea Murnik sets the dramatic scene for his design wares with black-and-white bricks and glass-tile wall. ♦ Closed M, Su, lunch. Via Giulianova 1. 806030

61 Al Matarel ★★$$ One of the most beloved of all Milanese restaurants, Matarel (*crazy*) serves definintive versions of the city's specialties, from *insaccati* antipasto to all the risotto dishes and *cassoeula* or pig's-foot stew. ◆ Closed Tu, W lunch, July. Via Solera Mantegazza. No credit cards. 654204

62 Casa Pacchetti (1903, **Gaetano Moretti**) A pleasantly eclectic residence incorporating elements from Egyptian to Lombard Renaissance. ◆ Via Legnano 28

63 Moscatelli A lovely old *enoteca* or wine bar, run for the past few decades by **Giuseppe Moscatelli.** ◆ Tu-Su 10:30AM-7:30PM, 9:30PM-2AM. Corso Garibaldi 93. 6554602

64 G. Asnaghi Sturdy, well-designed men's and women's clothing at affordable prices. ◆ Closed Su, lunch. Via Moscova 68. No credit cards. 6597706

65 Giovanni Battista Piatti This bit of outdoor sculpture, by **Salvatore Pisani**, commemorates Milanese inventor Giovanni Battista Piatti. ◆ Corso Garibaldi

66 Caffè Radetzky A trendy new old-style cafe for whiling away the hours over a newspaper

Brera

and/or a plate of oysters. ◆ M-Sa 7:30AM-1:30AM. Corso Garibaldi 105. 6572645

67 La Cartoleria An old-fashioned stationer for old-fashioned notebooks and pens as well as contemporary items of the shop's Creare label. ◆ Closed M morning, Su, lunch. Corso Garibaldi. 6570672

68 Grazia Montesi Owners **Grazia Montesi** and **Raimondo Garau** have assembled a collection of everything from Baroque to modern furniture and objects in this shop. ◆ Closed M morning, Su, lunch. Via Marsala 13. 6557657

69 Effebieffe Anglo and faux-Anglo clothes in various generic labels for men and women at reasonable prices. ◆ Closed Su, lunch. Via Marsala 7. 6598069

70 Santa Maria Incoronata (1461, 1468) A strange church composed of 2 separate churches united in architectural matrimony in 1484 and still going strong. ◆ Corso Garibaldi

71 Centro Bonsai Bonsai, the Japanese art of cultivating miniature trees, has only recently caught on in Italy, so if you're stuck for a gift this shop might give you some ideas. ◆ Closed M morning, Su, lunch. Corso Garibaldi 121. 6597961

72 Antonia Jannone The only gallery in Italy dealing exclusively in architectural and theatrical drawings, the designs of **Michael Graves, Aldo Rossi, Massimo Scolari, Ettore Sottsass** and others may be perused and/or purchased here. ◆ Closed M morning, Su, lunch. Corso Garibaldi 125. 6557930

72 Panino Giusto Milan's original *paninoteca*—the kind of sandwich shop that revolutionized the natives' eating habits—still makes some of the city's most original sandwiches. ◆ M-Sa 8AM-midnight. Corso Garibaldi 125. 6554728

73 Porta Garibaldi (1826, **Giacomo Moraglia**) Another Neoclassical city gate, this one marched through by none other than **Giuseppe Garibaldi.** ◆ Piazza XXV Aprile

74 Roca's Bar Lively music hangout with light snacks for grazing alla Milanese. ◆ Tu-Su 8AM-1:30AM. Viale Pasubio 16. 6599729

75 Piccolo Teatro Fuori Porta ★★$$ Old Milanese food in a new location, with special emphasis on rich desserts such as chocolate mousse and warm *zabaglione*. ◆ Closed Su, Aug. Viale Pasubio 8. 65752105

76 Caffè Novecento Much frequented by fashion-world denizens for coffee, cocktails and snacks. ◆ M-Sa 8AM-midnight. Corso Como 9. 6552090

77 Romeo Gigli The ample showroom of the renowned fasion designer. ◆ Closed M morning, Su, lunch. Corso Como 10. 655674

77 All'Isola ★★$$ Another fabulous fashion-world haunt, this one too serving a Milanese menu with diet-busting desserts like warm *zabaglione*. ◆ Closed Sa lunch, Su, 2 weeks in Aug, Christmas week. Corso Como 10. 6571624

78 Hollywood Americans in town for the collections flock to this disco, run by a local celebrity DJ named **Ringo**. ◆ Tu-Sa 10PM-3AM; Su 3-6PM. Corso Como 15. 6598996

79 Shockin' Club Celebrity DJ **Philippe Renaul** draws an international crowd of models and advertizing people to this 1970s-style disco. ◆ Bastioni di Porta Nuova 12. 6595407

80 Galleria Michel Leo Deco plastics and Lalique glass are just some among many 20th-century collectibles on sale at this shop. ◆ Closed M morning, Su, lunch. Via Solferino 35. 6598333

80 Galleria Paola e Rossella Columbari These sisters sell design objects for home and office from about the postwar period onward, and have their own line of contemporary commissioned pieces. ◆ Closed M morning, Su, lunch. Via Solferino 37. 650189

81 Dinner & Lunch Club ★★$$ A tiny cafe and eatery featuring the international (it just opened a branch in Los Angeles) gourmet items of Princess Hortensia Chigi della Rovere. ◆ M-F, Su 7:30AM-3PM, 5-11PM; Sa 7:30AM-3PM. Via Solferino 48. 657608

82 Emilio Boffi The workshop of one of Milan's leading young designers of leather goods. ◆ Closed M morning, Su, lunch. Via Milazzo 6

82 Giallo ★★$$ Fashionable (with the fashion world) dining on everything from nibbles of *pizzettine* (little pizzas) to *cotoletta alla parigina* (breaded veal cutlet smothered with melted cheese). Dinner only. ◆ Closed Su. Via Milazzo 6. 6571581

83 Traifiori An etheral veil-covered courtyard leads to knitwear heaven. ◆ Closed M morning, Su, lunch. Via Solferino 31. 655946

84 Enoteca Cotti Milan's most famous *enoteca* or wineshop, where a studied selection of great grapes may be tasted and purchased here with the expert advice of **Signor Cotti**. ♦ M-Sa 8:30AM-midnight. Via Solferino 42. No credit cards. 6572995

85 L'Arcivolto The best selection of books on design and architecture in this design- and architecture-obsessed city. There are also temporary exhibitions on those subjects in its gallery. ♦ Closed M morning, Su, lunch. Via Marsala 2. 6590842

86 Antica Locanda Solferino $$ The choice for inexpensive but stylish accommodations in Milan, this former *pensione* is booked months in advance, so be sure to reserve. Rooms have a lot of character, and the staff a bit too much, but the neighborhood is worth the attitude. ♦ Via Castelfidardo 2. 656905

86 Solferino ★★$$ A young crowd appreciates the inventive menu of such pairings of pasta with seasonal vegetables and truffled kidney as well as *carpaccio* of various types of raw meat. ♦ Closed Sa lunch, Su, 2 weeks in Aug. Via Castelfidardo 2. 6599886

86 La Tenda Gialla Antiques and knickknacks with an emphasis on collectibles from the first half of the century. ♦ Closed M morning, Su. Via Castelfidardo 2. 652981

87 Bebel's ★$$ What towers at Bebel's are the pizzas, made in an authentic wood-burning brick oven, though more expensive items like lobster are also available. ♦ Closed W, Aug. Via San Marco 38. 6571658

88 La Piazzetta A large cafe for a drink or a snack of a sandwich or the daily plate of pasta. ♦ M-Sa 8AM-9PM. Via Solferino 25. No credit cards. 6590176

88 La Briciola ★★$$ Another lively place (largely thanks to maitre d' **Giorgio**) popular with models and journalists and serving a full Milanese menu as well as the ever-popular *carpaccio* or thinly sliced raw beef, here drizzled in extra-virgin Tuscan olive oil. ♦ Closed M, Su, Aug, Christmas week. Via Solferino 25. 6551012

89 Casa Rigamonti (1889-90, **Simone Giuseppe Locati**) A handsome Neoclassical residence which has seen better days but should be seen nonetheless for a subtle sense of neighborhood gentility. ♦ Via Solferino 24

90 Pavillon ★★$$ Lombard and Piedmontese cuisine is featured here, with risottos and homemade pastas leading the list, which also includes game and truffles in season. ♦ Closed Tu, holidays. Via Statuto 16. 6552219

91 La Vetrina di Beryl Footwear based on historical styles that make them new again. ♦ Closed M morning, Su, lunch. Via Statuto 4. 654278

92 Enrico Massei Very contemporary clothes and accessories for the ladies. ♦ Closed M morning, Su, lunch. Via Palermo 8. 6552852

93 Silvi Sí Our lady friends love the original knits. Silvia embellishes with sequins and other adornments. ♦ Closed M morning, Su, lunch. Via Palermo 5. No credit cards. 802435

93 Grand'Italia ★$$ Spaghetti and pizza make this lively place one of the least expensive options in the area. ♦ Closed Tu, Sa lunch, Aug. Via Palermo 5. 877759

93 Legatoria Artistica Marbelized paper and paper products made on the premises. ♦ Closed M morning, Su, lunch. Via Palermo 5. No credit cards. 861113

94 Rigolo ★★$$ Always abuzz with a lively crowd of fashion and designer types as well as journalists from the nearby offices of **Corriere**

Brera

della Sera, Rigolo has a long list of Italian dishes (the *costoletta milanese* is easily enough for 2) and is one of the few places in town open for Sunday dinner. ♦ Closed M, lunch Tu, July. Largo Treves. 8059768

95 Argenteria Dabbene Finely-crafted silver in jewelry, serving trays, picture frames and other gift items. ♦ Closed M morning, Su, lunch. Largo Treves 2. 6598890

96 Carrano Shoes for women in the latest styles by Carrano; men in more conservative cuts. ♦ Closed M morning, Su, lunch. Via Solferino 11. 867733

96 Kiovu Housewares with the kind of inventive design Milan is all about. ♦ Closed M morning, Su, lunch. Via Solferino 11. 870258. Also at: Corso Europa 12. 790821; Via Cerva 13 and 25. 793098

97 Controbuffet Clever gifts such as Avant de Dormir plastic gear (you know, the ones with the toy fish sandwiched inside). ♦ Closed M morning, Su, lunch. Via Solferino 14. 6554934

97 Lo Scarabattolo Mostly British antiques if you're not going to Portobello Rd in the near future. ♦ M 4-7:30PM; Tu-Sa 9AM-1PM, 4-7:30PM. Via Solferino 14. 6590253

98 Penelopi 3 Lots of well-chosen housewares, from dishtowels to Alessi teapots and espresso makers. ♦ Closed M morning, Su, lunch. Via Solferino 12. 6599640

98 L'Altro Calafuria ★★$$ This perennially trendy restaurant serves a mean *costoletta milanese*, topped with chopped basil and tomato. ♦ Closed Tu, Aug. Via Solferino 12. 6559627

Milan...has seemed prosaic and winterish as if it were on the wrong side of the Alps. **Henry James**

99 Stendhal ★★★$$$ Named in honor of the French writer and Milanophile, this trendy restaurant, decorated in boudoir style, has an elegant menu to match. The *culatello* ham appetizer melts in your mouth. The focus is on dinner, though light meals are served at lunch. ◆ Closed M, holidays. Via San Marco. 6555587

99 Notorious Another club for the younger set, this one with a 1970s theme on Friday nights. ◆ Tu-Su 8PM-1AM. Via Ancona 4. 876960

100 Enoteca N'Ombra de Vin A peaceful wine bar for sipping and purchasing. You can also learn about the vintages in their wine appreciation classes. ◆ Closed M morning, Su, lunch. Via San Marco 2. 6552746

101 Brerarte Another of Milan's most important auction houses, which usually has a pre-auction viewing or 2 going on. ◆ Closed Su, lunch. Piazza San Marco 1. 6555040

Brera

101 Fashion Cafe A hangout for all types of fashion models at all hours. ◆ M-Sa 11AM-2AM. Piazza San Marco 1. 659823

101 Dilmos Furniture and objects by Italy's top designers. ◆ Closed M morning, Su, lunch. Piazza San Marco 1. 6559837

102 San Marco (13th-18th c) This church, restored in the 19th century, contains a number of 14th-century frescoes in the right transept and a *Baptism of St. Augustine* by **Cerano** in the presbytery. ◆ Piazza San Marco

103 La Lanterna Clothing, sportswear and sports equipment with agreeable prices if not agreeable service. ◆ Closed Su, lunch. Via Cernaia 1A. No credit cards. 6555752

104 Casa Fiocchi (1924-25, **Giuseppe Fiocchi**) Surprisingly, this handsome Neoclassical residence wasn't built until this century. ◆ Via Cernaia 6

105 Palazzo Landrini (16th c, attributed to **Cesare Cesariano**) A lovely palazzo with a don't-you-wish-you-lived-here courtyard. ◆ Via Borgonuovo 25

106 Civico Museo del Risorgimento (Risorgimento Museum) The Italian Risorgimento, when the country fought for unity during the last century, is little studied outside Italy, but this museum provides a nicely didactic introduction. Even if you're not particularly interested in history, the period costumes and memorabilia are enticingly displayed. ◆ Daily 9:30AM-7:30PM; closed New Year's, Easter, 1 May, 25 Aug, Christmas. Via Borgonuovo 23. 8693549

107 Claudio Silvestri Various glass objects, especially from the 1940s, '50s and '60s. ◆ Closed M morning, Su, lunch. Via Borgonuovo 26. 6592909

108 Via Annunciata 23/1 (1932-34, **Luigi Figini** and **Gino Pollini**) Modernist apartment building the architects defined as *superimposed villas* because of their modular nature.

109 Saint Laurent Rive Gauche An Italian outlet house for the French designer (much of whose stuff is made in Italy anyway). ◆ Closed Sa-Su, lunch. Piazza Sant'Erasmo 3. 6557795

110 A. Caraceni Made-to-measure men's clothing by the best tailors in Milan. ◆ Closed M morning, Su, lunch. Via Fatebenefratelli 16. No credit cards. 6551972

111 Tanzi Driade One of the chicest showrooms in the city, displaying the designs of all the Italians as well as such international enfants terribles as **Philippe Starck**. ◆ Closed M morning, Su, lunch. Via Fatebenefratelli 9. No credit cards. 652692

112 Cavour Wide selection of books in many languages, displayed in style and a pleasure to browse. ◆ Closed M morning, Su, lunch. Via Fatebenefratelli 23. 6595644

113 Cardi Jewelry in the styles of bigger names, smaller prices. ◆ Closed M morning, Su, lunch. Piazza Cavour 1. 6592495

113 Palazzo dei Giornali (1937-42, **Giovanni Muzio**) This building was originally designed for **Il Popolo d'Italia**, the newspaper founded by **Mussolini**. Today a number of Italian newspapers have offices here. Check out the bas relief called *Le Origini a lo Sviluppo delGiornal della Revoluzione* by **Mario Sirone** at the top. ◆ Piazza Cavour 2

114 Casa Kit Well-designed and inexpensive home furnishings. ◆ Closed M morning, Su, lunch. Via Carlo Porta 1. 6597916. Also at: Piazza Risorgimento 10. 7388419

115 Sinig's Home furnishings at low prices that make up for the high-anxiety service. ◆ Closed Su, lunch. Via Turati 5. 6597896

115 Il Discanto A small shop selling ethnic jewelry from around the world as well as antique and exotic fabrics and other accessories. ◆ Closed M morning, Su, lunch. Via Turati 7. 652557

116 Porta Nuova The *new gate* dates from the 12th century and is decorated with Roman tomb sculpture from the 1st century AD. ◆ Piazza Cavour

117 Piazza Cavour The piazza and its sculpture (by **Antonio Tantardini** and **Odardo Tabacchi**) are dedicated to **Count Camille Cavour**, the Risorgimento politician after whom so many streets and piazzas in Italy are named. ◆ Piazza Cavour

118 Galleria Milano Modern (and later) painting, sculpture, photography and design are the mixed palette of this gallery. ◆ Tu-Sa 10AM-1PM, 4-8PM. Via Manin 13. 650352

119 Spazio Krizia In a former stable, the headquarters of the famous designer known for his knits and animal motifs is also used for literary events. ◆ Via Manin 21. 6596415

20 Palazzo Montecatini (1935-38, **Studio Ponti**) A model of industrial architecture in its day, this building was among the first to use such technical tricks as climate control, pneumatic tubes, etc. ♦ Via Moscova 3

20 Ranieri One of the city's premiere *pasticcerie* or pastry shops, famed for its *panettone ripieno*, the Milanese cake stuffed with all sorts of creamy fillings. ♦ Tu-Sa 8AM-8PM; Su 7AM-1PM. Via Moscova 7. 6595308

21 Profumeria Leali Brand-name toiletries at a discount. ♦ Closed M morning, Sa afternoon, Su. Via Moscova 10. 6552663

22 Palazzo della Permanente (1883-85, **Luca Beltrami**; 1951-52 **Achille** and **Piergiacomo Castiglioni**) Check out this palazzo for the temporary exhibitions it often houses. ♦ Via Turati 34. 6599803

23 Via Manin 33 (1933-34, **Mario Asnago** and **Claudio Vender**) A residential version of Fascist-era architecture incorporating the reductionist geometric forms of its institutional counterpart which also foreshadow postmodern architecture.

24 Good Mood An older-generation club where some of Italy's most popular pop singers often turn up for a gig. ♦ Tu-Sa 9PM-2:30AM; Su 3-6PM. Via Turati 29. 6559349

25 Cá Brüta (1921-23, **Studio Barelli-Colonnese**) The name of this building is Milanese dialect for *ugly house*, affectionately given it because of the unusually idiosyncratic decoration on the facade. There's nothing ugly about the courtyard either. ♦ Via Moscova 12

26 Le Cinque Terre ★★$$ **Stefano** and **Elena Galligari** have created one of the most upscale seafood joints in town, serving everything from oysters to lobster at their absolute freshest. ♦ Closed Sa lunch, Su, Aug 10-22. Via Andrea Appiani 9. 6575177

27 Pucci Handmade handbags and other canvas and leather goods. ♦ Closed Sa-Su. Via Moscova 16. No credit cards. 6559451

28 Artform **Paolo** and **Anna Tilche**'s shop (designed by Paolo, a trained architect) sells a tasteful selection of design objects for home and office, with an emphasis on Scandinavian goods. ♦ Closed M morning, Su, lunch. Via Moscova 22. 652423

29 Bar Margherita A peaceful nightspot for an older jazz crowd with a fine selection of *grappa*, the Italian acquavit. ♦ M-Sa noon-2AM. Via Moscova 25. 6590833

30 El Timbun de San Marc An English-style pub that serves a mean bean soup. ♦ M-Sa noon-3PM, 5PM-1AM. Via San Marco 20. 6599507

31 Mirabello Bed and bath accessories in imaginative patterns and fabrics including rich silks from the factories of nearby Como. ♦ Closed M morning, Su, lunch. Via Montebello. 6559785

32 Raimondo Bianchi Plants are always an appropriate gift for business and other acquaintances in Milan, and this place has some of the best-looking ones in the city. ♦ Closed M morning, Su, lunch. Via Montebello 7. 6555108

133 San Fermo ★★$$ Old Milan 19th-century decor provides a backdrop for classic Milanese cuisine, with especially good value on the less-expensive lunch menu. ♦ Closed Su, M dinner, Aug, Christmas week. Via San Fermo della Battaglia 1. 6551784

134 Caffe Milano Light meals, snacks and pastries in a setting reminiscent of Vienna. Especially pleasant in warmer weather when a few tables spill out into the little piazza. ♦ M-Sa 11AM-3AM. Piazza Mirabello 1. 29003300

134 Il Verdi ★★$$ Milan's increasingly American-style eating habits (for better or worse) are in evidence here in one-course meals (called *piatti unici*) of meat, pasta and salads. ♦ Closed Sa lunch, Su, Aug, Christmas week. Piazza Mirabello 5. 6590797

135 Piazza Sant'Angelo Appropriately, the highlight of this peaceful piazza is a fountain by realist sculptor **Giannino Castiglioni** depicting *St. Francis of Assisi*. ♦ Piazza Sant'Angelo

Brera

136 Sant'Angelo (1552, **Domenico Giunti**) This church and its adjacent convent were built by the Franciscan brothers. Inside are 16th- and 17th-century frescoes of not outstanding importance in the history of art, but rather pleasant local interpretations of the stories of St. Francis and other saints. ♦ Piazza Sant'Angelo

Bests

Massimo Vignelli
Designer

The food is good in many restaurants—shops are fantastic (the best in the world...)—design is everywhere —fashion is everywhere—**Via Della Spiga** is great.

There are too many restaurants to mention. Some of my favorties are: **La Brisa—La Scaletta—La Pesa—La Torre de Pisa—Bice—Stenterello—Le Colline Pistoiesi**.

There are many good examples of pre-Rationalist and Rationalist architecture—works by **Ponti, Muzio, Terragni, Figini, Pollini, Gardella, BBPR**.

Berlioz complained that the music at **La Scala** could not be heard above the noise of the people eating in the boxes during performances.

Stazione Centrale

On the map, the area around Milan's central train station—**Stazione Centrale**—looks like a fuse connecting the round bomb of the rest of the city, as though the motion-obsessed Milanese Futurists had their hand at urban planning. Indeed, in its own way the station—designed at the same time as the Futurist movement was gaining momentum—glorifies motion and power (and Fascism) as much as the Futurist movement ever did. And the adjacent district, known as **Centro Direzionale** or the administrative center, provides

ore fuel for the explosive energy of the city. Most visitors arrive at the station om trains and the airport buses that stop there, and many check in at the city's rgest concentration of business hotels. Though there is little of more than ractical interest in the Stazione Centrale area, the Futurists would have been leased at the functionalism. Besides the hotels, it bristles with Modernist kyscrapers, including the **Pirelli** building—the tallest in Italy—as well as a umber of no-nonsense discount outlets. Even its art galleries seem to specialize the reductionist Italian art of the *arte povera* school.

1 Stazione Centrale (completed 1932, **Ulisse Stacchini**) Italy's busiest train station also kept workers busy for the longest period of time, since the 1912 project wasn't completed until 1932. That period coincides with the rise of Fascism in Italy, and it shows in this train station of a monumentality that rivals Nebuchadnezzar. Besides representations of the actual fasces or bundle of rods with an ax that symbolized the movement, there are a number of other works of art: **Giannino Castiglioni**'s medallions representing *Work*, *Commerce*, *Science* and *Agriculture* in the entrance hall; **Alberto Bazzoni**'s bas-reliefs, statues and medallions in the ticket hall; and **Basilio Cascella**'s ceramic panels with views of Milan, Turin, Florence and Rome by the tracks. ◆ Piazza Duca D'Aosta

Within Stazione Centrale:

Museo delle Cere (Wax Museum) In the not-unlikely event that your train has been delayed and you're really pressed for entertainment, take heart. Milan's wax museum is right in the station, its motionless dioramas a mocking counterpoint to Italy's train service. **George**

Stazione Centrale

Bush and **Margaret Thatcher** are some of the contemporary figures represented, but they can't hold a candle to such historical figures as **Napoleon**, **Albert Schweizer** and the like. ◆ Admission. 24 hrs. Piazza Duca D'Aosta. 6690495

2 McDonald's $ Somehow the golden arches gleam more stylishly at Milan's McDonald's, the most elegant of all the fast-food restaurants (*fest* as they're pronounced here) in Milan. It is decorated in chrome and travertine and staffed by personnel uncharacteristically eager for Italy or the chain elsewhere in the world. The fast-food concept fits right into Milan's work ethic, so you'll see middle management types biting burgers right alongside unadventurous American tourists. ◆ M-Sa 8AM-11PM. Piazza Duca D'Aosta 6/8. 66987850

Milan, in its newer quarters, is a little more like Zurich, Dusseldorf, and Madison Avenue than Zurich, Dusseldorf, and Madison Avenue themselves. You are in Italy after all. **Luigi Barzini**

Restaurants/Nightlife: Red **Hotels:** Blue
Shops/Parks: Green **Sights/Culture:** Black

Excelsior Hotel Gallia

3 Excelsior Hotel Gallia $$$$ What the Stazione Centrale is to Fascism, this hotel is to Art Nouveau. Recently refurbished, it is the grandest of Milan's hotels, its public rooms and banquet facilities the majestic setting for power events in Milan. Guest rooms are decorated in pale Postmodern splendor. ♦ Deluxe ♦ Piazza Duca d'Aosta 9. 6277

Stazione Centrale

Within the Excelsior Hotel Gallia:

Baboon Bar Bartender (or *barman* as the Italians say) **Francesco Frigerio** prides himself on such cocktails as his Kir Royal, Mimosa, Evelin (pomegranate juice and champagne) and Passion Flower (passion fruit and vodka), served to a loyal, mostly business, clientele. ♦ Daily 10AM-2AM. 6785

Gallia's Restaurant ★★★$$$ The chic English-language name sets the tone for this spacious and elegant restaurant, where chef **Nicola Magnifico** magnificently prepares a menu that ranges from Milanese classics at lunch to more inventive dishes such as *fiocco di cinghiale con ananas* (wild boar with pineapple) and *branzino farcito al pate di olive* (bass stuffed with olive pâté) at dinner. ♦ Daily. 6785

In 1529 the **Archibishop of Milan** gave a 16-course dinner that included caviar and oranges fried with sugar and cinnamon, brill and sardines with slices of orange and lemon, 1000 oysters with pepper and oranges, lobster salad with citrons, sturgeon in aspic covered with orange juice, fried sparrows with oranges...orange fritters, a soufflé full of raisins and pine nuts and covered with sugar and orange juice, 500 fried oysters with lemon slices, and candied peels of citrons and oranges.

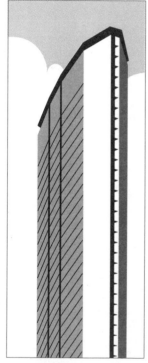

4 Grattacielo Pirelli (Pirelli Building) (1955-60, **Gio Ponti, Antonio Fornaoli, Alberto Rosselli, Giuseppe Valtolina, Edigio Dell'Orto, Arturo Danuso, Pier Luigi Nervi**) Designed by a team of architects and engineers almost as large as the building is high, Italy's tallest skyscraper (127.10 meters or 417 feet) symbolizes the dynamism of Milan. Built for the Pirelli rubber company, it was sold for 43 billion lire to the **Region of Lombardy** in 1979 for use as its headquarters. If you'd like to see the view of the city from high atop the pinnacle of the Pirelli, get permission to do so by contacting the Region of Lombardy (Regione Lombardy, Affari Generali, telephone 67651). ♦ Piazza Duca D'Aosta

5 Auriga $$$ A middle-priced, modern hotel with fairly soundproofed double rooms on the busy street and singles facing a quiet courtyard. ♦ Via Pirelli 7. 5692851

6 Porta Rossa ★★$$ Chef **Checchele** features the robust cuisine of his native region of Puglia in southern Italy, with such specialties as the tiny ear-shaped *orecchiete* pasta with *rabe* broccoli and roast kid and lamb being the best choices here. ♦ Closed Su, Christmas, Easter. Via Locatelli 2. 6705932

7 Piedra del Sol ★★$$ Milan-Mex, with simple south-of-the-border (not to mention across-the-Atlantic) dishes accompanied by tequila and live music to match. This was the first in a chain that now has links in Florence and Rome. ♦ Tu-Su 6PM-1:30AM. Via Cornalia 2. 6691901

8 Altopascio da Pietro ★★$$ Tuscan cuisine is the specialty of this restaurant, where **Eleanora** and **Pietro** prepare such dishes as *ribollita* (a white bean soup), ribbons of *tagliatelle* pasta, and robust roasts. ♦ Closed Sa, Su, Aug. Via Gustavo Fara 17. 6702458

9 Torre Galfa (1959, **Melchiorre Bega**) A sleek office skyscraper so acronymed because it rises from the corner of Via Galvani and Via Fara. ♦ Via Fara 41

10 Da Berti ★★$$ Another excellent Tuscan restaurant, this one run by **Enrica Colombi**, who also serves such personal dishes as *bifore alla Berti*, a square pasta accompanied by a sauce of tomato, peas and rocket. ♦ Closed Su, Aug, Christmas-New Year's. Via Algarotti 20. 6081696

11 Hilton $$$$ Milan's Hilton is all you'd expect of the chain, as busily efficient as the rest though less anonymous and more stylish than most, in keeping with the context of the city and the neighborhood. ♦ Via Galvani 12. 6983

Within the Hilton:

Valentino ★★$$ For a quick business lunch, this is the place, dishing up serviceable versions of Italian classics, from pasta to simple steaks and chops. Extensive wine list. ♦ Daily lunch only. Via Galvani 12. 6983

Giuseppe ★★★$$$ Dinner at the Hilton is more relaxed, with chef **Diego Rosa** preparing especially toothsome *risottos*. ♦ Daily dinner only. Via Galvani 12. 6983

12 Madison $$$ A simply decorated modern option in a surprisingly quiet street, this hotel serves a substantial American-style breakfast at no extra charge. ♦ Via Gasparotto 8. 6085991

13 Hong Kong ★★$$ One of the better Chinese restaurants in Milan in terms of both quality and variety. It serves not only Cantonese dishes but also specialties of Shanghai and Beijing. ♦ Closed M. Via Schiapparelli 5. 6890645

14 Rataplan Women's career apparel at a discount, supposedly from designer showrooms, at this bargain basement. ♦ M-Sa 10AM-7PM. Via Montepulciano 1. No credit cards. 6700746

15 Diffusione Moda This wholesaler is open to the public on Saturdays (though you can sometimes persuade them to let you in at other times), when women's clothes by such designers as **Laura Biagiotti** and **Krizia** are offered at a discount. ♦ M-F 9AM-12:30PM, 2:30-6PM; Sa 9AM-6PM. Via Andrea Doria 44. No credit cards. 6705145

16 Firme Designer signatures or *firme* by such names as **Krizia, Kamali** and others appear on discounted clothing for the entire family. ♦ M-Sa 9AM-7PM. Corso Buenos Aires 77. No credit cards. 66983113

17 Canevari Discount luggage, with everything from Samsonite to Delsey, a stylish French line the shop discounts even more (10 percent). ♦ Closed Su, lunch. Via Caretta 2. 29405888

18 Mercantini Michela Secondhand children's clothes and linens are the specialty of this discount outlet. ♦ Closed Su. Via Paganini 9. No credit cards. 228596

Stazione Centrale

19 Blue Point No oysters here, rather inexpensive jewelry of the semiprecious-stone variety. ♦ Closed Su. Corso Buenos Aires 58. 225852. Also at: Galleria Pattari 2. 808033

20 Via della Seta This *street of silk* is just that, offering brightly colored silk tops and dresses great for street and office if not the opera. ♦ Closed Su, lunch. Corso Buenos Aires 54. 2046750. Also at: Via Bramante 32. 33101081

21 El Tropico Latino This coffeebar popular with a prosperous young crowd doubles as a great place for tropical cocktails and light Mexican food and music well into the night. ♦ M-Sa 7AM-2AM. Via Ozanam 15. 201259

22 Libreria Buenos Aires A discount Italian-language bookshop where you can pick up the latest translation of Stephen King or Danielle Steele for your trash-loving Milanese friends (the word in Italian for such literature is *bestseller*) at a discount. ♦ Closed M morning, Sa lunch, Su. Corso Buenos Aires 42/3. No credit cards. 222987

Restaurants/Nightlife: Red	**Hotels:** Blue
Shops/Parks: Green	**Sights/Culture:** Black

23 Cascina Pozzobonelli (15th c) These ruins of a Lombard Renaissance oratory and portico, built when this part of town was in the countryside, look a bit bewildered surrounded by today's concrete-and-glass landscape. ♦ Via Andrea Doria

24 Michelangelo $$$$ This towering business hotel's high-tech aspect (zillions of television channels, push-button controls for everything imaginable) lends itself well to Milan's rep for modern design. ♦ Deluxe ♦ Via Scarlatti 33. 6755

Within the Michelangelo:

Bar del David A cocktaily lounge (with music after 10:30PM) serving a light menu of nouvellish Italian food designed by Milan's restaurateur impresario of gastronomy **Gualtiero Marchesi**. ♦ Daily 8:30AM-1AM. 6755

Ghirlandaio ★★$$$ A seamless restaurant with another unthreatening menu of Italian nouvellish food again put together by the busy hand of **Gualtiero Marchesi**. ♦ Closed F. 6755

25 Florida $$$ Convenient for airport and train departures, this clean, modern hotel attracts a loyal clientele of Germans. ♦ Via Lepetit 33. 6705921

26 I Mercanti Housewares of all sorts at a 30-percent discount off list price. ♦ Closed Su,

Stazione Centrale

lunch. Via Mauro Macchi 32. No credit cards. 6696638

27 Grazzini Toys galore from games to stuffed animals, with a 30-percent discount for members—you can sign up on the spot. ♦ Closed Su. Via Mauro Macchi 29. No credit cards. 6691319. Also at: Viale Romolo 9. 8370172; Via Pitagora 4. 257842

28 Atlantic $$$ Pleasant enough accommodations catering to a loyal business crowd. ♦ Via Napo Torriani 24. 670533

29 Flora $$$ Clean and efficient accommodations, popular as are most such places around here with a business clientele. ♦ Via Napo Torriani 23. 65042

30 San Camillo de Lellis (1912, **Spirito Maria Chiapetta**) This oddball brick-and-stone church demonstrates that, just as northern Gothic doesn't quite work in Italy, neither does Neo-Gothic. ♦ Via Ruggero Boscovich 25

31 Mennini $$$ This modern hotel has a lively breakfast room popular with its largely Italian clientele. ♦ Via Napo Torriani 14. 228951

32 Zefro Clothing for men, women and children in styles ranging from basic Italian to the ever popular faux Anglo. ♦ Closed Su. Via Ruggero Boscovich 14/18. No credit cards. 6571151

33 Profumeria Dorica Nice variety of discount perfumes and cosmetics in major international brands. ♦ Closed Sa, Su, lunch. Via Vittor Pisani 12A. No credit cards. 66983017

34 Telerie Ginetto Discount fabrics galore, including a nice selection of linens. ♦ Closed Sa afternoon, Su, lunch. Via San Gregorio 48. No credit cards. 6554443

35 Eugenio Medagliani Milan's best restaurant supply store, Medagliani stocks an astounding variety of pasta and espresso machines, cooking utensils and the like, and is especially good for copper pots in every shape imaginable. ♦ Closed Sa, Su, lunch. Via Luigi Razza 8. No credit cards. 66983073

36 Colzani Big-name baby clothes at a discount ♦ Closed Su, lunch. Via San Gregorio 43. 66983032

37 Rufus More practical clothing for men, women and (especially) children at a discount. ♦ Closed Su, lunch. Via Lazzaretto 7. No credit cards. 66983211

38 Calzature a Meta Prezzo While not exactly half-price as its name implies, the shoes here fit most budgets. Of special interest are women's high heels, sturdy men's shoes, and slippers for both sexes. ♦ Closed Su, lunch. Via Felice Casati 12. 206801

39 Da Lino Buriassi ★★$$ Lino's son **Guido** now runs this stylish restaurant serving such Italian classics as *spaghetti con le vongole* (spaghetti with clams) and *filetto con tartufo* (truffled filet of beef) as well as French-inspired snails and omelets. ♦ Closed Sa lunch, Su, holidays. Via Lecco 15. 228227

40 Studio Marconi One of the happeningest contemporary galleries in Milan, Marconi hold some of the hottest openings and represents such artists as **Lucio Fontana** and **Arnaldo Pomodoro**. ♦ Via Alessandro Tadino 15. 225543

41 Porta Portese Named after Rome's famous flea market, this used clothing store usually has a nice selection of men's hats (including **Borsalino**) in stock. ♦ Closed Su, lunch. Via Felice Casati 7. No credit cards. 29405010

42 Orea Malia One of Milan's chicest clip joints, Orea Malia is stylist to the stars and fashion models in town for the collections. ♦ M 4-7:30PM; Tu-Sa 9AM-1PM. Via Melzo 36. 2046584

43 Il Sahara ★★$$ As its name implies, this North African restaurant serves some of the only (and best) couscous in Milan, complemented by a nice array of teas, beers and wines. ♦ Closed M, Aug. Via Alessandro Tadino 2. 29400684

Restaurants/Nightlife: Red   **Hotels:** Blue
Shops/Parks: Green   **Sights/Culture:** Black

25% of Milan's residences were destroyed or rendered uninhabitable by WWII bombing.

44 Massimo De Carlo Another trendy gallery in the district, showing the work of **Amadeo Martegani** and more international artists. ♦ Via Panfilo Castaldi 33. 29406404

44 Lucca ★★$$ Another of the Tuscan restaurants which proliferate in Milan, this one serves the specialties of Lucca, including *minestra di farro* or wheat soup, and *budino di marron glace* or glazed chestnut pudding. ♦ Closed W, Sep. Via Panfilo Castaldi 33. 221668

45 Confezioni Berta Made-to-order lingerie, which will be shipped in about 2 weeks. ♦ Closed Su, lunch. Viale Tunisia. 211404

46 Joia ★★$ The subtitle of this place, *alta cucina naturale* (natural haute cuisine), says it all. **Nicla Nardi** has taken the lessons of nouvelle cuisine and applied them to natural foods, with an emphasis on wholesome ingredients presented with panache in tasty soups and *risotto* dishes. ♦ Closed Su, Aug. Via Panfilo Castaldi 18. 2049244

47 Galleria Christian Stein This dealer specializes in *arte povera*, a Minimalist movement begun in Turin in the mid-1960s and represented by **Mario Merz, Jannis Kounellis** and **Michelangelo Pistoletto**. ♦ Via Lazzaretto 15. 6704754

48 Palace $$$$ This boxy link in the CIGA hotel chain is '60s-modern on the outside, Empire on the inside and a class act through and through with period prints and 15th century-style furniture. ♦ Deluxe ♦ Piazza Repubblica 20. 6336

Within the Palace:

Casanova Grill ★★★$$$ Even in a city where hotel restaurants are actually good, the Casanova Grill is better than the rest. A creative Italian menu by chef **Sergio Mei** features such dishes as *macceroncini ai fiori di zucca* (macaroni with zucchini flowers) and *fegato d'oca con tartufo nero* (foie gras with black truffles), to the distinct pleasure of Milan's power lunchers. ♦ Daily. 650803

49 Principe di Savoia $$$$ The sprawling Principe is another of Milan's grand dames, its Old World public rooms complemented by the Empire-style guest facilities that are the hallmark of the CIGA chain. ♦ Deluxe ♦ Piazza Repubblica 17. 6230

Within the Principe di Savoia:

La Bella Fontana ★★$$$ Milan's newest hotel restaurant has an opulent setting in which international classics are complemented by such well-prepared regional specialties as *risotto giallo* (rice with saffron) and *costoletta alla milanese* (breaded veal cutlet). ♦ Daily. Piazza della Repubblica 17. 6330

50 Piazza della Repubblica This large piazza contains **Piero Cascella's** 1974 low-key monumental sculpture *Alla Repubblica* made of stacked stones meant to be walked on and touched. ♦ Piazza della Repubblica

51 Duca di Milano $$$$ This CIGA-chain hotel is smaller and more intimate than its big sister next door, combining comfortably elegant facilities with a full range of business services that make it popular with visiting execs. ♦ Deluxe ♦ Piazza Repubblica 13. 6284

52 Liquidazione Campionari Abbigliamento Monitor Men's clothing at unmanly prices. ♦ Closed Sa lunch, Su. Viale Monte Grappa 4. 6598157

Stazione Centrale

53 Cucine Economiche (1886, **Luigi Broggi**) A Neo-Romanesque edifice in brick and terra cotta surprisingly reminiscent of architecture in America at the time. ♦ Viale Monte Grappa 8

Trams

Though Milan has extensive and efficient bus and subway systems, its trams are one of the most entertaining forms of public transportation in the city. Typically Milanese in that they are practical rather than touristic, trams nonetheless have a romantic appeal owing to the original Art Nouveau-era character of the polished wooden seats and dim lighting fixtures in many of them—not to mention the fact that gorgeous models of both sexes often take the trams between their agencies and assignments. Maps of the tram routes are available in the ATM office in the Duomo metro station and at other ATM locations, providing a plan (actually one of the best city maps) for an unusual and smooth way of getting around town.

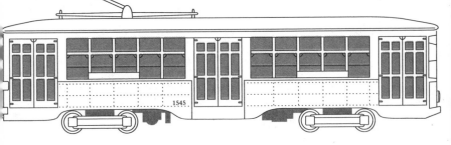

Porta Venezia

One of the most exclusive residential neighborhoods in Milan, **Porta Venezia** is just east of Centro, sandwiched between the Cerchia dei Navigli (the innermost ring) and the Viali or Bastioni ring built under the Spanish, whose city gates still give many of the neighborhoods their names. **Via Bellini, Via Mascagni, Via Mozart** and **Via Cappuccini** are where the upscale residences are located, but even if you don't live in one of them, you can still sample Porta Venezia's gentility by peeking into their courtyards and gardens. If that's not enough, some of the patrician palazzi—such as **Villa Reale** and **Palazzo Dugnani**—have been turned into public museums. And if it's public gardens you like, Porta Venezia also includes the **Giardini Pubblici**—Europe's oldest public park.

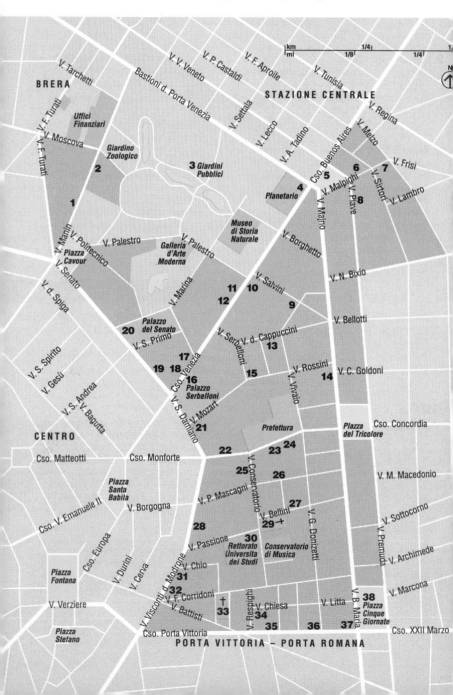

1 Manin $$$ This pleasant hotel has been in the **Colombo** family for generations. Rooms are plain but comfortable. The front ones have balconies overlooking the Giardini Pubblici; the rear ones are even more peaceful. Service is personal, accounting for the loyal clientele. ◆ Via Manin 7. 6596511

2 Palazzo Dugnani (late 17th c) This patrician residence contains 2 mythological frescoes by Gian Battista Tiepolo.

Within the Palazzo Dugnani:

Civico Spazio Baj A collection of prints by contemporary Italian artist **Enrico Baj**. ◆ Tu-Su 9:30AM-12:15PM, 2:30-5:30PM; closed M, New Year's Day, Easter, 1 May, 15 Aug, Christmas. Via Manin 2. 62085415

Museo del Cinema e Cineteca Italiana (Cinema Museum and Italian Cinematheque) Displays of cinema equipment and memorabilia are complemented by screenings here. ◆ Tu-F 3-6PM. Via Manin 2. 6554977

3 Giardini Pubblici (begun 1783, **Giuseppe Piermarini**) The first public park in Europe was laid out on land confiscated from the suppressed Carcanine and San Diogini religious orders. Its statuary is of little interest, as it is mostly of the 19th-century monumental variety celebrating war heroes like its Civil War equivalent in American town squares. What is of interest within the park are a little zoo, a relaxing cafe, and the chance to take in a bit of fresh air in this hectic city along with everyone from the *rampanti* or Milanese yuppies out for *il footing* (jogging) to their poor relations with pets and babies out for a *passeggiata* or promenade.

Within the Giardini Pubblici:

Villa Reale (1790, **Leopold Pollack**) **Ludovico Barbiano di Belgiojoso** commissioned this expansive Neoclassical villa, for which he himself designed the English-style garden. **Napoleon** and **Josephine** lived here for a spell, as did the Austro-Hungarian rulers of Milan. Today the villa houses the **Galleria d'Arte Moderna** (Gallery of Modern Art). This museum has an exhaustive collection of 19th-century Lombard painting, which went through stylistic changes similar to what was happening in the rest of the world: idyllic landscapes, Neoclassicism, Romanticism and plein-air painting. Also represented is 19th-century painting from Piedmont, the Veneto, Tuscany (including the *macchiaioli* plein-air painters) and Naples. Upstairs is the **Museo Marino Marini** (Marino Marini Museum), dedicated to the 20th-century Italian sculptor best known

for his variations on the horse-and-rider theme; and the **Raccolta Grassi** (Grassi Collection), a rich assemblage of mainly 19th- and 20th-century paintings from Italy and abroad, including some Impressionist and Post-Impressionist canvases. ◆ Daily 9:30AM-7:30PM; closed last M of month. Via Palestro 16. 76002819

Civico Padiglione d'Art Contemporanea A temporary exhibition space, usually of shows devoted to contemporary art. ◆ Daily 9:30AM-7:30PM; closed last M of month. Via Palestro 14. 784688

4 Casa Torre Rasini (Rasini Apartment Building) (1933-34, **Giò Ponti** and **Emilio Lancia**) One of the few Functionalist apartment buildings in Milan that takes aesthetics into consideration. ◆ Corso Venezia 61

5 Porta Venezia (1827-28, **Rodolfo Vantini**) Twin colonnaded buildings provide this gate to the no-longer-extant walls built under the Spanish who ruled Milan from 1535-1706. ◆ Piazzale Oberdan

6 Casa Galimberti (1903-06, **Giovan Battista Bossi**) This palazzo is interesting for its refined Art Nouveau detail. ◆ Via Malpighi 3

7 Casa Guazzoni (1905, **Giovan Battista Bossi**) Notice the ceramic floral motifs on this Art Nouveau apartment building. ◆ Via Malpighi 12

Porta Venezia

8 Diana Majestic $$$ An Art Deco link in the CIGA hotel chain, popular with models and others in the fashion trade, who appreciate its private garden. ◆ Viale Piave 42. 203404

9 Palazzo Civita (1933-36, **Gigiotti Zanini**) Stop at this massive American-style building to have a look at the mosaic pavement in the entrance vestibule. ◆ Piazza Duse 2

10 Palazzo Saporiti (1812, **Giovanni Perego**) A Neoclassical palazzo topped with stucco bas reliefs by **Pompeo Marchesi** of scenes from the history of Milan. ◆ Corso Venezia 40

11 Palazzo Bovara (1787, **Carlo Felice Soave**) A Neoclassical palazzo which served as the French embassy and the office of Milanophile Stendhal, who lived and loved in Milan. ◆ Corso Venezia 51

12 Palazzo Castiglioni (1900-04, **Ermenegildo Castiglioni** and **Giuseppe Sommaruga**) One of the outstanding Art Nouveau palazzi in Italy, dripping with crusty detail. ◆ Corso Venezia 47

13 Palazzo Berri-Meregalli (1911-14, **Giulio Ulisse Arata**) An eclectic and monumental building embellished with mosaics and a ceiling by **Angiolo D'Andrea**, sculpture by **Adolfo Wildt** and wrought iron by **Alessandro Mazzucotelli**. ◆ Via Cappuccini 8

14 Casa Moretti (**Gaetano Moretti**) This handsome residence shows a rare example of the use of bay windows in Milan. ◆ Viale Majno 15

15 Oldani A wide selection of traditional men's clothing with a smaller section set apart for women's wear. ◆ Closed lunch Sa, Su. Via Serbelloni 7. 76001087

16 Palazzo Serbelloni (1775-93, **Simone Cantoni**) This imposing Neoclassical palazzo was home to **Napoleon** and **Josephine Bonaparte** when they were in town for a few months in 1796. ◆ Corso Venezia 16

17 Il Girarrosto da Cesarina ★★$$ One of Milan's oldest Tuscan restaurants, this is the place to try *ribollita*, the white bean soup. ◆ Closed Sa, lunch Su, Aug, Christmas week. Corso Venezia 31. 76000481

18 Civico Museo di Storia Naturale (Natural History Museum) (1888-1919, **Giovanni Ceruti**) The first building in Milan built specifically to be used as a museum, this was one of the most important natural history museums in Europe before it was bombed during WWII. Reconstructed, the museum houses an extensive col-

Porta Venezia

lection of every animal, vegetable and mineral imaginable, including its own dinosaurs—Triceratops, Allosaurus and Kritosaurus the most kid-pleasing. ◆ Daily 9:30AM-7:30PM; closed last M of month. Corso Venezia 55. 62085407

18 Planetario Hoepli Milan's planetarium has regular program presenting peeks at celestial phenomena to the general public. ◆ Tu, Th 9-11PM; Sa-Su 3-6PM. Corso Venezia 57. 62085407

18 Bar Bianco (1930, **Piero Portaluppi**) This Neoclassical building houses a cafe much appreciated for its outdoor tables in the warm weather and for its hot chocolate in the winter Behind the Civico Museo di Storia Naturale an the Civico Planetario. ◆ Daily 8AM-8PM. Giardini Pubblici. No phone

19 San Pietro Celestino (1735, **Marco Bianchi**) This Baroque church sports a medieval campanile dating from 1317. ◆ Via di Senato

20 Collegio Elvetico (begun 1608, **Fabio Mangone**; completed 1629, **Francesco Maria Ricchino**) This curved palazzo today houses the **Archivio di Stato** or state archives. In fron of it is a sculpture by Joan Miró. ◆ Via di Senato 10

21 Dellera Furs and fur-lined raincoats often offered at discounts of 30 to 50 percent. ◆ Closed Su, lunch. Via San Damiano 4. 796151

22 Studio Casoli One of the best contemporar galleries in Milan, showing Italian and international artists in a high-concept setting. ◆ Cors Monforte 23. 793238

23 Palazzo della Prefettura (1779-1817) Constructed as a religious college, the facade of this palazzo was completed by **Pietro Gilardoni**. ◆ Corso Monforte 31

24 Palazzo Isimbardi (late 15th c) Behind the Neoclassical facade of this Renaissance palazzo is *The Triumph of Doge Francesco Morosini*, a grand painting by **Gian Battista Tiepolo**. ◆ Corso Monforte 35

Palazzo Isimbardi

25 Gallini Milan's music shop *per eccellenza*, pianist **Annalisa Gallini**'s emporium sells old and new sheet music, prints, and everything imaginable pertaining to music. ♦ Closed M morning, Su, lunch. Via Conservatorio 17. 702858

26 Sotheby's Italia The Milan branch of the international auction house, which holds sales of everything from 19th-century paintings to historical design. ♦ Closed Sa-Su. Via Mascagni 15. 783911

27 Casa Campanini (1904, **Alfredo Campanini**) This house is decorated in Milanese Art Nouveau in all its splendor. ♦ Via Vincenzo Bellini 11

28 Libreria Salto Here's the place to stock up on books pertaining to all that Italian design with which you're been surrounding yourself in Milan. ♦ Closed M morning, Su, lunch. Via Visconte di Modrone 18. 76001032

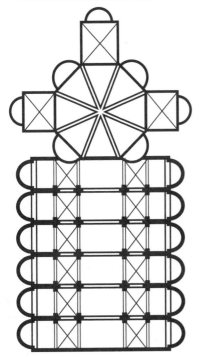

29 Santa Maria della Passione (begun 1486, **Giovanni Battagio**) This church, second only to the Duomo in size in Milan, has ample space for the paintings of **Daniele Crespi**, for whom it is practically a museum. The 17th-century Lombard painter expressed the pious ideals of the Counter-Reformation in his series of saints along the nave and especially in his masterpiece, *St. Charles Borromeus Fasting*, in the first chapel of the left aisle. Crespi also painted the organ shutters with *Scenes from the Life of Christ*. The left transept has a 16th-century *Last Supper* and *Crucifixion*, both by **Giulio Campi**; in the right transept are 15th-century painter **Bernardino Luini**'s *Deposition* and *Christ Rising from the Sepulchre*. In the former monastery next to the church is the **Museo della Basilica di Santa Maria della Passione**, the church

museum of which the series *Christ and the Apostles*, by 16th-century painter **Ambrogio da Fossano** (known as **Bergognone**), is the highlight. ♦ Admission to museum. M-Sa 10AM-noon, 3-5PM; Su and holidays 3-5PM; closed Sa, Aug. Via Vincenzo Bellini 2. 791370

30 Palazzo Archinto (1833-47, **Gaetano Besia**) This giant palazzo is home to the **Collegio delle Fanciulle**, a girl's academy founded by **Napoleon** in 1808. ♦ Via della Passione 12

31 Libreria Scientifica Italian books—on science and other subjects—at a 20 percent discount. ♦ Closed M morning, Su, lunch. Via Visconti di Modrone 8. 709734

31 Miss Loti Made-to-measure ladies' silk suits and dresses at relatively reasonable prices. ♦ Closed M morning, Su, lunch. Via Visconti di Modrone 8/6. 76000104

32 Taveggia An Art Deco tearoom that gathers upscale sippers from the nearby law courts. ♦ Tu-Su 7:30AM-9PM. Via Visconti di Modrone 2. 791257

33 San Pietro in Gessate (1447-75, attributed to **Pietro Antonio** and **Guinforte Solari**) This Renaissance church is noted for its **Cappella Grifi**, which contains 15th-century frescoes of *The Life of St. Ambrose* by **Bernardino Butinone** and **Bernardino Zenale**. ♦ V F Corridoni

Porta Venezia

34 Alias The showroom for furniture by designers **Mario Botta, Ginadomenico Belotti, Alberto Meda, Carlo Forcolini** and others. ♦ Closed M morning, Su, lunch. Via Ottorino Respighi 2. 76005672

35 L'Eliografica A trendy architect's dream, where all types of papers and pens may be purchased. ♦ Closed M morning, Su, lunch. Corso di Porta Vittoria 29. 791394. Also at: Via San Nicolao 10. 8693102

36 Marino This shop is awash with bath products at liquidation prices. ♦ Closed Su, lunch. Via Donizetti 1A. No credit cards. 795106

37 Coin The largest branch of one of Italy's nicest department store chains. Coin carries its own label, especially appealing on such items as woolen sweaters and men's cotton shirts. ♦ Closed M morning, Su, lunch. Piazza Cinque Giornate 1A. 782583

38 Alle Cinque Giornate This romantic, allegorical 1895 monument by **Giuseppe Grandi** commemorates the 5 days (*cinque giornate*) of 18-22 March 1848 when the Milanese overthrew Austrian rule in the **Castello Sforzesco**. The name Cinque Giornate appears on streets and piazzas throughout Lombardy the same way Garibaldi and Cavour do throughout the rest of the country. ♦ Piazza Cinque Giornate

Porta Vittoria/Porta Romana

Like Porta Venezia, the **Porta Vittoria/Porta Romana** area is sandwiched between the **Cerchia dei Navigli** and the **Viali**. But unlike that residential neighborhood, the Porta Vittoria/Porta Romana is institutional in nature—everything from churches and a synagogue to a major hospital may be found here. But for a rather nondescript part of town it does contain a few surprises—including Italy's only Russian restaurant!

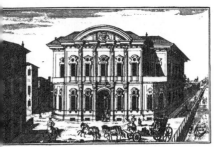

Palazzo Sormani-Andreani

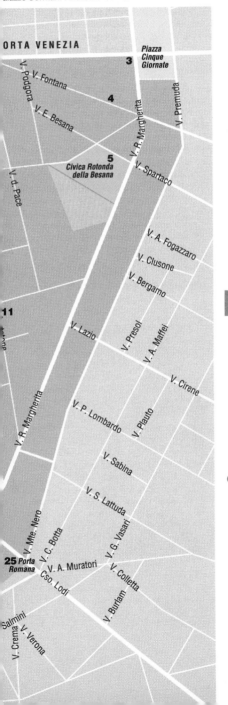

1 Palazzo Sormani-Andreani (17th c)
Francesco Croce restructured this pre-existing palazzo in 1736, to which the facade facing the garden was added by **Benedetto Alfieri** in 1756. Today it houses the **Biblioteca Comunale** or public library. ♦ Corso di Porta Vittoria 6

2 Palazzo di Giustizia (1932-40, **Marcello Piancentini** and **Ernesto Rapisardi**) A look at Fascist grandeur shows us that boxy marble buildings weren't invented as 1960s cultural centers. ♦ Corso di Porta Vittoria

3 Gelateria Umberto Elio Martinuzzi is the proprietor of this ice cream parlor, known in the land of tutti frutti for its sobering vanilla and a select few sorbets, as well as its *taglio di limone reale* or royal lemon slice served with champagne. ♦ Tu-Su 9AM-10PM. Piazza Cinque Giornate 4. 5458113

4 Niki Flashy women's apparel from slinky cocktail dresses to fabulous fake furs at affordable prices. ♦ Closed Su, lunch. Via Fontana 19. No credit cards. 55181284. Also at: Viale Montenero 78. 5468855

5 Civica Rotonda della Besana (1725, **Carlo Francesco Raffagno, Attilio Arrigoni** and **Francesco Croce**) The former cemetery of the **Ospedale Maggiore**, surrounded by a Neoclassical portico, has been converted by the city into a pleasant public park. ♦ Daily 9:30AM-7:30PM; closed last M of month. Via Besana 12. 5463254

6 San Barnaba e Paolo (begun 1558) This Renaissance church contains works from the

Porta Vittoria/Porta Romana

same period, notably a *Pietà* by **Aurelio Luini** on the second altar on the right and 2 paintings illustrating the story of **St. Paul** and **St. Barnabas** by **Simone Peterzano** on the presbytery walls. ♦ Via San Barnaba

7 Tempio Israelitico (1890-92, **Luca Beltrami** and **Luigi Tenenti**) Milan's synagogue is a florid Romanesque-Arabesque eclectic typical of turn-of-the-century architecture around the world. ♦ Via Guastalla 19

8 Giardino della Guastalla The grounds of this academy have been converted into a pleasant public park filled with venerable trees and decorated with a statuary group depicting **Mary Magdelene** surrounded by angels. ♦ Via Guastala, corner Via San Barnaba

9 Mila Schön Negozi The outlet for elegant women's clothes by the famous Milanese designer, known for her well-coordinated separates as well as her silk scarves. ♦ Closed Su. Piazza Umanitaria 2. 5457.611

10 Policlinco (19th-20th c) Milan's vast hospital complex was built on land confiscated from the **Knights of Malta** when religious orders were suppressed. It's a strong example of post-industrial institutional architecture. ♦ Via Francesco Sforza

11 Il Sole ★★$$ This modern-looking restaurant serves French-inspired cuisine as well as inventive variations on Italian standards, such as *risotto al limone* or lemon risotto. ♦ Closed M, Aug. Via Curtatone 5. 55188500

12 L'Acerba II ★★$$ An upscale Postmodern health restaurant where the food is accompanied by the strains of Mozart and a selection of magazines and newspapers. ♦ Tu-Su 8AM-10PM. Via Orti 4. 5455475

13 Lo Spiffero ★★$$ The varying menu of **Betty** and **Tony Vincenti**'s pleasant restaurant includes such seasonal treats as game and truffles as well as desserts made on the premises. ♦ Closed Su, Aug. Via Orti 1. 5484279

14 Great Perfumery Brand-name toiletries at bargain prices not implied by the trendy Anglo name. ♦ Closed Sa lunch, Su. Corso Porta Romana 57. 55180109

15 Calimerius Owner **Oreste**'s elegant and romantic cocktail lounge is made more so by live piano music by **Ernest Maccaro**. ♦ M-Sa 6PM-2AM. Via San Calimero 3. 5510049

Porta Vittoria/Porta Romana

16 San Calimero This church, which dates from paleochristian times, was redesigned through the ages by the likes of **Bishop Lorenzo** in 490 and **Francesco Maria Ricchino** in 1609. Unfortunately, a bad restoration in the 19th century took away most of what was interesting. Some of the older stuff may be seen in the canon's courtyard, which has some Roman marbles and tombstones. ♦ Via San Calimero

17 Casa della Meridiana (1924-25, **Giuseppe De Finetti**) One of the first Modern apartment buildings in Milan (De Finetti was a student of **Adolf Loos**) takes its name from the sundial painted high up on the facade by **Gigiotti Zanini**. ♦ Via Marchiondi 3

18 Yar ★★$$ **Natasha Garilskaya** has opened the first Russian restaurant in Italy. Chef **Nikolai Yakimov** prepares caviar, smoked sturgeon, borscht, beef Stroganov, chicken Kiev and other standards with love, while **Giuseppe Vaccarini** takes care of the largely Italian wine list, which works surprisingly well with the food. ♦ Closed Sa lunch, Su, Aug. Via Giuseppe Mercalli 22. 58309603

19 Santa Maria Presso San Celso (begun 1493, **Gian Giacomo Dolcebouno**; facade designs 1565, 1568, **Galeazzo Alessi**) Two of Milan's leading 17th-century painters, **Giulio Cesare Procaccini** and **Giambattista Crespi**, decorated the aisles of this church with Man-

Santa Maria Presso San Celso

nerist stuccoes and frescoes. Procaccini also painted the *Martyrdom of Saints Nazarius and Celsus* in the 4th bay on the right, which in turn influenced Crespi's *Martyrdom of St. Catherine* in the 2nd bay on the left. Also of interest are **Paris Bordone**'s *Holy Family with St. Jerome* in the right transept; **Gaudenzio Ferrari**'s *Baptism of Christ* and the *Conversion of St. Paul* by **Alessandro Bonvicino** (called **Moretto**) in the ambulatory; and *Madonna and Saints* by **Ambrogio da Fossano** (called **Bergognone**) at the beginning of the left aisle. The name of the church translates literally as *St. Mary c/o St. Celsus*, since it was built near the restored Romanesque church of San Celso, accessible through a door in the right aisle. ♦ Corso Italia

20 **Santa Maria al Paradiso** (1590, **Franciscan Brothers**) This recently restored church contains a few low-key examples of Rococo in Milan, namely the altar in the 3rd chapel on the right. ♦ Corso di Porta Vigentina

21 **Il Punto Malatesta** ★★$$ Satellite dishes with stock quotations from New York, London and Tokyo successfully attract a business crowd to this restaurant, which serves such inventive dishes as champagne *risotto* and curried kidney. ♦ Closed Su, Aug. Via Bianca di Savoia 19. 58300079

22 **Oriani Due** Secondhand clothes and showroom samples for women and children at reasonable prices. ♦ Closed Su, lunch. Via Beatrice d'Este. 55188550. Also at: Via Tobruk 4. 72023523

23 **Il Principe** 1960s-style disco with a 1970s-style door policy (foreigners usually pass muster), popular with visiting models and especially lively on Monday nights. ♦ M-Sa 8PM-2AM. Viale Bligny 52. No phone

24 **P.M. Cafe** Cocktails and snacks in a Postmodern cafe good for a fast lunch or a late-night snack. ♦ M-Sa 10AM-2AM. Corso di Porta Romana 131. No phone

25 **Porta Romana** (1598, **Aurelio Trezzi**) This city gate was built in honor of **Mary Margaret** of Austria, passing through town from Vienna on her way to marry **Philip III** of Spain in Madrid. ♦ Piazzale Medaglie d'Oro

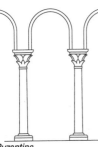

Byzantine

Romanesque

Renaissance

Bests

Inge Feltrinelli
President, Giangiacomo Feltrinelli Editore

First of all, pro domo: the 3 **Feltrinelli** bookstores.

La Scala.

Il Piccolo Teatro.

Lunch during summer at **Don Lisander** in the garden under trees.

Risotto al salto da *Alfredo* **Gran S. Bernado**.

Via S. Andrea with **Armani**'s new boutique.

A candlelight evening at Krizia's **Spazio** before Christmas—in gold or silver.

Via Monte Napoleone—drink at **Cova** and a tiny sandwich.

Via Monte Napoleone—scarves at **Missoni**.

Via Monte Napoleone—newest sweaters at **Benetton**.

Opening at **Galleria Marconi**, Via Tadini 15.

A winter-dinner at **Savini** (risotto con tartufi).

Bicycling around the inner city to see the lovely courtyards (Via Jesu, V. Bigli, Via S. Spirito)—the streets **Stendhal** loved and wrote about!

Summer party in our courtyard with writers, booksellers, designers, architects, painters—for an anniversary!

Italo Lupi
Architect, Art Director and Art Designer

Tour of Sacred Sights around Milan:

Certosa di Garegnano (exit autostrada Nord) for the frescoes of Daniele Crespi.

Abbazia di Chiaravalle (exit autostrada Sud) for the splendid tourer.

Abbazia di Viboldone and, 30 kilometers from the city, the **Certosa of Pavia**, the most important in Italy.

Villas along the Naviglio A few kilometers to the West, towards Robecco, at sunset.

All the Neoclassical gates of the city Porta Nuova, Porta Vittoria, Porta Garibaldi, Porta Romana, Porta Ticinese.

Courtyards of the houses of the ancient aristocracy of the centre They hide unexpected gardens.

20th-century Milanese architecture.

The small **Piazza Sant'Angelo** for the architecture of Muzio and nearby in Via Turati, Muzio's **Ca'Brutta** and the first head office of **Montecatini** by Giò Ponti.

Visit to the Bronze Horses on the summit of the **Arco della Pace** and nearby, the Neoclassical **Arena** (only during the restoration).

Ticinese/Navigli

Followers of urban renewal (not to mention real estate agents) have for some time had their eye on the adjoining **Ticinese** and **Navigli** neighborhoods of Milan. Once a strictly working-class district, the Ticinese has been increasingly settled by *rampanti* (Milanese yuppies) who are attracted to the charms of the sturdy and still-affordable *case di ringhiera*—apartment buildings characterized by *ringhiere* or railings which surround inner courtyards on each floor of the multiple-story dwellings. The Navigli, also low-rent until recently with similar architecture, gets its name from the *navigli* or canals which still run through it as they once connected much of Milan. As romantic as they look in the fog and at twilight, the canals should be thought of more as the gritty Canal St. Martin in Paris rather than the well-scrubbed canals of Amsterdam. The entire area—increasingly filled with trendy boutiques and a variety of restaurants and clubs which give Milan the reputation for Italy's liveliest nightlife—is the trendiest in the city and continues to expand as it extends itself beyond the Viali toward Milan's third

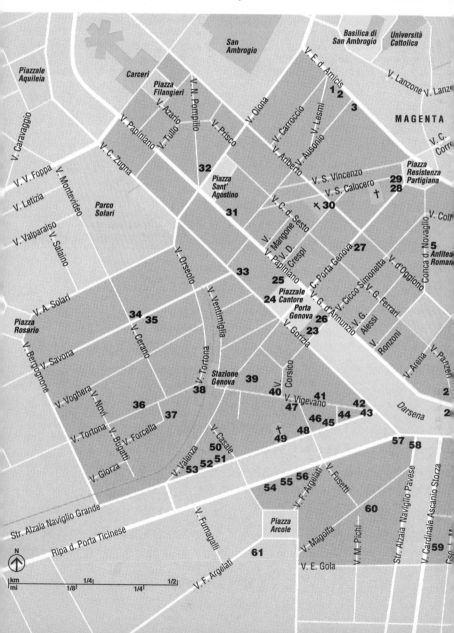

ng, the connecting road called the **Circonvalazione Esterna**. Besides increased roperty values, gentrification has brought new life to the Ticinese and Navigli istricts, most evident during the antiques flea market held along the **Naviglio Grande** the last Sunday of every month and in the nightlife which sparkles along he water well into the wee hours.

1 Bianca & Blu Monica Bolzoni's inventive women's clothing designs, based on cuts and cloths from the 1940s and 50s, have quite a following in Milan. ♦ Closed Su, lunch. Via Edmondo de Amicis 53. 836119

2 Franco Fiorentino Men's and women's shoes are the forte of Franco Fiorentino, who makes them in casual and fashionable styles at affordable prices. ♦ Closed M morning, Su, lunch. Via Edmondo de Amicis 51. 8354992

3 Oca Nera ★★$$ This trendy restaurant serves trendy variations of Italian classics in a trendy setting to a trendy crowd of journalists and television personalities. Needless to say, the menu changes according to the proprietor's whim and food trends. ♦ Closed Su, holidays. Via Edmondo de Amicis 45. 8361427

4 Portnoy Cafe Letterario High-tech, Postmodern trappings attract a crowd of literary types and the more literarily bent of Italian pop singers for snacks and cocktails. ♦ M-Sa 7PM-midnight. Via Edmondo de Amicis 1. 8378656

5 Anfiteatro Romano Peek into the courtyard of this building to see the surprisingly secret remains of Milan's Roman amphitheater. ♦ Via Edmondo de Amicis 17

6 Gelateria Ecologica Some of the ecological gelato served in this gleaming and popular spot are such flavors as *germe di grano* (wheat germ), *fico d'India* (prickly pear) and *fragoline di bosco* (wild strawberries). ♦ Daily 9AM-midnight. Corso di Porta Ticinese 40. 8351872

7 Nart & Abbiati The best bicycle shop in the neighborhood. ♦ Closed M morning, Su, lunch. Corso di Porta Ticinese 53. 8353678

HIGH-TECH

8 High-Tech One-stop shopping for the kind of design associated with Milan by many (you

Ticinese/Navigli

know, the kind of people who call it *Milano*), this shop stocks a number of European-designed housewares along with some American kitchen gadgets. ♦ Closed M morning, Su, lunch. Corso di Porta Ticinese 77. 8351263

9 Naj Oleari The original branch of the larger shops (in the Brera), selling cutely printed fabric and children's accessories made from same. ♦ Closed M morning, Su, lunch. Corso di Porta Ticinese 58. 8399857

10 Lo Specchio di Alice A recent peek in Alice's ever-changing looking glass revealed used dinner jackets and bowler hats among other natty castoffs. ♦ Closed Su, lunch. Corso di Porta Ticinese 64. No credit cards. 8370445

11 Stefania Guglielmo Trendy women's clothing in new, used and showroom varieties at bargain prices. ♦ M-F 3-7PM. Corso di Porta Ticinese 68. No credit cards. 8325282

Restaurants/Nightlife: Red	**Hotels:** Blue
Shops/Parks: Green	**Sights/Culture:** Black

12 Osteria dell'Operetta ★★$$ The menu at this Postmodern hangout changes regularly, but crepes, risotto and salads are usually among the staples. Live music until the wee hours. ♦ M-Sa 8PM-2AM. Corso di Porta Ticinese 70. 8375120

12 Lo Gnomo Fashionable bags in leather and canvas, seemingly produced at an endless rate by the shop's titular gnome, are the specialty here. ♦ Closed M morning, Su, lunch. Corso di Porta Ticinese 70. 8375163

13 Prem Legnodipinto Wooden everything—from jewelry to toys and gift items—are the specialty of Prem, who paints it all with a true artist's eye. ♦ Closed M morning, Su, lunch. Corso di Porta Ticinese 76. 8372934

14 Panca Men's and women's shoes, some of which are passable copies of designs by Ferragamo and Chanel and many of which are attractive originals, abound in this bargain store. ♦ Closed Su, lunch. Corso di Porta Ticinese 96. 8394543. Also women's branch at: Corso di Porta Ticinese 103. 8321361

15 Piazza Sant'Eustorgio The column in this piazza is dedicated to **St. Peter Martyr**, who was born in nearby Verona and is buried inside the church of Sant'Eustorgio. ♦ Piazza Sant'Eustorgio

16 Eliogabalo Stark and dark are the words for these women's clothes, sold at this factory outlet at bargain prices. ♦ Closed Su, lunch. Piazza Sant'Eustorgio 2. 8378293

17 Sant'Eustorgio This large Dominican basilica was founded in the 4th century, enlarged in the 9th and 13th centuries, and given a Neo-Romanesque facade in the 19th century. It once housed the relics of the **Three Magi**, donated by **Emperor Constantine** from Constantinople, and taken to Cologne by **Frederick Barbarossa** in the 12th century. The **Cappella dei Magi**, where the relics were kept in a still-extant sarcophagus, is located in the south transept. Of even greater interest is the **Cappella Portinari**, one of the best Renais-sance monuments in Milan, reached from behind the chancel. The chapel was designed for the Medici banker **Pigello Portinari** by the Florentine **Michelozzo**, who was inspired by Brunelleschi's circle-in-a-square plans for the Cappella Pazzi and the Sagrestia Vecchia in the churches of Santa Croce and San Lorenzo in his native city. It is dedicated to **St. Peter Martyr**, patron saint of Milan's ruling families (the **Torriani, Visconti** and **Sforza**), who is buried in the elaborate tomb in the center by the 14th-century Pisan sculptor **Giovanni di Balduccio**. The saint's life is depicted in 15th-century frescoes by **Vincenzo Foppa**, who is probably also responsible for the angels dancing around the dome.

For a donation, the sacristan will let you into the **Museo di Sant'Eustorgio** (Sant'Eustorgio Museum) to see numerous reliquaries and paintings connected with the church. An entrance in the museum leads to Milan's only *in situ* Roman and early-Christian cemetery. (Another entrance is in the left nave.) ♦ Piazza Sant'Eustorgio

Sant'Eustorgio

18 La Cucina di Edgardo ★★$$ Chef Ermanno is from the town of Treviso, so the cuisine of the Veneto is in evidence here in such dishes as *risotto al radicchio*, risotto made with the long-leafed radicchio from that very town. ◆ Closed Su, Aug. Via Col Di Lana 3. 8323373

19 Le Case d'Aste A contemporary art gallery designed to the hilt with Castiglioni lighting and Sotsass and Cibic furniture. Among the artists represented are **Sol Lewitt, Richard Prince** and **Victor Burgin**. ◆ Closed M, Su, lunch. Col di Lana 14. 8370407

20 Porta Ticinese (1801-14, **Luigi Cagnola**) This Neoclassical city gate was originally built as the entrance of Napoleon into the city after the Battle of Marengo. It was also called **Porta Marengo**, a name which, had it stuck, would have made it easier to distinguish this Porta Ticinese from the medieval one at the other end of Corso Ticinese. ◆ Piazza XXIV Maggio

21 Ipotesi This new club features an old-fashioned discotheque on the bottom floor, cocktails and more subdued live music on the top floor. ◆ Th-Su 8PM-1AM. Piazza XXIV Maggio 8. 8233160

22 La Darsena The confluence of some of the main *navigli* or canals is a great spot for waterfront watching of people and toy-boat regattas. ◆ Darsena

23 Al Porto ★★$$ One of Milan's finest fish restaurants, Porto has an ever-changing menu depending on the day's catch (of what husband-and-wife owners **Domenico** find at the fish market, that is), with an excellent wine list, primarily of whites. Daughter **Barbara** makes the desserts on the premises. ◆ Closed M lunch, Su, Aug. Piazzale Cantore. 8321481

24 Coin The local and less hectic branch of the Italian chain, where woolens and men's cotton shirts are best bets. ◆ Closed M morning, Su, lunch. Piazzale Cantore. 8324385

25 Pozzi A wonderful array of *gelato* here in all the old standard flavors as well as some unusual ones like *tè* (tea), *liquirizia* (liquorice) and *pompelmo* (grapefruit). ◆ Tu-Su 9AM-1AM. Piazzale Cantore 4. 8399830

26 Casa Reininghaus (1895-96, **Sebastiano Giuseppe Locati**) The influence of Viennese architecture is evident in this old relic of an office building, commissioned by beer importer **Pietro Reininghaus** and originally containing a beer hall on the ground floor. ◆ Piazzale Cantore

27 Funghi e Tartufi Milan's most pungent specialty shop stocks mushrooms and truffles from throughout Italy. Black truffles from Norcia in Umbria are available throughout the year, while the white truffles from Alba in Piedmont are in season from September to January. ◆ Closed M afternoon, Su, lunch. Corso di Porta Genova 25. 8391327

28 Biffi Terrific variety in men's and women's clothing by many top designers (as well as the shop's own label) draw shoppers from all parts of town. ◆ Closed M morning, Su, lunch. Corso di Porta Genova 6. 8397182

29 Floretta Coen Musil Silk blouses and other women's apparel at a discount are the drawing cards of this popular shop. ◆ M-Sa afternoon. Via San Calocero 3. No credit cards. 8397708

30 San Vincenzo in Prato The church that has stood on this site since early Christian times has gone though many uses, among them a chemical plant called the **Casa del Mago** (House of the Wizard). Restored to its Romanesque appearance between 1885 and 1889, it is now a church again—a peaceful pile of brick with a simple interior filled with light. ◆ Via San Calocero

31 La Frittata ★★$$ Another Tuscan restaurant (the city abounds with them) offering the usual specialties of *ribollita* (white bean soup), *tagliatelle* pasta and *trippa alla fiorentina* or tripe in a spicy tomato sauce. ◆ Closed Tu, Aug. Viale Papiniano 43. 89402643

32 Emporio 2 Casual clothes by **Enrico Coveri** and the like at discount prices. ◆ Closed Su, lunch. Piazza Sant'Agostino 22. No credit cards. 4989448

33 Supporti Fonografici Recordings of music in New Wave and beyond in authorized and pirated versions, popular with Milan's club set. ◆ Closed M morning, Su, lunch. Viale Coni Zugna 63. 89403947

34 Trattoria all'Antica di Domenico e Maria ★★$$ **Domenico Passera** prepares Lombard specialties such as *cassoeula* (a pig's-foot stew) as well as Spanish *paella* in an

upscale setting. ◆ Closed Su, Aug. Via Montevideo 4. 8372849

35 Aurora ★★$$ Piedmontese specialties from minestrone and a variety of pastas to boiled and roasted meats and a fine selection of cheeses. Sit in the outdoor garden in the warmer months. ◆ Closed M. Via Savona 23. 89402700

36 La Granseola ★★$$ The ever-changing menu at **Rocco Nisi**'s seafood restaurant does have some constants—fresh fish prepared in style at reasonable prices. ◆ M-Sa dinner; closed Su, Aug, Christmas week. Via Tortona 20. 89402445

37 Esprit The US clothing firm's Italian headquarters is a huge space of white-plaster walls and industrial carpeting that sets off the sprightly designs nicely. ◆ Closed M morning, Su, lunch. Via Forcella 5. 89401640

Restaurants/Nightlife: Red   Hotels: Blue
Shops/Parks: Green   **Sights/Culture:** Black

38 Osteria dei Binari ★★$$ This sprawling restaurant features crowd-pleasing regional food from various parts of Italy, with an emphasis on Piedmont and Lombardy in both food and wine. *Busecca* (cheese-covered tripe served on bread rounds), game and grilled meats are all good choices. ♦ M-Sa dinner; closed Su, Aug. Via Tortona 1. 89409428

39 La Scaletta ★★★$$$ In this small and refined restaurant, **Pina Bellini** creates grand and refined dishes using such Italian classics as lasagna, ravioli, tripe, foie gras and saddle of rabbit as her solid starting-point. Son **Aldo** keeps the atmosphere in the dining room hushed without being overly reverent, guaranteeing one of the best meals you'll have in Milan. ♦ Closed M, Su, Aug. Piazza Stazione Genova 3. No credit cards. 58100290

40 Selfservice dello Scampolo Fabric remnants from various manufacturers at rock-bottom prices, sold by length as well as weight. ♦ Closed Su, lunch. Via Vigevano 32. No credit cards. 58100866

41 Zeus A center representing many facets of contemporary design in this most designerly of cities, Zeus shows everything from fashion to objects and furniture. ♦ Closed M morning, Su, lunch. Via Vigevano 8. 8373257

42 Gambelin Pottery from throughout Italy— terra cotta, majolica and the like—at reasonable prices. ♦ Closed Su, lunch. Viale Gorizia 30. No credit cards. 8350880

43 Osteria del Pallone ★★$$ Though the name implies that it's an old-fashioned, rustic restaurant, light meals (sandwiches, desserts and the like) take second place to the cocktails at this hangout, which has a few tables overlooking the canal during the warmer months. ♦ Tu-Su 5PM-1AM. Viale Gorizia. 8373445

Ticinese/Navigli

43 Posto di Conversazione ★★$$ What purports to be a *conversation nook* turns out to be a comfortable restaurant, serving *crespelle* (crepes), *bistecca* (steak) with a variety of sauces (*paprika dolce* or sweet paprika, *fichi secchi* or dried figs, and *ginepro* or juniper) as well as copious salads, well into the night. ♦ Tu-Su dinner. Alzaia Naviglio Grande 6. 8326646

44 Vicolo della Lavandaia This tiny street is where the last remaining washerwoman's stand along the *navigli* is located. A reminder of when cleaner water flowed in the canals and appliance-crazed young professionals were yet to discover the area, it is near and dear to the hearts of the old-time residents. ♦ Vicolo Lavandai

45 El Brellin A small club for a late-night drink or a snack after sampling the nightlife in the *navigli*. ♦ M-Sa 10PM-2AM. Vicolo Lavandai. 58101351

46 Il Libraccio Bargain books, many of them are books not at all as off-putting as the shop's name (it means *ugly book*) might lead you to believe. ♦ Closed Su, lunch. Via Corsico 9 (also at Via Corsico 12) No credit cards. 8323230

47 Decio Carugati ★★$$ Signor Carguti puts together combinations that manage to be original without being pretentious, such as *spaghetti alle erbe e pomodoro* (spaghetti with herbs and tomato), *coniglio in casseruola con olive liguri* (rabbit with Ligurian olives) and *latte cotto in fondo di pere* (a creamy-rich milk-and-pear dessert). ♦ Closed Su, 1-10 Jan. Via Corsico 2. 8323970

48 Il Discomane A secondhand record shop especially good for European-label 45s. ♦ Closed Su, lunch. Alzaia Naviglio Grande 36. No credit cards. 89406291

48 Il Torchietto ★★$$ Owner **Sergio Ragazzi** is from Mantua, which although within the region of Lombardy is nearer to and more influenced by the cuisine of Emilia-Romagna. Thus *culatello* melt-in-your-mouth ham, boiled and stuffed meats and sausages are all good choices here. ♦ Closed Su, Aug. Alzaia Naviglio Grande 36. 89406068

48 Tornavento For an evening of musical standards by such Milanese favorites as **Mina** (called the Italian Barbra Streisand) and **Fred Buongusto** (sort of the Italian Tony Bennett) as interpreted by the cocktail pianist, this is the place. ♦ Tu-Su 9PM-1AM. Alzaia Naviglio Grande 36. 8390068

49 Santa Maria delle Grazie al Naviglio (1899-1909, **Cesare Nava**) A typically Italian Neo-Gothic church built on the site of a real Gothic church. Inside are 8 granite columns inside, which come from the basilica of San Paolo fuori le Mura in Rome. ♦ Alzaia Naviglio Grande

50 Osteria di Via Pre ★$$ Largely Ligurian cuisine here, meaning pesto sauce, lots of olives, and fried fish authentically prepared by **Mariangela Musi**. Photographer husband **Giancarlo** is responsible for the decor, which features huge blow-ups amusingly called *gigantografie* (gigantographs) in Italian. ♦ Closed M-Tu, Aug. Via Casale 4. 8373869

51 Asso di Fiori Osteria dei Formaggi ★★$$ Cheese is the theme of this restaurant. It comes in all shapes and sizes, melted on pasta, coupled with meat, and sliced up for dessert. Added to the experience is the fact that the restaurant is on 2 barges floating in the navigli. ♦ Closed Sa lunch, Su. Alzaia Naviglio Grande 54. 89409415

51 Martin Luciano Old jeans, new jeans, black jeans, blue jeans as well as piles and piles of international Army surplus. ♦ Closed Su, lunch. Alzaia Naviglio Grande 58. No credit cards. 58101173

Restaurants/Nightlife: Red   **Hotels:** Blue
Shops/Parks: Green   **Sights/Culture:** Black

52 Brinkhoff's ★★$$ This club and eatery features live music and snacks as well as some 100 varieties of risotto. ♦ Closed M. Alzaia Naviglio Grande 62. 8321235

53 Il Montalcino ★★$$ Named after the famed wine-producing town in Tuscany, Montalcino prides itself on its wine list. Upscale rustic decor matches the cuisine, mostly Lombard but offering other regional specialties (notably Tuscan, which go well with the titular grape) as well. ♦ Closed Su, Aug. Via Valenza 17. 8321926

54 Al Pont de Ferr ★★$$ Near an iron bridge from which it takes its name, this restaurant is a relaxed place to sample simple Milanese cuisine. Only a few dishes are offered daily (or rather, nightly, since it's only open for dinner), but such things as *pasta e fagioli* (pasta with beans), *cassoeula* (pig's-foot stew) and *osso buco* (veal shank) are reassuringly regular and dependable. ♦ M-Sa dinner; closed Su, Aug. Ripa di Porta Ticinese 55. No credit cards. 89406277

54 L'Arcobaleno One of the best options for *gelato* right on the *navigli*, with a full selection of cool fruity and creamy treats. ♦ M-Sa 8AM-midnight. Ripa di Porta Ticinese 53. 89402360

55 Sadler ★★★$$$ In a seamless, expense-account setting, young chef **Claudio Sadler** prepares an ever-changing nouvellish cuisine based on luscious regional Italian ingredients, from his zucchini-flower vegetable pâté to delicately presented pheasant and pigeon. Ask for the *gran menu* or full menu to sample the greatest variety of his wares. ♦ M-Sa dinner. Ripa di Porta Ticinese 51. 58104451

56 Warhouse Secondhand clothing with a military bent. ♦ Closed Su. Ripa di Porta Ticinese 49. No credit cards. No phone

57 Angelo Azzuro A high-tech club featuring jazz and crepes, a classic combination along the *navigli*. ♦ M-Sa 9AM-2AM. Ripa di Porta Ticinese 11. 58100992

58 Osteria del Pontell Music videos and occasional live music provide the backdrop for this club, where the snacks include 11 different types of *bruschetta* or toasts covered with various tasty things. ♦ Alzaia Naviglio Pavese 2. 58101982

59 Lento Battello This club is anything but a *slow boat*, filled as it is with the fast beat of some of the youngest navigators of Milan's club scene. ♦ Tu-Su 9PM-2AM. Via Ascanio Sforza 31. 8322747

60 La Magolfa ★★$$ Another relaxed place to sample some Milanese standards in this most relaxing of Milanese neighborhoods, Magolfa offers all the usual risotto dishes as well as *osso buco* (veal shank) in a canal-side setting. ♦ M-Sa dinner. Via Magolfa 15. No credit cards. 8321696

61 La Topaia ★★$$ Informal dining with a little Ligurian mixed in with the Lombard specialties on the menu, as seen by **Andrea** and **Anita**'s numerous risotto dishes, minestrone, and the seafaring *insalata tiepida di polipo* (warm octopus salad). ♦ M-Sa dinner; closed Su, Aug. Via Argelati 46. 8373468

Fashion Design

Having surpassed Paris as the fashion capital of the world (as the Milanese will be the first to tell you), Milan produces fashion ranging from playful to sophisticated but always stylish. To followers of fashion, shopping (or more likely window-shopping, given the prices) in Milan's boutiques is equivalent to an art historian's visit to the Louvre. From A to Z, from **Giorgio Armani**'s loose interpretations of American classics to **Ermenegildo Zegna**'s highly tailored menswear (not to mention the bright casual clothes of **Enrico Coveri**, the architectural silhouette of **Gianfranco Ferrè**, the whimsical knits of **Krizia**, the colorful knits of **Missoni**, and the fabric-conscious **Gianni Versace**), internationally acclaimed local designers are the main event for many in Milan. Their shops, often designed by leading architects and designers, are found primarily in and around **Via Monte Napoleone**.

Additional Milan Highlights

We had to tell you about the following even though they fall out of the bounds of our chapter maps. You will find them worth the detour.

1 Gualtiero Marchesi ★★★★$$$$ This restaurant from Milan's self-proclaimed gastronomical guru is often cited as Italy's best. Having introduced nouvelle cuisine-style eating to Italy years ago, Marchesi has since moved on (besides having begun his own line of food products and designed menus here and there) to a more personal cuisine based on regional Italian ingredients. Some of his more renowned dishes include *filetti di sogliola fritti a salsa agrodolce* (sweet-and-sour fried filet of sole), *soufflé di panettone con salsa al rum* (panettone soufflé with rum sauce) and *granita al té verde* (a green tea ice). Menus at various prices. ♦ Closed M lunch, Su, Aug. Via Bonvesin de la Riva 9. 741246

2 Soti's ★★★$$$ This intimate, elegant restaurant requiring jacket and tie for men features the *cucina creativa* of **Simone Francesco**, who makes such creations as *gnocchi al nero di seppia* (potato dumplings with cuttlefish ink) and *coniglio alle arachidi* (rabbit with walnuts). ♦ Closed Sa lunch, Su, Aug. Via Pietro Calvi 2. 796838

3 L'Ami Berton ★★★$$$ Remigio Bertone was one of the first restaurateurs in town to take an interest in international culinary trends, giving him more experience than most in perfecting such succulent pairings as *lasagnette pesto e frutti di mare* (pasta with pesto and seafood) and *fegatino con le mele* (liver with apples). The fish dishes are the most inventive in Milan. ♦ Closed Sa lunch, Su, Aug, Christmas week. Via F. Nullo 14

4 Calajunco ★★$$ The Aeolean Islands off the northern coast of Sicily are the unusual inspiration for much of the menu here. Fish, freshly brought back from the market and not cheap, reigns supreme, but such dishes as filet of beef and liver with Ala wine nicely round out the menu. ♦ Closed Sa lunch, Su. Via Stoppani 5. 2046003

5 Luna Park Varesine Milan's amusement park is close to the center of the city and a little rough around the edges, but makes a great place to take the kids or observe the Milanese version of same cavorting on merry-go-rounds and roller coasters (called *montagne russe* or Russian mountains in Italy). ♦ M-Sa 2:30-7:30PM, 8:30PM-midnight; Su 10AM-1PM, 2:30PM-midnight. Via Galileo Galilei 15. 6571149

Restaurants/Nightlife: Red   Hotels: Blue
Shops/Parks: Green   Sights/Culture: Black

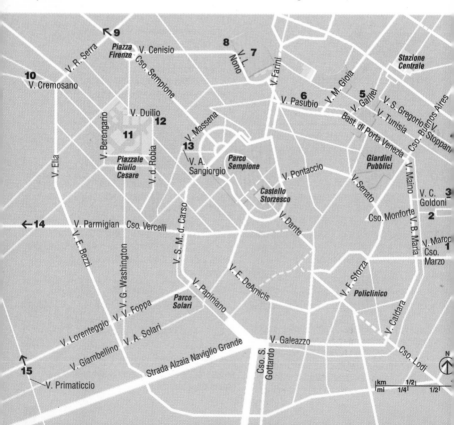

6 Antica Trattoria della Pesa ★★$$ One of the oldest restaurants in the city, it appropriately serves all the Milanese classics (*buseca, minestrone, risotto giallo, risotto al salto, osso buco, cazzoeula* in a charming old setting. ♦ Closed Su, Aug. Via Pasubio 10. 6555741

7 Cimitero Monumentale (1863-66, **Carlo Maciachini**) While hardly Paris' Pere Lachaise, Milan's extensive cemetery (it was put together from 5 suburban cemeteries) does contain the remains of Milanese notables such as writer **Alessandro Manzoni** and intellectual **Carlo Cattaneo**. Perhaps more interestingly, it is filled with a fascinating assemblage of fanciful 19th- and 20th-century funereal sculpture by obscure and less obscure sculptors such as **Giacomo Manzù, Fausto Melotti** and **Gio Pomodoro**. It is still the final resting place of choice for Milan's leading families, though admission is restricted to those whose ancestors are already buried here. ♦ Tu-Su 8:30AM-5:45PM, 1 Apr-30 Sep; 8:30AM-4:45PM, 1 Oct-31 Mar. Piazzale Cimitero Monumentale

8 Alfredo Gran San Berdnardo ★★★$$$ **Alfredo Valli**'s elegant eatery features all the Milanese classics (*nervetti con cipolla, risotto alla milanese, risotto alsalto, cotoletta alla milanese, cazzoeula osso buco*) followed by the city's current dessert trends of chocolate mousse and zabaglione. Excellent selection of *grappa*, the Italian aquavit. ♦ Closed Su, Jan, Aug. Via Borgese 14. 3319000

9 Franca, Paola e Lele ★★$$$ As homey (in everything but the price) as its name implies (the first names of its owners), this restuarant features *cucina creativa* or creative cuisine that changes according to chef **Paola Zanella**'s whim and what she finds at the market. Usually, though, you'll find mouthwatering *culatello* ham as an appetizer and a few good game dishes among the pastas and entrees. The chocolate desserts are terrific as well. ♦ Closed Sa, Su, Aug, Christmas week. Via Certosa 235. 305238

10 Ribot ★★$$ Named after a famous racehorse (it's near the track of San Siro), this restaurant features many photos of it and other such beasts, and at times seems as busy as the track. Stick with the classics—*risotto*, grilled and boiled meats, homemade desserts. ♦ Closed M, Aug. Via Cremosano 41. 33001646

11 Fiera di Milano Italy's most important trade fair was founded in 1920 and opened on its present site in 1923. Dozens of exhibitions (given the odd acronyms of which the Italians are so fond, such as MIFED for films and TV) are held regularly each year, the most internationally famous ones being the fashion and furniture fairs. Like much of Milan, the fairgrounds suffered heavily during WWII bombing, but a number of structures remain from the early days of the fair (the April edition is still something of a family outing opportunity among the locals), among them the **Via Domodossola** entrance and the **Palazzo dello**

Sport (1925, **Paolo Vietti-Violi**). Postwar construction includes the **Palazzo delle Nazioni** (1947, **Angelo Bianchetti** and **Cesare Pea**), **Emiciclo** (1947-53, **Pier Luigi Nervi**), **Padiglione dell'Agricoltura** (1956, **Ignazio Gardella**), **Padiglione della Meccanica** (1969, **Melchiorre Bega**). ♦ Largo Domodossola 1. 49971

12 Grand Hotel Fieramilano $$$ Across from the Porta Domodossola entrance to the fairgrounds. Such amenities as hairdriers and telephones in the bathrooms and air-conditioning in the warmer months (when you can also have breakfast in the outdoor garden) make it the hotel of choice for those going to the fair. ♦ Viale Boezio 20. 3105

13 Lancaster $$$ Also near the fairgrounds, the Lancaster is a less expensive option for those going to the fair. Its smaller size (there are only 29 rooms) and such personal touches as Pedro the parrot at the front desk ensure a regular clientele, which makes reservations a must. ♦ Via Sangiorgio 16. 313472

14 Grand Hotel Brun $$$$ This luxury hotel, located near the San Siro race track, is a practically self-contained environment for business travelers, containing all the amenities. ♦ Via Novara. 4526279

Within the Grand Hotel Brun:

Ascot ★★★$$$ A good spot for a business lunch (especially if one of the lunchers is a guest at the hotel), Ascot serves an especially good *pasta d'olive nere e carciofi* (pasta with black olives and artichokes), *orecchiette al ragu di agnello* (tiny ear-shaped pasta with a lamb ragout) and other southern Italian-influenced dishes under the direction of Apulian chef **Giuseppe Troiano**. ♦ Daily

15 Aimo e Nadia ★★★$$$ **Aimo** and **Nadia Moroni** have taken their native Tuscan appreciation for wholesome ingredients and put them together in imaginative and ever-changing

Additional Milan Highlights

ways, which makes it impossible to mention specific dishes but it's always pleasantly surprising to try them. Delicate pastries are made in-house by **Gabriele Grigolon**. ♦ Closed Sa lunch, Su, Aug. Via Montecuccoli 6. 416886

16 Hotel Quark $$$$ Another modern and efficient business hotel famous for its restaurant under the same ownership as Ascot in the Grand Hotel Brun. ♦ Via Lampedusa 11A. 84435005

Within the Hotel Quark:

Ascot Due ★★★$$$ Expense-account lunching here is based on a menu that ranges from international specialties to (more interestingly) such Italian regional dishes as the various pastas and truffles in season, all accompanied by a good selection of wines. ♦ Closed Su, Easter week, Aug, Christmas-New Year's

Florence Index

Florence Index

Florence RESTAURANTS

Only restaurants with star ratings are listed below. All restaurants are listed alphabetically in the main index. Always telephone as far in advance as possible to confirm your table and ensure that a restaurant has not closed, changed its hours, or booked its tables for a private party.

Venice Index

Milan INDEX

Milan Index

Credits

Research & Writing
Dwight V. Gast

Associate Editor
Karin Mullen

Editorial Assistants
Margie Lee
Daniela Sylvers

Word Processing
Jerry Stanton

Art Direction
Tom Beatty

Map Design
Cheryl Fitzgerald
Kitti Homme
M. Kohnke
Laurie Miller

Production Assistance
Michael Blum
Gerard Garbutt
Patricia Keelin
Chris Middour
Lynne Stiles

Scanning
Nisha Inalsingh

Film Production
Digital Pre-Press
International

Printing and Otabind
Webcom Limited

Special Thanks
Ron Davis
Ann Kook
Dieter Marx, Edizione Lidiarte
Margie's Sister (cover photo)
Stuart Silberman (cover photo)

ACCESS®PRESS

President
Mark Johnson

Director
Maura Carey Damacion

Project Director
Mark Goldman

Editorial Director
Jean Linsteadt

Dwight V. Gast (writer and researcher) has lived and worked in Italy on and off since 1979. He has written about the country for numerous publications, including *Art in America, Bon Appétit, Esquire, Food and Wine, The International Herald Tribune, The New Yorker, The New York Times,* and *Travel & Leisure.* He thanks Franco Dianda, Paolo Lanapoppi, Patricia Schultz, and friends of Bill W. for their assistance and support

Staircase of the Giants in the inner courtyard of the Palazzo Ducale

Printed in Canada

Distinctive features of **ACCESS**® Travel Guides

- Organized by neighborhood, the way natives know a city and visitors experience it.

- Color-coded entries distinguish restaurants, hotels, shops, parks, architecture, and places of interest.

- Easy to use and a pleasure to read.

- Generous use of detailed maps with points of interest identified.

- Each city's flavor is conveyed by descriptions of its history, by lists of the personal favorites of people who know and love the city, and by trivia and lavish illustrations.

BARCELONAACCESS®
An up-to-the-minute guide to Spain's avant-garde city, home of the 1992 Summer Olympic Games. 160 pages, $17.00

BOSTONACCESS®
A guide to the many charms of America's Revolutionary capital, from historic landmarks to where to shop, walk, stay, and dine. 208 pages, $16.95

CHICAGOACCESS®
The key to inimitable Chicago style, from its renowned architecture to its famous deep-dish pizza. 192 pages, $16.95

FLORENCE/VENICE/MILANACCESS®
A grand tour through Northern Italy's three major cities in one comprehensive guide. 240 pages, $17.00

HAWAIIACCESS®
Organized island by island . . . what to see . . . where to stay . . . what to do. 192 pages, $14.95

LAACCESS®
The city's characteristic urban sprawl and profusion of personalities rendered accessible. 224 pages, $16.95

LONDONACCESS®
The first winner from abroad of the London Tourist Board's Guidebook of the Year Award! 224 pages, $16.95

MIAMI & SOUTH FLORIDAACCESS®
A guide to all of sunny South Florida, including Miami, Ft. Lauderdale, Palm Beach, the Florida Keys, the Everglades, and Sanibel and Captiva Islands. Available in 1992. 192 pages, $17.00

NYCACCESS®
For natives and visitors...the ultimate guide to the city famous for everything except subtlety and understatement. 320 pages, $16.95

ORLANDO & CENTRAL FLORIDAACCESS®
A whirlwind tour of Central Florida from Orlando and Disney World to the JFK Space Center, Tampa, and much more. Available in 1992. 192 pages, $17.00

PARISACCESS®
For the first-time and the veteran visitor, a guide that opens doors to the city's magic and nuances. 216 pages, $16.95

ROMEACCESS®
An award-winning guidebook featuring favorite promenades of the Eternal City. 160 pages, $16.95

SAN DIEGOACCESS®
Discover the best of this vibrant young city, from its world-famous zoo to its sun-drenched beaches. 160 pages, $17.00

SFACCESS®
Our best-selling guide to the much-loved city includes daytrips around the Bay Area. 208 pages, $16.95

SUMMER GAMES 1992 ACCESS®
A TV viewer's guide to the Summer Olympics in Barcelona, with in-depth information and colorful illustrations for all the events. Available in 1992. 112 pages, $10.00

THE WALL STREET JOURNAL
Guide to Understanding Money & Markets
A best-selling book with details on buying stocks, bonds, and futures, spotting trends, and evaluating companies. 120 pages, $13.95

WASHINGTON DCACCESS®
A comprehensive guide to the nation's capital with descriptions of the beautiful and historic places that encircle it. 216 pages, $12.95

WINE COUNTRYACCESS®
Northern California
All the ingredients you need to create your own wine touring vacation. Available in 1992. 176 pages, $17.00

To order these **ACCESS**®Guides, please see the other side of this page.

Praise for **ACCESS**® Guides

In a radical approach to the genre, **ACCESS**® Press has reinvented the wheel with a series of compact volumes that open up cities through striking graphics, terse copy, and a tight format. **Time Magazine**

The **ACCESS**® Series offers literally thousands of bits of useful or surprising information, all color-coded and organized in odd but sensible ways that will satisfy both tourist and native. **New York Magazine**

For either the traveler or the armchair explorer who loves accurate detail and affectionate description, the **ACCESS**® Guides prove wonderful companions. **James A. Michener**